FAST STOCKS,
FAST MONEY

FAST STOCKS, FAST MONEY

How to Make Money Investing in New Issues and Small-Company Stocks

Robert S. Natale

McGraw-Hill

New York   San Francisco   Washington, D.C.   Auckland   Bogotá
Caracas   Lisbon   London   Madrid   Mexico City   Milan
Montreal   New Delhi   San Juan   Singapore
Sydney   Tokyo   Toronto

Library of Congress Catalog Card Number: 99-76292

McGraw-Hill

A Division of The McGraw·Hill Companies

1 2 3 4 5 6 7 8 9 0   AGM/AGM   9 0 9 8 7 6 5 4 3 2 1 9

ISBN 0-07-045980-0

*This book was set in Times New Roman by North Market Street Graphics. It was
printed and bound by Quebecor/Martinsburg.*

Contents

Preface

He who chooses the beginning of a road, chooses the place it leads to.

—Harry Emerson Fosdick

*F**AST STOCKS, FAST MONEY* **HAS BEEN** written for the mainstream investor who is interested in learning how to buy and sell small stocks and new issues intelligently. The book uses as its centerpiece an investment methodology developed at Standard & Poor's, one of the most respected names in the financial industry. The springboard for such honors is the firm's long-standing insistence on objectivity and its balanced approach to financial analysis, which sets apart its stock recommendations, financial indexes, and bond ratings, and which are found in abundance among these pages.

ORIGINS

The book is divided into three sections. The first section lays the groundwork for investing in small-cap stocks and new issues. It answers the following questions: What have been the historical returns over the long run? How much should anyone invest in such stocks? What returns can an investor expect to earn from such investments in the future? It does so by providing and interpreting returns analysis going back 75 years.

The second section concentrates on the new issues market. In 1982, S&P was one of the first financial information companies to offer investment advice on new issues and small-capitalization stocks through its publication, *Emerging & Special Situations*. As editor of that newsletter from 1983 to 1998, I had an opportunity to study the small-cap and IPO markets over many IPO cycles and to analyze literally hundreds of companies in virtually every major industry. This section hopefully reflects what was learned while closely monitoring this part of the U.S. equity market.

In 1987, in connection with S&P's launch of a new electronic financial information service to tens of thousands of account executives, the company decided to start categorizing the stock recommendations that had long been made by its equity research analysts. Five STARS meant a strong buy recommendation, three STARS a hold recommendation, and one STAR a sell recommendation. After almost 13 years, it is now clear that when it comes to stock selection, the analysts at S&P definitely are onto something. From January 1, 1987, through September 30, 1999, *S&P's 5-STAR stocks did more than twice as well as the S&P 500 index.* That's right, twice as well!

The third section of this book provides the methodology used by these analysts to construct this stellar record. The basic investment approach used can be most easily described as *growth at a reasonable price* (GARP) investing. It, along with S&P's successful Fair Value quantitative model, is applied to the selection of small-cap stocks in the third section of this book.

DISCIPLINE REALLY COUNTS

The best investment process in existence cannot help unless it is consistently practiced over many years. No investor can be right 100 percent of the time. The key is to be right more often than you are wrong. Similarly, no investment method works in all kinds of markets and with every stock, but what counts in the end is for it to work in most markets and with most stocks. And the earlier an investor starts using a tried-and-true approach, the better the final results are likely to be. GARP investing offers just such an opportunity.

SUMMARY POINTS

After reading *Fast Stocks, Fast Money,* investors should come away with an awareness and understanding of the following points:

- How well small stocks have done over the long term
- How the power of compounding can make a huge difference in total investment returns
- How much an investor should put into small stocks
- When to buy small cap stocks and IPOs
- What the main purchase rules are for IPOs
- How to get the most out of reading a prospectus
- How to develop relationships with the right brokers for IPO allocations

- How to invest in value or growth stocks by playing to your intuitive and personal strengths
- How S&P's GARP investment strategy to potentially add significantly to your investment returns
- How to develop a personal sell discipline applicable to a broad cross-section of stocks
- How to research a potential purchase fast

Acknowledgments

A LTHOUGH THE WORDS MAY COME from a single pair of hands, this book is a distillation of the best ideas culled during the 20 years I spent at what is as close to an objective think tank as Wall Street has to offer—the Equity Research Group at Standard & Poor's. Much of my investment thinking was developed there. And a great deal of the success of the fund I currently lead manage should rightfully be attributed to the investment process described in this book and practiced by the analysts at Standard & Poor's. Those I would like to thank for their many efforts over the years while at Analytical are quite numerous. They include Rob Gold, Megan Graham-Hackett, Tom Graves, Mike Jaffe, Cathy Seifert, and Ken Shea, who continue to offer sound investment recommendations based on many of the principles espoused in this book. I would like particularly to thank Tom, an individual with the rare combination of excellent analytical and editorial skills and generosity of spirit.

Bob Christie, Jim Dunn, and Stephen Sanborn are among the individuals who gave me the opportunity to broaden my horizons beyond specific stock selection into portfolio management. Jim Branscome offered me constant encouragement to develop and finally complete this book. His astute observations on human motivation provided food for thought well beyond the corporate office, but they were particularly useful when applied to finance.

Acting as research director of the equity analysts at S&P from 1991 to 1998 while continuing to follow IPOs and small-cap stocks required the support of many others if I were ever to find the time to complete this task. Mike Pizzi offered that and much more. While Mark Basham and Susanna

Lee toiled biweekly to put *Emerging & Special Situations* together, they also found the wherewithal to provide many of the new issues charts and tables in this book. The Quantitative Research Group, including Andre Archambault (Mr. Fair Value), David Braverman, Patrice Gueye, and Howard Silverblatt, provided a lot of the non-IPO data included here.

At Bear Stearns Asset Management, my new home, Mark Kurland and Bob Reitzes have offered many cogent tactical observations on the art of stock selection and the practical mechanics of portfolio management. Doni Fordyce also has been supportive in allowing this book to see the light of day. My current assistant, Carol Ann Baker, helped put the final pieces into place as we went to press.

Dolores Dean provided important insights on the original edits, and my father-in-law Nick Beldecos contributed the wisdom garnered after a long and distinguished career as a senior executive in the corporate and non-profit sectors. And as our friends know, my wife Ann and I were in a race to complete the gestation process, of our son Nicholas in her case, and this book in mine. Ann has long since won. I am profoundly grateful for her help as I struggled to put this book to bed and for her oft-mentioned words, "Any book worth writing once, is worth writing twice."

Finally, I would like to acknowledge my late father, who allowed a 12-year-old boy to buy his first shares of stock for his own account, which triggered an intellectual journey as exciting as any that could be enjoyed. For that and many other things, I will always be grateful.

Robert S. Natale, CFA

S E C T I O N

1

SMALL STOCKS, BIG PROFITS

MY INTRODUCTION TO the stock market was inauspicious. Every night my father would arrive home from the pharmacy he owned at a few minutes after 6 P.M. He would enter the kitchen, greet my mother, head for the refrigerator, get a beer or soda, and just before sitting at the dinner table, walk to the edge of the kitchen and turn on the radio.

Dad liked to dabble in the stock market. In the 1950s, he bought mining stocks. Now, in addition to a couple of blue chips, he was taking fliers on some tiny, little-known issues that his broker or customers had brought to his attention. He only bought shares in companies that he thought he understood.

At 6:25 P.M., conversation would stop as the Wall Street report came on. As in the 1990s, many Americans were playing the market back then. Each night the announcer would recount how the Dow did that day, followed by the performance of the most active stocks on the two major trading venues in the United States at the time, the New York and American Stock Exchanges. The whole process took about two minutes.

I am not sure how many weeks or months passed before I started asking questions, most of them having to do with the stocks my father listened for each evening. After a few months of this, I summoned up the courage to ask him if I could take some of the money I had gotten over the years as gifts and put it in the stock market. "Sure," he said. He told me how much to take out of the account and that weekend sold me 10 shares of Pacific Telephone & Telegraph from his own position. The total amount was about $250.

Each day I would check the evening paper (the New York *World Telegram & Sun*) to see how I was doing, but the utility stock hardly moved at all. After a couple of months of this lackluster experience, I went back to my broker and asked if I could sell PacTel back to him for something with a little more pizzazz.

This time, he let me make the pick. Among the choices were Burry Biscuit, Canada Dry, Chock Full O'Nuts, and IBM. But I chose Saxon Paper, a small company trading on the American Stock Exchange. The investment premise had something to do with manufacturing cheaper coated copier paper. I bought it at 20. Six months later it was at 40.

I was hooked.

SMALL STOCKS CAN MAKE YOU RICH

Small stocks can be absolutely great investments. Everyone loves to hear the story of the investor in oil wells who strikes it rich on the last well drilled out of 10. But what if the odds were 1 in 10 and you could only afford to drill 2? Most investors want the odds to be with them, not against them. As we will show, small stocks offer excellent odds. Unless you have outstanding personal expertise, throw out oil wells, real estate limited partnerships (LPs), coins, and baseball cards. Equity stocks in general and small-cap stocks in particular are the way to go.

Ibbotson's *Stocks, Bonds, Bills, and Inflation Yearbook* provides a definitive record of asset class returns since 1926. Its performance series for the 73 years through 1998 show that small stocks provided an average annual return of 12.4 percent, by far the best results of any type of financial instrument surveyed. That compares with 11.2 percent for stocks in general, 5.8 percent for long-term corporate bonds, and 3.8 percent for U.S. Treasury bills. This includes 1998, when large stocks advanced 28.6 percent, and small ones fell 7.3 percent, the greatest disparity on record. While large company equities may be peaking, small ones appear poised to provide above-average returns for many years to come. (Today most professionals define small stocks as those equities with market caps of $100 million to $2 billion.)

There is only one asset that can provide a better return than small stocks. That is your home. Real estate does not typically appreciate as fast as small stocks, but when you buy a house, the bank lets you borrow 5 to 10 times as much as your down payment. A $10,000 increase in the value of a house worth $200,000 represents a 50 percent return on the $20,000 you might have put down on it. That kind of financial leverage is not possible with stocks, at least not in the United States. But owning small stocks provides the best returns of any major potential investment.

Why do small stocks provide superior results? Put simply, there is a direct relationship between the variability of investment returns and the annual rate of return on that asset. The relative performance of cash, bonds, and stocks can be explained by the volatility of returns over long periods of time. Investments that offer the most predictable near-term returns, like bank passbook accounts and six-month certificates of deposit (CDs), provide the lowest returns over the long run. The higher the probable variation in returns from one year to the next, the higher the required rate of return needed to entice investors to assume those risks. Since small stocks have the most risk of declining quickly, they should provide the highest returns over the long run.

The extra rate of return needed to convince investors to buy stocks in general is called the *equity risk premium*. It varies over time, based on how risky stocks are perceived as an investment. All other things being equal, there are greater operational and financial risks assumed when owning shares in smaller companies. Their activities are not as diversified, there is less existing cash flow to support potential earnings shortfalls, and their balance sheets are usually not as strong. Because of the added risks of owning small stocks, the extra required return to convince investors to buy small stocks must be still greater. Nonetheless, *if your time horizon is more than five years, history tells us that small stock ownership is not all that much riskier than owning stocks in general.* As long as you buy a diversified portfolio of small stocks, the returns over time should be better than for equities in general and well worth the added risks assumed.

HISTORY POINTS TO SMALL STOCKS
Before getting into the nuts and bolts, let's get excited about the potential returns that can be achieved. One thing you should know is that you'll never get rich owning either bonds or T-bills. In only 2 years out of the last 73 did investors get better than 30 percent returns from owning bonds. In no year did the return on T-bills exceed 15 percent. Granted, long-term corporates never lost more than 10 percent, and in the case of T-bills, there was no year when returns were negative, but owning U. S. Treasuries won't make you wealthy.

In stark contrast, there have been 23 years since 1926 when annual total returns of small stocks exceeded 30 percent. In fact, in this period, they were the best-performing financial instrument in 32 of those 73 years. There were also 5 years when small stocks provided negative returns greater than 30 percent, but that was only slightly more frequent than the 2 years for large stocks. The worst year was 1937, when small stocks dropped 58 percent. However, the big difference between large and small stock returns is that there were more than 4 times as many big up years as down ones for small stocks. In the best one, 1933, small stocks provided a whopping 143 percent return over 12 months.

A little while ago we said that over the last 73 years, small stocks returned 12.4 percent annually, versus 11.2 percent for stocks in general, as measured by the Standard & Poor's (S&P) 500 index. The difference between 12.4 and 11.2 percent, or 1.2 percent, may not seem like much, but the power of compounding cannot be underestimated. With history as an excellent guide, though not a guarantor, of similar future returns, Table 1-1 outlines what an investor could expect to achieve at these average rates.

In each case we start with $10,000. But what if you were lucky enough to put in more? Just think of it—using the same assumptions, a $50,000 investment in small stocks over 25 years has a decent chance of growing to over $929,000! By contrast, investing in the S&P 500 index would give you $711,000, and corporate bonds $205,000. That could make a huge impact on your golden years or the amount you leave your children.

TABLE 1-1 $10,000 investment value: small stocks versus the S&P 500.

Year	Annual Return	
	Small Stocks, 12.4%	S&P 500, 11.2%
0	**$ 10,000**	**$ 10,000**
1	11,240	11,120
2	12,634	12,365
3	14,200	13,750
4	15,691	15,290
5	17,940	17,003
10	32,186	28,910
15	57,742	49,155
20	103,591	83,579
25	**$185,848**	**$142,108**

NOTE: These returns are *before* taxes, and assume that all stock proceeds were put back into the market. The after-tax return for taxable accounts would be lower but still in the double digits. Hence, these are the returns you could get in an IRA or Keough account.

SOURCE: *Stocks, Bonds, Bills and Inflation Yearbook,* © 1999 Ibbotson Associates, Inc. Based on copyrighted works by Ibbotson and Sinquefield. All rights reserved. Used with permission.

STARTING EARLY HELPS A LOT

Clearly, the sooner you start to invest, the larger the pot at the end of the rainbow will become. Compounding, of course, is the key that unlocks the treasure. For example, if one were to put $2000 a year for 8 years into small stocks, and then let that investment sit for another 17 years, the value of that portfolio at the end of year 25 would be $204,669. But if you waited to begin saving until year 9, and then put away $2000 for *17 years,* you'd end up with only $114,123. Table 1-2 shows the gains that would accrue over 25 years, assuming a 12.4 percent annual return.

This is, indeed, how fortunes are made. Individuals with long investment horizons are generally young to middle-aged adults with many current demands for cash. Although cash for savings may be limited, putting just $1000 to $2000 into small stocks each year is enough to produce a much larger payoff down the road. Just look at how that original investment of $2000 a year for 8 years compounded over the last 5 years of the 25-year period.

SMALL STOCKS CAN PROVIDE GOOD RETURNS EVEN IF YOUR TIMING IS OFF

Conventional wisdom says that small stocks beat or trail the market over five- to seven-year blocks. The time periods, however, are actually much longer, particularly the length of time when small stocks do really well. Since 1926 there have been nine extended periods when small stocks have either outperformed or underperformed (see Table 1-3). Only in the 1990s did the periods of out- or underperformance shorten.

If you had the misfortune to put $10,000 into small stocks at the end of 1968, and to sell them when you got disgusted with the returns over the next 5 years, you would have lost $4930. That is awful by any standard but particularly galling since the same amount put in the S&P 500 would have resulted in a gain of $1141. But consider this: If you had held on for *another* five years you would have come out ahead after all. For the 10 years through 1978, the same amount put in small stocks at year-end 1968 would have resulted in a $5530 gain, as against $3702 for the S&P 500.

THERE HAS NEVER BEEN A BETTER TIME TO BUY SMALL-CAP STOCKS

In 1998, small-cap stocks had their worst performance relative to the rest of the stock market since World War II. For the record, small-cap stocks fell 2.1 percent, as measured by the S&P SmallCap 600 index, while the S&P 500 rose 26.7 percent. In the first quarter of 1999, the S&P SmallCap 600 index fell an additional 10.3 percent, while the S&P 500 advanced 4.4 percent.

TABLE 1-2   Starting early: the early bird versus the procrastinator.

Year	Early-Bird Investor		Procrastinator	
	Investment	Value	Investment	Value
1	$2000	$ 2,248	0	0
2	2000	4,775	0	0
3	2000	7,615	0	0
4	2000	10,807	0	0
5	2000	14,395	0	0
6	2000	18,428	0	0
7	2000	22,961	0	0
8	2000	28,056	0	0
9	0	31,535	$2000	$ 2,248
10	0	35,445	2000	4,775
11	0	39,840	2000	7,615
12	0	44,781	2000	10,807
13	0	50,334	2000	14,395
14	0	56,575	2000	18,428
15	0	63,590	2000	22,961
16	0	71,475	2000	28,056
17	0	80,338	2000	33,783
18	0	90,300	2000	40,221
19	0	101,497	2000	47,456
20	0	114,083	2000	55,588
21	0	128,229	2000	64,729
22	0	144,130	2000	75,004
23	0	162,002	2000	86,552
24	0	182,098	2000	99,533
25	**0**	**$204,669**	**$2000**	**$114,123**

TABLE 1-3   Small stocks: major periods of underperformance and outperformance.

	CAGR*		
Years	S&P 500	Small Stocks	Performance
1926–1931	–2.5%	–20.2%	Underperformed
1932–1945	11.5	25.2	Outperformed
1946–1957	13.2	8.3	Underperformed
1958–1968	12.7	24.2	Outperformed
1969–1973	2.0	–12.3	Underperformed
1974–1983	10.6	28.4	Outperformed
1984–1990	14.6	2.6	Underperformed
1991–1994	11.9	22.1	Outperformed
1995–1998	30.5	15.8	Underperformed

* Compound annual growth rate.
SOURCE: *Stocks, Bonds, Bills and Inflation Yearbook,* © 1999 Ibbotson Associates, Inc. Based on copyrighted works by Ibbotson and Sinquefield. All rights reserved. Used with permission.

What caused the acceleration of poor relative performance? A select number of large companies—some call them the new Nifty 50—have generated consistent earnings growth far in excess of the average large and small company. It is the stocks of such large companies as Cisco Systems, MCI WorldCom, Microsoft, Pfizer, and Time Warner that kept driving the S&P 500 to all-time highs during the late 1990s, while the rest of the market lagged badly behind.

As of the end of 1998, small stocks had not fared well for four straight years (see Table 1-4). Since small stocks did 15 percentage points worse than the S&P 500 in the first quarter of 1999, it is a fairly safe bet that we are looking at another year of bad times for small caps. If you are a momentum investor, this is the last place you would put your money.

However, there are three important considerations which suggest that investing in small-cap stocks now could provide quite extraordinary returns to the astute investor. From this observer's vantage point, *the year 2000 could be a once-in-a-lifetime opportunity to get in at the beginning of an extended, multiyear upcycle for small-cap stocks.*

First, there appears to be a vague relationship between the degree to which small stocks underperform and then subsequently outperform. The two periods when small stocks did worst relative to the S&P 500 were followed by the best and the third-best periods of relative outperformance for

TABLE 1-4   Annual return: large versus small stocks during the 1990s.

	Annual Return	
Year	Large Stocks	Small Stocks
1990	−3.2%	−21.6%
1991	30.5	44.6
1992	7.7	23.3
1993	10.0	21.0
1994	1.3	3.1
1995	37.4	30.2
1996	23.1	17.6
1997	33.4	22.8
1998	28.6	−7.3
CAGR*	17.9%	13.6%

* Compound annual growth rate.
SOURCE: *Stocks, Bonds, Bills and Inflation Yearbook*, © 1999 Ibbotson Associates, Inc. Based on copyrighted works by Ibbotson and Sinquefield. All rights reserved. Used with permission.

small stocks. *Since small stocks have substantially underperformed over the last four years (1995–1998), going on five years, they stand to do quite well over the next five years.* The underperformance in the second half of the 1990s is setting the stage for potentially explosive outperformance in the first decade of the twenty-first century. Underlying this bold statement is the fact that the shortest period of underperformance was 5 years (1969 to 1973), while, until the 1990s, the shortest span of outperformance was 10 years.

Second, as of April 1999, small stocks, on a relative basis, were the cheapest they had been in more than 30 years. They were trading at lower price/earnings (P/E), price/cash flow, and price/sales levels relative to large caps than even during the last major bottoms for small-cap stock relative performance in 1973 and 1990. Indeed, the weighted average P/E ratio for stocks in the S&P SmallCap 600 index fell below that for the S&P 500 for the first time in its existence in mid-1998. This was still the case as of late 1999.

Third, and most important, *with small stocks having turned in returns more than 20 percentage points below the S&P 500 in 1998 and another 15 percentage points worse in just the first quarter of 1999, it certainly appears that we have experienced the capitulation phase of the current underperformance cycle for small stocks.* When a particular asset class lags behind for many years, even core believers give up. This is what kept stocks cheap during the 1940s and 1950s following the 1929 crash, and again after the 1973 to 1974 bear market, even after long-term fundamentals began to improve. But consider this: While some of the most diehard small-cap-oriented investors are throwing in the proverbial towel, institutions are reentering the small-cap market. Individual investor actions are reflected in the large amount of redemptions in most small-cap stock funds during 1998 and early 1999. But over the same time, institutions actually have been taking money out of the S&P 500 and putting proportionally more new money into broader market indexes like the S&P 1500, Wilshire 5000, and Russell 3000 indexes. All these indexes include more small-cap stocks.

Are you afraid to jump into small caps at the top of this roaring bull market? If so, here is one last point that may persuade you. *The last time Nifty-50 growth stocks held sway, small stocks subsequently provided substantially better returns.* For example, between 1976 and 1978, small-cap stocks rose 25 percent, while large caps fell 12 percent, the reverse of what happened in 1998 to 1999. Indeed, given their relative performance over the last five years, there may be less risk in buying small stocks now than in large-cap growth equities, which have now become extremely expensive investment vehicles.

No one can predict an absolute bottom for a particular kind of stock or asset class. Small stocks are no exception. What can be said, however, is that as of late 1999, small stocks are very, very cheap compared to their bigger brethren. They may take off immediately or stay cheap for another year or two, but based on their value relative to the current Nifty 50, by starting to buy now, you will be very well rewarded when the turn finally comes.

THE MOST CONSISTENT WAY TO BEAT THE PROS

When buying small stocks and new issues, you, the individual investor, have an important edge over the pros. That is because the small investor has the advantage of being able to get in and out of small stocks without moving their prices. Most money managers cannot buy a stock that is less than $100 million in market cap. Buying $500,000 worth of a $10 stock that trades 10,000 shares a day could drive the price 20 percent higher just in getting the position. Without another willing buyer, the stock will drift back to its original value. On the other hand, an individual investor can buy up to $10,000 worth without moving the price higher. This represents a huge advantage over the professional when trading small stocks.

Jeff Vinik did an absolutely phenomenal job during the two years he ran the giant Fidelity Magellan Fund by heavily overweighting technology stocks when they were beating the market. That successful sector bet powered the fund to the top of its class. Stocks like Cisco Systems, Compaq, IBM, Intel, Motorola, and Texas Instruments are big enough for even Fidelity Magellan to invest in without affecting the market—but what happens when Fidelity Magellan decides to get *out* of those stocks? Even those big names could underperform as word spread that Vinik was selling, and it was just about impossible to keep it a secret.

At mid-1999, the Fidelity Magellan Fund had almost $100 billion under management. That represents more than 25 percent of the combined value of all 600 stocks in the S&P SmallCap 600 index. With such a large amount of assets to manage, it becomes difficult for a money manager to invest in small niche industries—often those that are growing the fastest. As it gets harder to exploit these anomalous performance advantages, returns inevitably trend toward the mean—that is, toward the market average.

There have been other stars, managers such as Peter Lynch and George Vanderheiden at Fidelity, and Shelby Davis at the New York Venture Fund, who have run large portfolios and consistently beaten the market on a pretax basis over time. Like Vinik, they have been able to stay far enough ahead of the crowd by making the right sector bets using well-timed industry, capitalization, and value/growth weightings. But these are just a handful of the thousands of portfolio managers in the industry.

Despite what has occurred recently, the most predictable way to beat the market over the long run has been to buy small stocks. And there may never be a better time to get started. By running a smaller portfolio than professionals do, you can best capture what has come to be called the *small stock effect*. The next few chapters will give you a framework to judge better when to buy small stocks and IPOs, and when to get out.

2

HOW BIG A BET
SHOULD YOU MAKE
IN SMALL STOCKS?

MY UNCLE FRANKLIN bought mining stocks along with my dad in the 1950s, and, like most mining-stock buyers at the time, they lost their proverbial shirts. Uncle Franklin rarely bought another stock and essentially gave up on the market. As a New York City police officer, he was on a fixed salary and he did not know when he might be injured and forced to take early retirement. He stopped taking any financial risks at all.

Aunt Clara, Uncle Franklin's wife, on the other hand, was not afraid of taking risks, sometimes huge ones. In fact, legend has it that before she married my uncle she took just about everything she had gotten from an inheritance and bought a boxcar full of grapes in California for resale in New York. She expected to double her money in a month. But there was a railroad strike. The grapes spoiled outside Chicago and she lost every cent she put up.

Both relatives lost a fortune—my uncle by not taking on any risk at all (curious given his line of work), and my aunt by taking on too much of it. But what is the right level of risk to maximize returns without courting disaster? This chapter will give you some guidelines for that decision.

One of the basic questions you need to ask yourself is how much money you should put into small stocks. Informed allocation decisions require careful consideration. Your age, total wealth, stability of future income, and your comfort with stock-market risk are all important factors. But when you come right down to it, it is your investment time horizon— the period of time before the cash is needed—that should determine the amount you allocate to small stocks.

WITH SMALL STOCKS, TIME REDUCES RISK

When it comes to stocks, time is one of your greatest allies in managing investment risk. Small stocks benefit most from this rule. As mentioned in Chapter 1, huge returns in less than a year have been generated by buying small stocks at just the right moment, such as in 1974 and 1991. But even though the historical variation in payoffs from small stocks is higher than with stocks in general, you should never buy small stocks expecting to garner peak profits in any 12-month period. Indeed, a short-term focus is risky. Since 1926, according to Ibbotson Associates, there have been 21 one-year periods out of 72 when small stocks did worse than T-bills (see Table 2-1). That is 29 percent of the time. Returns have been negative a like number of times. Although the odds are a lot better than even that your stocks could outperform over a year, the chances are still decent that you could be a loser owning them, as well.

Owning small stocks for more than five years substantially reduces their added risk. From 1926 through 1998, there were 14 out of 71 three-year holding periods when returns were negative. That is 20 percent of the time. That is not bad, but a 1-in-5 chance remains troublesome. If you increase the holding period to five years, however, that risk comes down. As seen in Table 2-1, there were 9 five-year periods out of 65 (14 percent) when investors actually lost money owning small stocks—better than the 20 percent chance you had with a three-year holding period. And if you increase your holding period to 10 years, your odds improve even more: The chances of sustaining an absolute loss over any one 10-year period drops to just 3 percent, or a 1-in-33 possibility. That is a bet that just about any reasonable person would take.

But there are other considerations that could make it difficult for investors to sleep at night if the bulk of their net worth were in stocks like Eaton Vance, Global Marine, and SportsLine USA, however well they might do in the long run. Many individuals crave the predictability of future income streams from lower-risk investments (like blue chips and bonds). The following section discusses the issues that must be considered when deciding how much should be allocated to small stocks. After that are some concrete suggestions for dice rollers, middle-of-the-roaders, and scaredy-cat investors.

TABLE 2-1   Historical returns over different time periods, 1926 to 1998.

	S&P 500	Small Stocks	Salomon Bond Index	30-Day T-bills
No. of 1-year holdings	73	73	73	73
No. of annual losses	20	22	16	1
Percent of holding periods	27%	30%	22%	1%
Best annual return	54.0%	142.9%	42.6%	14.7%
Worst annual return	−43.3%	−58.0%	−8.1%	0.0%
Mean return	13.2%	17.4%	6.1%	3.8%
Standard deviation	20.3	33.8	8.6	3.2
No. of 5-year holding periods	69	69	69	69
No. of loss periods	7	9	3	0
Percent of holding periods	10%	13%	4%	Nil
Best 5-year average annual return	24.1%	45.9%	22.5%	11.1%
Worst 5-year average annual return	−12.5%	−27.5%	−2.2%	0.1%
No. of 10-year holding periods	64	64	64	64
No. of loss periods	2	2	0	0
Percent of holding periods	3%	3%	Nil	Nil
Best annualized return	20.1%	30.4%	16.3%	9.2%
Worst annualized return	−0.9%	−5.7%	1.0%	0.2%
No. of 20-year holding periods	54	54	54	54
No. of loss periods	0	0	0	0
Best annualized return	17.8%	21.1%	10.9%	7.7%
Worst annualized return	3.1%	5.7%	1.3%	0.4%

FOUR CONSIDERATIONS WHEN INVESTING IN SMALL STOCKS

Beyond the time horizon, there are four key factors that should always be considered as part of your asset allocation decision:

1.   Age
2.   Wealth
3.   Income predictability
4.   Risk tolerance

Age.   Although less important than your projected need for cash, your age and health affect how much you should allocate to small stocks. For example, a person who is 23 and expects to use available savings to buy a house 5 years from now can better afford the additional risk of small stocks than can, say, an 80-year-old who will need the funds to live on over the next 5 years. Both investors risk a short-term capital loss for the sake of likely higher results over the long term. But the risks are not the same for both investors. The retired person with little chance of generating additional capital from future income may experience a loss and find that basic living standards will have to be compromised over the next five years. Worse, there will be less money left, so an even greater percentage of the remaining assets will be spent over the next five years to maintain the current lifestyle, making it even more difficult to recoup losses should some remaining assets be left in small stocks. On the other hand, young wage earners who are just at the beginning of their earning years can suffer a loss but know that it only means happiness postponed.

To reduce risk as your investment period draws to a close, you should start to move your money out of small stocks and into those assets that will provide a surer return—albeit a smaller one—so that the required funds will be available when needed. Someone who has been 100 percent invested in small stocks between the ages of 35 and 55 and who wishes to retire in 5 years should probably reduce the small-stock allocation to about 30 percent, putting the rest into a combination of large-cap stocks, long-term corporate bonds, and cash. The remaining investment in small stocks is justifiable because, even for a retiree, the investment horizon can be quite long (essentially one's life expectancy or beyond).

A 60-year-old retiree is likely to live another 20 years. Hence, small stocks can logically remain a portion of a retiree's portfolio for most of that period.

Wealth.   Even for those strapped for cash, it makes sense to put some money into small stocks if the investment time horizon is apt to be greater than five years. But there is no denying that buyers with large cash reserves are better able to make one-time bets in small caps. Someone with reserves that will not be needed for awhile can "double up" toward the bottom of a bear market—something that most of us cannot afford to do. The less-wealthy buyer must hang on and keep the faith until the market turns higher.

It should be some consolation to a small investor, though, that whether a person is of modest means or extravagantly wealthy, the percentage gains or losses that can be achieved remain the same. Indeed, one could easily argue that a 100 percent gain on a $10,000 portfolio over 10 years could have a more positive impact on a person's lifestyle than the same return on a $100,000 portfolio for a wealthier person.

Income Predictability.   Even more important than your level of wealth is the predictability of your annual income stream when allocating assets. The lower the predictability of earnings, the less you should allocate to small stocks and other asset classes that have higher variations in annual investment returns. Take a self-employed artist who can make lots of money one year and very little the next. There could be certain years when savings have to be dipped into in order to meet current obligations. That could come just when small stocks have taken a swoon. Selling them then will chew up principal and could have a very adverse impact on portfolio performance over the years. By contrast, a two-income household of high school teachers working in a school district with a level student population can much more easily predict available disposable income over the following five years. Because of the relative steadiness of their earnings, they can establish financial requirements that would leave rainy-day assets undisturbed under all but the most dire circumstances.

Risk Tolerance.   Like most things in life, there are very few sure bets. Will a marriage work out? Was a home bought in the right town? Is it time for a job change?

One cannot ultimately be ruled by absolute surety. If that were so, no one would ever move beyond what they already know. We all play the odds and hope for the best. There are good odds that if small stocks are bought in the right way, the rewards will more than compensate for the risks assumed.

Fully armed with supporting statistics about the probable returns from stocks, bonds, money market funds, real estate, and collectibles, you should decide how much variation in results you are willing to accept over the near term in order to reach your long-term financial goals. Are you prepared to see 40 percent of your investment assets disappear in just 2 years, even though you will probably get it all back over the succeeding few years? If the answer is no, then you are not a candidate to make a big bet on small stocks.

Here is a simple gauge. If after perusing this book you are still paralyzed by the thought that investing in small caps could bring a lower return over the next 10 years than funds put in long-term T-bonds, then investing in this kind of asset is not for you. But if you are comfortable with the odds, as most people should be, then investing in small stocks should be a satisfying and profitable experience.

ASSET ALLOCATION DECISION MAKING

Table 2-2 presents a decision matrix that provides more specific guidelines for investing in small stocks. These allocation choices try to take into account all four of your key decision factors: investment time horizon, wealth, predictability of income, and risk tolerance.

For purposes of this model, the small-stocks category can be either a small-stocks mutual fund or a diversified portfolio of no less than 10 stocks. For large-cap stocks, an S&P 500 index fund can serve well, supplemented by an actively managed large-cap fund, or, of course, you can select the stocks yourself, most of which should be in the index. Bonds should be either investment-grade long-term corporates or municipal bonds, depending on your tax bracket.

Risk tolerance aside, since small stocks have excellent odds of outperforming when investment horizons are 10 years or better, small stocks should take preference over other asset classes whenever the time horizon is longer than that. When investors do have low risk tolerance, however, then a majority of equity investments should be in larger, more stable stocks. When the time horizon shortens and the investor's risk acceptance is low, the fixed-income and S&P 500 components rise. Except for the most willing risk takers with high income predictability, anyone with an investment horizon of less than one year should have most of their funds in fixed-income investments or cash or cash equivalents.

OPPORTUNITY COSTS OF NOT INVESTING IN STOCKS

Most investors put too little money into stocks, particularly into small stocks. Examples of investor timidity about buying equities are legion. Why is this the case? First, there are those investors (like my uncle Franklin) who've approached the market in an uninformed way, lost their shirt, and are subsequently very wary of doing it again. Then there are those investors who are simply so risk averse that they cannot rest easy if a stock drops in value, even overnight. These are the people who just cannot sleep at night if their portfolio takes any kind of short-term loss.

Investors in retirement accounts turn out to make some of the least propitious investment decisions of all. Analyses of how 401(k) participants invest in their funds show that most participants plan for their retirement by placing most of their savings in money market and bond funds. Worst of all, the lowest-income participants, those most in need of retirement savings, are avoiding equity investments in the largest numbers.

The irony of this is that by seeking to reduce their risk of capital loss by not investing in stocks, these investors incur the even larger problem of not

TABLE 2-2   Asset allocation guidelines.

Income and Comfort Level	Investment Horizon, Years				
	20	10	5	1	
High annual income, >$100,000					
High comfort	100%	80%	30%	10%	Small stocks
			30	20	Large stocks
		20	30	20	Corp. bonds, munis
			10	50	CDs, cash
Moderate comfort	80	40	10		Small stocks
	20	40	40	20	Large stocks
		20	40		Corp. bonds, munis
			10	80	CDs, cash
Low comfort	40	20			Small stocks
	40	40	40	20	Large stocks
	20	40	40		Corp. bonds, munis
			20	80	CDs, cash
Moderate annual income, $50,000 to $100,000					
High comfort	100%	60%	30%	10%	Small stocks
		20	30	20	Large stocks
		20	30		Corp. bonds, munis
			10	70	CDs, cash
Moderate comfort	80	40	10		Small stocks
		30	40	20	Large stocks
	20	30	30		Corp. bonds, munis
			20	80	CDs, cash
Low comfort	40	20			Small stocks
	40	40	40	20	Large stocks
	20	20	20		Corp. bonds, munis
		20	40	80	CDs, cash
Lower annual income, <$50,000					
High comfort	100%	60%	20%		Small stocks
		20	40	20	Large stocks
		20	20		Corp. bonds, munis
			20	80	CDs, cash
Moderate comfort	60	30			Small stocks
		20	40		Large stocks
	40	40	40		Corp. bonds, munis
		10	20	100	CDs, cash
Low comfort	30	10			Small stocks
	30	40	30		Large stocks
	40	40	20		Corp. bonds, munis
		10	50	100	CDs, cash

having enough money when they retire. Caution when buying stocks is under-standable, particularly given the bad experiences many have had at the hands of unscrupulous advisors. On the other hand, the penalties of not investing in stocks only compound with time, resulting in a devastating opportunity cost.

Consider the following illustration. If a risk-averse individual had allo-cated all of his or her retirement funds toward long-term government bonds for 20 years (1978 to 1997), the compound annual rate of return would have been 10.4%. Although this was an excellent period for such instruments, the results pall when compared to the 17.7% annual return that small stocks earned. If $10,000 had been put into the long-term government bonds dur-ing that period, it would have grown to $72,340, while the stock account would have burgeoned to $260,333, a difference of $187,993.

My dad lost a fortune in the 1973 to 1974 bear market just after his business failed. His biggest investment, Whittaker Corporation, went from 46 to 2. And he put the proceeds from the sale of his pharmacy into the Oppenheimer Time Fund right at the top of the market for growth stocks. He did not get even on that investment for a decade. In his fifties, it took a considerable degree of inner strength to stay the course and stick with stocks for retirement.

By 1980, Whittaker had recovered to the low 30s. Although Dad sold his fund in the early 1980s, he put the proceeds into a portfolio of individ-ual issues he and I had researched. The list included Coca-Cola, Du Pont, IBM, a bunch of utilities, and an assortment of smaller-cap names such as Metromail and good old Chock Full O'Nuts. Dad was not an exceptional stock picker, and his investment timing was average at best. But by the late 1980s, his considerable patience had brought him vindication.

Clearly, not buying stocks, and small stocks in particular, can mean missing out on above-average investment returns. With rare exceptions, small stocks should be a part of most investors' portfolios.

Here's a quick checklist for investors in three different risk-taking categories:

Advice for Risk-Takers

- Don't just look at what you can make, also consider what you can lose.
- Don't think that by taking the maximum risk, you will get the maxi-mum return.
- When buying risky stocks, diversify, diversify, diversify—own 10 to 20 stocks with none initially more than 10 percent of the portfolio.
- Don't just take someone's word for it. Make sure you are comfortable with an investment and understand the risks before committing to it.

Advice for Middle-of-the-Roaders

- Blessed are the patient investors with reasonable reward expectations, for they shall find great joy.

Advice for Scaredy-Cats

- Too much caution is harmful to your financial health.
- Just a small commitment to growth stocks can go a long way.
- Rely on trusted professionals running known, successful mutual funds to do the heavy lifting.
- Don't give up if your timing is off.

C H A P T E R

3

LIMITING RISKS AND BEATING THE MARKET

EVEN THOUGH SMALL stocks are good bets over the long run, any stock can always take a spill. Everyone can recall having had complete confidence in a stock pick, only to see it plummet in value. It happens all the time to the best investors. Who bought IBM at 175 in 1984, Digital Equipment at 200, and Discovery Zone at 34? "They" are us! Even Warren Buffett probably rues the day he bought USAir and Salomon Brothers.

But take faith in the knowledge that for all the sophistication, experience, and knowledge that a smart investor brings to the table, the better part of investment returns accrues from the original *asset allocation* decision. This means that your decisions about the major categories of your portfolio—such as big stocks, small stocks, and bonds—are much more important than the actual instruments you pick *within* those categories. As long as your stock portfolio is diversified, the decision to buy small stocks is the most important one you'll make. That's because the majority of a portfolio's investment performance comes from the original decision to own small stocks and not from the specific stocks bought.

Proof of this phenomenon is provided by a study published in mid-1986 in the *Financial Analysts Journal*. The authors, Gary Brinson, Brian Singer, and Gilbert Beebower, demonstrated that most of the returns achieved in stock portfolios are due to the asset allocation decision. Five years later, in a follow-up study, the authors reaffirmed their earlier findings. They analyzed the performance of 91 large pension plan investment portfolios and showed that fully 91.5 percent of investment returns are explained by basic asset allocation policy—that is, the original decision to own stocks. Individual stock selection came in a very distant second, accounting for 3.6 percent of performance. (Industry weightings accounted for 1.6 percent, with the remaining 3.2 percent of returns unexplained.)

The major implication of these studies is that a "top-down" approach—emphasizing asset allocation decisions rather than individual stock selection—is a better strategy than a stock-picking strategy. In fact, many professionals who try to beat the historical returns of the stock indexes (using different industry and stock weightings) usually fail. Of 82 equity funds that Brinson, Singer, and Beebower studied, 76 underperformed the S&P 500. (By contrast, two-thirds of the 70 funds that had invested in bonds beat their bond benchmark.) Since few professionals, let alone individual investors, have been able to beat their equity benchmarks for more than a few years at a time, it would appear that the effort required to beat overall small-cap stock performance (as measured by the S&P SmallCap 600, the Russell 2000, or Ibbotson's numbers) is not worth the risks assumed. The investment emphasis thus should be placed on owning a large enough list of stocks that will capture the small-stock effect in general. Any other bets should be made at the margin.

If being invested in small stocks is all that counts, buying a mutual fund like DFA's 9-10 Small Stock Fund or the Dreyfus Midcap 400 no-load fund would seem the best strategy. These truly diversified portfolios succeed at reducing the sometimes considerable risks associated with shifts in interest rates, currency exchange, inflation, and liquidity that all stock investors must assume. These funds *passively* invest—that is, they include in their portfolios all stocks within a certain capitalization sector of the market. (There are no industry and sector weightings that are different from the indexes they are intended to emulate.) In this way, these portfolios are most likely to match the historical returns for the small- to mid-cap sectors of the market.

One major problem, though, is that there is a $2 million minimum initial investment requirement for the DFA 9-10 fund. Vanguard has a few passively managed pure small-cap funds that aim to emulate the performance of the S&P SmallCap 600 or the Russell 2000, but the non-S&P small-cap index funds have had trouble mimicking the indexes they are supposed to track.

One could buy one or more of the actively managed small-cap growth and value funds but most of them have underperformed Ibbotson's historical returns for small stocks. Some exceptions include the RS Emerging Growth Fund, Weitz Hickory Fund, and Bear Stearns' Small Cap Value Fund.

The variation in returns for these small-cap equity funds has been quite wide. If you find a small-cap fund that consistently does better than other small-cap funds, stick with it, but remember most of them have significant style biases—some managers prefer *growth stocks* to *value stocks,* for example—that may or may not add to returns over an investor's time horizon. The fund owner's risk profile may also eventually diverge from that of the manager as time passes, or the portfolio manager may change.

There are a lot of good reasons why you might entrust your funds with professional portfolio managers. You might not have the time, interest, or, in the end, acumen to manage your own portfolio. If you do decide to invest in a small-cap mutual fund, don't expect most of them to match the returns of the small-cap indexes. But you *will* generally receive better returns than from most large-cap funds over time, and without spending a lot of time learning how to invest. Just buy one or two of the better performing small-cap funds and be done with it.

But bear in mind that it is small-cap stocks that offer the best chances for small investors to beat the professionals. Although the funds Bear Stearns runs are small enough to give its portfolio managers a decent shot at beating their benchmarks, most portfolio managers run such big funds that they cannot buy enough good small stocks to make much of a difference in their overall performances, or they must buy so many shares that they artificially move the market higher when they buy and lower when they sell. Of the more than 10,500 stocks that are in the S&P Stock Guide database, 5600 have market capitalizations of less than $100 million. Also, portfolio managers often don't have as much of an information edge when researching these companies. For example, many of the stocks in the S&P SmallCap 600 Index, which are typically the more liquid and well-known issues in the small-cap universe, are tracked by only one or two securities analysts. The majority of stocks with market capitalizations under $50 million have no research coverage at all. This more level playing field provides a good opportunity for individual investors to unearth undiscovered gems.

ACTIVE PORTFOLIO MANAGEMENT WITH SMALL STOCKS

To match or exceed small-cap index returns, avoid large sector bets by picking enough stocks in many different industries. You should also avoid trying to time the market—a tactic that pays off handsomely only once every 10 or 20 years.

Does major sector betting or market timing ever add significantly to investment returns? Sometimes. Now might be one of those historic moments to make a timely lump sum purchase of small stocks, but then, your weightings may be off. Unless you are very astute about the country's economic cycle, and good at picking the right industries, hedge your bets. Create a diversified portfolio. If you're wrong, the downside is limited. Otherwise, considerable damage could be wrought on your portfolio returns. Incorrect market calls or sector allocations, along with the investment management fees and portfolio turnover costs, cause most mutual funds to underperform the S&P 500. A well-diversified investor-picked portfolio without a lot of turnover has just as much potential to outperform the market.

One conservative and safe route to better returns is to put most of the money allocated to small stocks into one or two small-cap mutual funds that have good long-term track records, and the rest into a small-cap portfolio of one's own making. Section 3 of this book concentrates on individual stock selection. For the moment, our focus is on portfolio construction.

CREATING A DIVERSIFIED PORTFOLIO
The key to beating the market averages is making small sector bets and picking the right stocks within each industry. By diversifying your portfolio, you can ensure that your investment returns will at least approximate the results small stocks have turned in over the years. A portfolio of at least 10 to 20 stocks *that are not all in the same industries or industry sector* should do the trick. To be truly diversified, such a portfolio should include stocks that will go in different directions should interest rates rise and economic conditions change. Your portfolio should also reflect varied investment orientations. For example, a diversified portfolio should have both high-price-earnings (P/E) *growth* stocks and low-P/E *value* stocks, as well as cyclical, financial, and technology issues.

As mentioned before, professional investors often intentionally overweight certain segments of the market. They have their opinions about which parts of the economy will do well based on their forecasts of economic growth and the direction of interest rates. For most of us, too, sector bets are an integral part of the investment process. However, a highly skewed portfolio can diverge significantly from the benchmark indexes. The portfolio analysis tools I use to analyze analysts' stock-picking ability have revealed that it is easier for S&P analysts to pick good stocks than it is for them to properly weight those holdings within a portfolio.

If you are going to make sector bets, do so at the margin. That way, if you do pick the right industries, you can add a few percentage points to your returns. As has been pointed out, consistently adding a few percentage points to annual returns can have a profoundly favorable impact on investment profits over time. If you're wrong at the margin, you'll still probably beat the overall market over the long run because of your emphasis on small-cap stocks.

Also bear in mind that good stock picks in winning industries typically become larger percentages of the total portfolio. Hence, the better-performing stocks will automatically skew the industry concentration of a portfolio toward the better-performing groups. You generally would not rebalance the portfolio and sell such winners, but would concentrate on replacing stocks that are underperforming their peers. But if 1 name within a 10-stock portfolio starts to approach 20 percent of the total value of a portfolio, start to trim the position back. For a 20-stock portfolio, reduce your exposure when it gets above 15 percent. Otherwise, *cut your losses and let your profits run.*

The point of portfolio diversification is that you don't have to swing for the fences and risk striking out in order to win the game. Home runs are great to look at and provide a special thrill for the hitter, but most hitters strike out more often than they hit four-baggers. In investing as well as in baseball, the odds are against most investors becoming all-stars.

TIMING THE MARKET IS RARELY SMART
One-time bets can increase profits too, just as can choosing the right industries to invest in. But again, do it at the margin. Most professionals and individual investors fail to add anything to their investment returns by timing the market.

But you can try to add a little value by making prudent side bets, judiciously paring your exposure to small stocks as they get expensive or increasing your exposure when they are cheap. By making modestly active investment decisions on the market, be it small market-timing bets or slight changes in industry weightings, you can increase your investment returns without compromising the superior small-stock effect in general. Thus, you can still feel you are part of the game without risking a great deal to participate.

I have hopefully, by now, convinced you not to make major overall market-timing bets, but lest you think I am just trying to avoid a major decision, the next few sections of this chapter are devoted to providing a framework for beating the market. After that, some examples of diversified portfolios are provided. Picking the right stocks for inclusion in these portfolios once the industry weightings have been established is discussed in Sections 2 and 3.

A lump-sum investment should be made when stock market conditions dictate, not when you just happen to come into money. If no funds are readily available, you can make prudent use of your margin account. Any such decisions, of course, entail having some fairly strong understanding of and convictions about potential stock returns over the following few years.

THE GREAT VARIABLES: INFLATION, P/E RATIOS, AND FUTURE EARNINGS

When is it the best time to buy small stocks? Basically, the same time that it's best to buy all stocks, because the most important market-timing factors affecting small stocks are the same as those affecting all stocks.

Is it really possible for a nonprofessional investor to accurately time the market? Perhaps, but *clear signals to buy or sell the market are very rare.* The most visible flags of a major market bottom—moments when stocks are unbelievably cheap based on historical valuation methods—usually come only once or twice in a lifetime. The same is true for peaks. Acting on the courage of your convictions at crucial moments like these can provide major payoffs.

What are the factors that signal the need to act? And how should you evaluate them? There are plenty of variables that influence stock prices but they can be boiled down to three basic variables:

- Price/earnings (P/E) ratios
- Current earnings
- Inflation

Why is inflation important? Simply put, there is an inverse relationship between P/E ratios and inflation. The most important reason for this relationship is that the current price of a stock represents a firm's future earnings and dividend flows, discounted to come up with a *present value* for those earnings. The rate used to discount the future earnings and dividend streams is a function of inflation. Thus, the P/E of the market changes based on fluctuations in interest rates. If inflation expectations change from, say, 4 to 3 percent, the present value of future earnings increases. The result is that investors will raise the P/E that they are willing to pay for a firm's future earnings, say, from 14 to 18. These changes in valuation have the greatest impact on overall stock prices. Conversely, when inflation goes up, the P/E applied to company earnings goes down, and so do stock prices.

Are Stocks Expensive Now?

By many measures, the answer is yes, but there are three significant factors that suggest otherwise.

First, there is an inverse relationship between P/E ratios and inflation and interest rates. Lower long-term interest rates should keep P/E ratios high. Interest rates should remain low or drop further because of long-term demographic trends, which will be at work over the next 30 years throughout the industrialized world. The aging of the population, not only in the United States, but in Europe and Japan as well, has created a bubble of savings for college education, retirement, and estate purposes. It has been consistently the case that most people spend at the greatest rate relative to their incomes while in their twenties and thirties, and save the most when in their forties and fifties. The baby boom population bubble suggests that there will continue to be excess demand for equities coming from these quarters until at least 2005. This in and of itself could keep P/E ratios well above the historical average.

Second, continuing productivity improvements can keep production costs tame when they historically would be rising. Many providers of new products and services are choosing to increase profits by *cutting* prices to spur greater demand. Better inventory management is dramatically reducing working capital requirements.

Third, and most important, as investors become more comfortable owning stocks, the historical risk premium that stocks have typically traded at relative to supposedly less risky assets, such as bonds and savings certificates, will continue to decline. Research suggests that stock returns are no more volatile than those of long-term bonds. If this is the case, then the risk premium, relative to fixed income assets, could disappear altogether. That could further buoy P/E ratios and keep them well above their twentieth-century levels in the twenty-first century.

Because timing the market is more art than science (if not just plain luck), it is a good deal easier to just take a buy-and-hold strategy rather than time the tops and bottoms. The 12.4 percent historical annual return for small stocks is not hay.

THE RULE OF 20

One way of judging whether stocks are cheap or expensive on a near- to intermediate-term basis is by systematizing the inverse relationship that exists between inflation and P/E ratios. In the 1960s, some professional investors hit upon the notion that the underlying rate of inflation, as denoted by the Consumer Price Index (CPI), when added to the trailing P/E on the S&P 500, should equal 20. Although there is no firm theoretical underpinning to such an idea, there is quite a bit of empirical evidence to support this view.

Let's go back to 1981. Entering the year, inflation was running at about 10.1 percent, while the P/E of the S&P 500 was 9.2. The sum was 19.3. At mid-1982, inflation was clearly coming down. If investors could foresee it staying, say, consistently under 7 percent, the market P/E could rise to 13 (13 + 7 = 20), a whopping 41 percent jump. The variable here is the P/E based on inflation expectations. Investors may not have had a clear view of how far interest rates might drop, but when the Fed finally cut rates, it was clear that they were likely to enter a long-term period of decline from unusually high double-digit levels. Over the next 12 months, as interest rates fell, the stock market rose 53 percent even though the economy was still in recession and corporate profits had not turned substantially higher. At mid-1983 the market P/E was 13.4, inflation was 3.7 percent, and the interest rate of the long bond was down to 11 percent.

In mid-1987, just before the crash, interest rates were rising as earnings picked up steam. The market P/E was above 20. With inflation running at 3.3 percent, the market was trading well above what it should have been under the Rule of 20. With the trend in inflation and interest rates clearly up, the likelihood of a market decline was definitely high.

Table 3-1 illustrates these relationships. It includes the ending P/E ratio of the S&P 500 by each quarter, the trailing 12-month inflation rate, and the sum of those 2 numbers, for the 20 years, ending with June 1998.

Why does the Rule of 20 work? Because of the inverse relationship between P/E ratios and inflation. *P/E ratios and stock prices are likely to rise when interest rates are trending down and fall when rates are moving higher* (see Figure 3-1).

Of lesser significance, the market typically *rises* when projected real gross domestic product (GDP) growth is expected to be 2.5 percent or better (and inflation is not rising) and *declines* when GDP growth is headed lower (and inflation is flat or moving higher).

One other very long range tool is the measure of equities as a percentage of household assets. These statistics are provided by the government, and further refinements of the numbers are made by various private organizations. When stocks as a percentage of household assets fall below 20 percent, it's bullish, and when they are more than 35 percent, it's bearish. This means there are fewer and fewer potential new buyers out there to push prices higher.

TABLE 3-1   Rule of 20 relationships for quarters ending December 1972 to June 1998.

Date	Inflation Rate	S&P 500 P/E	Total
12/29/72	4.1	18.4	22.5
3/30/73	4.9	16.4	21.3
6/29/73	6.8	14.4	21.2
9/28/73	7.8	14.1	21.9
12/31/73	6.8	12.0	18.8
3/29/74	8.7	11.2	19.9
6/28/74	9.1	9.8	18.9
9/30/74	13.4	7.0	20.4
12/31/74	13.0	7.7	20.7
3/31/75	9.2	9.9	19.1
6/30/75	5.8	12.0	17.8
9/30/75	7.7	10.8	18.5
12/31/75	6.6	11.3	17.9
3/31/76	3.9	11.9	15.8
6/30/76	4.1	11.3	15.4
9/30/76	5.8	11.0	16.8
12/31/76	6.7	10.8	17.5
3/31/77	6.6	9.8	16.4
6/30/77	6.7	9.6	16.3
9/30/77	5.6	9.0	14.6
12/30/77	6.2	8.7	14.9
3/31/78	7.2	8.2	15.4
6/30/78	9.2	8.5	17.7
9/29/78	7.4	8.9	16.3
12/29/78	8.5	7.8	16.3
3/30/79	8.4	7.6	16.0
6/29/79	9.9	7.4	17.3
9/28/79	8.3	7.5	15.8
12/31/79	7.7	7.3	15.0
3/31/80	9.8	6.7	16.5
6/30/80	9.5	7.7	17.2

TABLE 3-1   Rule of 20 relationships for quarters ending December 1972 to June 1998 (*Continued*).

Date	Inflation Rate	S&P 500 P/E	Total
9/30/80	9.4	8.6	18.0
12/31/80	10.3	9.2	19.5
3/31/81	10.9	9.3	20.2
6/30/81	7.5	8.7	16.2
9/30/81	8.8	7.7	16.5
12/31/81	6.7	8.1	14.8
3/31/82	5.6	7.6	13.2
6/30/82	4.8	7.7	12.5
9/30/82	5.5	8.9	14.4
12/31/82	3.7	11.1	14.8
3/31/83	3.4	12.3	15.7
6/30/83	3.7	13.4	17.1
9/30/83	3.4	12.5	15.9
12/30/83	3.6	11.8	15.4
3/30/84	2.9	10.4	13.3
6/29/84	2.9	9.5	12.4
9/28/84	3.1	10.0	13.1
12/31/84	2.8	10.1	12.9
3/29/85	3.7	11.0	14.7
6/28/85	3.2	12.3	15.5
9/30/85	2.7	12.0	14.7
12/31/85	3.0	14.5	17.5
3/31/86	1.7	16.5	18.2
6/30/86	2.0	17.1	19.1
9/30/86	2.4	16.0	18.4
12/31/86	2.7	16.3	19.0
3/31/87	2.9	20.2	23.1
6/30/87	2.4	20.1	22.5
9/30/87	3.3	22.4	25.7
12/31/87	3.5	15.6	19.1
3/31/88	2.6	14.8	17.4

TABLE 3-1   Rule of 20 relationships for quarters ending December 1972 to June 1998 (*Continued*).

Date	Inflation Rate	S&P 500 P/E	Total
6/30/88	4.3	14.8	19.1
9/30/88	5.8	12.4	18.2
12/30/88	3.9	12.2	16.1
3/31/89	4.2	12.3	16.5
6/30/89	4.7	13.1	17.8
9/29/89	3.1	13.7	16.8
12/29/89	3.4	14.7	18.1
3/30/90	4.4	14.9	19.3
6/29/90	5.2	16.4	21.6
9/28/90	4.2	14.3	18.5
12/31/90	3.9	15.3	19.2
3/29/91	4.6	17.6	22.2
6/28/91	2.8	17.7	20.5
9/30/91	2.6	20.0	22.6
12/31/91	2.3	22.9	25.2
3/31/92	2.9	25.5	28.4
6/30/92	2.1	25.2	27.3
9/30/92	1.5	24.7	26.2
12/31/92	3.0	24.3	27.3
3/31/93	3.6	23.5	27.1
6/30/93	2.3	23.8	26.1
9/30/93	1.6	23.8	25.4
12/31/93	2.7	23.0	25.7
3/31/94	2.2	20.3	22.5
6/30/94	2.2	19.8	22.0
9/30/94	2.6	18.3	20.9
12/30/94	2.5	17.0	19.5
3/31/95	2.1	16.5	18.6
6/30/95	1.9	16.8	18.7
9/29/95	1.7	16.9	18.6
12/29/95	1.5	17.4	18.9

**TABLE 3-1   Rule of 20 relationships for quarters
ending December 1972 to June 1998 (*Continued*).**

Date	Inflation Rate	S&P 500 P/E	Total
3/29/96	1.9	18.9	20.8
6/28/96	2.0	19.3	21.3
9/30/96	1.7	19.7	21.4
12/31/96	1.4	20.8	22.2
3/31/97	2.5	19.9	22.4
6/30/97	1.8	22.4	24.2
9/30/97	1.2	24.0	25.2
12/31/97	1.0	24.5	25.5
3/31/98	0.5	28.0	28.5
6/30/98	0.5	27.3	27.8

At the end of the last great bull market in 1969, stocks were 38 percent of household assets. By 1982, that number had fallen to 18 percent. As of year-end 1998, stocks were a record 40 percent of household assets.

BASED ON THE RULE OF 20,
STOCKS ARE EXPENSIVE, BUT . . .

The rising amount of equities held by investors is worrisome. It is a definite sign that we are entering the latter stages of a bull market that began more than 13 years ago. By the Rule of 20, stocks are at best fairly valued. As of mid-1998, inflation was rising at about 0.5 percent and the S&P 500 P/E ratio on trailing 12-month earnings was 27.3. So, according to the Rule of 20, stocks were about 39 percent overvalued.

What might be the expected rate of return over the 12 months ending June 30, 2000? If you use trailing 12-month earnings per share and a projection of inflation of about 2.5 percent, the potential return for stocks would be quite negative (2.5 + 28 = 30.5). The potential return is −34 percent [(20/30.5) = 0.66 − 1 = −0.34].

Could things turn out better? Sure. Overall P/Es above 20 can be justified if earnings continue to grow at or above the historical rate of 7 percent a year *and* long-term interest rates drop to and remain well below 5 percent. Right now, with GDP apt to slow over time as the population in the major industrial economies ages, the U.S. government running a surplus, and the general Pax Americana holding firm, the likelihood for long-term interest

**FIGURE 3-1   Inverse relationship between the S&P 500 P/E ratio
and the rate of inflation.**
(Source: © FactSet Research Systems, Inc.. Printed with permission.)

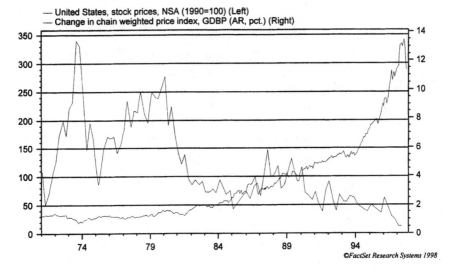

— United States, stock prices, NSA (1990=100) (Left)
— Change in chain weighted price index, GDBP (AR, pct.) (Right)

©FactSet Research Systems 1998

rates to trend well below 5 percent appears very good. The jury is out, however, on whether earnings will be able to grow at or above 7 percent as GDP
growth slows. More likely is that earnings growth will be lower, stock
returns will be less than the historic average, and the difference in real
return between long-term bonds and stocks, which has averaged 7.2 percentage points over the very long run, will be somewhat less going forward.
Nonetheless, should earnings grow at an average 5 percent, the dividend
yield hover at 2 percent, P/Es stay roughly where they are now, inflation
ease to 1 percent, and the long-term bond trade under 4 percent, small-
stock investors could still garner an extra 4 percentage points of return over
the long bond over the coming decade, without counting the favorable tax
effects from generating capital gains rather than interest or dividend
income. In other words, the *absolute level* of returns from stocks could easily be lower, but the *real return* to investors will continue to be better than
for other major financial asset classes. These market conditions have never
held over a sustained period of time. If they ever do, the Rule of 20 as an
accurate gauge of stock valuation would come to an end, and a new investment paradigm of high profit growth with low inflation would take over. It
is not yet certain that this scenario will materialize, but if the current high
level of productivity gains are sustainable, one can indeed foresee low
inflation accompanied by mid-single-digit real corporate profit growth.

Such an economic backdrop could justify currently high P/E ratios or even higher levels in the coming decades.

MARKET-TIMING SUMMARY

To summarize: Over a complete, secular market cycle, the *worst* time to make a one-time purchase is when inflation added to the P/E is above 20 and inflation and interest rates are rising. The *best* time to buy is when the market P/E is below 10 and interest rates have just started to come down. This usually signals the end of a protracted bear market. This was the case at the end of 1974 and again toward the close of 1981. Those would have been the best times to make a short-term bet on the market. Otherwise, the best thing to do is to steadily invest in annual increments regardless of recent market action.

BACKDROP FOR STOCKS IN THE LATE 1990s

A still more systematic rendering of the relationship between the beginning level of stock prices, corporate earnings, and interest rates was recently published by John C. Bogle, who also recently retired as head of the Vanguard group of investment companies. Back in the fall of 1991, Bogle published an article in the autumn issue of the *Journal of Portfolio Management* suggesting some tools for forecasting likely 10-year stock returns. In one of the most important practical contributions to the art of investing, Bogle persuasively argued that stock returns can be explained by three things:

1.   The dividend yield at the start of the period
2.   The rate of historical earnings growth
3.   The annual impact on returns as the market P/E moves back to the historical average

To come up with projected returns for stocks from 1990 to 1999, he added the beginning dividend yield of equities as measured by the S&P 500 (3.1 percent) to the average earnings growth for the last 30 years (6.6 percent) and the effect on annualized returns caused by the movement of P/E ratios from current levels to the historic norms for the previous 30 years (15.5). The result was as follows:

	1990 to 1999
Initial yield	3.1%
Earnings growth rate	6.6%
Impact of multiple change	−1.0%
Projected 10-year annual return	**8.7%**

Guess what the annual total return of the S&P 500 was for the first five years of the period? Exactly 8.7 percent. Lest you think that an aberration, here are the statistics for the decades beginning in 1970 and 1980, compared with actual returns:

	1970s		1980s	
	Model	Actual	Model	Actual
Initial yield	3.4%		5.2%	
Earnings growth rate	6.4%		6.4%	
Impact of multiple change	−1.4%		6.9%	
Projected 10-year annual return	**8.4%**	**5.9%**	**18.5%**	**17.6%**

Bogle wrote a follow-up article in 1995. What did he forecast for the following 10 years? Here were his targets:

	1995 to 2004
Initial yield	2.9%
Earnings growth rate	6.4%
Impact of multiple change	−0.9%
Projected 10-year annual return	**8.4%**

What could lower the results even further over the next few years is the subsequent run-up in stock prices—37 percent in 1995, 23 percent in 1996, and 33 percent in 1997. Averaging that out over the following 7 years reduces the potential annual return to just 2.2 percent. This return is historically very low but entirely possible since returns in the 1980s and early 1990s were well above the mean. But Bogle's second study was done at the end of 1994. At year-end 1998, the initial yield was down to 1.6 percent. Adding the earnings growth of more than 11 percent achieved in 1995 and 14 percent achieved in 1996 to the average for the last 30 years raised the earnings growth rate, but the favorable impact was small (about 0.6 percent). But the impact from a change in the P/E multiple was quite severe. By Bogle's model, projected annual returns over the next 10 years should be about 3.6 percent. If we are right that small-cap stocks are very undervalued, they should do a few percentage points better than that.

	1999 to 2008
Initial yield	1.6%
Earnings growth rate	7.0%
Impact of multiple change	−5.0%
Projected 10-year annual return	**3.6%**

Does all this make any intuitive sense? Sure. The initial yield of the S&P 500 is a good measure of how expensive stocks are relative to the historic norm; stock prices should rise when earnings growth increases; and P/E ratios should eventually return to the historical average over time.

SMALL STOCKS WILL OUTPERFORM EARLY IN THE TWENTY-FIRST CENTURY

This may be a good time to reprise our argument that stocks are cheap compared with larger ones. Toward year-end 1999, the P/E of the S&P SmallCap 600 index was 15 times the consensus 2000 estimates for companies that comprised it. That compares with 24 times for the S&P 500. Despite the substantially lower P/E, earnings for companies in the S&P SmallCap 600 were expected to rise 33 percent over the next year, compared with 9 percent for the S&P 500. Both these numbers appear unrealistic given that GDP growth was expected to slow in 1999, but the point here is that earnings growth for small companies should still be better than that for large-cap companies, yet their P/Es are much lower. That extra earnings growth is typically the case because small companies tend to grow faster than mature ones. With valuations very reasonable and the capital gains tax lower, small stocks have a better chance of rising over the next five years or so. Finally, we have entered the last and most speculative phase of a bull market that, arguably, began either in late 1974 or in mid-1982 and, despite what occurred in 1998, has yet to come to an end. Although they have not done so to date, small stocks tend to do best during these market phases.

If we are right that stocks will provide lower returns than has historically been the case—that is, slightly more than those of long-term fixed-income investments, but better than other forms of investment—and that stocks are entering the last, most speculative stage of an aging bull market, it means that small stocks will initially do quite well over the next few years, will tumble more during the inevitable bear market, and then will revive faster when the new bull market commences.

REVIEW OF MARKET-TIMING POINTERS

As is emphasized throughout this chapter, timing the market is a difficult task. The possibility that history will not serve us well remains a stubborn fact. It can be very rewarding when someone is able to read the tea leaves. But very few professionals have been able to consistently add value by timing when to get into and out of the stock market.

There is one way that we recommend aggressive investors time their small-cap stock-buying decisions. That is to purchase additional stock at the bottom of bear markets using margin. By this strategy investors do have to withstand the agony of enduring the tail end of a bear market fully invested, but by *adding* to fully invested positions when stocks are very cheap, *one can dramatically improve returns.* Eliminate the margin position when the market P/E gets into the midteens on current-year estimated earnings. This strategy is recommended because it is typically easier to perceive the bottom of a bear market than market tops. And by always being fully invested in stocks, the large opportunity cost of getting out at the wrong time is eliminated.

SECTOR BETTING: ANOTHER SIDE BET THAT CAN IMPROVE RETURNS

When deciding how to tilt one's portfolio toward different industries, the first item on the agenda is knowing the sector weightings of the overall market. Tables 3-2 and 3-3 show the important characteristics and sector weights of the S&P 500, S&P MidCap 400, and S&P SmallCap 600 indexes as of June 30, 1999. As you can see, there are small variations among them

TABLE 3-2   Important index characteristics.

	S&P Index*		
Characteristic	500	MidCap 400	SmallCap 600
Total capitalization, $ billion	11,232	927	357
U.S. capitalization, %	78	6	2
1-y trailing performance, %	23	17	−2
Annual average portfolio turnover as of 12/31/98, %	6	14	14
Average capitalization, $ million	22,463	2316	595
Median capitalization, $ million	8,452	1789	483

* Data as of June 30, 1999.

TABLE 3-3   Index sector weightings.

| | S&P Index* | | |
Sector	500	MidCap 400	SmallCap 600
Technology	22%	22%	18%
Consumer staples	13	9	10
Health care	11	9	9
Consumer cyclicals	9	16	21
Capital goods	8	9	13
Communications services	8	1	—
Energy	6	4	4
Basic materials	3	6	5
Financials	16	12	15
Utilities	3	9	5
Transportation	1	1	3

* Data as of June 30, 1999.

TABLE 3-4   Sample sector weights for small-cap portfolios.

| | Passive Portfolio Weights (S&P Small Cap 600) | | 20-Stock Active Portfolio Weights | |
Sector	10-Stock Portfolio	20-Stock Portfolio	Interest Rates Rising	Interest Rates Falling
Consumer cyclicals	2	3	2	4
Technology	2	4	3	4
Capital goods	1	2	1	2
Health care	1	2	4	2
Consumer staples	1	2	5	1
Basic materials	—	1	—	1
Energy	1	1	—	1
Communications services	—	1	2	—
Financials	2	3	1	4
Utilities	—	1	2	—
Transportation	—	—	—	1

that allow each index to accurately reflect the sector weightings of the stocks they are meant to represent.

We would adjust the weightings by overweighting the following sectors when interest rates are rising or falling:

Interest Rates Rising	*Interest Rates Falling*
Value stocks	Growth stocks
Consumer staples	Financials
Health care	Technology
Utilities	Consumer cyclicals (early in rate drop)
Communications services	Capital goods
Energy	Basic materials (early in drop)

The last step to take in portfolio creation is allocating the actual number of stocks that a portfolio should have in each industry group. Table 3-4 shows four model small-cap portfolios. The first two 10- and 20-stock portfolios are matched to the sector weightings of the S&P SmallCap 600 index. The third and fourth 20-stock portfolios reflect our sector weightings for rising and falling interest rate environments.

SECTION II

C H A P T E R

INVESTING IN IPOs: FINDING THE GAPs AND IBMs OF TOMORROW

NETSCAPE IS SCHEDULED to go public at 12 to 14 per share. The price is raised to 20, then to 28. The first trade is at 72 and it closes the first day of trading above 58. During the next few weeks, it drifts down as low as 46, and then skyrockets past 100 during the following 3 months. Incredibly, Goldman Sachs next recommends purchase of the stock at 125. It peaks at 174 within 30 days. If you had bought the stock on the first trade (72), and sold at 50, you would have lost 31 percent of your investment in just a matter of weeks. But whoever bought it from you would have tripled their money in just a few months.

Compaq Computer goes public in June 1983 at 11. It hardly moves when it opens. Ten months later it is at 4⅝, down 58 percent. Twelve years later it's at the equivalent of 474.

3DO, the video game maker, an April 1993 IPO, opens 23 percent above its initial offering price of 15, and then closes the year at 22. One year after the offering, buyers of the IPO are under water. One year after that, they're down 42 percent.

Most people think that buying new issues at the offering is the surest way to make a lot of money fast. They're right. For many market participants, particularly insiders, the new-issues market represents the pot of gold at the end of the rainbow. It is probably the most volatile segment of the U.S. stock market, and an arena where a well-informed investor with well-placed contacts could make a mint. Even a small allocation of a hot deal can be easy money if the timing's right.

In the *aftermarket*—the period of time immediately following the opening trade—IPOs are a speculator's paradise. But for normal mortals, buying in the aftermarket has plenty of pitfalls. Nonetheless, even if you are not well positioned to make a fast buck, there are still some ways to profitably participate in this dynamic segment of the equities market without taking undue risks.

There are three golden rules of IPO investing:

1. Sell within three months of the offering.
2. Invest in industries at the start of an IPO cycle.
3. Sell during a market correction.

The rest of this chapter is devoted to proving the importance of these axioms.

IPO INVESTING RULE 1: SELL WITHIN THREE MONTHS OF THE OFFERING

New issues are a different breed of small-cap stock, posing challenges of a special kind to investors. Typically, initial public offerings (IPOs) outperform the broader market near term and then underperform thereafter. Unlike small stocks in general, with their excellent overall long-term performance record, IPOs provide the most reward as short-term trades (see Table 4-1).

Most new issues do very well in the *first three months* of trading, with particularly strong advances occurring on the first day. But even if one removes first-day performance from the record, IPOs tend to do better than the S&P 500 over their first 90 days of public life. Of the 370 new issues appraised by Standard & Poor's during the years 1992 through 1994, 241 rose more than the S&P 500 from the first day of trading over the following 3 months. And not by a small amount—the average gain was 19.6 percent, versus an average increase of 1.7 percent for the S&P 500 and 2.6 percent for the NASDAQ Composite Index.

A comparison of the returns of the S&P New Issues index with the S&P 500 also provides evidence of significant near-term outperformance.

TABLE 4-1   Short-term IPO returns versus the S&P 500.

Year	No. of Offerings	Average Initial Return*	Gross Proceeds, $ Million	S&P 500 Return
1960	269	17.8%	$ 553	0.47%
1961	435	34.1	1,243	26.89
1962	298	−1.6	431	−8.73
1963	83	3.9	246	22.80
1964	97	5.3	380	16.48
1965	146	12	409	12.45
1966	85	7.1	275	−10.06
1967	100	37.7	641	23.98
1968	368	55.9	1,205	11.06
1969	780	12.5	2,605	−8.50
1970	358	−0.7	780	4.01
1971	391	21.2	1,655	14.31
1972	562	7.5	2,724	18.98
1973	105	−17.8	330	−14.66
1974	9	−7.0	51	−26.47
1975	14	−1.9	264	37.20
1976	34	2.9	237	23.84
1977	40	21.0	151	−7.18
1978	42	25.7	247	6.56
1979	103	24.6	429	18.44
1980	259	49.4	1,404	32.42
1981	438	16.8	3,200	−4.91
1982	198	20.3	1,334	21.41
1983	848	20.8	13,168	22.51
1984	516	11.5	3,932	6.27
1985	507	12.4	10,450	32.16
1986	953	10.0	19,260	18.47
1987	630	10.4	16,380	5.23
Total	**8668**	**16.4%**	**$83,984**	

* From 1960 to 1976, percentage returns are to month-end. From 1977 to 1987, returns are first-day.
SOURCES: Ibbotson & Jaffe (1960–1970); Going Public: The IPO Reporter *(1983–1985);* Venture
magazine (1986–1987). Proceeds data has been adapted from SEC Monthly Statistical Bulletin *and*
Going Public: The IPO Reporter.

Started in 1982, the S&P New Issues index has tracked the performance of investment-quality new issues in the immediate aftermarket. Included in the index are all initial public offerings with an offering price of at least $5 and an offering capitalization of at least $5 million. Through late 1986, it measured IPO price changes over the first three months of trading, and for six months after that. As Figure 4-1 graphically illustrates, the index has substantially beaten the S&P 500 since its inception.

Don't Hang On Too Long

Although IPOs greatly outperform the market during the first three months of trading, *they underperform the market when held longer.* To test this theory, Standard & Poor's took a look at the IPO class of 1990 to see how the issues did during the first 15 months after the offering. They rose an average 50.5 percent—more than the return of the S&P 500 during the same period, but less than that of the NASDAQ Composite Index. More worrisome is that only 47 issues or 46 percent of the IPOs did better then the S&P 500. In other words, a few big winners masked the fact that most IPOs performed far worse than the market after their initial trading period was over. The same proved true of the IPO class of 1991.

In summary, most of the easy money is skimmed off the top in the first day of trading by investors lucky enough to get in on the offering. There will always be a Microsoft, a Novell, an Oracle, or a Xilinx that provides

FIGURE 4-1   Historical performance of the S&P New Issues index versus the S&P 500.

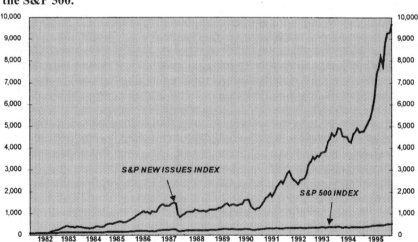

When Is the Best Time to Own IPOs?

As Table 4-2 shows, new issues do better during up market phases, and underperform when stocks are flat or decline. In the year following the bear markets of 1982 and 1990, the S&P New Issues index doubled. The predictability of these extra returns is borne out by a comparison of the monthly time series of the two indexes. Looking at the annual performance of the S&P New Issues index, it beat the S&P 500 in 14 out of the last 17 years. That is a whopping 82 percent of the time. The only exceptions were 1986, 1987, and 1990—years when small stocks underperformed.

TABLE 4-2   Comparison of S&P new issues index with the S&P 500 and the NASDAQ composite index.

Year	New Issues	S&P 500	NASDAQ Composite
1982	82.8%	14.7%	NA
1983	103.19	17.3	NA
1984	2.8	1.4	NA
1985	75.0	26.3	31.1%
1986	−2.5	14.6	7.5
1987	−13.9	2.0	−5.3
1988	20.7	15.7	15.4
1989	27.9	27.3	19.3
1990	−11.1	6.1	−17.8
1991	106.4	26.3	56.8
1992	42.7	4.5	15.5
1993	37.0	7.1	14.8
1994	2.5	−1.5	−3.2
1995	94.0	38.1	39.9
1996	27.7	20.3	22.7
1997	43.3	31.0	21.6
1998	37.3	28.6	39.6

prodigious returns if held for years, but the majority of new issues fade fast and do not come back. In the vast majority of cases, IPOs must be viewed strictly as short-term trading vehicles and we as investors should not look back after taking their gains. For every one we should have held, there will be two we were right to sell. Take the money and move on to the next idea.

To further show how short-term investing in IPOs is the most rewarding course, let's take a more real-world approach. It might be helpful to review the performance of a model portfolio of new issues over a long period of time. To that end, let's look at a 14-year track record of recommendations published in Standard & Poor's *Emerging & Special Situations* (*ESS*). *ESS* appraises more than 150 new issues each year, applying the following investment recommendations:

Avoid.	Not recommended for purchase.
Flip.	Sell within the first few days of trading, sometimes within the first hour.
Short-term buy.	Hold for less than three months.
Buy.	Three-month bet.
Long-term buy.	Hold from six months to a year.

From the inception of the publication in January 1982 through year-end 1995, 170 issues were recommended for purchase and placed in the publication's model portfolio (see Table 4-3). Of 135 closed positions, 83 advanced, 50 declined, and 2 were unchanged, for an average gain of 46 percent. The average holding period was one year, four months. That was certainly better than the S&P 500, which rose an average of 12 percent on a time-weighted basis.

But what would have happened if one had sold all of these new issues after the first three months of trading? Even with the names that S&P analysts thought would do best over a longer period of time, *most of the outperformance occurred during just the first three months of trading.* The average return for this period alone would have been a whopping 27 percent. Just as important, the capital employed could have been recycled more quickly and put back to profitable use. Using a three-month sale rule, the annual return of this portfolio would have been a truly astounding 264 percent.

Okay, we've proven the point that new issues are indeed good investments off the starting block. Now, what are the main reasons behind the stellar performance?

TABLE 4-3   S&P *Emerging & Special Situations* recommended IPO purchases.

Stock	Date	Pur-chase	Sale	Time Held, Months	Change Since IPO, %	S&P 500 Change, %
Technology for Com International	2/2/82	15½	8¼	32	−45%	45%
Vector Graphic	2/15/82	13¼	2⅞	21	−78	44
Seagate Technology	3/15/82	5⅛	17	17	232	50
Data Switch	4/27/82	5	31½	15	530	421
Convergent Technology	5/18/82	9	26	15	189	40
TERA	7/8/82	16	4½	27	−72	51
Diagnostic Products	7/19/82	7⅝	8¼	22	8	41
On-Line Software	9/29/82	15	8½	24	−43	37
InteCom	10/19/82	10	9⅝	27	−4	22
ARGOSystems	12/2/82	10¾	36⅝	54	241	108
Quantum	12/20/82	20	17	56	−15	129
Cooper Vision	1/21/83	18	26¾	35	49	47
Diasonics	2/23/83	22	8	9	−64	18
Televideo Systems	3/15/83	18	4⅛	19	−77	10
Integrated Software	3/23/83	16	16¼	7	2	9
MacNeal Schwendler	5/5/83	15¼	12¼	17	−18	−1
Daisy Systems	6/1/83	15½	11¼	33	−27	35
Marquest Medical	7/1/83	17	9½	43	−44	57
Comptek Research	7/14/83	13	9¾	29	−25	32
Stratus Computer	8/26/83	12	11	7	−8	−3
Equatorial Communications	9/13/83	14	18⅛	16	29	2
Provincetown-Boston Air	9/15/83	10	9¾	8	−3	−4
Lotus Development	10/6/83	13½	23¼	26	75	19
VLI	10/13/83	13	16¾	2	29	−3
Ashton Tate	11/10/83	14	7¾	11	−45	−1
Compaq Computer	12/9/83	11	4⅝	10	−58	−2

**TABLE 4-3   S&P *Emerging & Special Situations* recommended
IPO purchases (*Continued*).**

Stock	Date	Pur-chase	Sale	Time Held, Months	Change Since IPO, %	S&P 500 Change, %
Archive	12/16/83	10	4¾	10	−53	1
Medicine Shoppe International	12/16/83	5⅝	44⅝	21	693	259
Nico	2/1/84	11	16¼	16	48	14
Telco Systems	2/15/84	11	10¼	21	−2	27
Metromail	4/5/84	10	18	14	80	23
Russ Berrie	4/11/84	13½	24	11	78	15
Lam Research	5/4/84	10	20½	103	103	172
Silvar-Lisco	5/10/84	5	3¾	8	−25	5
Micron Technology	6/1/84	14	37⅜	3	167	7
Stuarts Dept. Stores	6/13/84	5	15½	19	210	36
Optrotech	8/9/84	7⁵⁄₁₆	10½	19	45	36
Ceradyne	8/15/84	7¼	15⅝	11	116	18
Direct Action Marketing	9/11/84	8½	6⅜	11	−25	15
Automated Systems	11/20/84	10¼	10⅛	13	−1	28
AST Research	12/20/84	7	30⅜	12	334	27
LSI Lighting	3/12/85	8⅜	13¼	18	59	28
PT Components	3/13/85	11½	12¼	4	7	8
Tri-Star Pictures	4/17/85	8½	14¾	7	74	9
Central Sprinkler	5/17/85	12¾	18¼	7	43	12
Maxtor	8/17/85	11	20¼	6	84	18
HomeClub	10/13/85	9	14	3	56	12
Doxsee Food	12/2/85	6¼	10¾	7	72	26
Concurrent Computer	1/24/86	20	12½	7	−38	21
Oliver's Stores	2/11/86	6	6⅛	9	2	9
Microsoft	3/13/86	21	50½	8	140	4
Price (T. Rowe)	4/2/86	24	42	1	77	—
SunGard Data Systems	5/3/86	11	18¼	27	66	16

TABLE 4-3   S&P *Emerging & Special Situations* recommended IPO purchases (*Continued*).

Stock	Date	Pur-chase	Sale	Time Held, Months	Change Since IPO, %	S&P 500 Change, %
Waterford Glass	7/1/86	20	15⅜	25	−23	8
Amer Cruise Lines	7/9/86	9½	4¼	4	−55	1
Steve's Ice Cream	7/11/86	8	15¾	2	97	−3
Golden Valley Microwave	9/16/86	14	39⅛	5	180	21
Chem Waste Management	10/16/86	17¼	39⅞	34	131	49
Convex Computer	10/17/86	7½	17⅜	4	132	20
Foodmaker	2/24/87	13½	13	18	−11	−4
Excelan	2/26/87	21¼	6½	29	25	19
Ecology & Environment	3/6/87	15	11⅛	23	−26	2
Forstmann & Co.	7/1/87	15	11¾	3	−22	8
EMCON Associates	9/16/87	12	24½	35	104	6
Liggett Group	10/18/87	12	8½	7	−29	12
NS Group	3/8/88	13¾	13¾	4	—	—
Mallard Coach	3/18/88	8	7¼	13	−9	13
Dell Computer	6/22/88	8½	7⅝	8	−10	6
Index Technology	6/23/88	12	11¾	2	−2	−5
Drug Emporium	6/30/88	14½	20¾	8	43	6
Casual Male	9/20/88	10	8¼	3	−18	3
Staples	4/27/89	19	25	23	32	21
GZA GeoEnvironmental	7/27/89	12	3⅞	68	−68	47
Sierra Tucson	10/20/89	12	22½	18	88	11
Tetra Technologies	4/2/90	10	15¾	16	58	14
Pool Energy Service	4/17/90	10¼	8¼	16	−20	12
K-Swiss	6/6/90	17½	28	1	60	−2
Micrografx	6/29/90	16	23¾	1	48	−1
Rocky Mountain Helicopters	9/11/90	7	3⅝	15	−48	18

**TABLE 4-3   S&P *Emerging & Special Situations* recommended
IPO purchases (*Continued*).**

Stock	Date	Pur-chase	Sale	Time Held, Months	Change Since IPO, %	S&P 500 Change, %
Symix Systems	3/2/91	15	19½	1	30	3
LXE	4/11/91	9½	19¾	7	108	4
AnnTaylor	5/17/91	26	20⅞	11	−20	12
Mediplex Group	8/13/91	20½	35⅛	34	71	21
Scherer, R. P.	10/11/91	18	30⅝	10	70	10
QUALCOMM	10/13/91	8	32¹⁄₁₆	35	301	23
Cardiopulmonics	1/17/92	11	6	5	−45	−4
Scholastic	2/25/92	22½	45	32	100	12
Coleman	2/26/92	19½	24½	8	26	1
Dames & Moore	3/5/92	20	20½	23	3	16
First Data	4/9/92	22	49	30	123	15
Waste Management International	4/14/92	23⅛	16⅛	23	−30	13
NetFrame Systems	6/4/92	9	20¾	5	131	1
Paco Pharmaceutical	8/20/92	10	7⅝	20	−24	6
Interphase	9/8/92	7¼	5	9	−31	7
Netrix	9/22/92	12	9⅝	5	−20	4
IQ Software	10/15/92	9	10	14	11	13
Hook SupeRx	11/10/92	11	7½	9	−32	7
Haggar	12/11/92	16½	19¼	30	17	22
Maybelline	12/11/92	23½	17¾	26	−24	11
SEACOR Holdings	12/16/92	15	25	11	67	8
Dr Pepper/7UP	1/27/93	15	33	26	120	15
Nathan's Famous	2/26/93	9	8⅜	10	−7	5
Payless Cashways	3/9/93	12¾	7¼	26	−43	15
Southern Energy Homes	3/12/93	13	18¾	9	44	3
Pillowtex	3/18/93	14	14⅞	16	6	1
Amtrol	3/19/93	15	20¾	6	38	2

**TABLE 4-3   S&P *Emerging & Special Situations* recommended
IPO purchases (*Continued*).**

Stock	Date	Pur-chase	Sale	Time Held, Months	Change Since IPO, %	S&P 500 Change, %
Rust International	5/10/93	17⅞	22¼	9	24	6
Discovery Zone	6/4/93	11	19	16	73	−1
MASISA	6/17/93	14⅛	18¾	3	33	2
Arethusa Offshore	8/4/93	10	12¾	18	28	13
Cornerstone Imaging	8/9/93	11	20⅝	12	88	2
Eckerd	8/10/93	17½	29⅞	15	71	3
Redman Industries	9/17/93	15	15⅞	10	6	−1
Gartner Group	10/5/93	12½	42⅜	17	239	5
Detroit Diesel	10/8/93	20	23⅛	16	16	5
IGEN	2/3/94	11½	5⅝	12	−51	—
Rock-Tenn	3/3/94	16½	16¾	5	2	—
Career Horizons	3/24/94	17½	17½	8	—	−3
Grupo Iusacell	6/14/94	27¼	14⅜	13	−47	21
Baby Superstore	9/27/94	18	35⅞	1	99	1
PRI Automation	10/13/94	13½	21⅞	5	62	5
Telex Chile	10/14/94	18¾	6¾	5	−64	5
HCIA	2/22/95	14	19¾	1	41	5
Tivoli Systems	3/10/95	14	36⅝	1	162	4
Premisys Communications	4/6/95	16	36¼	1	127	3
CBT Group	4/13/95	16	39½	2	147	5
Open Environment	4/13/95	15	22¾	2	52	5
Garden Ridge	5/9/95	15	33⅞	3	126	7
Astea International	7/27/95	15	18¾	1	25	−1
Red Lion Hotels	7/27/95	19	21⅞	1	15	−1
Netscape	8/9/95	28	58¼	1	108	2
Tower Automotive	8/25/95	11½	8	6	−25	18
133-company average				**16**	**46%**	**14%**

Power of the Sales Force

First, and by far the most important factor, is the concentrated selling power trained on the deal just prior to the IPO. There are significant incentives for brokers to push a new issue over another stock. There may be no commission paid by the buyer at the offering, but the broker gets an above-average payout from the issuer via the underwriting fee. Hundreds, sometimes thousands, of sales people are unleashed to simultaneously talk up the deal with their clients. Given that a typical offering entails the sale of only 1 to 3 million shares, it's not hard to see how interest in buying multiples of that amount is often generated for just an average deal. Broker sales efforts on behalf of a well-known brand name or franchise like Talbot's, Compaq, Steve's Ice Cream, or Boston Chicken can stir an avalanche of demand. Sometimes there are expressions of interest to purchase 20 times as many shares as there are available for sale. The less knowledgeable the buyers, the less particular they may be about the price paid, so the sky can sometimes be the limit after some of these stocks go public.

Limited Supply

The second reason most IPOs initially do well is the absence of additional shares in the marketplace. Just about every offering is subject to an underwriter's *lock-up agreement.* In order to maintain an orderly market once trading begins, the underwriter will usually insist that substantially all current holders of the shares sign an agreement that effectively prevents them from selling any of their holdings in the immediate future, usually for six months to one year. The underwriter then knows that only the shares sold through the offering will be available for trading in the aftermarket. After expiration of the lock-up agreement, the sale of stock is still limited by SEC Rule 144, which restricts the sale of certain shares held by an insider.

Underpricing the Deal

A third reason IPOs tend to do very well out of the box is that they are usually slightly underpriced by the underwriter. This ensures good demand for the stock and at least a small rise in the price of the shares. Slightly underpricing a deal also insures against lawsuits. There are plenty of lawyers who file class-action suits in the name of new owners if something goes wrong. They often accuse company managements and underwriters of withholding important pieces of information that should have been in the offering prospectus. Slightly underpricing a deal helps to keep the stock at or close to the offering price even if the underwriter's internal projections of future results prove somewhat too rosy.

Industry Upswings

The last factor that contributes to IPO outperformance in early trading is that most new issues are in industries that are currently in favor on Wall Street. Here's an example. After years of being in a depression, day rates for oil rigs spurt higher. Analysts start to predict that with no new rigs having been built for 10 years and many older ones being retired, demand is finally starting to outstrip supply. Profits are rising rapidly. Investors are suddenly clamoring to buy drilling stocks.

In this environment, any additional supply of drilling company shares can easily be absorbed, and the shares are apt to initially move higher due to the huge stream of equity capital trying to flow into an industry with good prospects to boost profits at a faster than average pace. IPOs are almost always in industries that are currently in favor with investors and are carried along by the same wave of investor enthusiasm as other stocks in those fields.

IPO INVESTING RULE 2: INVEST IN INDUSTRIES AT THE START OF AN IPO CYCLE

Just as important as selling early is choosing the right industry in which to do your IPO investing. Too many times, IPOs are in hot industries in which the valuations are already high—meaning that you'll be paying a premium.

The trick is to get in early. Let's say a new issue in an emerging industry meets with strong demand. The underwriter may have priced it at 20 times trailing 12-month per-share earnings. If it rises 50 percent, the P/E of the next IPO in that industry could be 30, which is what the first one is now trading at. An investor in the second IPO is much more susceptible to a downturn than the first buyer, because he or she has taken the same amount of risk for 1.5 times the price. Buying IPOs in industries that are already in favor means that at some point the industry fundamentals will move back toward the mean and valuations will come down.

Remember: All Companies Want to Sell High

Unfortunately for you, the buyer, it is exactly when their shares are valued highest that most companies try to go public. This makes intuitive sense—wouldn't you rather sell your company to investors when they're ready to pay a high price? That is exactly why there are very few offerings during a bear market. There is a general disinterest in adding to stock holdings, which usually causes stocks to trade at low P/E ratios. With valuations low, companies are disinclined to sell equity at discount prices.

Tables 4-4 to 4-6 clearly show that being early is best in an industry underwriting cycle. Table 4-4 displays the performance of larger chemical company IPOs in the 1980s, their prices one year after the IPO, their closing prices at decade-end, and their percent changes since the IPO. Tables 4-5 and 4-6 show the same data for IPOs in the gambling and Internet industries in the early and mid-1990s, respectively.

To gauge which industries are going in or out of favor, you could consult *Investor's Business Daily,* which publishes the relative stock performance of industry groups and subgroups on a daily basis. Prime candidates for investment are those groups that have the strongest relative strength and that have not had a large number of IPOs.

But by far the best gauge of industries can be found in Standard & Poor's *Industry Surveys.* Sam Stovall, director of industry information at Standard & Poor's, has come up with an industry scorecard. It shows which

TABLE 4-4 Performance of chemical industry IPOs.

Stock	IPO Price	IPO Date	Closing Price 1 yr Later*	Percent Change	Price 12/92*	Percent Change
Aristech Chemical	11.83	11/26/86	15½	31%	—	—
Vista Chemical	17	12/11/86	36½	115	—	—
Georgia Gulf	9½	12/17/86	23¹¹⁄₁₆	143	23⅜	133%
HIMONT	28	02/12/87	33⅛	18	—	—
Calgon Carbon	5½	06/02/87	10¹⁵⁄₁₆	99	17⅝	220
Melamine Chemical	12½	08/07/87	13½	8	6	–52
Cambrex	7.33	09/22/87	4⅞	–33	5¹¹⁄₁₆	–23
ARCO Chemical	32	09/29/87	30½	–5	43¾	37
Borden Chemicals L.P.	10	11/20/87	16¾	66	13¾	38
IMC Fertilizer	11	01/26/88	24¼	120	21⁵⁄₁₆	94
Rexene	925	07/28/88	295	–68	3⅞	–100
Sterling Chemicals	16	10/13/88	8⅜	–52	3⅞	–76
Hitox	8½	12/14/88	9	6	6	–29
Lyondell Petrochem	30	01/18/89	19	–37	24⅝	–18
Potash	15.33	11/02/89	14⅛	–8	25¾	68
Average return				**27%**		**24%**

* Prices adjusted for stock splits.

TABLE 4-5   Performance of gambling IPOs.

Stock	IPO Price	IPO Date	Closing Price 1 yr Later*	Percent Change	Price 12/95*	Percent Change
Grand Casino	5	10/09/91	9¹¹⁄₁₆	94%	23¼	365%
BoomTown	10	10/23/92	19¾	98	5	−50
Casino Magic	1.67	10/23/92	18	978	3⅛	87
Argosy Gaming	19	02/18/93	23⅜	23	7⅝	−60
Station Casinos	20	05/25/93	13⅞	−31	14⅝	−27
Hollywood Casino	16	05/28/93	7¾	−52	4¼	−73
Primadonna Resorts	18	06/22/93	23½	31	14¾	−18
Monarch Casino	7½	08/06/93	7	−7	3½	−53
Boyd Gaming	17	10/15/93	13⅛	−23	11⅝	−32
Ameristar Casinos	11	11/09/93	7	−36	6½	−41
Mikohn Gaming	15	11/18/93	10	−33	3¾	−75
Average Return				**95%**		**2%**

* Prices adjusted for stock splits.

TABLE 4-6   Performance of Internet IPOs.

Stock	IPO Price	IPO Date	Closing Price 1 yr Later*	Percent Change	Price 12/97*	Percent Change
Netcom On-Line	13	12/14/94	54⅜	318%	24	85%
Firefox Com	18	05/04/95	9¼	−49	—	—
Uunet Technologies	14	05/25/95	61¼	338	—	—
Spyglass	4¼	06/27/95	19¾	365	4¹⁵⁄₁₆	16
Netscape Com	14	08/09/95	44⅝	219	24⅜	74
Secure Computing	16	11/16/95	9¼	−42	11¹³⁄₁₆	−27
CyberCash	17	02/15/96	13⅝	−20	12¹¹⁄₁₆	−25
Cylink	15	02/16/96	11	−27	9¾	−35
Individual, Inc.	14	03/15/96	6½	−54	4¼	−70
Lycos	8	04/01/96	6¾	−16	20¹¹⁄₁₆	159
Excite	8½	04/03/96	4⅞	−43	15	76
Yahoo!	4.33	04/12/96	11⁷⁄₁₆	164	34⅝	700
Average Return				**96%**		**95%**

* Prices adjusted for stock splits.

industries are trading above or below their historical range. From a value perspective, investors should be buying when an industry's relative valuation is well below its historical average and be wary when an industry is trading well above its historical range. One particularly lucrative gambit is to buy IPOs in industries that are just beginning to attract investor attention. Stovall's sector scorecard (Exhibit 4-1 at the end of this chapter) lets you know what they are.

IPO INVESTING RULE 3: SELL DURING A MARKET CORRECTION

As shown by the performance of the S&P New Issues index over the last 10 years, when the stock market gets a cold, the new issues market gets pneumonia. For the 3-month period ending December 31, 1987 (which includes the October crash), the S&P 500 dropped 23 percent, and the New Issues index fell 40 percent. In the second half of 1990, when the pending Gulf War sent the U.S. economy into a temporary recession (triggering a short bear market), the S&P 500 declined 8 percent, and the S&P New Issues index skidded 22 percent.

Always remember: New issues do well when the overall market is rising, which is by far most of the time, and fall to a greater degree when stocks are dropping. Getting out of your IPO positions too quickly is better than staying in too long. IPOs should be sold at the first confirmation that the market may be in trouble. Should the decision prove wrong, there will be plenty of other new issues to invest in.

Here are a few signals that could mean it's time to get out:

1.   There are more stocks hitting 52-week lows than those hitting 52-week highs.

When the IPO Market Peaks, Stocks Underperform

Another critical signpost in deciding whether to buy IPOs is the number of recent IPOs. Underwriters time deals when investors have a favorable view of stock returns over the long term. Table 4-7 shows the number and dollar volume of offerings added to the S&P New Issues index by year. Note that dollar volume reached an interim peak in 1983. This is important because the S&P 500 returned just 6.1 percent in 1984, and small-cap stocks did even worse. The number of offerings peaked again in 1986—just before the crash of 1987. In either event, the S&P 500 in 1987 returned just 5.1 percent. The number of offerings peaked again in 1993, the year before the S&P 500 gained just 1.3 percent.

TABLE 4-7   Number and dollar volume of IPOs, 1982–1997.

Year	No. Offerings	Volume, $ Million
1982	54	1,046.3
1983	349	8,687.2
1984	134	2,637.9
1985	169	5,713.1
1986	372	16,943.0
1987	330	22,957.4
1988	167	23,006.0
1989	159	13,728.1
1990	144	9,872.5
1991	327	25,504.9
1992	492	37,626.2
1993	672	56,942.7
1994	496	34,008.6
1995	489	31,127.1
1996	737	49,203.7
1997	529	43,634.9
1998	307	42,833.8

2. The NASDAQ Composite Index has dropped below its 200-day (20-week) moving average. When the index goes through its moving average on the downside, the chances are good that a correction is in full swing. It usually breaks lower before the S&P 500 because the NASDAQ contains more volatile technology stocks.

3. The S&P 500 clearly slips below its 200-day moving average.

4. The dividend yield of the S&P 500 falls below 2.3 percent.

An IPO investor should consider the new issues market to be overextended on a short-term basis when the number of offerings surges past the previous monthly record for two months in a row. Incidentally, a major market buy signal occurs when the number of IPOs drops below five a month. That happened right after the 1987 crash and in late 1990.

EXHIBIT 4-1   S&P sector scorecard.

(From Standard & Poor's Industry Surveys, *September 1998. Copyright © 1998 by The McGraw-Hill Companies.)*

S&P Sector Scorecard (8/31/98) -- Available on S&P's investorinsight.com and personalwealth.com

	Index Value	% of S&P 1500	Price Changes (%)				Rankings 5=Best, 1=Worst			Analyst Recommendations Pos.(+), Neu.(0), Neg.(-)
			1 Mo.	3 Mos.	YTD	1997	STARS	Rel. Str.	Fair Val.	
S&P 500	957.28	88.3	(14.6)	(12.2)	(2.3)	31.0				
S&P MidCap 400	281.10	8.5	(18.7)	(21.5)	(14.0)	30.4				
S&P SmallCap 600	151.06	3.2	(15.7)	(21.0)	(14.9)	24.5				
S&P Super 1500	201.29	100	(15.1)	(13.6)	(4.2)	30.7				

(Performances and investment outlooks for the sectors and industries in the S&P 1500 Super Composite Index)

	Index Value	% of S&P 1500	1 Mo.	3 Mos.	YTD	1997	STARS	Rel. Str.	Fair Val.	Recommendations
Basic Materials	**102.51**	**4.1**	**(13.3)**	**(23.6)**	**(15.5)**	**8.5**	**3.0**	**2.4**	**2.0**	**Underweight**
Agricultural Products	143.66	0.28	(3.7)	(14.3)	(6.0)	21.3	3.4	3	1.6	0
Aluminum	93.42	0.22	(15.7)	(19.4)	(22.5)	(0.1)	3.2	2	3.2	0
Chemicals	131.57	1.40	(11.7)	(24.8)	(7.6)	18.9	3.1	3	1.7	0
Chemicals (Diversified)	134.32	0.57	(10.3)	(14.0)	2.1	11.0	3.2	3	1.8	+
Chemicals (Specialty)	92.50	0.43	(14.6)	(26.4)	(25.2)	20.0	3.3	2	2.6	+
Containers & Packaging (Paper)	97.64	0.13	(12.5)	(26.9)	(23.5)	9.5	3.0	2	2.4	-
Gold & Precious Metals Mining	40.80	0.14	(23.4)	(35.2)	(37.1)	(34.7)	3.9	1	2.9	+
Iron & Steel	66.35	0.18	(21.1)	(35.3)	(30.8)	2.6	2.9	1	3.5	0
Metals Mining	42.69	0.09	(22.1)	(33.1)	(35.5)	(34.5)	2.1	1	2.1	*
Paper & Forest Products	91.01	0.57	(15.0)	(23.7)	(22.8)	5.6	2.7	2	1.9	-
Capital Goods	**141.98**	**8.6**	**(13.4)**	**(17.0)**	**(10.5)**	**24.2**	**3.1**	**3.3**	**2.2**	**Underweight**
Aerospace/Defense	98.84	0.78	(16.2)	(28.9)	(27.4)	4.2	3.0	2	3.2	0
Construction (Cement & Aggregates)	175.86	0.10	(14.7)	(15.2)	(2.1)	54.5	3.0	4	2.3	0
Containers (Metal & Glass)	92.47	0.12	(24.3)	(31.3)	(21.8)	(2.6)	4.0	2	3.2	+
Electrical Equipment	183.01	3.94	(10.6)	(7.7)	(2.3)	37.0	3.0	4	1.4	+
Engineering & Construction	71.88	0.09	(12.1)	(25.5)	(11.4)	(7.5)	2.3	2	4.2	-
Machinery (Diversified)	115.29	0.59	(15.5)	(30.8)	(24.4)	27.9	2.8	2	3.6	0
Manufacturing (Diversified)	137.63	1.92	(15.5)	(21.8)	(11.2)	18.5	3.4	3	2.0	0
Manufacturing (Specialized)	100.54	0.43	(13.8)	(23.7)	(22.5)	18.5	3.1	2	3.1	
Metal Fabricators	97.96	0.04	(21.9)	(30.7)	(28.4)	29.5	3.0	2	3.6	-
Office Equipment & Supplies	143.97	0.24	(9.7)	(11.6)	(12.3)	33.5	3.1	3	2.3	+
Trucks & Parts	141.04	0.08	(17.6)	(27.7)	(23.9)	59.6	2.1	2	3.6	-
Waste Management	124.03	0.37	(17.6)	(5.4)	18.7	5.2	3.0	3	3.6	-
Communication Services	**141.52**	**7.0**	**(9.6)**	**(4.5)**	**0.0**	**37.0**	**3.6**	**5.0**	**1.4**	**Marketweight**
Telecommunications (Cellular/Wireless)	171.34	0.45	(10.3)	7.3	15.8	50.4	4.5	5	1.3	+
Telecommunications (Long Distance)	143.38	2.30	(17.8)	(12.4)	(4.7)	38.8	4.6	5	1.5	+
Telephone	138.62	4.21	(4.2)	(0.8)	1.3	34.8	3.0	5	1.4	0
Consumer Cyclicals	**156.05**	**10.3**	**(15.8)**	**(16.0)**	**0.9**	**33.2**	**3.3**	**3.9**	**2.5**	**Overweight**
Auto Parts & Equipment	120.34	0.60	(17.2)	(22.6)	(15.8)	21.0	3.4	3	2.7	0
Automobiles	166.51	1.39	(22.4)	(17.9)	18.8	27.1	3.0	4	2.4	0
Building Materials	113.61	0.14	(18.9)	(22.4)	(8.6)	17.0	3.2	3	2.0	0
Consumer (Jewelry, Novelties & Gifts)	110.65	0.08	(19.2)	(22.6)	(16.8)	20.3	3.0	3	2.6	0
Footwear	91.42	0.16	(22.9)	(29.8)	(20.3)	(29.3)	2.1	1	1.9	-
Gaming, Lottery & Parimutuel Companie	74.85	0.10	(27.2)	(33.8)	(36.4)	(1.7)	3.2	1	4.2	0
Hardware & Tools	128.45	0.10	(19.2)	(23.9)	(14.3)	46.2	3.1	3	1.2	0
Homebuilding	127.24	0.14	(14.6)	(13.4)	(10.8)	43.8	3.3	3	3.1	+
Household Furnishings & Appliances	145.52	0.16	(16.0)	(20.9)	(6.9)	37.9	3.0	3	3.0	0
Leisure Time (Products)	119.31	0.29	(17.7)	(21.3)	(18.0)	20.0	3.6	3	3.4	+
Lodging-Hotels	131.29	0.18	(17.0)	(27.9)	(24.5)	39.2	4.1	3	4.5	+
Publishing	137.56	0.24	(7.8)	(5.0)	2.5	37.1	3.1	4	1.7	0
Publishing (Newspapers)	177.61	0.50	(7.3)	(11.7)	(5.1)	56.8	3.1	4	2.1	0
Retail (Building Supplies)	211.90	0.87	(9.8)	(6.5)	23.4	52.9	3.8	5	2.2	+
Retail (Computers & Electronics)	200.46	0.18	(20.0)	0.4	4.5	52.7	3.0	4	2.3	0
Retail (Department Stores)	140.99	0.65	(13.6)	(19.3)	(3.6)	27.7	3.7	3	2.4	0
Retail (Discounters)	256.43	0.15	(23.0)	(25.1)	(14.4)	70.1	3.4	3	3.4	+
Retail (General Merchandise)	231.89	2.18	(10.3)	(4.7)	30.6	54.5	3.1	5	1.4	0
Retail (Home Shopping)	107.28	0.03	(25.4)	(21.1)	(12.5)	40.4	2.8	3	4.1	+
Retail (Specialty)	113.30	0.54	(24.0)	(25.9)	(16.6)	18.1	3.7	3	3.8	+
Retail (Specialty-Apparel)	267.19	0.39	(14.2)	(12.0)	18.8	53.2	3.0	5	2.9	+
Services (Advertising/Marketing)	198.09	0.25	(11.4)	(3.7)	13.1	42.8	3.7	4	2.4	+
Services (Commercial & Consumer)	94.61	0.66	(17.6)	(24.1)	(32.0)	34.2	3.7	3	3.6	+
Textiles (Apparel)	119.56	0.19	(22.2)	(32.2)	(15.9)	8.9	3.3	2	3.2	+
Textiles (Home Furnishings)	129.35	0.08	(17.3)	(22.1)	(2.0)	28.0	2.9	4	3.8	0
Textiles (Specialty)	80.75	0.04	(19.2)	(44.9)	(39.8)	23.1	3.0	1	4.5	0
Consumer Staples	**148.39**	**14.3**	**(13.9)**	**(13.2)**	**(3.6)**	**32.1**	**3.5**	**3.4**	**1.9**	**Overweight**
Beverages (Alcoholic)	124.24	0.46	(10.7)	(9.7)	0.4	3.4	3.0	3	2.4	+
Beverages (Non-Alcoholic)	156.98	2.47	(21.7)	(21.5)	(6.6)	32.0	3.8	3	1.4	0
Broadcasting (TV, Radio & Cable)	151.34	1.03	(19.3)	(3.4)	12.0	61.1	4.2	5	2.3	+
Distributors (Food & Health)	166.54	0.41	(11.8)	(6.2)	4.1	43.7	3.5	4	2.6	0
Entertainment	148.91	1.42	(18.2)	(15.1)	(4.0)	45.0	3.8	4	1.8	+

EXHIBIT 4-1   S&P sector scorecard.

	Index Value	% of S&P 1500	Price Changes (%)				Rankings 5=Best, 1=Worst			Analyst Recommendations Pos.(+), Neu.(0), Neg.(-)
			1 Mo.	3 Mos.	YTD	1997	STARS	Rel. Str.	Fair Val.	
Foods	143.57	2.45	(7.6)	(15.2)	(7.3)	38.4	3.5	3	1.8	+
Household Products (Non-Durables)	161.13	1.90	(8.9)	(12.9)	(6.8)	37.1	3.4	3	1.4	+
Housewares	113.47	0.21	(18.1)	(17.1)	(7.3)	6.6	4.2	3	2.3	0
Personal Care	153.26	0.67	(22.6)	(29.1)	(15.1)	26.5	3.9	3	1.4	+
Restaurants	117.05	0.74	(14.4)	(15.0)	8.3	10.4	3.2	4	3.3	0
Retail (Drug Stores)	244.20	0.50	(9.7)	5.8	14.5	53.0	4.3	5	1.0	+
Retail (Food Chains)	173.95	0.48	0.7	2.6	6.0	32.8	4.1	5	2.1	+
Services (Employment)	80.73	0.13	(23.8)	(38.0)	(30.3)	20.4	3.3	1	4.5	+
Services (Facilities & Environmental)	91.21	0.02	(13.4)	(25.1)	(45.8)	30.7	3.0	1	4.4	0
Specialty Printing	102.13	0.14	(16.1)	(16.2)	(5.7)	17.4	3.0	3	3.1	-
Tobacco	130.77	1.23	(5.0)	10.3	(1.5)	19.2	2.0	3	2.1	-
Energy	**123.67**	**6.7**	**(13.0)**	**(20.7)**	**(12.9)**	**21.6**	**2.4**	**2.6**	**1.5**	**Underweight**
Oil & Gas (Drilling & Equipment)	104.30	0.67	(29.6)	(49.2)	(45.2)	47.7	3.0	1	4.1	0
Oil & Gas (Exploration & Production)	73.65	0.33	(24.8)	(37.2)	(36.9)	(9.2)	2.9	1	2.3	-
Oil & Gas (Refining & Marketing)	124.92	0.16	(15.8)	(25.1)	(25.3)	34.4	3.9	2	2.9	+
Oil (Domestic Integrated)	106.12	0.66	(13.1)	(23.5)	(19.0)	15.5	2.4	2	1.8	-
Oil (International Integrated)	136.98	4.86	(8.9)	(11.7)	(0.7)	20.7	2.3	3	1.0	-
Financial	**257.39**	**16.2**	**(23.0)**	**(20.2)**	**(9.2)**	**48.4**	**3.8**	**3.3**	**1.7**	**Marketweight**
Banks (Major Regional)	161.29	3.56	(21.7)	(21.5)	(13.3)	46.8	3.6	3	1.3	0
Banks (Money Center)	170.20	3.25	(28.7)	(23.4)	(6.9)	31.7	3.9	3	1.8	+
Banks (Regional)	170.71	0.87	(21.6)	(21.6)	(17.2)	73.5	3.5	3	1.4	0
Consumer Finance	220.74	0.54	(25.5)	(17.7)	0.4	36.7	4.2	4	2.4	0
Financial (Diversified)	190.48	2.70	(20.0)	(15.6)	(6.5)	54.6	4.0	4	1.5	0
Insurance (Brokers)	169.79	0.28	(15.0)	(10.8)	4.1	40.8	3.0	4	1.6	-
Insurance (Life & Health)	142.53	0.70	(18.1)	(19.4)	(12.6)	26.4	3.4	3	2.5	0
Insurance (Multi-Line)	179.09	2.03	(23.7)	(14.9)	(1.4)	51.4	4.3	4	1.9	+
Insurance (Property-Casualty)	148.41	1.17	(13.8)	(19.4)	(13.7)	44.3	3.5	3	2.0	+
Investment Banking & Brokerage	223.74	0.58	(31.6)	(27.0)	(8.6)	85.3	3.0	3	1.8	0
Investment Management	207.16	0.14	(22.1)	(28.1)	(21.1)	75.4	4.4	3	2.4	0
Savings & Loans	155.35	0.39	(22.6)	(31.5)	(20.6)	68.0	3.2	3	1.9	0
Health Care	**172.14**	**11.8**	**(12.2)**	**(6.6)**	**2.2**	**37.1**	**4.5**	**4.6**	**1.6**	**Overweight**
Biotechnology	85.14	0.33	(17.6)	(9.4)	(0.8)	(4.3)	3.9	3	3.0	+
Health Care (Diversified)	201.05	4.33	(10.3)	(1.2)	6.0	43.1	4.5	5	1.4	+
Health Care (Drugs - Generic & Other)	96.99	0.17	(18.2)	(21.3)	(3.3)	17.0	3.9	4	3.2	0
Health Care (Drugs - Major Pharms.)	218.03	4.81	(9.5)	(2.8)	5.6	56.7	4.8	5	1.0	+
Health Care (Hospital Management)	87.22	0.35	(20.3)	(28.0)	(13.6)	(7.2)	3.6	3	3.3	+
Health Care (Long-Term Care)	93.81	0.16	(28.4)	(36.2)	(29.2)	32.1	4.2	2	4.3	0
Health Care (Managed Care)	50.20	0.20	(34.3)	(45.8)	(34.1)	(10.5)	3.0	1	4.8	0
Health Care (Medical Prods. & Supplies)	144.08	1.20	(15.4)	(8.4)	1.7	22.5	4.1	4	2.4	+
Health Care (Specialized Services)	103.39	0.21	(19.6)	(21.4)	(10.6)	10.6	3.0	3	3.0	0
Technology	**186.58**	**15.5**	**(17.0)**	**(7.1)**	**2.8**	**24.2**	**3.9**	**3.2**	**2.5**	**Marketweight**
Communication Equipment	174.81	2.08	(23.6)	(13.0)	13.1	26.9	3.3	3	1.8	+
Computers (Hardware)	217.04	3.49	(13.3)	(3.0)	8.7	44.4	4.0	3	2.6	0
Computers (Networking)	165.60	1.17	(15.4)	1.5	13.4	3.1	4.8	4	3.3	+
Computers (Peripherals)	208.52	0.43	(15.8)	(10.2)	6.5	3.8	4.2	3	3.2	+
Computers (Software & Services)	245.55	4.20	(17.0)	(3.8)	10.6	38.3	3.9	4	2.6	+
Electronics (Component Distributors)	89.53	0.09	(17.3)	(31.1)	(33.6)	16.9	3.0	2	3.6	0
Electronics (Defense)	110.34	0.21	(17.3)	(16.6)	(12.4)	10.0	4.0	3	2.9	+
Electronics (Instrumentation)	85.77	0.08	(13.1)	(30.3)	(26.3)	9.4	2.9	3	3.4	-
Electronics (Semiconductors)	164.66	1.98	(18.4)	(7.9)	(18.5)	6.0	3.9	2	2.5	0
Equipment (Semiconductor)	94.26	0.18	(26.4)	(29.5)	(34.0)	41.3	4.6	1	2.1	0
Photography/Imaging	126.72	0.65	(13.3)	(8.8)	4.7	(3.1)	4.4	3	2.1	0
Services (Computer Systems)	175.31	0.35	(19.7)	(16.2)	(6.5)	69.9	3.0	4	2.7	+
Services (Data Processing)	117.94	0.61	(14.1)	(13.0)	(4.9)	13.3	3.8	3	2.2	+
Transportation	**160.33**	**1.2**	**(15.7)**	**(18.2)**	**(16.1)**	**29.9**	**3.5**	**2.7**	**2.9**	**Marketweight**
Air Freight	136.71	0.13	(20.4)	(27.6)	(28.3)	49.2	3.4	2	3.5	0
Airlines	169.42	0.39	(20.4)	(16.8)	(8.3)	65.7	4.1	4	2.7	+
Railroads	107.66	0.57	(10.5)	(14.8)	(15.4)	13.1	3.1	2	2.7	0
Shipping	102.90	0.02	(9.9)	(17.5)	(16.5)	17.8	2.5	2	2.5	-
Truckers	97.78	0.07	(19.9)	(29.4)	(28.2)	34.6	3.8	2	3.8	-
Utilities	**154.54**	**4.4**	**(0.0)**	**(3.1)**	**2.0**	**20.4**	**3.3**	**3.8**	**1.7**	**Underweight**
Electric Companies	117.17	3.47	5.7	3.5	7.7	19.8	3.2	4	1.6	0
Natural Gas	123.12	0.85	(15.0)	(20.4)	(13.3)	18.6	3.5	3	1.9	0
Power Producers (Independent)	188.14	0.07	(34.7)	(37.9)	(30.1)	57.1	3.7	4	4.7	0
Water Utilities	144.40	0.05	(2.9)	3.8	3.3	27.6	2.5	4	1.6	0

Rankings: STARS and Fair Values are averages of company STARS and Fair Values. Relative strength is the index's 12-month performance versus the S&P 1500.
Recommendations: S&P analysts' investment outlooks for index and non-index companies. Weightings based on recommendations and Investment Policy Committee input.

EXHIBIT 4-1   S&P sector scorecard.

S&P 500 Industry Valuations (as of 8/31/98)

Sector/Industry	Index Value	% of 500	Earnings (% Change) 1998e	1999e	P/E 1998e	1999e	L-T Avg.	Relative P/E 1998e	1999e	Avg	Ind. Div'd Yield	Volatility Std Dev	Beta	Avgs Since
S&P 1500	201.29		10.8	NA	21.1	17.0	...	1.03	0.82	...	1.6	...	...	1994
S&P 500	957.28	100	17.0	18.2	20.6	17.4	16.3	NM	NM	NM	1.7	16	1.0	1982
Mid-Cap 400	281.10		8.1	NA	19.6	16.1	...	0.95	0.78	...	1.6	...	...	1995
Small-Cap 600	142.56		8.3	NA	16.5	13.3	...	0.80	0.65	...	1.0	...	...	1995
Basic Materials	102.94	3.81	10.4	22.0	22.6	18.5	24.2	1.10	1.06	NA	1.8	6	0.1	1992
Agricultural Products	118.37	0.23	8.5	10.5	25.8	23.3	25.3	1.25	1.34	1.55	1.2	...	...	1994
Aluminum	343.12	0.25	-2.1	46.7	13.4	9.1	17.9	0.65	0.52	1.10	2.2	23	0.6	1982
Chemicals	413.30	1.44	30.1	0.9	13.6	13.4	17.6	0.66	0.77	1.08	2.9	19	0.9	1982
Chemicals (Diversified)	121.04	0.63	20.6	24.4	25.5	20.5	17.4	1.24	1.18	1.06	1.0	14	0.6	1982
Chemicals (Specialty)	262.39	0.28	-13.3	15.7	15.7	13.6	19.1	0.76	0.78	1.17	2.3	14	0.9	1989
Containers & Packaging (Paper)	1153.27	0.11	NM	127.9	36.4	16.0	12.0	NM	0.92	0.73	3.0	24	0.9	1982
Gold & Precious Metals Mining	97.35	0.15	NM	82.6	32.0	17.5	51.2	NM	1.01	3.14	1.4	41	-0.3	1982
Iron & Steel	46.77	0.14	-11.6	11.8	8.4	7.5	15.0	0.41	0.43	0.92	2.9	23	0.4	1982
Metals Mining	127.91	0.10	-70.1	9.6	31.5	28.7	16.2	1.53	1.65	0.99	3.6	25	0.4	1982
Paper & Forest Products	918.90	0.50	NM	44.3	26.8	18.6	20.8	NM	1.07	1.27	2.9	18	0.8	1982
Capital Goods	719.04	8.47	-6.9	12.8	26.5	23.5	34.7	1.29	1.35	2.13	1.7	10	0.7	1992
Aerospace/Defense	891.31	0.77	144.1	11.1	13.9	12.5	13.3	0.67	0.72	0.82	1.8	26	1.1	1982
Containers (Metal & Glass)	402.40	0.13	21.7	13.9	13.1	11.5	19.4	0.64	0.66	1.19	1.4	19	0.5	1982
Electrical Equipment	3497.56	4.11	7.6	13.8	27.6	24.3	16.7	1.34	1.39	1.02	1.5	19	1.1	1982
Engineering & Construction	137.37	0.06	30.4	-9.8	11.3	12.6	52.4	0.55	0.72	3.21	2.3	19	0.4	1986
Machinery (Diversified)	518.52	0.61	56.5	3.5	9.7	9.4	20.3	0.47	0.54	1.24	2.4	20	0.7	1983
Manufacturing (Diversified)	699.74	1.89	-81.4	16.7	118.0	101.1	20.0	5.73	5.80	1.23	0.3	13	0.6	1983
Manufacturing (Specialized)	108.05	0.22	1048.6	14.6	2.6	2.2	29.3	0.12	0.13	1.80	11.8	11	0.7	1992
Office Products & Supplies	770.42	0.19	-6.1	34.3	28.2	21.0	23.5	1.37	1.21	1.44	1.8	...	...	1993
Trucks & Parts	136.96	0.08	14.1	-3.3	8.2	8.5	17.4	0.40	0.49	1.07	1.4	28	1.0	1982
Waste Management	305.14	0.40	NM	35.8	20.0	14.7	22.8	NM	0.84	1.40	2.1	38	1.7	1982
Communications Services	141.36	7.65	-26.9	20.7	39.0	32.3	23.7	1.90	1.86	1.45	2.1	19	1.2	1992
Telecommunications (Cellular & Wireless)	172.81	0.49	NM	NM	NM	NM	69.8	NM	NM	4.28	0.0	...	...	1996
Telecommunications (Long Distance)	560.50	2.59	55.9	18.0	22.1	18.7	27.5	1.07	1.07	1.69	1.6	23	1.4	1989
Telephones	592.17	4.57	5.9	24.4	23.5	18.9	15.1	1.14	1.09	0.93	2.7	18	1.0	1985
Consumer Cyclicals	161.37	9.42	1.2	15.8	19.4	16.8	20.6	0.94	0.96	1.26	1.3	15	0.9	1992
Auto Parts & Equipment	70.10	0.41	88.1	8.5	10.8	10.0	17.1	0.53	0.57	1.05	2.8	25	0.9	1982
Automobiles	400.42	1.58	-13.5	14.8	14.3	12.5	10.0	0.70	0.72	0.62	2.3	30	0.9	1982
Building Materials	397.14	0.15	34.5	14.5	13.4	11.7	21.2	0.65	0.67	1.30	2.1	24	1.1	1982
Consumer (Jewelry, Novelties & Gifts)	116.67	0.04	2.1	15.1	13.9	12.1	25.2	0.67	0.69	1.54	2.6	15	0.8	1992
Footwear	804.34	0.14	-50.7	35.3	24.5	18.1	15.6	1.19	1.04	0.96	1.3	38	1.4	1982
Gaming, Lottery & Parimutuel Companies	69.57	0.05	1.0	31.8	13.5	10.2	31.3	0.66	0.59	1.92	0.0	...	...	1995
Hardware & Tools	39.24	0.10	154.7	18.2	16.2	13.7	19.9	0.79	0.79	1.22	1.6	18	1.0	1982
Homebuilding	138.00	0.07	28.9	10.7	11.5	10.4	17.6	0.56	0.59	1.08	1.0	37	1.7	1982
Household Furnishings & Appliances	833.12	0.10	251.2	12.8	13.7	12.1	22.1	0.66	0.70	1.35	2.2	30	1.3	1982
Leisure Time Products	126.25	0.20	85.1	15.6	14.5	12.6	19.8	0.71	0.72	1.21	1.2	14	1.0	1982
Lodging-Hotels	453.69	0.16	19.5	17.5	17.2	14.6	22.9	0.83	0.84	1.40	1.1	43	1.7	1982
Publishing	3421.52	0.25	NM	76.1	35.3	20.0	24.2	NM	1.15	1.48	1.7	27	1.1	1982
Publishing - Newspapers	282.27	0.44	11.1	3.5	18.7	18.1	20.5	0.91	1.04	1.26	1.3	24	1.1	1982
Retail (Building Supplies)	2216.37	0.95	36.4	19.5	30.4	25.5	24.5	1.48	1.46	1.50	0.5	25	1.1	1982
Retail (Computers & Electronics)	177.71	0.11	40.9	26.8	21.9	17.3	13.6	1.07	0.99	0.84	0.6	16	0.3	1992
Retail (Department Stores)	1778.54	0.69	26.4	17.2	16.9	14.4	14.6	0.82	0.83	0.89	1.8	27	1.1	1982
Retail (Discount Stores)	56.76	0.09	57.1	28.8	20.4	15.9	25.7	0.99	0.91	1.58	0.0	...	...	1998
Retail (General Merchandise)	106.68	2.46	27.4	6.5	24.9	23.4	19.1	1.21	1.34	1.17	0.6	28	1.2	1982
Retail (Specialty)	91.01	0.15	26.0	18.2	12.5	10.6	27.6	0.61	0.61	1.69	0.1	24	0.2	1982
Retail (Specialty Apparel)	758.66	0.42	50.5	12.7	22.1	19.6	18.9	1.07	1.12	1.16	0.7	39	1.7	1989
Services (Advertising & Marketing)	197.94	0.21	17.7	19.2	27.3	22.9	23.4	1.33	1.31	1.43	1.1	...	...	1993
Services (Commercial & Consumer)	250.95	0.50	40.8	9.3	15.6	14.3	29.3	0.76	0.82	1.80	1.1	17	1.0	1985
Textiles (Apparel)	259.57	0.12	580.6	13.9	11.7	10.3	17.1	0.57	0.59	1.05	1.6	36	1.6	1982
Textiles (Home Furnishings)	79.91	0.01	22.3	45.6	12.7	8.7	14.9	0.62	0.50	0.92	4.0	8	0.5	1982
Consumer Staples	150.02	14.86	-19.8	53.3	39.4	25.7	26.8	1.91	1.47	1.64	1.4	14	1.0	1992
Beverages (Alcoholic)	566.79	0.51	29.4	-22.8	16.1	20.8	15.9	0.78	1.20	0.97	2.2	27	1.0	1982
Beverages (Non-Alcoholic)	3520.91	2.64	-7.8	16.1	36.3	31.2	21.2	1.76	1.79	1.30	1.1	26	1.2	1982
Broadcasting (TV, Radio & Cable)	14481.41	1.12	NM	NM	NM	NM	30.0	NM	NM	1.84	0.0	31	1.1	1982
Distributors (Food & Health)	815.40	0.27	4.3	22.3	26.3	21.5	19.0	1.28	1.24	1.17	1.0	16	0.7	1985

EPS % Chgs. -- The percent change in industry earnings (actual or S&P analysts' estimates). **P/E** -- Price to earnings ratios on actual and estimated earnings, plus a long-term average of trailing 4Q earnings. **Relative P/E** -- The industry P/Es compared with P/Es for the S&P 500. **Indicated Dividend Yield** -- Current indicated dividend payment divided by share price. **Volatility** -- Standard deviations and betas are shown, representing the absolute and relative measures of volatility for these industries. **Averages Since** -- Average P/Es and Relative P/Es are based on results since this year. **NM** -- Not Meaningful (e.g. division by zero). **...** -- No history.

EXHIBIT 4-1   S&P sector scorecard.

S&P 500 Industry Valuations (as of 8/31/98)

Sector/Industry	Index Value	% of 500	Earnings (% Change) 1998e	1999e	P/E 1998e	1999e	L-T Avg.	Relative P/E 1998e	1999e	Avg	Ind. Div'd Yield	Volatility Std Dev	Beta	Avgs Since
Entertainment	3550.46	1.61	−69.3	245.1	169.6	49.1	31.6	8.23	2.82	1.94	0.5	34	1.0	1982
Foods	1531.63	2.46	−12.5	45.7	30.0	20.6	17.0	1.46	1.18	1.04	2.0	20	0.9	1982
Household Products (Non-Durables)	2521.91	2.11	−24.0	15.0	41.3	35.9	17.5	2.01	2.06	1.07	1.4	18	0.7	1982
Housewares	901.21	0.23	60.5	6.0	17.4	16.5	21.3	0.85	0.94	1.31	2.4	21	0.8	1989
Personal Care	721.05	0.73	5.3	19.1	29.1	24.4	7.3	1.41	1.40	0.45	1.4	24	1.2	1982
Restaurants	587.02	0.64	55.8	10.4	21.0	19.0	17.2	1.02	1.09	1.06	0.6	35	1.3	1982
Retail (Drug Stores)	572.73	0.57	66.9	17.8	30.6	26.0	18.0	1.49	1.49	1.10	0.8	33	1.5	1982
Retail (Food Chains)	1163.71	0.50	13.1	15.3	23.2	20.1	16.7	1.13	1.15	1.02	1.1	20	0.6	1982
Specialty Printing	111.20	0.10	218.9	−2.3	13.7	14.1	19.1	0.67	0.81	1.17	3.2	...	...	1993
Tobacco	2072.03	1.38	9.5	11.4	14.4	12.9	12.1	0.70	0.74	0.74	3.9	19	0.7	1990
Energy	**630.64**	**7.11**	**−17.7**	**17.6**	**20.3**	**17.3**	**17.6**	**0.99**	**0.99**	**1.08**	**2.8**	**12**	**0.6**	**1988**
Oil & Gas (Drilling & Equipment)	2375.19	0.56	36.1	19.0	12.8	10.8	25.2	0.62	0.62	1.54	2.0	31	0.9	1982
Oil & Gas (Exploration & Production)	42.82	0.21	−51.6	76.8	26.1	14.8	27.6	1.27	0.85	1.69	1.8	20	0.4	1990
Oil & Gas (Refining & Marketing)	123.02	0.09	1.1	11.7	11.6	10.4	30.3	0.56	0.60	1.86	2.7	...	...	1993
Oil (Domestic Integrated)	680.68	0.75	3.5	21.5	15.4	12.7	24.3	0.75	0.73	1.49	3.8	22	0.6	1982
Oil (International Integrated)	720.61	5.51	−18.7	18.5	21.0	17.7	12.9	1.02	1.02	0.79	3.2	18	0.9	1982
Financial	**105.04**	**16.39**	**5.0**	**14.2**	**16.0**	**14.0**	**12.1**	**0.78**	**0.81**	**0.74**	**1.8**	**21**	**1.0**	**1982**
Banks (Major Regionals)	390.65	4.03	25.6	13.2	14.6	12.9	15.9	0.71	0.74	0.97	2.6	23	1.1	1981
Banks (Money Center)	392.96	3.68	15.6	16.7	12.2	10.4	9.4	0.59	0.60	-0.58	2.8	22	0.9	1982
Consumer Finance	1019.78	0.60	12.5	24.7	16.7	13.4	11.9	0.81	0.77	0.73	1.2	27	1.3	1982
Financial (Diversified)	147.04	2.90	−9.3	10.4	20.5	18.5	12.9	0.99	1.06	0.79	1.3	24	1.6	1982
Insurance Brokers	502.87	0.30	86.8	15.5	17.8	15.4	18.8	0.86	0.88	1.15	2.6	23	1.1	1990
Insurance (Life & Health)	1925.83	0.60	−17.7	17.3	14.3	12.2	10.7	0.69	0.70	0.66	1.5	23	1.0	1982
Insurance (Multi-Line)	191.92	2.27	−11.4	14.3	21.4	18.7	17.7	1.04	1.08	1.09	1.0	22	1.1	1982
Insurance (Property-Casualty)	899.83	1.09	−12.5	16.9	14.3	12.2	14.4	0.69	0.70	0.88	1.7	19	0.9	1982
Investment Banking & Brokerage	362.91	0.52	20.6	−2.9	11.7	12.1	9.7	0.57	0.69	0.59	1.2	31	2.0	1982
Investment Management	60.42	0.11	22.8	23.9	15.4	12.4	NM	0.75	0.71	NM	0.6	...	...	1998
Savings & Loans	131.91	0.30	67.6	15.7	11.0	9.5	15.3	0.53	0.55	0.94	2.0	33	1.5	1989
Health Care	**602.64**	**12.19**	**48.3**	**30.2**	**30.1**	**23.1**	**22.1**	**1.46**	**1.33**	**1.36**	**1.2**	**25**	**1.4**	**1987**
Biotechnology	102.53	0.20	31.1	11.9	19.8	17.6	35.7	0.96	1.01	2.19	0.0	...	...	1993
Health Care (Diversified)	1145.53	4.88	−37.1	22.9	54.4	44.2	19.5	2.64	2.54	1.20	0.8	18	1.1	1985
Health Care (Drugs - Major Pharmaceuticals)	4921.89	5.45	57.4	16.0	32.9	28.3	25.9	1.60	1.63	1.59	1.2	22	1.0	1992
Health Care (Hospital Management)	99.79	0.29	NM	31.8	18.5	14.1	18.2	NM	0.81	1.12	0.2	32	0.6	1982
Health Care (Long-Term Care)	114.34	0.12	14.4	25.9	15.8	12.6	36.8	0.77	0.72	2.25	0.1	...	...	1993
Health Care (Managed Care)	214.03	0.12	12.5	24.4	13.3	10.7	26.4	0.65	0.61	1.61	0.1	14	...	1992
Health Care (Medical Products & Supplies)	530.92	1.07	41.2	38.6	32.8	23.7	22.5	1.59	1.36	1.38	0.8	25	1.1	1982
Health Care (Specialized Services)	148.66	0.04	NM	22.2	27.5	22.5	35.2	NM	1.29	2.15	0.0	...	...	1993
Technology	**798.90**	**15.50**	**17.6**	**60.6**	**29.4**	**18.3**	**23.3**	**1.43**	**1.05**	**1.43**	**0.3**	**16**	**0.5**	**1982**
Communications Equipment	232.98	2.17	−82.6	668.1	337.7	44.0	21.9	16.40	2.52	1.34	0.3	22	0.8	1982
Computers (Hardware)	399.76	3.86	−24.0	36.0	34.1	25.1	18.5	1.66	1.44	1.13	0.3	22	0.8	1982
Computers (Networking)	170.69	1.31	−86.1	543.8	533.4	82.9	58.2	25.90	4.76	3.56	0.0	...	...	1994
Computers (Peripherals)	247.90	0.35	−52.7	542.3	141.7	22.1	27.6	6.88	1.27	1.69	0.0	...	...	1996
Computers (Software & Services)	607.12	3.95	−11.0	29.7	73.3	56.5	25.9	3.56	3.24	1.59	0.0	21	1.1	1982
Electronics (Component Distributors)	118.30	0.05	10.2	11.9	15.7	14.0	25.4	0.76	0.80	1.55	1.5	11	0.6	1992
Electronics (Defense)	538.70	0.20	62.8	15.5	12.9	11.1	16.6	0.62	0.64	1.02	1.8	25	1.2	1982
Electronics (Instrumentation)	255.14	0.06	−21.6	46.3	21.5	14.7	20.4	1.04	0.84	1.25	1.8	28	1.1	1982
Electronics (Semiconductors)	535.07	1.95	−46.6	84.2	35.6	19.3	23.8	1.73	1.11	1.46	0.3	31	1.0	1982
Equipment (Semiconductor)	110.11	0.14	−0.2	−39.2	18.4	30.3	25.7	0.89	1.74	1.57	0.0	...	...	1995
Photography/Imaging	232.55	0.73	145.3	16.8	17.3	14.8	26.6	0.84	0.85	1.63	1.9	19	0.5	1990
Services (Computer Systems)	93.71	0.23	11.7	24.0	19.2	15.5	27.5	0.93	0.89	1.69	1.8	25	0.8	1992
Services (Data Processing)	111.71	0.49	11.9	15.6	22.1	19.1	39.2	1.07	1.10	2.40	0.7	...	...	1994
Transportation	**578.75**	**1.07**	**0.8**	**23.2**	**12.4**	**10.1**	**21.6**	**0.60**	**0.58**	**1.32**	**1.3**	**20**	**1.2**	**1982**
Air Freight	33.53	0.10	8.1	26.1	14.8	11.8	20.2	0.72	0.68	1.24	0.0	24	0.6	1989
Airlines	471.52	0.39	3.7	4.7	9.1	8.7	14.0	0.44	0.50	0.86	0.1	32	1.4	1990
Railroads	519.93	0.57	−4.2	45.0	16.0	11.0	15.0	0.78	0.63	0.92	2.3	24	1.0	1983
Truckers	222.43	0.02	6.6	16.7	9.8	8.4	71.5	0.48	0.48	4.38	2.5	28	0.9	1982
Utilities	**236.62**	**3.53**	**12.1**	**15.1**	**16.7**	**14.5**	**12.3**	**0.81**	**0.83**	**0.75**	**4.3**	**16**	**0.8**	**1982**
Electric Companies	95.64	2.86	9.4	14.7	16.7	14.6	10.6	0.81	0.84	0.65	4.6	16	0.7	1982
Natural Gas	672.00	0.67	28.2	17.3	16.7	14.2	19.8	0.81	0.82	1.22	3.1	22	0.8	1982

EPS % Chgs. -- The percent change in industry earnings (actual or S&P analysts' estimates). **P/E** -- Price to earnings ratios on actual and estimated earnings, plus a long-term average of trailing 4Q earnings. **Relative P/E** -- The industry P/Es compared with P/Es for the S&P 500. **Indicated Dividend Yield** -- Current indicated dividend payment divided by share price. **Volatility** -- Standard deviations and betas are shown, representing the absolute and relative measures of volatility for these industries. **Averages Since** -- Average P/Es and Relative P/Es are based on results since this year. **NM** -- Not Meaningful (e.g. division by zero). **...** -- No history.

C H A P 5 T E R

HOW IPOs ARE SOLD

T
O TRULY UNDERSTAND the IPO market, it is helpful for the small investor to understand the process behind each new offering. First, let's consider how underwriters get ready to do an IPO.

THE FIRST LOOK AT THE DEAL

Notice of an intended public offering of shares to the public must be filed with the Securities and Exchange Commission (SEC). These filings usually occur anywhere from three to eight weeks before the company actually goes public.

The preliminary prospectus—or, as it is known in industry parlance, the *red herring*—is the most important part of the filing. It is the primary tool used to disseminate information about the deal. IPO prospectuses are now available via the Internet. The prospectus also can be obtained from the underwriter (ask for the prospectus department), usually a week or two after the SEC filing; through Disclosure, Inc; or free on the SEC Edgar website at www.sec.gove/edgarhp.htm. Access is by company name.

HOW A DEAL IS MARKETED AND SOLD

During the so-called "selling period," company executives and the firm's investment bankers formally market the deal. This usually includes "road show" meetings for institutional money managers in half a dozen important cities and one-on-one meetings with particularly important money managers in each town.

Information on upcoming deals, with the lead underwriter noted, can be found in investment newsletters such as *Emerging & Special Situations, IPO Value Monitor,* and *New Issues Outlook,* and on a variety of websites, including IPOhome.com, IPOmonitor.com, and IPOCentral.com, as well as in *Investor's Business Daily* and *Barron's.*

These presentations are then assessed by analysts and portfolio managers at money management firms, who begin to make their decisions about the attractiveness of the deal. This information is also broadly disseminated to brokers within the syndicate.

Now it is time for the institutional investors to make their decisions. After listening to the company's presentation, studying the prospectus, and consulting with industry analysts and other portfolio managers, they weigh in with indications of interest. If the deal is known to be hot, they may ask for anything they can get. In other cases, however, they provide indications to purchase stock on a sliding scale. For example, a money manager may offer to buy 100,000 shares if the stock comes out at 10, 50,000 at 11½, or none at all if the deal is priced at 13.

Following the road show meetings, the lead underwriter managing the deal will take its final solicitations of interest and add them up to see if there is enough demand for the offering. The ideal situation would be indications of interest for at least two to three times as much stock as the company wishes to sell. If this is the case, the shares are divided up, with preference given to investors according to account type and geography, and special attention given to influential investors, as mentioned earlier. The account executives then go back to their clients and tell them the amount of stock that has been "circled" for them.

At this point, the client may confirm or reject its purchase order. If the allocation is small compared to what was requested, it indicates a tight deal and the likelihood of quick trading profits. Most managers will take the allocation and *flip* it (sell it quickly), if it's possible to do so without unduly upsetting the account executive.

If a deal does turn out to be weak, there is typically a lowering of the offering price or cancellation of the IPO. Often, a syndicate manager will try to discretely solicit pricing information both from knowledgeable third parties within the syndicate and from important institutional portfolio managers before provisionally penciling other investors in for shares. If the manager knows the deal is not strong, the syndicate may go back to the company and argue for a lower price to ensure at least a 2:1 demand-to-supply ratio for the stock at the offering. The company is faced with the decision of whether to continue to go with the deal. If the purpose of the IPO is primarily to create a public market so that insiders can sell their shares, or if the company knows that it will have to tap the equity markets in the not-too-distant future and thus wants to keep shareholders happy, it may be more inclined to lower the offering price.

PRICING THE DEAL

At the heart of the IPO deal is the risky and challenging business of setting an offering price. As much art as science, pricing is no mean task since IPOs have no stock trading history. How then, does the underwriter arrive at it?

An underwriter derives the price of a new issue through good analysis and a great deal of finesse, balancing the interests of the company, its stockholders, and the public investors who will buy at the offering, and those of its own stockholders, partners, and/or investors. This must be done with at least the appearance of equanimity.

Meanwhile, the goal of the company's management would seem obvious—to get the highest price possible for its shares. After all, its responsibility is to nurture and safeguard the welfare of the firm, and it is presumably seeking to raise capital to develop the business or repay debt. But that goal can be tempered by the knowledge that the company will need additional funds down the road. If this is the case, the company could find it advantageous to sell shares at the IPO at a slightly lower price than it has to. This increases the likelihood that the shares will move higher, building management credibility with investors and making subsequent offerings easier.

Public investors are, of course, interested in getting the shares at the lowest price possible, but they also want to be able to get an allocation of the shares. At too low a price, there could be so many potential buyers that none but the largest institutional and most influential individual investors could get an allocation. Most investors would be satisfied to get a meaningful amount of stock at a price only slightly below what comparable company shares are trading at. In such a case, the IPO has a high probability of quickly rising to match the valuation levels of comparable stocks.

Last, the underwriter has its own mercantile interests that need to be satisfied. The underwriter wants to collect a good underwriting fee, but it must balance this profit motive against its need to maintain a good reputation. A higher price increases the underwriting fee (which typically comes to between 5 and 9 percent of the total amount raised), but too high an initial offering price may backfire. In this situation, the underwriter may lose potential trading profits as a "market maker" in the aftermarket. Once again, slightly underpricing the deal turns out to be the best compromise. That way the underwriter builds investor satisfaction and paves the way for future offerings by the company, all the while building its own reputation.

Consider what happens if a company goes public at 12 and then trades below that level. The underwriter is placed in the position of having to buy shares in order to support the price of the stock. One might think that buying low is an advantage to the firm, but if there are not enough buyers at or above the offering price after the huge selling effort tied to the IPO, there are not likely to be any for some time to come. This means the firm must put its own capital at risk and potentially keep it tied up to support the stock for awhile with no reasonable expectation of it getting out of its position at a higher price. On the other hand, if the stock is worth 11, and the IPO price is 10, the equity has a greater of chance of trading up in the aftermarket.

If this happens, the underwriter also has the opportunity of exercising the overallotment option—referred to as the *green shoe*. This option typically allows the underwriter to buy, from insiders or the company, 10 percent more shares *at the offering price* that can then be sold at the higher current price.

THE UNDERPRICING PUZZLE

Those investors who peruse the financial pages each day are well aware of stocks that skyrocket on their first day of trading. How could companies allow investors to earn so much easy money when the company could have sold the shares at the higher price and reaped the gains?

This is one of the most difficult questions behind the IPO market. Perhaps we can partially answer it by considering three recent examples of dramatic IPO underpricing: Genentech, Home Shopping Network, and Boston Chicken.

Did these companies really mean to underprice their shares by so much? Of course not. But all three were dealing with variables that made it difficult to accurately gauge the value of the shares in the marketplace. In the first place, in all three cases, there were no direct *comparables* (traded shares in similar types of companies) to use as benchmarks. That inherently meant more potential variation in the stock's valuation.

For example, Genentech was one of the first biotechnology companies to go public. Public investors were eager to put money into biotechnology, but there were almost no reputable "pure plays" in this new industry available. Genentech had no operating revenues, but it did have a number of research and development contracts with important drug companies. These industry allies were willing to share the investment risks to help fund their new genetic technology drug research—all for potentially large payoffs, of course.

Given this outlook, the underwriter chose to value the company based on the earnings potential of the company's drugs in development. Since no earnings were expected for five years or so, there was also a heavy discount built into that value.

But in Genentech's case, investors chose to disregard the risks attendant to owning those shares. They priced the stock as though the company's prospective success was completely assured. Genentech did deliver on its product development effort, and the company is now solidly profitable. The stock went public at 5.83 (adjusted for splits), and closed the first day of trading at 11⅞—but 5 years later, despite a very healthy stock market in the interim, the stock was lower than its closing price on the first day of trading (see Table 5-1 and Figure 5-1).

Home Shopping Network and Boston Chicken were no different. When Merrill Lynch priced HSN, there were no independent shopping channels to use as comparison. (MTV was the only pure-play cable-channel public that the shares could be valued against.) Merrill Lynch saw that there was tremendous pent-up demand that could not be satisfied on the first day. It raised the offering price to a presplit price of 24, equal to 3 on a postsplit basis. This was far above the original indicated range, but based on the available comparables, it could not reasonably set a price higher than that. HSN closed the first day of trading at $7.10, again adjusted for subsequent stock splits. Three months later, it was trading at well over 5 times its original IPO price. But five years after the IPO, again during a great bull market, the stock was trading below the price it closed at on the first day of trading (see Table 5-1 and Figure 5-2).

Boston Chicken is a much younger company. It went public toward the end of 1993. The only comparables that could be used were other restaurant

TABLE 5-1   Three underpriced IPOs.

High Flyer	IPO Date	IPO Price	1 Day Close	After 3 mo*	After 1 yr*	After 5 yr*
Boston Chicken	11/8/93	10	24¼	22⅛	19	¾
Genentech	10/14/80	5.83	11⅞	7.23	7.29	12¹⁄₁₆
Home Shopping Network	5/13/86	3	7.10	16.02	14⅝	5⅞

* Prices adjusted for stock splits.

FIGURE 5-1   Genentech trading history.

chains that were not growing as fast. But none of these "comparables" was truly a good benchmark for Boston Chicken's perceived short- and long-term growth prospects. It was selling a different kind of take-out food service, and its food was higher quality and more expensive. Members of management had a completely different approach to a restaurant enterprise, having come from businesses like Waste Management and Blockbuster Entertainment.

Merrill Lynch had published a range between 5 and 6 in the original prospectus (adjusted for a subsequent 2-for-1 stock split). The price was raised to 10 at the offering on May 13, 1986, and closed at $47^{11}/_{16}$ on June 30. Despite continued execution of its business plan, at year-end 1987, Boston Chicken's stock had fallen to the equivalent of 16, and then by mid-1988 had dropped to $4\frac{7}{8}$, not far from the original contemplated offering price (see Table 5-1 and Figure 5-3).

What all this suggests is that over the long run, the price suggested by underwriters in large deals often turns out to be a fairly good appraisal over time. IPO buyers tend to have very short holding horizons, and simply may not care what the price of a stock may be a year or two out. The company, the insiders, and the long-term holders do care. As a final point, all three of these companies sold shares at higher prices via secondary offerings within one year of the IPO.

FIGURE 5-2   Home Shopping Network trading history.

BLIND POOLS ARE FOR FOOLS

Tiny deals are almost always the exclusive domain of the retail investor. Many of these small company IPOs have a single underwriter, and proceeds often go into a *blind pool*. This term comes from the fact that the funds being raised represent pools of money that investors have blindly provided without an inkling as to their eventual use. All that the investors are typically buying is, hopefully, the management's expertise. These deals are usually too small and speculative to attract institutional interest. Almost none of them ever pan out.

Other small offerings are for companies that are trying to perfect a technology or product, or that are seeking funds to commence full-scale manufacturing of a product. As mentioned in Chapter 4, these deals are marketed by entire offices of brokers making cold calls to potential buyers. This highly concentrated selling effort often results in the stock moving higher in initial trading, but without additional sponsorship, few trade higher than their IPO price after the first few years.

CALLS FROM BROKERS ABOUT IPOs: BUYER BEWARE

Almost every investor has been called by a broker touting a hot new IPO. The sales conversation often runs along the lines of the broker being able to provide the shares at the offering price only if the client will buy an equal

FIGURE 5-3   Boston Chicken trading history.

amount at a *higher* price in the aftermarket. This selling strategy also
ensures that the stock moves higher in initial trading. The resultant price
spike helps to preserve the underwriter's standing as a provider of hit IPOs.
But at some point the sales force moves on and the stock drops. It is not
unusual for the underwriting firm, some of its affiliates, or its partners'
cronies to short the stock, knowing that once their selling effort ends the
stock will drop. As a rule, there are no investment fundamentals supporting
the shares beyond the usual hopes and dreams. One year later, they are all
too often trading at half the offering price. Two or three years out, the stock
has often disappeared from sight.

   One good example is Saratoga Brands. Underwritten by Thomas James
Associates, it was originally sold as a purveyor of potato chips. Indeed it
was. Its chips were positioned to sell in delis as a premium-priced chip. The
company was rolling its products out in the New York City area when the
offering occurred. Revenues did rise rapidly. But the chip market is highly
competitive, and there was really very little to differentiate its product from
others. Losses rose faster than sales. Because relatively little money was
raised via the IPO, it was not long before the company ran into financial
trouble. The offering was at the equivalent of 750, adjusting for a 1-for-10
split that occurred in 1995. As is typical, the stock rose in the immediate
aftermarket, hitting a high of 937½. But 1 year later it had sunk to 450, and

1 year after that, just 262½. By late 1995, the shares were trading at the equivalent of 10½. The company is now out of the potato chip business. As of September 30, 1998, the stock was changing hands at 1⅟₁₆.

It is such deals that most hurt the long-term performance of all IPOs. When evaluating the potential of these firms' products, investors should ask themselves: If the underlying technology or marketing value has so much profit potential, why isn't it being funded by venture capitalists? There is always the chance that a unique technology may have real value that escaped the studied investment expertise of venture fund managers, but this is much more likely to be the exception to the rule.

Owning small underwriter IPOs is, in the long run, very dangerous to one's financial health. Any position taken should be small in comparison to the total portfolio, and it should be *quickly sold* after the IPO.

ADVICE FOR THE SMALL INVESTOR

There are precious few sources of independent recommendations on IPOs available to the individual investor. Hard analysis takes time. With analyst salaries what they are, it is primarily the institutional marketplace that can afford to pay for professional actionable advice. One source of impartial analysis is Standard & Poor's *Emerging & Special Situations,* which publishes estimates and investment recommendations on about 13 offerings a month. Since 1991, S&P has kept tabs on the performance of all its IPO investment assessments, including those it said to avoid. These recommendations provided substantial value to readers.

IPO Value Monitor and *New Issues Outlook* also contain a good deal of factual information on pending offerings, but the number of IPOs assessed is small. Similarly, the stock advice provided by *New Issues* has outperformed the market over the years, but the number of IPOs analyzed each month is usually less than five.

The Advantages of the Big Guys

Brokers are legally barred from sharing earnings projections from the deal with interested individual investors. This means, of course, that what is probably the most important ingredient needed to assess a deal—this year's projected earnings—is available only to the underwriter's clients and not to the general public. This can make for a *very* uneven playing field.

Other IPO Facts for the Individual Investor
- Discount brokers never serve as lead underwriters because they don't have syndicate departments or investment banking units.
- IPOs cannot be bought on margin.
- Small IPOs can be good for your tax bill. The capital gains tax on an IPO profit, usually 20 percent if held for a year, may be cut in half if the market value of the company is less than $100 million, and you hang on to the shares for at least 5 years.

OVERVIEW OF THE UNDERWRITING PROCESS

The Underwriting Players

Investment bankers	Advise corporations on raising capital (i.e., public or private offering of stock, short-term or long-term loans, bonds) and on tax consequences of the offering.
	Raise capital for issuers by distributing new securities.
	Distribute shares via purchase from issuing corporation and resale to public.
	Distribute large blocks of stocks to public and private institutions.
SEC	Reviews registration statement.
	Sends deficiency letter suggesting changes to improve offering prospectus.
	Declares registration effective, allowing formal sale of shares to public.
Issuing company	Files registration with the SEC.
	Files registration with states where shares will be sold.
	Negotiates price of securities and under-writing fees with underwriter.
NASD	Reviews underwriting spread (fees) for fairness

| Individual states | Register of *blue sky* deals, allowing the sale and subsequent trading of the issue in that state. |

Types of Offerings

New issue	Initial public offering of shares to the public to raise capital and create an increased market for shares.
Additional stock sales in aftermarket	Part of the ongoing capital-raising and stock distribution process.
Primary offering	Proceeds go to the issuing corporation.
Secondary offering	Proceeds go to the current holders.
Shelf offering	Multiple offerings over a two-year period, typically used for bond sales.
Standby offering	Underwriter agrees to buy all shares not sold in rights offering to current holders and then attempts to resell shares to others.
Private placement	Exempt from registration requirements of the 1933 act.

The Underwriting Timeline

1. Syndicate formation—could be later in a negotiated underwriting.
2. Document preparation.
3. Cooling-off period—20 days to several months depending on SEC reaction to the filings. In rare instances, the SEC may issue a stop order at this point, preventing the issuer from proceeding with the deal.
4. Blue sky registration in the appropriate states—exemptions are allowed by most states if securities are to be listed on a regional or national exchange or on NASDAQ.
5. Due-diligence work by the investment banker—examining the use of proceeds, performing financial analyses, determining the stability of company and whether the investment risk being assumed by investors is reasonable. Due-diligence work also includes analyses of industry data, operation data, management and employee relations, financial stability, and the legal status of the issuer.

6. Due-diligence meeting—a formal meeting for the benefit of sell-
    ing agents (brokers) who want information on the deal; several are
    scheduled for national offering meetings. Due-diligence findings
    are presented.

7. New issue pricing—based on indications of interest (underwriter's
    book) and prevailing market conditions. Biggest valuation factors
    for interested parties are P/E ratios of similar companies and per-
    formance figures of recent offerings, and those of hot issues.

8. Effective date—the first date the issue can legally be sold to the
    public.

9. Issuance of final prospectus—issued to all buyers at the offering
    and potentially to others in the aftermarket.

10. Underwriter price stabilization efforts in the aftermarket—under-
    writer may buy shares in the aftermarket in an effort to keep the
    price close to the offering price while the syndicate is still together.
    However, stabilizing bids *cannot* be above the offering price.

11. Transaction settlement date—third day following the public offering.

Exhibit 5-1 following this overview presents a directory of lead underwriters.

EXHIBIT 5-1   Directory of lead underwriters.

(From Standard & Poor's Emerging & Special Situations. *Copyright © 1997 by The McGraw-Hill Companies.)*

▶ **DIRECTORY OF LEAD UNDERWRITERS**

Adams, Harkness & Hill, 60 State St., Boston, MA 02109 (617) 371-3900

BA Robertson, Stephens & Co., 555 California St.. San Francisco, CA 94104 (415) 781-9700

BT Alex. Brown, One South St.. Baltimore, MD 21202 (410) 727-1700

Baird (Robert W.) & Co., 777 E. Wisconsin Ave., Firstar Ctr., Milwaukee. WI 53202 (414) 765-3500

Bear Stearns & Co., 245 Park Ave., New York, NY 10167 (212) 272-2000

Blair (William) & Co., 222 W. Adams St., Chicago, IL 60606 (312) 236-1600

Bradford (J. C.) & Co., 330 Commerce St., Nashville, TN 37201 (615) 748-9000

CS First Boston, 11 Madison Ave., New York. NY 10010 (212) 325-2000

Capital West Securities, 211 N. Robinson, One Leadership Sq., Oklahoma City, OK, 73102 (405) 235-5700

Commonwealth Associates, 733 Third Ave., New York, NY 10017 (212) 297-6000

Cowen & Co., Financial Square, New York, NY 10005 (212) 495-6000

Cruttenden Roth, 18301 Von Karman Ave., Irvine, CA 92715 (714) 757-5700

Dain Bosworth, 60 S. Sixth St., Dain Bosworth Plaza, Minneapolis, MN 55402 (612) 371-2811

Deutsche Morgan Grenfell, 31 W. 52 St., New York, NY 10019 (212) 469-5000

Donaldson, Lufkin & Jenrette Securities, 277 Park Ave., New York, NY 10172 (212) 504-3000

Edwards (A.G.) & Sons, One N. Jefferson Ave., St. Louis, MO 63103 (314) 955-3000

Equitable Securities, 800 Nashville City Center, Nashville, TN 37219 (615) 780-9300

Friedman, Billings, Ramsay & Co., 1001 19 St., N., Potomac Tower, Arlington, VA 22209 (703) 312-9500

Furman Selz, 230 Park Ave., New York, NY 10169 (212) 309-8200

GKN Securities, 61 Broadway, New York. NY 10006 (212) 509-3000

Goldman, Sachs & Co., 85 Broad St.. New York. NY 10004 (212) 902-1000

Hambrecht & Quist, One Bush St., San Francisco, CA 94104 (415) 439-3300

Hampshire Securities, 640 Fifth Ave., New York, NY 10022 (212) 641-3500

ING Baring Securities, 667 Madison Ave., New York, NY 10021 (212) 350-7700

Janney Montgomery Scott, 1801 Market St., Philadelphia, PA 19103 (215) 665-6000

Jefferies & Co., 11100 Santa Monica Blvd., Los Angeles, CA 90025 (310) 445-1199

Josephthal Lyon & Ross, 200 Park Ave., New York, NY 10172 (212) 907-4000

Ladenburg Thalmann & Co., 590 Madison Sve., New York, NY 10022 (212) 409-2000

Lehman Brothers Inc., 200 Vesey St., Three World Financial Center, New York, NY 10285 (212) 526-7000

McDonald & Co. Securities, 800 Superior Ave., McDonald Investment Ctr., Cleveland, OH 44114 (216) 443-2300

Merrill Lynch, Pierce, Fenner & Smith, 250 Vesey St., World Financial Center, North Tower, New York, NY 10281 (212) 449-1000

Meyers, (H.J.) & Co., 1895 Mt. Hope Ave., Rochester, NY 14620 (716) 256-4700

Morgan (J.P.) Securities, 60 Wall St., New York, NY 10260 (212) 483-2323

Morgan Keegan & Co., 50 Front St., Morgan Keegan Tower, Memphis, TN 38103 (901) 524-4100

Morgan Stanley Dean Witter Discover, 1585 Broadway, New York. NY 10036 (212) 761-4000

NB Montgomery Securities, 600 Montgomery St., San Francisco, CA 94111 (415) 627-2000

National Securities, 1001 Fourth Ave., Seattle, WA 98154 (206) 622-7200

Needham & Co., 445 Park Ave.. New York. NY 10022 (212) 371-8300

Oppenheimer & Co., Oppenheimer Tower. World Financial Center. New York. NY 10281 (212) 667-7000

PaineWebber, 1285 Ave. of the Americas, New York. NY 10019 (212) 713-2000

Piper Jaffray Inc., 222 S. Ninth St., Minneapolis, MN 55440 (612) 342-6000

Prudential Securities, One Seaport Plaza, New York, NY 10292 (212) 214-1000

Raymond James, 880 Carillon Pkwy.. St. Petersburg, FL 33716 (813) 573-3800

Robinson-Humphrey Co., 3333 Peachtree Rd., N.E., Atlanta, GA 30326 (404) 266-6000

SBC Warburg Dillon Read Inc., 222 Broadway, New York. NY 10038 (212) 335-1000

Salomon Smith Barney, Seven World Trade Center, New York, NY 10048 (212) 783-7000

Schroder & Co., 787 Seventh Ave., The Equitable Center. New York, NY 10019 (212) 492-6000

Sutro & Co., 201 California St., San Francisco, CA 94111 (415) 445-8500

UBS Securities Inc., 299 Park Ave.. New York, NY 10171 (212) 821-7500

Unterberg Harris, 275 Battery St., San Francisco, CA 94111 (415) 399-1500

Volpe, Brown Whelan & Co., One Maritime Plaza, San Francisco, CA 94111 (415) 956-8120

Wheat First Butcher Singer, 901 E. Byrd St., Richmond, VA 23219 (804) 649-2311

Standard & Poor's   ⬚

A Division of The McGraw-Hill Companies

Emerging & Special Situations (ISSN: 0882-5440) is published twice a month by Standard & Poor's, 25 Broadway, New York, NY 10004. Annual subscription: $259. Second-class postage paid at New York, NY and additional mailing offices. POSTMASTER: Send address changes to Emerging and Special Situations. Standard & Poor's, 25 Broadway, New York, NY 10004. Copyright © 1997 by The McGraw-Hill Companies. Reproduction in whole or in part prohibited except by permission. All rights reserved. Officers of The McGraw-Hill Companies: Joseph L. Dionne, Chairman and Chief Executive Officer; Harold W. McGraw, III, President and Chief Operating Officer; Kenneth M. Vittor, Senior Vice President and General Counsel; Robert J. Bahash, Executive Vice President and Chief Financial Officer; Frank D. Penglase, Senior Vice President, Treasury Operations. Because of the possibility of human or mechanical error by S&P's sources, S&P or others, S&P does not guarantee the accuracy, adequacy, or completeness of any information and is not responsible for any errors or omissions or for the results obtained from the use of such information. Information on initial public offerings is primarily derived from registration statements filed under the Securities Act of 1933 and is subject to correction and amendment. These securities may not be sold nor may offers to buy them be accepted prior to the time when the registration statement becomes effective. More complete information is contained in the prospectus which must be furnished to purchasers. Emerging & Special Situations is a publication of Standard & Poor's Equity Information Services Department. This department operates independently of, and has no access to information obtained by Standard & Poor's Ratings Group, which may in its regular operations obtain information of a confidential nature.

6

DECODING
THE PROSPECTUS

THE FIRST STEP in evaluating an IPO is obtaining and reading the prospectus for the deal. You can request one from the lead underwriter—a prospectus must be delivered to any customer who expresses interest in purchasing shares. By law, it must be sent out at least 48 hours prior to the mailing of a customer purchase confirmation. It is also available through the SEC's website.

The prospectus is filed by the issuer. Among other things, it must include a business description, names and addresses of key people involved in the enterprise, the amount of securities owned by such individuals, the company's capitalization, a description of the use of proceeds, and whether the company is subject to any legal proceedings. Major sections include the following:

Description of offering

Business summary

Capitalization

Use of proceeds

Description of underwriting

SEC disclaimer

Financial statements

History of business

Risks to purchasers

Management discussion of recent corporate results and financial standing

Description of management

Material business arrangement and contracts

Legal opinions

Once an initial offering prospectus is filed with the SEC, there is a 20-day cooling-off period. While investors look the material over, the SEC studies it to make sure that proper disclosure is being made. During this period, a broker is not legally allowed to send anything other than the prospectus to potential investors. Because the offering has not yet taken place, this initial prospectus does not include the final price, commissions, and dealer fees. No sales are allowed unless and until a buyer is furnished with a final prospectus. Nonetheless, *the SEC simply clears the offering for distribution to the public. It does not guarantee that the prospectus is accurate.*

THE PROSPECTUS AS DETECTIVE NOVEL

As in any good detective novel, before solving the mystery, you have to find all the bodies. You never know when or where they will turn up, so that means just about every section of the prospectus has to be inspected. The fewer the bodies, the more attractive the deal. In other words, read through the entire prospectus before trying to value the shares.

An offering prospectus may at first appear to be a daunting document. It is usually more than 100 pages long, without exhibits (see Table 6-1). But like any other task, it takes less time the more often you do it. Seasoned professionals can run through a typical IPO prospectus in less than an hour. After reading this chapter you should be able to do the same.

It is important to remember that no one piece of information is apt to make your decision. It is the mosaic of information gathered by reading the prospectus that usually tips the scales one way or the other. It might be helpful to keep a scratch pad with two columns headed *Positives* and *Negatives*. As you read the document, list the obvious points on each side. When you are done, review your list, properly weighing each factor.

Finally, remember that you should read the prospectus with the goal of answering two questions:

1.   What is the appropriate price-to-earnings (P/E) valuation for this company?

2.   Can this company sustain its sales and earnings trends?

The initial offering prospectus is known as a *red herring* because of the legal red lettering that can be found on the print version. The required red-ink legend states that the prospectus has been filed with the SEC but has not yet become effective.

TABLE 6-1 Overview of a prospectus.

Section	Stated Purpose	Content	What to Look For
Cover page	Offering details	Amount of shares being offered Who is selling Offering price range Underwriters	Percentage of shares sold for company Percentage of shares sold by insiders Quality of underwriters
Inside cover page	Shows actual product or company facilities	Photos Tables	
Prospectus summary	Summary of most pertinent data of company and offering	Short corporate description Description of the market; corporate strategy and corporate background Basic facts of the actual offering Five years of selected income and balance-sheet data	Section most susceptible to marketing hype; description not intended to be balanced Use of proceeds Revenue and earnings trends Debt/equity ratio after offering
Risk factors	The major things that could go wrong and prevent the company from executing its business plan	Risks, ordered potentially most to least important	Competitive risks Product development risks Operating risks Customer concentration Contract risks Financial risks Absolute number of risks
Use of proceeds	What company will spend its portion of proceeds on	Specific dollar allocations of proceeds	Shares eligible for future sale How much is being reinvested in the business How much is directly or indirectly going to pre-IPO owners *(Continued)*

TABLE 6-1 Overview of a prospectus (*Continued*).

Section	Stated Purpose	Content	What to Look For
Dividend policy	Expected initial dividend payout, if any	Initial quarterly dividend First declaration date	Initial per-share dividend annualized as percentage of trailing 12-month EPS Long-term debt and other long-term liabilities as percentage of long-term debt, other liabilities, and stockholders' equity Short-term debt after offering
Capitalization	Changes in balance sheet caused by IPO	Most salient balance-sheet items before and after deal	
Dilution	Change in book value caused by IPO	Per-share dilution to new investors Total consideration paid by pre-IPO investors Total consideration to be paid by outside investors through IPO	Average per-share price paid by existing investors Percentage IPO investor consideration paid versus ownership interest acquired
Selected financial information	Full income statement Selected balance sheet information Income and balance sheet statements pro forma for the offering(s)	Five years of income and balance-sheet history, year-to-date stats	Sales and earnings trends Changes in profit margins Changes in costs as percentage of revenues R&D as percentage of revenues Changes in tax rate Nonoperating income and interest changes

Management's discussion of financial condition	Prose description of year-to-date and annual changes in sales, costs, and earnings	Reasons for revenue growth Components of revenue by product line and/or geography Reasons for changes in costs as percentage of revenues Major contributions to gains/declines in operating income Reasons for changes in interest income/expense and tax rate	Changes in revenue growth rate Changes in revenues from major customers Changes in gross profit margin Major trend-altering changes in costs as percentage of revenues Changes in rate of operating income growth Changes in rate of earnings growth Changes during periods closest to IPO more important than back years Back out nonrecurring items
Business description			
Company description	Basic description of company operations	Present business lines	Missing descriptions of current business lines
History	History of operations	Company's formation Changes in legal status	Missing years in prose version of business time line
Products and services	More specific descriptions of current business lines	Breakdown of product lines within each business segment	Full descriptions of lagging/cash cow operations Ratio of text devoted to hot business lines versus slower-growing ones versus their sales and earnings Length of product life cycles History of product introductions for each major and fast-growing business segment

(Continued)

TABLE 6-1 Overview of a prospectus (*Continued*).

Section	Stated Purpose	Content	What to Look For
Customers	Description of customers	Type of customer Major customers	Domination of a specific customer type Quality of customer list Percentages of revenues from major customers Lengths of contracts with major users
Product development	Description of process	Characterization of importance of R&D Success factors Amounts spent on R&D Number of employees in R&D	External or internal development Favorable follow-on R&D work beyond first generation R&D as percentage of revenues Success of new and continuing R&D efforts Hints of personnel changes that could affect future R&D success
Employees	Number of employees by type	Number of employees Union/nonunion status Union contract expirations	Near-term wage issues Management initiatives to maintain and improve relations Pending union contract expirations Changes in quality of management/employee relations

Competition	Qualitative review of competitive conditions	Recent changes in competitive conditions
	Important competitive factors	Factors emphasized by firm to gain competitive edge
	State of competition	Recent changes in competitive landscape
		Importance of technology versus price
		Company's relative emphasis of technology and price
		Competitive pressures that may affect firm's technology or price advantage
		Recent changes in intermediary relationships affecting near-term results
Manufacturing	Manufacturing process and facilities	Single sources of components or raw materials
	Factories by size, location, and year built	Importance of raw material prices to revenue growth and profit margins
	Sources of raw materials or components	Age of owned/leased manufacturing facilities

(Continued)

TABLE 6-1 Overview of a prospectus (*Continued*).

Section	Stated Purpose	Content	What to Look For
Properties	Description of physical plant	Corporate headquarters Distribution or manufacturing plants Expansion requirements to accommodate growth	Age of facilities Location of major plants to current and future customer base Current capacity utilization Expansion plans Foreign supply capabilities Potential effect of expansion plans on near-term capacity utilization Facility ownership by third parties or corporate insiders
Legal proceedings	Description of potential or existing legal proceedings	Description of nature of potential or existing legal liability Possible financial ramifications from potential or existing legal actions	Potential or existing patent suits that could affect competitive position Financial impact of possible adverse legal decisions Product-liability exposures
Environmental issues	Impact of corporate activities on the environment	Potential or existing exposures to cleanup costs due to previous or existing production activities	Potential or existing cleanup costs
Regulatory issues	Impact of federal and state regulations on business operations	Pending or existing laws that impact or potentially impact operations	Effect of potential regulatory actions on product sales Impact of changing industry regulations on future competition

Management		
Chief executives and board members	Quality of management	Five-year history and backgrounds of senior managers, board of directors; age, position with company
		Experience running large operations
		Entrepreneurial versus formal education levels
		Collective industry experience
		Tenure with company
		Amount of time devoted to company
		Quality of board—hands-on applicable business experience
		Filial relationships
		Business success of CEO
Compensation	Senior employee compensation	Cash compensation
		Stock option or stock purchase plans
		Retirement benefits
		Employment agreements
		Level of compensation versus industry
		Value of stock options granted each year
		Total stock options granted versus shares outstanding
		Impact of cumulative compensation on senior executive ambitions

(Continued)

TABLE 6-1 Overview of a prospectus (*Continued*).

Section	Stated Purpose	Content	What to Look For
Insider transactions	Description of insider transactions	Insider-owned properties leased by company Stock purchase arrangements Business transactions involving affiliates, corporate parents Operating contracts with affiliates, corporate parents	Potential impact of corporate profitability based on insider transactions Recent resignations of key executives Nature of insider transactions Potential or current impact on corporate profitability Potential conflicts of interest Potential compromise of insider's corporate loyalty
Share ownership	Current corporate ownership	Owners with or potentially with more than 5 percent of each preferred and common stock class before and after IPO Shares being sold via IPO by major holders Total amount of insider shares potentially available for sale in aftermarket	Share ownership after IPO by directors and officers Large insider sales Large sales of shares as percentage of holdings and exercisable stock options Ownership by investment partners managed by astute sponsors Ownership changes by limited partners

Shares eligible for future sale	Shares owned by insiders that can potentially be sold in aftermarket	Number of shares subject to underwriter lock-up agreements Expiration date of underwriter lock-up agreements Insider stock registration rights	Expiration date of lock-up agreements Number of shares not subject to lock-up immediately available for sale in aftermarket Dates when additional stock becomes available for sale
Financials	Two years of balance sheets Three full years plus partial current year Two years of cash-flow numbers Pro forma income and balance-sheet statements as required Income statements and balance sheets of predecessor firms and pending acquisitions	Full statements Pro formas as though recent reorganizations or acquisitions had occurred earlier	Footnotes for aggressive accounting methods Operating cash-flow trends Timing of stockholder contributions Reasons for existing tax rate Likely changes in tax rate Available tax loss credits Provisions and amortization requirements of debt agreements Segment revenue and operating income information
Other sections			
Description of common stock	Full description of rights and privileges of stockholders by individual class		Major differentiating factors
Registrar and transfer agent experts	Signoffs by financial professionals that had a hand in creating the prospectus		Should be reputable
Accountants' opinion			
Officer signatures			Essential that it be unqualified

The answer to the first question should help you come up with a fair price for the offering. Answering the second will help you to decide if these are shares you should hold for the long run.

COVER PAGE

The cover page lays out the details of the stock offering. Most of it is *boilerplate*—that is, standard information that does not vary from one prospectus to the next. But there are a few clues to be found here. The ones to look for are the total *number of shares* being sold, the *percent of shares being sold by the company,* the preliminary *offering price range,* and the quality of the *underwriters.*

The first paragraph usually explains *who is selling the shares.* Typically, the majority of shares are sold by the company, with additional stock sold by insiders. It should be a warning flag if all shares are being sold by insiders. That's because insiders have more knowledge about the company than just about any outside investor—if they are selling, why should you be buying?

Also in this section is a preliminary *offering price range.* This is the underwriters' best estimate of the potential price of the shares. They arrive at this price based on their due diligence work to this point. The actual offering price could be above or below this range, based on the receptiveness of investors, as well as the performance of the overall stock market and the stocks of the companies in that industry.

The absolute dollar amount—be it 3, 10, or 21—*has absolutely no importance as to the stock's investment merits.* That can only be found elsewhere in the prospectus. That is to say, a stock priced at 20 could be every bit as speculative as one priced to be sold at 5. The table in the middle of the cover page is left blank, to be completed in the final prospectus after the shares have been sold. It is only then that the underwriter will know exactly

---

At the top of the cover page is a notice of the *number of shares* that are expected to be sold through this offering. The higher the number of shares being sold, the more difficult it will be for the shares to pop on the first day of trading. The smaller the number, the easier it is for that to occur. More than 5 million shares should be considered high, and will require fairly significant institutional participation. Less than 1.5 million shares is a small deal.

how many shares have been sold, the underwriters' fee, and the proceeds to the company.

At the bottom of the page are the *lead underwriters* in the offering. This is one of the most important pieces of information on the cover page. The primary lead underwriter is at the top. (If there is more than one in the same row, then it is the first one on the left.) The other underwriters listed on the cover page are the major underwriting partners that will help market the deal. The larger the deal, the greater the supporting cast. In a huge offering, the total list of underwriters goes well beyond the lead ones noted here, and could include virtually every significant brokerage house in the country.

The quality of the lead underwriter(s) is a major clue as to the overall quality of a deal. IPOs underwritten by top-tier brokers do better over the long run than those brought by second- and third-tier underwriters. Generally speaking, the larger and more prestigious the firm, the more that firm's name and reputation could be adversely impacted by a bad IPO. The best underwriting houses get the largest and best deals. This does not mean that all the IPOs they underwrite will do well over time, but it does increase the odds for the better.

Small offerings by small underwriters tend to perform best, at least initially, in hot IPO markets, but worst over the longer term. This is because small deals are more likely to be affected most by the trading environment initially created by the lead underwriter. Small deals also involve companies that are typically very early in development and that have been unable to find financing from more reputable investment groups. Stick with the larger underwriters.

PROSPECTUS SUMMARY

If a portfolio manager or analyst has to get through 10 prospectuses in an hour, this section is what he or she reads first. Back in the 1980s, the prospectus summary was a small description of the company. Today, this first section of the prospectus is probably the most promotional part of the document. This is the section where the SEC most allows issuers to sell the deal. It is not intended to be balanced.

The prospectus summary has been lengthened and compartmentalized over the years. After a basic description of the company, there follows a description of the *addressable market,* followed by sections on *strategy* and *corporate background,* which usually involve the formation and financing of the company to the present.

Since this is essentially a promotional section, the company goals in the strategy section will always be admirable and agreeable to most investors. The strategy section will contain supporting commentary to show that the company is making real strides in executing its corporate business plan.

That is all well and good. But investors should be very careful to differentiate reality (company description, background) from intentions (market, strategy). The addressable market will typically be described as quite large compared with the current size of the firm. That might imply significant growth prospects. But keep in mind that the company probably does not have the products or current financing to address the entire market. Indeed, there will be nary a qualifier in this entire section. Along the same lines, the company may have a brilliant strategy, but your job is to determine whether it can execute it. Take what is contained in the market and strategy sections with a healthy grain of salt.

For example, in the IPO prospectus for Calpine, a major independent power producer, the first sentence of the market section of the prospectus summary reads, "The power generation business represents the third largest industry in the United States, with an estimated end user market of approximately $207.5 billion of electricity sales and 3 million gigawatt hours of production in 1995." What it does not say is that independent producers like Calpine have only a tiny portion of that market and that structural considerations within the electrical utility industry and a lack of financial capacity will prevent it from going after more than a tiny portion of the total market.

By far the most important information here is the *use of proceeds*. The use of proceeds provides a number of signals about the company's real growth prospects, and should tell you whether the IPO will move the company toward those growth goals. The *common shares to be outstanding* is also important in calculating the market capitalization of the company (shares outstanding times stock price). We like to compare this number to total revenues, a particularly important ratio for fast-growing firms.

The selected *consolidated information* table is a quick summary of the company's results for the last five-plus years. The most important line items from the income statement for the last five complete fiscal years are shown, plus results so far in the current fiscal year. Balance-sheet data is also shown at the end of the most recently completed fiscal quarter. The balance sheet is now also shown on a pro forma basis—that is, with new numbers which assume that the IPO is completed, and that the shares were sold at the middle range of the indicated price range. This gives investors an idea of how the balance sheet will look after the offering. (Also be careful to read whatever footnotes may exist. Most tables will contain footnotes that refer to nonrecurring items that may have been taken during one or more of the reporting periods shown, or that provide definitions of certain line items, including those that are industry specific.)

The most important things to bear in mind here are *revenue and earnings trends* and the *debt-to-equity ratios* after the offering. Although the calculations are often done for you in the prospectus, one should pay particular attention to the yearly change in revenue and earnings growth for each period. We would list slowing revenue and/or earnings growth as definite negative factors. Exceptions could be when a company has higher research and development expenses as a percent of revenues as it tries to stay ahead of the competition in a rapidly evolving market, or when a company is still developing its marketing infrastructure.

The balance-sheet data allows you to quickly calculate debt as a percentage of capitalization—an important measure of a company's debt load. This calculation is sometimes known as *committed capital* [long-term debt/(long-term debt + other long-term liabilities + stockholders' equity)].

COMPANY DESCRIPTION

This is another description of the company, which has recently become highly duplicative with the prospectus summary at the beginning of the document. There is some additional discussion about specific products, but that is covered in more detail in later sections. The final paragraph usually describes the firm's corporate transformations (i.e., founding, move to corporate status, and major acquisitions or sales of business lines). For the record, the corporate address and phone number can usually be found here.

RISK FACTORS

This is absolutely essential reading. This is where most of the bodies are buried. Underwriters rely on this section to fulfill the SEC requirement that they provide *full and fair disclosure* of the risks of investing in a particular company. It also helps to avoid lawsuits brought by disappointed investors. You will find that the smaller the deal, the less respected the underwriter, and the shorter the corporate history, the longer the list of risk factors. The cleaner the corporate history, the steadier the revenue and earnings, and the more predictable the industry fundamentals, the shorter the list of risks.

There is boilerplate in this section—that is, risk factors that have to be mentioned in every prospectus—but the first few of them usually apply to the company itself. These are known risks that the investor will be assuming when buying the shares. These "concerns" represent the most likely reasons that a stock could go down in subsequent trading. Just one of these risk factors, if severe enough, can be enough for Standard & Poor's to recommend avoiding an IPO. Pay particular attention to competitive, product development, operating, customer contract, and financial risks.

USE OF PROCEEDS
This concept is reviewed to some extent in the section on the prospectus summary. In essence, you want to be sure that the company is using proceeds for the betterment of the firm, and for new as well as existing shareholders. An example of an *undesirable* use of proceeds would be big dividend payouts—for example, to other stockholders or a parent company.

The use of proceeds to repay debt is good if it frees up financial capacity for the firm to grow through acquisition. However, again, if the goal is to get down to a more normal debt level, then very little benefit will accrue to future stockholders. One way or another, reinvestment in the business is what counts, not the return of previously invested capital or even the reduction of debt.

DIVIDEND POLICY
Unless the company is a real estate investment trust (REIT) or a high-dividend-paying limited partnership, the dividend policy usually has very little bearing on the initial value of a firm or the pricing of an IPO. Most companies going public are trying to raise capital to grow their businesses. Paying it out in the form of dividends would be counterproductive. For growth companies, the return on every dollar of capital retained in the business should be higher than that to an investor if they put it elsewhere. In other words, as a shareholder, you should not really *want* a dividend from a growth company. That money should be used to grow the business and thus increase the stock price.

In the case of REITs, oil and gas pipeline companies and partnerships, and closed-end bond funds, the name of the game is dividend coverage. Here, payout as a percentage of cash flow (net income plus depreciation) is the crucial ratio. A payout above 90 percent of cash flow could be an invitation for trouble. A payout below 75 percent offers opportunities for dividend increases or growth through reinvestment in the business—a real plus when it comes to total-return stocks. Also, look for clues to the company's ability to maintain and grow the payout. Avoid those with *wasting assets* (i.e., oil and gas production and shipping partnerships). Last, these kinds of stocks trade as much on changes in interest rates as on their own fundamentals. They will tend to rise when rates are falling and decline when rates are moving up.

CAPITALIZATION

This is a more complete version of the company's balance sheet before and after the offering. There are breakdowns of both long-term liabilities and stockholders' equity. The capitalization section gives a more complete picture of how the balance sheet will change as a result of the IPO. (Keep in mind that it almost always changes for the better. Stockholders' equity goes up as a result of the equity infusion and debt often drops, helping debt/equity ratios.)

DILUTION

The first table in this section describes the changes that will occur to the company's book value; the second table details the amount of money that has been contributed and the price paid per share by various shareholder groups. (Book value has diminished in importance over time. In the days of Graham and Dodd, when there was little inflation, book value was considered an important measure of how much a company and its stock might be worth. But that was before inflation in the 1970s and financial engineering techniques in the 1990s, including large stock buybacks and writedowns from corporate takeovers, undermined the validity of the statistic as a measure of economic value.)

Nonetheless, one potential red flag that can be found in this section is when net tangible book value is negative after the offering. A company might still be attractive despite a negative book value, but the lack of stockholders' equity could make it more difficult for the company to tap credit lines should the company's cash flow or industry conditions deteriorate.

Of more interest to you is the table showing the relative contributions of existing and new investors. Of particular note is the average price paid per share. For existing stockholders, this is the amount paid per share less cash amounts that might subsequently have been distributed. Existing stockholders typically contribute significantly less than those putting in money at the IPO and wind up with the lion's share of the equity.

Another warning flag is when the average insider cost is just below or above the prospective offering price. This often means that insiders overpaid for their investment and may be looking to public stockholders to bail them out of a difficult situation. The investment could still be a sound one, but more often than not, the problems that prevented the company from increasing in value as a *private concern* will restrain its progress as a *public one.*

SELECTED CONSOLIDATED FINANCIAL DATA

The two tables that make up the bulk of this section expand upon the *historical income* and *balance sheet data* introduced in the prospectus summary. The most important items introduced here are the complete income statements, which allow for better analysis of earnings growth. Scrutiny of revenue growth trends and each cost and expense line is the best way to project future profit levels. The rate of profit growth is the most important factor driving the P/E ratio, both at the IPO and in the aftermarket.

As in the earlier sales and earnings summary, pay particular attention to sales and earnings trends as well as changes in each cost and expense line as a percentage of revenue. (Be sure to exclude any one-time events when you are measuring year-to-year performance.)

MANAGEMENT'S DISCUSSION AND ANALYSIS
OF OPERATIONS AND FINANCIAL CONDITION

After the prospectus summary and risk factors sections, this is the third most important part of the prospectus. The management discussion section contains the most detailed information available on historical results. When reading this section, you should be trying to determine whether sales and earnings growth can be sustained. This is the key factor behind choosing the appropriate P/E to apply to the firm's earnings. This will also affect how long you want to hold the shares.

The section is usually composed of two required and two optional parts. Management discusses each major revenue and cost line item, one at a time. The next section is entitled "Liquidity and Capital Resources." It contains management's discussion of the firm's recent capital requirements, the company's needs to execute its business plan over the foreseeable future, and the sources of capital that will be available.

An optional section is a table showing each line item in the income statement as a percentage of revenues. This section can be invaluable. To fully understand an income statement, you need the yearly percentage change in revenue, as well as the expense and profit lines calculated *as a percentage of revenue.* This table does the latter task for you. By looking at changes in expenses as a percentage of revenues, along with revenue growth trends, you can begin to form your earnings projections. These will be a primary tool in deciding what the stock should be worth at the offering.

A second optional section is a quarterly sales and earnings table. This is usually included in the prospectus for very fast growing tech companies that have short operating histories, or other companies that have a great deal of seasonality within annual results (i.e., construction and swimming pool companies).

To do a good job with the management discussion, you should spend a fair amount of time studying the following items: the *revenue growth rate* and *gross profit margin, costs as a percentage of revenues,* and *operating income and net earnings growth.* Also, pay particular attention to changes that have occurred in periods closest to the IPO, back out nonrecurring items, and carefully consider any discussion of changes in revenues from major customers. Try to compare the company's profit margins with those of comparable companies by getting on the Internet and accessing 10-Qs and 10-Ks on the SEC EDGAR website, or Standard & Poor's and Value Line stock reports.

BUSINESS DESCRIPTION

According to Peter Lynch, one of Fidelity Management's most successful portfolio managers, the first thing one should gauge when buying stocks is one's comfort level with the basic business. If you were thinking of buying a gas marketer and its station down the road from you was up for sale, would you buy it? If you were looking to invest in a tax software company, would you buy its tax package?

The business description provides invaluable information for an IPO. It describes in much greater detail the evolution of the firm's products and services, the markets and customers served, any competitive advantages, how the products are sold, and environmental and legal issues. This section should be one of the first you read, because if you are not comfortable with the business and the firm's growth strategies, then there is little reason to read on.

Many prospectuses today start this section by repeating points from the prospectus summary, and then offer an overview, comments on the market, and the firm's development strategy. Following that should be an extended discussion of the firm's products. There should be a thorough description of each product line and its evolution, as well as current prices and development activities. You should get a good sense of each major product's life span and where it currently is on the curve. There should also be a full listing of industries served and representative customers, as well as a breakdown of revenues by distribution channel. International sales and marketing efforts should also be included.

The amount of copy devoted to competition can vary, but it is important that major competitors be mentioned by name for each product line. The discussion of manufacturing facilities should include mention of the geographical location of facilities and important component costs. Mention should also be made of the quality of relationships between management and employees, how many of them are unionized, and the number that might be subject to incentive programs. The discussion of legal proceedings should also include the general climate of litigation that exists in this business.

When reading this section, what is *not* included is as important as what is. In particular, look for missing descriptions of business lines that account for a fair amount of revenues. Often the amount of text devoted to different business lines is out of kilter with their relative contributions to sales and earnings. Does this mean that they are outmoded? Has the company properly mapped out a future without these products, or is the deemphasis based on the failure of the products themselves? If you suspect it is the latter case, how culpable was current management in not properly designing and marketing the line? Could this happen again with the company's current main activities? Do not be misled by extended descriptions of rapidly growing product lines which represent only a small portion of total revenues.

Be careful to note the length of product life cycles and where the company may be with its major products. Revenues rise fastest just as a new product is introduced, and then tend to lag in anticipation of next-generation competition. Note the history of product introductions. Has the company shown success in handling product transitions? Many technology companies exploit an emerging technology, but fail to follow through on the timely development of next-generation versions.

Look for missing years in the description of the company's business development. That could mean the company took a detour. It may not have much relevance to the current business, but it could reflect on management's overall business acumen.

There are always legal proceedings of one kind or another. Make sure to take note of those suits that could have a materially adverse impact on the company's long-term viability. It could be a patent suit, for example, or an environmental suit, which, if lost, could mean big losses. Of less importance is legislation that has to do with events that occurred in the past and do not have a bearing on current or future operations. The one-time judgment might be large, but as long as the company has the financial resources to pay it, most investors will look past it. Remember that the present value of a company is, for the most part, the present value of future earnings. As long as the one-time judgment does not threaten the firm's future, it should not significantly impact the value investors currently place on the company. Indeed, a settlement often triggers a rise in stock price, as investors see that the potential liability has been quantified and dealt with.

MANAGEMENT
There are many important kernels of information buried in the small biographies of *key executives*. However, do not count on the most significant business events of an officer's past appearing here. Although most go

back farther, biographies are legally required to cover only five years. More responsible underwriters with reputations to protect will provide fuller disclosure here. There have been many instances, however, when legal infractions, compliance problems, or an unsuccessful past business have not appeared here. Nefarious characters who may be intimately involved in the company's affairs often do not show up because they are neither officers nor directors. They can, however, appear in the stock ownership table or in the footnotes to that table.

The first thing to do is review the backgrounds of the chief executive officer (CEO), chief operations officer (COO), and the head of research and development (R&D). Successful, intelligent, and motivated senior managers do not get on rickety ships. As professional managers go, the best jockeys tend to wind up with the best horses. A sound business concept for profitable growth will attract the attention of smart, savvy senior executives.

Are the original founders willing to cede authority as the business gets bigger? Many of them have the entrepreneurial skills to develop a product, but once the technology has been proven, another set of executives may be required to raise additional capital, manage full-scale production, and create a full-fledged marketing infrastructure. Once a company gets to be a certain size—about the time when the CEO no longer recognizes the names of everyone at the firm—resource management and strategic planning take precedence over entrepreneurship and the CEO's own customer relationships. Perfecting a product, developing a working prototype, and attracting initial sales personnel are vastly different tasks than managing a large corporation. This takes professional managers with an ability to study a market, develop long-term growth plans, and execute them efficiently. The founder may still be able to grow the business, but someone else may be better able to maximize the firm's potential.

Take a look at the ages of the senior executives. There is nothing intrinsically wrong with senior managers being either very young (under 35) or approaching retirement age (over 60), but in the former case it often does mean a lack of experience in running a large business through an entire product or economic cycle. When senior executives are older, there could be succession issues. This is particularly important for the CEO position, as that individual's vision may be difficult to replace.

Scrutinize recent departures of top executives. They may have been important to the success of the firm—will their absence hinder future growth? Abrupt departures of CEOs and COOs are rare just before an IPO. If one occurs, you should be satisfied that the replacement is a potentially stronger player.

The COO should have experience running a large organization. Consider the collective industry experience of key executives and directors. Do not be taken in by well-known retired executives serving on the board of directors. These supposedly independent directors were nominated by current management and probably are very supportive of its activities. Look for current or new board members who represent venture capital or those nominated by the underwriter to represent the interests of new public stockholders. More important, these executives should have hands-on experience in the company's field in order to provide advice. Too often, boards are filled with dignitaries to fulfill certain political or filial purposes. This is usually just window dressing and should be viewed as such. Colin Powell does not pretend to have a lot of business experience, but he is on more than one corporate board.

Try to intuit why founders have remained an integral part of the enterprise, or why they have not. Was it good for the company that they left or stayed? Why and when did new managers come on board? Was it after the firm missed certain operating or financial targets?

The quality of the board of directors is extremely important. Board members do not get involved in day-to-day affairs, but subcommittees do pass judgment on compensation levels, strategic business plans, and audit controls. Board members are also the primary agents of management change at the top when it is warranted. In ideal situations, a majority of board members should be independent directors. Independent directors, in theory, act on behalf of outside stockholders. Beware of family relationships or managements dominated by relatives. That could be a sign of an unwillingness to share corporate decision making, which could prove a major deterrent to long-term success and prevent the natural flow of better managers to the top.

Executive compensation gives important clues about the stakes of top management. What are the incentives to grow the business? Salary levels vary widely based on the industry and firm size. Compare executive salaries against those at comparable companies in the same industry. Retailing and entertainment companies pay some of the highest salaries, while technology companies have the most generous stock-option programs.

It is important that management have some kind of stake in the company's future. Give careful attention to the number of shares available for stock-option programs. In general, it is better that a CEO have a low salary and a large number of stock options. This should be within reason, of course—every stock grant at a discount to the current share price causes dilution to current and future stockholders' holdings. With that in mind, the total number of shares available for options should not exceed 10 percent of total current shares outstanding. Be wary of companies that set aside more than 20 percent of outstanding shares for stock-option programs.

There are always insider transactions. Some are fairly innocuous occurrences. Often, one or more of the officers own a building that the company occupies. Just make sure that there is a statement to the effect that rents being paid approximate the going rate. There are also instances when the company may contract for a service provided by entities controlled or owned by officers or large shareholders. This can be stickier. There should be a statement similar to that for rental agreements. Be on the lookout for agreements large enough to have the potential to impact profitability. Consider this example: Suppose that, a year or so before the IPO, the CEO of an auto rental company grants the firm a sweetheart deal to lease cars from another firm he controls. That way, earnings would be spruced up before the offering. But he could reverse the deal after the IPO has been completed, penalizing shareholders of the public company.

PRINCIPAL AND SELLING STOCKHOLDERS
The share ownership table lets the reader of a prospectus know how committed managers may be to the success of the venture. Professional investors like it when corporate principals have large sweat equity stakes. More important is whether they are voting with their feet and selling shares at the IPO. It is normal for executives with almost all of their assets in company stock to try to diversify their financial assets by selling some stock at the offering, but it should not be a majority of available shares. The remaining holdings should still represent the major portion of their net worth. Let intuition be your guide to an executive's possible worth based on their previous business positions and connections. Sale of a total stake by a corporation or an individual is a significant warning sign.

Look for reputable venture capital investors. The most successful managers and venture capital investors tend to be offered the best deals. They also have the best analytical skills, management expertise, and financial resources that can be used to promote successful execution of an upstart company's plans. (Some of those with good noses for investment are listed in Table 6-2.) Their presence is an important endorsement of the basic business enterprise. Although it does not guarantee success, it does show that smart-money individuals saw enough here to warrant investment.

SHARES ELIGIBLE FOR FUTURE SALE
The most important thing to look for here is the *expiration date of the underwriter's lock-up agreement.* Virtually every underwriting has one. In an age when many IPOs soar in price on the first day of trading, it may

TABLE 6-2   Smart Venture Investors.

Acadia Partners	Mayfield Funds
Accel Partners	Menlo Ventures
Acorn Ventures	New Enterprise Associates
Apollo Partners	Norwest Equity Partners
Battery Ventures	Oak Investment Partners
Benchmark Capital	Odyssey Partners
Brentwood Venture Capital	Omega Advisers
Canaan Partners	Sequoia Capital
Charles River Partnership	Sigma Partners
CMG, Inc.	Summit Partners
Greylock Partners	Sutter Hill Ventures
Hancock Venture Partners	TA Associates
International Venture Partners	Trident Partners
Internet Capital Group	Weiss, Peck & Greer
Kleiner, Perkins	Welsh Carson Anderson & Stowe

seem hard to believe that one of the lead underwriter's most important jobs is to stabilize prices in the aftermarket. If the stock jumps in price, the underwriter might short the stock (sell into the rising market), in an effort to reduce the rapid advance. (The short position would then be covered by exercise of the "green shoe" at the offer price.) By going short at a higher price and covering at the offering price with additional shares purchased from the company or insiders at the offer price, the underwriter turns a trading profit while also trying to limit price appreciation.

However, the underwriter might be reluctant to make these price stabilization moves if there are a lot of insider shares eligible for sale in the open market, particularly at the higher price. This is where the lock-up agreement comes in. Insiders agree not to sell any of their shares for a specific period of time, usually 180 days, without the express consent of the underwriter. This is good for the IPO buyer because the total number of shares eligible for trading in the aftermarket is limited to those offered in the deal (possibly supplemented by up to 15 percent through exercise of the green shoe).

The total number of shares subject to lock-up is often many multiples higher than the amount sold through the offering. For this reason, *be very careful to note the number of shares subject to the agreement.* There are occasionally instances when not all insider shares are tied up. The amount of insider shares eligible for sale (i.e., not covered by the lock-up) should not exceed 50 percent of the shares sold through the IPO.

FINANCIALS
The full financials at the end of the prospectus contain much the same information found elsewhere. Be careful to check for pro forma numbers, which assume that a recent or ensuing event has already occurred when calculating past results. That way investors can get an idea of what the new company's revenues, profits, and growth rates look like. Pro forma results are usually provided when an acquisition or reorganization is planned or has occurred just prior to the IPO. Pro forma results in this section sometimes also take into account the effects of the IPO—that is, the sale of the new shares. This gives investors a sneak peak at the effects on profitability.

Finally, take a quick look at the accounting statement to be sure that the accountant's opinion is *unqualified*. It should also be signed by a recognizable firm with a reputation to lose if its audit proves faulty. Also visit the footnotes to the main financial statement. Glance at the first lengthy footnote, particularly the section covering depreciation methods. Check for any changes, being sure that they are industry standards. A change in the depreciation method could have a very large effect on reported earnings and cause a company to appear more profitable than it really is compared to other companies in its field.

Tech companies often play around with the amount of R&D capitalized. (Generally speaking, the less the better.) Other kinds of companies may require closer scrutiny of revenue recognition. Also check the changes in tax rates. Maybe you can see a trend that could favorably impact or hurt future results—something that is often not discussed anywhere else in the prospectus. And look at long-term debt agreements—what are the amounts available for borrowing, the amounts subject to changing interest rates, and the debt agreement expiration dates? Lease agreements could also affect profitability if favorable ones expire early.

Those of you who would like to study the investment process still further should profit from studying the materials in the appendix at the end of the book. It contains a selection of pages from the IPO prospectuses for Microsoft (1984) and for Worlds of Wonder (1986), the creator and marketer of the Teddy Ruxpin doll that was fabulously popular for Christmas 1985, along with some short commentary, comparisons, and tables illustrating how one could have differentiated success from failure. Also found there are the original recommendation of Microsoft and pan of Worlds of Wonder that were published in Standard & Poor's *Emerging & Special Sit-*

uations at the time the initial offerings occurred. Table 6-3 suggests a reading order for the sections when analyzing a prospectus.

TABLE 6-3   Reading order for sections of a prospectus for analysis.

Prospectus summary

Risk factors

Managements' discussion and analysis
of operations

History of business

Financial statements

Description of management

Use of proceeds

Description of offerings

Capitalization

Material business arrangements

Legal opinions

Description of underwriting

SEC disclaimer

C H A P T E R

7

IPO POINTERS
ON SPECIFIC INDUSTRIES

EVERY INDUSTRY HAS different business and competitive characteristics. Most IPOs are of companies that occupy small niches.
There are too many of these industry niches to adequately
cover here, but some general observations can be noted for
some of the more important categories.

The largest categories of new issues are technology (computer software, services, networking, the Internet, emerging telecommunications,
semiconductors and semiconductor equipment, and biotech), specialty
retailers, medical products and services, American Depositary Receipts
(ADRs), bank and savings and loan (S&L) conversions, leveraged buyouts
(LBOs), and energy. Each industry has its own valuation models, and analysts write entire books about each group. This chapter is confined to the
most salient points to consider when investing in one of these IPOs.

AMERICAN DEPOSITARY RECEIPTS (ADRs)
American Depositary Receipts (ADRs) are stock offerings of companies
domiciled outside the United States. Although ADRs are traded on U.S.
exchanges, they are not really shares of stock. They simply represent shares
that physically exist somewhere else. In this arrangement, shares are placed on
deposit at a U.S. bank to equal the number of shares held by American owners,
who are then issued ADRs representing that ownership claim. When the
American owner sells the shares, they can be cleared just like any other stock.

Foreign stocks, particularly British ones, often trade at very low prices. This might give the impression to American investors that the stocks are speculative, so many ADRs and American Depositary Shares (ADSs) are for more than one ordinary share. For example, the Telefonos de Mexico ADR that trades on the New York Stock Exchange is equal to 20 ordinary shares that trade on the Mexican Bolsa.

Evaluating foreign stocks is in many ways quite complex. There are currency translation considerations, as well as significant differences in accounting principles. Most important, one is likely to be less aware of certain basic business characteristics in another country, such as labor relations, regulations, the tax environment, and local economic conditions. The huge Deutsche Telecom offering in late 1996, for example, presented all of these issues. In addition, almost all of its operations were in Germany, which would have made it more difficult for American investors to evaluate the company against other global leaders such as AT&T.

Fortunately, most ADRs are of large concerns with fairly long operating histories—longer ones than for most IPOs here. These extended track records make it somewhat easier to understand the intricacies of the business. It also helps if the firm has global operations, which could make it more comparable to U.S.-based global companies. For British Telecom, for example, a fair comparable would be Mercury Telecommunications, a British competitor, or even the former Bell local phone companies in the United States. For ENI, an Italian integrated oil and gas exploration and production company, the comparable could be AGIP, also based in Italy. (In the United States, one might use BP Petroleum or Exxon.)

Another important issue is the location of revenues. Your analysis should be weighted toward the country where the company collects most of its sales. For Deutsche Telecom it would be Germany; for STMicroelectronics, it would be western Europe first, the United States second, and then the Far East; and for Gucci, it would be western Europe and the United States. Table 7-1 lists representative offerings.

BANKING

At last count, there were 8975 banks in this country. Although there is a continuing trend to consolidate, there are still thousands of privately owned banks that may seek to convert to a public corporation.

Conversions are usually good deals for depositors. In order to induce them to agree to a conversion to public stock, shares are often offered below their perceived value, typically about 10 percent. Most banks traded between 1.0 and 2.0 times *book value* (book value is a company's assets minus its liabilities divided by the number of shares outstanding), with

TABLE 7-1 Representative ADR offerings.

IPO	Symbol	IPO Date	Price	Offering Size	6/30/98 Price	Return Since IPO	S&P 500 Since IPO
AXA S.A.	AXA	06/25/96	26.40	8,000,000	56¹⁵⁄₁₆	115.7%	69.6%
British Sky Broadcasting	BSY	12/08/94	24.05	18,222,452	42⅝	77.2	154.5
Deutsche Telecom	DT	11/16/96	18.89	85,000,000	27½	45.6	53.7
ENI	E	11/27/95	32.88	20,000,000	54⁵⁄₁₆	65.2	88.6
Estee Lauder	EL	11/16/95	26	11,482,338	69¹¹⁄₁₆	168.0	89.8
Fila	FLH	05/26/93	18	7,500,000	15	−16.7	150.1
Gucci Group	GUC	10/24/95	22	14,700,000	53	140.9	93.3
New Holland	NH	11/01/96	21½	34,900,000	19⅝	−8.7	61.1
Panamerican Beverages	PB	09/21/93	*12¼	*20,700,000	31¹⁄₁₆	156.7	150.3
Royal PTT Nederland	KPN	10/23/95	35.41	22,000,000	63⅝	79.7	93.8
Scania AB	SCV.A	04/01/95	27.08	25,000,000	24	−11.4	151.8
SGS Thomson†	STM	12/08/94	22.25	21,000,000	69⅞	214.0	154.5
Shanghai Petrochemical	SHI	07/26/93	20⅜	5,040,000	11³⁄₁₆	−45.1	152.5
YPF	YPF	06/29/93	19	65,000,000	30¹⁄₁₆	58.2	151.6
Average						**2%**	**113.9%**

* Adjusted for stock split.
† Now STMicroelectronics.

most of the conversions coming in at the lower end of the scale. Now the range is more like 2.0 to 3.0. You can become eligible for shares by becoming a depositor of the institution. There are also agents that specialize in marketing shares that become available for sale when some number of depositors decide not to participate in the offering. If you are disciplined about holding the shares for just a short period of time, the return on invested capital is often quite satisfying.

Analysis of banks is quite different from that of industrial firms. Historical earnings growth is certainly a factor, but because banks maintain very leveraged balance sheets it is even more important to understand what level of financial risk senior management has taken on to achieve those returns. Lenders make money on the *yield spread*—their cost of funds compared to the average rate they charge on loans. That spread must be positive; that is, the interest rate received must be higher than that paid for funds. The most conservative way to run a bank is to match the maturity dates of liabilities with the loans made. That way the positive yield spread is locked in for the life of the loan. If this is not done, banks and S&Ls can get into big trouble. For example, a bank might try to increase returns by borrowing short at a low interest rate and then lending long. But if short-term interest rates rise above long-term rates, as they occasionally do, this strategy can trigger losses. Because of the significant financial leveraging done by all banks, serious mismatching of assets with liabilities can often lead to insolvency.

The makeup of the loan portfolio is also an important factor in this analysis. (For example, single family home mortgages are more likely to be repaid on time than construction loans on commercial properties.) An investor should also consider the possibility of a takeover by a larger bank in the same region—almost always a positive event for the shareholder. Table 7-2 lists representative offerings.

BIOTECHNOLOGY

Biotech offerings rank among the most speculative IPOs of all. Most biotechnology firms filing for IPOs have no operating revenues and are chewing through cash as they try to develop a viable drug and then wend it through the FDA approval process, which usually takes many years.

There are three phases to these approvals. Phase I concentrates on proving nontoxicity, and essentially seeks to prove that the drug won't kill anyone. (As you might imagine, these study sizes are small.) Phase II studies attempt to prove efficacy. Does the drug work? Are there any side effects? The patient numbers for these studies are greater but still not large, and typically last at least a year. A fair number of potential drugs get through these two phases, but Phase III is the most important. In this phase,

TABLE 7.2 Representative banking offerings.

IPO	Symbol	IPO Date	Price	Offering Size	6/30/98 Price	Return Since IPO	S&P 500 Since IPO
Bank United	BNKU	08/09/96	20.00	10,500,000	47⅞	139.4%	71.2%
Bell Bancorp	BELL	11/12/91	25.00	7,480,000	*	—	—
Capital Bancorp	CABK	08/08/91	14.50	1,030,195	*	—	—
Excel Bancorp	XCEL	09/17/86	10.63	3,009,841	*	—	231.68
First Charter	FCTR	06/04/87	5.875	500,000	20⅛	242.6	294.2
Money Store	MONE	09/20/91	2.84	2,200,000	33¹⁵⁄₁₆	1095.3	192.3
Average						**492.4%**	**182.6%**

* Acquired prior to December 31, 1998.

111

larger studies are done which seek to prove that the drug not only works, but works *better* than those already on the market. This phase also attempts to show that the drug has no important side effects on the larger patient population. The length of Phase III studies will depend on the type of drug being tested. (In a cancer study, for example, it will typically take many years to track survivability rates and long-term side effects.) It is only after a drug passes Phase III that it becomes eligible for sale in the United States.

Very few drugs ever get to the point of being licensed for sale. As of late 1998, fewer than 20 pharmaceutical companies had succeeded in winning drug approvals. But that has not prevented hundreds of would-be drug developers from going public over the last 10 years. Biotech companies are more likely to eventually succeed the further they are along in the cycle, but virtually any technology can get derailed anywhere along the line. If it does, the typical single-product company is often not worth more than remaining cash on hand. This is why these offerings are so speculative—because the investor is really making all-or-nothing bets.

As with other technology IPOs, an investor should consider the confidence level in the company from other sources. Did major venture capital firms infuse funds? What is the caliber of the management that has been attracted to the firm? What about the research team that developed the drug? How much more cash will be needed before the drug is approved? If the prospectus yields favorable answers to these questions, the company *might,* just might, be worthy of investment. But remember—for every major hit in the biotechnology IPO world, there are probably two or three that had below-market returns and another five that were total duds. Table 7-3 lists representative offerings.

CLOSED-END FUNDS
We have a very definite opinion about closed-end funds, which is that most of them are sucker bets. Brokers love selling these types of IPOs to unsophisticated buyers. Typically, they will tell you that this is a way to invest in an asset class (i.e., small-cap stocks or intermediate-term bonds) without having to pay a front-end, back-end, or general transaction charge. This is extremely misleading because you *do* pay a sales charge, although somewhat indirectly. The underwriter's fee, usually 5 to 9 percent of the total amount raised, is paid from the proceeds of the offering. If the offering price of the fund is 15, the underwriter's fees will be, say, 7 percent of that. On day 1, the shares are now worth $13.95 ($15 minus the 7 percent underwriter's fee). This "haircut" is significantly worse than buying a similar fund already trading in the aftermarket (as opposed to an IPO), and even worse than buying a mutual fund with a front-loaded charge equal to less than 7 percent (most are below 4 percent).

TABLE 7-3 Representative biotechnology offerings.

IPO	Symbol	IPO Date	Price	Offering Size	6/30/98 Price	Return Since IPO	S&P 500 Since IPO
Amgen	AMGN	06/17/83	*9	*4,700,000	65⅜	726.4%	570.4%
Biogen	BGEN	03/22/83	*11.50	*5,000,000	49	426.1	652.6
Centocor	CNTO	07/22/83	*8.125	*600,000	36¼	446.2	571.3
Chiron	CHIR	02/18/86	*1.99	*12,096,000	15¹¹⁄₁₆	788.3	415.5
Genentech	GNE	10/14/80	7.78	1,000,000	67⅞	872.4	758.8
Genetics Institute	GENI	05/19/86	29.75	2,500,000	†	†	†
Genzyme	GENZ	06/05/86	5	2,826,000	25⁹⁄₁₆	511.4	486.2
Immune Response	IMNR	05/02/90	7	2,200,000	13	85.7	339.0
Regeneron	REGN	04/01/91	22	4,500,000	8½	−61.4	305.4
Average						**421.7%**	**512.4%**

* Adjusted for stock splits.

† Acquired prior to date.

113

Even worse, most closed-end funds trade at discounts to their net asset value. Usually, a few weeks after the offering, the underwriter stops its price-stabilization efforts and the stock price goes to the *discounted value,* dropping by about 5 to 10 percent. This means that between the underwriter's fee and the drift to a discount, many holders are quickly out 15 percent on their money.

As of this writing, there are closed-end funds covering just about every segment of every asset class, from intermediate-term municipal bond funds to biotech stock funds. All typically trade at a discount. There are also many closed-end funds for countries, including Argentina, Chile, China, Hungary, India, Malaysia, Russia, Singapore, Taiwan, and Thailand. In any case, we have the same recommendation for all closed-end funds: Stay away from the IPOs, wait a few months to get your discount, and then buy if you like the asset class. Table 7-4 lists representative offerings.

COMPUTER NETWORKING AND TELECOMMUNICATIONS

This is one of the fastest-growing segments of the technology sector. Fueled by burgeoning development of corporate networked databases, e-mail systems, Intranets, and Internet traffic, market growth is projected to be 30 to 35 percent over the next 3 to 5 years. There are some former IPOs that are now big players in this field, including Cisco Systems, 3Com, and Bay Networks (now part of Nortel Network).

Data is also converging with voice and video traffic. Computer networking companies and telecommunications equipment makers such as Alcatel, Lucent, and L. M. Ericsson are facing off against each other. That will mean more competition but a bigger addressable market for all. Goliaths will win this multifront war.

But there are still plenty of niche products that may develop into big winners at the periphery. Excellent examples from the past include some big winners in the asynchronous transfer mode (ATM) switch field, including Stratacom (now part of Cisco Systems) and Ascend and Cascade Communications (both now part of Lucent). The latest upstarts include Juniper Networks and Sycamore Networks.

Management, product quality, competitive position, demonstrated sales and earnings growth, and venture capital sponsorship are all key factors to consider. Companies going public in this field should be rapidly ramping up sales and earnings.

The major point here is that this is very fertile ground for startups to carve a sizable niche for themselves. There will be other home runs here, so keep your eye out for them as they file over the next few years. Table 7-5 lists representative offerings.

TABLE 7-4 Representative closed-end fund offerings.

IPO	Symbol	IPO Date	Price	Offering Size	6/30/98 Price	Return Since IPO	S&P 500 Since IPO
Argentina Fund	AF	10/11/91	12	5,000,000	$10\frac{7}{8}$	−9.4%	252.7%
Black Rock 2001 Term	BLK	08/20/92	10	130,000,000	$8\frac{3}{16}$	−11.9	171.1
Chile Fund	CH	09/26/89	7½	4,666,667	$*13\frac{5}{16}$	*80.8	229.3
Global Health Sciences Fund	GHS	01/17/92	15	20,000,000	$*19\frac{11}{16}$	*31.3	170.7
H&Q Life Science	HQL	05/01/92	15	3,700,000	$*13\frac{3}{16}$	*−8.8	174.9
Korea Fund	KF	08/22/84	4	5,000,000	$6\frac{5}{16}$	57.8	578.7
New Age Media	NAF	10/13/93	15	13,000,000	$21\frac{5}{8}$	43.8	145.6
Nuveen Muni Value	NUV	06/17/87	10	150,000,000	$9\frac{1}{2}$	−5.0	270.9
Royce OTC Microcap Fund	OTCM	12/14/93	7½	8,000,000	$*9\frac{3}{8}$	*25.0	144.9
Scudder New Asia	SAF	06/18/87	12	7,000,000	$*8\frac{7}{8}$	*−26.0	272.0
Templeton Russia	TRF	06/15/95	15	4,600,000	$*30\frac{3}{4}$	*38.3	111.1
Templeton Vietnam	TVF	09/15/94	15	7,000,000	$5\frac{13}{16}$	−61.3	145.8
Average						**12.9%**	**222.3%**

Note: Prices are adjusted for ordinary and capital gains distributions and for stock splits.

* Large d stributions have occurred relative to S&P 500.

COMPUTER SERVICES

For technology investors, these stocks can be safe ports in a storm. Service companies such as data and specialized transaction-processing firms tend to have high recurring revenues, which make their earnings streams more predictable. The higher the predictability of earnings, the higher the price-to-earnings multiple that may be applied to those profits.

Service companies in the computer industry enjoy an important advantage over their hardware counterparts. A hardware company, like Compaq, depends almost entirely on current hardware sales—which can disappear if the hardware becomes obsolete or in the event of a recession. But a service firm, on the other hand, typically has a multiyear contract which protects it from this kind of near-term risk.

Service companies have also benefited from the trend to outsourcing. Companies are now realizing the economies of scale which can come from farming out departments such as payroll, 401(k) plan, mutual fund accounting, and credit card processing. Companies such as Automatic Data Processing, DST Systems, First Data, Paychex, and SunGard Data Systems have all grown their businesses tremendously by taking on these tasks for other firms.

Many of these firms have been excellent investments over the last few years, and we believe that favorable trend will remain in place through the next five years. We expect a number of additional IPOs in this area going forward—particularly spin-offs from existing public computer service companies. Table 7-6 lists representative offerings.

COMPUTER SOFTWARE

Successful computer software companies trade at generally high P/E ratios, because of their high profit margins and cash flows. It is not surprising to see 20 to 25 percent net profit margins for some software companies, versus well under 10 percent for the average industrial firm. Those software companies with the highest margins and valuations sell products into markets with very high barriers to entry. Microsoft is phenomenally profitable and is likely to remain that way because of its entrenched position as the provider of Windows and related operating systems for personal computers. The software is relatively cheap to develop and keep fresh, but there are thousands of software packages expressly designed to run on Windows, making the company virtually impossible to dislodge from its market position. On the other hand, there could be a firm that has successfully carved a niche providing certain utility software. It may not be that technologically difficult for others to provide the same product. It could become a marketing game. That often reduces margins. And if Microsoft were to incorporate its functionality within Windows, the business could disappear virtually

TABLE 7-5 Representative computer networking and telecommunications offerings.

IPO	Symbol	IPO Date	Price	Offering Size	6/30/98 Price	Return Since IPO	S&P 500 Since IPO
Ascend Communications	ASND	05/12/94	*1.625	16,000,000	49⁹⁄₁₆	2,950.3%	155.5%
Banyan Systems	BNYN	08/06/92	10.50	2,670,000	8¼	−21.4	169.6
Cabletron Systems	CS	05/30/89	*3.10	*27,000,000	13⁷⁄₁₆	333.5	240.0
Cisco Systems	CSCO	02/15/90	*0.25	*134,400,000	61⅜	23,550.0	238.6
Lucent Technologies	LU	04/03/96	*13.50	*196,074,000	83⁵⁄₁₆	516.2	72.9
Pairgain Technology	PAIR	09/15/93	*3.50	*16,600,000	17⁷⁄₁₆	398.2	145.6
Picturetel	PCTL	10/29/84	*1.00	*2,200,000	9¼	825.0	578.1
Teleport Communications TCGI	TCGI	06/26/96	16	18,800,000	54¼	239.1	70.7
3Com	COMS	03/31/84	*1.50	*8,520,000	30¹¹⁄₁₆	1,945.8	617.3
Average						**3,415.2%**	**253.7%**

* Adjusted for stock splits.

TABLE 7-6 Representative computer services offerings.

IPO	Symbol	IPO Date	Price	Offering Size	6/30/98 Price	Return Since IPO	S&P 500 Since IPO
DST Systems	DST	10/31/95	21	20,240,000	56	166.7	95.0
FactSet	FDS	06/27/96	17	3,125,000	32½	91.2	69.6
First Data	FDC	04/09/92	*11	*700,000,000	$33\frac{5}{16}$	202.8	183.0
Paychex	PAYX	08/26/83	*0.29	*25,628,906	$40\frac{11}{16}$	13,929.2	599.3
SunGard Data	SDS	03/13/86	*2.75	*9,280,000	38⅜	1,295.5	386.2
Transaction Systems Architects	TSAI	02/23/95	*7.50	*5,500,000	38½	413.3	152.5
Average						**2,683.1%**	**247.6%**

* Adjusted for stock splits.

overnight. The point here is that the more complex the software, the more likely that high profit margins can be sustained.

Another factor to closely monitor is the product life cycle. There are usually leapfrogs in software technology every few years. A dominant player selling computer-aided engineering (CAE) or database management software could lose its favorable competitive position if it is late in coming up with a better version. This is what happened to Mentor Graphics in CAE and IBM in database management software. Cadence Design Systems ate Mentor's lunch in CAE, and Oracle did the same to IBM in database management.

Most software company IPOs will be exploiting a new market. They often do not have significant current competition, probably because the sales potential is not yet big enough to attract the larger players. The upstart firm must quickly exploit its market opportunity, get significant market share via a superior product, and then maintain R&D leadership. It must also rapidly develop the sales and marketing skills to fully exploit the growing worldwide market opportunity. This is what Netscape attempted to do with Internet browsers and intranet management software. It was ahead of Microsoft for about 18 months and owned the markets in many respects. But the company was hard pressed to withstand the onslaughts of Microsoft, and eventually sold out to AOL.

The critical factors in a software company's growth after the IPO are the potential size of the market, R&D leadership, continuing timely product improvements and line extensions, and sales and marketing support. Again, an investor should also check out the venture groups that invested in the firm, as well as the company's management experience. Table 7-7 lists representative offerings.

CYCLICAL COMPANIES

There are not a lot of IPOs in traditional industries such as electrical equipment, paper products, and steel. (These industries are called *cyclical* because their earnings are closely tied to the vagaries of the economy.) Those that do are typically *reverse LBOs*—that is, companies that underwent a management-led LBO a few years back, restructured, became more profitable, and are now going public again. Reverse LBOs tend to hit the public markets when there is a clearly positive trend in cash flow, a year or two of profitability, and favorable industry fundamentals.

Most industrial companies generate average to low returns on assets and equity. This is because they require a lot of assets to produce their goods, and they are more dependent on the economic cycle, making sales and earnings volatile. Hence, valuations (like P/E ratios) will be deservedly lower. Look for companies that are growing unit volume in a new product category or that are growing market share because of new manufacturing technology.

TABLE 7-7 Representative computer software offerings.

IPO	Symbol	IPO Date	Price	Offering Size	6/30/98 Price	Return Since IPO	S&P 500 Since IPO
Adobe Systems	ADBE	08/12/86	*1.375	*4,000,000	42⅟₁₆	2,986.4%	361.5%
Borland	BORL	12/19/89	10	102,252,000	7⅜	−26.3	231.1
Computervision	CVN	08/14/92	12	25,000,000	†3¹⁵⁄₁₆	−67.2	123.7
Daisy Systems	DAZY	06/01/83	15.50	2,000,000	Nil	−100.0	597.5
Informix	IFMX	09/24/86	7.50	1,380,291	7²⁹⁄₃₂	5.4	379.9
Microsoft	MSFT	03/13/86	*0.25	*201,240,000	108⅜	43,250.0	386.2
Oracle	ORCL	03/12/86	*0.28	*113,400,000	24⁹⁄₁₆	8,672.2	425.0
Sterling Commerce	SE	03/27/96	24	11,500,000	48½	102.1	74.7
Average						**6,852.8%**	**322.5%**

* Adjusted for stock splits.

† Price when acquired by Cadence Design Systems, January 12, 1998.

Most cyclical company IPOs occur at the beginning and just past the middle of an economic upcycle. Managements are eager to create markets for their companies' shares, and often do so at the first opportunity when the economy turns up.

When evaluating IPOs in cyclical industries, the stage of the economy is critical. Cyclical company stocks typically trade at high multiples when the economy is coming out of recession, and low multiples when at the top. Nonetheless, it is important to buy during the beginning stages of an economic upswing—these purchases will enjoy the most upside. We recommend avoiding cyclical IPOs more than three years into a business cycle. Table 7-8 lists representative offerings.

INTERNET

As just about everyone knows these days, the Internet is a rapidly evolving technological revolution. The Internet has moved from the realm of computer jocks, to business users searching for information, and now to consumers for knowledge, e-commerce, and entertainment. With the proliferation of broadband access over the next few years, the Internet will become a major pipeline for video entertainment. Data transmission speeds will improve to the point where home computers will become entertainment centers, and television monitors will also become knowledge and transaction centers, receiving all kinds of video transmissions on a real-time basis.

There are three kinds of Internet stocks that have gone public so far. The first category included companies like Netscape and NetCom, which provided software and services to facilitate access to the Internet. Netscape did not make any money selling browsers, but its business plan was always to emphasize the sale of server software to businesses (where it made inroads). The provision of Internet access service has very low barriers to entry, with many major vendors such as AT&T, Sprint, and your local regional Bell operating company (RBOC) interested in providing the same service. We would steer clear of all independent Internet access companies for IPO investment. They are too late to the party. About 4500 companies provided Internet access services in the United States in 1998, according to Gartner Group.

The second kind of Internet stock has been the content provider. This category includes the electronic "yellow page" providers such as Yahoo!, Lycos, @ Home, and Excite, as well as information providers such as CNET, FactSet, Hoovers, Sportsline, and Broadcast.com. Some of these services will use advertiser-revenue business models, while others will charge access fees for specialized information that cannot be found elsewhere.

There is a tremendous opportunity for the advertising-driven model. At the end of 1995, Forrester Research, a technology think tank, estimated that

TABLE 7-8 Representative cyclical company offerings.

IPO	Symbol	IPO Date	Price	Offering Size	6/30/98 Price	Return Since IPO	S&P 500 Since IPO
AK Steel	AKST	03/30/94	*11.75	*28,144,444	$17\frac{7}{8}$	52.1%	154.5%
American Standard	ASD	02/02/95	20	10,000,000	$44\frac{11}{16}$	123.4	139.8
Birmingham Steel	BIR	1126/85	*5.22	*4,500,000	$2\frac{3}{8}$	–54.5	465.0
Calgon Carbon	CCC	06/02/87	*5.50	*18,000,000	$9\frac{15}{16}$	80.7	293.1
ConRail	CRR	03/26/87	28	52,000,000	$15\frac{1}{4}$	–45.5	276.8
Geon	GON	04/29/93	18	10,500,000	$22\frac{15}{16}$	27.4	158.3
Georgia Gulf	GGC	12/17/86	*9.75	*8,000,000	$22\frac{13}{16}$	134.0	358.0
Gulfstream Aerospace	GAC	10/09/96	24	29,600,000	$46\frac{1}{2}$	93.8	62.7
Interstate Hotels	IHC	06/20/96	21	9,350,000	†$31\frac{15}{16}$	52.1	64.8
J&L Specialty Steel	JL	12/15/93	14	11,000,000	$5\frac{15}{16}$	–57.6	145.5
Lyondell Petrochemical	LYO	01/18/89	30	32,000,000	$30\frac{1}{16}$	1.5	295.7
Polymer Group	PGH	05/09/96	18	11,393,939	$11\frac{3}{8}$	–36.8	75.7
Rouge Steel	ROU	03/29/94	22	5,600,000	$12\frac{3}{4}$	–42.0	150.6
Titanium Metals	TIMT	06/04/96	23	12,325,000	$22\frac{1}{16}$	–4.1	68.6
UCAR International	UCR	08/09/95	$23\frac{3}{4}$	13,760,000	$29\frac{3}{16}$	22.9	102.6
World Color Press	WCR	01/25/96	19	13,103,034	35	84.2	83.8
York International	YRK	10/01/91	23	10,700,000	$43\frac{9}{16}$	89.9	191.3
Average						**30.7%**	**181.6%**

* Adjusted for stock splits.

† As of June 1, 1998.

Internet advertising would total $75 million in 1996. That estimate proved to be extremely conservative, since that much was spent in the first half alone. More important, advertising for consumer products began to proliferate, and in fact became the dominant type of advertiser by the end of that year.

The Internet is uniquely attractive to advertisers. It can deliver a very specialized audience, and advertisers can also closely monitor the number of people actually seeing and reacting to their advertisements. Advantages like these point to tremendous growth in Internet advertising—recent estimates are that it will rise more than 30 percent a year through 2003. At that point, advertising could exceed $11.5 billion—more than what is currently being spent on magazine space.

Look for companies that have a dominant share of the market for a particular Internet service or type of information. For example, Yahoo! has a 50 percent share of the Internet yellow pages market. Also, the first one into the market often establishes a lead that can be hard to overtake. *TV Guide* is an excellent example in the print market. By being first to develop a television guide, and then rapidly developing it throughout the country, the Annenbergs were able to dominate the TV listings market for 20 years until local newspapers improved their offerings in the 1980s. Yahoo! is following the same model of growth in the Internet. Others will establish themselves as dominant providers of particular kinds of content. Some will be familiar names such as ESPN and the *Wall Street Journal,* while others will be relative upstarts such as FactSet and Sportsline.

The third and most recent wave of Internet stock offers have been e-commerce plays. They include Amazon.com, Cyberian Outpost, CNET, ebay, and ubid. Amazon.com is a good example of a first-in company exploiting a new communications medium to sell traditional merchandise. Although very early in development, the combination of convenience, attendant information, wide selection, and, in some cases, lower prices could allow Internet e-commerce sales to capture 15 to 20 percent of overall retail revenues over the long run.

Valuations are very high, so the payoff with these companies will likely be a few years out. The best IPO investment opportunities will occur during a major market correction or bear market. Because these stocks tend to sell at high valuations, they will not fare well during market downturns. Table 7-9 lists representative offerings.

OIL EXPLORATION, PRODUCTION, AND SERVICES

Although oil stocks were perennial Dow dogs during the 1980s, the recovery in oil and natural gas prices, along with improved exploration and development technology, has made them attractive again. There are two

TABLE 7-9 Representative Internet offerings.

IPO	Symbol	IPO Date	Price	Offering Size	6/30/98 Price	Return Since IPO	S&P 500 Since IPO
Amazon.com	AMZN	05/15/97	*3	18,000,000	99¾	3,225.0%	34.7%
America OnLine	AOL	03/19/92	0.69	32,000,000	105⅛	15,135.5	176.7
@ Home	ATHM	07/11/97	10.50	9,000,000	47⁵⁄₁₆	350.6	23.7
Excite	XCIT	04/03/96	8.50	4,000,000	46¾	550.0	72.9
Infonautics	INFO	04/29/96	14	2,250,000	3⅜	−75.6	73.3
Infoseek	SEEK	06/11/96	12	3,454,500	35⅝	199.0	69.1
Lycos	LCOS	04/02/96	*8	*6,000,000	37¹¹⁄₁₆	371.1	73.0
Netscape	NSCP	08/09/95	*14	*10,000,000	27⁵⁄₁₆	93.3	102.6
Sportsline	SPLN	11/13/97	8	3,500,000	36⁹⁄₁₆	357.1	23.7
Spyglass	SPYG	06/27/95	4¼	8,000,000	11⁷⁄₁₆	169.1	109.0
Yahoo!	YHOO	04/12/96	*4.33	*7,800,000	78¾	1,718.7	78.1
Average						**695.8%**	**66.0%**

* Adjusted for stock splits.

major factors driving the improved fundamentals. First, many oil companies drew down on their reserves. Production exceeded reserve replacement throughout the 1980s to the point that by the early 1990s, in many cases, reserves were down to very low levels. Second, the advent of three-dimensional seismic studies, horizontal drilling, and improved drill bits has driven development costs significantly lower.

The trend to higher exploration activity should continue well into the next century. Demand for oil is burgeoning in emerging countries and regions, such as China, Latin America, and Eastern Europe. That should keep oil and natural gas prices climbing slightly in excess of the U.S. inflation rate (world oil trading is done in U.S. dollars).

The biggest beneficiaries will be the service companies—particularly the drillers and three-dimensional seismology companies. The drilling industry went into a severe depression when oil prices broke down in 1983. There was a glut of oil rigs, and most drilling companies either went bankrupt or suffered severe out-of-court restructurings. Not a single new rig was built in more than 10 years. Many others rusted away and disappeared from the marketplace.

But in the mid-1990s demand for rigs and other services began to come into balance with supply. Starting in 1995, both day rates (the price an exploration company pays per day to use a rig and its crew) and rig utilization started to climb. They have continued to rise, but, except in 1997 to 1998, have remained substantially below the price that would support the construction of new rigs.

When considering the purchase of an IPO in the oil and gas exploration and production industries, look for companies that are increasing production, lowering exploration costs, and have a demonstrated ability to find oil. We also recommend that the company have enough debt capacity and cash flow to sustain growth. Service companies should either be introducing new technology or have a significant share of a service segment that is not likely to see additional competition.

There should be plenty of IPOs in the oil and gas market during the next few years. To get a good idea of the level of service activity, pay careful attention to the trend in day rates and rig utilization. (These numbers are reported by most drilling companies each quarter in the 10-Qs they file with the SEC.) Table 7-10 lists representative offerings.

REAL ESTATE INVESTMENT TRUSTS (REITs)
Real estate investment trusts (REITs) have become increasingly popular in the 1990s, with many investors believing them to be more attractive total-return investments than electric utilities. Conservative investors liked elec-

TABLE 7-10 Representative oil exploration, production, and services offerings.

IPO	Symbol	IPO Date	Price	Offering Size	6/30/98 Price	Return Since IPO	S&P 500 Since IPO
Burlington Resources	BR	07/07/88	25.50	20,000,000	43 3/16	68.9%	317.2%
Chesapeake Energy	CHK	02/04/93	*1.33	*20,700,000	4	200.8	152.2
Diamond Offshore Drilling	DO	10/10/95	*12	*20,800,000	40 5/16	235.9	98.4
Flores & Ruckes†	OEI	11/30/94	*4.27	*13,455,000	19 5/16	361.1	149.9
Sonat Offshore Drilling	RIG	05/28/93	*11	*27,116,000	44 1/2	304.5	151.99
Union Pacific Resources	UPR	10/10/95	21	37,000,000	17 5/16	−16.3	96.3
Vastar Resources	VRI	06/28/94	28	15,000,000	43 11/16	56.0	154.2
Average						**173.0%**	**160.0%**

* Adjusted for stock splits.

† Now Ocean Energy.

126

tric utilities because, in a regulated operating environment, they provided very stable increases in earnings and cash flows. No more. The government has slowly been deregulating the electricity market during the last 10 years and will complete the task during the next 10. There will be winners and losers, but individual company returns will be less predictable and many firms will not be able to survive in a more competitive environment.

In the meantime, real estate markets have slowly recovered from the overbuilding that occurred in the 1980s. When evaluating a REIT IPO, the most important number to follow is *funds from operations*. This is essentially the REIT's cash flow, and is the key measure of its financial health. Growth in cash flow is primarily a function of two factors: rent increases and occupancy levels. If real estate markets are strong and the REIT has been keeping up its properties, cash flow should rise. With that being the case right now and the utility industry continuing to be roiled by deregulation, more investors will be turning to REITs as investments.

REITs are categorized by the kind of real estate they own. Most REITs specialize in a certain type of property, so a REIT might focus on shopping malls, discount outlets, office buildings, or medical properties. These subgroups go in and out of relative favor based on each group's evolving fundamentals. An investor should expect to see IPOs in those subgroups which are currently in favor. In 1993, for instance, the apartment, shopping center, and discount mall REITs were most popular, while in 1996, it was hotel and office REITs.

During the next decade, we believe that there will be an unfolding opportunity to develop assisted-living apartment centers for elderly Americans—a rapidly growing segment of the population. There is also likely to be a continuing trend toward sun-belt apartment living. With those trends in mind, we would emphasize REIT IPOs in the medical property, assisted-living, and sun-belt apartment markets.

In all cases, an investor should be sure that there are a diversified number of operators that lease the properties from the REIT and that funds from operations have shown steady growth during recent years. In addition, one should check that the current dividend is no higher than 85 percent of those funds from operation, and that debt is less than 60 percent of total capitalization. Be particularly wary of REITs that offer high current yields but carry high debt. These REITs are more apt to run into financial difficulties or exhibit poor dividend growth. Table 7-11 lists representative offerings.

REVERSE LEVERAGED BUYOUTS (LBOs)

Leveraged buyouts (LBOs) are transactions whereby a company is purchased almost entirely with borrowed funds. This can be done if a company gener-

TABLE 7-11 Representative REIT offerings.

IPO	Symbol	IPO Date	Price	Offering Size	6/30/98 Price	Return Since IPO	S&P 500 Since IPO
Arden Realty	ARI	10/04/96	20	18,800,000	25⅛	29.4%	61.6%
Carr Realty	CRE	02/08/93	22	6,800,000	28⅜	29.0	153.2
Crown American Realty	CWN	08/10/93	17¼	19,640,000	9¹¹/₁₆	−43.8	152.3
Factory Stores of America	FAX	06/02/93	23	5,300,000	8	−65.2	149.8
General Growth Properties	GGP	04/07/93	22	15,180,000	37⅜	69.9	156.1
Patriot American Hospitality	PAH	09/27/95	12.45*	19,578,320	23¹⁵/₁₆	92.3	95.1

Post Properties	PPS	07/16/93	25½	10,580,000	38½	51.0	154.4
Prentiss Properties	PP	10/17/96	20	20,000,000	24⁵⁄₁₆	21.6	60.4
Simon Property Group	SPG	12/14/93	22¼	32,087,000	32½	46.1	144.9
Taubman Centers	TCO	11/20/92	11	22,800,000	14¼	29.5	165.8
Average						**26.0%**	**129.4%**

* Adjusted for stock splits

ates very steady profits year in and year out. Very successful LBOs have included AutoZone, Duracell, and Safeway. The vast majority of the debt is typically borrowed from institutions, with a small part of the equity being put up by private and institutional investors, borrowers, and management.

The lenders are typically looking to receive 10 percent or more on their funds for about 5 years. The equity holders are typically looking for 20 percent or better annual returns during the same time period. There are two exit strategies for these constituencies. One is to pay down debt over a few years and then sell the business. The other, more lucrative, pursuit is to take the company public (again) via what is called a *reverse LBO*. The company sells enough stock to retire high-interest-rate debt, replacing it with equity capital and traditional borrowings at lower interest rates. With lower interest expenses, the company generates higher profits, and with the balance sheet repaired, the stock can trade at more typical valuations against comparable firms.

In the event of such a happy outcome, the big winners are usually the equity investors that took the risk of putting up that small sliver of equity in the original LBO. A quadruple return on investment over five years is fairly common on deals that work out in this fashion.

But is it wise to buy shares in the IPO? That depends on the stage of recovery at the time. Some poorly structured LBOs are desperate to go public in order to survive. These are companies that have been unable to pay down debt because cash flow has not been as high as anticipated. To avoid such situations, look for companies that have shown consistent growth in profits and that have paid down debt while private.

The best reverse LBOs are those that are already paying down debt, but not too much. Because debt will still be high compared to similar firms, the shares will go public at an attractive P/E multiple. But as profits continue to expand and debt is paid down, the stock price will benefit from both per-share earnings growth and an increase in its market valuation.

Returns are likely to be lackluster if a slow-growing company pays down all of its excess debt at the IPO. Most LBOs are of companies that generate a lot of cash flow but exhibit slow earnings growth. (Cigarette companies are good examples of this trait.) If the IPO is completed, and earnings growth is sluggish, the stock will probably underperform. Table 7-12 lists representative offerings.

SEMICONDUCTORS AND SEMICONDUCTOR EQUIPMENT

Semiconductor technology is probably the greatest miracle of our age. The ability to place thousands of tiny circuits on a piece of silicon smaller than

TABLE 7-12 Representative reverse LBO offerings.

IPO	Symbol	IPO Date	Price	Offering Size	6/30/98 Price	Return Since IPO	S&P 500 Since IPO
AutoZone	AZO	04/01/91	*5.75	*13,000,000	31¹⁵/₁₆	455.4%	205.4%
Barnes & Noble	BKS	09/28/93	*10	*4,470,000	37⅝	276.3	145.7
Burlington Industries	BUR	03/19/92	14	33,530,000	14¹/₁₆	0.4	176.7
Bradlees	BLE	07/01/92	13	11,018,625	⁵/₃₂	−98.8	174.6
Caldor	CLDRQ	04/24/91	21	5,150,000	29/64	−97.8	196.2
Gartner Group	IT	10/05/93	*2.75	*21,280,000	35	1172.7	145.8
General Instrument	GIC	06/10/92	*7.50	*35,200,000	27³/₁₆	262.5	145.8
Interstate Bakeries	IBC	07/24/91	*8	*31,250,000	33³/₁₆	314.8	199.5
Levitz Furniture	LFI	07/02/93	14	10,400,000	29/64	−96.8	154.3
OfficeMax	OMX	11/02/94	*8.44	65,700,000	16½	95.5	143.1
Payless Cashways	PCS	03/09/93	12¾	25,700,000	2¹⁵/₁₆	−77.0	149.4
RJR Nabisco	RN	04/11/91	*56.2	20,000,000	23¾	−57.8	200.3
Safeway	SWY	04/25/90	*2.81	*40,000,000	40¹¹/₁₆	1346.7	241.5
Average						**268.9%**	**175.3%**

* Adjusted for stock splits.

131

the tip of a finger is probably the greatest manufacturing feat of the twentieth century. It is the driving factor behind virtually all of the revolutionary technology proliferating today.

There are many different kinds of semiconductor companies. There are microprocessor makers such as Intel and Motorola; analog chip makers such as Analog Devices, Linear Technology, and Maxim Integrated Products; and dynamic random-access memory (DRAM) chip makers such as Micron Technology. Companies with the widest profit margins have proprietary technology or very high barriers to entry because of economies of scale. Intel is an excellent example of a company with exactly those advantages. All Windows-based personal computers can use its microprocessors, and its market share is more than 90 percent, so it can make the part cheaper than anyone else. That is tough to beat.

Then there are the commodity part makers. DRAM chip manufacturers use technology that is more in the public domain—a fact that has been successfully exploited by Japanese and Korean companies. There is usually so much available manufacturing capacity out there that prices are constantly moving lower.

In general, we believe that demand for semiconductors will continue to grow. One major problem for investors, though, is that the average part has a design life of about 18 to 24 months before production peaks. At that point, revenues begin to fall. The company must then vie for the next design to maintain revenue growth in the product line. Hence, a chip company is usually only as good as its design engineers.

Going forward, most IPOs in this industry will be of small companies which have a unique chip design. (It also helps if they are in a newly emerging market.) But these are high-risk endeavors. A highly successful business could go sour in a matter of months if competitors come up with a better design.

Semiconductor equipment makers are another, more visible segment of this market. A number of equipment companies are being created to develop the specialized equipment needed to reduce circuit line widths. The downside of this business is that it is more dependent on overall semiconductor industry growth. Companies will only be willing to spend more than $1 billion on a new plant when they absolutely know demand growth justifies it. And like most companies in cyclical industries, P/E ratios applied to semiconductor equipment stocks tend to be lower than average to account for this added risk.

However, because there are just a few potential customers and the price per machine is usually in the millions of dollars, there are typically only a few competitors. Competition is based less on price than on functionality. Most important, a technology lead in this industry can often be exploited over a number of years (as opposed to the 18 months or so for chip design). Recent successful IPOs of equipment makers such as these include Brooks Automation, Du Pont Photomasks, and PRI Automation. Table 7-13 lists representative offerings.

SPECIAL RETAILERS

Most new retailers are big-box, category killers—that is, stores such as Toys "R" Us, Staples, Barnes & Noble, and The Sports Authority that specialize in providing a wide array of a specific kind of merchandise at a very low price. They are destination stores in that customers will search them out when they need something, as opposed to food stores, which consumers will frequent for basic necessities based on price or location. A number of big-box concepts have proliferated over the last 10 years, and we believe there are more to come.

A crucial factor in evaluating these companies is same-store sales, or the percentage increase in sales of stores which have been open for at least one year. A healthy retailer should have same-store sales that exceed the rate of inflation over the long run. Many fast growing chains show big revenue growth as they put capital to work adding stores, but it is same-store sales growth that is the best measure of management's ability to grow the business over time.

America is for the most part, "overstored," which means that there is more per-capita retail space than there should be. This does *not* mean that there isn't room for a new store concept. But it *does* mean that much retailing in America has become a zero-sum game. For every Starbucks and Wal-Mart that opens, there will be a Chock Full O'Nuts and Zayres that closes. With that reality in mind, investors should look for IPOs of companies bringing a fresh new concept to market—preferably a concept which has already been proven.

The chain should also be profitable, and have a large enough store base that same-store sales figures are not subject to local aberrations. This is also a category in which the backgrounds of the major players in the IPO should be given particular attention. The underwriter should be a top-tier firm.

Besides these specialty discounters, we would also pay careful attention to high-end restaurant IPOs. As people get older, they tend to have more disposable income and prefer to frequent sit-down eateries rather than fast-food outlets. The aging of the U.S. population is increasing the number of potential attendees of such restaurants. Restaurant IPOs have been mixed, with Outback Steakhouse and Starbucks meeting with great success, and Boston Chicken, Lone Star Steakhouse, and Planet Hollywood among the more spectacular disasters. Table 7-14 lists representative offerings.

TABLE 7-13 Representative semiconductors and semiconductor equipment offerings.

IPO	Symbol	IPO Date	Price	Offering Size	6/30/98 Price	Return Since IPO	S&P 500 Since IPO
Altera	ALTR	03/30/88	*1.375	*16,000,000	$29\frac{9}{16}$	2043.1%	339.4%
AVX	AVX	08/14/95	$25\frac{1}{2}$	15,200,000	$16\frac{1}{16}$	−37.0	102.6
Exar	EXAR	06/12/91	*12.33	2,250,000	21	70.3	201.0
KLA Instruments	KLAC	10/08/80	*1.50	*4,920,000	$27\frac{11}{16}$	1745.8	761.2
Lam Research	LRCX	05/04/84	*6.67	*2,550,000	$19\frac{1}{8}$	186.9	612.6
Maxim Integrated Products	MXIM	02/29/88	*0.69	*18,400,000	$31\frac{11}{16}$	4492.4	323.4
MEMC Electronic Materials	WFR	07/13/95	24	13,600,000	$10\frac{3}{8}$	−56.8	102.1
Micron Technology	MU	06/01/84	5.60	5,250,000	$24\frac{13}{16}$	343.1	572.6
Xilinx	XLNX	06/12/90	3.33	8,625,000	34	921.0	209.6
Average						**1078.8%**	**358.3%**

* Adjusted for stock splits.

134

TABLE 7-14 Representative special retailer offerings.

IPO	Symbol	IPO Date	Price	Offering Size	6/30/98 Price	Return Since IPO	S&P 500 Since IPO
Borders Group	BGP	05/24/95	*7.25	57,448,000	37	410.3%	114.5%
Crazy Eddie	CRZY	09/13/84	*2	*8,000,000	0	-100.0	575.1
Discovery Zone	ZONE	06/03/94	*5.50	*10,000,000	0	-100.0	146.4
Donna Karan International	DK	06/27/96	24	10,750,000	$14\frac{11}{16}$	-38.8	69.6
General Nutrition	GNCI	01/21/93	*2	*33,600,000	$30\frac{3}{8}$	1406.3	160.4
Gitano Group	GIT	09/30/88	$20\frac{1}{2}$	2,500,000	0.07	-99.7	317.0
Gymboree	GYMB	03/31/93	*10	*4,330,000	$15\frac{3}{16}$	51.9	151.0
Intimate Brands	IBI	10/24/95	17	34,000,000	$27\frac{9}{16}$	62.2	93.3
Lone Star Steakhouse	STAR	03/12/92	$*1\frac{11}{16}$	11,200,000	$13\frac{13}{16}$	718.5	180.7
Nine West	NIN	02/02/93	$17\frac{1}{2}$	7,360,000	$26\frac{13}{16}$	53.2	156.2
Office Depot	ODP	06/01/88	*1.48	*14,175,000	$31\frac{3}{8}$	2041.0	325.2
Outback Steakhouse	OSSI	06/18/91	*2.22	7,065,000	39	1656.8	199.5
PetSmart	PETM	07/16/93	*6	*20,520,000	10	66.7	154.4
Saks Holding	SKS	05/21/96	$*12\frac{1}{2}$	*22,000,000	$40\frac{3}{8}$	223.0	67.1
The Sports Authority	TSA	11/17/94	*12.67	16,974,000	$14\frac{15}{16}$	17.9	144.6
Average						**424.6%**	**90.5%**

* Adjusted for stock splits.

TABLE 7-15 Representative wireless telecommunications offerings.

IPO	Symbol	IPO Date	Price	Offering Size	6/30/98 Price	Return Since IPO	S&P 500 Since IPO
AirTouch International	ATI	12/02/93	23	*60,000,000	$58\frac{7}{8}$	154.1%	144.8%
COLT Telecom PLC	COLTY	12/10/96	*4.50	53,400,000	$40\frac{7}{8}$	808.3	51.7
Korea Mobile Telecommunications	SKM	06/27/96	16.13	20,955,150	$5\frac{1}{6}$	−65.5	69.6
Omnipoint	OMPT	01/25/96	16	7,000,000	$22\frac{15}{16}$	43.4	83.8
PanAmSat	SPOT	09/22/95	17	15,136,000	$56\frac{7}{8}$	234.6	94.9
Telecommunications International	TINTA	07/13/95	16	14,000,000	$30\frac{3}{32}$	25.6	102.1
TeleWest Communications PLC	TWSTY	11/22/94	$22\frac{1}{4}$	13,650,000	$23\frac{3}{4}$	6.7	151.9
Orange PLC	ORNGY	03/27/96	15.63	26,000,000	$43\frac{15}{16}$	181.2	74.7
Western Wireless	WWCA	05/22/96	$23\frac{1}{2}$	8,800,000	$19\frac{5}{16}$	−15.2	67.1
Average						**152.6%**	**93.4%**

* Adjusted for stock splits.

WIRELESS TELECOMMUNICATIONS SERVICES

This is one of the most exciting areas of current technological development. By 2005, about half of all phone calls in the United States will be done over wireless systems, and wireless technology will increasingly be viewed as the standard system. Indeed, many emerging countries are encouraging the development of wireless local calling systems in both urban and rural settings. It is entirely possible that by 2005 the cost of placing and receiving a call over a wireless system could be less than over current wire lines. We also expect many IPOs in this area because wireless services chew up cash quickly as systems are developed, meaning that lots of capital needs to be raised via the debt and equity markets.

These companies trade on cash flow rather than earnings. Because of their high fixed costs and long buildout periods, wireless companies do not tend to post profits for a number of years. Revenue growth is important, but it is cash flow that will make or break the enterprise. It is cash flow, otherwise known as EBITDA (earnings before interest, taxes, depreciation, and amortization), supplemented by secondary stock and convertible debt offerings, that will provide most of the additional capital to further develop the infrastructure once the initial buildout is complete. When the systems have been fully developed, profits usually take off. As the operation matures, the company is then valued based on earnings growth.

The key ingredients to look for here are financial capacity, transmission costs, the number of existing and likely competitors, and revenues per customer. It appears that satellite dish technology will prove a big winner, not only for video transmissions but for voice and data as well. We also think that PCS vendors will garner excellent returns on investment over time. Emphasize those firms that operate in the best calling districts (i.e., Los Angeles and New York), and that have plenty of capital to go toe-to-toe with the likes of AT&T and MCI WorldCom. Table 7-15 lists representative offerings.

C H A P T E R 8

HOW TO GET ALLOCATIONS OF CHOICE DEALS

THE MOST DIFFICULT issue facing new-issue investors is getting allocations of hot deals, or even decent distributions of lesser favorites. These allocations can be very hard to come by, and typically go to only the best customers of the highest-producing account executives. There are, however, ways in which an investor can become such a client.

That having been said, developing that special relationship (and maintaining it) is no easy task. But once it has been established, it can be very profitable.

TARGETING THE RIGHT BROKERAGE HOUSE

Table 8-1 lists underwriters by the number of IPOs they led over the three years ending December 31, 1997. It does *not* include deals in which they may have been involved less directly, usually as members in the underwriting syndicate.

The more IPOs you wish to participate in, the more brokers you need to recruit to your cause. No one broker will have access to every deal, so work to develop relationships with several. Also keep in mind that the larger bro-

TABLE 8-1   Leading IPO managing underwriters, 1995–1997.

Underwriter	IPOs Led
Goldman, Sachs	120
Morgan Stanley Dean Witter	116
Salomon Smith Barney	111
Deutsche Banc Alex. Brown	107
Merrill Lynch	94
Banc of America Securities	85
Banc Boston Robertson, Stephens	82
Donaldson, Lufkin & Jenrette	77
Hambrecht & Quist	70
Lehman Brothers	58
CS First Boston	37
S.G. Cowen	33
CIBC Oppenheimer	30
Bear Stearns	29
PaineWebber	27
Prudential Securities	26
Friedman, Billings	23
William Blair	21
Warburg Dillon Read	20
J. P. Morgan	20
UBS Securities	20
Volpe Brown Whelan	17

kerage houses will likely be involved in the most IPOs. Merrill Lynch, for example, will participate in many more deals than Warburg Dillon Read.

To begin your search, review recent offerings that you would have bought if you had had an allocation. Does a specific brokerage house come up more often than the others? If so, start there. Also, check the "tombstones" (announcements of deals successfully completed) in the *Wall Street Journal* each day, and note the firms mentioned that you might be able to target. In general, the larger the print used for their name, and the higher they are on the list, the larger their allocation of shares for distribution.

Take another look at Table 8-1. The more active underwriters primarily cater to institutions, but virtually all of them, from Goldman, Sachs on down, have private client groups that serve high-net-worth individuals (defined as individuals with more than $100,000 in assets beyond the equity they have in their home and in their retirement plans). There usually is a minimum deposit required to open an account, and bear in mind—the larger the amount placed, the more attention you will receive for allocations. If you are fortunate enough to have that much money to commit to the project, you will also be able to qualify for more than one brokerage account.

For individuals with less money to put to work, all is not lost. You should concentrate on the large retail brokerage firms, often called *wire houses* because they have lots of branches wired to the home office. You may not get large allocations, but if you get to the right broker, you should still be able to play the game. Focus first on the large brokerage houses such as Merrill Lynch and Salomon Smith Barney, and start with the larger deals coming public. All of the major retail brokers will get allocations of these big offerings, so even small investors should be able to get allocations from time to time. A small but increasing number of shares are being distributed through discount brokers via the Internet. It is worth pursuing, but the line is long for a hot deal, and your allocation is likely to be quite small.

As is noted later in this chapter, small investors should take particular care to do their own homework. Sometimes an allocation of a good stock becomes available because the industry is out of favor or there is a glut of similar deals that has bumped it from the institutional spotlight. But beware—small players are most likely to get allocations of the weakest deals when the IPO market is strong. Some of these deals can be profitable, but they offer substantially less likelihood of a good payoff. If you are a smaller investor, make sure you are getting allocations of IPOs you

---

It is sometimes easier to find receptive and reputable brokers when the IPO market is in the doldrums. The only problem with this environment is that it is often a drag on near-term performance—IPOs launched in such a market usually do not jump on the first day of trading. But by exercising more selectivity, you should be able to get allocations to some very attractive deals that can work out quite well over the long run.

have researched and *want* (or that at least have been recommended by an independent research firm such as Standard & Poor's, Renaissance Capital, or IPO Market Monitor). If you are unduly pressured by your broker to buy unattractive IPOs, then it's probably time to move on to another account executive.

Remember, among the dozens of reputable major retail, regional, and specialty brokerage houses, there are thousands of brokers. All you need are two or three good contacts to develop a steady deal flow. Be persistent and you will be rewarded.

DEVELOPING THE RIGHT RELATIONSHIP WITH THE RIGHT BROKER

After targeting the right brokerage houses to fit your needs, the next step is to find the broker to fulfill your IPO requests. This is no trivial task, and is probably the most important factor affecting your chances at winning the IPO game. (The second most important, of course, is buying the right new issues.) But before addressing a broker's ability to get new issues, we should run through some principles for finding reputable, intelligent brokers in general.

Start by asking everyone you know—business associates, relatives, friends, and golf partners—whether they invest in IPOs, and if so, the name of their broker. Call the local branch offices of larger brokerage firms and ask for the manager. Explain that you would like to develop a *long-term relationship* with the broker at that office who has the most success gaining IPO allocations for his or her clients. Make sure that you emphasize your interest in developing a relationship, and that you have a certain amount of capital to commit (and possibly a much larger amount if things work out). The subsequent conversation can at least give you an idea of what you are up against.

The Internet can also provide good leads. Virtually every brokerage firm now has a website, and, as you might suspect, is eager to hear from you. But stick to reputable corporate sites when perusing the Internet—chat sites on the Internet are a poor way to find good brokers. A stranger is unlikely to share an excellent source for IPOs with you. The "investor" on the other end of the chat line is just as likely to be a disreputable broker fishing for uninformed potential clients who is masquerading as an impartial observer or successful investor.

Individual investors gain access to good brokers for three reasons, all of which directly or indirectly have to do with increasing trade commissions. The first and most direct benefit for the broker is the size of the brokerage account you might be willing to move to the firm. The second is your ability to influence others to direct commissions to the broker, and the third is your willingness to trade, thereby generating steady commissions.

Although you should indicate a willingness to trade your portfolio, you should never insinuate that you will accept unlimited portfolio turnover in order to get access to IPOs. You will soon regret having made such a verbal assurance. There are plenty of rogue brokers even in the best retail wire houses, so if you have characterized yourself as an aggressive investor, be aware that the smaller your account, the greater the chance that *churning* could occur (churning is an unacceptable level of stock trading simply to generate commissions). Ultimately, the level of transactions you are willing to accept will be up to you. In general, even in the most aggressive accounts, turnover should not exceed 150 percent annually.

Account executives live to work with high-net-worth individuals, since they know that they might eventually supply such people with a whole array of financial services and investments. And good brokers know that creating a relationship of trust can result in substantial commissions and fees over the years. Emphasis will then be placed on continuing the relationship, over and above any short-term commissions. In a capitalist world, the profit motive is the best incentive to do well by a client.

Pay very careful attention to what your prospective financial advisor says when queried about potential access to IPOs. Many office managers give the office's IPO allocations to their most productive brokers or to those with the most active clients. Try to get the names of people they helped to get IPO allocations. Go the extra mile and speak with them. Was it an occasional thing? What was the ratio of requests to actual allocations? What were the sizes of the allocations? And did the client actually get a good return on investment?

Influence is also an important factor. You might not have a large account yourself, but, without dropping any specific names, you might have family or business relationships that could convince the broker to work with you. There are other reasons a broker might value you as a contact: You might be self-employed and come into contact with a large number of potential brokerage clients. Or perhaps you're a member of a country club, or an officer in a fraternal or religious organization.

> There are only very restricted circumstances when a discretionary account might be appropriate. Getting more IPO allocations is not one of them.

Last, before committing your hard-earned money to a new brokerage relationship, you should have at least one face-to-face meeting. You can learn a great deal about an organization and an individual by their offices and overall presentation skills.

Once you are thoroughly satisfied that you will be working with a trust-worthy individual, commit only a portion of your total funds to see how the broker operates. A reputable broker will understand this strategy and refrain from talking you out of it. Give the broker enough to execute two or three transactions of the size you expect to trade in the future. (Unused cash balances should be placed in a money market fund until actually used.)

As a general gauge, if you define yourself as a very aggressive investor—that is, someone willing to take on a fair amount of risk for potentially above-average gains—and you have $100,000 to work with, you should commit about half of that to the broker. Depending upon the investment firm, you probably have about an even chance of getting a reputable and savvy broker to work with you in exchange for at least some IPO access.

The initial contacts and transactions are just the start of what hope-fully will be a long and mutually rewarding relationship. Just as in any business relationship, there must be a willingness for give and take. It is important for the broker to know that an investor is willing to be a regular and reliable buyer of new issues, just as it is important for the investor to feel secure that the broker values the relationship more than short-term commissions.

Set goals that are reasonable. Do not expect a large allocation of the next Yahoo! right out of the box. Do not be disappointed if the first one or two requests are not filled. In any case, you should have a running conver-sation with your broker about the IPO market and get a sense of how well he or she will be able to fill your future IPO requests. It should not take long before you know if the chemistry is there. If it isn't, move on.

Although the relationship should mean more to both parties than any gains that might accrue from a single transaction, do not be pressured into making a large commitment to a single IPO against your better judgment.

In an increasing number of instances, broker commissions from sell-ing an IPO can be confiscated if the shares are quickly flipped. Assur-ance that you will hold all but the most successful deals for at least a few weeks could make it easier to get initial allocations and keep your broker out of trouble with the home office.

If, for the good of the game, a broker asks you to go into a deal that you may feel ambivalent about, take a small allocation, and sell it within a few weeks. The law of averages show that as long as you are not buying in a rapidly deteriorating IPO market, most of these transactions will result in small if any losses and should be more than offset by gains from the better deals. Only flip those stocks you absolutely abhor, or that have skyrocketed on the first day of trading. (Brokerage houses do not care if a stock is flipped after it has soared. They only mind if clients sell while they struggle to keep the price of a recent IPO at or near the offering price.)

As long as you are doing well executing your strategy and earning an attractive return on your committed capital, you can survive one or two bad calls brought your way by the broker. Do not, however, overweight your portfolio with the broker's ideas. If the ratio of good to bad deals is unfavorable, either limit the exposure to such adverse deals or move on to another broker. In all cases, there should be a healthy mix of offerings the investor personally wants and gets allocations for, along with those that the broker offers for purchase. If at any time the atmosphere of mutual trust is broken, it is probably time to shift gears and concentrate on some of your other allocation options. In any case, when it comes to IPOs, *you should always be cultivating at least one other broker relationship just in case your main one dries up.*

Always express satisfaction for a job well done. Everyone likes to be appreciated, particularly if they are doing a good job for you. If you are satisfied, do not be shy to express your pleasure. That will make it easier for you to communicate disappointment with a trade or recent account performance without destroying the relationship.

Remember: One important way to reward a broker (and keep him or her supplying what you want) is to provide sales leads. If someone you know has an investment style similar to yours and you think could benefit from your broker's counsel, call the individual up first. If the person is interested in the idea, mention it to your broker. The promise of additional clients, particularly influential ones, should reinforce the relationship.

DEVELOPING RELATIONSHIPS WITH MORE THAN ONE BROKER
Not every brokerage house is part of every IPO, so it will be important to develop relationships with other brokers from different investment houses. As mentioned earlier, larger broker-dealers are more likely to generate a steady flow of good IPOs. But there are always exceptions—you never know when an office of a smaller firm will have trouble fulfilling allotments, perhaps because it simply does not have clients interested in IPOs.

Take, for example, one investor's experience with the Duff & Phelps IPO in 1991. This investor tried to get an allocation of the stock through brokers working for Prudential and Kemper with whom he had long-standing relationships. As it turned out, this was not a hot deal. Although both account executives came up with some shares, the Prudential associate offered more. The stock did not trade up at the offering, but by buying via the IPO, transaction costs were avoided. After a slow start, the stock rose more than 50 percent in just over a year. By having accounts in two places, the investor was able to build a larger position in the stock than would otherwise have been the case.

This story is a perfect illustration of the advantage of working with more than one broker. If you have enough money to spread around, start off working with a number of brokers and narrow the list to just two or three as you get a feel for their performance. Three to nine months should be enough time to gauge the relationship. In the end, you should be working with one main supplier of IPOs that suit your interests, and at least one or two backup sources.

PAYING FOR RESEARCH AND GOOD ADVICE

The better brokerage houses publish weekly research that outlines their views on the economy, the stock market, and companies in specific industries. Because of possible bias caused by the company's investment-banking activities, the favorable investment recommendations contained in these research reports should be subject to further scrutiny. You and your account executive should decide together if action is appropriate. These reports can, however, be invaluable for building up a body of knowledge and an analytical framework to judge specific industries that attract your attention. You never know when an analysis of the computer networking industry or a piece of information from a company research report will come in handy when evaluating an IPO. If your account is too small to warrant the firm mailing you lots of reports, tell your broker that you would like to drop by the office at a specific time of the week to pick up relevant research. (If you are in a position to generate a fair amount of commissions, you might be able to wheedle the Internet access code to all the company's current investment research.)

Full-service brokers charge much more for a trade than discounters. It is this research information, along with access to IPO allocations, proper order execution, and sound personal advice, which can justify the added expense.

PLACING AN ORDER

There are a number of cat-and-mouse games that go on when playing the IPO market. One occurs when an investor places an order. Because the order cannot be executed immediately, the investor puts in an *indication of interest,* which is essentially an order request. This order may be substantially greater than what the investor really wants to purchase, since even institutional clients might get only 5 or 10 percent of their requested allotments.

As the actual offering date approaches, the institutional or retail account executive goes back to the client with the number of shares and the likely offering price. This is the number of shares that the client has been *circled* to receive. The client then has the opportunity to take the designated amount at that price, a portion of it, or none at all.

The smaller the percentage of requested shares penciled in for major clients, the stronger the deal is likely to be. Most underwriters initially want at least twice as many shares requested as there are shares available, knowing that some buyers may drop out of the deal at some point before the IPO.

If there are not enough buyers within the price range, the lead under-writer will try to cut the price to entice more purchasers. The problem is that dropping the price will chase out short-term traders looking for a quick buck. If the mix of traders and longer-term investors attracted to the deal is unfa-vorable, demand for the shares could deteriorate further. If a broker comes back with a full allocation or states that the offering price has been cut, you should think twice before buying the stock. At the least, we recommend that you consider cutting your order in half. If you really like the company, you may be able to buy the remaining shares at a cheaper price in the aftermarket.

On the other hand, do not be so disappointed with a small stock alloca-tion that you pass it up. Take the small allocations. Fifty shares of a stock that jumps 50 percent on the first day is still a favorable event.

READING BETWEEN THE LINES WHEN A BROKER CALLS

Any cold call (i.e., an unsolicited one) from a broker trying to market an IPO should typically be disregarded. If a deal must be actively marketed to small investors, it is most likely a dud. Here are typical lines used to entice buyers to commit to a deal:

> *"You have to act fast."*   From a cold caller, this means the deal is so full of holes that if you thought twice about it, you would proba-bly rescind the trade. A trusted broker may ask you to act quickly on recent news, but coming from a stranger, the words should immediately make you suspicious.

> *"I can only guarantee an allocation at the offering if you are willing to buy more in the aftermarket."*   This is covered in the box on the aftermarket trap. Listeners who fall for this line might also be inter-ested in buying limited partnership interests in the Brooklyn Bridge.

Beware the Aftermarket Trap

Under no circumstance should you promise to buy more shares of an IPO in the aftermarket other than with a broker with whom you have had a highly satisfactory, multiyear realationship. This ploy is often used by disreputable brokers working for unscrupulous brokerage organizations. The goal of these "bucket shops" is to bring a company public with questionable fundamentals and manipulate the issue in the aftermarket for their own profit. The brokers initially tout the stock, promising that they have found enough buyers to send it higher in the aftermarket, but that they can get you in on the "sure thing" if you agree to purchase additional shares then as well. This amounts to a modified pyramid scheme. But this scam is only a sure thing for the broker-dealer and other insiders. With ready acquirers of the stock, the IPO moves higher, as promised—but when the investor seeks to cash in, the broker often makes excuses not to sell the position. The investor is caught in a bind, because even if he or she were to transfer the stock to another broker or request that a stock certificate be issued, it can often take so long that the stock moves down in the interim. The reason that the brokers seek to delay the sale is that they are busy selling the stock short, knowing exactly when the bubble will burst. When that happens, the stock drops and the brokerage house covers its short position at a lower price. At that point, the investor is allowed to sell. Usually, this results in a loss, sometimes a sizable one. In this zero-sum game, the big winner is always the house.

"If you wait for the prospectus it will be too late."   Without the prospectus, there is little chance of understanding what one is getting into and whether the rewards are worth the risks assumed. Although the sooner the request for shares is made the better, it does not guarantee preferable treatment.

"Investors feel that this stock has very bright prospects. That's why we've priced the deal at $5."   Chances are the deal has been given that price for a very specific reason: because a price *below* $5 is a pain in the neck to a broker. This is because of an SEC ruling stating that an order for an IPO price below $5 must be followed up with a note from the investor confirming the trade. Penny-stock brokers are so loath to allow investors a second thought that they try to price even the riskiest deals at $5 or better.

"I liked the deal at 12 when I first pitched it to you. I love it at 10."
A lower price means there were not enough buyers to get the deal done at 12. Even if you come to the independent conclusion that the company is attractive for investment, buy only half of the desired position at the offering. The stock might get even cheaper in the immediate aftermarket.

"If you take this IPO, I'll give you all you want of the next one."
Again, coming from a broker you trust, this might be an honest statement (though your broker still can't *guarantee* an allocation for your next favorite IPO). Coming from a stranger, it is highly suspicious. The next deal is apt to be just as lousy a company as the one he or she is trying to foist on you now.

"I did the trade because I knew that you'd want me to do it."
Unless you have signed away investment discretion to a broker, making a trade without your approval is against the law. Talking to your spouse does not count unless their name is also on the account and they have investment discretion as well. Unless your broker is your best friend (or very close to it), favorite son, or closest sibling, signing over investment discretion can result in financial disaster. It should be provided only to your most trusted associates, friends, and family, and only if you are in danger of losing your faculties or dying. Without the power of discretion, a broker cannot execute a transaction without your prior knowledge or approval. A reputable broker (there are plenty of them) would never do it, and that goes for IPO purchases as well.

TELLING WHETHER A BROKER IS REPUTABLE

As previously mentioned, references are your most important source when trying to gauge the honesty of your broker. Look for trusted individuals who will vouch for a broker's honesty *and* investment acumen. Then use your judgment. Is the broker well informed? Does he or she know what the stock market has done over the last few weeks or for the year to date? Can the broker articulate the firm's current investment policy? If so, how does the investment he or she is selling fit into that perspective?

In addition, ask yourself if the account executive makes reasonable assertions about the potential returns of investments. Does he or she level with you about the possible risks of owning more speculative investments? And remember: Anyone who *promises* a specific return on any investment in stocks probably should not be trusted.

A respected broker should also be concerned with your investment goals, financial condition, age, and salary level. Understanding the suitability of various investments for a broad range of clients is a cardinal virtue of any financial advisor. A cold caller should ask certain basic questions about an investor's financial standing before posing a specific investment idea.

Will the broker readily sell a position if you insist upon it? Convincing you to change your mind for your own good is one thing. Refusing to execute an instruction is quite another. (That includes the immediate sale of an IPO in the aftermarket.) Stubborn resistance in the face of a customer's firm desire for a specific order execution is cause for ending the relationship right there. (Incidentally, if you are having trouble getting the broker to make the sale, you should call the branch manager. If that does not work, try NASDAQ's compliance department. It can sometimes put pressure on the broker-dealer to let the trade go through.) But by far the best course of action is to avoid getting involved with a broker like this in the first place.

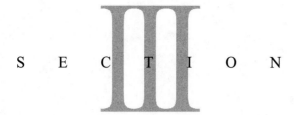

S E C T I O N

9

BUYING SMALL-CAP STOCKS: THE WORLD ACCORDING TO GARP

THIS AND THE FOLLOWING chapter show how a specific investment style, *growth at a reasonable price* (GARP), has allowed
Standard & Poor's equity analysts to pick stocks and create
portfolios that have consistently beaten the market by wide
margins. There are obviously many factors behind this success,
but much of the strategy can be summed up very simply: Their *strong buy*
recommendations have been, for the most part, companies with above-
average sales and earnings growth, *and* with price/earnings (P/E) ratios at
or below that of the S&P 500. It is this *Stock Appreciation Ranking System*
(STARS) model, along with Standard & Poor's *Fair Value* model (a STARS
quantitative correlative), that is the subject of Chapters 9 and 10.

Simply put, STARS is based on fundamental analyses done by Standard
& Poor's 50 equity analysts. Fair Value, on the other hand, is a quantitative
model that uses regression analysis to come up with *valuation anomalies*—
that is, stocks that are trading above or below their current intrinsic value, at
least based on statistics. STARS began covering about 600 issues in 1987, and
now appraises about 1100 stocks. Fair Value assesses more than 2000 names.

The two models complement each other in that both systems emphasize relative value, that is, stocks that are not being properly priced by
investors. STARS recommendations are subjective assessments, albeit by
experienced professionals, while Fair Value goes strictly by the numbers.

STARS stock recommendations, as well as Fair Value rankings, are published in most Standard & Poor's equity research products, including *Stock Reports, Personal Wealth, The OUTLOOK* investment newsletter, and *MarketScope.*

WATCHING THE STARS FOR INVESTMENT GUIDANCE

In late 1985, in an effort to compete more effectively with Value Line, Standard & Poor's decided to begin tracking its specific stock recommendations. It also set about designing a *quantitative* model to pick stocks, as well. In 1986, the two systems were compared. After 12 months, the analysts clearly won, beating both the statistical model and the S&P 500 by a wide margin. In early 1987, S&P announced its new STARS system, continuing to rely on its analysts rather than a "black box" for investment guidance.

The company made the right decision. During the last 12-plus years, S&P's analysts have done an amazing job of consistently beating the market. In contrast, Value Line's top-rated buys have beaten the market in fewer than half of the last 10 years.

Because it relies on humans for its recommendations, STARS is not really a *system* at all. It is not computer driven, it does not use technical analysis, nor does it draw from a static index universe. It *does* represent the collective wisdom of 25 industry and supervisory analysts, who make the bulk of the recommendations, as well as of 25 nonindustry analysts. These professionals use basic fundamental analysis to find their best picks, focusing on potential stock performance over the intermediate term and emphasizing capital appreciation (i.e., stock price appreciation) instead of total return (which might also include dividends).

The analysts are asked to judge every company they follow based on its potential for stock price appreciation over the next 6 to 12 months. Their recommendations can fall into five different categories:

Recommendation		*Expectation*
*****	Buy	Offers potentially high returns relative to the market
****	Accumulate	Could generate above average returns
***	Hold	Market performer
**	Avoid	Likely to underperform market
*	Sell	High potential to drop in value

Before divulging some of the secrets to their success, it might be interesting to review the actual performance of the stocks on the 5-STAR buy list, or the names with the highest ratings. Table 9-1 shows just how well the analysts have done predicting stock performance over 12-plus years. (When looking at these results, bear in mind they are before dividends and transaction costs. The average dividend yield of a 5-STAR stock is about half that of the S&P 500, and portfolio turnover is about 125 percent a year, which is about average for a growth-stock portfolio. Adjusting for these transaction costs and dividends would slightly reduce the outperformance of the list, but most of the excess returns would remain.)

Table 9-2 isolates the performance of the 5-STAR buy list and shows how $100,000 invested in it would have grown compared with the S&P 500. (Again, this is before transaction costs and dividends.)

In summary, the annual returns of the 5-STAR buy list exceeded the S&P 500 in 8 out of 12 full years, and for the first 9 months of 1999. The size of the 5-STAR portfolio has generally ranged between 30 and 110 stocks, with the number rising over the years in line with the number of stocks ana-

TABLE 9-1   Relative returns of STAR categories.

Year	1 STAR	2 STAR	3 STAR	S&P 500	4 STAR	5 STAR
1987	−24.9%	−0.1%	−4.1%	2.0%	−2.8%	21.3%
1988	13.0	18.3	19.5	12.4	17.0	19.4
1989	−5.1	8.3	16.0	27.3	26.9	28.5
1990	−43.2	−23.8	−12.9	−6.6	−6.1	−12.8
1991	−7.5	28.0	28.5	26.3	41.2	47.7
1992	20.3	14.3	14.7	4.5	12.2	12.8
1993	11.5	16.4	15.1	7.1	12.3	22.4
1994	1.0	2.3	−5.3	−1.5	−2.3	−2.4
1995	10.2	20.9	26.4	34.1	29.8	32.4
1996	−14.6	14.0	13.3	20.3	18.4	27.8
1997	14.5	13.4	22.1	31.0	30.4	31.5
1998	−0.7	1.9	4.8	26.7	11.3	26.7
1999*	3.6	9.0	0.2	4.4	4.7	15.5
Cumulative return	−28.4%	199.1%	239.8%	429.7%	450.3%	950.7%
Compound return	−2.6%	9.0%	10.1%	14.0%	14.3%	20.3%

* Through September 30.

TABLE 9-2   5-STAR historical returns.

Year	5-STARS Portfolio	$100,000 Invested	S&P 500	$100,000 Invested
1987	21.3%	$121,300	2.0%	$102,000
1988	19.4	144,832	12.4	114,648
1989	28.5	186,109	27.3	145,947
1990	−12.8	162,287	−6.6	136,314
1991	47.7	239,698	26.3	172,165
1992	12.8	270,380	4.5	179,913
1993	22.4	330,945	7.1	192,686
1994	−2.4	323,002	−1.5	189,796
1995	32.4	427,655	34.1	254,516
1996	27.8	546,543	20.3	306,183
1997	31.5	718,704	31.0	401,100
1998	26.7	910,595	26.7	505,194
1999*	15.5	1,051,741	4.4	530,554
Cumulative return	950.7%		381.1%	
Compound annual return	20.3%		13.4%	

* Through September 30.

lytically followed. The average beta (a measure of volatility) of the portfolio is about 1.2, slightly higher than that of the market.

Because the STARS universe is made up of approximately 1100 companies, the majority of its stocks are small- and midcapitalization. But there is also a subset of the portfolio known as the S&P SmallCap/IPO Buy List. This list, which has been regularly published in S&P's *Emerging & Special*

For non-do-it-yourselfers, we should mention the existence of the Bear Stearns S&P STARS Portfolio Fund. Launched in April 1995, the fund is designed to emulate the 5-STAR buy list. (Under most circumstances, at least 85 percent of the portfolio has to be made up of stocks that were designated 5-STAR at their time of purchase.) From its inception through June 30, 1999—a little more than four years— the fund generated a total return well above the average large-cap stock fund.

Situations newsletter since 1982, contains IPOs (priced upon inclusion *after* the first day of trading) and small-cap growth stocks. Since we started tracking the performance of this subgroup at the end of 1987, returns have also been impressive against its benchmark, the S&P SmallCap 600 Index, as shown in Table 9-3.

So, then, how do S&P's analysts do so well? As it turns out, by sticking to sound, old-fashioned strategies. S&P's analysts pick the best stocks within the industries they monitor, and recommend them only when the stocks' P/E multiples are at a discount to the companies' earnings growth rates.

In late 1994, in connection with the launching of the Bear Stearns S&P STARS Portfolio Fund, the company did a major analysis of STARS returns. This analysis revealed that the most significant factor affecting positive performance was analyst stock selection within each industry. *Top-down* economic considerations were also important, as was accurate industry selection. Other factors that contributed to outperformance included emphasis on superior growth, as well as on accurate earnings projections. All these attributes were consistent with a GARP style of investment.

TABLE 9-3   S&P's small-cap buy list and performance history.

Year	*ESS* Portfolio	S&P SmallCap 600	S&P 500
1988	13.6%	17.0%	12.4%
1989	25.2	11.5	27.3
1990	−19.9	−25.4	−6.6
1991	43.8	45.9	26.3
1992	32.1	19.4	4.5
1993	18.9	17.6	7.1
1994	−9.3	−5.8	−1.5
1995	28.9	28.6	34.1
1996	25.1	20.1	20.3
1997	22.6	24.5	31.0
1998	−6.4	−2.1	−26.7
1999*	22.0	−0.7	4.4
Cumulative return	426.8%	251.2%	429.7%
Annual return	15.2%	11.3%	15.3%
$100,000	$526,810	$351,210	$533,150

* Through September 30.

This all made sense to us. Since most analysts focus on one industry, their knowledge bases are deep, but narrow. They concentrate on the relative worth of stocks *within* each industry and not on the relative weighting of their industries in a portfolio.

GROWTH AT THE RIGHT PRICE (GARP)

The next thing S&P needed to know was the collective investment characteristics of the 5-STAR buy list as a portfolio. When put together, what were the most unique statistical differences which were driving performance? The analysis revealed a consistency in investment profiles, meaning that the analysts seemed to be adhering to a specific investment style.

Table 9-4 shows that, on average, the analysts chose and the fund owned stocks that were growing faster than those in the S&P 500, and which had

TABLE 9-4   5-STAR portfolio characteristics versus S&P 500*.

Characteristic	5-STAR Buy List	Bear Stearns S&P STARS Portfolio Fund	S&P 500
Beat, 60 mo	1.2	1.2	1.0
Price/earnings, trailing	26.9	29.8	27.5
Price/book value	6.6	6.5	7.4
Price/sales, trailing	4.1	3.5	3.7
Price/cash flow, trailing	22.2	21.6	22.4
IBES[†] 5-yr estimated earnings/share growth	18.4%	19.6%	14.7%
P/E to IBES[†] 5-yr growth	1.6	1.6	1.9
Median market capitalization, $ billion	$5.1	$11.0	$6.7
Return on equity, trailing 12 mo	18.5%	23.8%	23.5%
Capitalization[‡]			
Large cap, >$5.0 billion	50.0%	65.1%	61.2%
Midcap, $1.0–$5.0 billion	37.0%	27.9%	33.2%
Small cap, <$1.0 billion	13.0%	7.0%	5.6%

* As of October 26, 1998.
[†] Institutional Broker's Estimate System.
[‡] Based on an equal-weighted portfolio.

higher levels of profitability, but that were still cheaper based on standard valuation ratios. Compared to the S&P 500, the 5-STAR stocks and the Bear Stearns S&P STARS Portfolio Fund held stocks of companies growing earnings faster than the S&P 500, but which had close to the same P/E and price/cash-flow ratios, lower price/book-value ratios, and, most important, lower P/E-to-growth rates. Also of note: The cap size distribution was virtually the same as that of the S&P 500.

STANDARD & POOR'S FAIR VALUE MODEL

Although S&P's analysts handily beat the computer's stock rankings in 1986, S&P was not about to abandon its search for a superior quantitative model. In 1991, after four years of labor and exhaustive backtesting, the S&P Fair Value model was unveiled. This time the model provided returns highly competitive with those of the analysts.

Like the Coca-Cola formula, quantitative methodologies that consistently beat the market are highly valuable and are vigilantly kept under lock and key, so we will only speak in general terms here. In summary, the model looks for stocks that are trading at a discount to their "fair value," based on consensus earnings growth expectations over the next three to five years. Using earnings projections, the Fair Value model evaluates likely returns on book value, as well as returns on equity over the next five years. It then compares these statistics with historical average returns for each stock, those of the overall industry, and those of the S&P 500. A fair value is then calculated for each stock in the universe, and the final stock list is broken down into quintiles. Those equities considered most attractive are ranked 5, and the least attractive are ranked 1.

As Table 9-5 illustrates, top-ranked stocks by this model have done quite well. Of course, this should be no surprise, because, like the STARS system, the Fair Value model essentially emphasizes growth at a reasonable price.

In early 1997, some major enhancements were made to the Fair Value model. The most important was the addition of an *earnings surprise* factor. Research has shown that companies that have recently exceeded earnings expectations will probably do so again in the next quarter. Similarly, companies that have recently reported earnings *disappointments* are likely to repeat that performance, too. To account for this phenomenon, stocks were divided into quintiles based on their likelihood to report an earnings surprise in the coming quarter. When incorporated into the model, the backtested results showed that this enhancement would have added 5 percentage points (or 500 basis points) of annual return to the portfolio.

TABLE 9-5   Returns of Standard & Poor's fair value model.*

Year	1	2	3	4	5	S&P 500
			Quintile			
1987	−3.9%	−1.1%	2.2%	−0.4%	6.7%	5.1%
1988	21.0	19.3	26.3	24.9	30.7	16.6
1989	17.3	23.1	22.5	22.0	24.8	31.7
1990	−17.1	−11.1	−10.4	−9.3	−4.1	−3.1
1991	27.7	29.6	43.9	45.1	59.7	30.5
1992	15.8	14.3	15.2	23.1	23.8	7.6
1993	17.3	16.4	21.6	15.0	12.7	10.1
1994	−2.8	−4.6	0.2	1.6	9.7	1.3
1995	25.9	23.7	28.8	28.7	33.7	37.6
1996	16.4	17.6	22.0	20.6	28.3	23.0
1997	23.1	31.4	24.5	31.4	37.7	33.4
1998	2.7	3.4	11.6	5.3	8.0	28.6
1999[†]	5.6	1.7	1.0	5.3	9.6	5.3
Cumulative return	256.8%	321.8%	515.8%	567.6%	654.6%	529.7%
Annual return	11.0%	11.9%	15.6%	15.7%	20.7%	15.6%
$100,000 invested	$256,800	$321,800	$515,800	$567,600	$654,600	$529,700

* Prior to 1997 enhancement.
[†] Through September 30.

STANDARD & POOR'S PLATINUM PORTFOLIO: A PERFECT MARRIAGE

It did not take long for the company to set about combining the best of its human and quantitative systems to create a model portfolio of top stocks. The performance of S&P Platinum Portfolio, as shown in Table 9-6, has been impressive. To be included, a stock must have a 5 ranking in both the STARS and Fair Value systems. To be removed from the list, the stock must no longer be ranked 5 according to *both* models.

Although not by design, most of the stocks in this portfolio have mid- and small capitalizations. Why? Larger-capitalization stocks have so many analysts following them that their stock prices more or less reflect their long-term prospects. It is among the less-followed stocks that the S&P ana-

TABLE 9-6   Standard & Poor's platinum portfolio performance history.

Year	Platinum Portfolio	S&P 500*
1987	9.1%	2.0%
1988	26.4	12.4
1989	36.5	27.3
1990	2.6	−6.6
1991	42.3	26.3
1992	8.0	4.5
1993	17.8	7.1
1994	3.8	−1.5
1995	37.7	34.1
1996	34.3	20.3
1997	17.4	31.0
1998	20.5	26.7
1999[†]	21.1	4.4
Cumulative return	1051.7%	429.7%
Annual return	21.1%	14.0%

* Excluding dividends.
[†] Through September 30.

lysts and the Fair Value model tend to make their most important discoveries. (Sample S&P 5-STAR, Fair Value 5, and Platinum Portfolio reports can be seen in Exhibits 9-1 to 9-3.) As the current portfolio manager of the S&P STARS Portfolio Fund, I pay careful attention to the Fair Value ranking, the Platinum Portfolio, and the 5-STAR buy list when selecting and weighting stocks within the fund.

INDEPENDENT CORROBORATION
In mid-1997, David Lipschutz, a Morgan Stanley Dean Witter analyst, completed a study of stock performance based on P/E-to-growth rates. It looked at the performance of the 1000 biggest stocks during the 11½ years ending June 30, 1997. The study found that stocks trading at low P/E-to-growth rates significantly beat the market, while high P/E-to-growth stocks

EXHIBIT 9-1   Sample S&P 5-STAR recommendations listing.

(From Standard & Poor's. Copyright © 1998 by The McGraw-Hill Companies.)

```
                    Five STAR Recommendations - (S&P) 23-Nov-98 Pg. 75      Seg 1
SYM    CO. NAME           DATE/PRICE      CURRENT REASON
ALK    Alaska Air         04/30/98-55 3/4Growing faster than industry
AMAT   Applied Matrls     02/11/98-36    Oversold on Asian worries
AMP    AMP Inc            11/23/98-47 3/4Acquisition by TYC
ARTS   Media Art          11/04/98-12 1/2Rapid expansion of new store openings
AS     Armco Inc          10/29/97-5 1/16Improved sales mix
ATI    AirTouch Comms     08/14/96-27 1/8Strong wireless demand
AXP    Amer. Express      01/25/94-30 5/8Card volume, managed assets growth
BDX    Becton, Dick       07/22/98-84 3/8New product launches
BGEN   Biogen Inc         07/14/98-53    Strong growth in Avonex MS drug
                              * Adjusted for stock split
SYM    CO. NAME           DATE/PRICE      CURRENT REASON
BGP    Borders Group      08/13/98-30 1/4Strong sales, improving margins
BK     Bank of N.Y.       01/16/96-11.47*Strong growth in fee business
BKS    Barnes&Noble       08/20/98-37 1/4Expect boost from IPO of internet unit
BMY    Bristol-Myers      12/19/97-92.562Strong drug pipeline, R&D boost
CAI.B  Continental Air    12/17/97-47.687Low P/E despite strong EPS growth
CBRNA  Canandaigua Bds    09/29/98-39    New products benefits, lower costs
CCE    Coca-Cola Ent.     01/20/98-36.44 Steady cash flow growth
CDN    Cadence Design     10/07/97-26.16*Stronger sales, more consulting
CEN    Ceridian Corp      02/20/98-46.562See 15%-20% earnings growth
                              * Adjusted for stock split
SYM    CO. NAME           DATE/PRICE      CURRENT REASON
CI     CIGNA Corp.        07/31/98-64 3/4Improved business mix
CMCSK  Comcast Corp       08/12/98-44.44 Takeover of JOIN very positive
CMS    CMS Energy         10/06/98-45 1/2Int'l growth, attractive valuation
COST   Costco Cos         11/05/98-59 3/4See strong cash flow, prospects
CSCO   Cisco Systems      05/01/97-51 3/4Dominates its industry
CVC    Cablevision        01/28/98-45.34*Wiz acquisition is long-term plus
CVG    Convergys Corp     08/13/98-16 3/8Benefits from telecom ind. outsourcing
CVS    CVS Corp           02/09/98-35.28*Strong sales gains, wider margins
DCN    Dana Corp          08/05/98-51    See as winner in consolidated ind.
                              * Adjusted for stock split
SYM    CO. NAME           DATE/PRICE      CURRENT REASON
DELL   Dell Computer      02/19/98-55.66*Consistent strong revenue growth
DH     Dayton Hudson      10/02/98-34.187See discount stores doing well
DL     Dial Corp          10/20/98-24    Undervalued vs. peers
DUK    Duke Energy        10/05/98-67.125Expansion of non-regulated operations
ECILF  ECI Telecom        02/08/96-25 3/8Revenue strength
EFS    Enhance Fin'l      02/12/98-28.94*Diversifing into high growth business
EMC    EMC Corp.          01/29/97-18.31*Client/server, mainframe prods demand
FBN    Furntr Brands      10/29/98-20    See strong revenue growth
FMY    Fred Meyer         10/19/98-49    Reflects acquisition by Kroger
                              * Adjusted for stock split
SYM    CO. NAME           DATE/PRICE      CURRENT REASON
FTU    First Union        01/16/98-39.81*Dynamic business mix
GDT    Guidant Corp       09/19/97-51 1/2Ambitious R&D program
HDI    Harley-Davidson    06/30/95-23 1/4Demand still above supply
HIG    Hartford Fin'l     01/07/98-46.03*Solid gains in annuities
HMA    Health Mgmt        03/29/96-10.3* Cost controls, targeted acquisitions
HRC    Healthsouth        03/31/98-27.562'99 impact of acquisitions
IBM    Int'l Business     10/22/98-142.69See P/E expansion
JBHT   Hunt (JB) Trans    11/20/98-17.312Fast growing truckload carrier
JNJ    Johnson&Johnson    10/19/95-39.06*Stream of new products
                              * Adjusted for stock split
SYM    CO. NAME           DATE/PRICE      CURRENT REASON
KLAC   KLA-Tencor         02/11/98-41.312Attractive niches in weak sector
KR     Kroger Co          01/07/98-35.63 Industry pickup; improved efficiency
```

EXHIBIT 9-1   Sample S&P 5-STAR recommendations listing (*Continued*).

```
                 Five STAR Recommendations - (S&P) 23-Nov-98 Pg. 75      Seg 1
KRB   MBNA Corp.           09/07/95-15.72*Evista potential, strong R&D
LLY   Lilly (Eli)          10/20/97-62 3/4Strongest EPS outlook among group
MCK   McKesson Corp        07/28/98-79    Strong grwth propects, ind fundamentals
MRA   Meritor Auto         08/14/98-21.562Increased outsourcing by manufacturers
MRK   Merck & Co           04/30/98-116   New wave of drugs to aid growth
MSFT  Microsoft            10/21/98-100.25New product cycle
NETA  Network Assoc.       08/21/98-44 1/2Price decline, good prospects
                                 * Adjusted for stock split
SYM   CO. NAME             DATE/PRICE     CURRENT REASON
NFB   North Fork           03/03/98-22.75*Strong local economy, acq strategy
NOK.A Nokia Corp           10/23/98-86 1/4Strong growth in mobil phone sales
NT    Northern Telecm      03/02/98-26.57*Benefits from wireless, Internet grwth
NWS   News Corp            11/07/97-20.375Strong outlook at films, internet units
OMX   OfficeMax            06/22/95-12.9* Better sales mix, more stores
PFE   Pfizer Inc           11/08/94-37.19*Strongest new drug pipeline
QCOM  QUALCOMM Inc         06/23/97-49 3/4Outlook for co's CDMA technology
REY   Reynold&Reynlds      04/23/98-22 7/8All business units improving
RHBC  RehabCare Group      01/12/98-23 3/8Growing earnings, low P/E
                                 * Adjusted for stock split
SYM   CO. NAME             DATE/PRICE     CURRENT REASON
RNT   Aaron Rents          08/15/94-6*    Strong earnings uptrend
RX    IMS Health           07/01/98-59-1/2See 20%+ EPS growth
SBUX  Starbucks Corp       10/02/98-36.187Broader prod line, new distrbtn chanels
SKS   Saks Inc.            09/18/98-27    See strong FY2000 earnings
SLE   Sara Lee             01/06/98-55.687Benefits of outsourcing
SOI   Solutia Inc          03/31/98-29 7/8Lower raw material costs
SPLS  Staples Inc          08/16/96-12.19*Strong fundamentals, rising margins
SSW   Sterling Sftwre      05/18/95-17.81*Strength in all segments
SWY   Safeway Inc          01/07/98-30.91*Better sales mix, efficient buying
                                 * Adjusted for stock split
SYM   CO. NAME             DATE/PRICE     CURRENT REASON
T     AT&T                 07/27/98-59.937Venture with BTY positive
TCOMA Tele-Commncts        03/23/98-31.78 Higher revs., lower debt, costs cuts
TOS   Tosco Corp           09/15/97-33.187Lower oil prices, summer gas demand
TRH   Transatlantic        07/01/97-66.17*Well-managed by 49%-owner AIG
TX    Texaco Inc           10/09/98-62.312Strong production profile, cost cuts
TXU   Texas Utilits        10/02/98-46.562Attrctv divs, outlook in this market
TYC   Tyco Int'l           10/16/96-22.56*Benefits of U.S. Surgical acquisition
USB   US Bancorp           07/15/98-47.062Strong rev. generating capability
USFC  USFreightways        04/30/98-35 3/8Gaining market share
                                 * Adjusted for stock split
SYM   CO. NAME             DATE/PRICE     CURRENT REASON
UVN   Univision Comms      10/27/98-26.062Reflects porgramming breadth & diversity
WCOM  MCI WorldCom         08/14/96-28    To thrive in new telecom mkt
WDFC  WD-40 Co             10/22/98-27.312Strong cash generation, high margins
WLA   Warner Lambert       04/23/98-62.60*Success of Lipitor cholestrol drug
WPI   Watson Pharma        04/02/98-37 7/8Makes hard-to-produce generics
XIRC  Xircom Inc           11/20/98-34 3/8Leader in PC cards for laptops
YELL  Yellow Corp          08/18/98-15    Undervalued after drop, share buybacks
YHOO  Yahoo! Inc           01/20/98-32.63*Leading position in industry
ZBRA  Zebra Tech           11/16/98-33.312Sales, earnings outlook
```

EXHIBIT 9-2   Sample S&P fair value portfolio 5-ranked listings.
(From Standard & Poor's. Copyright © 1998 by The McGraw-Hill Companies.)

```
        Fair Value Portfolio ------ (S&P) 17-Nov-98 Pg. 82      Seg 1
           Return Year to Date through 10/31/98:
        Fair Value Portfolio: 3.54%   S&P 500: 13.21%.
           See Below For Historical Performance
                                  Nov. 13  1998
Company Name            Ticker| Fair Val | Price | Rank
----------------------  ------|----------|-------|------
ADVO, Inc.              AD         41.50   23.90   5A+
Anchor Gaming           SLOT      102.00   46.60   5A+
Andrew Corp.            ANDW       26.80   17.30   5A+
Applebee's Internationa APPB       35.90   18.80   5B+
Autodesk, Inc.          ADSK       55.90   34.60   5B+
                                  Nov. 13  1998
Company Name            Ticker| Fair Val | Price | Rank
----------------------  ------|----------|-------|------
Avado Brands            AVDO       19.90    7.50   5N+
Avondale Industries     AVDL       37.10   28.00   4A+
Beazer Homes USA        BZH        45.80   25.10   5A+
Checkpoint Systems      CKP        19.00   12.80   5A+
Commercial Metals       CMC        42.20   27.50   5A+
DSP Communications      DSP        22.80   10.40   5B
Darden Restaurants      DRI        22.10   16.40   4A+
Department 56           DFS        42.30   31.80   4A+
                                  Nov. 13  1998
Company Name            Ticker| Fair Val | Price | Rank
----------------------  ------|----------|-------|------
Fluor Corp.             FLR        69.50   43.80   5A+
Harrah's Entertainment  HET        34.40   16.90   5D
Health Management Syste HMSY       12.90    6.25   5N
International Game Tech  IGT        37.70   23.60   5B+
Jones Apparel Group     JNY        36.80   21.30   5A+
Keane, Inc.             KEA        69.30   35.30   5A
Nautica Enterprises     NAUT       34.00   18.60   5A
Oracle Corporation      ORCL       60.30   33.20   5A
                                  Nov. 13  1998
Company Name            Ticker| Fair Val | Price | Rank
----------------------  ------|----------|-------|------
Planar Systems          PLNR       18.60   10.30   5C+
Promus Hotel            PRH        49.30   30.30   5C
Shuffle Master          SHFL       15.90    8.00   5N+
Stride Rite             SRR        12.30    9.44   4A+
Sundstrand Corp.        SNS        78.10   50.80   5A+
Taco Cabana             TACO        5.66    6.25   1A+
Xilinx, Inc.            XLNX       80.00   51.40   5A+
Zale Corp               ZLC        42.50   26.30   5A
        Fair Value Portfolio Performance
Year   Fair Value    Fair Value    S&P 500
       (Total Ret.) (Cap. Appr.) (Cap. Appr.)
1997    50.28%        48.91%        31.01%
1996    33.90%        32.50%        20.26%
1995    40.70%        38.80%        34.11%
1994    24.00%        21.70%        -1.54%
1993    11.60%        10.00%         7.06%
1992    17.90%        16.30%         4.46%
Returns (Total Return and Capital Appreciation)
      based on backtesting prior to 1997.
Year   Fair Value    Fair Value    S&P 500
       (Total Ret.) (Cap. Appr.) (Cap. Appr.)
1991    46.80%        44.70%        30.40%

        Fair Value Portfolio ------ (S&P) 17-Nov-98 Pg. 82      Seg 1
1990     8.60%         6.70%        -6.56%
1989    36.70%        34.10%        27.25%
1988    25.70%        23.20%        12.40%
1987    30.90%        28.80%         2.03%
Returns (Total Return and Capital Appreciation)
      based on backtesting prior to 1997.
```

EXHIBIT 9-3   Sample S&P platinum portfolio listings (ranked 5 by both the STARS and fair value models).
(From Standard & Poor's. Copyright © 1998 by The McGraw-Hill Companies.)

```
      Platinum Portfolio -------- (S&P) 24-Nov-98 Pg. 27      Seg 1
           Return Year to Date through 10/31/98:
        Platinum Portfolio: -1.23%   S&P 500: 13.21%
      Return in October: Platinum: 11.25%  S&P 500: 8.03%.
           See Below For Historical Performance
```

Company Name	Ticker	Nov. 20 1998 FairVal	Price	Ranking FVal	Star
Aaron Rents	RNT	18.90	14.60	4	5
Alaska Air Group	ALK	58.00	33.30	5	5
Applied Materials	AMAT	51.70	39.30	4	5
Borders Group	BGP	37.10	23.30	5	5
Cadence Design Systems	CDN	39.40	29.00	4	5
Canandaigua Brands*Cl'A	CBRNA	72.30	48.80	4	5
Cisco Systems	CSCO	96.00	74.60	4	5
EMC Corp.	EMC	85.00	70.00	3	5
Gartner Group'A'	IT	44.40	20.10	5	3
HEALTHSOUTH Corp.	HRC	23.60	11.90	5	5
Health Management Assoc	HMA	32.10	22.40	4	5
KLA-Tencor Corp.	KLAC	38.10	36.90	2	5
Lone Star Steakhouse &	STAR	21.80	7.44	5	3
MBNA Corp.	KRB	23.60	21.60	3	5
Modis Professional Svcs	MPS	23.20	14.00	5	4
Network Associates	NETA	88.90	43.10	5	5
News Corp.	NWS	43.70	29.00	5	5
OfficeMax, Inc.	OMX	16.50	10.60	5	5
Oracle Corporation	ORCL	61.90	34.80	5	3
Parametric Technology	PMTC	39.20	15.30	5	4
Precision Castparts	PCP	75.00	46.20	5	3
QUALCOMM Inc.	QCOM	94.20	55.40	5	5
Roper Industries	ROP	30.40	17.10	5	4
Safeway Inc.	SWY	62.40	52.80	3	5
Saks Inc.	SKS	38.10	27.80	4	5
Staples, Inc.	SPLS	48.00	35.60	4	5
Sterling Software	SSW	13.80	25.90	1	5
Symantec Corp.	SYMC	34.70	19.10	5	4
Transatlantic Holdings	TRH	87.00	76.60	3	5
Tyco International Ltd.	TYC	82.50	65.10	4	5
USFreightways	USFC	28.80	26.40	3	5
Yellow Corp.	YELL	18.80	17.00	3	5

```
        Platinum Portfolio Performance
        Year   Platinum      S&P 500
        1997    17.42          31.01
```

EXHIBIT 9-3   Sample S&P platinum portfolio listings (ranked 5 by both the STARS and fair value models) (*Continued*).

```
Platinum Portfolio -------- (S&P) 24-Nov-98 Pg. 27     Seg 1
       1996    34.32%        20.26%
       1995    37.72%        34.11%
       1994     3.78%        -1.54%
       1993    17.81%         7.06%
       1992     8.02%         4.46%
* - Returns are capital appreciations only
Prior to mid-1995, returns based on backtesting

       Platinum Portfolio Performance
       Year    Platinum    S&P 500
       1991    42.28%       26.31%
       1990     2.64%       -6.56%
       1989    36.53%       27.25%
       1988    26.39%       12.40%
       1987     9.12%        2.03%
* - Returns are capital appreciations only
Prior to mid-1995, returns based on backtesting
```

did quite poorly. The results were as shown in Table 9-7, with Group 1 representing the 100 stocks with the lowest P/E-to-growth rates, and Group 10 representing the 100 stocks with the highest. (The P/E was based on projected 12-month operating earnings per share, and the growth rate was based on consensus projected earnings for the next 5 years.) Rebalancing

TABLE 9-7   Morgan Stanley Dean Witter Study: Stock-price performance by P/E-to-growth rate plus yield, stocks equally weighted*

Group	Average Forecast EPS Growth	Annual Return	Average P/E-growth Rate, 09/30/97
Group 1	17.7%	21.7%	0.5
Group 2	15.3	20.1	0.6
Group 3	14.9	18.1	0.7
Group 4	14.3	16.6	0.8
Group 5	13.7	16.7	0.9
Group 6	13.0	15.2	1.0
Group 7	12.5	12.4	1.0
Group 8	12.0	10.3	1.1
Group 9	11.5	10.0	1.3
Group 10	12.4	4.3	3.8
All 1000 stocks	13.7	14.9	1.2

* Annualized compound return, December 31, 1985 to September 30, 1997.

SOURCE: *Morgan Stanley Dean Witter.*

TABLE 9-8   Morgan Stanley Dean Witter Study: Most and least expensive stocks by P/E-to-growth rate.

Rank	Company	Recent Price	P/E*	Long-term Earnings Growth Rate[†]	P/E-to-Growth Rate
		Most expensive			
1	General Electric	67	24	13%	1.8
2	Microsoft	138	39	23	1.7
3	Intel	99	21	21	1.0
4	Exxon	63	21	7	3.2
5	Coca-Cola	61	34	18	1.9
6	Merck	95	22	15	1.5
7	Royal Dutch Petroleum	53	20	8	2.5
8	Philip Morris	45	14	16	0.9
9	IBM	108	15	12	1.3
10	Procter & Gamble	138	22	13	1.7
11	Wal-Mart	37	21	13	1.6
12	Bristol-Myers	79	22	11	2.0
13	Johnson & Johnson	59	21	14	1.5
14	Du Pont	66	17	10	1.7
15	Pfizer	55	27	16	1.7
		Least expensive			
1	Seagate Technology	43.00	9.5	23.3%	0.4
2	Falcon Drilling	27.56	17.4	32.4	0.5
3	Western Digital	54.00	11.7	20.7	0.6
4	Corporate Express	17.25	23.6	41.0	0.6
5	Quantum	37.00	12.7	19.5	0.6
6	Cooper Cameron	58.63	22.1	34.4	0.6
7	US Cellular	30.88	21.9	34.0	0.6
8	Medpartners	20.50	16.0	26.3	0.6
9	USX-US Steel	35.13	9.1	14.0	0.7
10	Santa Fe International	43.50	14.6	22.3	0.7
11	Iomega	24.13	23.4	35.7	0.7

168

FAST STOCKS FAST MONEY

TABLE 9-8 Morgan Stanley Dean Witter Study: Most and least expensive stocks by P/E-to-growth rate (*Continued*).

Rank	Company	Recent Price	P/E*	Long-term Earnings Growth Rate[†]	P/E-to-Growth Rate
12	Republic Industries	23.38	26.3	40.0	0.7
13	Diamond Offshore Drilling	44.00	17.7	26.8	0.7
14	Tidewater	51.06	13.2	19.7	0.7
15	Ensco International	63.00	17.0	25.0	0.7

* Based on projected 1998 profits as of July 31, 1997.
[†] Based on projected five-year profit growth from July 31, 1997, using Institutional Broker's Estimate System consensus.
SOURCE: *Morgan Stanley Dean Witter; adapted from Andrew Bary, "New Value in Old Saw," Barron's, August 25, 1997. Republished by permission of Dow Jones, Inc. via Copyright Clearance Center, Inc. © 1997 Dow Jones and Company, Inc. All rights reserved worldwide.*

(movement of stocks from one decile to another) occurred every month. Although this study is of large-cap stocks, we believe the results also apply to small-cap stocks.

Table 9-8 shows the most expensive stocks in the study's 1000-issue universe, as well as the cheapest.

10

C H A P T E R

GARP AND THE INDIVIDUAL INVESTOR

THE LAST CHAPTER takes a quick peek at the methodologies behind the Fair Value and STARS systems. But how can they be applied to individual stocks, particularly those that are not covered in the STARS and Fair Value systems?

This chapter provides a framework for understanding when a stock is or is not attractive. The stocks selected—Symantec, Kellogg, USFreightways, and Intergraph—run the gamut in terms of growth and value, price/earnings (P/E), and capitalization characteristics, and so are good illustrations of each category.

Standard & Poor's distinguishes between *growth* and *value* stocks by using book value. Those companies with the highest price/book values are placed in the *growth* subgroup, and those with the lowest in the *value* subgroup. As of mid-1999, the S&P 500 index was trading at almost 5 times book value. By this measure, Symantec and Kellogg would be defined as *growth* stocks, and USFreightways and Intergraph deemed *value* stocks.

The P/E ratios for these four companies ranged from 29 times for Kellogg to 13 times earnings per share (EPS) for USFreightways. Kellogg is the only large-cap stock of the bunch, with a market capitalization of over $16 billion. The other three were small cap sized, with the smallest, Intergraph, at $428 million.

Let's start with a quick review of our system. The goal is to use projected earnings estimates and long-term growth expectations to come up

169

with a fair valuation, or P/E, for the stock. That P/E may then be used to derive a target stock price 12 months from now. The next step is to compare that stock price with the current price to derive the stock's appreciation potential over the next 12 months. Finally, that appreciation potential is added to the current dividend yield, and compared to the historical return of the market. From this process, the stock is ranked in one of the following categories based on potential return:

20 percent and up return	Buy
13 to 20 percent	Accumulate
8 to 13 percent	Market performer
0 to 8 percent	Avoid
Negative return	Sell

If you apply this system and rank the stock a buy, find out as much about the company as possible. The key here is to develop a degree of confidence that the analyst's growth projections are realistic. Remember, small company growth rates almost always trend down over time. Growth rates also eventually revert to the growth rate of the overall product category. If the mainframe computer market is growing at 3 percent a year, a company that comes out with a better one might be able to enjoy a short spurt of growth as it takes market share away from the leader, but the growth rate will eventually drop back toward 3 percent over time.

As you might guess, the long-term earnings growth rate is the most important statistic in this analysis. There are a number of sources for analyst estimates of three- to five-year earnings growth. The primary vendors are Institutional Broker's Estimate System (IBES), First Call, and Zacks. They can be found in a number of Standard & Poor's products, on the Internet, on America Online (AOL), and on Compuserve. None of these vendors allows you to screen their earnings databases within the free portions of their Internet websites but all provide some valuable individual stock information gratis. For example, at the First Call site (www.firstcall.com) you can find earnings surprises, earnings revisions, companies expected to report the following week, and consensus earnings on the Dow Industrials. (Consensus earnings estimates, along with other information on particular stocks, can be obtained via its "Estimates on Demand" service at $1.50 to $3.00 per company, or $199 a year for access to the entire database.)

Other websites that supply similar free earnings estimates include E*Trade and Quote.com. As of mid-1999, Quote.com charged $24.95 a month for its Extra Subscription service, which includes First Call earnings information, other company information, customized daily charts, news, insider trade information, and portfolio-tracking information. Thomson's Investor's Network service (www.thomsoninvest.net) charges $9.95 a month for a variety of information, including up to 25 consensus earnings reports per month, $2.50 each after that. Or, for $12.95 a month, you can receive consensus earnings data via Nelson's Earnings Outlook.

As of mid-1999, Zacks Investment Research offered the best deal for studied users. Free information included unlimited access to brief company reports. These reports included Zacks's earnings estimates for the current and next fiscal year, as well as the current quarter. Last quarter's actual earnings are also there, along with any earnings surprises. Zacks's "Analyst Watch" also includes other fundamental data, screening capability, and e-mail alerts for $295 a year. *Barron's* rated Quote.com as the most economical for heavy users at $24.95 a month, followed by Zacks for the most sophisticated investors.

Now let's review some hard examples to prove our point. For companies increasing earnings by more than 30 percent a year, the target P/E should be below the growth rate. The higher the growth rate, the greater the discount that should be applied to that growth rate to come up with the target P/E. Always use a three- to five-year growth rate (preferably five). And remember: Even the fastest-growing companies typically come down to more realistic levels over that time span. Many companies that are doubling earnings now will not do so for long.

We should also point out that any cyclical companies (those that are more subject to the economic cycle) will inevitably experience down years. These companies should receive lower target P/E multiples than stocks operating in noncyclical industries (see Table 10-1). Sectors most subject to the economic cycle are basic materials, industrials, transportation, consumer durables, financials, and technology. Sectors less subject to the earn-

TABLE 10-1   Target P/E ratios and growth rates for cyclical and noncyclical industries.

	Target P/E	
5-yr Target Growth Rate	Cyclical Industry	Noncyclical Industry
50%	38	45
40	32	37
30	25	30
25	21	28
20	17	25

NOTE: Data as of September 30, 1999.

ings cycle are consumer staples, communications services, and healthcare services. Energy tends to run on its own cycle.

For companies likely to grow earnings at *less* than a 20 percent annual rate (which encompasses the vast majority of firms), the P/E should be a function of that currently being applied to the S&P 500. For example, in the beginning of 1997, analysts were projecting that earnings for the S&P 500 would expand about 13 percent over the next year. The S&P 500 was trading at 19 times that earnings expectation. A company expected to grow earnings above that 13 percent rate should then get a slightly higher P/E than 19 times. If earnings growth is expected to be less, then a lower P/E should be used. Raise the target P/E slightly for large companies with a consistent record of earnings growth; lower it a bit for troubled companies that are less likely to hit earnings-growth targets or that have low returns on equity.

Finally, once the P/E is derived, it should be applied to the company's potential earnings for the *succeeding* 12 months. As of the beginning of 1999, that would mean coming up with potential 2000 earnings. (Some analysts will not have derived a next-year estimate so early in the current calendar year, but you can come up with a rough guide by using the five-year projected growth rate. If projected 1999 earnings per share are $2.00, and the company's long-term earnings growth rate is 30 percent, then adding 30 percent would give you a quick-and-dirty estimate of $2.60 for 2000.) Once you have next year's earnings estimate, you can use the P/E to come up with a *target* for the year-end 1999 stock price. If that price is more than 20 percent above the current level, the stock could be a real winner. Of course, if the target price is close to the current one (or lower), it is less likely to generate much of a return (see Table 10-2).

Some details regarding Table 10-2 should be explained:

- Our analysis took place in June 1998, so the 13- to 24-month projected earnings-per-share (EPS) target was essentially a blend of calendar 1998 and 1999 estimates.
- For Symantec, the forward 12-month target price is our sense of where the stock should trade in June 1999 in anticipation of projected 1999 per-share earnings. (Symantec has a fiscal year that ends in March, so we had to interpolate a bit to get a calendar year estimate.)
- Return on equity (ROE) was based on beginning ROE for the current fiscal year.
- Net profit margin was for the most recently completed fiscal year, except for Intergraph which had a deficit for the quarter.

TABLE 10-2   Comparative value chart.

Characteristic	SYMC	K	USFC	INGR
			Stock (ticker)	
Trailing 12-mo earnings growth	86.8%	16.4%	43.5%	Deficit
Projected 3–5-yr growth rate	37%	9%	13%	8%
Target P/E on 5-yr growth rate	30×	19×	14×	10×
Consensus projected 12-mo EPS	$1.81	$1.89	$2.68	$0.59
Estimated 13–24-mo forward EPS	$2.48	$2.06	$3.03	$0.64
12-mo forward target price	$74.40	$39.14	$42.42	$6.40
June 1998 price	$26.13	$39.88	$30.88	$8.88
Percent difference	184.8%	−1.9%	13.7%	−27.9%
Dividend rate	Nil	2.3%	1.2%	Nil
Potential return	184.8%	0.4%	14.9%	−27.9%
Recommendation	Buy	Avoid	Accumulate	Sell
Fair Value ranking	5	2	4	1
Fair Value	$41.88	$39.63	$38.25	$6.13
STARS ranking	5	2	5	2
Earnings/dividend rank	B−	A	B+	C
P/E trailing 12-mo EPS	18	29	13	NM
Market cap/sales	2.6	2.4	0.5	0.4
Stock price/tangible book value	5.3	15.8	2.7	1.0
Debt/capital	2%	59%	21%	13%
ROE	32%	50%	17%	NM
Net profit margin	15%	8%	4%	NM
Beta	1.80	0.53	0.46	1.08
Stock relative strength	64	48	39	63

If an investor simply took a snapshot of the two growth stocks, Symantec and Kellogg, Symantec would appear to have the fastest growth, and hence be more likely to provide better returns during the next 6 to 12 months. Yet Symantec's P/E is lower than Kellogg's on a trailing 12-month basis. Symantec's stock is more volatile, as evidenced by its beta of 1.80. Still, by purchasing a stock at a P/E below the five-year growth rate, there is a sizable margin of error built into the equation. If growth remains strong, the stock will rise because the current P/E does not fully reflect it. If growth slows, it must slow appreciably below current long-term growth expectations before the stock will suffer.

USFreightways and Intergraph are both value stocks because they are trading at low stock price/book values and low price/sales, but these two firms appear to be going in different directions. USFreightways has been consistently profitable in a highly cyclical business. Intergraph has posted deficits for five straight years. USFreightways' revenues and earnings were up in each of the last five years, while Intergraph's revenues have been virtually flat for seven years. It has a lower projected long-term growth rate, and has had a lower return on stockholders' equity since 1992, yet it trades at a higher P/E on forward projected earnings. Go figure.

Clearly, the more attractive of the four stocks are Symantec and US-Freightways. Indeed, at the time this analysis was made, each stock was rated a buy by S&P's analysts and buy and accumulate, respectively, by its Fair Value model. (Exhibits 10-1 to 10-4 at the end of this chapter present S&P's *Stock Reports* analyses of the four stocks.) Try this valuation method out on some of the stocks you own. You might be surprised at the results.

Having a stock price well below the target price does not necessarily mean that Symantec and USFreightways will work out, but they certainly seem a better bet than Kellogg and Intergraph. The key point to remember is that stock-price movements are a function of two things—earnings growth and P/E ratios. *The stock of a fast-growing company is only a good buy if the P/E does not already reflect those growth prospects.* And a "value" stock cannot be considered cheap unless its P/E is low *given the company's long-term prospects.* A company with a below-market P/E is not cheap unless the company increases earnings at or above the average company in the S&P 500.

What about the really small stocks, sometimes referred to as the *microcap* stocks? Most of these companies are not followed by any brokerage house analysts, making their analysis somewhat more problematic. In this case, you will need to develop your own long-term growth rates. Unless you are a true student of the investment game, this could prove a daunting task. Nonetheless, even though you might not be able to come up with a target price, you should still be able to review a company's P/E versus the market.

EXHIBIT 10-1 Report on Symantec.

(From Standard & Poor's Stock Reports, *June 27, 1998. Copyright © 1998 by The McGraw-Hill Companies.)*

STANDARD
&POOR'S
STOCK REPORTS

Symantec Corp.   5354K
Nasdaq Symbol **SYMC**
In S&P MidCap 400

27-JUN-98   Industry:
Computer (Software & Services)

Summary: Symantec provides application and system software products designed to enhance individual and workgroup productivity.

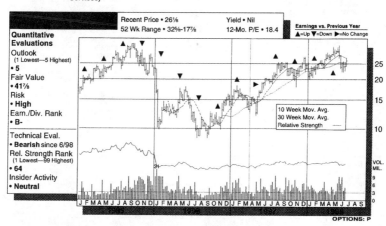

Quantitative Evaluations

Outlook
(1 Lowest—5 Highest)
• **5**

Fair Value
• 41⅞

Risk
• **High**

Earn./Div. Rank
• **B-**

Technical Eval.
• **Bearish** since 6/98

Rel. Strength Rank
(1 Lowest—99 Highest)
• **64**

Insider Activity
• **Neutral**

	Recent Price • 26⅛	Yield • Nil
	52 Wk Range • 32⅝-17⅞	12-Mo. P/E • 18.4

Earnings vs. Previous Year
▲=Up ▼=Down ►=No Change

10 Week Mov. Avg.
30 Week Mov. Avg.
Relative Strength   —

OPTIONS: P

Overview - 11-JUN-98

Revenues should increase 20% in FY 99 (Mar.), aided by contributions from new products, including products for the mobile market. Revenues will also benefit from strength in core products, led by Norton utility and antivirus offerings, and from strength in international markets, which continue to grow faster than the domestic market. Margins should widen, on volume efficiencies and a lower cost structure, but will be hurt by a higher tax rate. EPS comparisons in FY 98 benefited from the absence of FY 97 charges of $0.15 in the fourth quarter, associated with the sale of the company's networking business to Hewlett-Packard, and $0.14 in the second quarter, to reflect costs associated with acquisitions, a headcount reduction, and the consolidation of certain facilities.

Valuation - 11-JUN-98

The shares of SYMC declined recently on weakness in the retail antivirus software market. We believe this presents a good buying opportunity, and have upgraded the shares to strong buy, from accumulate. We expect this market to rebound in the second half of the year, and still expect 20% EPS growth for FY 99. Symantec is the leader in antivirus software, and dominates the market for mobile, remote and telecommuting software. New products in these areas should add to strong revenue growth. We expect the recent deal with IBM to provide upside potential, as IBM will recommend SYMC's antivirus software to its large corporate customer base. Despite a competitive market, the company possesses an array of award winning products across several product lines. With its strong growth outlook, and a P/E ratio trading significantly below the market, we recommend purchase of the shares.

Key Stock Statistics

S&P EPS Est. 1999	1.70	Tang. Bk. Value/Share	4.91
P/E on S&P Est. 1999	15.4	Beta	1.80
Dividend Rate/Share	Nil	Shareholders	900
Shs. outstg. (M)	56.6	Market cap. (B)	$ 1.5
Avg. daily vol. (M)	1.235	Inst. holdings	83%

Value of $10,000 invested 5 years ago: $ 19,219

Fiscal Year Ending Mar. 31

	1998	1997	1996	1995	1994	1993
Revenues (Million $)						
1Q	135.0	109.2	109.9	83.11	67.20	61.50
2Q	139.0	109.2	108.5	79.08	63.60	44.50
3Q	148.2	124.1	111.1	84.13	67.05	48.66
4Q	156.1	129.7	116.0	88.55	69.87	51.32
Yr.	578.4	472.2	445.4	334.9	267.7	206.0
Earnings Per Share ($)						
1Q	0.32	0.06	0.13	0.03	-0.32	0.20
2Q	0.35	0.02	-0.34	0.22	0.01	-0.48
3Q	**0.37**	0.25	-0.69	0.25	-0.31	-0.17
4Q	**0.40**	0.15	0.15	0.27	0.23	-0.06
Yr.	**1.42**	0.47	-0.76	0.77	-0.37	-0.49

Next earnings report expected: late July

Dividend Data

No cash dividends have been paid.

   A Division of The McGraw-Hill Companies

EXHIBIT 10-1 Report on Symantec (*Continued*).

STANDARD &POOR'S STOCK REPORTS

Symantec Corporation

5354K
27-JUN-98

Business Summary - 11-JUN-98

Symantec Corporation designs, markets and supports a line of application and system software products designed to enhance individual and workgroup productivity. Since 1989, SYMC has acquired 15 companies.

Symantec's business is organized into three major product groups: Remote Productivity Solutions, Security and Assistance, and Emerging Business and other.

Remote Productivity Solutions focus on customer needs to access information, applications and data from any location. Products include ACT!, a contact management software line; Internet FastFind, which allows the user to use all of the top Internet search engines at once; WinFax PRO, the world's best selling fax software to help send, receive and manage faxes; and pcANYWHERE, which enables reliable, fast and flexible PC-to-PC remote computing via serial or modem connection.

Security and Assistance products help increase productivity and keep computers safe and reliable. The primary product lines include AntiVirus software for the protection, detection and elimination of computer viruses; Norton Your Eyes Only, a data protection program that automatically decrypts files when authorized users open them; Norton Utilities, a set of tools designed to address the system-level operations of operating systems by incorporating powerful recovery and repair capabilities for troubleshooting and diagnostics. Other products include Norton Commander, Healthy PC.com, PC Handyman and CrashGuard.

The Emerging Business and Other segment includes Internet products providing an easy to use Java development environment, including Symantec Cafe, Visual Cafe, Visual Cafe PRO, and Visual Page

Approximately 80% of FY 97 (Mar.) revenues came from products that operate on MS-DOS, Windows, Windows 95 and Windows NT operating systems; other software products utilize the Apple Macintosh, Power Macintosh and IBM's OS/2 operating systems.

International revenues accounted for 29% of the total in FY 97, versus 32% in FY 96.

In the fourth quarter of FY 97, Symantec recorded a charge of $10 million ($0.15 a share), associated with the sale of its networking business to Hewlett-Packard. It also recorded a charge of $8.5 million ($0.14 a share) in the second quarter of FY 97, to reflect costs associated with acquisitions, a headcount reduction, and the consolidation of certain facilities.

Per Share Data ($) **(Year Ended Mar. 31)**	**1998**	**1997**	**1996**	**1995**	**1994**	**1993**	**1992**	**1991**	**1990**	**1989**
Tangible Bk. Val.	5.56	3.93	3.35	2.77	2.23	2.91	3.35	2.10	1.77	-1.53
Cash Flow	1.83	0.06	-0.38	1.12	Nil	-0.05	0.98	0.63	0.65	0.04
Earnings	1.42	0.47	-0.76	0.77	-0.37	-0.49	0.77	0.47	0.53	-0.04
Dividends	Nil	Nil	Nil	Nil	Nil	Nil	Nil	Nil	Nil	Nil
Payout Ratio	Nil	Nil	Nil	Nil	Nil	Nil	Nil	Nil	Nil	Nil
Cal. Yrs.	1997	1996	1995	1994	1993	1992	1991	1990	1989	1988
Prices - High	27¾	23⅛	33¼	19⅝	20½	51	44¾	14¾	9	NA
- Low	12	8¾	16⅛	9⅞	9¼	5⅞	13	7½	5½	NA
P/E Ratio - High	20	49	NM	25	NM	NM	46	32	17	NA
- Low	8	19	NM	13	NM	NM	13	16	10	NA
Income Statement Analysis (Million $)										
Revs.	578	472	445	335	268	206	217	116	50.0	40.0
Oper. Inc.	126	57.6	-0.9	60.0	30.2	4.6	40.2	22.9	9.7	5.2
Depr.	25.2	22.7	19.7	13.3	11.1	10.4	5.2	3.3	1.6	0.9
Int. Exp.	1.2	1.4	1.5	2.4	2.3	NA	0.5	0.5	0.9	0.1
Pretax Inc.	112	30.3	-44.3	38.3	-16.0	-17.2	28.8	14.3	8.7	4.1
Eff. Tax Rate	24%	14%	NM	26%	NM	NM	35%	34%	23%	23%
Net Inc.	85.1	26.0	-39.7	28.5	-11.1	-11.5	18.7	9.4	6.7	3.2
Balance Sheet & Other Fin. Data (Million $)										
Cash	226	160	129	105	51.5	53.3	31.9	24.9	21.5	4.3
Curr. Assets	329	238	237	180	120	110	95.7	52.5	30.7	11.7
Total Assets	476	342	298	221	158	142	123	65.0	38.0	18.0
Curr. Liab.	153	109	102	84.5	52.7	45.9	45.5	22.8	10.8	5.5
LT Debt	6.0	15.0	15.5	25.4	25.6	26.2	1.6	1.6	6.1	1.3
Common Eqty.	318	218	180	111	80.1	69.6	75.6	41.0	21.3	-7.1
Total Cap.	323	233	196	137	106	95.8	77.3	42.6	27.4	12.5
Cap. Exp.	26.3	27.1	35.8	17.7	7.3	15.4	12.7	5.5	2.8	1.8
Cash Flow	110	48.8	-20.0	41.8	-0.1	-1.1	23.9	12.7	8.3	0.4
Curr. Ratio	2.1	2.2	2.3	2.1	2.3	2.4	2.1	2.3	2.8	2.1
% LT Debt of Cap.	1.8	6.4	7.9	18.6	24.2	27.4	2.1	3.8	22.3	10.4
% Net Inc.of Revs.	14.7	5.5	NM	8.5	NM	NM	8.6	8.1	13.4	7.9
% Ret. on Assets	20.8	8.2	NM	13.9	NM	NM	18.8	14.8	15.7	20.8
% Ret. on Equity	31.8	13.0	NM	32.5	NM	NM	30.4	24.9	NM	NM

Data as orig. reptd.; bef. results of disc. opers. and/or spec. items. Per share data adj. for stk. divs. as of ex-div. date. Bold denotes diluted EPS (FASB 128). E-Estimated. NA-Not Available. NM-Not Meaningful. NR-Not Ranked.

Office—10201 Torre Ave., Cupertino, CA 95014-2132. **Tel**—(408) 253-9600. **Website**—http://www.symantec.com **Chrmn**—C. D. Carman.**Pres & CEO**—G. E. Eubanks Jr. **CFO**—H. A. Bain, III. **Secy**—G. K. Davidson. **Investor Contact**—Lori Barker (800-883-4497).**Dirs**—C. Boesenberg, W. W. Bregman, C. D. Carman, R. R. B. Dykes, G. E. Eubanks Jr., R. Miller. **Transfer Agent**—Bank of Boston. **Incorporated**—in Delaware in 1988. **Empl**— 2,300. **S&P Analyst:** Brian Goodstadt

EXHIBIT 10-1 Report on Symantec (*Continued*).

STOCK REPORTS
Symantec Corp

WALL STREET CONSENSUS   26-JUN-98
Analysts' Recommendations

Stock Prices

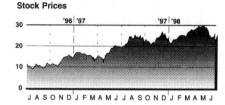

Analysts' Opinion

	No. of Ratings	% of Total	1 Mo. Prior	3 Mo. Prior	Nat'l	Reg'l	Non-broker
Buy	2	25	3	3	0	2	0
Buy/Hold	4	50	4	3	2	1	0
Hold	1	12	1	2	1	0	0
Weak Hold	0	0	0	0	0	0	0
Sell	0	0	0	0	0	0	0
No Opinion	1	12	1	1	0	0	1
Total	8	100	9	9	3	3	1

Analysts' Opinions

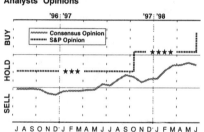

Analysts' Consensus Opinion

The consensus opinion reflects the average buy/hold/sell recommendation of Wall Street analysts. It is well-known, however, that analysts tend to be overly bullish. To make the consensus opinion more meaningful, it has been adjusted to reduce this positive bias. First, a stock's average recommendation is computed. Then it is compared to the recommendations on all other stocks. Only companies that score high relative to all other companies merit a consensus opinion of "Buy" in the graph at left. The graph is also important because research has shown that a rising consensus opinion is a favorable indicator of near-term stock performance; a declining trend is a negative signal.

Number of Analysts Following Stock

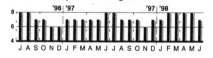

Standard & Poor's STARS
(Stock Appreciation Ranking System)

★★★★★	Buy	Standard & Poor's STARS ranking is
★★★★	Accumulate	our own analyst's evaluation of the
★★★	Hold	short-term (six to 12 month)
★★	Avoid	appreciation potential of a stock.
★	Sell	Five-Star stocks are expected to
		appreciate in price and outperform
		the market.

Analysts' Earnings Estimate

Annual Earnings Per Share

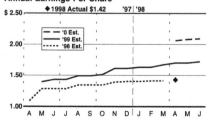

Current Analysts' Consensus Estimates

Fiscal years	Avg.	High	Low	S&P Est.	No. of Est.	Estimated P-E Ratio	Estimated S&P 500 P-E Ratio
1999	1.72	1.75	1.70	—	6	15.2	20.3
2000	2.09	2.20	1.95	—	5	12.5	—
1Q'99	0.41	0.41	0.41		4		
1Q'98	0.32 Actual						

A company's earnings outlook plays a major part in any investment decision. S&P organizes the earnings estimates of over 2,300 Wall Street analysts, and provides you with their consensus of earnings over the next two years. The graph to the left shows you how these estimates have trended over the past 15 months.

Copyright © 1998 The McGraw-Hill Companies, Inc. This investment analysis was prepared from the following Sources: S&P MarketScope, S&P Compustat, S&P Stock Reports, S&P Stock Guide, S&P Industry Reports, Vickers Stock Research, Inc., I/B/E/S/ International, Inc., Standard & Poor's, a division of The McGraw-Hill Companies, 25 Broadway, New York, NY 10004.

EXHIBIT 10-1 Report on Symantec (*Continued*).

Symantec Corp.

■■■■■■
STOCK REPORTS   27-JUN-98

INDUSTRY OUTLOOK

The computer software and services markets are some of the fastest growing segments of the computer industry. Earnings for the S&P Computer Software & Services Index are projected to rise 40% in 1998, on top of the 36% gain in 1997. The price appreciation for this index was 38% in 1997, versus 31% for the S&P 1500. Year to ·date through June 12, the industry index rose 29.4%, versus a 12.0% advance for the S&P 1500. The investment outlook for this industry remains positive. We believe the best strategy lies with investing in the market leaders of the major market segments.

Sales should remain solid for software vendors tied to mainframe software markets. Gains in the mainframe segment are expected to provide a firm foundation. In addition, vendors are using their mainframe expertise to develop and promote products that help manage, administer, and support large distributed (client/server) systems.

The PC software segment is attractive, aided by higher PC shipments. PC software sales should continue to rise strongly in 1998 with products for Microsoft's Windows 95 and Windows NT growing at the expense of the competition. Revenues for all versions of Windows and related software products should rise rapidly in 1998, aided by the expected introduction of Windows 98, by mid-1998. In contrast, other major PC software environments including DOS, and Apple Computer's Macintosh, are in decline.

The database market is slowing down, but is still being driven by the need to access, manipulate and display ever-increasing amounts of information, both "structured" (text and numbers) and "unstructured" (graphics, video and sound) from different computing environments. Huge opportunities exist for software relating to the Internet market, including electronic commerce.

Demand for computer services is strong, fueled by difficulties in integrating hardware from different vendors, advances in technology, complex network configurations, and inefficiencies associated with maintaining an in-house information services staff. Computer service stocks have strong and stable growth characteristics: they have a high level of repeat business and long contract life cycles, leading to recurring revenue and earnings predictability.

Industry Stock Performance
Related S&P 1500 Industry Index

Computer (Software & Services)

Month-end Price Performance As of 05/29/98

OTHER INDUSTRY PARTICIPANTS

Principal Peer Group	Stock Symbol	Recent Stock Price	P/E Ratio	12-mth. Trail. EPS	30-day Price Chg %	1-year Price Chg. %	Beta	Yield %	Quality Ranking	Stk. Mkt. Cap. (mil. $)	Ret. on Equity %	Pretax Margin %	LTD to Cap. %
Symantec Corp.	SYMC	26¼	18	1.42	6%	36%	1.80	Nil	B-	1,482	13.0	6.4	6.4
American Management Systems	AMSY	29¼	36	0.81	6%	15%	0.72	Nil	B+	1,236	14.1	5.9	9.9
Autodesk, Inc.	ADSK	38⅜	19	2.01	-11%	NA	1.53	0.6	B+	1,804	14.2	13.0	Nil
CSK Corp ADS	CSKKY	18⅜	53	0.35	-15%	-51%	0.23	0.4	NR	1,178	NM	NM	NA
Cognos Inc	COGNF	26¼	30	0.88	-1%	-19%	1.09	Nil	B-	1,158	32.9	23.1	3.0
Excite Inc	XCIT	76	NM	-1.78	31%	426%	NA	Nil	NR	1,781	NM	NM	NA
Gemstar Intl	GMSTF	35⅜	47	0.76	-14%	91%	NA	Nil	NR	1,706	31.9	37.2	NA
Informix Corp.	IFMX	8	NM	-1.41	14%	-15%	0.98	Nil	B-	1,335	NM	NM	Nil
Learning Company	TLC	26¾	NM	-9.84	1%	214%	1.28	Nil	NR	1,428	NM	NM	118.0
Legato Systems	LGTO	39⅜	86	0.46	40%	294%	NA	Nil	NR	1,431	19.4	30.4	NA
Lycos Inc	LCOS	66½	NM	-6.26	16%	427%	NA	Nil	NR	1,232	NM	NM	NA
Mastech Corp	MAST	26	59	0.44	36%	122%	NA	Nil	NR	1,231	26.2	10.4	NA
NOVA Corp.	NIS	35⅛	63	0.57	11%	44%	NA	Nil	NR	1,228	18.5	8.7	23.8
Rational Software	RATL	16⅛	NM	-0.44	11%	1%	1.93	Nil	C	1,426	NM	NM	0.7
Sapient Corp	SAPE	45¾	86	0.53	5%	89%	NA	Nil	NR	1,148	18.4	23.7	NA
Visio Corp	VSIO	44⅜	62	0.71	-1%	28%	NA	Nil	NR	1,302	22.9	20.5	NA

EXHIBIT 10-1 Report on Symantec (*Continued*).

Symantec Corporation

STOCK REPORTS   26-JUN-98

NEWS HEADLINES

■ **06/09/98** UP 1 7/8 to 24 1/2...
Sets 5% stock buyback... S&P upgrades to buy from accumulate...

■ **06/09/98** 3:10 pm... UPGRADING
SYMANTEC (SYMC 24-1/2******) TO
BUY FROM ACCUMULATE... Stock
down 25% from recent high on concerns about weak retail antivirus market... However, we see improvement in
2nd half, still expect 20% EPS growth
in FY 99 (Mar.).. IBM deal offers upside, since will recommend co.'s Norton AntiVirus to large corporate customer base... New growth opportunities
exist in mobile, remote and telecommuting markets, where SYMC dominates... See FY 99 EPS of $1.70...
SYMC set 5% buyback today... Given
growth expectations and 15% net margin, SYMC attractive at only 13X our
calendar 1999 estimate, 2X revenues. /
B.Goodstadt

■ **01/21/98** 1:30 pm... CONTINUE
TO ACCUMULATE SYMANTEC
CORP. (SYMC 23-3/4****)... Posts FY
Q3 EPS of $0.37 vs. $0.25, above expectations... Revenues grew 20%,
showing strength across several product lines, solid international growth...
Several product launches contributed
to growth, expect further introductions... SYMC building brand equity
with several award-winning offerings
across its broad product line... Raising
our FY 98 (Mar.) EPS estimate to
$1.40 from $1.35, FY 99's to $1.65
from $1.55... Shares attractive at only
15 times calendar '98 EPS. /
B.Goodstadt

■ **01/21/98** Jan. 20, 1998, Symantec Corp., announced Dec. '97
three-month diluted earnings of $0.37
vs. $0.25 for the same period a year

ago, and six-month diluted earnings of
$1.02 vs. $0.32 for the same period a
year ago. Results for the 1996
nine-month period include acquisition,
merger & other non-recurring charges
of $0.16 per diluted share.

■ **10/30/97** 2:55 pm... UPGRADING
SYMANTEC TO ACCUMULATE FROM
HOLD (SYMC 21-3/4****)... Posts FY
Q2 EPS $0.35, vs. $0.16 before acquisition charges... Revenues grew 27%,
showing strength across several product lines, including Norton AntiVirus,
pcANYWHERE and WinFax software...
Two new product launches in Q2 contributed to growth, expect further introductions... SYMC building brand equity
with several award-winning offerings
across broad product line... Estimate
FY 98 (Mar.) EPS at $1.35, FY 99's at
$1.55... Attractive at only 14 times cal-
endar '98 EPS. /B.Goodstadt

■ **08/25/97** Aug. 22, 1997, McAfee
Associates Inc. (MCAF) said it filed suit
against Symantec Corp. (SYMC),
charging it with defamation and "trade
libel." MCAF said it also "has already
filed similar suits in Japan." MCAF
said the suits "are in response to the
latest press release from Symantec,
which blatantly lies about the facts of
on-going litigation between the companies." MCAF said the suit it filed in
California Superior Court in Santa
Clara County requests $1 billion in
compensatory and punitive damages.
As reported, Symantec Corp. SYMC
said on April 23 that it it filed suit
against MCAF, charging it with copyright infringement. The suit accused
MCAF of "stealing code from Norton
CrashGuard, a crash protection and recovery program," and "incorporating it
into" MCAF"s PC Medic product,

SYMC said. On July 21 SYMC said it
filed a motion to amend the suit as a
result of MCAF's allegedly using additional SYMC code in other MCAF products. In announcing its lawsuits,
MCAF said it "has not used copied
code from Symantec."

■ **07/30/97** UP 1 3/4 to 23 1/8...
Posts $0.32 vs. $0.08 1Q EPS on 24%
revenue rise... Sands Bros. raises estimates... 5.

■ **07/30/97** UP 1 3/4 to 23 1/8...
Posts $0.32 vs. $0.08 1Q EPS on 24%
revenue rise... Sands Bros. raises estimates... 5.

■ **07/30/97** 3:05 pm... SYMANTEC
(SYMC 23-3/8) UP 2, POSTS $0.32
VS. $0.08 1Q EPS ON 24% REV.
RISE... SANDS BROS. RAISES ESTI-
MATES... Analyst Aaron Scott tells
MarketScope 1Q EPS ahead of his
$0.30 estimate... Notes upside surprise
on top-, bottom- lines (revs. about $3M
better than expected)... Also says
gross margins increased to 85% from
83% in 4Q FY 97, 80% year ago... Co.
back on track, showing ability to increase margins... Adds DSO were 29
days in 1Q vs. 46 days in 1Q FY 97...
Co. has a lot of good new products in
pipeline, gives visibility for next 6-8
months... Raises $1.25 FY 98 (Mar)
EPS estimate to $1.30, $1.50 FY 99 to
$1.60... Rates buy, has $30-$32 long
term target./J.Freund

■ **07/30/97** July 29, 1997, Symantec Corp. announced June '97
three-month earnings per share of
$0.32 vs $0.06 for same period a year
ago. Results for 1996 include an after-tax charge of $1,165,000 from ac-
quisition and restructuring expenses.

EXHIBIT 10-2 Report on Kellogg.

(From Standard & Poor's Stock Reports, June 27, 1998. Copyright © 1998 by The McGraw-Hill Companies.)

STANDARD &POOR'S
STOCK REPORTS

Kellogg Co.   **1289**

NYSE Symbol **K**

In S&P 500

27-JUN-98 | Industry: Foods | Summary: Kellogg is the world's leading producer of ready-to-eat cereal products, with a dominant 40% global market share. The W.K. Kellogg Foundation Trust holds 34% of the stock.

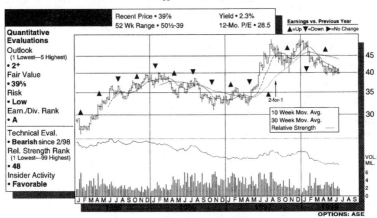

Recent Price • 39⅞	Yield • 2.3%
52 Wk Range • 50½–39	12-Mo. P/E • 28.5

Quantitative Evaluations

Outlook (1 Lowest—5 Highest)
• **2+**

Fair Value
• **39⅞**

Risk
• **Low**

Earn./Div. Rank
• **A**

Technical Eval.
• **Bearish** since 2/98

Rel. Strength Rank (1 Lowest—99 Highest)
• **48**

Insider Activity
• **Favorable**

Earnings vs. Previous Year
▲=Up ▼=Down ▶=No Change

2-for-1

10 Week Mov. Avg.
30 Week Mov. Avg.
Relative Strength —

OPTIONS: ASE

Overview - 28-APR-98

Net sales in 1998 are projected to be essentially unchanged, as very modest unit volume growth and price increases are largely offset by negative currency exchange translations. Increased marketing spending behind additional promotional activity beginning in the 1998 second quarter should be mitigated by cost saving benefits realized from a continuing streamlining of manufacturing facilities, allowing for margin stability. Interest expense is expected to be higher, reflecting increased borrowings for share repurchases. Overall, we anticipate EPS (before non-recurring items) rising to $1.75 in 1998, up only 3% from 1997's $1.70 (before unusual charges). Over the next few years, annual EPS growth of approximately 5% to 10% is seen, buoyed mostly by share repurchases.

Valuation - 28-APR-98

As a result of the intensely competitive state of the U.S. ready-to-eat cereal industry, we remain cautious on Kellogg's near-term fortunes. Competition in the ready-to-eat cereal industry remains fierce, stemming mainly from a greater number of low-price competitors over the past few years, despite soft cereal demand. Nevertheless, with cereal category margins still high relative to those of other grocery products, more price competition is possible in the future. Kellogg is somewhat insulated from domestic pressures by its large overseas presence, but near-term earnings could still suffer. The shares have commanded a large valuation premium relative to the S&P 500 over the years, because of K's financial strength and its relatively wide margins. However, this premium could narrow in coming periods, reflecting rising investor concerns about the company's future prospects.

Key Stock Statistics

S&P EPS Est. 1998	1.75	Tang. Bk. Value/Share	2.52
P/E on S&P Est. 1998	22.8	Beta	0.53
S&P EPS Est. 1999	1.90	Shareholders	26,800
Dividend Rate/Share	0.90	Market cap. (B)	$ 16.3
Shs. outstg. (M)	409.2	Inst. holdings	74%
Avg. daily vol. (M)	0.409		

Value of $10,000 invested 5 years ago: $ 13,407

Fiscal Year Ending Dec. 31

	1998	1997	1996	1995	1994	1993
Revenues (Million $)						
1Q	1,643	1,689	1,786	1,716	1,611	1,518
2Q	—	1,720	1,651	1,780	1,617	1,542
3Q	—	1,804	1,682	1,845	1,742	1,669
4Q	—	1,618	1,558	1,663	1,592	1,566
Yr.	—	6,830	6,677	7,004	6,562	6,295
Earnings Per Share ($)						
1Q	0.42	0.38	0.48	0.44	0.40	0.38
2Q	E0.38	0.39	0.19	0.31	0.34	0.31
3Q	E0.53	0.50	0.38	0.52	0.48	0.45
4Q	E0.42	0.04	0.21	-0.17	0.35	0.33
Yr.	E1.75	1.32	1.25	1.12	1.58	1.47

Next earnings report expected: early August

Dividend Data (Dividends have been paid since 1923.)

Amount ($)	Date Decl.	Ex-Div. Date	Stock of Record	Payment Date
2-for-1	Aug. 01	Aug. 25	Aug. 08	Aug. 22 '97
0.225	Oct. 31	Dec. 25	Dec. 28	Dec. 15 '97
0.225	Feb. 20	Feb. 26	Mar. 02	Mar. 13 '98
0.225	Apr. 24	May. 27	May. 29	Jun. 15 '98

EXHIBIT 10-2 Report on Kellogg (*Continued*).

STANDARD & POOR'S STOCK REPORTS

Kellogg Company

1289

27-JUN-98

Business Summary - 28-APR-98

Kellogg Co., incorporated in 1922, is the world's leading producer of ready-to-eat cereal products, with an approximate 34% market share in North America and 40% globally (both measured by volume). In recent years, the company has expanded its operations from ready-to-eat cereals to also include other grain-based convenience food products, such as Pop-Tarts toaster pastries, Eggo frozen waffles, Nutri-Grain cereal bars, Rice Krispies Treats squares, and Lender's bagels. Sales and profit contributions by geographic region in 1997 were:

	Sales	Profits
U.S.	58%	70%
Europe	25%	16%
Other	17%	14%

Products are manufactured in 19 countries and distributed in more than 160. Ready-to-eat cereals include Corn Flakes, Rice Krispies, Special K, Frosted Flakes, All-Bran, Corn Pops, Raisin Bran, Frosted Mini-Wheats, Bran Flakes, and Low Fat Granola. Cereals are generally marketed under the Kellogg's name and are sold principally to the grocery trade through direct sales forces for resale to consumers and through broker and distribution arrangements in less developed market areas.

The company's U.S. manufacturing facilities include four cereal plants and warehouses, in Battle Creek, MI; Lancaster, PA; Memphis, TN; and Omaha, NE. Other non-cereal foods are also manufactured in the U.S. at various plant locations. Manufacturing facilities outside the U.S. are in Argentina, Australia, Brazil, Canada, China, Colombia, Ecuador, Germany, Great Britain, Guatemala, India, Italy, Japan, Mexico, South Africa, South Korea, Spain, Thailand and Venezuela. The principal ingredients in K's products include corn grits, oats, rice, various fruits, sweeteners, wheat and wheat derivatives.

During 1997, Kellogg incurred non-recurring charges and other unusual items totaling $140.5 million, after tax ($0.34 a share), primarily for streamlining initiatives related to management's plan to optimize the company's pan-European operations, as well as continuing productivity programs in the U.S. and Australia. Charges consisted of manufacturing asset production redeployment, associated management consulting and similar costs.

The W. K. Kellogg Foundation Trust holds 34% of the common shares.

Per Share Data ($) (Year Ended Dec. 31)	1997	1996	1995	1994	1993	1992	1991	1990	1989	1988
Tangible Bk. Val.	2.42	2.15	3.66	4.06	3.63	3.98	4.39	3.81	3.28	2.91
Cash Flow	2.07	1.86	1.72	2.15	2.04	1.92	1.72	1.45	1.21	1.26
Earnings	1.32	1.25	1.12	1.58	1.47	1.43	1.26	1.04	0.87	0.98
Dividends	0.87	0.81	0.75	0.70	0.66	0.60	0.54	0.48	0.43	0.38
Payout Ratio	66%	65%	67%	44%	45%	42%	43%	46%	50%	39%
Prices - High	50½	40⅜	39¾	30⅜	34	37¾	33½	19⅜	20⅜	17⅛
- Low	32	31	26¼	23¾	23⅝	27¼	17½	14¾	14½	12¼
P/E Ratio - High	38	32	35	19	23	26	27	19	24	18
- Low	24	25	23	15	16	19	14	14	17	13
Income Statement Analysis (Million $)										
Revs.	6,830	6,677	7,004	6,562	6,295	6,191	5,787	5,181	4,652	4,349
Oper. Inc.	1,480	1,347	1,519	1,419	1,334	1,294	1,251	1,086	900	934
Depr.	287	252	259	256	265	232	223	200	168	140
Int. Exp.	108	70.0	70.0	52.3	40.4	33.6	60.7	84.5	72.6	60.4
Pretax Inc.	905	860	796	1,130	1,034	1,070	984	815	667	775
Eff. Tax Rate	38%	38%	38%	38%	34%	36%	38%	38%	37%	38%
Net Inc.	564	531	490	705	681	683	606	503	422	480
Balance Sheet & Other Fin. Data (Million $)										
Cash	173	244	222	266	98.0	126	178	101	80.0	185
Curr. Assets	1,467	1,529	1,429	1,434	1,245	1,237	1,173	1,041	906	1,063
Total Assets	4,877	5,051	4,415	4,467	4,237	4,015	3,926	3,749	3,390	3,298
Curr. Liab.	1,657	2,199	1,265	1,185	1,215	1,071	1,324	1,110	1,037	1,184
LT Debt	1,416	727	718	719	522	315	15.0	296	371	272
Common Eqty.	998	1,282	1,591	1,808	1,713	1,945	2,160	1,902	1,634	1,483
Total Cap.	2,414	2,235	2,511	2,725	2,424	2,445	2,514	2,544	2,295	2,048
Cap. Exp.	312	307	316	354	450	474	334	321	509	538
Cash Flow	851	783	749	962	946	914	829	703	590	620
Curr. Ratio	0.9	0.7	1.1	1.2	1.0	1.2	0.9	0.9	0.9	0.9
% LT Debt of Cap.	58.7	32.5	28.6	26.4	21.5	12.9	0.6	11.6	16.2	13.3
% Net Inc.of Revs.	8.3	8.0	7.0	10.7	10.8	11.0	10.5	9.7	9.1	11.0
% Ret. on Assets	11.4	11.2	11.1	16.4	16.8	17.3	15.8	14.2	12.7	16.1
% Ret. on Equity	49.5	37.0	28.8	40.6	38.0	33.5	29.9	28.6	27.2	35.7

Data as orig. reptd.; bef. results of disc. opers. and/or spec. items. Per share data adj. for stk. divs. as of ex-div. date. Bold denotes diluted EPS (FASB 128). E-Estimated. NA-Not Available. NM-Not Meaningful. NR-Not Ranked.

Office—One Kellogg Square, P.O. Box 3599, Battle Creek, MI 49016-3599. **Tel**—(616) 961-2000. **Website**—http://www.kelloggs.com **Chrmn & CEO**—A. G. Langbo. **Vice Chrmn**—W. A. Camstra. **Treas & Investor Contact**—John Bolt. **Dirs**—B. S. Carson, C. S. Fiorina, C. X. Gonzalez, G. Gund, W. E. LaMothe, A. G. Langbo, R. G. Mawby, A. McLaughlin, J. R. Munro, H. A. Poling, W. C. Richardson, D. Rumsfeld, J. L. Zabriskie. **Transfer Agent & Registrar**—Harris Trust & Savings Bank, Chicago. **Incorporated**—in Delaware in 1922. **Empl**— 14,339. **S&P Analyst:** Kenneth A. Shea

EXHIBIT 10-2 Report on Kellogg (*Continued*).

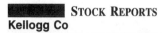 STOCK REPORTS
Kellogg Co

WALL STREET CONSENSUS   26-JUN-98
Analysts' Recommendations

Stock Prices

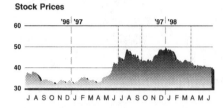

Analysts' Opinion

	No. of Ratings	% of Total	1 Mo. Prior	3 Mo. Prior	Nat'l	Reg'l	Non-broker
Buy	1	5	1	2	0	0	1
Buy/Hold	3	14	3	2	1	2	0
Hold	14	64	14	13	8	5	0
Weak Hold	0	0	0	0	0	0	0
Sell	0	0	0	0	0	0	0
No Opinion	4	18	4	5	1	0	3
Total	22	100	22	22	10	7	4

Analysts' Opinions

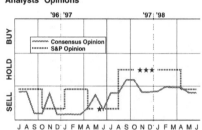

Analysts' Consensus Opinion

The consensus opinion reflects the average buy/hold/sell recommendation of Wall Street analysts. It is well-known, however, that analysts tend to be overly bullish. To make the consensus opinion more meaningful, it has been adjusted to reduce this positive bias. First, a stock's average recommendation is computed. Then it is compared to the recommendations on all other stocks. Only companies that score high relative to all other companies merit a consensus opinion of "Buy" in the graph at left. The graph is also important because research has shown that a rising consensus opinion is a favorable indicator of near-term stock performance; a declining trend is a negative signal.

Standard & Poor's STARS
(Stock Appreciation Ranking System)

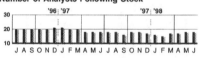

★★★★★	Buy	Standard & Poor's STARS ranking is
★★★★	Accumulate	our own analyst's evaluation of the
★★★	Hold	short-term (six to 12 month)
★★	Avoid	appreciation potential of a stock.
★	Sell	Five-Star stocks are expected to
		appreciate in price and outperform
		the market.

Number of Analysts Following Stock

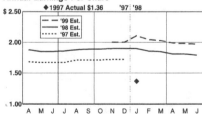

Analysts' Earnings Estimate

Annual Earnings Per Share

Current Analysts' Consensus Estimates

Fiscal years	Avg.	High	Low	S&P Est.	No. of Est.	Estimated P-E Ratio	Estimated S&P 500 P-E Ratio
1998	1.79	1.85	1.75	1.75	21	22.3	23.7
1999	1.97	2.10	1.90	1.90	19	20.2	20.3
2Q'98	0.39	0.43	0.35		14		
2Q'97	0.39 Actual						

A company's earnings outlook plays a major part in any investment decision. S&P organizes the earnings estimates of over 2,300 Wall Street analysts, and provides you with their consensus of earnings over the next two years. The graph to the left shows you how these estimates have trended over the past 15 months.

EXHIBIT 10-2 Report on Kellogg (*Continued*).

[redacted]

STOCK REPORTS

Kellogg Co.

27-JUN-98

INDUSTRY OUTLOOK

The S&P Food Index trailed the S&P 1500 index through June 25, 1998, but outperformed the index in 1997 by a significant margin. S&P attributes the latter performance at least partially to the group's improving profit growth following recent high agricultural commodity cost pressures. Industry profit margins are likely to improve further from the benefits accruing from recent aggressive restructuring actions undertaken by most of the major companies, such as H.J. Heinz, Campbell Soup and Sara Lee. With only projected modest U.S. economic growth ahead, S&P is bullish on the group's fortunes over the next 12 months.

The value of the nation's biggest crop -- corn -- has eased sharply from the high levels recorded in 1996 and much of 1997, thanks to replenished reserves. However, given continued strong demand in both the U.S. and abroad for corn, prices still remain high by historical measures. Also, the price of soybeans, another important raw material for food processors, is at or near record highs, primarily reflecting strong demand abroad. The impact of these raw material cost pressures will vary among companies, but will nonetheless dampen industry profitability in the near term. Companies that are the most sensitive to grain prices may continue to be pressured in coming periods, particularly for corn and soybean refiner Archer-Daniels-Midland.

The shares of branded packagers, which are much more insulated from the effects of changes in agricultural commodity costs (like Campbell Soup, Sara Lee, Hershey Foods, and H.J. Heinz), have risen steadily since mid-1994, helped largely by consistent double-digit earnings growth. Given our expectations of further positive earnings trends ahead in a slowing economy, these issues should moderately outperform the broader market averages.

Longer term, the packaged food industry's ability to meet evolving consumer life-styles and tastes should enable these companies to sustain their long, successful record of higher sales and profits. In addition, rising U.S. and world standards of living, increasing world trade liberalization, and the significant adoption of progressive economic policies throughout the world should provide U.S. food packagers adequate opportunities for long-term growth.

Industry Stock Performance

Related S&P 1500 Industry Index

Foods

Month-end Price Performance As of 05/29/98

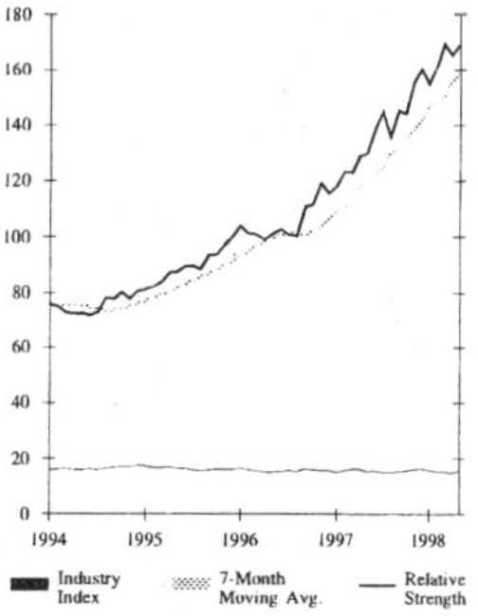

OTHER INDUSTRY PARTICIPANTS

Principal Peer Group	Stock Symbol	Recent Stock Price	P/E Ratio	12-mth. Trail. EPS	30-day Price Chg %	1-year Price Chg. %	Beta	Yield %	Quality Ranking	Stk. Mkt. Cap. (mil. $)	Ret. on Equity %	Pretax Margin %	LTD to Cap. %
Kellogg Co.	**K**	**39 7/8**	**28**	**1.40**	**-1%**	**-4%**	**0.53**	**2.3**	**A**	**16,317**	**49.5**	**13.3**	**58.7**
Bestfoods	BFO	59 1/4	47	1.26	6%	29%	0.86	1.5	A	17,110	30.0	8.4	61.1
Campbell Soup	CPB	54 1/2	36	1.50	0%	12%	0.66	1.5	B+	24,474	34.3	14.0	43.4
ConAgra, Inc.	CAG	31 1/2	22	1.41	7%	-1%	0.86	2.0	A+	15,163	26.0	4.5	44.0
Dole Food	DOL	48 3/8	21	2.32	4%	11%	0.89	0.8	B	2,920	26.3	4.5	51.7
General Mills	GIS	70 1/4	28	2.50	2%	8%	0.71	3.0	A-	11,116	110.7	12.5	62.7
Groupe Danone	DA	57 1/2	32	1.78	11%	NA	NA	0.8	NR	20,327	8.8	7.6	34.2
Heinz (H.J.)	HNZ	56 1/4	26	2.15	4%	21%	0.88	2.2	A	20,546	11.7	5.1	45.8
Hershey Foods	HSY	71 1/2	31	2.30	4%	27%	0.63	1.2	A	8,057	33.4	12.9	47.9
Hormel Foods	HRL	34 3/4	20	1.78	2%	31%	0.66	1.8	A	2,598	13.8	5.2	19.8
Interstate Bakeries	IBC	32 1/8	19	1.71	0%	13%	0.56	0.9	NR	2,345	19.5	5.3	27.5
Quaker Oats	OAT	56	33	1.67	-2%	26%	1.03	2.0	B	7,750	NM	NM	75.7
Ralston Purina	RAL	113	11	10.65	3%	37%	0.81	1.1	B+	11,933	46.9	9.3	40.3
Sara Lee	SLE	56 5/8	NM	-1.16	-4%	36%	1.06	1.6	A	26,449	22.9	7.5	26.1
Tyson Foods	TSN	22 1/2	30	0.74	7%	16%	0.86	0.4	A-	2,905	11.8	5.2	42.3
Wrigley (Wm.) Jr.	WWY	101 7/8	41	2.46	7%	49%	0.49	0.8	A+	9,449	28.9	20.4	Nil

EXHIBIT 10-2 Report on Kellogg (*Continued*).

STOCK REPORTS
Kellogg Company
26-JUN-98

NEWS HEADLINES

■ **06/23/98** June 23, 1998, Kellogg Co. (K) said it appointed Carlos M. Gutierrez as president and chief operating officer.

■ **04/28/98** Apr. 24, 1998, the Kellogg Co. (K) said Dorothy A. Johnson was elected to the board, succeeding Russell G. Mawby, who retired.

■ **04/24/98** Apr., 24, 1998, Kellogg Co. announced Mar. '98 three-month earnings per share of $0.42 vs $0.38 for·same period a year ago.

■ **01/30/98** DOWN 2 3/8 to 46 3/8... Posts lower than expected $0.39 vs. $0.39 4Q EPS as higher cost of good sold, SG&A expenses offset 4% sales rise.

■ **01/30/98** Jan. 30, 1998, Kellogg Co., announced Dec. '97 fourth quarter earnings per diluted share of $0.08 vs $0.21 for the same period a year ago, and annual earnings of $1.36 vs $1.25 for the prior year. Results are adjusted for 2-for-1 stock split. Results include charges from restructuring, streamlining & plant closings which reduced share earnings by $0.31 & $0.34 for the 1997 fourth quarter & year and $0.18 & $0.28 for the like periods of 1996. Also, they exclude a charge of $0.04 for both periods of 1997 from an accounting change.

■ **12/16/97** Dec. 12, 1997, Kellogg Co. (K) announced that it named John R. Hinton executive vice president of administration and chief financial officer.

■ **11/21/97** 12:20 pm... STILL HOLD KELLOGG CO. (K 46***)... Tells analysts in NY today that remains committed to retaining cereal industry cost advantage, through past production capacity adjustments, more global approach to material sourcing and new product launches... Says has stepped up product innovation, cites establishment of new nutrition research lab... Pegs 5-year 7%-9% annual volume

growth, low-teen EPS growth... Given shortfall of past goals and clouding of emerging market economies, we are skeptical of success... But strong brands and balance sheet make worth holding at 27X '97 estimate $1.70. / K.Shea

■ **11/03/97** Oct. 31, 1997 Kellogg Co. announced a Sept. '97 three-month earnings per share of $0.50 vs $0.38 for same period a year ago. Nine-month earnings of $1.28 vs $1.04 for same period a year ago. Based on avge. shs., adjusted for Aug. '97 two-for-one stock split Results includes net charges of $0.02 and $0.04 per share for the three & nine-month periods of 1997 & $0.05 and $0.10 per share for the three & nine-month periods of 1996, from cost of productivity and streamlining initiatives.

■ **08/01/97** UP 5 1/2 to 97 3/8... Posts $0.83 vs. $0.45 2Q EPS from ops. on 4% sales rise... Sets 2-for-1 stock split... Raises quarterly dividend 7%... Deutsche Morgan upgrades to hold... 5.

■ **08/01/97** 1:30 pm... KELLOGG CO. (K 96-7/8) UP 5, POSTS $0.83 VS. $0.45 2Q EPS FROM OPS. ON 4% SALES RISE... SETS 2-FOR-1 STOCK SPLIT, RAISES QUARTERLY DIVIDEND 7%... DEUTSCHE MORGAN UPGRADES TO HOLD FROM SELL... Analyst Timothy Ramey tells salesforce operating income was up 2.5% over 2Q '95, which was big snap back from depressed 2Q '96... Raises $3.25 '97 EPS estimate to $3.37... Maintains $3.45 '98 EPS estimate./ K.Lipani

■ **08/01/97** 1:15 pm... UPGRADING KELLOGG CO. (K 97***) FROM SELL TO HOLD... Posts Q2 EPS of $0.83 vs. $0.45 (both before charges), better than expectations... Rise led by better-than-expected 6.6% U.S. cereal volume growth, margin gains and fewer shares... K expects good margin performance next few quarters, assum-

ing continued new product volume gains... Raising '97 EPS estimate $0.10, to $3.40, '98's $0.15, to $3.75... But at 28 times our revised '97 estimate, stock amply priced for near term. /K.Shea

■ **08/01/97** Aug. 1, 1997, Kellogg Co., announced June '97 three-month earnings per share of $0.79 vs $0.37 for same period a year ago, and Six-month earnings of $1.56 vs $1.33 for same period a year ago. Results include non-recurring charges of $0.04 per share for both periods of 1997 & $0.08 and $0.11 per share for the three- and six-month periods of 1996 relating primarily to productivity and operational streamlining initiative.

■ **08/01/97** Aug. 1, 1997, Kellogg Co. (K) said its board approved a two-for-one stock split, payable August 22 to holders of record at the close of business on August 8. Kellogg also announced a higher quarterly dividend of $0.225 on post-split shares, payable September 15 to shareholders of record at the close of business on August 29. Kellogg previously paid $0.42 on pre-split shares..

■ **07/03/97** UP 4 to 91... Merrill upgrades to long term buy from accumulate... GENERAL MILLS to raise cereal prices by about 2.6%...

■ **07/03/97** 10:40 am... KELLOGG (K 92-1/4) UP 5-1/4, MERRILL UPGRADES TO LONG TERM BUY FROM ACCUMULATE... Analyst Eric Katzman tells salesforce believes K will benefit over intermediate term as it gains some volume from GIS... Raises $3.30-$3.40 '97 EPS estimate to $3.40, $3.60-$3.70 '98 to $3.70, long term EPG growth rate estimate to 9%-10% from 8%-9%... Maintains near term neutral./J.Freund

■ **06/30/97** UP 2 7/8 to 85 5/8... Goldman adds to recommended list, was rated market performer... Details, co. unavailable.

EXHIBIT 10-3   Report on USFreightways.

(From Standard & Poor's Stock Reports, *June 27, 1998. Copyright © 1998 by The McGraw-Hill Companies.)*

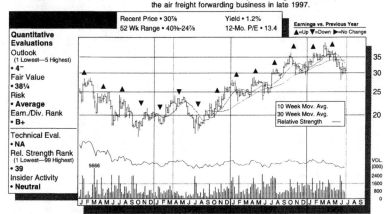

STANDARD
&POOR'S
STOCK REPORTS

USFreightways   **5531G**

Nasdaq Symbol **USFC**

In S&P SmallCap 600

27-JUN-98   **Industry:**
Truckers

Summary: This company operates a family of five regional less-than-truckload carriers, provides logistics services, and entered the air freight forwarding business in late 1997.

Recent Price • 30⅞	Yield • 1.2%
52 Wk Range • 40⅜-24⅞	12-Mo. P/E • 13.4

Quantitative Evaluations

Outlook
(1 Lowest—5 Highest)
• 4⁻

Fair Value
• 38¼

Risk
• Average

Earn./Div. Rank
• B+

Technical Eval.
• NA

Rel. Strength Rank
(1 Lowest—99 Highest)
• 39

Insider Activity
• Neutral

Earnings vs. Previous Year
▲=Up ▼=Down ▶=No Change

10 Week Mov. Avg.
30 Week Mov. Avg.
Relative Strength —

5666

VOL. (000)

Overview - 01-MAY-98

Less-than-truckload tonnage could advance 12% in 1998, versus 1997's 11% gain. USFC will not repeat the UPS business picked up in August when that carrier was strikebound, but will gain shipments from the acquisition of Mercury Distribution in January 1998. Single-digit traffic gains are projected for USF Bestway, as it shifts its focus to yield management. Margins will widen, particularly at Red Star, which will see improvement in load density as it integrates Mercury's operations. Lower fuel costs will also aid profits. Labor costs will increase somewhat less than revenues. The major sore spot is rapidly increasing insurance and claims. LTL yields should improve in 1998, as industry capacity remains tight. Logistics will benefit from new contracts with Western Star and Alberto-Culver. A positive contribution is anticipated from recently acquired Seko Worldwide. Comparisons will benefit from the absence of losses from recently sold truckload carrier Comet, and from lower interest expense.

Valuation - 01-MAY-98

In March 1998, the shares of this regional LTL carrier exceeded their October 1997 high. USFC's stock has outperformed that of other truckers, reflecting the company's ability to grow consistently at a double-digit pace. Management is also quick to deploy capital where it can earn the highest returns, as illustrated by the sale of the troubled truckload venture, and the recent acquisition of Seko Worldwide. With Seko, USFC moves a step closer to its goal of being a single-source provider of transportation services. A new Teamsters contract was signed in February 1998, covering two carriers. While USFC's P/E multiple is at a premium to that of other carriers, we think it is justified by above average growth potential, and recommend the purchase of the shares by aggressive investors.

Key Stock Statistics

S&P EPS Est. 1998	2.55	Tang. Bk. Value/Share	11.46
P/E on S&P Est. 1998	12.1	Beta	0.46
S&P EPS Est. 1999	2.90	Shareholders	6,300
Dividend Rate/Share	0.37	Market cap. (B)	$0.807
Shs. outstg. (M)	26.1	Inst. holdings	92%
Avg. daily vol. (M)	0.311		

Value of $10,000 invested 5 years ago: $ 23,903

Fiscal Year Ending Dec. 31

	1998	1997	1996	1995	1994	1993
Revenues (Million $)						
1Q	442.3	355.8	313.7	279.0	251.0	207.0
2Q	—	380.8	332.1	287.0	221.0	220.0
3Q	—	393.5	343.2	290.0	274.0	236.0
4Q	—	435.2	342.0	288.0	271.0	236.0
Yr.	—	1,565	1,331	1,144	1,016	899.0
Earnings Per Share ($)						
1Q	0.52	0.40	0.20	0.37	0.27	0.16
2Q	—	0.56	0.37	0.44	0.20	0.38
3Q	—	0.67	0.49	0.40	0.57	0.42
4Q	—	0.56	0.35	0.30	0.47	0.32
Yr.	E2.55	2.19	1.40	1.51	1.51	1.25

Next earnings report expected: mid July

Dividend Data (Dividends have been paid since 1992.)

Amount ($)	Date Decl.	Ex-Div. Date	Stock of Record	Payment Date
0.093	Sep. 05	Sep. 17	Sep. 19	Oct. 03 '97
0.093	Dec. 03	Dec. 23	Dec. 26	Jan. 09 '98
0.093	Mar. 12	Mar. 25	Mar. 27	Apr. 10 '98
0.093	Jun. 04	Jun. 24	Jun. 26	Jul. 10 '98

EXHIBIT 10-3 Report on USFreightways (*Continued*).

STANDARD &POOR'S STOCK REPORTS

USFreightways Corporation

5531G
27-JUN-98

Business Summary - 01-MAY-98

USFreightways (formerly TNT Freightways) primarily provides regional LTL (less-than-truckload shipments of less than 10,000 lbs) freight service. USFC's objective is to become a single-source provider of transportation services. Accordingly, USFC entered the air freight forwarding business in October 1997 through the acquisition of Seko Worldwide. Other transportation services offered include logistics and ocean cargo consolidation. USFC sold its unprofitable truckload carrier, Comet, in September 1997.

USFC operates a family of five regional LTL freight carriers. Collectively, these carriers generated 90% of revenues in 1997. Regional LTL carriers primarily handle shipments moving under 500 miles that are routed directly between origin and destination terminals.

High capital costs for terminals and equipment serve as a barrier to entry to competition. Operating through a network of 217 terminals at 1997 year-end, USFC provides freight service throughout the U.S. and parts of Canada.

USFC's largest regional carrier is USF Holland (45% of total revenues), which serves the Midwest and Southeast. USF Red Star (12% of revenues), which operates in the eastern U.S. and parts of Canada, underwent a major restructuring in 1996, requiring the company to record a $4.1 million pretax charge. In January 1998, USFC acquired Mercury Distribution Carriers, a LTL carrier serving six Mid-Atlantic states. Mercury's operations will be integrated with Red Star, in an effort to improve margins through increased load density.

During 1996, USFC integrated the operations of Transus, Inc., a Southeastern-based carrier acquired in January 1996, into USFC Dugan (11% of revenues). Also in 1996, the company consolidated the operations of USF United, which served the Northwest and Rocky Mountain states, with those of USF Reddaway (13% of revenues). USF Bestway (9% of revenues) serves the Southwest and California.

Over the past few years, USFC has consistently recorded operating ratios (operating expenses divided by operating revenues) lower than those of its peers. In 1997, the operating ratio was 92.7%, versus 94.5% in 1996.

Logistics services (7% of total revenues), conducted primarily through Logix, involve the total management of the transportation, distribution and warehousing supply chain.

Remaining operations (3% of revenues) include cargo consolidation services for shipments moving between the U.S. mainland and Hawaii, Guam and Puerto Rico. USFC entered the air freight forwarding market in October 1997, with the acquisition of SEKO Worldwide, which generated revenues of $105 million in 1996.

Per Share Data ($) (Year Ended Dec. 31)	**1997**	**1996**	**1995**	**1994**	**1993**	**1992**	**1991**	**1990**	**1989**	**1988**
Tangible Bk. Val.	11.24	8.40	7.45	6.19	4.75	5.32	NA	NA	NA	NA
Cash Flow	4.91	4.25	3.78	3.51	2.97	1.99	1.62	NA	NA	NA
Earnings	2.19	1.41	1.51	1.51	1.25	0.78	0.59	NA	NA	NA
Dividends	0.37	0.37	0.37	0.37	0.37	0.28	Nil	NA	NA	NA
Payout Ratio	17%	26%	25%	25%	30%	36%	Nil	NA	NA	NA
Prices - High	36¾	28¼	28⅝	29¾	27½	14⅜	NA	NA	NA	NA
- Low	22⅞	16¾	16¼	19¼	12	9⅜	NA	NA	NA	NA
P/E Ratio - High	17	20	19	20	23	18	NA	NA	NA	NA
- Low	10	12	11	13	10	12	NA	NA	NA	NA
Income Statement Analysis (Million $)										
Revs.	1,565	1,331	1,144	1,016	899	775	NA	NA	NA	NA
Oper. Inc.	175	131	118	114	101	72.0	NA	NA	NA	NA
Depr.	70.1	63.9	50.3	44.3	39.4	32.8	NA	NA	NA	NA
Int. Exp.	8.5	12.1	8.9	9.1	7.6	2.0	NA	NA	NA	NA
Pretax Inc.	97.5	54.9	58.5	59.2	52.1	36.8	NA	NA	NA	NA
Eff. Tax Rate	42%	43%	43%	44%	45%	44%	NA	NA	NA	NA
Net Inc.	56.6	31.5	33.3	33.4	28.5	20.8	NA	NA	NA	NA
Balance Sheet & Other Fin. Data (Million $)										
Cash	6.5	4.1	1.7	2.1	2.3	NA	NA	NA	NA	NA
Curr. Assets	237	204	159	145	123	NA	NA	NA	NA	NA
Total Assets	800	689	578	501	461	NA	NA	NA	NA	NA
Curr. Liab.	182	144	128	118	98.0	NA	NA	NA	NA	NA
LT Debt	115	178	137	106	124	NA	NA	NA	NA	NA
Common Eqty.	392	269	233	208	181	NA	NA	NA	NA	NA
Total Cap.	560	494	411	350	334	NA	NA	NA	NA	NA
Cap. Exp.	129	0.3	117	68.8	84.2	63.3	NA	NA	NA	NA
Cash Flow	127	95.4	83.7	77.7	67.9	53.6	NA	NA	NA	NA
Curr. Ratio	1.3	1.4	1.2	1.2	1.3	NA	NA	NA	NA	NA
% LT Debt of Cap.	20.5	36.0	33.3	30.3	37.2	NA	NA	NA	NA	NA
% Net Inc.of Revs.	3.6	2.4	2.9	3.3	3.2	2.7	NA	NA	NA	NA
% Ret. on Assets	7.6	5.0	6.2	6.9	6.6	NA	NA	NA	NA	NA
% Ret. on Equity	17.1	12.5	15.1	17.2	14.0	NA	NA	NA	NA	NA

Data as orig. reptd.; bef. results of disc. opers. and/or spec. items. Per share data adj. for stk. divs. as of ex-div. date. Bold denotes diluted EPS (FASB 128). E-Estimated. NA-Not Available. NM-Not Meaningful. NR-Not Ranked.

Office—9700 Higgins Rd., Suite 570, Rosemont, IL 60018. **Tel**—(847) 696-0200. **Fax**—(847) 696-2080. **Website**—http://www.usfreightways.com **Chrmn & CEO**—J. C. Carruth. **Pres & COO**—J. G. Connelly III. **SVP & CFO & Investor Contact**—C. L. Ellis.**Secy**—R. C. Pagano. **Dirs**—J. C. Carruth, J. G. Connelly III, R. V. Delaney, M. Koffman, R. P. Neuschel, A. J. Paoni, J. W. Puth, N. A. Springer, W. N. Weaver. **Transfer Agent & Registrar**—Harris Trust and Savings Bank, Chicago. **Incorporated**—in Delaware in 1991. **Empl**— 16,843. **S&P Analyst:** Stephen R. Klein

EXHIBIT 10-3 Report on USFreightways (*Continued*).

[redacted]

USFreightways

STOCK REPORTS **27-JUN-98**

INDUSTRY OUTLOOK

We believe that the rally in shares for less-than-truckload (LTL) carriers has ended and that the advance for truckload players (TL) is in its terminal phase. The fourth-quarter 1997 correction in trucking shares marked a shift in leadership from the LTL to the more speculative TL companies. Valuations for TL carriers are now excessive, while those for LTL carriers are unduly depressed. We recommend that trucking shares be traded only by the most nimble of investors. While we continue to believe that the best long-term values remain with the LTL carriers, we concede that these shares may lag the market as investors ignore good fundamentals and fret about an economic downturn. Through June 12, the S&P Trucking Index rose 0.2% while the S&P 1500 Index was up 12%. Among the various segments of the trucking industry, truckload carriers gained 3.5% in 1998, while LTL carriers have slid 13.6%.

The truckload (TL) segment, the industry's largest, is beginning to undergo a major consolidation. The chronic driver shortage has prompted large carriers to gobble up smaller players simply to tap their workforce. The magnitude of the driver shortage was illustrated by large increases in pay implemented in 1997 by J.B. Hunt and Schneider National. Truckload rates have finally stabilized. In 1997, rates climbed about 1%, year to year, and are seen advancing 2% or more in 1998. Consolidation through mergers and bankruptcy may accelerate once the economy slows. Fuel prices remain in a freefall; in early June, diesel fuel sold at an average $1.04 a gallon, down 12% from year-earlier levels.

The LTL segment, which includes only a couple dozen major players, is one-third the size of the TL group. The outlook for LTL currently is more favorable now than it has been in several years. Rates have firmed and show few signs of weakness. Additionally, carriers have made great strides in paring costs and boosting margins. Long-haul carriers, which radically restructured their terminal systems in 1995, appear to have succeeded in repositioning themselves to handle faster-growing regional cargo. Coming off a depressed base, we believe profits for LTL carriers increased 152% in 1997, on top of a 57% gain recorded in 1996. A 5-10% profit gain is projected for 1998, reflecting freight diversion and an inventory correction during the year's first half.

Industry Stock Performance

Related S&P 1500 Industry Index

Truckers

Month-end Price Performance As of 05/29/98

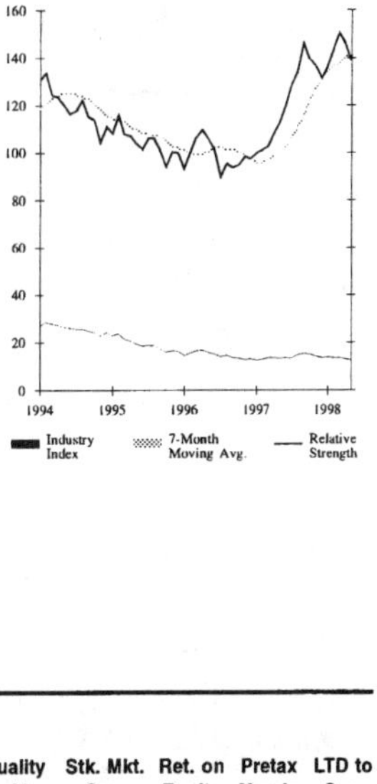

OTHER INDUSTRY PARTICIPANTS

Principal Peer Group	Stock Symbol	Recent Stock Price	P/E Ratio	12-mth. Trail. EPS	30-day Price Chg %	1-year Price Chg. %	Beta	Yield %	Quality Ranking	Stk. Mkt. Cap. (mil. $)	Ret. on Equity %	Pretax Margin %	LTD to Cap. %
USFreightways	**USFC**	**30⅞**	**13**	**2.31**	**-3%**	**23%**	**0.46**	**1.2**	**B+**	**807**	**17.1**	**6.2**	**20.5**
American Freightways	AFWY	10¼	17	0.61	-6%	-33%	0.32	Nil	B	324	8.2	3.4	42.3
Arnold Industries	AIND	15¼	12	1.23	-4%	-12%	0.02	2.9	A	395	15.1	13.3	1.0
C.H. Robinson Worldwide	CHRW	24½	36	0.68	7%	NA	NA	1.0	NR	1,008	NM	3.3	NA
Consolidated Freightways	CFWY	13¼	13	1.03	-5%	-17%	NA	Nil	NR	305	9.0	1.8	5.8
Dispatch Management Svcs	DMSC	24¼	NM	0.19	1%	NA	NA	Nil	NR	256	NM	NM	NA
Heartland Express	HTLD	21¼	20	1.04	2%	-7%	1.00	Nil	B+	636	21.5	17.9	Nil
Hunt (J.B.) Transport Services	JBHT	35½	64	0.55	23%	138%	0.56	0.6	B	1,258	3.3	1.2	40.3
Knight Transportation	KNGT	18	25	0.72	-7%	8%	NA	Nil	NR	269	20.0	17.6	NA
Landstar System	LSTR	34⅞	17	2.10	13%	32%	-0.02	Nil	NR	395	16.5	3.2	19.1
M.S. Carriers	MSCA	27⅞	17	1.64	-3%	16%	1.05	Nil	B+	342	11.4	7.1	31.1
Roadway Express	ROAD	18⅜	10	1.85	-1%	-14%	NA	1.1	NR	377	10.2	1.8	Nil
Rollins Truck Leasing	RLC	12¾	16	0.77	13%	28%	0.22	1.3	A	765	14.9	12.6	60.3
Swift Transportation	SWFT	19⅛	18	1.05	-10%	-4%	0.32	Nil	B+	817	15.2	8.4	NA
Werner Enterprises	WERN	19	18	1.07	7%	24%	0.12	0.5	A	730	13.0	9.9	11.0
Yellow Corp.	YELL	18¾	12	1.58	1%	-19%	0.49	Nil	C	513	12.5	2.7	25.5

EXHIBIT 10-3 Report on USFreightways (*Continued*).

STOCK REPORTS
USFreightways

WALL STREET CONSENSUS   26-JUN-98
Analysts' Recommendations

Stock Prices

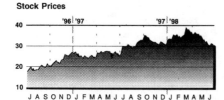

Analysts' Opinion

	No. of Ratings	% of Total	1 Mo. Prior	3 Mo. Prior	Nat'l	Reg'l	Non-broker
Buy	4	36	3	2	2	1	0
Buy/Hold	4	36	4	5	2	1	0
Hold	1	9	1	1	0	0	0
Weak Hold	0	0	0	0	0	0	0
Sell	0	0	0	0	0	0	0
No Opinion	2	18	2	2	1	0	1
Total	11	100	10	10	5	2	1

Analysts' Opinions

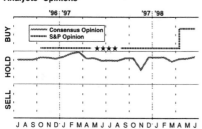

Analysts' Consensus Opinion

The consensus opinion reflects the average buy/hold/sell recommendation of Wall Street analysts. It is well-known, however, that analysts tend to be overly bullish. To make the consensus opinion more meaningful, it has been adjusted to reduce this positive bias. First, a stock's average recommendation is computed. Then it is compared to the recommendations on all other stocks. Only companies that score high relative to all other companies merit a consensus opinion of "Buy" in the graph at left. The graph is also important because research has shown that a rising consensus opinion is a favorable indicator of near-term stock performance; a declining trend is a negative signal.

Standard & Poor's STARS
(Stock Appreciation Ranking System)

Number of Analysts Following Stock

★★★★★	Buy	Standard & Poor's STARS ranking is
★★★★	Accumulate	our own analyst's evaluation of the
★★★	Hold	short-term (six to 12 month)
★★	Avoid	appreciation potential of a stock.
★	Sell	Five-Star stocks are expected to
		appreciate in price and outperform
		the market.

Analysts' Earnings Estimate

Annual Earnings Per Share

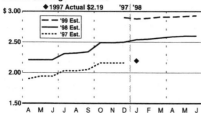

Current Analysts' Consensus Estimates

Fiscal years	Avg.	High	Low	S&P Est.	No. of Est.	Estimated P-E Ratio	Estimated S&P 500 P-E Ratio
1998	2.60	2.75	2.55	2.55	11	11.9	23.7
1999	2.93	3.15	2.70	2.90	11	10.5	20.3
2Q'98	0.68	0.71	0.65		9		
2Q'97	0.56 Actual						

A company's earnings outlook plays a major part in any investment decision. S&P organizes the earnings estimates of over 2,300 Wall Street analysts, and provides you with their consensus of earnings over the next two years. The graph to the left shows you how these estimates have trended over the past 15 months.

EXHIBIT 10-3 Report on USFreightways (*Continued*).

USFreightways Corporation

STOCK REPORTS

26-JUN-98

NEWS HEADLINES

■ **04/30/98**   1:50 pm... UPGRADING USFREIGHTWAYS (USFC 36*****) TO BUY FROM ACCUMULATE... USFC operates one of the fastest growing regional less-than-truckload carriers and has recently entered air freight forwarding via the acquisition of Seko Worldwide... USFC's truck business is benefiting from a trend in manufacturing to move supplies in smaller shipments over shorter distances... Its logistics business also is growing rapidly as more manufacturers and retailers outsource the management of their entire supply chain... Trading at 12X the $2.90 seen for '99, believe USFC is undervalued. /S.Klein

■ **04/16/98**   Apr. 16, 1998, US-Freightways Corp., announced Mar. '98 three-month earnings per diluted share of $0.52 vs. $0.40 for the same period a year ago.

■ **01/21/98**   Jan. 21, 1998, US-Freightways Corp. announced Dec. '97 fourth quarter earnings per diluted share of $0.56 vs $0.35 for the same period a year ago and annual earnings of $2.19 vs $1.40 for the prior year.

■ **12/02/97**   UP 1 1/8 to 31 7/8... Salomon Smith Barney upgrades to buy from outperform... Co. unavailable...

■ **12/02/97**   12:08 pm... US-FREIGHTWAYS (USFC 31-1/2) UP 3/4, SALOMON SMITH BARNEY UPGRADES TO BUY FROM OUTPERFORM... Analyst James Valentine tells salesforce primary reason for upgrade is strengthening rate environment in regional LTL sector... Notes upgrade makes USFC only buy rated stock in trucking, railroad universe... Raises $2.55 '98 EPS estimate to $2.75... Thinks recent weakness in stock has been due to confusion with regard to potential Teamsters strike;

says strike at USFC unlikely... Maintains $0.56 4Q EPS estimate, $2.18 '97 EPS... Has $41 target for end of '98./K.J.Wolfe

■ **10/31/97**   UP 2 1/2 to 32 3/8... BT Alex Brown upgrades to strong buy from buy... Co. unavailable...

■ **10/31/97**   12:30 pm... US-FREIGHTWAYS (USFC 31-3/4) UP 1-7/8, BT ALEX BROWN UPGRADES TO STRONG BUY FROM BUY... Analyst Anthony Gallo tells salesforce upgrade based on attractive valuation... Since co. reported strong 3Q on Oct. 9, shares have fallen 15.8% vs. 7.3% drop in S&P 500... Thinks co.'s announcement to seek early resolution to Teamsters' contract may have caused confusion... Says management execution has been strong, delivering both internal growth, accretive acquisitions... Has 6-12 month $40 target, 16x $2.50 '98 EPS estimate, offers 34% upside potential... Sees $2.15 '97 EPS, $2.50 '98, excl. any unannounced acquisitions./S.Trombino

■ **10/09/97**   11:50 am... CONTINUE TO ACCUMULATE USFREIGHTWAYS (USFC 36****)... Posts Q3 EPS of $0.67 vs. $0.49 on 14% fewer shares... in line with Street expectations... Shipments climbed 9.8% on strong economy, market share gains and some benefit from UPS strike... Logistics unit growing at 15% rate... USFC's decision to dump troubled truckload unit, Comet, will aid returns in '98... Pending acquisition of air freight forwarder SEKO Worldwide reflects plan to offer broader array of transport services... Lifting our '97 EPS estimate to $2.15 from $2.00, '98's to $2.40 from $2.25. / S.Klein

■ **10/09/97**   Oct. 9, 1997, US-Freightways Corp., announced Sept.

'97 three-month earnings per share of $0.67 vs $0.49 for same period a year ago, and nine-month earnings of $1.63 vs $1.05 for same period a year ago.

■ **07/15/97**   July 11, 1997, Standard & Poor's said it raised its senior unsecured and corporate credit rating on USFreightways Corp. (USFC) to A- from BBB+.

■ **07/11/97**   1:20 pm... CONTINUE TO ACCUMULATE USFREIGHTWAYS (USFC 30****)... Posts Q2 EPS $0.56 vs. $0.37, despite 18% more shares... better than expected... Less-than-truckload volume climbed 10.1%, yields up 5.4%... USFC tells analysts that making progress at all divisions but Red Star unit, which serves Northeast and is still struggling... Looking to make acquisition of small northeastern L-T-L carrier to build up Red Star's freight density... Got some benefit from demise of competitor Merchants... Lifting our '97 estimate to $2.00 from $1.95 and '98's to $2.25 from $2.20... USFC still attractively priced. /S.Klein

■ **07/11/97**   July, 11, 1997, Us-freightways Corp. announced June '97 three-month earnings per share of $0.56 vs $0.37 for same period a year ago. Six-month earnings of $0.96 vs $0.56 for same period a year ago.

■ **06/03/97**   UP 3/8 to 26... To be added to Dow Jones Transportation Average effective June 3, replacing CONRAIL.

■ **04/10/97**   April 10, 1997 US-Freightways Corp. announced a Mar. '97 three-month earnings per share of $0.40 vs $0.20 for same period a year ago. Results are based on average shares of 24,591,349 for '97 & 22,159,747 for '96.

EXHIBIT 10-4 Report on Intergraph.

(From Standard & Poor's Stock Reports, *June 27, 1998. Copyright © 1998 by The McGraw-Hill Companies.)*

STANDARD
&POOR'S
STOCK REPORTS

Intergraph Corp.   **4250**

Nasdaq Symbol **INGR**

27-JUN-98   **Industry:**   **Summary:** This company develops and sells software, hardware and
Computers (Hardware) services for technical professionals, particularly those in CAD/CAM/
CAE and GIS disciplines.

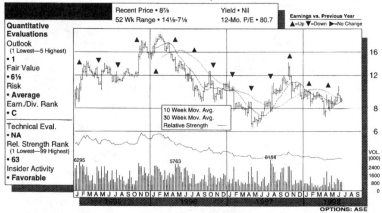

Quantitative Evaluations	Recent Price • 8⅞
	52 Wk Range • 14⅛-7⅛
Outlook (1 Lowest—5 Highest) • 1	Yield • Nil
Fair Value • 6⅛	12-Mo. P/E • 80.7
Risk • Average	
Earn./Div. Rank • C	
Technical Eval. • NA	
Rel. Strength Rank (1 Lowest—99 Highest) • 63	
Insider Activity • Favorable	

Overview - 08-MAY-98

Recent results have been adversely affected by a legal dispute with Intel which has led to delays in shipments of workstation graphics cards and other products, and has led to customer uncertainty and increased R&D costs as INGR tries to develop products without help from Intel. Due to a recent injunction against Intel, INGR feels it can start to regain lost momentum. However, the company faces an uphill battle. In the fourth quarter of 1997, INGR split its computer systems unit into a separate segment, called Intergraph Computer Systems, in order to make the company easier to understand, and increase measurability of results. We forecast sales growth in the mid-single digits for the year as a whole, as the company continues to try to build a brand name for itself in its underserved markets. Margins should narrow, on price competition and increased trade show and advertising activity.

Valuation - 08-MAY-98

Intergraph posted a loss of $0.67 a share in the first quarter of 1998, excluding non-recurring charges and a one-time gain of $2.13 on the sale of certain product lines, sharply worse than expected. Revenues fell 2.7%, and margins narrowed. Results in all four of the company's operating divisions were worse than anticipated, with Intergraph Computer Systems posting a $19.9 million loss, the graphics business reporting a $2 million loss, VeriBest showing a $4.8 million loss and Public Safety reporting a minor profit. The main issue at work was the dispute with Intel, and with an injunction in place, the company should start to get on the right track. However, results should continue to be impacted by INGR's attempt to move into the intensely competitive, high-volume, lower-margin hardware business. With revenue and earnings visibility limited, we recommend the stock be avoided.

Key Stock Statistics

S&P EPS Est. 1998	0.50	Tang. Bk. Value/Share	8.68
P/E on S&P Est. 1998	17.8	Beta	1.08
Dividend Rate/Share	Nil	Shareholders	6,100
Shs. outstg. (M)	48.3	Market cap. (B)	$0.428
Avg. daily vol. (M)	0.216	Inst. holdings	44%

Value of $10,000 invested 5 years ago: $ 6,698

Fiscal Year Ending Dec. 31

	1998	1997	1996	1995	1994	1993
Revenues (Million $)						
1Q	245.8	252.8	256.7	257.3	240.1	282.1
2Q	—	288.6	268.2	260.2	242.4	249.1
3Q	—	282.1	276.3	279.2	262.2	250.6
4Q	—	300.9	294.1	301.3	296.7	268.5
Yr.	—	1,124	1,096	1,098	1,041	1,050
Earnings Per Share ($)						
1Q	1.02	-0.55	-0.14	-0.49	-0.31	-0.21
2Q	—	-0.33	-0.32	-0.48	-0.45	-0.44
3Q	—	-0.15	-0.29	-0.17	-0.39	-0.43
4Q	—	-0.43	-0.71	0.15	-0.41	-1.54
Yr.	E0.50	-1.46	-1.46	-0.98	-1.56	-2.56

Next earnings report expected: late July

Dividend Data

No cash has been paid. A poison pill stock purchase rights plan was adopted in 1993.

EXHIBIT 10-4 Report on Intergraph (*Continued*).

STANDARD
&POOR'S
STOCK REPORTS

Intergraph Corporation

4250

27-JUN-98

Business Summary - 08-MAY-98

Intergraph has seen the future, and its name is Wintel. That high-tech duopoly (the Microsoft Windows operating system running on Intel microprocessors) has now penetrated the high end workstation segment of the computer industry. The company saw this change coming, and in 1992 decided to focus on developing products based on Wintel technology, and to shift from using its proprietary Clipper microprocessor in favor of Intel chips. In 1997, Intel systems represented 100% of hardware sales, and Windows-based systems represented 87% of software revenues. INGR is separated into four business entities: Industry Solutions, Computer Systems, Public Safety and VeriBest.

Intergraph Industry Solutions integrates both hardware and software platforms to meet engineering, design, modeling, analysis, mapping, information technology, and creative computing needs. Primary customers are in the process and building, infrastructure (transportation, utility and state and local government), and federal government. Applications include plant design, process control, product design, transportation network management, mapping and civil engineering, environmental and natural resource management, and energy exploration and production, to name a few.

Intergraph Computer Systems is a supplier of high performance, Intel/Windows NT-based graphics work-

stations and PCs, servers and 3D graphics subsystems. The workstation product line includes the TD personal computer, which is used for 2D design, office automation and business management tasks, and the TD personal workstation, for 3D design, engineering analysis, image processing and rendering. Other systems are also available for specialized needs, including the StudioZ workstation, which creates computer generated images and digital quality video for the entertainment market, and ExtremeZ 2D graphics workstations for prepress and publishing professionals. Graphics accelerators are also available, as well as large format production scanners, imaging systems for scanning and plotting images, and laser imagesetters for electronic map publishing.

Intergraph Public Safety provides public safety solutions on a global basis, including computer hardware and software systems, training, maintenance, customer support and outsourcing services. These are used by public safety agencies such as emergency medical and rescue units, fire departments and law enforcement organizations.

Veribest, formerly the electronics division of INGR, provides electronic system design solutions to the computer, telecommunications, automotive, industrial control and consumer industries. Core competencies include simulation, signal integrity, PCB implementation and enterprise-wide design process management.

Per Share Data ($)

(Year Ended Dec. 31)	1997	1996	1995	1994	1993	1992	1991	1990	1989	1988
Tangible Bk. Val.	7.66	9.38	10.76	11.66	12.98	15.49	15.80	14.35	12.58	11.72
Cash Flow	-0.21	0.14	0.76	0.08	-1.15	1.54	2.87	2.40	2.37	2.16
Earnings	-1.46	-1.46	-0.98	-1.56	-2.56	0.18	1.47	1.28	1.48	1.55
Dividends	Nil	Nil	Nil	Nil	Nil	Nil	Nil	Nil	Nil	Nil
Payout Ratio	Nil	Nil	Nil	Nil	Nil	Nil	Nil	Nil	Nil	Nil
Prices - High	14¹/₈	20⁵/₈	18¹/₈	11¹/₄	11¹/₄	13¹/₂	22⁵/₈	31¹/₂	23¹/₂	22³/₄	32¹/₂
- Low	6¹/₄	8⁵/₈	8¹/₈	7³/₈	8¹/₂	11	13	10¹/₂	13³/₄	19¹/₄
P/E Ratio - High	NM	NM	NM	NM	NM	NM	21	18	15	21
- Low	NM	NM	NM	NM	NM	NM	9	8	9	12

Income Statement Analysis (Million $)

Revs.	1,124	1,095	1,098	1,041	1,050	1,177	1,195	1,045	860	800
Oper. Inc.	6.5	17.6	32.0	-3.8	-9.0	95.0	165	149	140	167
Depr.	60.3	75.8	80.1	73.6	65.4	65.7	68.1	55.1	48.3	34.5
Int. Exp.	6.6	5.1	4.2	2.4	2.1	3.0	2.1	1.6	0.9	0.6
Pretax Inc.	-66.2	-66.1	-45.0	-74.0	-172	12.0	112	98.0	119	139
Eff. Tax Rate	NM	NM	NM	NM	NM	32%	37%	36%	33%	37%
Net Inc.	-70.2	-69.1	-45.0	-70.0	-118	8.4	71.1	62.6	79.5	88.0

Balance Sheet & Other Fin. Data (Million $)

Cash	46.6	50.6	56.0	62.0	76.0	93.0	116	90.0	91.0	180
Curr. Assets	502	504	542	575	585	648	710	640	574	638
Total Assets	721	756	826	840	855	987	997	907	808	831
Curr. Liab.	297	273	281	292	236	217	208	197	160	157
LT Debt	54.3	29.7	37.4	23.4	17.5	19.8	23.4	16.9	7.1	2.8
Common Eqty.	369	447	504	522	589	737	755	682	630	667
Total Cap.	424	483	545	548	619	769	789	710	648	674
Cap. Exp.	24.8	30.5	56.0	68.0	66.2	83.4	91.6	79.6	74.1	66.5
Cash Flow	-9.9	6.7	35.0	3.0	-53.0	74.0	139	118	128	122
Curr. Ratio	1.7	1.9	1.9	2.0	2.5	3.0	3.4	3.2	3.6	4.1
% LT Debt of Cap.	12.8	6.1	6.9	4.3	2.8	2.6	3.0	2.4	1.1	0.4
% Net Inc.of Revs.	NM	NM	NM	NM	NM	0.7	5.9	6.0	9.2	11.0
% Ret. on Assets	NM	NM	NM	NM	NM	0.9	7.4	7.5	10.3	11.4
% Ret. on Equity	NM	NM	NM	NM	NM	1.1	9.9	9.8	13.1	14.2

Data as orig. reptd.; bef. results of disc. opers. and/or spec. items. Per share data adj. for stk. divs. as of ex-div. date. Bold denotes diluted EPS (FASB 128). E-Estimated. NA-Not Available. NM-Not Meaningful. NR-Not Ranked.

Office—Huntsville, AL 35894-0001. **Tel**—(256) 730-2000. **Website**—http://www.intergraph.com **Chrmn & CEO**—J. W. Meadlock. **EVP & CFO**—L. J. Laster. **Secy**—J. R. Wynn. **Investor Contact**—Mary Beth Medley (205-730-2629). **Dirs**—L. J. Laster, T. J. Lee, S. L. McDonald, J. W. Meadlock, K. H. Schonrock Jr., J. F. Taylor Jr., R. E. Thurber. **Transfer Agent & Registrar**—Harris Trust & Savings Bank, Chicago. **Incorporated**—in Alabama in 1969; reincorporated in Delaware in 1984. **Empl**— 7,700. **S&P Analyst**: Jim Corridore

EXHIBIT 10-4 Report on Intergraph (*Continued*).

STOCK REPORTS
Intergraph Corp

SELL

WALL STREET CONSENSUS   26-JUN-98
Analysts' Recommendations

Stock Prices

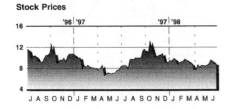

Analysts' Opinions

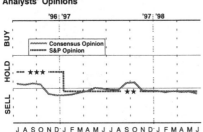

Number of Analysts Following Stock

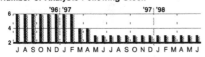

Analysts' Opinion

	No. of Ratings	% of Total	1 Mo. Prior	3 Mo. Prior	Nat'l	Reg'l	Non-broker
Buy	0	0	0	0	0	0	0
Buy/Hold	1	25	1	1	1	0	0
Hold	2	50	2	2	1	1	0
Weak Hold	0	0	0	0	0	0	0
Sell	0	0	0	0	0	0	0
No Opinion	1	25	1	1	0	0	1
Total	4	100	4	4	2	1	1

Analysts' Consensus Opinion

The consensus opinion reflects the average buy/hold/sell recommendation of Wall Street analysts. It is well-known, however, that analysts tend to be overly bullish. To make the consensus opinion more meaningful, it has been adjusted to reduce this positive bias. First, a stock's average recommendation is computed. Then it is compared to the recommendations on all other stocks. Only companies that score high relative to all other companies merit a consensus opinion of "Buy" in the graph at left. The graph is also important because research has shown that a rising consensus opinion is a favorable indicator of near-term stock performance; a declining trend is a negative signal.

Standard & Poor's STARS
(Stock Appreciation Ranking System)

★★★★★	Buy
★★★★	Accumulate
★★★	Hold
★★	Avoid
★	Sell

Standard & Poor's STARS ranking is our own analyst's evaluation of the short-term (six to 12 month) appreciation potential of a stock. Five-Star stocks are expected to appreciate in price and outperform the market.

Analysts' Earnings Estimate

Annual Earnings Per Share

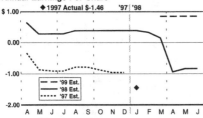

Current Analysts' Consensus Estimates

Fiscal years	Avg.	High	Low	S&P Est.	No. of Est.	Estimated P-E Ratio	Estimated S&P 500 P-E Ratio
1998	-0.84	0.50	-1.25	0.50	4	NM	23.7
1999	0.85	0.85	0.85	—	1	10.4	20.3
2Q'98	-0.26	-0.17	-0.34		2		
2Q'97	-0.33 Actual						

A company's earnings outlook plays a major part in any investment decision. S&P organizes the earnings estimates of over 2,300 Wall Street analysts, and provides you with their consensus of earnings over the next two years. The graph to the left shows you how these estimates have trended over the past 15 months.

Copyright © 1998 The McGraw-Hill Companies, Inc. This investment analysis was prepared from the following Sources: S&P MarketScope, S&P Compustat, S&P Stock Reports, S&P Stock Guide, S&P Industry Reports, Vickers Stock Research, Inc., I/B/E/S/ International, Inc., Standard & Poor's, a division of The McGraw-Hill Companies, 25 Broadway, New York, NY 10004.

EXHIBIT 10-4 Report on Intergraph (*Continued*).

Intergraph Corp.

STOCK REPORTS **27-JUN-98**

INDUSTRY OUTLOOK

Our investment outlook for the S&P Computers (Hardware) industry remains positive. The index's recent underperformance reflects near-term worries as PC makers expect early 1998 results to be under pressure. We believe this pressure is a function of a temporary problem of excess supply and not reduced demand. Long-term prospects remain bright, led by the continued proliferation of the Internet/intranets. Still, we expect share prices to remain volatile near term, as the market reacts to this recent weakness in sales, and projects the impact of weak Southeast Asian markets. We advise investors to approach this sector with a longer-term perspective.

The fundamentals in the computer industry remain strong, mainly due to a growing global appetite for technology products that increase productivity. Worldwide competition is forcing companies to become more productive, a task being accomplished largely through the employment of technology. While this trend is favorable for computer system vendors, the industry is still dominated by intense competition that can quickly turn today's leaders into tomorrow's losers. The new computing paradigm demands that vendors constantly introduce new, more powerful, and cheaper versions of successful products, while keeping a tight rein on operating expenses.

A profitable trend in the computer industry is expected to be the continued movement toward client-server computing. This model promotes the use of networks of cheap, yet powerful, PCs and servers, versus larger, more expensive, and proprietary mainframe computers. Companies that specialize in migrating customers to this new model -- like Hewlett Packard and Sun Microsystems -- are expected to be key beneficiaries. Another key trend is the growing implementation of corporate "intranets," which are internal corporate networks based on existing Internet technologies. These intranets require high-powered servers that are fueling a new product class for many hardware companies. Fundamentals in the PC industry will remain challenging to all participants, as price pressures remain intense. Still, we expect that strong international growth and a strong upgrade cycle, fueled by conversion to Microsoft's Windows NT operating system, will boost prospects. We view Compaq and Dell as attractive investments, with Compaq benefiting from growing demand for PCs priced less than $1,000.

Industry Stock Performance

Related S&P 1500 Industry Index

Computers (Hardware)

Month-end Price Performance As of 05/29/98

OTHER INDUSTRY PARTICIPANTS

Principal Peer Group	Stock Symbol	Recent Stock Price	P/E Ratio	12-mth. Trail. EPS	30-day Price Chg %	1-year Price Chg. %	Beta	Yield %	Quality Ranking	Stk. Mkt. Cap. (mil. $)	Ret. on Equity %	Pretax Margin %	LTD to Cap. %
Intergraph Corp.	**INGR**	**$8\frac{7}{8}$**	**81**	**0.11**	**5%**	**12%**	**1.08**	**Nil**	**C**	**428**	**NM**	**NM**	**12.8**
ATL Products	ATLPA	$25\frac{1}{2}$	31	0.83	1%	201%	NA	Nil	NR	247	NM	10.9	NA
Anacomp Inc	ANCO	$23\frac{7}{8}$	NM	-4.40	33%	85%	NA	Nil	NR	335	NM	NM	NA
Auspex Systems	ASPX	$5\frac{1}{2}$	NM	-0.41	6%	-42%	1.12	Nil	NR	139	11.3	12.0	NM
Bell & Howell	BHW	26	NM	-0.15	-2%	-10%	NA	Nil	NR	608	NM	4.9	144.0
Brooktrout Technology	BRKT	$14\frac{1}{4}$	59	0.24	-12%	15%	1.43	Nil	NR	153	18.9	20.4	Nil
Concurrent Computer	CCUR	$3\frac{3}{4}$	26	0.14	-7%	146%	0.71	Nil	C	176	29.8	5.0	NA
Data General	DGN	$14\frac{7}{8}$	22	0.67	6%	-43%	1.09	Nil	B-	731	13.2	3.8	29.1
Genesis Microchip	GNSSF	$8\frac{7}{8}$	31	0.29	-32%	NA	NA	Nil	NR	119	NM	NM	NA
Sequent Computer Systems	SQNT	12	12	1.02	-29%	-44%	1.82	Nil	B-	526	7.9	6.1	1.7
Splash Technology Hldgs	SPLH	$16\frac{1}{4}$	54	0.30	-2%	-50%	NA	Nil	NR	225	11.4	19.0	NA
Stratus Computer	SRA	$24\frac{1}{4}$	8	3.08	-34%	-51%	1.87	Nil	B	581	13.2	13.8	0.2
Telxon Corp.	TLXN	32	32	1.01	0%	79%	0.98	0.0	B-	509	NM	NM	42.4
Tera Computer	TERA	$12\frac{1}{8}$	NM	-2.13	6%	146%	NA	Nil	NR	141	NM	NM	NA
Visual Networks	VNWK	$33\frac{1}{8}$	NM	0.15	-4%	NA	NA	Nil	NR	589	NM	NM	NA
Vitech America	VTCH	$18\frac{3}{4}$	15	1.28	1%	29%	NA	Nil	NR	208	28.8	11.8	52.4

EXHIBIT 10-4 Report on Intergraph (*Continued*).

Intergraph Corporation

STOCK REPORTS   26-JUN-98

NEWS HEADLINES

■ **04/28/98**   Apr. 27, 1998, Intergraph Corp., announced Mar. '98 three-month diluted earnings of $1.02 vs. a loss of $0.55 for the same period a year ago. Results for 1998 include a gain of $102,767,000 or $2.13 per share from sale of assets and a charge of $14,761,000 or $0.31 per share primarily from employee termination costs and write-off of intangible assets.

■ **04/13/98**   UP 1 1/4 to 9... Says it has won federal court order in its antitrust suit against INTEL, INTC prohibited from terminating INGR's rights as a "strategic customer in current, future programs."

■ **01/30/98**   DOWN 1 to 8 3/4... Posts $0.43 4Q loss vs. $0.50 loss from ops. on 2.4% revenue rise... Notes 4Q orders for new systems down 6% from year ago.

■ **01/30/98**   10:10 am... STILL AVOID INTERGRAPH CORP (INGR 8-5/8**)... Posts Q4 loss of $0.43 vs. loss of $0.71, much worse than expected... revenues rose only 2.4%, operating margin narrowed... INGR hurt by dispute with Intel that caused delays in shipment of workstation graphics cards and higher legal expenses... Other problems included delay in closing sale of mechanical design and software business to EDS, which led to delayed purchase decisions by customers, and Asia problems, which produced $1.5 mln. currency loss. / J.Corridore

■ **01/30/98**   Jan. 29, 1998, Intergraph Corp. announced a Dec. '97 fourth quarter loss per diluted share of $0.43 vs a loss of $0.71 for the same period a year ago, and an annual loss of $1.46 vs a loss of $1.46 for the prior year. Results for the 1997 year include a charge of $6,126,000 from adverse arbitration award and a gain of

$4,858,000 from sales of investments in affiliates. Results for 1996 include a charge for write-down of assets of $10,545,000 for the fourth quarter and year, offset by gain on sale of investments in affiliated companies of $11,173,000, or $0.23 per share, for the year only.

■ **10/22/97**   Oct. 21, 1997, Intergraph Corp., announced Sept. '97 three-month loss per share of $0.15 vs loss of $0.29 for same period a year ago, and a nine-month loss of $1.03 vs loss of $0.75 for same period a year ago. Results include gains of $4,858,000 for both periods of 1997 and $316,000 & $9,689,000 for the three- and nine-month periods of 1996 from sale of an investments. Results for the nine-month period of 1997 include a charge of $6,100,000 or $0.13 per share from adverse contract award.

■ **07/23/97**   July 22, 1997, Intergraph Corp., announced a June '97 three-month loss per share of $0.33 vs loss of $0.32 for same period a year ago, and a six-month loss of $0.88 vs loss of $0.46 for same period a year ago. Results for both periods of 1997 include a charge of $0.13 resulting from an adverse contract arbitration award. Results for the six-month period of 1996 includes a gain of $.20 from sale of an investment.

■ **04/22/97**   9:55 am... STILL AVOID INTERGRAPH CORP. (INGR 7-1/2**)... Posts Q1 loss of $0.55 vs. year-ago loss of $0.14... Co. continues to disappoint, results well below estimates... Revenues fell 1.5%, as 11% decline in maintenance and service revenues outweighed 3.6% rise in hardware... Hurt by delayed software rollout, competitive pricing, strong dollar... Gross margins narrowed on adverse mix... Co. disposed of Optronics and Best Info units during qtr., with re-

lated $1.1 mln. loss... Quarter end orders up 10% to $159 mln... 3 new software releases in current quarter... See '97 loss of $0.80. /T.Groesbeck

■ **04/22/97**   Apr. 21, 1997, Intergraph Corp., announced a Mar. '97 three-month loss per share of $0.55 vs loss of $0.14 for same period a year ago. Results for 1996 include a gain of $0.20 from sale of an investment.

■ **01/31/97**   DOWN 2 to 8... Posts $0.50 4Q loss from ops. vs. $0.18 EPS from ops. on slightly lower sales...

■ **01/31/97**   9:15 am... DOWNGRADING INTERGRAPH (INGR 10-1/8***) TO AVOID FROM HOLD... posts Q4 loss of $0.71 (includes $0.21 asset write-down charge) vs. EPS of $0.15... '96 posted $1.46 loss vs. loss $0.98... Co. continues to disappoint, results well below estimates... Revenues for year fell slightly, hurt by weak software sales, pricing pressure for hardware... Gross margins narrowed to 37% from 39%... Positive note year end orders up 4.3% to $210.9 million... Co. sees break even in Q3, profitability in Q4, though we are skeptical... See '97 loss of $0.80. /T.Groesbeck

■ **01/31/97**   Jan. 30, 1997, Intergraph Corp. announced a Dec. 1996 fourth quarter loss per share of $0.71 vs earnings of $0.15 for same period a year ago. Annual loss, $1.46 vs loss of $0.98 for the prior year. Results for the 1996 fourth quarter and year include a charge of $0.21 per share, from write down of assets, and for the year only, a gain of $0.23 per share, on sale of investments in affiliated companies. Results for the 1995 fourth quarter and year include a credit of $0.03 per share and a charge of $0.13 per share, from reversal of/provision for restructuring. Also, results for the 1995 year only, include a gain of $0.14 per share, from sale of subsidiary.

Out of every 100 stocks, 80 will be worth roughly their current stock price. It's the outliers that should be bought or avoided. By this methodology, all you need are 20 or so attractive stocks in different industries to create a sound, diversified stock portfolio. The STARS, Fair Value, and Platinum Portfolio choices are good starting points. We recommend that you fill out your list with good small-cap ideas using the method outlined in this chapter.

11

GROWTH VERSUS VALUE

G ARP INVESTING USING the STARS and Fair Value systems is an excellent framework, but most investors will want to learn more about a stock before investing in it. The next few chapters discuss additional ways that investors can analyze small stocks.

One way to divide up the market is by industry. Most analysts working for brokerage houses and investment management firms have narrow and deep knowledge of a specific industry group, be it steel and other ferrous metals, or biotechnology. They try to determine whether their industry group is likely to do well against certain benchmarks, and to select the best companies within each industry.

Portfolio managers must necessarily take a more general approach. They quiz analysts and study industry and company reports across the board. They will utilize a variety of investment approaches. One might like to buy equities that are trading at low P/Es, while another might favor companies that are growing rapidly, regardless of the P/E. Another manager might prefer to buy mature companies with known track records, while someone else might prefer young companies developing emerging technologies.

Of course, no single investment approach can be singled out as best. A manager might excel at one style of investing but not others. Most investment firms try to align the investment style of an investment manager with the investment goals of the portfolio being managed. For example, a large-cap, low-P/E manager would be ill-suited for a small-cap growth fund.

This concept applies to the individual investor too. There are many investment styles that can serve an investor well. Although some strategies perform better than others, it is more important to choose one that fits your personality and that you will feel comfortable with over the long run. It makes little sense to invest in growth stocks, for instance, if you are inclined to bail out of the group at the first sign of trouble.

It is all right to experiment in the beginning, but in the end, sticking with an investment discipline is just as important as choosing the right one. Staying with a theoretically solid investment discipline is essential if you want to beat the stock market. Although you may make slight adjustments to your portfolio to reflect changing economic conditions, never abandon your core discipline.

Just about all of the most common quantitative and qualitative investment disciplines can be divided into the two categories of growth and value. Of course, for both categories, the key is to find stocks that are trading at prices that do not already reflect their future earnings power. But there are differences in the two types of equities—namely, differing financial ratios and fundamental factors that trigger buy and sell decisions (see Table 11-1).

MEASURING GROWTH

How should you evaluate a company's potential growth? The most common answer to this question is to assess historical and future sales and earnings growth. A *growth* company would be one that is growing at an above-average rate by these measures. If companies in the S&P 500 increased earnings at a 13 percent rate over a 12-month period, and a particular firm within that group showed earnings growth of 25 percent, then most investors would characterize it as a growth stock. Be careful, however, to watch out for one-time events that could be anomalies in the earnings pattern. A true growth company should maintain this above-average pace over a *number* of years, and be likely to continue to do so for a long time. Cisco Systems, Intel, and Microsoft are just such companies.

There are also plenty of growth stocks which have no earnings at all. Companies with strong revenue growth combined with significantly declining losses could still be deemed good growth companies—they are simply in an early stage of development. America OnLine (AOL), Qualcomm, and Yahoo! were good examples of early-stage growth stocks when they went public. On the other hand, companies with higher earnings on

The worst thing an investor can do is buy stocks based on what has worked best over the previous year. This is almost always a recipe for poor performance.

TABLE 11-1   Growth versus value stocks: positive buy signals.

Growth Disciplines	Value Disciplines
Above-average earnings growth	Low book value
High relative strength	Low P/E
High return on equity (ROE)	ROE above P/E
High profit margins	Low but improving margins
Rapid sales growth	Stock buybacks
Stock above moving average in emerging industries	Stock just crossed moving average
	Low stock capitalization/sales
No dividend	Rising cash dividend

declining revenues are *not* growth stocks. Maybe a money-losing division was jettisoned. That might make these firms' shares interesting special situations, but they would not be growth stocks.

One could also use annual increases in sales, cash flow, market value, or operating profit to measure growth. Sales and operating profit trends are good reflections of overall company growth over time, along with, of course, per-share earnings.

ASSESSING VALUE
Defining a value stock is just as tough a task. Most investors consider them to be stocks that are cheap by certain evaluative standards. What measurement of values should one use to define value stocks? Should it be a low return on equity (ROE), a high dividend yield, or some other statistic? There are many opinions on this point. Low price/sales and low price/cash flow are excellent value gauges, but low price/book value remains the primary standard to differentiate value stocks from growth stocks.

PRICE/BOOK VALUE AS A MEASURE OF GROWTH AND VALUE
In 1992, Standard & Poor's, in collaboration with BARRA, Inc., decided to categorize S&P's major indexes by growth and value (see Table 11-2). The statistic that it decided to use was book value. BARRA studied the issue at great length, and concluded that book value best reflects the contrasts of growth and value. The price/book value ratio was deemed the best indication of what the market believes a company's assets are worth today. This view is based on what the company might earn not over the next year or so, but over many decades. Hence, it also tends to be more stable over time.

Exhibits 11-1 and 11-2 at the end of this chapter present sample S&P/BARRA value and growth lists.

TABLE 11-2 S&P/BARRA growth and value index categories.

S&P/BARRA List

Factor	500 Growth	500 Value	MidCap 400 Growth	MidCap 400 Value	SmallCap Growth	Value
Mean market cap, $ Million	44,347	13,161	2913	1613	810	409
Barra beta	1.1	0.9	1.2	0.9	1.0	0.9
P/E	39.2	25.4	34.8	21.4	33.3	29.6
Price/book value	9.8	2.9	5.3	1.7	4.3	1.5
Dividend yield	0.8%	1.8%	0.5%	2.0%	0.5%	1.2%
ROE	30.1%	13.1%	19.22%	10.2%	14.8%	7.7%
ROA	20.1%	5.3%	15.6%	5.9%	14.3%	5.2%
Price/sales	3.6	1.3	2.0	0.8	1.7	0.6
Price/cash flow	42.2	15.8	34.2	12.4	29.7	14.6
Dividend payout	26.7%	39.1%	8.9%	29.5%	10.0%	18.1%
5-yr annualized EPS growth rate	17.5%	8.4%	21.0%	8.5%	15.8%	9.2%

NOTE: Data as of September 30, 1998.

EXHIBIT 11-1   Stock components of the S&P/BARRA SmallCap 600 Value Index.

(From Standard & Poor's, www.spglobal.com. Copyright © 1998 by The McGraw-Hill Companies.)

STANDARD & POOR'S   INDEX SERVICES

Home | Current Stats | News | Indices | Licensing | Sector Scorecard | FAQ

S&P/BARRA SmallCap 600 Value List

S&P 500
S&P 100
MidCap 400
SmallCap 600
S&P REITs
SuperComp 1500
Euro & Euro Plus
S&P/TSE 60

Growth & Value
500 Growth
500 Value
MidCap Growth
MidCap Value
SmallCap Growth
► SmallCap Value

search

	TICKER	COMPANY
1	ABM	ABM Industries
2	ADAC	ADAC Laboratories
3	ALO	ALPHARMA Inc.
4	ACO	AMCOL Int'l. Corp.
5	AMMB	AMRESCO Inc.
6	AEIC	Air Express International
7	ALN	Allen Telecom Inc.
8	ALLP	Alliance Pharmaceutical
9	AIZ	Amcast Industrial
10	AFWY	Amer Freightways
11	AORI	American Oncology Resources
12	AWR	American States Water Co.
13	ALOG	Analogic Corp.
14	ABCW	Anchor Bancorp Wisconsin
15	AGL	Angelica Corp.
16	AXE	Anixter International
17	ANN	AnnTaylor Stores Corp.
18	APOG	Apogee Enterprises
19	APPB	Applebee's Intl
20	APZ	Applied Industrial Technologies
21	APM	Applied Magnetics
22	WTR	Aquarion Co
23	ACAT	Arctic Cat Inc
24	ABFS	Arkansas Best
25	ASTE	Astec Industries
26	ASFC	Astoria Financial
27	ATO	Atmos Energy Corp
28	ABPCA	Au Bon Pain'A'
29	ASPX	Auspex Systems
30	ASM	Authentic Fitness
31	AZR	Aztar Corp
32	JBAK	Baker(J.) Inc
33	BTC	BancTec, Inc.
34	BGR	Bangor Hydro Electric
35	BKNG	Banknorth Group, Inc.
36	B	Barnes Group
37	BRR	Barrett Resources Corp.
38	BSET	Bassett Furniture
39	BI	Bell Indus
40	BHE	Benchmark Electronics
41	BNO	Benton Oil & Gas
42	BDY	Bindley Western Industries
43	BIR	Birmingham Steel
44	BBA	Bombay Company
45	BAMM	Books-A-Million
46	BNE	Bowne & Co
47	BRCOA	Brady Corp.
48	BG	Brown Group
49	BW	Brush Wellman
50	BMHC	Building Materials Hldg. Corp.
51	BBR	Butler Manufacturing
52	CER	CILCORP, Inc.
53	CPY	CPI Corp.
54	CTS	CTS Corp.
55	CDT	Cable Design Technologies

56	COG	Cabot Oil & Gas 'A'
57	CMIC	Calif Microwave
58	CBM	Cambrex Corp.
59	CBRNA	Canandaigua Brands
60	KRE	Capital Re
61	CKE	Carmike Cinemas'A'
62	CAFC	Carolina First Corp.
63	CGC	Cascade Natural Gas
64	CASY	Casey's Gen'l Stores
65	PWN	Cash Amer Intl
66	CACOA	Cato Corp'A'
67	CGRM	Centigram Communicatio
68	CNH	Central Hudson Gas&El
69	CV	Central Vt Pub Svc
70	CKP	Checkpoint Systems Inc.
71	CAKE	Cheesecake Factory
72	CEM	ChemFirst Inc.
73	CHE	Chemed Corp
74	CQB	Chiquita Brands Int'l
75	CCON	Circon Corp
76	CDE	Coeur d'Alene Mines
77	COHR	Coherent Inc.
78	CFB	Commercial Federal Corp.
79	CMC	Commercial Metals
80	CES	Commonwealth Energy System
81	CMIN	Commonwealth Industrials Inc.
82	CPDN	CompDent Corp.
83	COE	Cone Mills
84	CNE	Connecticut Energy
85	CONW	Consumers Water
86	CPO	Corn Products Int'l
87	ATX.A	Cross (A.T.) CO.
88	CFR	Cullen Frost Bankers
89	CUST	CustomTracks Corp.
90	CYRK	Cyrk Inc.
91	DHI	D.R. Horton
92	DRC	Dain Rauscher Corp.
93	DS	Dallas Semiconductor
94	DMRK	Damark International'A
95	DM	Dames & Moore Group
96	DAN	Daniel Indus
97	DSCP	Datascope
98	DFG	Delphi Financial Grp.
99	DLW	Delta Woodside Ind
100	DVN	Devon Energy
101	DP	Diagnostic Products
102	DGII	Digi International
103	DMIC	Digital Microwave
104	DAP	Discount Auto Parts
105	DXYN	Dixie Group Inc.
106	DSL	Downey Financial Corp.
107	DBRN	Dress Barn
108	EGRP	E*Trade Group
109	EAGL	Eagle Hardware & Garde
110	EUA	Eastern Util Assoc
111	ESIO	Electro Scientific Inds.
112	EGLS	Electroglas, Inc
113	EGN	Energen Corp
114	EFS	Enhance Financial Svcs
115	EXBT	Exabyte Corp.
116	ER	Executive Risk
117	FGCI	Family Golf Centers
118	FJC	Fedders Corp.
119	BSMT	Filene's Basement
120	FMBI	First Midwest Bancorp

121	FLM	Fleming Companies
122	FRK	Florida Rock Industries
123	FLOW	Flow International
124	FC	Franklin Covey Co.
125	FMT	Fremont Gen'l
126	FRTZ	Fritz Companies
127	FTR	Frontier Insurance Gr
128	FFEX	Frozen Food Express Ind. Inc.
129	GCX	GC Companies
130	GNL	Galey & Lord Inc.
131	GNCMA	General Communication
132	GHV	Genesis Hlth Ventures
133	GON	Geon Co.
134	GRB	Gerber Scientific
135	GGO	Getchell Gold Corp.
136	GIBG	Gibson Greetings Inc.
137	GLG	Glamis Gold Ltd
138	GIX	Global Industrial Technologies, Inc.
139	CSTM	Global Motorsport Group
140	GOT	Gottschalks Inc
141	GND	Grand Casinos
142	GMP	Green Mountain Pwr
143	GFF	Griffon Corp.
144	GFD	Guilford Mills
145	GYMB	Gymboree Corp.
146	HDCO	HADCO Corp.
147	HSE	HS Resources
148	HGGR	Haggar
149	HKF	Hancock Fabrics Inc.
150	JH	Harland (J.H.)
151	HAR	Harman Int'l Industries
152	HMX	Hartmarx Corp.
153	HAUS	Hauser Inc.
154	HL	Hecla Mining
155	HPK	Hollywood Park
156	HOLX	Hologic Inc.
157	HUF	Huffy Corp
158	HUG	Hughes Supply
159	HTCH	Hutchinson Technology
160	IDXX	IDEXX Laboratories
161	IHOP	IHOP Corp
162	IMR	IMCO Recycling
163	IO	Input/Output Inc.
164	INSUA	Insituform Technol'A'
165	III	Insteel Industries Inc
166	IAAI	Insurance Auto Auction
167	ICST	Integrated Circuit Sys
168	IHS	Integrated Health Svcs
169	INTV	InterVoice
170	IFSIA	Interface Inc'A'
171	IS	Interim Services Inc.
172	IMG	Intermagnetics Gen'l
173	INMT	Intermet Corp
174	IRF	Intl Rectifier
175	ION	Ionics Inc
176	ITRI	Itron, Inc.
177	JJSF	J & J Snack Foods
178	JSB	JSB Financial
179	JBM	Jan Bell Marketing
180	JAS.A	Jo-Ann Stores
181	JII	Johnston Industries
182	JUNO	Juno Lighting
183	FEET	Just For Feet
184	JSTN	Justin Indus
185	KSWS	K Swiss Inc 'A'

186	KTO	K2 Inc.
187	KCS	KCS Energy Inc
188	KMET	KEMET Corp
189	KAMNA	Kaman Corp Cl'A'
190	KWD	Kellwood Co
191	KNT	Kent Electronics
192	KEX	Kirby Corp
193	KMAG	Komag Inc
194	KLIC	Kulicke & Soffa Ind.
195	LZB	LA-Z Boy
196	LDRY	Landry's Seafood
197	LSTR	Landstar Systems Inc.
198	LSCC	Lattice Semconductor
199	LAWS	Lawson Products
200	LECH	Lechters Inc
201	LVC	Lillian Vernon
202	LCE	Lone Star Industries
203	LUB	Luby's Cafeterias
204	LDL	Lydall Inc.
205	MDC	M.D.C. Hldgs
206	MSCA	M.S. Carriers
207	MAFB	MAF Bancorp
208	MCS	Marcus Corp
209	MPN	Mariner Post-Acute Network
210	MI	Marshall Indus
211	MSC	Material Sciences
212	MWT	McWhorter Technologies
213	MESA	Mesa Air Group Inc.
214	METHA	Methode Electronics 'A'
215	MIKE	Michaels Stores
216	MICA	MicroAge Inc
217	GRO	Mississippi Chemical Corp.
218	MK	Morrison Knudsen Corp.
219	MYE	Myers Indus
220	NRC	NAC Re Corp.
221	NCSS	NCS Healthcare Inc.
222	NAFC	Nash Finch Co
223	NSH	Nashua Corp
224	NPK	National Presto Ind.
225	NWK	Network Equip Tech
226	NJR	New Jersey Resources
227	NFX	Newfield Exploration
228	NRL	Norrell Corp.
229	NWNG	Northwest Natural Gas
230	NWSW	Northwestern Steel & Wire
231	OSL	O'Sullivan Corp
232	OMP	OM Group, Inc.
233	OH	Oakwood Homes
234	OII	Oceaneering Int'l
235	OLOG	Offshore Logistics
236	ORU	Orange/Rockland Util
237	OC	Orion Capital
238	GOSHA	Oshkosh B'Gosh
239	OXM	Oxford Indus
240	PKE	Park Electrochemical
241	PXR	Paxar Corp
242	PENX	Penford Corp.
243	PNT	Pennsylvania Enterprises
244	PMRX	Pharmaceutical Marketing
245	PSC	Phila Suburban
246	PVH	Phillips-Van Heusen
247	PHYC	PhyCor Inc
248	PCTL	PictureTel Corp
249	PNY	Piedmont Nat'l Gas
250	PIOS	Pioneer Std Electr

251	PZX	Pittston BAX Group
252	PLX	Plains Resources
253	PLAY	Players International
254	PESC	Pool Energy Services
255	POP	Pope & Talbot
256	PDE	Pride Int'l Inc.
257	PRMA	Primadonna Resorts
258	PMK	Primark Corp
259	PDQ	Prime Hospitality
260	PDLI	Protein Design Labs
261	PGS	Public Service of North Carolina
262	KWR	Quaker Chemical
263	NX	Quanex Corp
264	RTI	RTI Intl. Metals Inc.
265	RTEX	RailTex Inc.
266	RAH	Ralcorp Holdings
267	RDRT	Read-Rite Corp
268	REGN	Regeneron Pharmaceutic
269	RS	Reliance Steel & Aluminum
270	ROILB	Remington Oil & Gas 'B'
271	RGC	Republic Group Inc.
272	RIGS	Riggs Natl Corp
273	RIVL	Rival Company
274	RBN	Robbins & Myers
275	RPC	Roberts Pharmaceutical
276	RLC	Rollins Truck Leasing
277	RAM	Royal Appliance Mfg
278	RI	Ruby Tuesday, Inc.
279	RURL	Rural/Metro Corp.
280	RUS	Russ Berrie & Co
281	RYAN	Ryan's Family Steak Hse
282	RYL	Ryland Group
283	SIII	S3 Inc
284	SFR	Santa Fe Energy Resources
285	SWM	Schweitzer-Mauduit Inc.
286	SCTTA	Scott Technologies
287	SMG	Scotts Co. 'A'
288	SEI	Seitel, Inc.
289	SIGI	Selective Insurance Gr
290	SKO	Shopko Stores
291	SIE	Sierra Health Services
292	SRP	Sierra Pacific Resourc
293	SIVB	Silicon Valley Bancshares
294	SMPS	Simpson Indus
295	SKYW	SkyWest Inc
296	SKY	Skyline Corp.
297	AOS	Smith (A.O.)
298	SFDS	Smithfield Foods
299	SNY	Snyder Oil Corp
300	SONC	Sonic Corp
301	SEHI	Southern Energy Homes
302	SWX	Southwest Gas
303	SWN	Southwestern Energy
304	SLMD	SpaceLabs Medical
305	SPAR	Spartan Motors
306	SFAM	SpeedFam Int'l Inc.
307	TSA	Sports Authority
308	MARY	St. Mary Land & Explor
309	SPBC	St. Paul Bancorp
310	SMSC	Standard Microsystems
311	SMP	Standard Motor Prod
312	SPF	Standard Pacific
313	SPD	Standard Products
314	SXI	Standex International
315	STTX	Steel Technologies

316	SW	Stone & Webster
317	SRR	Stride Rite
318	BEAM	Summit Technology
319	SMD	Sunrise Medical
320	SUPR	Superior Services
321	SUSQ	Susquehanna Bancshares
322	SABI	Swiss Army Brands Inc.
323	SYMM	Symmetricom Inc
324	SCOR	Syncor Int'l
325	SSAX	System Software
326	TJCO	T J International
327	TBCC	TBC Corp.
328	TBY	TCBY Enterprises
329	TCSI	TCSI Corp.
330	TTI	TETRA Technologies
331	TNP	TNP Enterprises
332	TACO	Taco Cabana'A'
333	TXI	Texas Industries
334	EGR	The Earthgrains Company
335	UIL	The United Illuminating Co.
336	TII	Thomas Indus
337	TNM	Thomas Nelson
338	THO	Thor Industries
339	TFS	Three-Five Systems
340	TWI	Titan Int'l. Inc.
341	TOL	Toll Brothers
342	TTC	Toro Co
343	TREN	Trenwick Group
344	TRMB	Trimble Navigation Ltd.
345	TTX	Tultex Corp
346	UH	U.S. Home
347	USFC	USFreightways Corp.
348	UTEK	Ultratech Stepper Inc.
349	UWR	United Water Resources
350	UTR	Unitrode Corp.
351	UFPI	Universal Forest Products
352	UHS	Univl Health Svs Cl'B'
353	VLSI	VLSI Technology
354	VALM	Valmont Indus
355	VRTX	Vertex Pharmaceuticals
356	VICR	Vicor Corp
357	VPI	Vintage Petroleum
358	VITL	Vital Signs
359	VOL	Volt Information Sciences
360	WHX	WHX Corp.
361	WIC	WICOR Inc.
362	WNC	Wabash National
363	WALB	Walbro Corp
364	WALL	Wall Data
365	WJ	Watkins-Johnson
366	WSO	Watsco Inc.
367	WERN	Werner Enterprises
368	WGO	Winnebago Indus
369	WZR	Wiser Oil
370	WLV	Wolverine Tube
371	WRC	World Color Press
372	WN	Wynn's Int'l
373	XRIT	X-Rite Inc
374	XIRC	Xircom Inc
375	YELL	Yellow Corp.
376	ZLC	Zale Corp.
377	ZNT	Zenith Natl Insurance

EXHIBIT 11-2   Stock components of the S&P/BARRA SmallCap 600 Growth Index.

(From Standard & Poor's, www.spglobal.com. Copyright © 1998 by The McGraw-Hill Companies.)

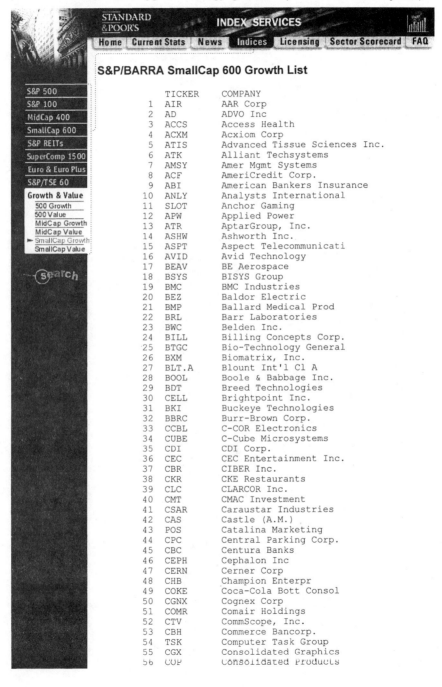

	STANDARD & POOR'S	INDEX SERVICES	
	Home	Current Stats	News	Indices	Licensing	Sector Scorecard	FAQ

S&P/BARRA SmallCap 600 Growth List

	S&P 500	
	S&P 100	
	MidCap 400	
	SmallCap 600	
	S&P REITs	
	SuperComp 1500	
	Euro & Euro Plus	
	S&P/TSE 60	
	Growth & Value	
	500 Growth	
	500 Value	
	MidCap Growth	
	MidCap Value	
►	SmallCap Growth	
	SmallCap Value	
	search	

	TICKER	COMPANY
1	AIR	AAR Corp
2	AD	ADVO Inc
3	ACCS	Access Health
4	ACXM	Acxiom Corp
5	ATIS	Advanced Tissue Sciences Inc.
6	ATK	Alliant Techsystems
7	AMSY	Amer Mgmt Systems
8	ACF	AmeriCredit Corp.
9	ABI	American Bankers Insurance
10	ANLY	Analysts International
11	SLOT	Anchor Gaming
12	APW	Applied Power
13	ATR	AptarGroup, Inc.
14	ASHW	Ashworth Inc.
15	ASPT	Aspect Telecommunicati
16	AVID	Avid Technology
17	BEAV	BE Aerospace
18	BSYS	BISYS Group
19	BMC	BMC Industries
20	BEZ	Baldor Electric
21	BMP	Ballard Medical Prod
22	BRL	Barr Laboratories
23	BWC	Belden Inc.
24	BILL	Billing Concepts Corp.
25	BTGC	Bio-Technology General
26	BXM	Biomatrix, Inc.
27	BLT.A	Blount Int'l Cl A
28	BOOL	Boole & Babbage Inc.
29	BDT	Breed Technologies
30	CELL	Brightpoint Inc.
31	BKI	Buckeye Technologies
32	BBRC	Burr-Brown Corp.
33	CCBL	C-COR Electronics
34	CUBE	C-Cube Microsystems
35	CDI	CDI Corp.
36	CEC	CEC Entertainment Inc.
37	CBR	CIBER Inc.
38	CKR	CKE Restaurants
39	CLC	CLARCOR Inc.
40	CMT	CMAC Investment
41	CSAR	Caraustar Industries
42	CAS	Castle (A.M.)
43	POS	Catalina Marketing
44	CPC	Central Parking Corp.
45	CBC	Centura Banks
46	CEPH	Cephalon Inc
47	CERN	Cerner Corp
48	CHB	Champion Enterpr
49	COKE	Coca-Cola Bott Consol
50	CGNX	Cognex Corp
51	COMR	Comair Holdings
52	CTV	CommScope, Inc.
53	CBH	Commerce Bancorp.
54	TSK	Computer Task Group
55	CGX	Consolidated Graphics
56	COP	Consolidated Products

57	CORR	Cor Therapeutics
58	CVTY	Coventry Health Care Inc.
59	XTO	Cross Timbers Oil
60	CURE	Curative Health Services
61	CYGN	Cygnus, Inc.
62	DV	DeVRY Inc.
63	DLP	Delta and Pine Land
64	DMN	DiMon Inc.
65	DLGC	Dialogic Corp.
66	DNEX	Dionex Corp
67	EV	Eaton Vance
68	ENVY	Envoy Corp.
69	ENZ	Enzo Biochem
70	ETEC	Etec Systems
71	ETH	Ethan Allen Interiors
72	EXPD	Expeditors Int'l
73	ESRX	Express Scripts 'A'
74	FIC	Fair Isaac & Co.
75	FNF	Fidelity Nat'l Fin'l
76	FILE	FileNet Corp
77	FAF	First Amer'n Fin'l
78	FBP	First Bancorp Hldg. Co.
79	FMER	FirstMerit Corp.
80	FM	Foodmaker Inc
81	FTS	Footstar Inc.
82	GKSRA	G & K Services Cl'A'
83	AJG	Gallagher(Arthur J.)
84	GDI	Gardner Denver, Inc.
85	SEM	General Semiconductor
86	GNTX	Gentex Corp
87	GDYS	Goody's Family Clothing
88	GGG	Graco Inc.
89	HMK	HA-LO Industries
90	HNCS	HNC Software Inc.
91	HUBC	HUBCO Inc.
92	HLX	Halter Marine Group
93	HRBC	Harbinger Corp.
94	HRMN	Harmon Indus
95	HTLD	Heartland Express
96	HELX	Helix Technology
97	JKHY	Henry (Jack) & Assoc.
98	HRH	Hilb,Rogal & Hamilton
99	HYSL	Hyperion Solutions
100	INCY	INCYTE Pharmaceuticals
101	IMNR	Immune Response Corp
102	INVX	Innovex, Inc.
103	NSIT	Insight Enterprises, Inc.
104	INTL	Inter-Tel Inc.
105	IVCR	Invacare Corp
106	JLG	JLG Industries, Inc.
107	JMED	Jones Pharma Inc.
108	KRON	Kronos Inc.
109	KUH	Kuhlman Corp
110	LSB	LSB Industries
111	LM	Legg Mason Inc
112	LBY	Libbey Inc.
113	LI	Lilly Industries 'A'
114	LNN	Lindsay Mfg. Co
115	LIN	Linens 'n Things Inc.
116	LIPO	Liposome Co
117	MCRS	MICROS Systems
118	MRD	MacDermid Inc.
119	MACR	Macromedia Inc.
120	MGL	Magellan Health Services
121	MTW	Manitowoc Co

EXHIBIT 11-2   Stock components of the S&P/BARRA SmallCap 600 Growth Index (*Continued*).

122	MEDI	MedImmune Inc
123	MEDQ	MedQuist, Inc.
124	SUIT	Men's Wearhouse Inc.
125	MNTR	Mentor Corp.
126	MERQ	Mercury Interactive
127	MRLL	Merrill Corp
128	MTNT	Metro Networks
129	MWY	Midway Games Inc.
130	MHK	Mohawk Industries Inc.
131	MB	Molecular Biosystems
132	MLI	Mueller Industries
133	MM	Mutual Risk Management
134	NBTY	NBTY Inc.
135	NFO	NFO Worldwide Inc.
136	NLCS	National Computer Systems
137	NATI	National Instruments
138	NDC	Natl Data
139	NATR	Nature's Sunshine Prod
140	NAUT	Nautica Enterprises
141	NEB	New England Bus. Svc.
142	NVX	North American Vaccine
143	NVLS	Novellus Systems
144	NOVN	Noven Pharmaceuticals
145	ORLY	O'Reilly Automotive
146	OAK	Oak Indus(New)
147	ORB	Orbital Sciences Corp.
148	ORG	Organogenesis, Inc.
149	OCA	Orthodontic Centers of America
150	OMI	Owens & Minor
151	PCMS	P-COM Inc.
152	PRXL	PAREXEL International
153	PSUN	Pacific Sunwear of California
154	PDCO	Patterson Dental
155	PDX	Pediatrix Medical Group
156	PPDI	Pharmaceutical Product Dev.
157	PLAB	Photronics, Inc.
158	PIR	Pier 1 Imports
159	PTX	Pillowtex Corp
160	PIOG	Pioneer Group
161	PSQL	Platinum Software
162	PLXS	Plexus Corp
163	PPP	Pogo Producing
164	PII	Polaris Industries
165	PPD	Pre-Paid Legal Svcs.
166	PMB	Premier Bancshares
167	PRGS	Progress Software
168	QCSB	Queens County Bancorp
169	RJF	Raymond James Finl
170	RBC	Regal-Beloit Corp.
171	RGIS	Regis Corp.
172	RCGI	Renal Care Group
173	RSND	Resound Corp
174	RESP	Respironics Inc
175	RFH	Richfood Hldgs.
176	ROP	Roper Industries
177	SEIC	SEI Corp.
178	ST	SPS Technologies
179	SFSK	Safeskin Corp.
180	SANM	Sanmina Corp
181	SEQU	Sequus Pharmaceutical
182	SVE	Service Experts, Inc.
183	SHN	Shoney's Inc.
184	SWD	Shorewood Packaging
185	SOL	Sola International
186	SJK	St. John Knits

EXHIBIT 11-2   Stock components of the S&P/BARRA SmallCap 600 Growth Index (*Continued*).

```
187  SMRT    Stein Mart
188  SWC     Stillwater Mining Co.
189  RGR     Sturm Ruger
190  TNL     Technitrol, Inc.
191  TSCC    Technology Solutions
192  TALK    Tel-Save.Com, Inc.
193  TLXN    Telxon Corp
194  WATR    Tetra Tech
195  COO     The Cooper Companies
196  THRT    TheraTech Inc
197  TBL     Timberland Co Cl'A'
198  TG      Tredegar Indus
199  TRY     Triarc Cos Cl'A'
200  TNO     True North Communications
201  TRST    TrustCo Bank Corp NY
202  TBI     Tuboscope Inc.
203  UBS     U.S. Bioscience
204  USTC    U.S. Trust Corp.
205  USAD    USA Detergents
206  USTB    UST Corp.
207  UBSI    United Bancshares, Inc.
208  VISX    VISX Inc
209  VCI     Valassis Communication
210  VLNC    Valence Technology
211  VST     Vanstar Corp.
212  VNTV    Vantive Corp.
213  VTSS    Vitesse Semiconductor
214  WDFC    W D-40 Co
215  WONE    Westwood One, Inc.
216  WTNY    Whitney Holding
217  WKR     Whittaker Corp
218  WHIT    Whittman-Hart Inc.
219  WFMI    Whole Foods Market
220  WSM     Williams-Sonoma Inc.
221  WWW     Wolverine World Wide
222  XYLN    Xylan Corp.
223  ZBRA    Zebra Technologies'A'
```

RELATIVE PERFORMANCE OF GROWTH AND VALUE STOCKS

Table 11-3 shows that growth significantly beat value among large stocks over the last five years, but even after the worst relative performance of any previous three-year period, value still edged out growth over the very long term. Over the past 24 years, the S&P/BARRA 500 Value index edged out its growth counterpart by a 1 percentage point margin.

But in the 1990s, small-company growth has beaten value, right? The answer is not as clear-cut as you might think. Small-company growth stocks did better for the year ending September 30, 1999, but the value portion of the S&P SmallCap 600 still outperformed the growth composite over the last three and five years.

Value has beaten growth over the long run because the average investor tends to overestimate the persistence of fast earnings growth. Sooner or later, even the fastest-growing companies slow down, and their P/Es suffer.

TABLE 11-3   S&P/BARRA Value versus Growth returns, 1975–1999.

Index	1 yr	3 yr	5 yr	10 yr	24 yr
600 Value	13.6%	12.5%	15.5%	NA	NA
600	17.5	9.4	13.8	NA	NA
600 Growth	20.9	6.0	11.7	NA	NA
400 Value	10.0	13.5	15.9	NA	NA
400	25.5	17.8	18.6	NA	NA
400 Growth	42.9	22.2	21.1	NA	NA
500 Value	21.5	19.1	20.7	14.4%	17.1%
500	27.8	25.1	25.0	16.8	16.8
500 Growth	33.4	30.6	29.1	18.9	16.1

NOTE: These are annual returns through September 30, 1998.

All too often, the P/Es of growth stocks reflect typically higher estimated forward 12-month earnings growth rather than more conservative 3- to 5-year growth rates. Hence, the damage to the P/E ratio is often greater over time than the positive impact of continued earnings expansion. (Later chapters revisit this phenomenon.).

In the 1990s, growth stocks have been helped by the extended decline in interest rates. As we have previously seen, when interest rates drop, the value of future earnings goes up. This is better for growth stocks, which have more of their earnings value based on the out years than do value stocks. Value typically does well when interest rates are rising, and much better during bear markets triggered by recessions, when earnings of most companies decline. Since growth stocks usually have higher betas, they drop more in a protracted market fall.

The other big factor helping growth stocks during the 1990s has been the increasing fearlessness of investors to accept risk in exchange for potentially higher investment returns. By 1999, most investors had never experienced a double-digit decline in the S&P 500 during a calendar year—you would have had to go back to 1974 to have experienced the pain first hand. This fearlessness is apt to continue until the penalties of greater risk taking become all too real.

But even during these go-go years, small cap value stocks still did better than growth equities. Despite these truly halcyon years for the American economy, most small growth companies do not fulfill their promise. Larger, more established growth firms, however, are better bets because they have already succeeded in pulling away from the field. The most apt analogy is of many hardwood seedlings germinating and then bursting out of the ground, nature's new issues. They grow to a certain height in the shade of their much more mature predecessors, but very few become saplings—successful, growing midcap stocks—and ever fewer still truly reach the sun to continue growing for many years to come.

Ultimately, given how close the returns have been over the years, your decision to concentrate on value or growth should primarily be based on your own psychological makeup. It is more important to play to your intuitive strengths, so you should never work in an investment universe that is not to your liking. If growth stocks excite you, your acumen and intuition could certainly help you to beat the market with a growth-stock portfolio. The same can be true for value. No preference? Do a mix of both. The GARP approach espoused in this book is appropriate for appraising the shares of both growth and value companies.

C H A P T E R

12

HOW TO BUY A GROWTH STOCK

S THE PREVIOUS chapter shows, it is somewhat more difficult to beat the market buying small-cap growth stocks. However, GARP investment tools are just as useful in picking attractively priced growth companies. This chapter applies a number of these strategies to the selection of growth stocks. This chapter emphasizes three basic principles:

1.   Buy stocks with price/earnings (P/E) ratios that are less than the three- to five-year projected earnings growth rate.
2.   Invest in industries that are just coming into favor, not ones that are already in favor.
3.   Combine these two screens with Graham and Dodd's test for relative value.

Why the emphasis on P/E-to-growth rate and the Graham and Dodd formula? Because *in order to create a portfolio of stocks that can beat the market, it is essential to emphasize investment candidates with the potential for P/E expansion as well as the capacity to grow earnings at an above-average rate.* The rest of this chapter illustrates each of these investment concepts.

Let's start with the first rule. The key to beating the market is investing in companies with above-average earnings growth rates, when their stocks are trading at P/E multiples at or below the market average. The most

213

important thing to remember when looking at stocks of fast-growing companies is to pick those that trade at a P/E that is less than their estimated three- to five-year earnings growth rate. The gravest mistake a growth-stock investor can make is assuming that very high sales and near-term earnings growth is sustainable. This is why we emphasize that the *three- to five-year projected earnings growth rate* should be used to assess corporate growth.

A reasonable goal when buying growth stocks is to choose those with the potential to generate a 40 percent return within 18 to 24 months. To achieve this sort of appreciation, earnings must grow while the P/E remains stable or slightly expands. Of course, not all growth stocks selected by the value and GARP methodologies mentioned in this chapter will meet the aggressive 40 percent return target, so the overall return of your portfolio will likely be lower. However, you should not buy a growth stock unless you think that such returns could be achieved.

The target turnover of a growth-stock portfolio should be anywhere from 50 to 100 percent a year, meaning that more than half of the stocks in the portfolio will probably be replaced each year. This is higher turnover than a typical value-stock portfolio, but growth stocks are more likely to disappoint, requiring more frequent replacement. If your portfolio is doing well, there is no need to aggressively change names. If you find that your stocks have underperformed by a wide margin for at least a quarter, you should certainly analyze why that has been the case and at least consider replacing some issues. But, as a rule, let your profits run until they are overvalued, and sell your mistakes as soon as you recognize them.

THE GROWTH PARADOX

In his book *What Works on Wall Street* (McGraw-Hill, 1997), Jim O'Shaughnessy provides confirmation of a long-running, and surprising, observation: Fast-growing companies are not the best investments—particularly the smallest, fastest-growing firms. Table 12-1 tells the story. O'Shaughnessy tested two portfolios, the S&P 500 and all stocks in the Compustat universe, from 1954 to 1994. The results noted in Table 12-1 are for the smaller-cap, all-stocks portfolio.

O'Shaughnessy's work stopped before 1998, when growth stocks did better than their value counterparts by a staggering 28 percentage point margin. Nonetheless, even the inclusion of this outlier year would not tip the balance in favor of growth as measured by the strategies in Table 12-1.

The sad truth is that high flyers—the stocks of the most rapidly growing companies—are generally not good investments. As can be seen from Table 12-1, stocks with strong growth characteristics such as high one-year

TABLE 12-1   Returns of the S&P compustat all-stocks universe, 1954–1994.

Strategy	$10,000 Becomes	Compound Annual Return	Standard Deviation	Sharpe Ratio*
High 1-yr relative strength	$1,905,842	14.0%	30.3%	41
All stocks	1,091,933	12.5	19.8	43
High ROE	968,912	12.1	26.4	36
Large stocks, > $ billion	643,667	11.0	15.88	41
High 1-yr EPS gain	571,829	10.7	26.9	31
High profit margin	476,182	10.1	21.2	31
High 5-yr EPS gain	353,446	9.3	27.1	26
High P/E	254,601	8.4	27.1	23
High stock price/book value	178,166	7.5	29.0	20
High stock price/cash flow	138,791	6.8	27.8	17
High stock price/sales	50,910	4.2	27.6	8

* The Sharpe ratio is an indication of relative risk, which measures the annual return of a stock minus the risk-free rate of interest. The results are then divided by the standard deviation of returns over the years studied. A high score is good, and means a strategy provided excellent returns without a substantially higher variation in annual returns. Strategies with good returns but higher variations from one year to the next will rank lower than others that have the same annual return but a lower variation.

EPS gain, high P/E, and high profit margin all did worse than the average return for all stocks. The only exception among all these growth factors was relative strength. The chances are good that you will beat the market if you invest in stocks that rose strongly over the last year. But even these strong relative-strength stocks did better when combined with value factors, not the growth factors just listed. Exhibit 12-1 at the end of this chapter presents a list of stocks screened by this first principle.

Now that you know that the direct approach—screening for specific growth factors—will not work, can you really make money buying growth stocks? Despite the evidence that *taken as a group, growth stocks underperform over the very long term,* by using a variety of relative valuation methods *you can move the odds back in your favor.* One normally would not use the word *contrarian* in the same breath as *growth stock,* but that is exactly what we propose. The following strategy is meant to coax into view equities that are reasonably priced, *despite* their good growth prospects.

BEING A GROWTH-STOCK CONTRARIAN

Many growth-stock investors believe they will find gold at the end of the rainbow as long as they are early in discovering a new trend. Recent examples include steamboat casinos located where gambling has been newly legalized, natural vitamins, computer games, and the need for year-2000 computer software solutions. Depending on your timing, you would have lost in almost every case while the general market was zooming to new highs. That's because investment bankers are usually way ahead of you. They see the possibilities years in advance and are in early via venture-capital investments in start-up companies. They also spread the extremely high ownership risks across a much larger number of deals than you can.

The stocks of companies in these emerging industries typically hit their highs within three to six months of their IPOs. They are often good trades at the IPO price, but after that, they are generally horrible investments. It is never wise to get on a surfboard just as the beach approaches. This is what many investors did when they bought shares of companies in these industries just after their IPOs.

In short, be practical, not visionary. Avoid the really hot, just-emerging industries. Instead, take a step back. Extensive work at Standard & Poor's indicates that the most attractive groups are those that are *not* in favor. And remember: A company does not have to be in the hottest market to be part of a trend. Indeed, buying stocks in industries that are currently in vogue is usually a sure-fire way to underperform. What counts is participating in an industry that is moving in the *right direction,* but which has not been completely discovered.

Boston Chicken was deemed the best way to invest in the trend to healthy fast food. But when it was in the news, the stock was overvalued. Instead, one could have gotten an *Investors Business Daily* that contained a list of companies in the restaurant industry. There, one could have discovered some firms such as Starbucks or Brinker International (a franchisee of Boston Chicken) that were not as well known, but that could benefit from the same trend. In late 1994, Brinker International was trading at 24 times its estimated 1994 earnings and had a projected 3- to 5-year EPS growth rate of 24 percent. On the other hand, Boston Chicken, after 1 year of being public, was still trading at 59 times its projected 1994 EPS—much higher than its estimated growth rate of 40 percent. Even though Boston Chicken was growing faster, the chances were good that if the concept really delivered, Brinker would be the better stock.

Table 12-2 was drawn from data as of April 22, 1997, a time when interest rates were rising and stock prices were at least temporarily on the defensive. The groups to target would have been those shown in boldface. These are industries that enjoyed rising relative performance over the previous nine months but that are still well below their long-term highs.

The fundamentals of the industries recommended in Table 12-2 may not have been great, but, barring a recession, they were likely to improve. Consider where the economy is and where it might be 6 to 12 months from now. If interest rates are rising (which is generally bad for banks and the like), it is probably not a good idea to invest in financial stocks.

The list in Table 12-2 is fairly representative of our "underdog but improving" methodology. The industries selected are not necessarily the fastest-growing ones, nor are they likely to be the most hyped at the moment. They *are* likely to be in turnaround, and where a number of IPOs could appear in another year. Exhibit 12-2 at the end of the chapter presents a list of stocks screened by this second principle.

GOING FOR THE SAFEST SMALL-CAP AND MIDCAP PURE PLAYS

Take another look at the industries in boldface in Table 12-2. Growth-oriented investors might be drawn to semiconductor stocks or computer software issues even though the group is not cheap by our primary signal, because they are trading at P/E levels below their historical levels relative to the S&P 500. We would recommend, however, that you consider growth segments of industries that are just turning around. For example, in homebuilding, that might be manufactured housing; or, in publishing, you might consider Internet plays or Spanish-language magazines. Table 12-3 provides some examples.

Within these fastest-growing segments, pick the stock of the leading company in that niche as the first company to research. You are likely to find that most of these companies will be growing at rates well above the average for the S&P 500 and their overall industry, but are trading at lower P/E multiples than the average high flier because their industry is not fully in favor.

Here are two examples. Restaurant stocks were out of favor in 1995 because of the perception that the United States is *overstored*—that is, that there are too many restaurants chasing too few customers. For this reason, industrywide same-store revenue growth had lagged inflation over the previous 12 months. In addition, profit margins had suffered because of an increase in the minimum wage. There were also signs that gains from recent declines in food costs, particularly beef, could be coming to an end. Hence, near-term earnings expectations were cut for many restaurant chains.

In 1996, the average restaurant stock actually fell even though earnings rose slightly. But this is because the aforementioned problems affected only the large fast-food chains. These restaurants were also hurt by the aging of the population—this older crowd typically has more money to spend, and prefers to be waited on. But this provided growth opportunities for chains such as Consolidated Products (Steak 'n' Shake), Applebee's, and Outback Steakhouse. Mostly because the overall industry fell out of favor, and because it experienced a 1.1 percent decline in same-store sales, Outback Steakhouse's common shares fell from 35 to 27 in 1996, while the S&P 500 rose 23 per-

TABLE 12-2 Relative performance of stock groups.

Sector and Group	Relative Performance			Historical Average			Relative P/E		Major Stock
	Current	9-mo Average	3-mo Change	Low	High	1997	Average	Beta	
Basic materials	85	NA	NA	NA	NA	0.89	1.24	0.32	
Aluminum	**94**	**91**	**-3**	**83**	**112**	**0.97**	**0.81**	**0.72**	**Alcoa**
Iron and steel	**76**	**75**	**8**	**70**	**117**	**0.72**	**0.92**	**0.38**	**USX**
Capital goods	100	NA	NA	NA	NA	1.10	1.94	0.80	
Machinery, diversified	101	99	7	82	112	0.81	1.32	0.73	Caterpillar
Trucks and parts	102	98	3	81	111	1.11	1.55	0.85	Navistar
Communications services	81	NA	NA	NA	NA	0.86	1.78	1.01	
Consumer cyclical	90	NA	NA	NA	NA	0.78	1.42	0.76	
Building materials	100	97	3	85	115	0.73	1.15	1.11	Owens-Corning
Homebuilding	**87**	**82**	**10**	**70**	**124**	**0.62**	**1.25**	**1.66**	**Centex**
Publishing	**95**	**88**	**12**	**87**	**115**	**1.36**	**1.36**	**1.09**	**Times Mirror**
Consumer staples	107	NA	NA	NA	NA	1.40	1.30	0.93	
Beverages, alcoholic	**102**	**98**	**7**	**91**	**121**	**1.22**	**0.90**	**1.16**	**Seagram**
Beverages, nonalcoholic	115	112	1	99	125	1.88	1.15	1.24	Coca-Cola
Distributors, food and health	**89**	**85**	**8**	**90**	**111**	**0.99**	**1.15**	**0.62**	**Fleming Cos.**
Entertainment	**93**	**84**	**10**	**86**	**123**	**2.76**	**1.60**	**1.00**	**Disney**
Foods	110	100	18	95	120	1.29	1.03	0.89	ConAgra
Household products, nondurable	124	110	17	94	118	1.40	1.00	1.04	Procter & Gamble
Personal care	121	118	1	93	119	1.70	1.14	1.20	Gillette
Restaurants	**88**	**86**	**15**	**94**	**118**	**1.17**	**1.02**	**1.44**	**McDonald's**
Retail, drug stores	116	107	20	93	114	1.28	1.07	1.47	Walgreen

Tobacco	114	100	14	89	129	0.83	0.73	0.69	Philip Morris
Energy	100	103	−3	89	107	1.03	1.17	0.85	
Oil, international integrated	103	102	1	90	111	1.03	0.78	0.90	Exxon
Financials	111	109	1	89	112	0.76	0.72	1.01	
Financial, diversified	106	105	6	94	116	0.80	0.73	1.49	Fannie Mae
Insurance brokers	101	94	7	82	116	0.94	1.24	1.04	Marsh&McLennan
Insurance, life and health	104	99	10	88	118	0.78	0.63	1.03	Aetna
Insurance, multiline	113	105	7	87	115	0.80	0.92	1.01	CIGNA
Insurance, property-casualty	112	101	12	89	111	0.76	0.84	0.84	Allstate
Investment, banks and brokerages	116	109	8	94	124	0.64	0.66	1.63	Merrill Lynch
Savings and loans	126	110	14	75	128	0.86	1.07	1.40	H.F. Ahmanson
Health care	109	NA	NA	NA	NA	1.32	1.30	1.40	
Health care, diversified	117	110	11	93	116	1.30	1.14	1.06	Johnson & Johnson
Health care, major pharmaceuticals	115	109	10	92	121	1.39	1.11	0.91	Merck
Technology	108	110	−17	91	115	1.21	1.50	0.44	
Computers, software and services	125	122	−7	93	124	2.00	1.52	1.15	Microsoft
Electronics, instrumentation	**98**	**97**	**−3**	**83**	**122**	**1.09**	**1.24**	**1.14**	**Tektronix**
Electronics, semiconductors	154	137	−37	81	138	1.07	1.33	1.09	Intel
Transportation	91	82	−2	90	108	0.73	1.22	1.27	
Air freight	113	104	1	79	115	1.10	1.15	0.46	Federal Express
Airlines	**88**	**87**	**3**	**81**	**115**	**0.56**	**1.25**	**1.30**	**AMR**
Truckers	**78**	**67**	**8**	**77**	**114**	**0.91**	**1.45**	**0.82**	**Con Freightways**
Utilities	81	84	2	88	108	0.68	0.78	0.80	

NOTE: Data as of April 22, 1997. Best groups to target shown in boldface.

TABLE 12-3   Subsegments of industries.

Industry	Faster-growing Segment	Representative Company
Aluminum		
Iron and steel	Compressed metal	Sinter Metals
Homebuilding	Manufactured housing	Clayton Homes
Publishing	Electronic and print publications on computer technology	Gartner Group
Beverages, alcoholic	Craft brewing	Red Hook Ale
Distributors, food and health	Health product distribution	Cardinal Health
Entertainment	The Internet	Yahoo!
Restaurants	Sit-down restaurants for older crowd	Outback Steakhouse
Electronics, instrumentation	Laser equipment	Spectra-Physics
Airlines	Discount regionals	Southwest Airlines
Truckers	Transportation logistics	U.S. Freightways

cent. Yet per-share earnings were up 22 percent that year, on the strength of new store openings. With additional units also opening in 1997, analysts expected earnings to advance another 17 percent. Over the first 9 months of 1998, the shares jumped to 42, and then slid back below 25 when the overall market corrected before recovering to the mid-30s. In the first quarter of 1999, the shares jumped another 40 percent. But even at that price, the company was buying back shares. Given the lack of investor expectations during 1998, the downside on this growth stock was quite limited.

Consider another attractive subcategory: that of laser equipment within the larger electronics instrumentation industry. The laser business had been growing by more than 15 percent, and Spectra-Physics—a leading maker of laser systems—had seen more than 30 percent growth during the previous two years. Sales and earnings growth over the next three to five years was likely to slow down, but still be higher than those of the S&P 500. Despite these favorable trends, the stock at the end of October 1998 was trading at just 7, down from its IPO price of 10. Earnings faltered due to the declining value of the dollar, the recession in Japan, and the downturn in the semiconductor industry. Those investors that expected 30 percent growth to continue were surely disappointed. But current growth expectations are much more reasonable and achievable. By October 1999, the stock had recovered to 12 but was still trading at a significant discount to the overall market and its long-term growth rate.

We emphasize the bigger players within a niche, because larger companies have sustainable cash flow that helps them to stay on top of technological trends over the long haul. They also have more diversified product lines, which helps them to even out product transitions in a specific product line. A smaller company selling just a single product may be able to show very high sales and earnings growth if it hits the sweet spot in an emerging application, but it can easily falter when other firms leapfrog its technology. Many small companies never recover. Larger firms have enough diverse revenue sources to even out the rough spots.

INVESTING IN GROWTH STOCKS THE GRAHAM AND DODD WAY

As has been pointed out before, once it is established that a company will exhibit strong growth, there is the more difficult task of deciding whether the current stock price already reflects such growth prospects. We have reviewed a number of ways to find the fair value of a stock, but there is still another method you can use.

The following Graham and Dodd stock-valuation formula was introduced in 1954. Like the other valuation tools we have reviewed, it can be used on either growth or value stocks. Graham and Dodd's equations will also help narrow the field when stocks are generally overvalued because fewer stocks pass the screen. Using this equation you will learn that *the key to successful growth-stock investing is not picking the biggest winners, but avoiding the big losers.* We think that this Graham and Dodd valuation tool is also an excellent complement to GARP investment strategies.

Stated simply, Graham and Dodd worked out an equation that measures the relative value of stocks against the fixed-income markets. The idea is that you, as a stock investor, should be receiving *at least* what you would have gotten in the bond market, and then some.

Here's the general formula:

$$\text{Share price} = \frac{\text{next year's EPS} \times [8.5 + (2 \times \text{annual growth rate})] \times 4.4}{\text{expected long-term AAA corporate bond yield}}$$

Graham and Dodd used long-term corporate bonds as the fixed-income proxy, and in the preceding equation, the 8.5 equals the normal return of corporate bonds over an extended period of time. The 4.4 equals the average dividend yield of stocks, which is then divided by the corporate bond

yield. By using this equation, Graham and Dodd created a model for valuing growth stocks relative to corporate debt and other growth stocks.

All this seems very complex, so let's try an example. Tractor Supply
runs retail stores catering to the needs of farmers and would-be farmers.
The consensus estimate for next year's earnings (1999) was $1.90. The 3-
to 5-year growth rate was estimated at 20 percent. The existing expectation
was for long-term corporate bond yields to average about 6.3 percent in
1999. Now let's plug these three numbers into the equation and see what
happens:

$$\text{Share price} = 1.90 \times [8.5 + (2 \times 20)] \times \frac{4.4}{6.3}$$

$$= 1.90 \times 48.5 \times 0.70$$
$$= 65$$

Stock price: 26

Why did the stock look so cheap? Although not in the formula, the
shares were trading at a P/E ratio of 16, when the average for the S&P 500
was about 30. The P/E was also quite low when considering the company's
growth rate. The 20 percent growth rate was quite high compared to the 11
percent average for companies in the S&P 500, and high relative to the
stock's P/E. This Graham and Dodd equation captures both of these undervalued concepts.

Now let's look at other stocks—Computer Task Group, a growing
provider of information technology solutions; Outback Steakhouse, which
runs the Outback and Carabba restaurant chains; and Microsoft.

Computer Task Group (November 1998)

$$\text{Share price} = 1.75 \times [8.5 + (2 \times 29)] \times \frac{4.4}{6.3}$$

$$= 1.75 \times 66.5 \times 0.70$$
$$= 81$$

Stock price: 30

Outback Steakhouse (November 1998)

$$\text{Share Price} = 2.30 \times [8.5 + (2 \times 19)] \times \frac{4.4}{6.3}$$

$$= 2.30 \times 46.5 \times 0.70$$

$$= 75$$
Stock price: 36

Microsoft (November 1998)

$$\text{Share price} = 3.10 \times [8.5 + (2 \times 23)] \times \frac{4.4}{6.3}$$

$$= 3.10 \times 54.5 \times 0.70$$
$$= 118$$
Stock price: 114

As of October 1998, growth stocks were just coming out of a severe correction. Three of the four stocks looked very cheap. In mid-1997, three of four stocks also appeared undervalued. Here is how they looked:

Tractor Supply (June 1997)

$$\text{Share price} = 1.95 \times [8.5 + (2 \times 15)] \times \frac{4.4}{7.5}$$

$$= 1.95 \times 38.5 \times 0.59$$
$$= 44$$
Stock price, June 30, 1997: 24

Computer Task Group (June 1997)

$$\text{Share price} = 1.20 \times [8.5 + (2 \times 29)] \times \frac{4.4}{7.5}$$

$$= 1.20 \times 66.5 \times 0.59$$
$$= 47$$
Stock price, June 30, 1997: 38

Outback Steakhouse (June 1997)

$$\text{Share price} = 1.95 \times [8.5 + (2 \times 24)] \times \frac{4.4}{7.5}$$

$$= 1.95 \times 56.5 \times 0.59$$
$$= 67$$
Stock price, June 30, 1997: 24

Microsoft (June 1997)

$$\text{Share price} = 1.95 \times [8.5 + (2 \times 23)] \times \frac{4.4}{7.5}$$

$$= 1.95 \times 54.5 \times 0.59$$
$$= 63$$

Stock price, June 30, 1997: 83

Microsoft's long-term earnings growth rate must be significantly greater than analysts believe will be the case. Microsoft did confound the experts in 1997 on the strength of the successful introduction of Windows NT, and again in 1998 with Windows 98. But Microsoft is now a $15-billion company. It would need to dominate at least one, if not two additional very large, major markets (i.e., Internet delivery and content, enterprise network and e-commerce enabling software) for the shares to continue to appreciate at these above-average rates.

On the other hand, Tractor Supply still looks cheap—in fact, cheaper than it was in mid-1997. Although their results are somewhat subject to the

---

Check List for the Growth-Stock Investor

Do	*Why*
Use Graham and Dodd and GARP valuation tools.	Helps to avoid overpaying for growth.
Concentrate on industries just coming into favor.	Potential P/E expansion and/or positive earnings surprises.
Look for stocks with P/Es on forward 12-month EPS below projected long-term earnings growth rate.	Helps to avoid overpaying for growth.
Remember that reasonable value is more important than very fast growth.	Most growth stocks do not beat market.
Buy only companies that are already profitable.	Helps to avoid big losers.
Remember that momentum works best with other value measures.	Small cap stocks with very strong momentum often get that way via manipulation.

vagaries of the weather, the company has shown higher revenues and earnings in each of the last five years. Tractor Supply and Outback Steakhouse appear to offer the best upside opportunities from here.

Exhibit 12-3 at the end of the chapter presents a list of stocks screened by this third principle.

SMALL-STOCK MOMENTUM INVESTING: THE FIRST REFUGE FOR SCOUNDRELS

Small growth stocks are the favored stomping ground of momentum investors. We view momentum trading as the purchase and sale of stock purely based on price movement without regard to underlying business fundamentals. There may be no P/E in the newspaper, no S&P stock report, nor any other information readily available other than what the broker tells you, but "the chart looks great."

Momentum traders represent the hot money in the stock market. These are what we call *first-in, first-out (FIFO)* stocks. That is, the first one in on the way up and the first one out on the way down can make a killing. Unfortunately, anyone paying retail for their shares (buying in the open market through a broker) is unlikely to be one of those winning investors. Momentum stocks are also a favorite haunt for stock manipulators because they play on investor desires to participate in a particular industry with bright growth prospects. There is seldom anything underneath the surface.

The *greater fool* theory, which holds that in a rising market there is usually a greater fool out there willing to buy an overvalued stock from you, often does work during speculative periods. Thus, a lot of money can be made quite quickly via momentum trading. There are occasional periods when there are enough naive investors willing to bid up stocks to unreasonable values. But owners of momentum stocks must be very careful to bail out quickly should demand for speculative issues turn down, lest they give back what they have earned, and more. Gains from momentum invest-

---

Because growth stocks have not performed as well as their value counterparts over the past 45 years, great care must be taken when evaluating them. Overpaying, even for a good company, can keep you from beating the market. Certainly Snapple and Baby Superstores had bright futures when they went public, and the companies more or less met investor expectations, but both stocks traded down six months beyond their IPOs.

ing are also generally short-term, which means they are taxed as ordinary income.

Strong momentum stocks with little weak fundamentals are the first refuge of scoundrels. These are the stocks that give Wall Street a bad name and can deep-six portfolio returns. These stocks are not necessarily frauds, but they are generally trading far above their intrinsic value by any measure, and often get there through unscrupulous hyping by unsavory broker-dealers and individuals through Internet chat. Momentum investing also generates a lot of trades, which will keep your broker happy. But churned portfolios usually do not generate very high returns.

The main point here is that *you should, in general, avoid pure momentum investing when buying small-cap stocks.* Stock charts can be useful when used in tandem with fundamental analysis, but never alone.

Let's review an example: In the wake of the TWA crash off Long Island in early 1996, there was a sudden upsurge of interest in airport security devices. Suddenly, Comparator Systems, a tiny company trading on the NASDAQ, announced that it had developed a new device in this area. The firm had almost no employees, and no working model of the device. The stock promptly went from $0.06 to $2.00. What investors had not bothered to notice was that the company had less than $250,000 in assets, most of which were intangible in nature, which meant they did not really exist at all. Indeed, as soon as the SEC got wind of this, it quickly realized that the company did not even fit NASDAQ listing requirements. When trading resumed, the stock quickly went back to $0.06.

Who were the winners in this sad tale? The folks at the company and at La Jolla Securities, the small brokerage firm that was hyping it. La Jolla had been quietly accumulating the shares at or below $0.06 in anticipation of working the stock when the time was right. It was so successful, however, that it attracted the attention of the SEC, and was closed down.

Need another example? At about the same time in 1996, Diana Corporation, a company that had been trading on the New York Stock Exchange, decided that it was going to sell its money-losing meat-packing business and invest in a start-up company that was introducing a new computer network switch. A multimillion-dollar investment was made in the firm. Diana had only about 4 million shares outstanding.

At year end 1995, its stock closed at 25⅜, which was already well above its historical range, despite the absence of any profits. But when the market got wind of the new network product (albeit with no prototype), Diana promptly rose to more than 125. At that price, the company was valued at more than $600 million. Meanwhile, a deal to sell the meat-packing unit for less than $20 million had fallen through for lack of financing. Could a start-up company in the highly competitive networking field with no working product and no revenues have been valued by a reputable underwriter at $600 million? No way. Yet that is exactly what investors did. The company never generated much in the way of revenues or earnings from the networking product, and about a year after hitting an all-time high, the stock was delisted by the exchange. The last trade was at 4.

The Software 2000 Hype

Late in 1996, headlines were proliferating in the business press about the huge problems expected to befall computers when the clock strikes 2000. The problem was real—billions of dollars have since been spent on the problem. But most of the money has been expended with large service organizations and mainframe software companies such as Computer Associates, EDS, and IBM. There were a few small, viable companies that announced efforts to develop "software 2000" solutions, such as KeaneTSR and Viasoft, that had investment value even without such prospects, but there were also a slew of tiny software companies with little operating history that were unlikely to be successful at exploiting the year-2000 opportunity, and that had been hyped to investors as major software 2000 plays. What is so amazing is that investors could place such a high value on these firms knowing that the business would disappear in only three years.

One of these companies was a small computer concern named Zitel. At the end of 1996, Zitel was losing money. Its major product was marketed through IBM, but those royalties were on a down slide. The company had indicated that the trend was irreversible. Hence, total revenues were dropping, as were earnings. The hype was that it would soon start reselling software 2000 solutions created by a 33-percent-owned subsidiary. The problem, however, was that the software was still in development and no sales had been made to date. Nonetheless, the stock hit a peak of 72, and Zitel had a market capitalization of $1.1 billion in early 1997. This meant, assuming Zitel's main business had little residual value, that investors had placed a value of $3.2 billion on its new start-up subsidiary, which had no revenues, no earnings, and a business that would effectively disappear in three to four years anyway. Could anyone reasonably expect this small company to generate even $100 million over the life of the product?

Similar stories can be told about other software 2000 plays. Acceler8 is a provider of legacy software for the aging DEC VAX and UNIX software platforms. Its president is a former stockbroker. Prior to a public offering through the underwriting firm of Janco Partners, it had traded in the pennies on the Bulletin Board. Even though it had fewer than 25 employees, it announced a major software 2000 solution. It earned $0.18 in fiscal 1996, and just $0.01 for the three months ended in January 1997. The sole estimate that existed for fiscal 1997 was $0.27, which did not appear to be very realistic. Nonetheless, as of April 1997, the stock was trading at 13, and had a market capitalization of over $85 million. At its all-time high of 30⅝ shortly after an October 1996 stock offering, the company had a market capitalization of more than $200 million, although its revenues were under $5 million.

Last, there is Data Dimensions. Unlike the other two stocks, it does have sales and earnings. Nonetheless, in 1996, sales were just $15 million. Adjusted for a 3-for-1 stock split in early 1997, per-share earnings were $0.09. The company had never generated revenues of more than $6.2 million in any of the prior five years. But when it announced that it had received a contract from MCI to assess its software 2000 compliance requirements, the company's stock peaked at 40¾. That gave it a market capitalization of over $500 million, and a very high P/E of 394 times trailing 12-month EPS.

As Table 12-4 illustrates, an equal-weighted portfolio of these three stocks would have badly underperformed the small-cap universe over the following year. Six months later, the results were dramatically worse. As the millennium approached, all three stocks were trading at under $2.

INVESTING IN EMERGING COUNTRY MARKETS

In the early 1980s, the Association of Investment Management Research (AIMR) began recommending that a diversified investment portfolio for a U.S. investor contain at least a small amount of foreign stock exposure. Today, most advisors suggest that 10 to 20 percent of a U.S. investor's portfolio could justifiably be placed in foreign equities. This means that for a 20-stock portfolio that is equal-weighted, 2 to 4 large ADRs or closed-end country funds should be included.

TABLE 12-4 Hyped Software 2000 stocks.

Stock	1996 Price Range	Price 12/31/96	Market Cap, $ Million	P/E	Forward 12-mo EPS, Estimated	Forward 12-mo P/E	Actual 1997 EPS	Price 12/31/97	12-mo Return	Price 6/30/98
Acceler8	30⅝–7¼	19⁹⁄₁₆	129	Def.	$0.27	72	$0.19	27	38%	12¼
Data Dimensions	18⁹⁄₁₆–4¼	11⅞	135	132	0.67	18	Nil	17¼	46	17¹⁄₁₆
Zitel	72⅞–4¹¹⁄₁₆	44⅜	675	222	NA	NA	1.23	9½	–79	4¼
S&P 500									33	
S&P SmallCap 600									26	

Check List of What Not to Do When Buying Growth Stocks	
Don't	*Why Not*
Invest in the hottest industry.	P/E ratios will be at their highest for a generation.
Invest in pure plays in just-emerging, not-yet-profitable industries.	They are the first refuge of scoundrels.
Be visionary—instead, be practical.	Aim for companies with new technologies or services in existing industries that are available at reasonable prices.
Indiscriminately buy the fastest growing companies	The valuations are too high and the growth ultimately slows.

An interesting benefit of owning foreign stocks is that, by adding them to an investment portfolio, an extra return can be achieved without adding overall risk. This is because some foreign markets have very little correlation to what happens in the United States. Of course, the *individual* risks of owning such foreign stocks may still be high, even though some of that risk is counteracted by this diversity.

In theory, foreign stocks should also provide better overall returns because, like small stocks in the United States, investors need to be compensated for investing in financial instruments that have highly variable annual returns. Most mature foreign economies have generated stock market returns below those of the United States. The real action is in the emerging markets. There are many emerging countries that are experiencing faster economic growth, and there are now vibrant stock markets all over the globe. However, as good as some of these countries can be in providing above-average returns, they can also be highly volatile in the short term.

Foreign Stock Market Returns from Index Services

Most emerging countries have fragile political institutions. Revolutions are still possible even without a Marxist opposition. It is essential that these governments manage their economies so that the right balance is struck between a stable currency to attract foreign investors and improving the welfare of the general population. Ideological divisions may not be as severe, but ethnic ones still remain.

Emerging market economies can be very fragile as well. They may grow faster, but they will also be subject to more sudden and violent downdrafts. An investor must have a long investment horizon to withstand these anxiety-ridden downturns.

There is also currency risk. In addition to the occasional large currency breaks that occur from time to time (such as the Mexican peso devaluation of 1995), almost all emerging country currencies gradually depreciate against the dollar over time. Spectacular returns in the home currency may look anemic to a U.S. investor after currency conversion. Inflation exists in even the most successful emerging economies, such as China and Chile.

We recommend that investors focus on countries with stable political environments that are friendly to capitalist enterprise. There also should be a large middle class with more political clout than that of the underclass. Avoid countries that are still susceptible to ethnic or class conflict. For example, Brazil may have a bigger economic market than Chile or Argentina, but it also has a larger underclass that may never fully participate in a capitalist economic resurgence. The political and economic underpinnings for growth have recently been put into place, and it has finally managed to bring runaway inflation under control. A turnaround there could trigger large rewards, but the risks are also very high, especially now that the easy money has been made.

Once you are satisfied with the political and social environment, pick countries where GDP growth is greater than that of the United States, plus the home country's inflation rate. GDP should be rising fast enough to trigger earnings growth, which should compensate for any currency devaluation. For example, if Argentina's GDP is expected to expand 6 percent this year and that of the United States is expected to expand 3 percent,

There are some excellent information sources to help you in evaluating foreign stocks and funds. Two leading are *The Economist* and the *Financial Times.* Over the course of a year, *The Economist* offers in-depth features on individual countries. Each issue includes economic data on mature and emerging economies, including projected GDP and inflation rates. The *Financial Times,* based in London, provides background commentary on changing economic conditions around the globe. *Global Finance* offers recent country stock market results and shows how some large foreign stock investors are weighting their portfolios by country.

Argentina could be attractive to a U.S. investor if inflation there is not running at more than 3 percent above the U.S. rate of inflation.

Another good way to invest wisely in foreign economies and avoid paying the onerous up-front loads and commissions found in foreign company mutual funds is to buy one of the many closed-end global country funds that are already trading. Try to buy them when they are trading at least 10 percent below their asset values. (Country funds can be found in the exchange tables every day, but the *Wall Street Journal* and *The New York Times* list them together on Mondays. Included there are the funds' asset values and premiums/discounts-to-asset values based on the current stock prices.) A listing of closed-end regional and country funds is shown in Exhibit 12-4 at the end of the chapter.

When analyzing companies in emerging markets one should be keenly aware of a few things. First, an investor should look for earning that are in compliance with U.S. generally accepted accounting principles (GAAP). (U.S. GAAP results must be reported at least once a year by companies listed on the NYSE, ASE, and NASDAQ exchanges, either in an annual report or in the 20-F filing with the SEC.) Most of the disparities between home-country and U.S. GAAP reported results have to do with intangible assets. Without becoming too technical, this accounting difference can trigger big disparities in valuations. Table 12-5 illustrates how certain investment ratios of media ADRs looked according to local accounting and U.S. GAAP principles.

TABLE 12-5. Media ADR profit/earnings and profit/book value ratios by local and U.S. accounting principles.

Company (Country)	P/E Ratio Local	P/E Ratio U.S.	P/B Ratio Local	P/B Ratio U.S.
Carlton Communications (U.K.)	20.9	42.4	4.1	1.5
Grupo Radio Centro (Mexico)	18.4	20.1	5.2	5.6
Grupo Televisa (Mexico)	103.9	122.4	23.1	31.1
Hollinger (Canada)	33.2	30.9	1.8	3.1
News Corp. (Australia)	17.2	34.9	1.4	3.1
Polygram (Netherlands)	22.8	23.8	7.2	5.2
Quebecor (Canada)	15.2	17.1	1.6	NA
Reuters (U.K.)	27.3	31.5	12.6	9.5
Saatchi & Saatchi (U.K.)	45.6	NM	NM	NM

SOURCE: *Morningstar ADR Service, October 7, 1994, p. S2.*

EXHIBIT 12-1   Growth screen 1.

(From Standard & Poor's Stock Reports, *October 27, 1998. Copyright © 1998 by The McGraw-Hill Companies.)*

Search Expression	Passed	Total
EPS_5_Yr_Gr_Rate > 15	2166	2166
Return_on_Equity_-_Last_year_ > 17	1261	733
ROE_5yr_Avg > 17	955	368
Return_on_Assets_-_Last_year_ > 10	901	250
EPS_%_Change_FY1_/_FY0 > 25	2101	62
Search Results:		62

Ticker	Company Name	EPS Gr 5 Yr / PE	EPS 5 Yr Gr Rate	Return on Equity	Return on Equity 5 Yr Avg	Return on Assets	EPS % Change FY1 / FY0
VOD	Vodafone Group ADR	0.31	16.13	40.60	44.60	17.30	25.80
WLA	Warner-Lambert	0.38	22.12	32.10	32.80	11.40	40.40
WPI	Watson Pharmaceuticals	0.44	19.39	19.00	20.00	15.30	44.60
HD	Home Depot	0.45	21.35	17.10	17.90	11.20	35.10
KSS	Kohl's Corp	0.56	24.36	23.00	21.70	10.60	25.30
GPS	Gap Inc	0.57	21.58	27.50	27.00	18.20	43.10
MSFT	Microsoft Corp	0.57	35.86	41.20	34.30	28.20	29.30
AMGN	Amgen Inc	0.64	19.18	30.60	33.10	21.90	32.30
EMC	EMC Corp	0.64	29.50	26.80	34.80	18.60	38.50
BBBY	Bed Bath ,Beyond	0.70	30.27	30.10	30.90	19.50	29.40
CPWR	Compuware Corp	0.73	31.93	25.40	24.10	14.80	60.00
PSDI	Project Software ,Dvlp	0.78	22.77	17.20	20.40	12.40	25.20
DG	Dollar General	0.79	25.62	24.90	24.90	16.50	28.40
SFSK	Safeskin Corp	0.79	28.02	39.30	30.60	32.30	41.40
ASGN	On Assignment	0.80	29.43	24.70	26.50	21.50	29.30
BMCS	BMC Software	0.80	31.05	35.20	28.70	22.60	85.70
ACXM	Acxiom Corp	0.81	28.15	19.70	17.30	11.10	26.70
HMA	Health Management Assoc	0.85	28.48	22.10	21.70	16.40	25.60
CEFT	Concord EFS	0.86	38.00	17.50	20.80	13.00	44.40
CPC	Central Parking	0.89	32.86	22.40	23.90	11.80	28.60
JKHY	Henry(Jack) ,Assoc	0.95	32.09	34.90	33.40	22.10	33.90
SNPS	Synopsys Inc	1.00	28.28	22.30	17.20	13.90	44.80
FLC	RB Falcon	1.01	48.55	31.10	17.20	12.10	3450.00
ORCL	Oracle Corp	1.02	27.02	38.70	39.60	20.50	49.40
RFH	Richfood Hldgs	1.14	16.15	26.80	22.50	10.70	41.70
HBOC	HBO Co	1.17	67.95	20.10	20.70	13.20	112.10
SUNW	Sun Microsystems	1.21	31.28	30.50	21.60	17.90	42.00
DLTR	Dollar Tree Stores	1.26	47.48	37.80	53.50	21.90	34.70
GNTX	Gentex Corp	1.29	30.52	23.40	23.50	21.30	28.60
GDT	Guidant Corp	1.29	45.44	29.10	28.80	13.40	135.00
FAST	Fastenal Co	1.45	32.56	27.90	30.00	22.80	35.20
NMTX	Novametrix Med Sys	1.48	21.95	31.90	36.40	21.30	29.00
RHI	Robert Half Intl	1.49	48.85	25.70	19.00	19.10	37.00
JNY	Jones Apparel Group	1.51	24.65	29.90	26.10	22.70	27.40
KCP	Kenneth Cole Productions'A'	1.63	23.13	23.30	36.80	17.30	30.80
NOBH	Nobility Homes	1.76	27.43	22.00	25.50	17.90	30.90
APOL	Apollo Group'A'	1.78	82.32	32.60	56.70	20.10	34.90
PSFT	PeopleSoft Inc	1.85	74.04	32.20	20.30	15.00	50.00
SNS	Sundstrand Corp	1.90	25.70	35.60	22.50	11.40	26.80
CATP	Cambridge Technology Ptnrs	2.02	51.95	27.10	28.20	17.90	63.20
ALCD	Alcide Corp	2.06	25.79	22.30	21.00	19.90	72.40
BTH	Blyth Industries	2.19	46.02	24.20	25.60	16.00	36.40
COMR	Comair Holdings	2.24	37.41	30.50	26.40	14.80	25.80
IT	Gartner Group'A'	2.24	60.61	34.80	29.10	13.40	31.00
TLAB	Tellabs, Inc	2.38	57.08	34.50	26.90	27.30	32.40
DELL	Dell Computer Corp	2.42	165.59	59.90	41.60	20.70	62.50
BARZ	BARRA Inc	2.48	31.50	32.80	20.40	19.00	187.30
BKE	Buckle Inc	2.64	33.21	19.50	20.70	14.80	35.20
COGNF	Cognos Inc	2.99	51.43	32.90	21.70	19.20	91.50
TMBS	Timberline Software	3.18	54.33	40.80	29.60	20.70	48.40
NHL	Newhall Land/Farming	3.37	40.72	33.40	23.80	11.40	32.00
DCO	Ducommun Inc	3.76	39.95	21.50	22.50	14.20	28.30
ASIS	ASI Solutions	3.89	54.88	64.20	43.80	28.20	69.70
NRVH	Natl R.V.Holdings	3.95	40.55	27.20	24.00	18.60	39.60
CDN	Cadence Design Sys	4.45	163.41	31.40	24.90	20.80	43.40
SANM	Sanmina Corp	5.25	134.16	31.50	26.20	15.30	30.60
LOJN	LoJack Corp	5.53	92.82	23.10	32.20	18.00	41.70
PPD	Pre-Paid Legal Svcs	5.93	118.12	32.30	30.40	25.10	43.40
USNA	USANA Inc	8.21	174.71	41.60	43.00	27.70	34.00
MTW	Manitowoc Company	8.22	87.51	31.80	19.30	10.20	40.20
ITGI	Investment Tech Group	11.93	164.43	33.40	21.00	27.40	47.20
LXK	Lexmark Intl Group'A'	31.22	735.85	31.30	21.90	13.40	47.90

EXHIBIT 12-2   Growth screen 2.

(From Standard & Poor's Stock Reports, *October 27, 1998. Copyright © 1998 by The McGraw-Hill Companies.)*

Search Expression	Passed	Total
Return_on_Equity_-_Last_year_ > 18	1125	1125
ROE_5yr_Avg > = 15	1230	635
P/E_Ratio_ < 18	2875	380
P/E_Ratio_FY1_Est < 18	2872	274
Book_Value_5yr_Gr_Rate > = 15	851	107
EPS_5_Yr_Gr_Rate > 15	2166	83
Cap_Exp_5yr_Gr_Rate > 10	1315	53

Search Results: 53

Ticker	Company Name	P/E Ratio (Trail 12)	Return on Equity	Return on Equity 5 Yr Avg	P/E FY1 Estimate	Book Val 5 Yr Gr Rate	EPS 5 Yr Gr Rate	Cap Exp 5 Yr Gr Rate
ELXS	ELXSI Corp	3.80	39.80	28.40	7.70	37.90	37.42	20.30
DAVX	Davox Corp	4.80	47.70	17.00	9.00	32.30	267.50	34.60
CTI	Chart Industries	5.20	43.20	29.20	5.50	18.70	197.33	37.20
FOTO	Seattle FilmWorks	5.70	31.50	35.00	5.30	31.10	26.40	37.00
COHU	Cohu Inc	5.90	26.20	28.30	8.40	32.40	25.82	47.30
SJK	St. John Knits	6.30	30.20	32.60	6.40	38.40	27.51	39.90
WIRE	Encore Wire	6.40	37.10	17.20	6.10	23.50	67.48	16.70
MSCC	Microsemi Corp	6.90	30.90	19.10	8.90	21.40	160.51	24.10
INVX	Innovex Inc	7.80	51.90	29.70	10.10	38.90	53.69	37.70
GLM	Global Marine	8.20	49.80	21.60	8.60	32.20	390.69	69.10
LCSI	LCS Industries	8.30	20.20	20.60	8.40	22.90	56.90	12.10
C	Chrysler Corp	8.40	24.50	31.40	8.30	43.80	463.96	12.60
CAS	Castle (A.M.)	9.40	18.40	20.20	10.20	18.80	22.26	58.60
ORBKF	Orbotech Ltd Ord	9.40	29.70	24.20	9.20	44.30	55.18	23.10
WDHD	Woodhead Indus	9.50	19.60	18.70	11.30	16.80	15.90	14.10
TNL	Technitrol Inc	9.50	23.60	18.10	9.20	17.30	52.98	28.80
TOL	Toll Brothers	9.60	19.30	19.50	9.60	22.50	21.74	27.80
BSH	Bush Indus Cl'A'	9.60	22.40	23.30	14.70	27.20	21.47	58.80
AMES	Ames Department Stores	9.80	19.60	16.90	9.00	31.60	50.97	37.90
SMRT	Stein Mart	9.90	23.40	25.00	11.00	25.90	17.39	30.20
DCN	Dana Corp	10.00	23.50	23.50	10.20	18.90	19.75	26.30
XRIT	X-Rite Inc	10.10	22.60	22.40	15.20	15.30	15.64	20.90
UK	Union Carbide	10.20	29.60	29.40	14.10	16.10	29.06	18.00
WCLX	Wisconsin Central Trans	10.40	23.10	19.70	10.20	22.80	29.66	16.60
JOB	Genl Employ Enterpr	10.40	39.60	47.20	9.90	81.60	95.28	79.70
DCO	Ducommun Inc	10.60	21.50	22.50	9.70	151.00	35.95	25.70
OH	Oakwood Homes	11.50	18.70	15.90	7.60	19.70	19.00	48.50
ROP	Roper Industries	11.70	23.00	27.40	10.60	36.10	15.85	28.90
CHB	Champion Enterprises	11.70	27.90	31.00	10.90	18.00	30.35	72.00
ANDW	Andrew Corp	12.00	22.30	19.60	12.30	26.00	28.44	28.90
NHL	Newhall Land/Farming	12.10	33.40	23.80	12.80	20.10	40.72	24.90
AMWD	Amer Woodmark	12.40	25.70	17.80	11.50	17.60	44.08	17.70
ALCD	Alcide Corp	12.50	22.30	21.00	8.00	82.60	25.79	16.20
GCHI	Giant Cement Holding	12.80	19.50	18.90	10.20	20.80	24.57	36.50
CHP	CD Technologies	12.80	20.80	21.80	12.20	46.10	26.41	19.30
LCE	Lone Star Indus	12.80	21.90	24.30	12.90	93.80	494.60	20.20
ECILF	ECI Telecom Ltd	12.80	24.00	24.30	11.70	26.20	21.84	20.40
MAN	Manpower Inc	13.00	26.90	22.80	14.30	54.10	301.33	34.90
NAUT	Nautica Enterprises	13.20	23.40	21.40	11.30	26.20	27.74	57.80
NATR	Nature's Sunshine Prod	13.20	30.90	30.10	12.20	23.80	26.41	31.40
B	Barnes Group	14.20	23.90	19.00	11.20	17.80	41.57	23.20
DS	Dallas Semiconductor	14.50	20.50	17.20	15.40	17.80	17.94	32.40
TOM	Tommy Hilfiger	14.60	24.80	23.30	11.10	40.00	32.16	47.40
CLE	Claire's Stores	15.30	25.90	24.50	13.90	23.85	23.85	25.70
SWD	Shorewood Packaging	15.40	29.70	33.80	13.80	31.10	18.40	38.20
NTZ	Industrie Natuzzi ADS	15.50	19.40	31.20	12.50	34.40	23.76	55.10
NOBH	Nobility Homes	15.60	22.00	25.50	14.90	41.00	27.43	73.60
JNY	Jones Apparel Group	16.30	29.90	26.10	14.60	26.00	24.65	38.20
CRVL	CorVel Corp	16.60	18.40	18.60	15.00	16.90	18.13	14.20
COMR	Comair Holdings	16.70	30.50	26.40	14.50	22.30	37.41	17.60
PLXS	Plexus Corp	17.00	27.70	16.40	17.10	19.20	48.13	16.40
TMBS	Timberline Software	17.10	40.80	29.60	16.20	33.20	54.33	46.60
COGNF	Cognos Inc	17.20	32.90	21.70	12.10	16.20	51.43	14.90

EXHIBIT 12-3   Growth screen 3.

(From Standard & Poor's Stock Reports, *October 27, 1998. Copyright © 1998 by The McGraw-Hill Companies.)*

Search Expression	Passed	Total
STARS_Ranking > = 4	412	412
Fair_Value_Rank > 4	431	48
Earnings_and_Dividend_Ranking < = 5	1705	27
EPS_%_Change_FY1_/_FY0 > 10	2970	18

Search Results: 18

Ticker	Company Name	STARS Ranking	EPS % Change FY1 / FY0	Fair Value Ranking	Earnings _Div Ranking	EPS Gr 5 Yr / PE
TIF	Tiffany .Co	4	17.30	5	5	18.86
APPB	Applebee's Intl	4	19.60	5	3	2.12
ANV	Aeroquip-Vickers Inc	4	21.10	5	4	7.30
ROP	Roper Industries	4	21.60	5	4	1.36
VSH	Vishay Intertechnology	4	25.30	5	4	NA
HET	Harrah's Entertainment	4	26.40	5	5	78.66
CNK	Crompton _Knowles	4	27.00	5	3	11.73
TLAB	Tellabs, Inc	4	32.40	5	5	2.38
AFWY	Amer Freightways	4	35.70	5	5	NA
SNPS	Synopsys Inc	4	44.80	5	5	1.00
TRN	Trinity Indus	4	66.10	5	4	1.85
CNS	Consolidated Stores	4	89.60	5	5	0.23
KEA	Keane Inc	4	104.40	5	4	1.36
STJ	St. Jude Medical	4	144.10	5	5	NA
ADSK	Autodesk, Inc	4	571.00	5	4	NA
HRC	HEALTHSOUTH Corp	5	23.10	5	4	7.05
CDN	Cadence Design Sys	5	43.40	5	5	4.45
SKS	Saks Inc	5	104.90	5	5	17.26

EXHIBIT 12-4 Closed-end regional and country funds.

(From Barron's, *November 23, 1998. Reprinted by permission of Dow Jones, Inc. via Copyright Clearance Center, Inc. © 1998 Dow Jones and Company, Inc. All rights reserved worldwide.)*

Friday, November 20, 1998

Fund Name (Symbol)	Stock Exch	NAV	Market Price	Prem /Disc	52 week Market Return
General Equity Funds					
Adams Express (ADX)-a	♣N	30.65	25 1/2	−16.8	17.8
Alliance All-Mkt (AMO)	N	37.25	38 3/8	+3.0	43.3
Avalon Capital (MIST)	O	17.52	16 1/4	−7.2	25.0
Baker Fentress (BKF)-a	♣N	19.11	16 9/16	−13.3	2.8
Bergstrom Cap (BEM)	A	182.54	160	−12.3	23.0
Blue Chip Value (BLU)	♣N	9.79	9 7/16	−3.6	2.4
Central Secs (CET)	A	27.54	24 7/16	−11.3	−16.4
Corp Renaissance (CREN)-c	O	8.63	6 1/8	−29.0	4.3
Engex (EGX)	A	9.92	7 7/8	−20.6	−23.1
Equus II (EQS)	♣N	23.84	18	−24.5	−19.2
Gabelli Equity (GAB)	N	11.40	11 5/8	+2.0	16.2
General American (GAM)	♣N	32.31	29 7/16	−8.9	32.0
Librty AllStr Eq (USA)-a	♣N	13.38	12 9/16	−6.1	10.9
Librty AllStr Gr (ASG)-a	♣N	12.18	11 1/16	−9.2	1.6
MFS Special Val (MFV)	N	14.42	16 13/16	+16.6	−1.3
Morgan FunShares (MFUN)-c	O	7.37	6 3/4	−8.4	35.7
Morgan Gr Sm Cap (MGC)	♣N	10.48	9 1/2	−9.4	−8.5
NAIC Growth (GRF)-c	C	12.29	11 7/8	−3.4	−26.2
Royce Micro-Cap (OTCM)	♣O	10.02	9 1/4	−7.7	−6.3
Royce Value (RVT)	♣N	15.21	14 1/8	−7.1	−0.1
Salomon SBF (SBF)	N	20.57	18 5/8	−9.4	14.4
Source Capital (SOR)	N	45.84	52	+13.4	12.0
Tri-Continental (TY)	♣N	35.36	29 1/16	−17.8	17.2
Zweig (ZF)	♣N	11.74	11 1/4	−4.2	−2.9
Specialized Equity Funds					
C&S Realty (RIF)	♣A	9.09	10 1/8	+11.4	−0.3
C&S Total Rtn (RFI)	♣N	14.45	14 3/8	−0.5	−5.6
Chartwell D & I (CWF)	N	14.06	14 3/8	+2.3	N/A
Delaware Gr Div (DDF)	N	16.12	17 1/2	+8.6	5.7
Delaware Grp Gl (DGF)	N	15.53	15 1/2	−0.2	−4.0
Duff&Ph Util Inc (DNP)	N	10.28	11 5/16	+10.0	20.9
Emer Mkts Infra (EMG)	♣N	9.91	7 11/16	−22.4	−27.6
Emer Mkts Tel (ETF)	♣N	13.36	10 3/4	−19.5	−7.8
First Financial (FF)	N	12.56	14 1/8	+12.5	−27.7
Gabelli Gl Media (GGT)	N	11.46	9 5/8	−16.0	28.1
H&Q Health Inv (HQH)	♣N	18.41	14 7/16	−21.6	−12.2
H&Q Life Sci Inv (HQL)	♣N	15.23	12	−21.2	−11.5
INVESCO Gl Hlth (GHS)	♣N	19.68	18 9/16	−5.7	35.0
J Han Bank (BTO)	♣N	11.60	11 7/16	−1.4	8.4
J Han Pat Globl (PGD)	♣N	15.08	13 1/2	−10.5	14.1
J Han Pat Sel (DIV)	♣N	16.85	15 3/4	−6.5	10.9
Nations Bal Tgt (NBM)	N	10.67	9 5/8	−9.7	11.9
Petroleum & Res (PEO)-a	♣N	35.15	31 7/8	−9.3	−13.2
SthEastrn Thrift (STBF)	♣O	25.92	24 1/8	−6.9	−5.8
Thermo Opprtunty (TMF)	A	8.73	6 11/16	−23.4	−30.9
Tuxis Corp (TUX)	A	16.59	16 1/4	−2.0	22.3
Preferred Stock Funds					
J Han Pat Pref (PPF)	♣N	14.03	14 3/4	+5.1	13.1
J Han Pat Prm (PDF)	♣N	10.64	10	−6.0	14.7
J Han Pat Prm II (PDT)-a	♣N	13.22	11 7/8	−10.1	11.4
Preferred Inc Op (PFO)	♣N	13.36	12 7/16	−6.9	6.5
Preferred IncMgt (PFM)	♣N	15.89	13 7/16	−15.4	−3.1
Preferred Income (PFD)	♣N	16.28	15 9/16	−4.4	8.2
Putnam Divd Inc (PDI)-a	N	11.50	10 11/16	−7.0	8.5
Convertible Sec's. Funds					
Bancroft Conv (BCV)	♣A	N/A	27 1/4	N/A	7.9
Castle Conv (CVF)	A	25.94	23 1/4	−10.4	3.8
Ellsworth Conv (ECF)	♣A	N/A	9 1/2	N/A	10.7
Gabelli Conv Sec (GCV)	N	11.23	10 9/16	−6.0	14.7
Lincoln Conv (LNV)-c	♣N	16.19	15 3/16	−6.2	−3.7
Putnam Conv Opp (PCV)-a	N	24.11	23 5/8	−2.0	−2.0
Putnam Hi Inc Cv (PCF)-a	N	8.68	10 1/4	+18.1	8.3
TCW Conv Secs (CVT)	♣N	9.14	9 3/8	+2.6	6.5
VK Conv Sec (VXS)	N	22.99	19 15/16	−13.3	4.2
World Equity Funds					
AIM Eastern Euro (GTF)	N	7.59	6 5/16	−16.9	−29.3
ASA Limited (ASA)-acv	N	19.92	20 5/8	+3.6	−7.3
Argentina (AF)	N	13.69	10 3/8	−24.2	−15.0
Asia Pacific (APB)	N	8.12	7 5/16	−10.0	−8.4
Asia Tigers (GRR)	N	7.89	6 11/16	−15.2	−12.3
Austria (OST)	♣N	11.97	10 11/16	−10.7	19.9
BGR Prec Metals (BPT.A)-cy	T	14.51	10	−31.1	−11.5
Brazil (BZF)	N	20.31	15 13/16	−22.2	−10.8
Brazilian Equity (BZL)	♣N	6.13	5 1/16	−17.5	−12.3
Cdn Genl Inv (CGI)-y	♣T	15.06	13 3/4	−8.7	−8.4
Cdn Wrld Fd Ltd (CWF)-cy	T	5.85	4 35/64	−22.2	−3.2
Central Eur Eqty (CEE)	♣N	16.33	13 5/16	−18.5	−20.5
Central Eur Value (CRF)	N	13.44	11	−18.2	−7.7
Centrl Fd Canada (CEF)-c	♣A	3.90	3 7/8	−0.5	7.4
Chile (CH)	♣N	14.31	10 11/16	−25.3	−25.3
China (CHN)	N	11.36	9 1/2	−16.4	−27.3
China, Greater (GCH)	♣N	9.43	7 7/16	−21.1	−19.3
Clemente Global (CLM)	N	13.20	11 3/8	−13.8	27.4
Dessauer Glbl Eq (DGE)	N	13.09	12 1/16	−7.9	7.7
Economic Inv Tr (EVT)-cy	T	149.32	104 1/4	−30.2	16.2
Emer Mkts Grow (N/A)	z	42.48	N/A	N/A	N/A
Emerging Mexico (MEF)-c	N	6.62	5 3/4	−13.1	−37.4
Europe (EF)	♣N	22.18	19 7/8	−10.4	27.9
European Warrant (EWF)-c	N	19.97	17 5/8	−11.7	36.8
F&C Middle East (EME)-c	N	16.30	13 3/16	−19.1	−13.4
Fidelity Em Asia (FAE)	♣N	10.34	9 1/8	−11.7	3.2
Fidelty Ad Korea (FAK)	♣N	5.48	4 7/8	−10.9	8.4
First Australia (IAF)	A	8.77	6 7/8	−21.6	7.1
First Israel (ISL)	♣N	14.82	12 1/16	−18.6	−8.0
First Philippine (FPF)	N	6.95	5 3/4	−17.3	−29.2
France Growth (FRF)	N	16.66	14	−16.0	46.1
Germany Fund (GER)	♣N	15.64	13 7/8	−11.3	41.8
Germany, Emer (FRG)	♣N	15.29	14 1/8	−7.6	46.2
Germany, New (GF)	♣N	16.22	13 1/2	−16.8	26.0
Global Small Cap (GSG)	A	15.87	13 1/4	−16.5	−2.8
Growth Fd Spain (GSP)	♣N	24.73	23 5/8	−4.4	55.1
Herzfeld Caribb (CUBA)	O	5.80	4 3/4	−18.1	−3.5
India Fund (IFN)	N	8.35	6 5/8	−20.6	−7.8
India Growth (IGF)-d	N	10.33	7 3/4	−25.0	−15.1
Indonesia (IF)	♣N	2.98	4 1/16	+36.2	−30.2
Irish Inv (IRL)	N	22.63	19 15/16	−11.9	28.9
Italy (ITA)	N	17.09	14 1/8	−17.3	39.8
Jakarta Growth (JGF)	N	2.25	2 5/8	+16.9	−41.6
Japan Equity (JEQ)	♣N	6.38	8 15/16	+40.1	22.3
Japan OTC Equity (JOF)	N	N/A	6 1/4	N/A	11.1
Jardine Fl China (JFC)	♣N	8.02	6 3/8	−20.4	−38.9
Jardine Fl India (JFI)-c	♣N	6.85	5 5/16	−22.5	−19.9
Korea (KF)	N	7.90	8 7/16	+6.8	11.6
Korea Equity (KEF)	N	3.23	3 1/8	−3.1	−15.1
Korean Inv (KIF)	N	3.63	3 5/8	0.0	−18.2
Latin Am Sm Cos (LLF)	♣N	6.95	6 1/8	−11.8	−31.3
Latin Amer Disc (LDF)	N	9.09	7 5/8	−16.1	−8.9
Latin Amer Eq (LAQ)	♣N	11.45	8 3/4	−23.6	−26.1
Latin Amer Inv (LAM)	♣N	12.98	10	−23.0	−17.9
Malaysia (MF)	N	2.53	5 1/16	+100.0	−29.7
Mexico (MXF)-c	N	N/A	11 5/8	N/A	−32.0
Mexico Eqty&Inc (MXE)-c	N	7.97	6 1/16	−24.0	−20.7
Morgan St Africa (AFF)	N	13.12	10 1/8	−22.8	−16.8
Morgan St Asia (APF)	N	8.41	7 11/16	−8.6	2.1
Morgan St Em (MSF)	N	10.67	8 11/16	−18.6	−20.1
Morgan St India (IIF)	N	8.98	7 1/4	−19.3	−10.1
Morgan St Russia (RNE)	N	12.44	11 1/4	−9.6	−39.3
New South Africa (NSA)	♣N	11.39	9 7/16	−17.1	−14.2
Pakistan Inv (PKF)	N	2.57	1 15/16	−24.5	−58.1
Portugal (PGF)	♣N	23.68	20 3/8	−13.9	42.6
ROC Taiwan (ROC)	N	8.34	7 1/16	−15.3	−0.1
Royce Global Trust (FUND)	♣O	5.51	4 7/8	−11.4	−5.9
Scud Spain & Por (IBF)	N	14.99	13 7/8	−7.4	33.5
Scudder New Asia (SAF)	N	11.94	10 3/16	−14.7	4.3
Scudder New Eur (NEF)	N	22.87	19 1/2	−14.7	34.5
Singapore (SGF)-c	♣N	7.40	7 5/16	−1.2	−4.1
Southern Africa (SOA)	N	12.70	10 1/4	−19.3	−15.1
Spain (SNF)	N	21.86	19 1/8	−12.5	50.8
Swiss Helvetia (SWZ)	♣N	19.69	16 1/8	−18.1	32.2
Taiwan (TWN)-c	N	18.14	14 11/16	−19.0	0.6
Taiwan Equity (TYW)-c	♣N	13.31	10 7/16	−21.6	1.2
Templeton China (TCH)-c	N	8.72	7 3/16	−17.5	−15.4
Templeton Dragon (TDF)	N	11.11	8 7/8	−20.1	−18.8
Templeton Em App (TEA)-c	N	11.49	10 1/4	−10.8	−0.9
Templeton Em Mkt (EMF)-a	N	9.37	10 9/16	+12.7	−20.4
Templeton Russia (TRF)-c	N	8.31	12	+44.4	−58.3
Templeton Vietnm (TVF)	N	9.26	7 5/16	−21.1	−19.8
Thai (TTF)	N	3.91	7 3/8	+88.7	−8.4
Thai Capital (TC)	♣N	3.33	4 5/8	+39.0	−7.4
Third Canadian (THD)-cy	T	20.50	16 1/2	−19.5	−11.8
Turkish Inv (TKF)	N	5.37	4 3/8	−18.4	−39.3
United Corps Ltd (UNC)-cy	T	64.68	44 1/2	−31.2	8.1
United Kingdom (UKM)	♣N	16.18	15	−7.3	15.4
Z-Seven (ZSEV)	O	7.60	8 1/4	+8.6	9.7

13

HOW TO BUY VALUE STOCKS

V *ALUE STOCKS* ARE so designated because they typically have low valuations. This is because sales and earnings growth are often, but not always, below average. Evaluative measures such as price/earnings (P/E) and price/sales ratios and return on equity (ROE) are lower than the norm. With such low profitability scores, it would seem odd that value stocks outperform growth equities. You would naturally think that by investing in fast-growing companies, your portfolio would more rapidly increase in value. After all, such companies increase earnings faster and their returns on stockholders' equity are higher.

And if the valuation (i.e., P/E level) of all stocks was the same, faster-growing companies *would* provide better returns over time. But stocks most certainly do not trade at the same P/E level. Investors naturally prefer to own stocks of companies with good stories to tell. But when it comes to investment equities, it's the tortoises that usually beat the hares. *Value beats growth over the long run because investors systematically overvalue the growth of well-positioned companies in rapidly expanding industries. They just as systematically overstate the persistence of poor earnings growth for companies in a downtrend.* Put another way, investors overpay for faster-growing companies, while value stocks tend to trade at lower prices because they lack sex appeal or are in out-of-favor industries.

High-flying stocks are also susceptible to big drops. With expectations very high, when earnings in a particular quarter fall short, there can be a very large impact on the stock's P/E. The double whammy of a lower earnings projection, combined with a lower P/E, is all that is needed for a growth stock to take a big hit.

There are the nimble few who manage to beat the market using short-term trading strategies. They usually buy growth stocks on the way up and bail out before earnings disappointments or high P/Es start causing damage to returns. But most investors do not have the time or the trading acumen to do well with this investment strategy. All too often, momentum-driven gains disappear in a flash when a company fails to meet an overly optimistic earnings projection.

At the other end of the spectrum, investors too often assume that companies with subpar earnings growth will stay that way for the long run. Of course, there are those companies with moribund management, or permanently altered industry conditions, for which this is true. The stocks of these companies deserve below-average P/Es. But there are also a good number of *underpriced* value stocks which understate the ability of management to turn things around.

Just as fast-growing companies revert to the corporate mean over time, so do slow-growing ones as long as cash flow remains strong. That is particularly true for companies with revenues over $1 billion. Studies have shown that companies with ROEs in the lowest quintile improve the most over the following five years, while ROEs which drop the most are those with the highest current rankings.

But not all value approaches do well when applied to the small-stock universe. For example, the low-P/E, high-dividend approach, which often works for large stocks, is not generally successful with their smaller counterparts.

AVOIDING CHEAP STOCKS THAT DESERVE TO BE CHEAP
There is no shortage of low-priced stocks of companies with deteriorating market positions, declining or static markets, poor balance sheets, or lackluster management that are unable to improve business. There are a lot of walking wounded out there. Most firms do manage to survive, but some eventually end up stiffing creditors and relying on the bankruptcy courts for reorganization.

There are even sorrier tales to tell when small, rapidly growing companies fail to fulfill their original promise. Most of these firms will not have the financial wherewithal to make another run. Lacking capital to grow, they are unable to retain strong managers to get the most out of their business potential. These companies also deserve to have below-average P/E ratios.

Only a Matter of Time: Great Assets Destroyed by Bad Management

One good example of a perennially cheap stock that deserved to be cheap was Dart Group. After selling off the Dart Drug chain in the mid-1980s, the autocratic Herbert Haft ruled over a cash-rich holding company with majority interests in Trak Auto (an auto parts retailer), Crown Books, and a small supermarket chain based in the Baltimore area. As of January 31, 1994, it also had cash equal to more than $95 a share, net of long-term debt. Yet, over the following four years the shares fluctuated between $60 and $90, a huge discount to liquidation value.

Why? The problem was truly poor management that was squandering the firm's corporate assets, but was unlikely to be dislodged. Dart Group earned very little money for 10 years. This is because earnings were eaten up by exorbitant salaries paid to Haft family members. The shares went nowhere. Investors astutely ascertained that as long as Herbert Haft remained in control, the company's ability to grow would be severely hampered. For the 7 years through October 15, 1997, the stock rose just 21 percent, while the S&P 500 went up 84 percent.

However, a pivotal event occurred in 1994 that could have altered control of the company. Herbert Haft's remaining family ally, his younger son Robert, tried to wrest control from him. To succeed he had to side with more progressive family members. Although the elder Haft continued to fight to keep control of his fiefdom, there did appear to be a very reasonable chance that the company would eventually be placed in more capable hands.

Assume that the transition would take 5 years, that earnings would average just $5 million a year, and that the ROE 5 years out would be a below-par 10 percent. This would imply per-share earnings at that time of about $17. Putting a P/E of 12 on the shares implies an ending price of over $200—great potential upside.

What happened? There were only five members on the board of directors. After a great deal of soul searching, a long-time ally of Herbert Haft changed sides in late 1996 and agreed to help set up a separate management council. He died of a heart attack within the month, but the wheels had been put in motion for the company to set an independent course.

Unfortunately, while the Hafts had been feuding, the competitive landscape changed dramatically in both the book and auto parts retailing businesses. Both Crown and Trak Auto were well behind their competitors in transitioning to a discount-superstore format. Both chains struggled to catch up and were only marginally profitable in 1996, even before some significant write-downs. The company was also saddled with a huge legal judgment from a lawsuit by Herbert's oldest son. Costs continued to mount. Dart basically got stuck with paying for Herbert Haft's rash and vindictive actions as its CEO.

This is all by way of saying that even the most asset-laden companies, like Dart, may turn out to be horrible investments due to management problems. Lousy management can destroy the best assets. And mediocre managements allow companies to trundle along without a concerted effort to maximize shareholder value.

LOOKING FOR SMALL INCREASES IN EARNINGS PLUS P/E EXPANSION

Most value stocks do not have clean stories. There is usually something that keeps them out of favor. It could be that earnings are down because of poor products, or because of poor economic or industry fundamentals. There could be mild or potentially severe financial problems, or the firm might have an unattractive market position. In each case, one must decide if the problem is temporary or ripe for resolution in the not-too-distant future. Assume that the average company in the S&P 500 index is growing earnings at a 12 percent rate, and the average P/E of all stocks in the index is 16. If a value company that is growing earnings at 8 percent a year and trading at a P/E of 12 can convince investors that it is capable of growing at 12 percent, the stock will not only increase in value along with earnings, but will often experience P/E expansion relative to that of the market P/E as well. The typical stock might gain 12 percent over the coming year, but the value stock with improved growth prospects will gain 45 percent!:

$$\text{Earnings growth} + \text{P/E expansion} = \text{Stock appreciation}$$

$$12 \text{ percent} + \frac{16}{12}$$

$$12 \text{ percent} + 33.3 \text{ percent} = 45.3 \text{ percent}$$

For many growth stocks the opposite occurs. If a company is growing at 30 percent a year and trading at a P/E of 25, and growth slows down to 25 percent, its P/E might drop to 22. The following occurs:

Earnings growth − P/E compression = Stock appreciation

$$25 \text{ percent} - \frac{25}{21}$$

25 percent − 16 percent = 9 percent

Not only has the value stock done better than the growth stock, but if the average equity in the S&P 500 index increases earnings by the expected 12 percent, and the P/E of the market remains stable, then the growth stock will have done worse than the market, as well. It is this phenomenon that often causes value to beat growth.

WHAT TO LOOK FOR IN A VALUE STOCK
It is reasonable to expect that if you own a cross section of value companies you will at least match the market, and probably will do a little better than you would have by overpaying for growth. The following pointers should increase the odds of garnering better-than-average returns.

Industry Turns
Some of the most fabulous investment gains occur when an industry with poor fundamentals finally turns positive. What were the worst investments in the late 1980s? Hotel and oil and gas drilling stocks. What were some of the best stocks in the early 1990s? Hotel and oil and gas drilling stocks. This is where most of Peter Lynch's "10-baggers" lie—among the hundreds of stocks that will benefit from both good earnings growth *and* P/E expansion as investors climb back on board.

In the hotel industry, massive numbers of rooms were added throughout the country in the 1980s, well in excess of growth in room demand. Even the best hotel operators had to live through tough industry conditions, cutting prices per room to cover costs. For more than three years, hotel room occupancy fell. Earnings dropped across the board. Indeed, so many available rooms came on stream during the latter half of the decade that those operators that had leveraged their balance sheets to expand found themselves in considerable financial difficulty.

Prime Motor Inns was one such company. The company went bankrupt in 1990, but stockholders got a piece of the reorganized firm. It emerged in 1992 with substantially lower revenues, but positive cash flow, and some earnings. The stock was under 2. However, industry fundamentals were improving. Because of all the previous overbuilding, there was virtually no new construction of hotels. With the U.S. economy humming along, demand for rooms rose. By 1993, it was clear even to the casual observer that things were looking up for hoteliers. That would have been the ideal time for investors to get back into hotel stocks. Buying Prime Motor back at 2, when the industry was just turning, did take a strong stomach, but one year later there was a clear trend to hang your hat on. In 1993, Prime's stock rose to 6. But that was not the end. The economy continued to grow, and Prime had the wherewithal to start building again. The company continued to expand, and, by mid-1997, Prime's stock moved past 20.

A similar story can be told for Global Marine. The collapse of oil and natural gas prices in 1983 had a devastating impact on demand for oil-drilling rigs. Industry rig utilization and day rates plummeted. The industry descended into a depression. Global Marine had the newest fleet of off-shore oil rigs—if any rig would be used, it would be one of Global's. But most sat idle for years. With so little demand for rigs, most companies were able to negotiate enough debt forgiveness to survive. Many were financially restructured so that there would be just enough cash flow for most drillers, including Global, to stay alive, while the banks at least got paid interest on the debt that remained.

During the late 1980s and early 1990s, day rates did climb a bit for off-shore rigs, but it was not until 1996 that a combination of increased demand, technological advances, and rig retirements caused day rates and rig utilization to turn favorable for good. Global Marine's common stock entered that year trading at 8, up from 4 one year earlier. In August 1997, the stock was changing hands at 28, and had more than tripled in just over 18 months. There are dozens of oil-drilling and oil-service companies that enjoyed the same kind of price rise.

Temporary Earnings Setbacks
There are some fine companies that will sometimes experience temporary earnings slides. Wall Street typically disregards or looks favorably upon one-time write-downs. Examples of temporary profit setbacks which could represent excellent buying opportunities include late product introductions, missed earnings expectations (but within an uninterrupted earnings uptrend—like 3 Com and Cisco Systems had in early 1997), or an ill-conceived marketing campaign (like McDonald's with its ill-fated $0.50 Big Mac offer).

Scholastic is a good example of a company that generated very steady sales and earnings growth based on its dominant position in children's books and teachers' learning tools. The shares went public on February 25, 1992, at 22½ and rose steadily, hitting a high of 78½ in November 1996. During that 4-year period, sales rose at a powerful 17 percent annual rate, while per-share earnings expanded at a 16 percent pace. Most of the gain was in children's books, lead by the *Goosebumps* series. However, in late 1996 and early 1997, sales of some of these titles faltered, and the company had to take some one-time inventory write-downs. Investors focused on the problems at *Goosebumps,* cutting the stock price by two-thirds to 25. As it gradually became apparent that the basic business was still sound (and quite profitable), the shares recovered to 36 a few months later.

Strong Earnings Power

In the early 1980s, cyclical industries fell far out of favor. Steel, chemical, paper, and railroad companies suffered from overcapacity, high labor costs, increased foreign competition, and declining revenues. But those firms with good balance sheets and proactive managements downsized, reinvested, reduced labor costs, and waited for the eventual industry upturn. It finally happened in the early 1990s.

One measure to consider when an industry is out of favor is each company's peak earnings power. What would USX or Dow Chemical be able to earn at the peak of the economic cycle, assuming full-capacity utilization and record product prices? By then applying a conservative P/E ratio to those earnings, you should come to a target price which is likely well above the current level. Next, consider how long it took the industry to revive over the last few economic upcycles and figure out the compound annual return based on the number of years it might take for peak earnings to be achieved. The annual return should be 20 percent or better to justify the business and timing risks assumed. Cyclical groups that experienced big gains during the late 1980s to early 1990s were aerospace, defense, autos, chemicals, home construction, and paper.

Favorable Business Position in an Out-of-Favor Industry

Companies in noncyclical industries may also be attractive if they are well positioned for an industry upturn. Does the company have a dominant share of growing segments of its market? Is it reinvesting in its plant and equipment (or products and brands) at an adequate rate? Is the firm's operating profit ratio at least as good as its competitors'? Is it in low-end or value-added profit segments? If the answers to these questions indicate the presence of a solid business that provides immediate cash flow and opportunities for growth, the stock is capable of doing better than the average one in a depressed industry.

As alluded to earlier, the S&P 500 jumped 22 percent in 1996, but the S&P Restaurant index hardly moved at all. Mind you, this was not an industry that was headed for serious financial trouble. Investors were concerned, however, that America was overstored with fast-food outlets. Although many chains continued to show modest revenue and profit gains, chain-wide same-store sales for units open more than one year faltered. Nonetheless, faster-growing sit-down restaurants such as Consolidated Products were painted with the same broad brush by investors. Same-store sales were down modestly at COP's Steak 'n' Shake restaurants, but it was still experiencing 20 percent earnings growth and had a very strong balance sheet.

From a high of 14 in mid-1996, Consolidated's stock slid to 9, even though earnings continued to climb during the period. Per-share earnings at Consolidated were projected to grow 22 percent to $0.82 a share, and another 16 percent in 1998 to $0.95, but because the industry was out of favor, the stock was trading at a P/E ratio of less than 10 times those projections. Inevitably, the industry, and investor enthusiasm for it, turned up again. Sure enough, at the end of 1997 Consolidated Products was trading at 16, up more than 60 percent from its 52-week low.

Companies in Favorable Industries That Are Poised to Be Restructured

It takes less time for a poorly run but financially stable company to be turned around than for good companies in troubled industries. Often, the best bang for the investment buck comes from playing non-family-controlled companies that have just replaced poor management. These are often companies with basic operating and marketing strengths that are ripe for restructuring, such as H. J. Heinz, IBM, B. F. Goodrich, and W. R. Grace.

Scott Paper is a good example of a company that had been carrying a lot of excess baggage. In early 1994 there was a management change, and the company set about selling underperforming assets, paying down debt, and reducing head count at remaining operations. The result was a dramatic increase in profitability. Further aided by improving industry fundamentals, the stock rose steadily following the announcement of the change in corporate direction. Indeed, the revamped company became so attractive that it became a strong takeover candidate, and agreed to a lucrative buyout in 1996.

Companies with Strong Products, Brands, or Retail Positions

Peter Lynch often counsels investors to buy companies with operations or products that can be readily understood. A well-known product with a dominant market share often trades at a premium to other companies because of the higher perceived value of its franchise, one that is often impossible to duplicate. Once a company dominates a business, it can be very difficult to dislodge. IBM ruled the roost for many decades until the personal computer came along. Intel, Microsoft, and, increasingly, Cisco Systems come to mind today.

These companies typically trade at high P/Es, although at lower P/E-to-growth rates than the S&P 500. There are also smaller companies with dominant market shares that for some reason or other trade at low multiples to growth. Even in the overvalued stock market of today, investors are still overlooking such stocks. One example at the time was Coherent, the leading manufacturer of laser systems for industrial and medical purposes. The company was the acknowledged industry granddaddy, and was expected to grow per-share earnings 19 percent over the following 3 to 5 years. But the stock was trading at a P/E ratio of 15, while the S&P 500 was trading closer to 20.

Companies with Large Amounts of Free Cash Flow and Strong Balance Sheets

A company needs enough cash flow (net income plus depreciation) to fund working capital needs, meet interest payments on debt, and fund required capital expenditures. A firm is particularly attractive when it meets all these obligations without skimping on business reinvestment A strong balance sheet allows the company to reinvest in the business, either through internal expansion or acquisition, without diluting current shareholder ownership via the sale of additional shares. It also allows a firm to withstand industry downturns and position itself for an industry upswing.

This is particularly important if the firm is in a slow-growing industry. Such companies need to diversify and increase earnings by buying related companies cheaply in order to enhance prospects for long-term earnings growth and to improve returns on stockholders' equity, thereby increasing the P/E multiple the stock can trade at. The result could be a 10-bagger for stockholders. Hanson PLC, a large British company, grew earnings significantly and provided shareholders well-above-average returns for many years by taking cash out of its British tobacco operations and putting it to work in stodgy businesses that also generated significant free cash flow. Once the strategy stopped working, the company was rightfully dismantled.

Stockholder Representation

Consider who owns the stock. Are outside stockholders properly represented on the board of directors? Many boards act in the best interests of the entrenched managements that nominated them to their posts. When Snapple went public, the major stockholder was R. H. Lee, a leveraged buyout firm. LBO partnerships are not long-term investors, so it would be reasonable to assume that it would dispose of its shares, either through secondary offerings or outright sale of the company. The shares skyrocketed after the IPO, but fell just as sharply when earnings faltered. Rather than wait until earnings recovered, the LBO outfit chose to find a buyer right away. Although it made a handsome return on its original LBO investment, most public shareholders incurred heavy losses.

We would also recommend staying away from family-owned businesses until the families themselves become restive. Norcen Energy, a Canadian oil and gas producer, was part of the Bronfman empire. The Bronfmans had been in disrepute among Canadian investors for a number of years. Many of their real estate firms became overleveraged, wiping out the interests of public investors. There was also continuing concern that Norcen's preferred holdings in other Bronfman-controlled companies would have to be written down. That did not occur, and the portfolio was just about completely liquidated. Nonetheless, because Canadian investors were reluctant to invest alongside the Bronfmans, Norcen's stock consistently traded at a discount to comparable Canadian exploration companies. After a few years sprucing up the company, the Bronfmans eventually opted to sell the company at a substantial premium to the then-prevailing stock price.

Undervalued Assets

There are a number of instances when assets are carried on the balance sheet for less than they are worth. This is can be especially true for real estate investments. During cyclical downswings, companies may be forced to write down assets to the lower of cost or market value. (Market value often proves then to be the lower mark.) However, when the market value of these assets begins to appreciate from cyclical lows, these assets are not written up and their true value is concealed.

Consider Alexander & Baldwin, an ocean shipping concern and sugarcane grower. Its major operations include ocean shipping, container leasing, and sugar-cane growing, but it also the largest private land owner in Hawaii, with extensive plantations and property on the islands of Kauai and Maui. The stock has been in the doldrums because of Hurricane Iniki and an ill-conceived forward integration effort in its agriculture business, but the underlying real estate values remain. Other types of companies that can often have hidden asset values include banks, S&Ls, oil and gas companies, media, and mining companies. But be careful to find companies that possess potential catalysts for change. Otherwise, these hidden values will always stay locked up. Alexander & Baldwin is not one of them.

SCREENING FOR VALUE STOCKS

There are many ways to screen for value stocks. Computer screens are efforts to mine an equity database in order to unearth those stocks deserving further study. Through what is known as *factor analysis,* a financial analyst can screen a list of stocks for characteristics that have caused them to do better or worse than average. The first thing that usually comes to mind is that, with thousands of analysts mining the same data, wouldn't enough of them find the best factors, sometimes termed *anomalies,* so that the stocks would no longer generate excess returns in the future? The fact is that certain stock factors still provide excess returns. One growth factor that still works—stock momentum—has already been mentioned. There are, however, quite a number of value factors that work, as well. Some provide better returns when applied to large-cap stocks, others when applied to smaller stocks.

In *What Works on Wall Street,* (McGraw-Hill, 1997), James O'Shaughnessy, using the S&P Compustat database, isolated a number of factors to show how stocks with value characteristics provided favorable returns. Table 13-1 shows the returns offered by various value factors on an isolated basis. The returns provided are for both the large-cap S&P 500 and the all-stocks portfolio, which mostly contains small-cap stocks. Note that most factors provided excess returns (in boldface) compared to the S&P 500 and provided even better absolute returns when applied to small-cap stocks.

With the exception of relative strength, all of the factors that consistently beat their respective stock universe were traditional value measures. Stocks with low stock-capitalization/sales ratios (better known as price/sales) provided the best returns for the small-cap stock universe, followed by low price/book value and low price/cash flow. Curiously, a low P/E strategy did not work for small-cap stocks. Nonetheless, three of the five value factors studied provided returns in excess of the all-stocks (small-cap) portfolio.

It is our view that the best strategy is to marry the best value and growth factors to come up with low-priced stocks that *also* have strong

TABLE 13-1 Summary compound annual returns for various value factors, 1954–1994.

	Return	
Factor	Large-Cap Portfolio (>$1 Billion)	All-Stocks Portfolio
Low stock capitalization/sales	13.2%	15.4%
Low stock price/book value	14.0	14.4
Low price/cash flow	14.1	13.6
Low P/E	12.9	11.1
High yield	12.7	10.6
Overall portfolio	11.0	12.5

Again, please keep in mind that the difference between 15.4 and 12.5 percent may not sound like a lot, but compounded over many years it can make a huge difference in the final value of your portfolio. If one had invested $10,000 in a low-price/sales stock portfolio for the 41 years from 1954 to 1994, it would have grown to *$3.1 million,* versus just *$1.1 million* for the all-stocks universe.

growth characteristics. Our emphasis on buying faster-growing companies at reasonable valuations combines the best tenets of value investing with those of growth investing.

In the meantime, here are some value screens devised to help you find sound small-cap value stocks. Each of these strategies has provided favorable returns on a backtested basis.

Screen 1 (See Exhibit 13-1)	Stocks with market caps of $100 million to $1.5 billion
	Price/sales ratio less than 0.5
	Ranked by price/sales ratio

EXHIBIT 13-1   Value screen for stocks with market caps of $100 million to $1.5 billion: price/sales ratio less than 0.5. Ranked by price/sales ratio.
(From Standard & Poor's Stock Reports, *October 30, 1998. Copyright © 1998 by The McGraw-Hill Companies.)*

Ticker	Company Name	Price / Sales	Market Cap ($ Mil)
FLM	Fleming Cos	0.03	420.07
MICA	MicroAge Inc	0.04	203.51
CMPC	CompuCom Systems	0.06	133.06
ICO	InaCom Corp	0.06	270.97
ABFS	Arkansas Best	0.07	107.85
UWW	Unisource Worldwide	0.07	507.79
BDY	Bindley Western Indus	0.08	632.78
NS	Natl Steel 'B'	0.09	127.12
PIOS	Pioneer Std Electr	0.09	171.26
VC	Vencor Inc(New)	0.09	285.57
CFWY	Consolidated Freightways	0.10	230.49
ROAD	Roadway Express	0.10	262.05
IAD	Inland Steel Indus	0.10	435.26
NOV	NovaCare	0.11	183.66
YELL	Yellow Corp	0.11	327.57
OLS	Olsten Corp	0.11	399.63
IMC	Intl Multifoods	0.12	301.70
SHG	Sun Healthcare Group	0.12	338.69
CLST	CellStar Corp	0.13	228.45
MXM	MAXXAM Inc	0.13	346.98
VST	Vanstar Corp	0.13	362.07
AG	AGCO Corp	0.13	401.76
HPH	Harnischfeger Indus	0.14	376.41
JAII	Johnstown America Indus	0.15	125.77
OMI	Owens _Minor	0.15	480.00
CYRK	Cyrk Inc	0.16	120.09
NTK	Nortek Inc	0.16	244.51
VOL	Volt Info Sciences	0.16	256.60
STFF	Staff Leasing	0.16	334.52
AMES	Ames Department Stores	0.16	375.58
SFDS	Smithfield Foods	0.16	607.61
AAS	AmeriSource Health'A'	0.16	1234.98
BCU	Borden Chem/Plastics L.P.	0.17	107.93
GNL	Galey _Lord Inc	0.17	130.09
BBR	Butler Mfg	0.17	158.58
PKT	Pinkerton's Inc	0.17	173.91
MPN	Mariner Post-Acute Network	0.17	288.52
Z	Venator Group	0.17	1084.20
DDC	Detroit Diesel	0.18	409.11
CAST	Citation Corp	0.19	134.15
MVII	Mark VII	0.19	136.19
RYL	Ryland Group	0.19	311.75
AXE	Anixter Intl	0.19	568.93
HOC	Holly Corp	0.20	120.71
HUF	Huffy Corp	0.20	138.67

EXHIBIT 13-1   Value screen for stocks with market caps of $100 million to $1.5 billion: price/sales ratio less than 0.5. Ranked by price/sales ratio (*Continued*).

Ticker	Company Name	Price / Sales	Market Cap ($ Mil)
AEPI	AEP Industries	0.20	146.46
INT	World Fuel Services	0.20	164.99
PFGC	Performance Food Group	0.20	276.07
CDI	CDI Corp	0.20	298.86
KLU	Kaiser Aluminum	0.20	484.78
TRA	Terra Industries	0.20	514.92
NAV	Navistar Intl	0.20	1487.57
LADF	LADD Furniture	0.21	121.36
TBCC	TBC Corp	0.21	132.72
TTC	Toro Co	0.21	231.62
SAVO	Schultz Sav-O Stores	0.22	105.60
HMX	Hartmarx Corp	0.22	156.92
AFWY	Amer Freightways	0.22	209.58
UWZ	United Wisconsin Svcs	0.22	276.50
CUM	Cummins Engine	0.22	1328.25
XC	Cross-Continent Auto Retaile	0.23	132.34
OTRKB	Oshkosh Truck	0.23	189.82
SGE	Stage Stores	0.23	266.37
BYL	Brylane Inc	0.23	308.32
HMS	Host Marriott Services	0.23	311.35
MLG	Musicland Stores	0.23	422.24
PMRY	Pomeroy Computer Resources	0.24	138.31
CWC	Caribiner International	0.24	149.19
SSSS	Stewart Stevenson	0.24	304.32
NVR	NVR Inc	0.24	319.62
LSTR	Landstar System	0.24	321.63
CEI.C	Co-Steel Inc	0.24	427.50
CQB	Chiquita Brands Intl	0.24	633.22
RBK	Reebok Intl	0.24	843.11
OMX	OfficeMax Inc	0.24	967.96
BS	Bethlehem Steel	0.24	1085.58
CSE	Case Corp	0.24	1493.51
PKOH	Park-Ohio Holdings	0.25	129.28
AMN	Ameron Intl	0.25	138.26
WSTF	Westaff Inc	0.25	158.39
MHO	M/I Schottenstein Homes	0.25	163.00
MDC	M.D.C. Hldgs	0.25	273.61
MAG	MagneTek Inc	0.25	299.09
CVTY	Coventry Health Care	0.25	392.08
SEB	Seaboard Corp	0.25	455.32
BUR	Burlington Industries	0.25	495.17
KELYA	Kelly Services 'A'	0.25	884.72
NSS	NS Group	0.26	122.44
VCD	Value City Dept Stores	0.26	301.35
BOR	Borg-Warner Security	0.26	367.04

EXHIBIT 13-1   Value screen for stocks with market caps of $100 million to $1.5 billion: price/sales ratio less than 0.5. Ranked by price/sales ratio (*Continued*).

Ticker	Company Name	Price / Sales	Market Cap ($ Mil)
FHT	Fingerhut Companies	0.26	471.68
DTG	Dollar Thrifty Auto Grp	0.27	235.24
DIIG	DII Group	0.27	250.52
SPD	Standard Products	0.27	294.94
MME	Mid Atlantic Medical Svcs	0.27	303.88
PDM	Pitt-DesMoines Inc	0.28	142.71
GFF	Griffon Corp	0.28	249.58
ASF	Administaff Inc	0.28	406.02
MK	Morrison Knudsen	0.28	483.92
AWA	America West Holdings'B'	0.28	535.89
HUG	Hughes Supply	0.28	613.00
AVI	Avis Rent A Car	0.28	635.40
REMX	RemedyTemp Inc 'A'	0.29	100.67
JAS.A	Jo-Ann Stores'A'	0.29	155.72
SW	Stone Webster	0.29	379.20
KWD	Kellwood Co	0.29	518.76
MAH	Hanna(M.A.)Co	0.29	659.69
UVV	Univl Corp	0.29	1255.17
CNF	CNF Transportation	0.29	1335.60
GYMB	Gymboree Corp	0.30	125.38
SCR.A	Sea Containers Ltd Cl'A'	0.30	301.73
WBB	Webb (Del) Corp	0.30	351.96
AS	Armco Inc	0.30	546.08
FLE	Fleetwood Enterpr	0.30	959.00
BY	BWAY Corp	0.31	124.19
ENGL	Engle Homes	0.31	150.70
FA	Fairchild Corp 'A'	0.31	200.17
SMGS	SEMCO Energy	0.31	224.11
REV	Revlon Inc'A'	0.31	295.98
DRYR	Dreyer's Gr Ice Cr	0.31	313.03
USFC	USFreightways	0.31	552.49
SFE	Safeguard Scientifics	0.31	634.65
SKO	Shopko Stores	0.31	776.32
MRA	Meritor Automotive	0.31	1151.83
ODFL	Old Dominion Freight Line	0.32	115.32
SIND	Synthetic Industries	0.32	117.03
POP	Pope Talbot	0.32	126.38
ALN	Allen Telecom	0.32	140.40
DTII	D T Industries	0.32	164.03
HLX	Halter Marine Group	0.32	236.26
GON	Geon Co	0.32	407.76
DGN	Data General	0.32	470.26
NC	NACCO Indus Cl'A'	0.32	626.01
RDK	Ruddick Corp	0.32	775.78
OXM	Oxford Indus	0.33	255.89

EXHIBIT 13-1   Value screen for stocks with market caps of $100 million to $1.5 billion: price/sales ratio less than 0.5. Ranked by price/sales ratio (*Continued*).

Ticker	Company Name	Price / Sales	Market Cap ($ Mil)
DANKY	Danka Business Systems ADR	0.33	270.15
HXL	Hexcel Corp	0.33	337.46
MWL	Mail-Well Inc	0.33	422.66
AR	ASARCO Inc	0.33	832.88
POOL	SCP Pool	0.34	133.73
CAE	Cascade Corp	0.34	138.73
KEG	Key Energy Group	0.34	141.70
JASN	Jason Inc	0.34	155.84
IV	Mark IV Industries	0.34	785.95
LAYN	Layne Christensen Co	0.35	112.04
URS	URS Corp	0.35	247.36
STLTF	Stolt-Nielsen S.A.	0.35	275.08
KAMNA	Kaman Corp Cl'A'	0.35	344.05
MZ	Milacron Inc	0.35	666.82
ABF	Airborne Freight	0.35	1068.45
RAZR	Amer Safety Razor	0.36	107.47
VRES	VICORP Restaurants	0.36	120.62
PESC	Pool Energy Services	0.36	174.94
PRMX	Primex Technologies	0.36	175.33
MOG.A	Moog Cl'A'	0.36	186.45
RCOT	Recoton Corp	0.36	206.86
PGI	Polymer Group	0.36	244.00
THO	Thor Industries	0.36	249.80
BUS	Greyhound Lines	0.36	293.08
DOSE	PharMerica Inc	0.36	303.49
SQNT	Sequent Computer Sys	0.36	303.94
AVDO	Avado Brands	0.36	334.14
TEX	Terex Corp	0.36	373.08
WLM	Wellman Inc	0.36	383.03
SXC	Essex Intl	0.36	575.79
FTS	Footstar Inc	0.36	662.47
GLE	Gleason Corp	0.37	157.21
SAFM	Sanderson Farms	0.37	188.60
SKY	Skyline Corp	0.37	237.03
TJCO	T J International	0.37	270.91
CELL	Brightpoint Inc	0.37	471.81
WLT	Walter Industries	0.37	663.40
ARV	Arvin Indus	0.37	883.08
APM	Applied Magnetics	0.38	111.48
GUAR	Guarantee Life Cos	0.38	139.43
CKE	Carmike Cinemas'A'	0.38	156.58
SMRT	Stein Mart	0.38	316.91
FTT.C	Finning Intl	0.38	949.09
FFEX	Frozen Food Express	0.39	128.65
NEW	Nvest L.P.	0.39	170.30

EXHIBIT 13-1   Value screen for stocks with market caps of $100 million to $1.5 billion: price/sales ratio less than 0.5. Ranked by price/sales ratio (*Continued*).

Ticker	Company Name	Price / Sales	Market Cap ($ Mil)
RDRT	Read-Rite Corp	0.39	368.43
ABM	ABM Industries Inc	0.39	570.62
DTC	Domtar, Inc	0.39	784.75
KBH	Kaufman _Broad Home	0.39	886.75
TKR	Timken Co	0.39	1063.61
BMC	BMC Industries	0.40	127.92
MCLL	Metrocall Inc	0.40	139.49
HVT	Haverty Furniture	0.40	164.01
CMCO	Columbus McKinnon	0.40	221.83
LE	Lands' End	0.40	529.18
VALN	Vallen Corp	0.41	124.15
CUB	Cubic Corp	0.41	156.98
WES	Westcorp, Inc	0.41	169.91
TEC	Commercial Intertech	0.41	235.40
TBL	Timberland Co Cl'A'	0.41	273.38
ICP	Intl Comfort Products	0.41	274.29
WTS	Watts Industries'A'	0.41	298.45
DZTK	Daisytek Intl	0.41	326.98
GFD	Guilford Mills	0.41	371.00
BD	Budget Group'A'	0.41	765.45
SILI	Siliconix Inc	0.42	129.48
ABCR	ABC Rail Products	0.42	134.64
SCOR	Syncor Int'l	0.42	171.65
MSCA	M.S. Carriers	0.42	209.95
CFN	ContiFinancial Corp	0.42	277.54
SOC	Sunbeam Corp	0.42	491.52
CSI	Chase Industries	0.43	119.20
LUFK	Lufkin Industries	0.43	129.99
ADV	Advest Group	0.43	138.76
IFSIA	Interface Inc'A'	0.43	472.91
AEIC	Air Express Intl	0.43	664.31
SWFT	Swift Transportation	0.43	789.76
NMG	Neiman-Marcus Group	0.43	1026.27
SSAX	System Software	0.44	190.37
KTTY	Kitty Hawk	0.44	215.83
SCL	Stepan Co	0.44	262.08
BTC	BancTec,Inc	0.44	265.90
STAR	Lone Star Steakhouse/Saloon	0.44	276.95
GND	Grand Casinos	0.44	285.47
RS	Reliance Steel _Aluminum	0.44	509.46
CHX	Pilgrim's Pride'B'	0.44	586.26
BCF	Burlington Coat Factory	0.44	796.53
BLL	Ball Corp	0.44	1090.23
MCCO	Monaco Coach	0.45	223.68
WGO	Winnebago Indus	0.45	236.24

EXHIBIT 13-1   Value screen for stocks with market caps of $100 million to $1.5 billion: price/sales ratio less than 0.5. Ranked by price/sales ratio (*Continued*).

Ticker	Company Name	Price / Sales	Market Cap ($ Mil)
AMMB	AMRESCO INC	0.45	254.59
FRTZ	Fritz Companies	0.45	255.65
BWC	Belden Inc	0.45	345.48
WSO	Watsco, Inc	0.45	364.36
FM	Foodmaker Inc	0.45	538.13
GY	GenCorp	0.45	757.88
LVC	Lillian Vernon	0.46	121.98
WND	Windmere-Durable Hldgs	0.46	122.95
FINL	Finish Line 'A'	0.46	161.88
PKE	Park Electrochemical	0.46	178.12
TXI	Texas Indus	0.46	546.90
WRC	World Color Press	0.46	1005.47
BAR	Banner Aerospace	0.47	167.54
ACAT	Arctic Cat	0.47	174.06
FIZ	Natl Beverage	0.47	189.40
IRIC	Information Resources	0.47	229.50
SMG	Scotts Co 'A'	0.47	509.00
ALK	Alaska Air Group	0.47	863.17
DRRA	Dura Automotive Sys'A'	0.48	101.00
KWR	Quaker Chemical Corporation	0.48	120.34
GRDG	Garden Ridge	0.48	154.64
FTO	Frontier Oil	0.48	165.38
HKF	Hancock Fabrics	0.48	189.39
MWT	McWhorter Technologies	0.48	208.35
BHE	Benchmark Electronics	0.48	224.82
LSS	Lone Star Technologies	0.48	251.64
SPF	Standard Pacific	0.48	277.19
KNT	Kent Electronics	0.48	310.35
NCH	NCH Corp	0.48	376.58
PDE	Pride International	0.48	394.97
CENT	Central Garden _Pet	0.48	540.94
NOI	Natl-Oilwell Inc	0.48	556.46
DEX	Dexter Corp	0.48	608.94
CKR	CKE Restaurants	0.48	809.31
BSH	Bush Indus Cl'A'	0.49	141.24
CVTI	Covenant Transport 'A'	0.49	145.16
RESC	Roanoke Electric Steel	0.49	145.24
XPRSA	U.S. Xpress Enterprises'A'	0.49	146.59
AMPI	Amplicon, Inc	0.49	153.84
MCC	Mestek Inc	0.49	160.56
ESSF	ESSEF Corp	0.49	202.96
AD	ADVO Inc	0.49	516.65

Screen 2   Stocks with market caps of $100 million
(See Exhibit 13-2)   to $1.5 billion

                            Price/sales ratio less than 1.0

                            ROE less than 20 percent

                            Above-average profit margins

                            Ranked by price/sales ratio

EXHIBIT 13-2   Value screen for stocks with market caps of $100 million to $1.5 billion: price/sales ratio less than 1.0; ROE less than 20 percent; above-average profit margins. Ranked by price/sales ratio.

(From Standard & Poor's Stock Reports, *October 30, 1998. Copyright © 1998 by The McGraw-Hill Companies.)*

Ticker	Company Name	Price / Sales	Return on Equity	Net Profit Margin	Market Cap ($ Mil)
GYMB	Gymboree Corp	0.30	22.20	10.50	125.38
STLTF	Stolt-Nielsen S.A.	0.35	23.50	15.00	275.08
APM	Applied Magnetics	0.38	50.50	19.40	111.48
NEW	Nvest L.P.	0.39	44.70	17.00	170.30
BMC	BMC Industries	0.40	22.10	11.40	127.92
SILI	Siliconix Inc	0.42	24.80	10.20	129.48
CFN	ContiFinancial Corp	0.42	30.10	25.30	277.54
PDE	Pride International	0.48	23.40	14.80	394.97
TIE	Titanium Metals	0.59	22.50	11.30	450.24
MSX	MascoTech, Inc	0.59	59.70	12.40	759.40
COHU	Cohu Inc	0.65	26.20	15.50	131.43
ICII	Imperial Credit	0.65	31.90	35.40	238.24
CTI	Chart Industries	0.68	43.20	11.70	151.41
SRI	Stoneridge Inc	0.69	38.80	10.40	335.95
BDG	Bandag, Inc	0.74	27.90	14.80	301.44
AAP	Amway Asia Pacific	0.78	33.70	12.30	504.42
SJK	St. John Knits	0.82	30.20	14.20	227.31
RSYS	RadiSys Corp	0.88	23.20	12.20	110.58
RJF	Raymond James Finl	0.89	26.30	10.80	950.34
SVR	Silverleaf Resorts	0.91	22.90	14.00	108.16
CIG	Consolidated Cigar Hldgs'A'	0.94	191.40	17.90	102.19
CDG	Cliffs Drilling	0.99	26.00	17.80	312.84
ELY	Callaway Golf	0.99	31.40	15.70	821.54

Screen 3   Stocks with market caps of $100 million to
(See Exhibit 13-3) $1.5 billion

                           Yield greater than mean

                           Price/book-value ratio less than 1.5

**EXHIBIT 13-3   Value screen for stocks with market caps of $100 million to
$1.5 billion: yield greater than mean; price/book-value ratio less than 1.5.**
(From Standard & Poor's Stock Reports, *October 28, 1998. Copyright © 1998 by The McGraw-Hill
Companies.)*

Ticker	Company Name	Market Cap ($ Mil)	Dividend Yield	Price / Book Ratio
AIR	AAR Corp	512.57	1.80	1.87
AKS	AK Steel Holding	943.59	3.10	1.06
AVX	AVX Corp	1253.87	1.80	1.55
ANV	Aeroquip-Vickers Inc	817.09	3.00	1.92
ALG	Alamo Group	132.65	3.20	1.34
AIN	Albany Intl 'A'	442.28	2.30	1.92
ALEX	Alexander _Baldwin	908.77	4.40	1.27
AIZ	Amcast Industrial	131.19	3.90	1.19
ACO	AMCOL Intl	293.06	2.20	1.88
ABP	Amer Business Prod	269.10	3.60	1.82
AII	Amer Ins Mtge Inv Ser 85	157.02	9.60	0.94
AIK	Amer Ins Mtge Inv Ser 88	105.62	9.10	0.82
AIP	Amer Israeli Paper Ord	119.82	16.10	0.66
AMN	Ameron Intl	138.26	3.70	0.97
AP	Ampco-Pittsburgh	119.12	2.80	0.87
AGL	Angelica Corp	144.27	6.10	0.86
APZ	Applied Indus Technologies	265.22	4.00	1.10
ACI	Arch Coal	647.58	2.80	1.02
ACAT	Arctic Cat	174.06	2.80	1.39
AIND	Arnold Indus	314.02	3.60	1.43
AR	ASARCO Inc	832.88	3.80	0.51
ASL	Ashanti Goldfields Ltd GDS	987.93	1.90	1.74
AVT	Avnet, Inc	1433.43	1.50	1.68
BPT	BP Prudhoe Bay Royalty	159.15	2.90	0.72
BDG	Bandag, Inc	301.44	3.50	1.49
BIR	Birmingham Steel	142.38	2.00	0.34
BL	Blair Corp	230.49	3.40	1.06
BLOCA	Block Drug'A'non-vtg	495.25	3.50	1.66
BOBE	Bob Evans Farms	859.23	1.50	1.92
BNE	Bowne _Co	430.40	1.80	1.44
BG	Brown Group	261.66	2.70	1.29
BW	Brush Wellman	219.29	3.50	0.97
BBR	Butler Mfg	158.58	2.90	0.99
CAE.C	CAE Inc	999.93	1.70	NA
CCC	Calgon Carbon	240.92	5.20	1.68
CZM	CalMat Co	530.93	1.70	1.76
CCJ	Cameco Corp	1035.39	2.70	0.58
CMW	Canadian Marconi	268.25	3.70	0.83
CRS	Carpenter Technology	836.77	3.60	1.79
CAS	Castle (A.M.)	214.17	5.10	1.48
CACOA	Cato Corp'A'	222.28	2.00	1.59
CCL.C	Celanese Canada	904.25	3.60	1.99
CENX	Century Aluminum	180.00	2.20	1.03
CEM	ChemFirst Inc	337.19	2.20	1.20
CSK	Chesapeake Corp	711.82	2.30	1.87
CQB	Chiquita Brands Intl	633.22	2.00	1.53
CHCO	City Holding	241.54	2.10	1.92
CLF	Cleveland-Cliffs	456.53	3.70	1.10
CEI.C	Co-Steel Inc	427.50	2.80	0.70
COKE	Coca-Cola Bott Consol	415.65	1.60	NA

EXHIBIT 13-3   Value screen for stocks with market caps of $100 million to $1.5 billion: yield greater than mean; price/book-value ratio less than 1.5 (*Continued*).

Ticker	Company Name	Market Cap ($ Mil)	Dividend Yield	Price / Book Ratio
COHU	Cohu Inc	131.43	2.30	0.95
CMCO	Columbus McKinnon	221.83	1.70	NA
CLT	Cominco Ltd	923.34	1.70	0.70
CMC	Commercial Metals	367.86	2.10	0.97
CMIN	Commonwealth Industries	127.55	2.50	0.81
CSII	Communic Sys	102.15	3.50	1.63
CTB	Cooper Tire Rubber	1248.75	2.30	1.57
CGW	Cristalerias de Chile ADS	237.33	3.70	0.79
CUB	Cubic Corp	156.98	2.10	1.08
CUM	Cummins Engine	1328.25	3.10	1.71
CW	Curtiss-Wright	345.66	1.50	1.59
CYM	Cyprus Amax Minerals	1217.63	6.10	0.54
DRC	Dain Rauscher	378.39	2.80	1.77
DANKY	Danka Business Systems ADR	270.15	4.60	NA
DLW	Delta Woodside Ind	126.30	1.90	0.78
DES	Desc S.A. ADS	234.40	3.60	NA
DP	Diagnostic Products	281.66	2.30	1.58
DTC	Domtar, Inc	784.75	2.60	0.66
EFU	Eastern Enterprises	974.89	3.70	1.71
ELRNF	Elron Electrn Ind Ord	263.86	1.80	1.21
EQT	Equitable Resources	1071.26	4.00	1.41
EXC	Excel Industries	159.50	3.90	1.07
FIT	Fab Indus	117.32	3.30	0.85
FVH	Fahnestock Viner Hldgs'A'	173.14	2.00	1.04
FGP	Ferrellgas Partners L.P.	292.16	10.00	NA
FLH	Fila Holdings ADS	209.36	2.40	0.68
FHT	Fingerhut Companies	471.68	1.60	0.78
FTT.C	Finning Intl	949.09	1.60	1.56
FFS	Fletcher Challenge Forest AD	258.70	10.50	0.39
FCX	Freep't McMoRan CopperGold'	1347.87	1.60	NA
FFEX	Frozen Food Express	128.65	1.50	1.33
FULL	Fuller (HB)	482.13	2.30	1.64
GAN	Garan Inc	127.58	3.20	1.21
GET	Gaylord Entertainment	754.58	2.60	1.81
GBND	Genl Binding	366.76	1.50	NA
GON	Geon Co	407.76	2.80	1.79
GI	Giant Industries	131.22	1.60	1.16
GLT	Glatfelter (P. H.)	498.66	5.80	1.42
GLE	Gleason Corp	157.21	1.60	1.45
GRC	Gorman-Rupp	142.47	3.60	1.77
GAP	Great Atl Pac Tea	865.47	1.70	0.92
GBX	Greenbrier Cos	193.19	1.70	1.67
IMY	Grupo Imsa ADS	609.48	2.80	0.95
GSH	Guangshen Railway ADS	612.35	10.00	0.55
GFD	Guilford Mills	371.00	3.00	0.87
HKF	Hancock Fabrics	189.39	4.30	1.98
HPH	Harnischfeger Indus	376.41	5.00	1.88
HVT	Haverty Furniture	164.01	1.80	1.39
HPS	HealthPlan Services	144.50	5.30	NA
HRH	Hilb,Rogal Hamilton	207.67	3.70	NA

EXHIBIT 13-3   **Value screen for stocks with market caps of $100 million to $1.5 billion: yield greater than mean; price/book-value ratio less than 1.5** (*Continued*).

Ticker	Company Name	Market Cap ($ Mil)	Dividend Yield	Price / Book Ratio
HLR	Hollinger Intl'A'	1107.90	4.40	NA
HOC	Holly Corp	120.71	4.30	1.11
HBC.C	Hudson's Bay Co	1450.51	3.60	NA
HUF	Huffy Corp	138.67	2.90	1.98
IRS	IRSA Inversiones y Rep GDS	265.13	4.80	0.93
IEX	IDEX Corp	711.51	2.20	NA
IKN	Ikon Office Solutions	999.72	2.10	NA
IAL	Intl Aluminum	115.02	4.40	1.01
IMC	Intl Multifoods	301.70	4.90	1.54
ISH	Intl Shipholding	107.76	1.50	0.62
IBI	Intimate Brands 'A'	889.99	2.40	NA
KTO	K2 Inc	154.27	4.70	0.80
KAMNA	Kaman Corp Cl'A'	344.05	2.90	1.18
KT	Katy Indus	127.53	1.90	0.86
KWD	Kellwood Co	518.76	2.60	1.85
KELYA	Kelly Services'A'	884.72	3.60	1.93
KBALB	Kimball Intl Cl'B'	460.38	3.70	1.58
KOR	Koor Indus Ltd ADS	1152.53	3.20	NA
LAWS	Lawson Products	267.26	2.30	1.83
LAW	Lawter Intl	219.03	6.20	1.82
LEE	Lee Enterprises	775.32	2.30	NA
LCUT	Lifetime Hoan	108.56	2.80	1.52
LVC	Lillian Vernon	121.98	2.40	1.08
LI	Lilly Industries'A'	386.86	1.80	NA
LFB	Longview Fibre	613.66	2.60	1.47
LUB	Luby's Cafeterias	334.52	5.50	1.48
LUFK	Lufkin Industries	129.99	3.60	0.85
MTSC	MTS Systems	227.43	1.90	1.67
MAD	Madeco S.A. ADS	231.87	5.40	0.63
MTW	Manitowoc Company	510.08	1.50	NA
MCS	Marcus Corp	256.91	1.50	1.46
MSX	MascoTech, Inc	759.40	1.70	NA
MAV	Mavesa, S.A. ADS	153.75	2.10	0.60
MHX	MeriStar Hospitality	779.01	11.70	0.91
MKS	Mikasa Inc	203.63	1.70	1.12
MNES	Mine Safety Appl	375.99	1.80	1.57
GRO	Mississippi Chemical	316.66	3.40	1.16
MND.A	Mitchell Energy/Dev'A'	277.60	3.80	1.54
MOL.A	Molson Cos Cl'A'	967.11	3.40	NA
MCL	Moore Corp Ltd	939.77	1.80	1.15
NCH	NCH Corp	376.58	2.00	1.26
NFC	NFC plcADS (New)	864.10	8.70	1.00
NTAIF	Nam Tai Electronics	119.90	2.60	0.81
NPK	Natl Presto Indus	275.00	5.30	1.15
NLP	Natl Realty L.P.	127.62	2.40	NA
NS	Natl Steel 'B'	127.12	4.60	0.30
NET	North Europn Oil Rty Tr	140.22	9.70	NA
CBRYA	Northland Cranberries'A'	172.06	1.60	1.70
OEA	OEA Inc	166.03	4.00	0.95
OGLE	Oglebay Norton	114.31	3.30	1.44

EXHIBIT 13-3   Value screen for stocks with market caps of $100 million to $1.5 billion: yield greater than mean; price/book-value ratio less than 1.5 (Continued).

Ticker	Company Name	Market Cap ($ Mil)	Dividend Yield	Price / Book Ratio
OLN	Olin Corp	1220.20	4.60	1.40
OV	One Valley Bancorp	986.48	3.10	1.79
OS	Oregon Steel Mills	330.25	4.30	1.06
OSH.A	Oshawa Grp Cl'A'	1025.97	2.00	1.22
OTRKB	Oshkosh Truck	189.82	2.10	NA
OSL	O'Sullivan Corp	111.11	4.40	0.97
OSG	Overseas Shiphldg	632.37	3.40	0.80
OXM	Oxford Indus	255.89	2.70	1.60
PKE	Park Electrochemical	178.12	2.00	1.04
PVA	Penn Virginia	176.43	4.20	1.07
PNT	Pennsylvania Enterpr	230.60	5.20	1.82
PBY	Pep Boys-Man,Mo,Ja	984.84	1.60	1.18
PIC	Piccadilly Cafeterias	104.36	4.80	1.54
PIR	Pier 1 Imports	732.92	1.60	1.92
PIOS	Pioneer Std Electr	171.26	1.80	1.90
PDM	Pitt-DesMoines Inc	142.71	3.00	1.10
PZX	Pittston BAX Group	109.53	4.40	0.80
POP	Pope _Talbot	126.38	8.10	0.69
PCH	Potlatch Corp	1069.70	4.70	1.13
PRMX	Primex Technologies	175.33	1.70	1.51
PTS.C	Prudential Steel	193.36	3.10	1.59
PRN	Puerto Rican Cement	217.51	1.80	1.38
NX	Quanex Corp	259.64	3.40	1.27
LQU	Quilmes Ind(Quinsa) ADS	305.35	2.70	1.20
LQ	Quinenco S.A. ADS	662.52	6.80	1.03
RES	RPC Inc	253.66	1.60	1.83
RMA	Rauma Oy ADS	609.50	4.30	1.46
RYN	Rayonier Inc	1126.88	3.10	1.75
RGC	Republic Group	162.27	2.60	1.76
REXI	Resource America'A'	174.18	1.50	0.85
REXYD	Rexam Plc ADR	1176.69	4.30	1.47
ROM	Rio Algom Ltd	825.38	3.30	0.51
ROAD	Roadway Express	262.05	1.50	1.05
RESC	Roanoke Electric Steel	145.24	2.90	1.27
ROU	Rouge Industries 'A'	106.62	1.60	0.36
RDK	Ruddick Corp	775.78	1.90	1.92
RUS	Russ Berrie _Co	384.62	4.40	1.18
RML	Russell Corp	894.11	2.20	1.36
SPM	Saga Petroleum ADS	1353.49	4.00	1.39
SAFM	Sanderson Farms	188.60	1.50	1.59
SHS	Sauer Inc	174.65	4.30	1.24
SHLM	Schulman (A.)	544.17	2.90	1.45
SAVO	Schultz Sav-O Stores	105.60	2.00	1.99
SWM	Schweitzer-Mauduit Intl	255.23	3.70	1.32
SCR.A	Sea Containers Ltd Cl'A'	301.73	3.90	1.23
SY	Shelby Williams Ind	109.27	3.00	1.71
SKY	Skyline Corp	237.03	2.30	1.32
SMF	Smart _Final Inc	186.92	2.40	1.28
AOS	Smith (A.O.)	269.62	2.60	1.25
PCU	Southern Peru Copper	136.01	6.40	0.71

EXHIBIT 13-3   Value screen for stocks with market caps of $100 million to $1.5 billion: yield greater than mean; price/book-value ratio less than 1.5 (*Continued*).

Ticker	Company Name	Market Cap ($ Mil)	Dividend Yield	Price / Book Ratio
SWX	Southwest Gas	667.24	3.70	1.57
SWS	Southwest Securities Grp	180.20	1.60	1.44
SWN	Southwestern Energy	163.28	3.60	0.74
SMI	Springs Industries'A'	371.67	4.00	0.83
SPF	Standard Pacific	277.19	1.70	0.95
SPD	Standard Products	294.94	3.90	1.59
SR	Standard Register	594.74	3.30	1.51
SCX	Starrett (L.S.)'A'	170.43	2.40	1.24
SSSS	Stewart .Stevenson	304.32	3.10	0.73
SW	Stone .Webster	379.20	2.00	1.10
SRR	Stride Rite	372.55	2.50	1.48
SDP	SunSource Inc	105.98	2.70	NA
TECUA	Tecumseh Products Cl'A'	734.67	2.50	1.03
TEK	Tektronix Inc	827.52	2.90	1.15
TRA	Terra Industries	514.92	2.90	0.99
TDW	Tidewater Inc	1350.17	2.50	NA
TKR	Timken Co	1063.61	4.20	1.16
TTC	Toro Co	231.62	2.60	1.17
TGS	Transportadora De Gas ADS	730.93	10.00	1.45
TNZRY	Tranz Rail Hlds ADS	633.50	4.20	0.77
TRN	Trinity Indus	1419.93	2.00	1.52
TUSC	Tuscarora Inc	124.67	1.60	1.80
UC	United Cos Financial	127.83	7.20	0.33
UIC	United Industrial	114.45	4.30	1.09
UWR	United Water Res	695.36	5.10	1.34
USFC	USFreightways	552.49	1.70	1.73
VALM	Valmont Indus	393.16	1.70	1.79
VCO	Vina Concha y Toro ADS	300.25	1.80	1.87
VTO	Vitro,Sociedad Anonima ADS	555.00	2.50	0.57
WTS	Watts Industries'A'	298.45	1.90	1.89
WMO	Wausau-Mosinee Paper	839.28	1.90	1.86
WMK	Weis Markets	1433.28	2.90	1.64
WLM	Wellman Inc	383.03	2.90	1.05
WGR	Western Gas Resources	253.16	2.50	0.85
WSH	Western Star Trucks Hldg	148.41	2.40	0.67
WGO	Winnebago Indus	236.24	1.90	1.97
WTHG	Worthington Indus	1353.19	4.00	1.98
ZAP	Zapata Corp	167.20	4.00	0.80
STLTF	Stolt-Nielsen S.A.	275.08	4.60	NA
CBI	Chicago Bridge .Iron N.V.	113.77	2.50	1.41
TK	Teekay Shipping	571.59	4.70	NA

Screen 4 (See Exhibit 13-4)	Stocks with market caps of more than $20 million
	Stock-price/book-value ratio less than 1.0
	Stock price less than $5
	Debt less than 30 percent of capital
	Current ratio greater than 2.0
	Ranked alphabetically

EXHIBIT 13-4 Value screen for stocks with market caps of more than $20 million: price/book-value ratio less than 1.0; stock price less than $5; debt less than 30 percent of capital; current ratio greater than 2.0. Ranked alphabetically.

(From Standard & Poor's Stock Reports, October 28, 1998. Copyright © 1998 by The McGraw-Hill Companies.)

Ticker	Company Name	Price / Book Ratio	Stock Price	Debt % Tot Cap	Current Ratio	Market Cap ($ Mil)
BIOI	BioSource Intl	0.84	2.84	4.40	7.03	24.05
DMIC	Digital Microwave	0.81	2.81	0.10	3.37	172.64
DIO	Diodes, Inc	0.81	4.25	11.50	2.84	21.44
MCON	EMCON	0.52	2.59	16.40	2.14	22.62
FSTR	Foster (LB)	0.59	3.93	19.80	3.71	39.51
GSE	Gundle/SLT Environmental	0.75	3.25	29.60	2.31	42.98
SPTR	SpecTran Corp	0.51	4.06	29.70	2.43	28.45
BEAM	Summit Technology	0.77	3.12	6.64	4.71	97.76

261

Screen 5   Stocks with market caps of less than
(See Exhibit 13-5) $1 billion
                            Stock-price/cash-flow ratio less than 5.0
                            Debt less than 30 percent of capital
                            Current ratio greater than 2.0
                            Price/sales ratio less than 1.0
                            ROE greater than 10 percent
                            Ranked by price/cash-flow ratio

EXHIBIT 13-5 Value screen for stocks with market caps of less than $1 billion: price/cash-flow ratio less than 5.0; debt less than 30 percent of capital; current ratio less than 2.0; price/sales ratio less than 1.0; ROE greater than 10 percent. Ranked by price/cash-flow ratio.

(From Standard & Poor's Stock Reports, October 30, 1998. Copyright © 1998 by The McGraw-Hill Companies.)

Ticker	Company Name	Price / Cash Flow	Debt % Tot Cap	Current Ratio	Price / Sales	Return on Equity	Market Cap ($ Mil)
CECX	Castle Energy Corp	2.60	8.00	2.99	0.75	39.90	52.00
CFI	Culp Inc	2.65	23.60	3.11	0.17	14.40	83.64
BMC	BMC Industries	2.76	28.70	3.13	0.40	22.10	127.92
ELXS	ELXSI Corp	2.95	20.50	2.38	0.51	39.80	47.40
STAF	Lone Star Steakhouse/Saloon	2.97	0.05	4.16	0.44	12.90	276.95
GFD	Guilford Mills	3.18	23.90	2.38	0.41	12.00	371.00
SPTF	SpecTran Corp	3.30	29.70	2.43	0.46	11.30	28.45
SEEQ	SEEQ Technology	3.35	14.70	3.78	0.69	28.00	21.10
RAM	Royal Appliance Mfg	3.36	17.70	2.13	0.21	21.30	65.67
INFS	In Focus Systems	3.39	0.70	4.26	0.30	16.60	95.02
HTCH	Hutchinson Technology	3.40	21.30	2.52	0.73	20.10	284.29
TXI	Texas Indus	3.43	23.60	2.57	0.46	17.30	546.90
DRCO	Dynamics Research	3.51	20.30	2.22	0.22	11.10	38.41
BTC	BancTec,Inc	3.58	4.30	2.42	0.44	18.30	265.90
DWSN	Dawson Geophysical	3.58	16.80	9.38	0.91	12.90	54.22
DA¨M	Datum Inc	3.64	22.90	5.17	0.31	10.50	32.59
AMK	Amer Techi Ceramics	3.76	12.00	3.91	0.57	13.80	22.93
HTXA	Hitox Corp	3.80	6.42	3.56	0.53	10.90	5.82
CAE	Cascade Corp	3.80	10.90	2.28	0.34	18.40	138.73
DIC	Diodes, Inc	3.80	11.50	2.84	0.33	23.30	21.44
WIRE	Encore Wire	3.84	24.00	2.77	0.57	37.10	146.70
KAMNA	Kaman Corp Cl'A'	3.89	9.40	2.22	0.35	31.40	344.05
MLI	Mueller Industries	3.99	9.60	3.08	0.72	18.20	656.59
WMD	Windmere-Durable Hldgs	4.04	7.80	2.07	0.46	11.00	122.95
MOSX	Mosaix Inc	4.22	0.10	2.46	0.51	17.20	58.17
BNE	Bowne Co	4.38	0.70	2.41	0.55	20.60	430.40
TLI	Twin Disc	4.42	21.30	3.16	0.32	10.30	64.98
LSS	Lone Star Technologies	4.45	16.50	3.23	0.48	23.80	251.64
MAVK	Maverick Tube	4.47	18.70	3.04	0.30	22.00	89.71
BDG	Bandag, Inc	4.49	17.50	2.48	0.74	27.90	301.44
TJCO	T J International	4.53	23.50	3.99	0.37	12.40	270.91
C-IP	CD Technologies	4.56	18.10	2.22	0.88	20.80	281.05
U·C	United Industrial	4.71	3.90	2.80	0.52	15.40	114.45
PZA	Provena Foods	4.78	8.10	4.40	0.27	15.80	8.66
UFI	Unifi, Inc	4.81	29.90	2.32	0.69	20.40	951.36
CCAM	CCA Industries	4.89	1.00	2.45	0.26	15.70	8.97

263

14

C H A P T E R

KNOWING WHEN TO SELL

DECIDING WHEN TO sell is usually the hardest decision an investor makes. Of course, this can be a simple decision if the stock was a good buy in the first place. The stock rises for all of the reasons that the buyer expected, the favorable ramifications are understood by other investors, and the stock is sold at a huge profit one year after purchase to take advantage of lower tax rates for long-term gains. Simple, right?

You do not need to be told that most investment calls do not work out that way. Just as in other aspects of life, what actually happens may be better or worse than predicted but will rarely turn out exactly as originally contemplated. Perhaps it will take longer for the story to develop than you had anticipated—of course, you cannot know if this is a delay or a missed call. Maybe the stock will not work out at all, and you will sustain a loss. Or maybe the individual company will provide a good story, but the overall stock market will drag the stock down.

Most often, an investor will be only partially right. The stock will rise, but only by half as much as was anticipated because the company's business does not develop as expected; or investors do not react to events as was thought. Should the stock be sold? In answering this question, the key is to ask yourself whether your original investment premise, whether based on GARP or other investment tools, has been or could still be achieved.

But before dealing with your specific stock, you should first evaluate the state of the overall market—is it over- or undervalued? As noted in Chapter 2, if you have more than a five-year time horizon, we would never recommend selling all of your stocks, nor do we generally recommend trying to time the market. Nonetheless, understanding the valuation level of U.S. stocks as a group is necessary in order to understand the relative value of each stock in your portfolio.

WHEN TO CUT BACK YOUR STOCK EXPOSURE

Earlier chapters counsel *against* trying to time the market. It is easier to pick individual stocks than to judge when to get in or out of the market. Of course, it is true that investment returns could be improved substantially if major downturns are avoided, but they could also suffer greatly if even a few big days on the upside are missed.

Similarly, it is easier to know when to get out of the market—usually due to short-term trading imbalances—than when to get back in. Many smart investors saw that the market was overvalued just before the 1987 crash. But because it came back so fast, most failed to return quickly enough to take full advantage of the drop.

Nonetheless, if you are interested in market timing—either because you are a very aggressive investor or, perhaps, because you have a short time horizon—here are some important signals that bear watching.

Value Line has made a habit of comparing the overall cheapness or expensiveness of the market based on projected earnings for all stocks it follows, and posting the rolled-up results for its stock universe on the first page of its biweekly print publication. By this P/E-to-growth-rate measure, stocks were most expensive in 1973 (just before the great bear market of 1973 to 1974), in 1987 (just before the October crash), and at mid-1998, just before the September quarter drop.

High Valuations: The Rule of 20

This is another theme reviewed in Chapter 3. The stock market is most overvalued when equity returns are very strong, economic fundamentals are favorable, and profit growth is well above the historical average. Investors get so enthusiastic about owning stocks that they drive stock prices well above mean valuation levels. This is the kind of rosy scenario in which the Rule of 20 can be very helpful.

As you will recall from Chapter 3, by this measure the market is generally fairly valued when the P/E of the S&P 500 added to the rate of inflation equals 20. For example, in early 1982, inflation was running at 8 percent and the P/E of the S&P 500 was 8. Stocks were a definite buy. Alternatively, just before the 1987 crash, the P/E of the market was 24—stocks were a sell *even before adding the inflation component.* As of November 1999, the P/E of the S&P 500 was 24 and the inflation rate was 2 percent, implying that the market was about 30 percent overvalued. Could this measure be wrong this time? Only if real earnings growth remains very high for a number of years. This can happen only if inflation remains low for the next 5 to 10 years *and* real earnings growth stays well above the historical average. Could this occur? Sure. But the combination of low inflation and high real earnings growth has rarely gone on long enough to justify such a high valuation. Indeed, stock prices fell in the third quarter of 1998 precisely because of dramatic cuts in earnings expectations for the rest of the year and into 1999 for companies in the S&P 500. They would fall even further if such cuts were extended to include reduced earnings growth expectations or higher inflation prospects for 2000 and beyond.

Spread Between 30-Year T-Bond and S&P 500 Yields of More than 6.0 Percent

This high spread usually occurs when the market P/E is historically high and interest rates and inflation fears are on the rise. For example, in the summer before the 1987 crash, the yield on the long bond was moving higher and eventually hit 9.5 percent. In the meantime, the dividend yield of the S&P 500 dropped below 3.0 percent.

Of course, this situation was an easier call for investors to make when interest rates were running high. This was a more difficult call as of mid-1998, when inflation and yields were down. After all, if 30-year Treasuries yield *less* than 6.0 percent, then this measure can never give a sell signal.

Standard & Poor's keeps track of this comparison via its Asset Allocation Model, which can be found within its Marketscope service (the model is more complicated than what is described here, but it follows the same logic). The model recommended being out of stocks in mid-1987 and late 1989, and getting back into them just after the crash and in early 1991. In July 1997, for the first time since, the model gave a sell signal again. However, it again recommended going back into stocks in October 1998.

Of course, it should be emphasized that the model is primarily for use by traders, not long-term investors. But it does provide a good quantitative measure of equities versus the fixed-income markets. At any given point in time, it has also been a good predictor of short- to intermediate-term price swings in stock prices. For long-term investors, we suggest that it be used when timing lump-sum investments in equities, and when rebalancing portfolios. For example, if the model is giving a caution signal, you might want to consider committing only a portion of the amount you have targeted for stocks.

Sell Signals from the Fed

You cannot fight the Fed. *Stocks do well when interest rates are falling, move sideways as interest rates initially move higher, and decline as they continue to move up.* This is because a decline in interest rates usually triggers economic growth and P/E expansion. Interest rate increases eventually choke it off.

The best move on the upside occurs when the markets begin to antici- pate a cut in rates by the Fed, and especially if it has been raising rates over an extended period of time. The biggest drops occur when the first rise in short-term rates is executed, and during subsequent months. Although there is usually a 6- to 12-month lag between the initial rate increase and its effect on the economy, stock investors react immediately. This initial rise in interest rates need not be a disaster. If the Fed is *early* in raising rates, growth may slow but should not be wholly eliminated—this is what as known as a *soft landing*. When a soft landing occurs, the market corrects but there is no significant bear decline. (A *bear market* is defined as a dip in the S&P 500 of more than 20 percent from its peak.) Earnings will be flat for a while, but damage to the market P/E is modest. (Soft landings have been tricky to orchestrate in the past, but the Fed has had better luck [or skill] during the 1990s.)

However, if the Fed has not reacted early enough, and has let inflation rise too high, then higher interest rates will be needed to cool the economy off. This scenario usually triggers a recession.

As of late 1999, the interest rate on the 30-year Treasury was fluctuat- ing above 6.25 percent, with the market dropping as rates rose above 6 per- cent. The latest moves by the Fed have been to raise rates, which should result in slower economic growth. This is good for stocks in the long run, but not over the short term.

Major Breach of the S&P 500's 200-Day Moving Average

Studies have shown that investors can add a few percentage points of annual return if they get out of stocks when the S&P 500 index drops below its 200-day moving average. Unfortunately, it is inherently not a particu- larly early sell signal—stocks must already have fallen by a certain amount for the moving average to cross the index.

The breach must also be a decisive one—at least 10 to 15 points on the S&P 500—in order to be a good sell signal. (On the upside, investors would get back in when the index recrosses the moving average by 10 to 15 points on the way up.) This is because there are many times that stocks will approach the moving average without significantly penetrating it. For example, the S&P 500 neared but never seriously penetrated its 200-day moving average between 1990 and 1998. On the other hand, the index deci- sively fell through its moving average on the Friday before the crash. Investors had just a few precious hours to act before the biggest drop occurred on the following Monday. As of early November 1999, the S&P

500 index had fallen just below its 200-day moving average as a reaction to moves by the Fed to raise interest rates and slow economic growth.

HEDGING THE PORTFOLIO

What if you like stocks for the long term, but are nervous about a near-term correction? There are a number of ways to hedge against a downturn without creating taxable events. One of the most common is to go short on Standard & Poor's Depositary Receipts (SPDRs, referred to as "spiders"). SPDRs are depositary receipts that trade based on the underlying value of an index. The price of an S&P 500 SPDR very closely tracks that of the underlying index. It is traded on the American Stock Exchange, and is quoted in sixty-fourths. (One can also buy puts on the S&P 500 index itself, but this means that you must be right on the *timing* as well as the direction of the market, since most puts have a duration of less than 9 months.)

MOST STOCKS ARE NOT THE MARRYING KIND

When considering the purchase of a stock, a keen distinction must be made between *investments* and *trades*. A stock is an investment when it is attractive based on underlying economic, industry, and company fundamentals. For this kind of equity, the most important issue is the P/E level that is acceptable when considering the purchase.

Consider Microsoft and Intel, two classic growth stocks with excellent fundamentals. Are they good buys at current P/E levels? Strong underlying fundamentals can bail you out if you modestly pay too much for a company, but you should never substantially overpay for any stock. You should keep your perspective concerning the stocks of even the best companies in America.

There is also the possibility that the fundamentals of a company are not what you thought they were. Long-term investments can become short-term trades in that kind of scenario, particularly if other investors share your surprise. Of course, you should never sell in a panic. But once the dust has settled, you should put the stock through a serious GARP analysis once again. *If you believe you have made a mistake, take the loss and move on.* Holding on to your losers to "get even" is a sure way to underperform the market.

Some investors use stop-loss orders to limit their downside. Trades are placed at, say, 10 to 20 percent below the current price to prevent large losses. Another strategy is to sell a stock whenever it drops a certain percentage below its 200-day moving average. (In order to avoid being whipsawed, the sale should occur once the stock is at least 10 percent below the average.) But these strategies should be used cautiously, since they could result in your being sold out of an otherwise good stock (not to mention triggering a potentially adverse taxable transaction).

When Getting Married to a Stock Is Okay

Although we do recommend a continual assessment of your portfolio holdings, there are some stocks that an investor may decide should be a core holding to be held for a number of years. (There are also tax advantages to this strategy. As of this writing, stocks held 5 years or more are subject to a very low 18 percent capital-gains tax beginning in 2002 for most investors and no higher than 20 percent even in the highest tax bracket.)

Although the 5-STAR and Fair Value-5 portfolios do turn over quite a bit, there are many stocks that have remained 5s for very long periods of time. Many 5-STAR stocks have become core holdings in the Bear Stearns S&P STARS Portfolio Fund. Similarly, there are many stocks that have been top-ranked by the S&P's Fair Value model for a number of years, including Express Scripts, Foodmaker, Gartner Group, OfficeMax, Outback Steakhouse, Oracle, Photronics, and Xilinx.

Table 14-1 lists 50 widely held stocks, their returns for 1994, and their returns for the succeeding 3 years. Of the 50 stocks that out- or underperformed in 1994, 32 trended the same way over the succeeding 3 years (i.e., if they beat the market in 1994, they did so during the next 3 years, and vice versa). This is a significantly high percentage, and illustrates the advantage of having a long-term focus.

TABLE 14-1   3-Year total return of selected stocks in the S&P 500.

Stock	12-mo Return 12/31/94	3-yr Return 12/31/97
Alcoa	24.9%	19.5%
Ameritech	3.9	30.8
AMR	−21.1	34.1
Bethlehem Steel	−9.4	−21.6
Bristol-Myers	−0.8	53.6
Burlington Northern	−16.7	26.6
Carolina Power & Light	−12.3	23.2
Caterpillar	22.3	23.2
Chase Bank	−11.7	49.7
Chevron	1.3	24.2
Chrysler	−8.4	17.8
Citicorp	11.5	48.0
Coca-Cola	14.8	38.9
Compaq Computer	59.3	53.1
Consolidated Edison	−21.7	25.0
Digital Equipment	−3.3	3.7

Stock	12-mo Return 12/31/94	3-yr Return 12/31/97
Disney, Walt	5.1	29.9
Dow Chemical	18.0	19.2
Dow Jones & Co.	−13.6	23.0
Easton	−4.3	24.8
Exxon	−4.5	30.8
Federal National Mortgage	−7.3	53.8
Federated Department Stores	−6.7	30.8
Ford Motor	−13.9	25.6
General Electric	−3.6	45.6
Global Marine	−6.5	89.2
GTE	−13.5	25.5
IBM	29.0	43.4
Intel	1.4	64.3
Johnson & Johnson	21.7	36.2
Kmart	−38.8	−2.3
McDonald's	1.5	18.5
MCI Communications	−31.9	32.8
Merck & Co.	9.7	43.8
Merrill Lynch	−15.4	62.7
Microsoft	50.5	61.8
Motorola	25.2	0.3
Novell	−18.0	−24.1
Oracle Systems	51.5	20.0
Penney, J. C.	−14.8	15.2
Pfizer	11.6	59.6
Philip Morris	2.9	39.7
SBC Communications	−10.6	26.0
Sun Microsystems	21.9	65.1
Telefonos de Mexico A ADRs	−41.3	14.1
Time Warner	−20.6	21.9
Toys "R" Us	−24.5	0.9
Wal-Mart	−15.8	23.9
Westinghouse Electric (CBS)	−13.3	35.4
Weyerhaeuser	−16.7	13.1
Average	**−2.3%**	**29.7%**
S&P 500	**1.4%**	**31.2%**

In summary, many are called but few are chosen. There are very few stocks eligible for marriage, but as your mother or father may have said, they are out there. And the longer one has owned the stock, the greater the deliberation required before closing out the position.

top-loss order trigger a sale, an analysis should *still* be made as ~~erlying~~ fundamentals have changed. Indeed, if the fundamen- ~~........ in~~ place, then the stock could represent a buying opportunity.

IMPORTANT SELL DISCIPLINES

The following sell disciplines are in order of importance, although you should choose those that work best for you. Studies have shown that all six disciplines can enhance portfolio returns over time.

1. *Original investment premise is no longer true.* Probably the worst drags on individual investor portfolio performance come from holding onto lousy stocks. You may have purchased it because of strong anticipated earnings growth, or because of an attractive P/E compared to the underlying earnings growth rate. Whatever the reason, if your original investment premise is no longer true, sell the stock. There will always be exceptions to this rule, but we are focusing on likelihoods, not possibilities. Most of these equities won't rebound any time soon.

2. *The stock is trading at a P/E that is more than 2.5 times its projected 3- to 5-year earnings growth rate.* It is extremely difficult for even the fastest growth stock to continue expanding earnings at a meteoric rate. There are very few product markets large enough to support it. Stocks that trade at big premiums to their growth rates are always strong sell candidates. There are many large-cap stocks in the S&P 500 with excellent track records that are trading well above their earnings growth rates, but most of them are below 2.5. Stocks with P/E-to-growth ratios above 2.5 may be attractive core holdings, but we would not add substantially to positions until they become more attractive from a GARP perspective. And for very high P/E small-cap stocks, we would be even more aggressive in paring them from a portfolio.

3. *The stock has a Fair Value ranking of less than 3.* In a way, this could be seen as another GARP tool, since the model incorporates many of the same valuation techniques. But the model adds in other important valuation measures, which make its signals worthy of attention. Stocks with fair values below 3 will likely underperform the market.

4. *The industry group is expensive on an historical basis.* Chapter 4 shows how the industry scorecard published as part of Standard & Poor's *Industry Surveys* can reveal *undervalued* industries—those

with favorable growth prospects compared to their current P/E valuation. This is important information to consider when deciding on individual stocks, as well. You will be surprised by the number of stocks that are unattractive individually that are also in industries for which the scorecard is negative.

5. *The stock has a STARS ranking of less than 3.*   Standard & Poor's equity analysts have not only done a fine job of picking attractive stocks, they have also been very good at identifying the lemons. Their avoid (2-STAR), and sell (1-STAR) recommendations have consistently underperformed the market as a group. A 1- or 2-STAR ranking is based on what the analyst thinks the stock will do over the next 6 to 12 months. Even if your time horizon is longer, such STARS designations should trigger a thorough review of the stock.

6. *There is heavy insider selling on a dollar basis.*   Insiders often sell their stock for reasons other than company fundamentals; often, they simply want to exercise their stock options. However, a very large exercise of options or straight stock sale could indicate that an insider believes that the shares are overvalued in the near term. If there is more than one such seller of large chunks of stock (valuing in the millions of dollars, for instance), it is a strong signal to reassess your position.

When to Sell a Growth Stock: The IBM Case Study

Most professionals have a hard time judging when to get out of a successful growth stock. The key lies in identifying important industry inflection points. For retailing, it was the creation of discount superstores such as Wal-Mart and Toys "R" Us. For technology, it was the creation of the WinTel personal computer in the early 1980s. These turns are often difficult to pinpoint exactly, but they can often be seen before it is too late—that is, before the losers have touched bottom and the winners have hit their peak.

Consider IBM's experience during the 1980s. It may have been difficult early in the decade to see that IBM was about to lose its preeminent position in the computer world, but by 1987 it was clear. Between the end of 1987 and the close of 1996, IBM's stock advanced just 9 percent—major underperformance compared to the S&P 500, which rose 293 percent.

What were the main factors behind IBM's fall from grace? Despite its significant presence in the PC market, IBM derived most of its sales and profits from mainframe computers. During the late

1980s, after the stock hit its all-time high of almost 88, management contended that mainframes should remain the company focus. Astute observers could see the handwriting on the wall. Mainframe sales generated the highest profit margins for the company, but only because the firm had a captive audience. But suddenly this was no longer true. Those investors who heeded this fundamental change in IBM's future business bailed out.

15

PUTTING IT ALL TOGETHER: HOW TO RESEARCH THE LATEST TIP

A S WE ALL KNOW, the most valuable commodity we have is time. This chapter uses what you have learned to show how a potential equity investment can be quickly researched, analyzed, and acted on in as little as an hour or two.

Deciding to buy a stock is a three-step process: *research, company analysis,* and *valuation analysis.* Suppose that an acquaintance who works for a store chain remarks to you that a slew of bar code printers are being installed as part of a companywide supply chain management program. But he does not know if other retailers are doing so, or have already done so, or whether the company's stock already has risen to reflect this new opportunity. Should you buy the shares?

Not before you do your research. In fact, the batting average of stocks researched to those *bought* should be quite low. But by looking at some key statistics early on in the research phase, you can significantly reduce the hours spent fruitlessly analyzing the wrong stocks. Hence, it is essential to develop some quick-and-dirty tools to speed the initial screening process. (Having fast access to company information via the Internet is very helpful at this stage.)

PHASE 1: GENERAL RESEARCH

Let's use your friend's bar code printer as an example—suppose that the printers being installed carry the Eltron brand. The first thing you would find is that there is no publicly owned stock for such a company. End of story? You should never give up at this point, because often the company you're interested in is owned by another company. Finding out the parent company of subsidiaries can be time consuming, but one place to look is the most recent volume of S&P's mammoth *Corporation Records,* which is available in most business libraries. If that turns nothing up, try Dun & Bradstreet's, or an open search on the Internet. And don't forget—your friend can always call up his sales purchase agent.

In this case, you would find that Eltron was recently purchased by another company called Zebra Technologies, which is indeed public. What follows is a step-by-step guide through the research and company-analysis process. What you will need are Standard & Poor's *Electronic Stock Reports, Investors Business Daily,* and the S&P *Earnings Guide.* The following list shows what to look for in each publication.

Publication	Key Stats
S&P *Electronic Stock Reports*	STARS ranking, Fair Value ranking, ROE, and risk level
Investors Business Daily	Earnings strength, relative strength, industry relative strength table, and P/E on forward earnings
S&P *Earnings Guide*	Estimated five-year earnings compound annual growth rate (CAGR)

The first publication to review is S&P *Stock Reports* (see Exhibit 15-1 at the end of the chapter). What are the STARS and Fair Value rankings? Hopefully, they are either 4s (accumulate) or 5s (buy). Next, look at the historical return on equity (ROE) at the bottom of page 2. The latest ROE should be greater than 10 percent and trending higher from the previous year. Quickly check the text on the first 2 pages to make sure there were no extraordinary items over the last 18 months that might have skewed the numbers.

Next, turn to your issue of *Investors Business Daily.* Look up the company on the stock tables. (Start with the New York Stock Exchange. If the company is not listed there, try the NASDAQ listings, then the American Stock Exchange.) Check the company's relative strength and earnings strength. Relative strength and earnings strength should both be above 80.

If the stock passes most of these hurdles, turn next to the S&P *Earnings Guide.* What is the estimated five-year earnings growth rate? Next, find the price/earnings (P/E) ratio from page 3 of S&P *Electronic Stock Reports* and calculate your P/E-to-growth ratio. (Remember, your P/E should always be calculated on forward 12-month projected earnings.) Generally speaking, if this ratio is below 1.5 it should be viewed as positive; 1.5 to 2.25 is average, and higher than 2.25 is poor. The whole process should take less than 10 minutes.

How would your test company, Zebra Technologies (ticker symbol ZBRA), have fared in this process? Table 15-1 shows the relevant statistics for ZBRA as of September 18, 1999. If the majority of these indicators are positive, the stock warrants additional attention. If most of the indicators are neutral to negative, chances are you should move on. There could always be some crucial information that would change your mind, but the chances are slim—is it really worth your time? (By the way, you should go through this exercise once every six months with your current holdings.)

PHASE 2: COMPANY ANALYSIS

Seven of the eight indicators flashed positive for Zebra Technologies in Table 15-1, so you should certainly look into the company and its stock. The next action to take is to get on the Internet, go to the government's Internet site at www.EDGAR.com, and download the most recent 10-K, 10-Q, and proxy statement. If you are not on the Internet, call the company using the phone number provided at the bottom of page 2 of S&P *Stock Reports*. Ask for the investor contact if a name is not already supplied. Make sure to ask for copies of recently published brokerage house stock reports. Not every company sends them, but it is worth a try. The company's website can also be useful. Portions of the annual report and press releases are usually available there.

TABLE 15-1   Statistics for Zebra Technologies (ZBRA), September 18, 1999.

Data Item	ZBRA	Comment
STARS ranking	5	Buy
Fair Value ranking	4	Accumulate
Risk	Average	Neutral
ROE	25%	Above average
Relative strength	87	Above average
Earnings strength	84	Above average
5-yr estimated earnings CAGR	20%	Above average
P/E-to-growth rate	0.9	Good

While your computer is downloading the information to your drive or printer, look at the "Industry Performance" tables in *Investors Business Daily*. Now that you know that the company is categorized as photography/imaging, you can look up some vital statistics on that industry. In a table that lists 197 industry indexes, look up photography/imaging (the category is actually called "computer-peripheral equipment"). You see that since January 1, this index was up 31.5 percent, an excellent performance, since the S&P 500 rose just 8.7 percent over the same period. Why was this the case?

One way to find out is to consult S&P *Industry Surveys,* which provides comprehensive analyses of more than 50 industries. (Many libraries have it.) A summary industry outlook is also supplied as page 4 of the electronic stock report of a company. But assume that you are unable to find one. Try to imagine the kind of economic changes that could impact specialty printer companies. Well, demand for computer hardware in general is way up this year. Part of that demand stems from the need to switch out non-Y2K-compliant hardware. There is also accelerated interest in installing supply chain management software that fosters greater use of bar codes further back in the inventory pipeline. This is what your friend is witnessing. The table also shows that computer peripheral equipment was number 11 in performance since January 1 out of the 197 groups ranked. (The industry's relative strength is a high A ranking.)

These are very good scores, and given the variety of information you have considered thus far, they encourage you to spend more time getting to know this company. (However, when you perform this exercise, bear in mind the overall makeup of the industry and whether it reflects the business of the firm you are looking at. For example, most of the market capitalization of the computer peripherals industry is comprised of disk-drive makers, such as EMC, Seagate, and Quantum, and printer companies, such as Xerox and Lexmark, but ZBRA's bar code printers address a very small subsegment of these markets—none of these players make bar code printers. Hence, you should use the general industry measures in an informed way.) One last item on the industry table in *Investors Business Daily* is titled "Sales % Growth Rate." This section provides the industry's three- to five-year compound sales growth rate.

Next, go through the company documents. Most of the important information in these filings can be found in S&P *Stock Reports.* For example, looking at the corporate description on page 2 of ZBRA's stock report you see that revenues rose in every one of the last eight years, as has operating income.

But the 10-K goes into much further depth. Reading it you find that ZBRA's main growth strategy is to expand revenues by capitalizing on rising industrywide demand and acquisitions of related businesses. Growth is being fueled by mandated standardization of product manufacturing and distribution tracking around bar coding, and increased demand for improvements in productivity and product quality in commercial and service organizations as part of enterprisewide resource planning (ERP) systems. Its card-printer business is being driven by the rapid growth in smart-card applications and increased use of computerized personal identification systems.

The 10-K also tells you that earnings in 1998 were hurt by integration issues stemming from the firm's purchase of Eltron International, one of its most important former competitors, and from a temporary pause in orders from UPS, its largest customer. The most recent 10-Q shows that revenue growth has since accelerated, while profit margins have recovered almost to preacquisition levels. As it is, the company's net profit margin of 17.6 percent for the most recent quarter is one of the highest for any company in the technology hardware sector.

So far you have not found anything that would undermine your intial attraction to the company's shares. The business has had a long history of revenue and profit growth, high profit margins, few direct competitors, and relatively high barriers to entry. So far, so good.

The next thing to do is to drill a little deeper and perform some statistical sensitivity analysis. In general, you are looking for some numerical support for your favorable reading of the company. Table 15-2 shows the statistics that bear watching, ZBRA's numbers, and our interpretation of them.

The results here are quite favorable, so you can move to the next phase of your study of ZBRA, that of valuation analysis.

PHASE 3: VALUATION ANALYSIS

This is where many growth stocks falter, particularly in the high-P/E stock market that is about to greet the next millennium. Some, but not all, of the ratios shown in Table 15-3 are incorporated into the S&P Fair Value Model. By far the most important statistic for us is P/E to long-term growth. As of mid-1999, the P/E-to-long-term-growth rate of the S&P 500 was 2.3. That is high by historical standards; the norm is 1.8. Price/sales is next in importance. As of mid-1999, this statistic for the S&P 500 was about 2.1. That is high by historical standards; the norm is about 0.8. Somewhat above-average price/sales ratios can be acceptable if a company is growing rapidly or if operations generate high profit margins. But when the price/sales ratio is above 3.0, it is cause for some concern for even the most well-positioned stocks.

Tallying up the trends, you wind up with 22 favorables, 2 unfavorables, and 4 neutrals. These numbers reflect a company that has exhibited consistently above-average sales and earnings growth and high levels of

TABLE 15-2 Statistics, trends, and comments for Zebra Technologies (ZBRA).

Key Statistic	Source*	ZBRA	Trend	Comment
Last 12-mo year-over-year sales growth	SR/AR/K	†9.2%	Unfavorable	Hurt by acquisition
3-yr compound trend	SR/AR/K	18.0%	Favorable	Very strong by any measure
5-yr compound trend	SR/AR/K	28.6%	Favorable	Very strong by any measure
5-yr projected EPS CAGR	Internet	20.0%	Favorable	Substantially better than S&P 500 estimated growth
Year-over-year estimated EPS growth	SR/AR/K	‡35.9%	Favorable	Inflated due to acquisition issues, but still well above average
Trailing 12-mo growth	SR/AR/K	†2.9%	Unfavorable	Hurt by one-time acquisition issues
3-yr compound trend	SR/AR/K	19.2%	Favorable	Consistent above-average growth, except for 1998
5-yr compound trend	SR/AR/K	15.9%	Favorable	Consistent above-average growth
Year-over-year annual cash flow	SR/AR/K	6.8%	Neutral	Growth limited by acquisition-related charges
3-yr compound trend	SR/AR/K	26.5%	Favorable	Better than profit growth
5-yr compound trend	SR/AR/K	21.0%	Favorable	Still stellar, but less than revenue and profit levels
Latest full-year net profit margin	SR/AR/K	11.9%	Favorable	Way over average, but less than historical margins due to acquisition
Net profit margin 3 yr ago	SR/AR/K	17.0%	Favorable	Very high by any standard
Latest 12-mo operating profit margin	SR/AR/K	22.3%	Favorable	High, particularly for technology hardware firm, despite acquisition costs

Operating margin 3 yr ago	SR/AR/K	25.6%	Favorable	Stable at high level
Gross profit margin last FY	AR/K	‡47.2%	Favorable	Stable
Gross margin 3 yr ago	AR/K	‡46.3%	Favorable	Stable
Debt as percent of long-term debt plus equity	SR/AR/K	7.5%	Favorable	Low
Debt (debt + equity) 3 yr ago	SR/AR/K	1.5%	Favorable	Low
Debt (debt + equity) 5 yr ago	SR/AR/K	0.3%	Favorable	Low
Current ratio	SR/AR/K	8.0	Favorable	Outstanding; reflects $194 million cash
Current ratio 3 yr ago	SR/AR/K	7.4	Favorable	Outstanding
Current ratio 5 yr ago	SR/AR/K	7.1	Favorable	Outstanding
ROE	SR/AR/K	35.0%	Favorable	Substantially above average and rising
ROE 3 yr ago	SR/AR/K	23.3%	Favorable	Still higher than average for S&P 500
ROE 5 yr ago	SR/AR/K	29.5%	Favorable	Substantially above average
Cap expenditure/depreciation	SR/AR/K	2.5	Neutral	Higher than historical rate
Cap expenditure/depreciation 3 yr ago	SR/AR/K	1.6	Neutral	Average for industrial company
Cap expenditure/depreciation 5 yr ago	SR/AR/K	1.5	Neutral	Average for industrial company

* SR—S&P *Stock Reports*; AR—annual report; K—10-K; Internet—*Zacks* or IBES web pages.
† Adjusted to include Eltron. Unless noted, all historical statistics exclude Eltron.
‡ Excludes $0.30 merger charges in 1998.

TABLE 15-3   Valuation statistics for Zebra Technology (ZBRA).

Key Statistic	ZBRA	Comment
P/E on projected EPS/estimated 5-y growth	1.0	Positive
P/E to projected year-over-year EPS growth	0.6	Positive
Price/sales	4.6	Negative
Price/cash flow	22.6	Negative
P/E on estimated next FY EPS	20.0	Positive
P/E on trailing 12-mo EPS	27.0	Positive
Price/book value	5.0	Negative

profitability. Such trends have resumed following the Eltron deal. A large cash hoard along with little internal need for capital suggests that already healthy internal growth can be further supplemented by additional acquisitions for cash. Occasional share buybacks could also boost EPS growth.

The votes are in, and they point toward the purchase of ZBRA. Management has clearly met aggressive growth goals for many years. With industry fundamentals excellent, that trend should continue. The stock is trading at somewhat high valuations by some measures—market cap/sales, market cap/cash flow, and price/book value among them. But on the basis of forward earnings, ZBRA is attractive compared to the rest of the market. At the time of this analysis, the S&P 500 is trading at a P/E ratio of 29 times trailing 12-month per-share earnings. Analysts are also projecting that companies in the S&P 500 will expand earnings at a 13 percent annual rate in 1999. Hence, ZBRA's shares are trading at a slight discount to the market, while also having better near-term and long-term earnings growth prospects. The Fair Value-5 and 5-STARS rankings give additional comfort that these shares could exceed the performance of the S&P 500. We would buy the shares.

Note that for a stock like this, you should carefully monitor revenue growth each quarter. Revisit this analysis every six months.

FINDING INVESTMENT IDEAS

Where else might a determined investor find investment information? The Internet is an obvious source, with this medium exploding with new information in the past few years. There are plenty of excellent databases available, but there is also a great deal of information that is worthless. Table 15-4 lists some websites that could prove useful. The first group provides some interesting free information. The second group charges a fee, and the quality of content is generally much better. But keep in mind, there are very few places to find truly objective information.

For $10 a month you can gain access to S&P *Personal Wealth.* There are a variety of modules available. You can screen the S&P *Stock Guide* database for investment leads, and gain access to S&P *Stock Reports.* You can also tap into Standard & Poor's objective portfolio evaluation expertise. Using a CD-based professional edition, you can gain access to all of the stock reports (there are currently more than 3500) and a screening engine, as well as to the *Outlook* and *Emerging & Special Situations* investment newsletters. (Value Line also has a stock database screening program available.)

There are also plenty of valuable print sources for stock screens. Financial magazines such as *Business Week, Fortune, Smart Money,* and *Worth* often publish lists of stocks designed to provide research leads to large-cap-, midcap-, small-cap-, value-, or growth-oriented investors. The S&P *Earnings Guide* regularly supplies screen ideas based on consensus earnings projections.

Finally, there are the ubiquitous investment newsletters. Just about all of them offer model investment portfolios. Check *Hulbert Financial Digest* for the five investment letters with the best performance track records over the last five years.

IPO INFORMATION

There are a number of good sources for IPO information, many of which can save a lot of legwork. The first is *Investors Business Daily.* Each issue contains tables showing recent IPOs and filings and those that have been registered over the last 60 days or so. The completed offerings list is the most comprehensive in print, with information such as the date the company went public, the stock symbol, the P/E ratio based on trailing 12-month earnings, the high filing price, and the offering price.

Other helpful sources of factual information include *IPO Digest* and *IPO Reporter,* which often provide short descriptions of what the company does and how it has done financially in recent quarters. *Securities Data* has the most comprehensive historical IPO database, and is typically used by academicians studying IPO investment performance. *SmartEdgar.com* offers an intelligent screening tool for the SEC website for timely access to recent filings.

Last, there are the publications that offer specific recommendations. The best known is Standard & Poor's *Emerging & Special Situations* newsletter. In our view, it is one of the best short cuts to earning investment profits in the IPO market. *Emerging & Special Situations* has been providing investment advice on new issues for more than 17 years. It offers more IPO investment recommendations than any other publication; more than 150 deals are appraised each year.

Other sources for finding IPOs include *New Issues,* which is published by the Institute of Econometric Research, Fort Lauderdale, Florida. It provides recommendations of one to five IPOs a month. There is also *Barron's*, which does not offer formal investment recommendations, but certainly gives an editorial slant on roughly one IPO a week.

FITTING THE LEVEL OF RESEARCH TO THE AVAILABLE TIME

The amount of time spent on personal research should reflect the importance of these investments within the framework of an investor's portfolio. Here are some suggested research and information steps that investors could complete based on the amount of time they have every week. The lists are not meant to be exhaustive, but should help investors maximize their time in the research process.

5 Hours

> *Wall Street Journal* (daily)
> *Investors Business Daily* (Friday)
> *Value Line*
> *Barron's*
> *Wall Street Week*
> 1 hour individual stock research

10 Hours

> All of the preceding, plus:
>> CNN/FN *Capital Ideas*
>> *Investors Business Daily* (two days a week)
>> S&P *Emerging & Special Situations*
>> *Research Digest*
>> *Business Week*
>> *Fortune*
>> 2 hours individual stock research (including IPO prospectuses)

20 Hours

> All of the preceding, plus:
>> *Investors Business Daily* (daily)
>> CNBC *Nightly Business Report* or CNN *Money Line Market Wrap*
>> S&P *Industry Surveys* or brokerage house industry reports
>> Access to *Dow Jones News*
>> *The Economist*
>> S&P *Earnings Guide*
>> 6 hours individual stock research

TABLE 15-4 Useful investment websites.

Website	Developer	Primary Focus
	Free websites	
www.bear.cpu.ufl.edu/ritter/index/	University of Florida	IPO information and links
www.biz.yahoo.com	Yahoo!	Tech stocks
www.bloomberg.com	Bloomberg	Daily market and IPO information
www.bridge.com	Dow Jones Markets	Stocks and fixed income
www.businessweek.com	*Business Week*	Business articles
www.byte.com	*Byte* magazine	Technology
www.cbsmarketwatch.com	CBS/DBC	News and stocks
www.cnnfn.com	CNN Financial Network	Daily market
www.dailyrocket.com	Daily Rocket	Market summaries
www.economist.com	*The Economist*	Business articles
www.fool.com	Motley Fool	Company chat pages
www.hoovers.com	Hoover's Online	Company information
www.info.wsj.com/headlines	*Wall Street Journal*	Daily market
www.investorama.com	Investorama	Web links
www.investorhome.com	Investor Home	IPO information
www.investorlinks.com	Investor Links	Daily market
www.investors.com	*Investors Business Daily*	Daily market
www.IPO.com	IPO.com	IPO information
www.IPODATA.com	IPO Data Systems	IPO information
www.ipohome.com	Renaissance Capital	IPO information
www.ipomaven.com	Otiva	IPO information
www.irs.ustreas.gov	Internal Revenue Service	Tax information

TABLE 15-4 Useful investment websites (*Continued*).

Website	Developer	Primary Focus
http://linux.agsm.ucla.edu/ipo/	UCLA	IPO information
www.moneycentral.com	Microsoft	News, stocks, and po.
www.moodys.com	Moody's	Bond ratings
www.morningstar.com	Morningstar	Funds
www.multexinvestor.com	Multex	Databases
www.nasdaq.com	NASDAQ	Daily market
	NASDAQ Exchange	Company information
www.page.top	IPO Professor	Daily market
www.personalwealth.com	Standard & Poor's	Daily market
http://prnewswire.com	PR Newswire	Company announcements
www.quicken.com	Intuit	News and stocks
www.reportgallery.com	Annual Report Gallery	Stocks
www.reuters.com	Reuters	Stocks, fixed income, and international
www.sec.gov	U.S. Securities and Exchange Commission	Company information
www.siliconinvestor.com	Silicon Investor	Tech chat
www.stockguide.com	Stockguide	Small-stock profiles
www.stockinfo.standardpoor.com	Standard & Poor's	Stock data
www.stockpoint.com	Stockpoint	Stocks and commentary
www.techweb.com	CMP Media	Technology trends
www.thestreet.com	The Street.com	Daily market and research tools
www.thomsoninvest.net	Thomson Financial	Stocks
www.vanguard.com	Vanguard	Funds and annuities
www.Vardem.com	Deutsche Bank	Economic commentary

		Historical data
Telescan	www.wallstreetcity.com	Historical data
Zacks	www.zacks.com	Analyst estimates

Websites charging a fee

Briefing.com	www.briefing.com	Market news
Dataquest	www.dataquest.com	Tech trends
First Call	www.firstcall.com	Analyst estimates
Gartner Group	http://gartnerweb.com	Tech stocks
I/B/E/S	www.ibes.com	Earnings estimates
INVESTools	www.investools.com	Baseline reports, Zacks, and *Market Guide*
Microsoft	www.investor.com	Broad coverage
IPOMonitor.com	www.ipomonitor.com	IPO information
Standard & Poor's	www.personalwealth.com	Stock reports
Quote.Com	www.quote.com	Stock and index quotes
James Cramer	www.thestreet.com	Original news
Wall Street Journal	http://wsj.com	General financial and company news

EXHIBIT 15-1   Report on Zebra Technologies.

(From Standard & Poor's Stock Reports, *September 18, 1999. Copyright © 1999 by The McGraw-Hill Companies.)*

STANDARD
&POOR'S
STOCK REPORTS

Zebra Technologies

Nasdaq Symbol **ZBRA**

In S&P SmallCap 600

18-SEP-99 Industry:
Photography/Imaging

Summary: Zebra Technologies is an international provider of demand label printers and supplies for users of automatic identification and data collection systems.

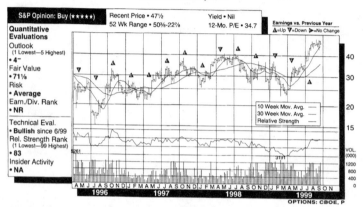

S&P Opinion: Buy (★★★★★)

Recent Price • 47½
52 Wk Range • 50⅜–22⅞

Yield • Nil
12-Mo. P/E • 34.7

Quantitative Evaluations

Outlook
(1 Lowest—5 Highest)
• **4⁻**

Fair Value
• **71⅛**

Risk
• **Average**

Earn./Div. Rank
• **NR**

Technical Eval.
• **Bullish** since 6/99

Rel. Strength Rank
(1 Lowest—99 Highest)
• **83**

Insider Activity
• **NA**

Earnings vs. Previous Year
▲=Up ▼=Down ▶=No Change

10 Week Mov. Avg. ——
30 Week Mov. Avg. ——
Relative Strength ——

OPTIONS: CBOE, P

Overview - 27-JUL-99

We see revenues advancing about 15% in 1999, driven by strength across all geographies and product lines. Following stronger than anticipated results in the first two quarters of 1999, it appears that the majority of challenges associated with integration of the Eltron merger are behind the company, allowing management to focus on growing the business. In future quarters, we expect ZBRA to further penetrate promising new markets, such as the plastic card business. We expect margins to widen in 1999, reflecting increased purchasing power of the combined company, as well as the elimination of inefficiencies related to integrating the acquisition. We have raised our 1999 operating EPS estimate $0.19, to $2.18, which represents a 37% increase over 1998 EPS (excluding merger costs), and see earnings rising 19%, to $2.58 a share, in 2000.

Valuation - 27-JUL-99

Shares of ZBRA have risen sharply sharply since early April 1999, and were recently trading at 20 times our upwardly revised 1999 EPS estimate of $2.18 (17X our 2000 EPS estimate of $2.58), which represents a discount to the P/E multiple of the broader markets. We believe the disruptions associated with the Eltron merger are behind Zebra, evidenced by two consecutive quarters of earnings that beat analysts' expectations. We believe this strong operating momentum will carry into the latter half of 1999 and, consequently, continue to recommend that investors buy the shares. Our long-term revenue outlook is strong, reflecting the expectation of continued strength in North America and improving Asian economies. In addition, with about $190 million of cash on the balance sheet and no debt, an acquisition in the early part of 2000 is possible.

Key Stock Statistics

S&P EPS Est. 1999	2.18	Tang. Bk. Value/Share	9.69
P/E on S&P Est. 1999	21.8	Beta	1.13
S&P EPS Est. 2000	2.58	Shareholders	600
Dividend Rate/Share	Nil	Market cap. (B)	$ 1.1
Shs. outstg. (M)	31.3	Inst. holdings	55%
Avg. daily vol. (M)	0.232		

Value of $10,000 invested 5 years ago: $ 16,777

Fiscal Year Ending Dec. 31

	1999	1998	1997	1996	1995	1994
Revenues (Million $)						
1Q	89.82	50.21	42.42	38.35	34.39	21.98
2Q	97.32	55.35	47.84	40.49	35.49	25.89
3Q	—	57.35	49.89	43.76	37.48	28.25
4Q	—	80.08	53.33	47.12	41.23	30.99
Yr.	—	336.0	192.1	169.7	148.6	107.1
Earnings Per Share ($)						
1Q	0.41	0.43	0.48	0.23	0.27	0.17
2Q	0.55	0.46	0.40	0.28	0.29	0.21
3Q	—	0.46	0.41	0.36	0.04	0.23
4Q	—	-0.01	0.48	0.40	0.33	0.26
Yr.	—	1.29	1.76	1.27	1.22	0.87

Next earnings report expected: late October

Dividend Data

No cash dividends have been paid. A two-for-one stock split was effected in December 1995.

EXHIBIT 15-1 Report on Zebra Technologies (*Continued*).

STANDARD
&POOR'S
STOCK REPORTS

Zebra Technologies Corporation

18-SEP-99

Business Summary - 27-JUL-99

Heading into 1999, Zebra Technologies' biggest challenge is the successful integration of its merger with Eltron International, previously a major competitor of ZBRA. The transaction was completed in October 1998 and called for the exchange of 0.90 shares of Zebra Class B common stock for each Eltron common share. The combined company generated pro forma sales of nearly $340 million in 1998.

ZBRA products consist of a broad line of computerized on-demand bar code label printers, print engines, plastic card printers, specialty bar code labeling materials, ink ribbons and bar code label design software. In 1998, hardware sales represented 79% of revenues, while supplies accounted for 19% of revenues. Working together, ZBRA's products provide identification labeling solutions for customers within the manufacturing, service and government sectors. Zebra's products are instrumental in many processes, including inventory control, small package delivery, baggage handling, automated warehousing, Just-In-Time (JIT) manufacturing, employee records and hospital management systems, among others.

The company believes that the advantages afforded by thermal transfer printing, including the ability to print high-resolution images on a wide variety of label materials at a lower cost than that of competing technologies, make it the technology of choice in ZBRA's target markets for the foreseeable future. The company's printers are designed to operate at the user's location to produce and dispense bar coded labels in environments ranging from fiery steel mills to the icy interiors of freezer compartments. Bar codes printed with Zebra printers are also used to control the movement of goods through warehouses.

One of the fastest growing areas in the bar code labeling industry is plastic card printers, which have the ability to produce on-site, full color, photographic quality plastic cards. These cards can typically be created in less than 30 seconds for under one dollar. The company believes that personalized card applications, such as driver's licenses, loyalty cards, school and work identification cards, and financial transaction cards, are well-suited to benefit from plastic printer card technology.

ZBRA's products are sold in over 90 countries, and in 1998 sales to foreign customers accounted for 41% of net sales. ZBRA believes that international sales growth will outpace growth in the U.S. because of the lower penetration of bar code systems in foreign markets.

In July 1997, ZBRA announced the discontinuation of its retail software business, which it had acquired two years earlier. The action resulted in a $2.4 million charge in the second quarter of 1997.

Per Share Data ($) (Year Ended Dec. 31)	1998	1997	1996	1995	1994	1993	1992	1991	1990	1989
Tangible Bk. Val.	8.67	7.39	5.79	4.47	3.41	2.53	1.76	1.28	0.58	NA
Cash Flow	0.16	1.94	1.35	1.03	0.94	0.81	0.53	0.50	0.53	NA
Earnings	1.29	1.76	1.19	0.94	0.88	0.76	0.49	0.48	0.52	NA
Dividends	Nil	Nil	Nil	Nil	Nil	Nil	Nil	Nil	Nil	NA
Payout Ratio	Nil	Nil	Nil	Nil	Nil	Nil	Nil	Nil	Nil	NA
Prices - High	$44\frac{5}{8}$	$38\frac{1}{4}$	$35\frac{3}{4}$	$35\frac{1}{4}$	$28\frac{5}{8}$	$30\frac{3}{8}$	$12\frac{3}{8}$	$9\frac{1}{2}$	NA	NA
- Low	25	$21\frac{1}{4}$	15	18	$11\frac{3}{4}$	$10\frac{1}{8}$	$7\frac{1}{4}$	$7\frac{1}{4}$	NA	NA
P/E Ratio - High	35	22	30	37	33	40	25	20	NA	NA
- Low	19	12	13	19	13	13	15	15	NA	NA
Income Statement Analysis (Million $)										
Revs.	336	192	170	149	107	87.5	58.7	45.6	38.0	NA
Oper. Inc.	80.0	57.0	43.5	40.8	31.7	25.9	16.2	13.2	10.9	NA
Depr.	10.2	4.3	3.8	2.2	1.4	1.0	0.8	0.5	0.4	NA
Int. Exp.	0.4	0.0	0.1	0.1	0.3	0.2	0.2	0.1	0.0	NA
Pretax Inc.	65.0	66.7	44.6	38.0	32.9	28.5	17.8	13.3	10.7	NA
Eff. Tax Rate	38%	36%	35%	41%	36%	36%	34%	19%	1.60%	NA
Net Inc.	40.1	42.8	28.9	22.6	21.1	18.3	11.8	10.8	10.5	NA
Balance Sheet & Other Fin. Data (Million $)										
Cash	163	7.2	94.5	71.9	54.2	41.5	33.7	31.2	1.0	NA
Curr. Assets	266	187	149	119	88.7	71.5	51.4	46.8	14.2	NA
Total Assets	310	204	163	131	95.0	76.7	54.8	48.9	16.2	NA
Curr. Liab.	36.8	22.6	20.2	19.0	12.4	15.5	12.0	17.1	3.8	NA
LT Debt	0.0	0.3	2.2	2.2	0.2	0.3	0.3	0.4	0.5	NA
Common Eqty.	271	180	140	108	82.0	60.6	42.2	30.7	11.9	NA
Total Cap.	273	181	143	112	82.3	60.9	42.7	31.7	12.4	NA
Cap. Exp.	25.6	5.3	6.0	4.3	2.1	2.5	2.2	0.7	1.0	NA
Cash Flow	50.3	47.1	32.8	24.8	22.5	19.3	12.7	11.3	10.9	NA
Curr. Ratio	7.2	8.3	7.4	6.3	7.1	4.6	4.3	2.7	3.7	NA
% LT Debt of Cap.	0.0	0.1	1.5	2.0	0.3	0.5	0.8	1.3	3.6	NA
% Net Inc.of Revs.	11.9	22.3	17.0	15.2	19.7	20.9	20.2	23.8	27.7	NA
% Ret. on Assets	15.6	23.3	19.6	20.0	24.5	27.7	22.8	31.9	NA	NA
% Ret. on Equity	17.8	26.8	23.3	23.7	29.5	35.5	32.5	48.5	NA	NA

Data as orig reptd.; bef. results of disc opers/spec. items. Per share data adj. for stk. divs. Bold denotes diluted EPS (FASB 128)-prior periods restated. E-Estimated. NA-Not Available. NM-Not Meaningful. NR-Not Ranked.

Office—333 Corporate Woods Pkwy., Vernon Hills, IL 60061. **Reincorporated**—in Delaware in 1991. **Tel**—(847) 634-6700. **Fax**—(847) 634-1830. **Website**—http://www.zebra.com **Chrmn & CEO**—E. L. Kaplan. **Pres**—C. E. Turnbull. **SVP & Secy**—G. Cless. **CFO, Treas & Investor Contact**—Charles R. Whitchurch. **Dirs**—G. Cless, E. L. Kaplan, C. Knowles, D. R. Riley, M. A. Smith. **Transfer Agent & Registrar**—Harris Trust & Savings Bank, Chicago. **Empl**— 627. **S&P Analyst:** Stephen J. Tekirian

EXHIBIT 15-1   Report on Zebra Technologies (*Continued*).

<u>STANDARD</u>
<u>&POOR'S</u>   **Zebra Technologies Corporation**
STOCK REPORTS   **17-SEP-99**

NEWS HEADLINES

■ **07/22/99**   UP 3 1/2 to 44... Posts $0.57 vs. $0.45 2Q EPS on 12% higher sales... S&P maintains buy...

■ **07/22/99**   July 21, 1999, Zebra Technologies Corp., announced June '99 3 mos. EPS, $0.55 vs $0.45 and 6 mos. EPS, $0.95 vs $0.87. Results for 1999 incls. charges of $1.3M & $3.2M for the 3 & 6 months from merger-related costs   Results for 1998 were restated.

■ **04/28/99**   Apr. 26, 1999, Zebra Technologies Corp., announced Mar. '99 3 mos. EPS, $0.41 vs $0.42.

■ **03/01/99**   Feb. 25, 1999, Zebra Technologies Corp., announced Dec. '98 3 mos. loss, $0.01 vs EPS $0.44 and annual EPS $1.29 vs $1.65. Results for 1997 are restated to reflect merger with Eltron International on October 28, '98. Results for 1998 incl. chge. $13M related to Eltron merger.

■ **02/26/99**   7:55 am... STILL BUY ZEBRA TECHNOLOGIES (ZBRA 26*****)... Posts Q4 EPS $0.29 (excl. merger costs) vs. $0.44, below mean... Sales and margins came in below our expectations, as disruptions associated with 10/98 acquisition of Eltron hurt results... But co. says bookings are up strongly in Q1 and sees gross margins improving in '99... With $160 million of cash on bal. sheet, no debt, we expect share buybacks once restrictions related to pooling are lifted... Lowering '99 EPS est. $0.30, to $1.90... But with 15+% net margins, strong cash flow, favorable industry fundamentals, shares attractive at 14X est. /S.Tekirian

■ **02/26/99**   DOWN 3/4 to 25 3/4... Posts $0.29 vs. $0.44 4Q EPS from cont. ops. on 2.4% sales decline, lower than expected investment income, higher tax rate... S&P, Bear Stearns rate buy, cut ests... 5.

■ **02/26/99**   8:44 am... ZEBRA TECHNOLOG (ZBRA 26-5/8) POSTS $0.29 4Q EPS FROM CONT. OPS... BEAR STEARNS CUTS EST., REITERATES BUY... Analyst Peter Barry tells MarketScope stock likely to trade lower due to lower than expected 4Q... Says miss largely due to integration distraction (Eltron acquis.)... Although co. had clean-up Q, now expects slower than expected revenue start... However, EPS progression likely to accelerate as '99 unfolds, should be impressive... Lowers $2.19 '99 EPS est. to $2.11... Believes new '99 EPS supports stock price above $20... Raises $2.57 '00 EPS est. to $2.60... Raises $49 target to $52./S.Trombino

■ **01/15/99**   2:35 pm... ZEBRA TECH. (ZBRA 33-1/4) UP 2-1/2, BEAR STEARNS INITIATES WITH BUY... Analyst Peter Barry tells salesforce ZBRA is world leader in designing, manufacturing, marketing thermal, thermal transfer bar code labeling printers... Says catalyst for rating is integration of ZBRA with archrival Eltron, which believes creates powerhouse competitor offering broadest product line, largest market share (25%) in fast growing, fragmented, global automatic information, data collection market... Expects qrtly EPS momentum to accelerate as '99 unfolds, driving y/y comps progressively faster throughout '99... Sees $1.75 '98 EPS, $2.19 '99... Has $49 target./J.Freund

■ **12/14/98**   11:10 am... STILL BUY ZEBRA TECHNOLOGIES (ZBRA 29*****)... Shares have pulled back over last few trading days, as Q4 sales are likely to come in a bit light, reflecting mgmt. focus on integration of Eltron merger... As a result, we have lowered our Q4 estimate $0.02, to a conservative $0.47... Company remains upbeat on '99, as fundamentals

of business remain strong, merger integration going well... At just 13X our unchanged '99 EPS estimate of $2.20, would use recent weakness as opportunity to add to positions of far-sighted, financially healthy provider of bar code labeling solutions. /S.Tekirian

■ **11/16/98**   2:45 pm... ADDING ZEBRA TECHNOLOGIES (ZBRA 32*****) TO STARS WITH BUY RECOMMENDATION... Provider of bar-code labeling solutions (printers, supplies, software) should grow revenues 15%-20% over next few years on strong demand, both in U.S. and elsewere (40% of revenues)... With only 7% of revenues from Asia, ZBRA is well insulated from woes there... View recent merger with Eltron International favorably, since deal will add over $100 mln. to top line... No debt and $140 mln. cash gives ZBRA flexibility to pursue more acquisition's and expand into growing markets... At 15 times our '99 EPS est. $2.20, stock attractive. /S.Tekirian

■ **10/22/98**   Oct. 21, 1998, Zebra Technologies Corp. announced Sept. '98 3 Mos. EPS, $0.46 vs $0.41 and 9 Mos. EPS, $1.35 vs $1.28. Results for the 1997 9 months incl. a one-time pre-tax investment gain of $5.5M. Results for 1997 excl. a loss of $0.11 per share for the 9 mos. from discontinued operations.

■ **07/23/98**   July 22, 1998, Zebra Technologies Corp. announced July 1998 three-month earnings per share of $0.46 vs $0.30 for same period a year ago. Six-month earnings of $0.89 vs $0.76 for same period a year ago. Results for 1997 include losses of $0.10 and $0.11 per share for the three- and six-month periods from discontinued operations.

EXHIBIT 15-1 Report on Zebra Technologies (*Continued*).

STANDARD
&POOR'S
STOCK REPORTS

Zebra Technologies

18-SEP-99

INDUSTRY OUTLOOK

Our investment outlook for the photography/imaging industry is neutral. We see Kodak and Polaroid having success with cost-cutting efforts, but view recent revenue levels as lackluster. Each company, and the industry as a whole, face opportunities and threats from what is likely to be a long-term movement toward capturing and displaying images in a digital form, rather through traditional silver-halide or more chemical-based photography. Our favorite is Xerox, which is capitalizing on trends in digital and networked imaging. Year to date through August 3, 1999, the S&P Photography/Imaging Index declined 9.2%, versus a 7.0% rise for the S&P 1500. In 1998, this industry modestly outperformed the market.

New products that encourage consumers to create more pictures are important for industry growth, since the conventional U.S. consumer photo industry is very mature. Most households already own a camera. Spending on photography is also likely to be affected by factors such as consumer confidence and the amount of vacation travel occurring. In the past we've viewed U.S. photography companies as having above-average growth opportunities in various foreign markets, where access to U.S. consumer products was increasing and/or income levels were

likely to grow faster than they were in the U.S. But, during the past year, economic problems in a number of countries, including Russia and Brazil, have weakened the near-term outlook.

In the past decade, U.S. photo activity has been stimulated by the relatively easy-to-use 35-millimeter cameras, as well as quick-service photofinishing outlets. Film use has been encouraged by the widespread availability of single-use, pocket-size cameras, selling for $6 to $20. These cameras offer convenience for consumers who forgot to bring their more expensive, permanent equipment, or did not feel like carrying a larger camera.

When looking at a photography/imaging manufacturing company, factors to consider include its competitive position, including the extent to which it is facing pricing pressure, and the strength of the company's technology. Particularly with the expected growing importance of digital imaging and the speed at which digital technology can change, attention should be given to new products efforts, and the success that a company is likely to have in converting research and development efforts into profits.

Industry Stock Performance

Related S&P 1500 Industry Index

Photography/Imaging

Month-end Price Performance As of 08/31/99

INDUSTRY: PHOTOGRAPHY/IMAGING
*PEER GROUP: BASED ON MARKET CAPITALIZATION WITHIN INDUSTRY

Peer Group	Stock Symbol	Recent Stock Price	P/E Ratio	12-mth. Trail. EPS	30-day Price Chg %	1-year Price Chg. %	Beta	Yield %	Quality Ranking	Stk. Mkt. Cap. (mil. $)	Ret. on Equity %	Pretax Margin %	LTD to Cap. %
Zebra Technologies	ZBRA	47½	35	1.37	1%	71%	1.13	Nil	NR	1,144	17.8	19.4	Nil
Concord Camera Corp.	LENS	9⅜	14	0.67	27%	178%	1.98	Nil	B-	106	18.3	6.3	9.5
Eastman Kodak	EK	75½	18	4.15	4%	-10%	0.33	2.3	B	23,895	38.9	15.7	11.1
Fuji Photo Film	FUJIY	35⅝	30	1.19	-5%	2%	0.63	0.4	NR	9,167	6.2	12.8	3.5
IKON Office Solutions	IKN	11¾	NM	0.04	-4%	56%	1.91	1.4	B-	1,743	NM	NM	54.4
Imation Corp.	IMN	30½	17	1.77	8%	76%	NA	Nil	NR	1,112	7.9	5.4	4.1
Lason Inc	LSON	46½	NM	0.46	0%	-6%	NA	Nil	NR	872	8.8	10.8	17.4
PSI Industries	PSII	1/16	1	0.07	60%	-98%	NA	Nil	NR	1	13.5	2.6	8.6
ParkerVision, Inc.	PRKR	24⅝	NM	-0.48	-9%	101%	1.09	Nil	NR	290	NM	NM	Nil
Photo Control	PHOC	2⅞	NM	-0.29	-8%	92%	0.13	Nil	C	5	NM	NM	Nil
Polaroid Corp.	PRD	28	NM	-1.39	13%	1%	0.61	2.1	B-	1,240	NM	NM	56.1
Quik Pix	QPIX	1/16	NM	-0.03	0%	13%	NA	Nil	NR	1	NM	NM	NA
Xerox Corp.	XRX	39⅜	17	2.56	-12%	1%	1.26	1.8	B	28,761	10.7	4.3	67.0

EXHIBIT 15-1   Report on Zebra Technologies (*Continued*).

STANDARD
&POOR'S
STOCK REPORTS
Zebra Technologies'A'

| SELL | | | | | | BUY/HOLD | | | | BUY |

WALL STREET CONSENSUS   17-SEP-99
Analysts' Recommendations

Stock Prices

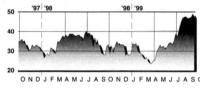

Analysts' Opinion

	No. of Ratings	% of Total	1 Mo. Prior	3 Mo. Prior	Nat'l	Reg'l	Non-broker
Buy	3	43	3	2	1	1	1
Buy/Hold	3	43	3	2	0	2	0
Hold	1	14	1	2	0	1	0
Weak Hold	0	0	0	0	0	0	0
Sell	0	0	0	0	0	0	0
No Opinion	0	0	0	1	0	0	0
Total	7	100	7	7	1	4	1

Analysts' Opinions

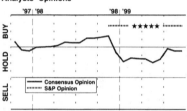

Analysts' Consensus Opinion

The consensus opinion reflects the average buy/hold/sell recommendation of Wall Street analysts. It is well-known, however, that analysts tend to be overly bullish. To make the consensus opinion more meaningful, it has been adjusted to reduce this positive bias. First, a stock's average recommendation is computed. Then it is compared to the recommendations on all other stocks. Only companies that score high relative to all other companies merit a consensus opinion of "Buy" in the graph at left. The graph is also important because research has shown that a rising consensus opinion is a favorable indicator of near-term stock performance; a declining trend is a negative signal.

Standard & Poor's STARS   ★★★★★
(Stock Appreciation Ranking System)

★★★★★	Buy
★★★★	Accumulate
★★★	Hold
★★	Avoid
★	Sell

Standard & Poor's STARS ranking is our own analyst's evaluation of the short-term (six to 12 month) appreciation potential of a stock. Five-Star stocks are expected to appreciate in price and outperform the market.

Number of Analysts Following Stock

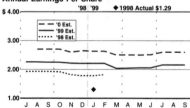

Analysts' Earnings Estimate

Annual Earnings Per Share

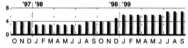

Current Analysts' Consensus Estimates

Fiscal years	Avg.	High	Low	S&P Est.	No. of Est.	Estimated P-E Ratio	Estimated S&P 500 P-E Ratio
1999	2.16	2.20	2.10	2.13	7	22.0	25.7
2000	2.60	2.70	2.50	2.58	7	18.3	22.5
3Q'99	0.55	0.57	0.53		7		
3Q'98	0.46 Actual						

A company's earnings outlook plays a major part in any investment decision. S&P organizes the earnings estimates of over 2,300 Wall Street analysts, and provides you with their consensus of earnings over the next two years. The graph to the left shows you how these estimates have trended over the past 15 months.

A Division of The McGraw-Hill Companies

MS-DOS VERSUS
TEDDY RUXPIN

PLEASE READ THROUGH Exhibits A-1 and A-2, the prospectuses for Microsoft and Worlds of Wonder, respectively, at the end of this appendix. While doing so, write on a pad in one column the pluses you see in each deal, in another, the negatives. Then come back and take a look at the report card we came up with when the deals actually went public.

Figure A-1 shows our report card for Microsoft. Not only does the absolute number of positives offset the negatives, but the number of major favorable characteristics, noted in bold, far exceed the negative ones. Clearly this was a stock to buy at the IPO and, depending on how high the stock might go on the first day of trading, even in the aftermarket. The recommendation published by Standard & Poor's in *Emerging & Special Situations* prior to the offering (Exhibit A-3 at the end of this appendix) shows that the offering was deemed highly attractive and that it was the Spotlight IPO Recommendation of the month. The bottom line is that Microsoft had proven technology, already profitable products, and a market position with DOS that virtually guaranteed continued sales for years to come.

Now consider Worlds of Wonder. Crazed parents sometimes drove hundreds of miles to satisfy a tot's fascination for the lovable bear. Capitalizing on this, its maker, Worlds of Wonder, decided to go public to raise money in order to meet extremely strong demand for Ruxpin as well as to develop a creative infrastructure for follow-on successes. When the stock went pub-

FIGURE A-1   Microsoft report card.

Positives

Top-notch underwriters (front page)

Multiple successful product lines (inside front cover)

IPO proceeds reinvested in business (Offering summary)

Dominant provider of proprietary PC operating system (business
summary)

Consistent revenue and earnings growth (income table in business
summary)

High profit margins (income table)

No debt (balance sheet data in business summary)

Short risk-factors section

**Application software revenues rising as percentage of total
revenues**

Develops software using proprietary tools (competitive advantage)

Doing well developing add-on software to DOS and Windows
(business)

Entrenched with most major OEMs (business)

No price competition

Negatives

Possible loss of MS-DOS' dominant market position (risk factors)

Slowing revenue growth (income table)

Dependence on one person's technological and corporate vision

Low insider cost of ownership (dilution section)

Trend of higher profit margins could be ending (management's
discussion)

lic, it immediately went to a first-day premium which, on a percentage
basis, was even higher than Microsoft achieved.

Figure A-2 shows our report card for Worlds of Wonder. As you can
see, there were some positives. The Ruxpin mania did, of course, exist;
follow-on sales of Teddy's World items were also possible; and the Lazer
Tag game did seem promising. But look at all the negatives, and look at all
the ones in bold. This company could easily have been a one-trick pony

with little staying power. The most important clue to this was that management already had a history of riding a fast wave in but getting caught in the surf. Much of the senior management came out of Atari, a video game company that had a few great years but fell on very bad times shortly after Warner Communications bought it.

The write-up that was published by Standard & Poor's when Worlds of Wonder originally went public (Exhibit A-4 at the end of this appendix) acknowledged and correctly called that the stock would do very well at the offering, with the first stop over 20. It actually hit almost 30. But S&P emphasized that the risks of failure were much too great for anyone to hang onto the shares for more than the first few days.

FIGURE A-2   Worlds of Wonder report card.

Positives

Leading product still experiencing strong demand.

High level of profitability for start-up company.

Broadcast licensing profits possible (Teddy Ruxpin and Lazer Tag)

Pending broadcast publicity could keep interest in Teddy Ruxpin at healthy level over long run.

Negatives

One-product toy company.

Rest of line unproven.

Very short operating history.

Low barriers to direct competition.

At competitive disadvantage due to small size of company.

Did not design Teddy Ruxpin. Done by third party.

Insiders paid just $0.20 a share for holdings ($1.5 million). Getting $29 million at offering.

Management unafraid to go to debt limits.

Very short product cycles for most toys.

Five senior managers involved with rapid rise of ill-fated Atari.

Executive compensation all cash—no corporate pension, retirement, annuity or savings plans.

Considerable insider stock purchase transaction just before IPO at highly favorable prices.

Table A-1 shows a comparison of the two companies based solely on the information that was in the prospectuses. Point for point, Microsoft is the winner. If one just looks past the hoopla and considers the publicly disclosed facts, an astute reader can, indeed, separate good deals from bad ones.

Everyone knows what has happened to Microsoft. As it turned out, sales of Teddy Ruxpin bears were strong during the Christmas selling season in late 1986 after the IPO. But it soon became clear that the mania had peaked. In addition, none of the company's other toy concepts were successful. The company was stuck with huge inventories of unwanted merchandise after the holidays. By the end of 1987, the firm was in deep financial trouble and filed for bankruptcy. Common stockholders wound up with nothing. Teddy Ruxpin is now but a memory, and a bad one for most poor souls who bought the stock.

TABLE A-1 Comparison of Microsoft with Worlds of Wonder.

Business Factor	Microsoft	Worlds of Wonder
Competition	High technological barriers	Low barriers
	Few competitors	Many competitors
	Dominant market share	Very small market share
Product	Proprietary barriers	No barriers
	Multiple successful product lines	Only one product
	Long, multiyear product cycles	Short product cycles
	Internally designs products	Product design farmed out
Operating trends	Highly profitable over many years	In existence one year
	Established sales and earnings growth	No sales and earnings trend yet
	Healthy profit margins	Healthy profit margins
	Strong balance sheet	Strong balance sheet after IPO
	Always cash-flow positive	High seasonal debt levels to finance inventories
Management	Opportunistic decision-making climate	Opportunistic
	Long-term perspective	Short-term focus
	Normal executive compensation packages	All cash compensation

EXHIBIT A-1   Microsoft prospectus.

TABLE OF CONTENTS

2,795,000 Shares

Microsoft Corporation

Common Stock

Goldman, Sachs & Co.

Alex. Brown & Sons

Incorporated

Representatives of the Underwriters

EXHIBIT A-1   Microsoft prospectus (*Continued*).

2,795,000 Shares

Microsoft Corporation

Common Stock

Of the 2,795,000 shares of Common Stock offered hereby, 2,000,000 shares are being sold by the Company and 795,000 shares are being sold by the Selling Stockholders. See "Principal and Selling Stockholders." The Company will not receive any of the proceeds from the sale of shares by the Selling Stockholders.

Prior to this offering, there has been no public market for the Common Stock of the Company. For the factors which were considered in determining the initial public offering price, see "Underwriting."

See "Certain Factors" for a discussion of certain factors which should be considered by prospective purchasers of the Common Stock offered hereby.

THESE SECURITIES HAVE NOT BEEN APPROVED OR DISAPPROVED BY THE SECURITIES AND EXCHANGE COMMISSION NOR HAS THE COMMISSION PASSED UPON THE ACCURACY OR ADEQUACY OF THIS PROSPECTUS. ANY REPRESENTATION TO THE CONTRARY IS A CRIMINAL OFFENSE.

	Initial Public Offering Price	Underwriting Discount (1)	Proceeds to Company (2)	Proceeds to Selling Stockholders (2)
Per Share	$21.00	$1.31	$19.69	$19.69 ·
Total (3)	$58,695,000	$3,661,450	$39,380,000	$15,653,550

(1) The Company and the Selling Stockholders have agreed to indemnify the Underwriters against certain liabilities, including liabilities under the Securities Act of 1933.

(2) Before deducting expenses of the offering estimated at $541,000, of which $452,000 will be paid by the Company and $89,000 by the Selling Stockholders.

(3) The Company has granted to the Underwriters an option to purchase up to an additional 300,000 shares at the initial public offering price, less the underwriting discount, solely to cover over-allotments. If such option is exercised in full, the total Initial Public Offering Price, Underwriting Discount and Proceeds to Company will be $64,995,000, $4,054,450 and $45,287,000, respectively.

The shares are offered severally by the Underwriters, as specified herein, subject to receipt and acceptance by them and subject to their right to reject any order in whole or in part. It is expected that the certificates for the shares will be ready for delivery at the offices of Goldman, Sachs & Co., New York, New York on or about March 20, 1986.

Goldman, Sachs & Co.   Alex. Brown & Sons
                                                      Incorporated

The date of this Prospectus is March 13, 1986.

ilestones in Microsoft History.

January 1975 Microsoft develops a BASIC Interpreter for the first commercially available personal computer, the MITS Altair. Over the next four years Microsoft licenses the BASIC Interpreter to Apple Computer, Commodore International, and Tandy Corporation; and introduces the Microsoft® FORTRAN and Microsoft® COBOL Compilers and the Microsoft® Macro Assembler.

October 1978 Microsoft retains ASCII Corporation as its sales representative in Japan for the Far Eastern Market.

February 1980 Microsoft introduces Microsoft®XENIX®, a UNIX®-based operating system for 16-bit multi-user computer systems.

August 1980 Microsoft begins development of systems and language software for the IBM® Personal Computer.

Microsoft releases the Microsoft® SoftCard® system, a software/hardware enhancement product that adds the CP/M® operating system to the Apple® II.

August 1981 IBM introduces the IBM Personal Computer, which offers the Microsoft® MS-DOS® operating system and the Microsoft BASIC Interpreter. At the same time, Microsoft introduces other language products for the IBM PC.

April 1982 Microsoft expands sales operations to the European market and offers localized products.

August 1982 Microsoft introduces its first application software program, the Microsoft® Multiplan® electronic worksheet.

March 1983 Microsoft forms Microsoft Press to publish and market computer-oriented books.

July 1983 Microsoft introduces the Microsoft® Mouse, a hand-held pointing and editing device.

October 1983 A graphics-based word processor, Microsoft® Word, is added to the applications product line. Three additional MS-DOS business applications are released over the next two years: Microsoft® Chart, Microsoft® Project and Microsoft® Access.

January 1984 Microsoft releases versions of the Microsoft BASIC Interpreter and Microsoft Multiplan simultaneously with Apple's introduction of the Apple® Macintosh™. Macintosh versions of Microsoft Word, Microsoft Chart, and Microsoft® File for the Apple Macintosh follow within a year.

August 1984 IBM introduces an advanced version of the Personal Computer called the IBM PC AT. Systems software offered on the PC AT includes MS-DOS, Microsoft® Networks, and Microsoft XENIX.

October 1985 Microsoft begins shipping Microsoft® Excel, a spreadsheet integrated with business graphics and database modules, for the Apple Macintosh.

November 1985 Microsoft begins shipping Microsoft® Windows, a graphical operating environment that runs on the Microsoft MS-DOS operating system.

The Company intends to furnish its stockholders with annual reports containing audited financial statements certified by an independent public accounting firm and quarterly reports for the first three quarters of each fiscal year containing unaudited interim financial information.

EXHIBIT A-1   Microsoft prospectus (*Continued*).

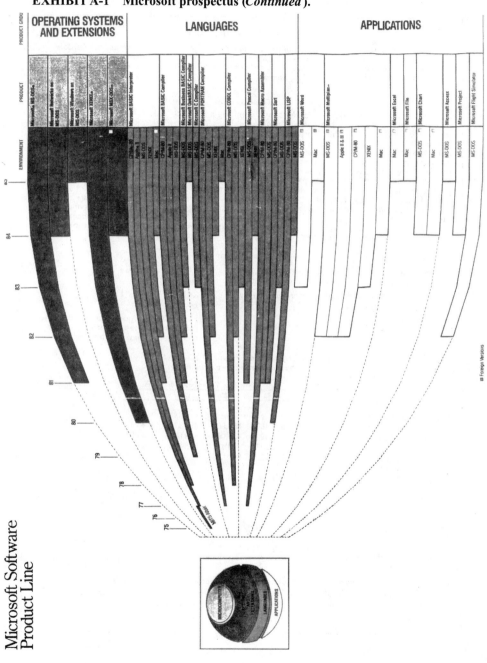

Microsoft Software
Product Line

EXHIBIT A-1   Microsoft prospectus (*Continued*).

PROSPECTUS SUMMARY

The following summary is qualified in its entirety by the more detailed information and Consolidated Financial Statements appearing elsewhere in this Prospectus. All information relating to the Company's Common Stock contained in this Prospectus, except as presented in the Consolidated Financial Statements, reflects the conversion of all outstanding shares of Preferred Stock into Common Stock on the date of this Prospectus.

The Company

Microsoft designs, develops, markets, and supports a product line of systems and applications microcomputer software for business and professional use. The Microsoft Software Product Line chart inside the front cover of this Prospectus illustrates the evolution and diversity of the Company's product line. Microsoft's systems software products include Microsoft® MS-DOS®, a 16-bit microcomputer operating system used on the IBM PC and IBM compatible computers, and computer language products in six computer languages. The Company offers business applications software products in the following categories: word processing, spreadsheet, file management, graphics, communications, and project management. The Company's products are available for 8-bit, 16-bit, and 32-bit microcomputers, including IBM, Tandy, Apple, COMPAQ, Olivetti, AT&T, Zenith, Wang, Hewlett-Packard, DEC, Siemens, Philips, Mitsubishi, and NEC. Microsoft develops most of its software products internally using proprietary development tools and methodology. The Company markets and distributes its products domestically and internationally through the original equipment manufacturer ("OEM") channel and through the retail channel primarily by means of independent distributors and dealers and by direct marketing to corporate, governmental, and educational customers.

The Offering

Common Stock offered by the Company...............	2,000,000 shares(1)
Common Stock offered by the Selling Stockholders	795,000 shares
Common Stock to be outstanding after the offering	24,715,113 shares(1)
Proposed NASDAQ symbol...........................	MSFT
Use of Proceeds....................................	For general corporate purposes, principally working capital, product development, and capital expenditures.

Selected Consolidated Financial Information
(In thousands, except per share data)

	Year Ended June 30,				Six Months Ended December 31,	
	1982	1983	1984	1985	1984	1985
					(Unaudited)	
Income Statement Data:						
Net revenues......................	$24,486	$50,065	$97,479	$140,417	$62,837	$85,050
Income before income taxes	5,595	11,064	28,030	42,843	18,219	29,048
Net income	3,507	6,487	15,880	24,101	9,996	17,118
Net income per share	$ .17	$ .29	$ .69	$ 1.04	$ .43	$ .72
Shares used in computing net income per share	21,240	22,681	22,947	23,260	23,253	23,936

	December 31, 1985	
	Actual	As Adjusted(1)(2)
	(Unaudited)	
Balance Sheet Data:		
Working capital..	$57,574	$ 96,502
Total assets...	94,438	133,366
Total long-term debt	—	—
Stockholders' equity...................................	71,845	110,773

(1) Assumes the Underwriters' over-allotment option is not exercised. See "Underwriting."

(2) Gives effect to the sale of shares offered by the Company hereby. The net proceeds have been added to working capital pending their use. See "Use of Proceeds."

EXHIBIT A-1   Microsoft prospectus (*Continued*).

THE COMPANY

Microsoft designs, develops, markets, and supports a product line of systems and applications microcomputer software for business and professional use. The Microsoft Software Product Line chart inside the front cover of this Prospectus illustrates the evolution and diversity of the Company's product line. Microsoft markets over 40 software products, including three operating systems, computer language products in six computer languages, and business applications products in six categories: word processing, spreadsheet, file management, graphics, communications, and project management. The Company's products are available on 8-bit, 16-bit, and 32-bit microcomputers, including IBM, Tandy, Apple, COMPAQ, Olivetti, AT&T, Zenith, Wang, Hewlett-Packard, DEC, Siemens, Philips, Mitsubishi, and NEC. Microsoft develops most of its software products internally using proprietary development tools and methodology.

Microsoft® MS-DOS®, introduced in 1981 as a 16-bit operating system for Intel microprocessor architectures, is running on approximately four million IBM PC and IBM compatible microcomputers, according to industry publications. Microsoft® XENIX®, a UNIX®-based multi-user operating system for microcomputers, is designed to accommodate transaction oriented data processing tasks. The Company's most widely used language product, Microsoft® BASIC Interpreter, is running on an estimated eight million microcomputers, according to industry publications. The Company markets compiler products in the following computer languages: BASIC, "C", FORTRAN, COBOL, and Pascal, and machine language assembler products. Microsoft® Word, a word processing product, Microsoft® Multiplan®, an electronic spreadsheet, and Microsoft® Chart, a graphics program, are business applications products which run on Microsoft MS-DOS-based computers and on the Apple Macintosh™. Microsoft® Excel, an integrated spreadsheet, and Microsoft® File, a file management product, run on the Apple Macintosh. Microsoft® Access, a communications product, and Microsoft® Project, a project management tool, are MS-DOS applications.

Microsoft markets and distributes its software products domestically and internationally through both the OEM and retail channels. In the OEM channel, Microsoft generally provides an OEM with master copies of the software and documentation which the OEM duplicates, packages, and distributes, although there is increasing OEM marketing of Microsoft's packaged language and application products. Domestic retail marketing involves the distribution of Microsoft's packaged software products primarily through independent distributors, large volume dealers, corporate key dealers, and other dealers, and direct marketing to corporate customers, government agencies, and colleges and universities. International OEM and retail marketing and distribution of domestic and foreign language versions of Microsoft's systems and applications software products are conducted through seven foreign subsidiaries and several independent sales representatives.

The Company was founded as a partnership in 1975 and was incorporated in the state of Washington on June 25, 1981. The principal executive offices of Microsoft are located at 16011 NE 36th Street, Redmond, Washington 98073-9717, and its telephone number is (206) 882-8080. Unless the context otherwise requires, the terms "Microsoft" and the "Company" are used herein to refer to Microsoft Corporation and its subsidiaries.

EXHIBIT A-1   Microsoft prospectus (*Continued*).

CERTAIN FACTORS

The following factors should be carefully considered in evaluating the Company and its business before purchasing the shares offered hereby.

Market Acceptance of Microsoft MS-DOS Operating System.   The Company believes Microsoft MS-DOS is the most widely used operating system for the IBM PC and IBM compatible microcomputers. If another developer were to produce and successfully market an operating system that competes against MS-DOS, the Company could lose substantial revenues. In addition, since IBM has been the leader in sales of microcomputers since its introduction of the IBM PC in 1981, a decision by IBM not to offer MS-DOS or to indicate a preference for another operating system on its current or future microcomputers would have an adverse impact on the Company's revenues. Finally, the Company's reputation in the microcomputer industry is partially based on its position as a major supplier of systems software to many microcomputer OEMs, and if MS-DOS were to lose its position as the most widely used operating system for the IBM PC and IBM compatibles it could adversely affect the Company's relationships with its customers.

Reliance on Key Officer.   William H. Gates III, a founder of Microsoft and its chairman and chief executive officer, plays an important role in the technical development and management efforts of the Company. Mr. Gates participates actively in significant operating decisions, leads deliberations concerning strategic decisions, and meets with OEM customers. Mr. Gates also has overall supervisory responsibility for the Company's research and development work. The loss of his services could have a material adverse effect on the Company's position in the microcomputer software industry and on its new product development efforts. There is no employment agreement between Mr. Gates and the Company.

Price Competition.   To date price competition has not been a major factor in the microcomputer software market. It seems likely to management, however, that price competition, with its attendant reduced profit margins, will emerge in the next few years as a significant consideration. The recent increase of "site licenses" (permitting copying of the program and documentation) and discount pricing for large volume retail customers is evidence of such competition.

Change in Marketing Structure in Japan.   The Company's exclusive sales representative agreement with its Japanese agent terminates on or before March 17, 1986. A wholly-owned subsidiary, Microsoft K.K., was formed by the Company in Japan in February 1986 to handle OEM and retail business. The transition could adversely affect net revenues in Japan. In fiscal 1985, customers in Japan accounted for approximately 12% of the Company's net revenues. See "Business—Marketing and Distribution—International OEM Distribution."

Tax Considerations.   In the course of a current examination of the years ended June 30, 1983 and 1984 by the Internal Revenue Service, a field agent has proposed that Microsoft is subject to the personal holding company ("PHC") tax. The PHC tax is 50% of after-tax income and through December 31, 1985 could be as much as approximately $30,000,000 plus interest. At its option, a corporation subject to the PHC tax may declare a "deficiency dividend" to its stockholders of record at the time such a dividend is declared in an amount equal to the corporation's undistributed PHC income. For Microsoft this could be as much as approximately $60,000,000 as of December 31, 1985. The payment of a deficiency dividend avoids a PHC tax to the corporation but is taxable to the stockholders. If a PHC tax were to be assessed and the Company elected to pay the tax, the payment of tax would be recorded as a charge to operations and would reduce net income accordingly. If a PHC tax were to be assessed and the Company elected to declare a deficiency dividend, retained earnings would be reduced by the amount of such a dividend. Although management and counsel presently believe there is a small risk that the Company might have to either pay a PHC tax or declare a deficiency dividend, they believe that it is more likely than not that neither a material payment of a PHC tax nor a material deficiency dividend will be required. Because the total amount of any PHC tax that might be assessed could vary significantly based upon the specific year for which such an assessment might occur and other facts and circumstances and because management and counsel

EXHIBIT A-1 Microsoft prospectus (*Continued*).

presently believe that it is more likely than not that neither a material payment of a PHC tax nor a material deficiency dividend will be required, management has not formulated specific intentions as to how the Company will proceed in the event such a tax is assessed. For additional information see Note 4 of Notes to Consolidated Financial Statements.

A corporation not subject to the PHC tax may be subject to the accumulated earnings tax ("AET"), a penalty tax assessed against corporations that avoid income tax at the stockholder level by unnecessarily accumulating funds in the corporation rather than paying dividends. The tax, at approximately 38.5%, is assessed on excess income after adjustments for regular corporate taxes and the reservation of funds reasonably required for normal business operations. Although Microsoft has and expects to continue to have significant retained earnings, management believes the accumulated funds together with the proceeds of this offering are necessary for working capital, product development, capital expenditures and potential acquisitions, and that the AET will not be applicable. However, the AET involves subjective questions and there is some risk that the Company might be subject to the AET in the future.

Shares Eligible for Future Sale. Approximately 230,000 shares of Common Stock held by current stockholders are eligible for sale in the open market without restriction and approximately 21,766,000 additional shares will be eligible for sale under Rule 144 under the Securities Act of 1933 beginning 90 days after the date of this Prospectus. Of these 21,766,000 shares, approximately 21,070,000 shares are subject to an agreement with the Underwriters which restricts their sale without the prior written approval of the Underwriters for 120 days after the date of this Prospectus. Prior to the end of this 120 day period, the Company also intends to register approximately 2,900,000 shares of Common Stock issuable under its 1981 Stock Option Plan and 300,000 shares of Common Stock issuable under its 1986 Employee Stock Purchase Plan. Sales of substantial amounts of Common Stock in the public market could adversely affect the market price of Common Stock. See "Shares Eligible for Future Sale."

Absence of Previous Trading Market. Prior to this offering there has been no public market for the Common Stock. Consequently the initial public offering price has been determined by negotiations among the Company, the Selling Stockholders, and the Representatives of the Underwriters. See "Underwriting" for factors considered in determining the initial public offering price.

USE OF PROCEEDS

The net proceeds to be received by the Company from the sale of the Common Stock offered by the Company are estimated to be $38,928,000 ($44,835,000 if the Underwriters' over-allotment option is exercised in full). The net proceeds are expected to be used for general corporate purposes, principally working capital, product development, and capital expenditures. The Company presently has no specific plans for any significant portion of the proceeds. Proceeds may also be used to acquire companies, products, or expertise which complement the business of Microsoft. No such transactions are being planned or actively negotiated as of the date of this Prospectus. Pending such uses, the proceeds will be invested in marketable securities. The Company will not receive any of the proceeds from the sale of the shares of Common Stock being sold by the Selling Stockholders. See "Principal and Selling Stockholders."

DIVIDEND POLICY

The Company has never paid cash dividends on its Common Stock. The Company presently intends to retain earnings for use in its business and therefore does not anticipate paying any cash dividends in the foreseeable future. Payment of any cash dividends will be dependent upon the earnings and financial condition of the Company, tax considerations discussed under "Certain Factors," and any other factors deemed relevant by the Board of Directors.

EXHIBIT A-1   Microsoft prospectus (*Continued*).

CAPITALIZATION

The following table sets forth the capitalization of the Company as of December 31, 1985, and as adjusted to reflect the sale of 2,000,000 shares of Common Stock by the Company.

	December 31, 1985	
	Actual	As Adjusted(1)
	(Unaudited, in thousands)	
Long-term debt	$ —	$ —
Stockholders' equity:		
Common stock — $.001 par value, 60,000,000 shares authorized, 22,715,113 shares outstanding, 24,715,113 shares outstanding as adjusted(2)(3)	23	25
Paid-in capital	5,281	44,207
Retained earnings	67,092	67,092
Translation adjustment	(551)	(551)
Total stockholders' equity	71,845	110,773
Total capitalization	$71,845	$110,773

(1) Assumes the Underwriters' over-allotment option is not exercised. See "Underwriting."

(2) Assumes conversion of the Company's outstanding Preferred Stock into 1,000,000 shares of Common Stock.

(3) Excludes 2,771,757 shares of Common Stock reserved for issuance under the Company's 1981 Stock Option Plan (the "Option Plan"), under which options for 2,667,861 shares were outstanding at December 31, 1985, and 300,000 shares of Common Stock reserved for issuance under the Company's 1986 Employee Stock Purchase Plan (the "Purchase Plan"). See Note 7 of Notes to Consolidated Financial Statements.

EXHIBIT A-1 Microsoft prospectus (*Continued*).

DILUTION

The net tangible book value of the Company at December 31, 1985 was $71,210,000, or $3.14 per share. "Net tangible book value per share" represents the amount of total tangible assets less total liabilities, divided by the number of shares of Common Stock outstanding, after giving effect to the automatic conversion of all outstanding Preferred Stock into Common Stock. After giving effect to the sale by the Company of 2,000,000 shares of Common Stock (at the initial public offering price and before deduction of offering expenses and the Underwriters' discount), the pro forma net tangible book value of the Company at December 31, 1985, would have been $113,210,000, or $4.58 per share, representing an immediate increase in net tangible book value of $1.44 per share to existing stockholders and an immediate dilution of $16.42 per share to the persons purchasing shares at the initial public offering price ("New Investors"). The following table illustrates the per share dilution in net tangible book value per share to New Investors:

Price to public		$21.00
Net tangible book value at December 31, 1985	$ 3.14	
Increase attributable to New Investors	1.44	
Pro forma net tangible book value		4.58
Dilution to New Investors		$16.42

The following table summarizes at December 31, 1985 the difference between existing stockholders and New Investors with respect to the number of shares purchased from the Company, the total consideration paid to the Company and the average price paid per share (for New Investors, at the initial public offering price):

	Shares Purchased(1)		Total Consideration Paid to Company		Average Price Per Share
	Number	Percent	Amount	Percent	
Existing stockholders	22,715,113	91.9%	$ 6,100,000	12.7%	$ .27
New Investors	2,000,000	8.1	42,000,000	87.3	21.00
Total	24,715,113	100.0%	$48,100,000	100.0%	

(1) Sales by the Selling Stockholders in the offering will cause the number of shares held by existing stockholders to be reduced to 21,920,113 or 88.7% of the total shares of Common Stock to be outstanding after the offering. See "Principal and Selling Stockholders."

The above computations assume no exercise of the Underwriters' over-allotment option or of outstanding employee stock options. See "Underwriting" and "Management—1981 Stock Option Plan."

EXHIBIT A-1   Microsoft prospectus (*Continued*).

SELECTED CONSOLIDATED FINANCIAL DATA

The selected consolidated financial data set forth below with respect to the Company's income statements for the years ended June 30, 1983, 1984, and 1985 and the Company's balance sheets at June 30, 1984 and 1985 are derived from the audited Consolidated Financial Statements included elsewhere in this Prospectus and should be read in conjunction with those financial statements and footnotes thereto. The selected income statement data for the year ended June 30, 1982 and the selected balance sheet data at June 30, 1982 and 1983 are derived from audited consolidated financial statements which are not included in this Prospectus. The selected consolidated financial data for the six month periods ended December 31, 1984 and 1985 are unaudited, but in the opinion of the Company include all adjustments, consisting of normal recurring adjustments, necessary for a fair presentation thereof. The results for the six months ended December 31, 1985 are not necessarily indicative of the results to be expected for the full fiscal year. See "Management's Discussion and Analysis of Results of Operations and Financial Condition—Quarterly Results."

(In thousands, except per share amounts)						
	Year Ended June 30,				Six Months Ended December 31,	
	1982	1983	1984	1985	1984	1985
					(Unaudited)	
Income Statement Data:						
Net revenues.....................	$ 24,486	$ 50,065	$ 97,479	$140,417	$ 62,837	$ 85,050
Costs and expenses:						
Cost of revenues	8,647	15,773	22,900	30,447	15,507	18,270
Research and development	3,597	7,021	10,665	17,108	7,414	8,720
Sales and marketing.............	4,009	11,916	26,027	42,512	18,268	24,429
General and administrative	3,037	4,698	8,784	9,443	3,831	6,980
Total costs and expenses	19,290	39,408	68,376	99,510	45,020	58,399
Income from operations	5,196	10,657	29,103	40,907	17,817	26,651
Non-operating income (loss)	399	407	(1,073)	1,936	402	2,397
Income before income taxes	5,595	11,064	28,030	42,843	18,219	29,048
Provision for income taxes.........	2,088	4,577	12,150	18,742	8,223	11,930
Net income	$ 3,507	$ 6,487	$ 15,880	$ 24,101	$ 9,996	$ 17,118
Net income per share	$ .17	$ .29	$ .69	$ 1.04	$ .43	$ .72
Shares used in computing net income per share	21,240	22,681	22,947	23,260	23,253	23,936

	June 30,				December 31, 1985
	1982	1983	1984	1985	
					(Unaudited)
Balance Sheet Data:					
Working capital........................	$ 5,305	$ 9,952	$ 21,458	$ 41,442	$ 57,574
Total assets...........................	14,784	24,328	47,637	65,064	94,438
Total long-term debt	—	—	705	650	—
Stockholders' equity....................	8,299	14,639	30,712	54,440	71,845

(1) See Note 4 of Notes to Consolidated Financial Statements for information concerning personal holding company tax.

EXHIBIT A-1 Microsoft prospectus (*Continued*).

MANAGEMENT'S DISCUSSION AND ANALYSIS OF
RESULTS OF OPERATIONS AND FINANCIAL CONDITION

Results of Operations

The following table sets forth consolidated results of operations as a percentage of net revenues.

	Percentage of Net Revenues For Year Ended June 30,			Percentage of Net Revenues For Six Months Ended December 31,	
	1983	1984	1985	1984	1985
Net revenues.......................................	100%	100%	100%	100%	100%
Costs and expenses:					
Cost of revenues	32	23	22	25	22
Research and development	14	11	12	12	10
Sales and marketing...............................	24	27	30	29	29
General and administrative	9	9	7	6	8
Total costs and expenses	79	70	71	72	69
Income from operations	21	30	29	28	31
Non-operating income (loss)	1	(1)	1	1	3
Income before income taxes	22	29	30	29	34
Provision for income taxes...........................	9	13	13	13	14
Net income	13%	16%	17%	16%	20%

The following charts show net revenues by product group for the years ended June 30, 1983, 1984, and 1985 and by product group and distribution channel for the six months ended December 31, 1984 and 1985.

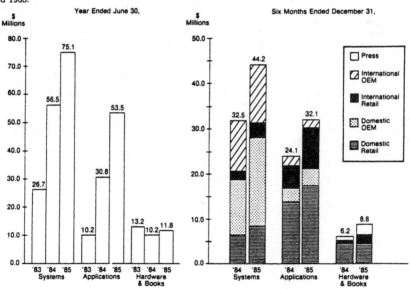

EXHIBIT A-1   Microsoft prospectus (*Continued*).

Revenue growth for the years ended June 30, 1984 and 1985 and the six months ended December 31, 1985 resulted from several factors, including the introduction of new products, the expansion of the market for microcomputer software, and the expansion of the Company's operations to new geographic market areas. As the microcomputer software industry and market mature it should not be expected that the Company's growth will continue at or approach the rate which occurred from 1983 to the present.

International net revenues for the years ended June 30, 1983, 1984, and 1985 were $10 million, $29.5 million, and $44.7 million and for the six months ended December 31, 1984 and 1985 were $22.1 million and $29.0 million. These amounts represented 20%, 30%, 32%, 35%, and 34% of net revenues for the respective periods. This growth is primarily the result of the establishment of additional foreign subsidiaries. Profit margins on international sales are similar to profit margins on domestic sales. For additional information concerning international sales and operations for the years ended June 30, 1983, 1984 and 1985, see Note 8 of Notes to Consolidated Financial Statements. The recent termination of an exclusive sales representative in Japan could adversely affect net revenues in Japan. See "Business — Marketing and Distribution — International OEM Distribution."

The reduction in cost of revenues for the years ended June 30, 1984 and 1985 and the six months ended December 31, 1985 was principally the result of a shift in the sales mix from lower margin hardware products to higher margin software products and, to a lesser degree, a decrease in the percentage of revenue attributable to Microsoft XENIX which has lower margins. Research and development expenses have increased, although not as dramatically as net revenues, as a result of planned software development staff increases and expenditures to create development tools. Sales and marketing expenses as a percentage of net revenues have increased as a result of (i) expanding the Company's domestic and international sales and marketing staff, (ii) the opening of local, regional, and international sales facilities, (iii) higher advertising and related expenditures, and (iv) increases in the provision for doubtful OEM accounts, primarily in 1985. During 1984 and 1985, and the six months ended December 31, 1985, the Company's general and administrative expenses were $8,784,000, $9,443,000, and $6,980,000, respectively. Such expenses increased as operations expanded.

Non-operating income includes interest income of $407,000, $427,000, and $952,000 for the years ended June 30, 1983, 1984, and 1985, and $402,000 and $1,151,000 for the six months ended December 31, 1984 and 1985. In addition, in 1984 the Company realized a short term capital loss of $1,500,000 from the write-off of the entire value of a minority interest in a closely held company. In 1985 the Company realized a short term capital gain of $984,000 upon the sale of marketable equity securities. During the six months ended December 31, 1985 the Company realized a foreign currency transaction gain of $1,245,000 resulting from the repayment of debt from certain international subsidiaries.

The effective tax rates for the years ended June 30, 1983, 1984, and 1985 were 41.4%, 43.3%, and 43.7%, and for the six months ended December 31, 1984 and 1985 were 45.1% and 41.1%, respectively, of income before income taxes. For an analysis of the differences between the statutory and the effective income tax rates for the years ended June 30, 1983, 1984, and 1985, see Note 4 of Notes to Consolidated Financial Statements. The effective tax rate for the six months ended December 31, 1985 was affected by foreign operating profits with no associated income tax expense due to the usage of foreign operating loss carryforwards.

See Note 4 of Notes to Consolidated Financial Statements for information concerning personal holding company tax.

EXHIBIT A-1   Microsoft prospectus (*Continued*).

Quarterly Results

The following table contains selected unaudited consolidated financial results for the six quarters ended December 31, 1985. In management's opinion this unaudited information has been prepared on the same basis as the audited information and includes all adjustments (consisting only of normal recurring adjustments) necessary for a fair presentation of the information for the periods presented.

| | Quarter Ended (Unaudited) | | | | | |
	September 30, 1984	December 31, 1984	March 31, 1985	June 30, 1985	September 30, 1985	December 31, 1985
	(In thousands, except per share data)					
Net revenues.............	$26,004	$36,833	$40,662	$36,918	$35,153	$49,897
Total costs and expenses ..	18,911	26,108	25,323	29,168	25,190	33,209
Income from operations ...	7,093	10,725	15,339	7,750	9,963	16,688
Non-operating income	128	273	148	1,387	553	1,844
Income before income taxes	7,221	10,998	15,487	9,137	10,516	18,532
Provision for income taxes	3,259	4,964	6,990	3,529	4,346	7,584
Net income	$ 3,962	$ 6,034	$ 8,497	$ 5,608	$ 6,170	$10,948
Net income per share	$ .17	$ .26	$ .37	$ .24	$ .26	$ .46
Shares used in computing net income per share ...	23,253	23,253	23,261	23,272	23,926	23,946

Historically, the Company's operating results have been influenced by the timing of new product introductions, holiday season purchases, the signing of license agreements with OEMs, the calendar year cycle of distributor and dealer contracts, and the mix of revenues between retail and OEM. Operating results for the quarter ended March 31, 1985 were influenced by the introduction of new products for the Apple Macintosh (Microsoft Word, Microsoft File, and Microsoft Business Pack) and the introduction of Microsoft Word 2.0 for the IBM PC and IBM compatible computers. Operating results for the quarter ended June 30, 1985 were affected by the mix of revenue which resulted in significant commission expense, bonuses awarded under the Company's bonus program, and significant discretionary expenditures, primarily advertising and contract product development. The quarter ended December 31, 1985 was a record quarter for the Company and included significant revenue from new product introductions, principally Microsoft Excel for the Apple Macintosh, and from the receipt of orders from distributors prior to the Company's reduction of distributor discounts in calendar year 1986. The Company does not expect results for the quarter ending March 31, 1986 to equal the results for the quarter ended December 31, 1985.

Liquidity and Capital Resources

Since its inception, the Company has funded its activities almost entirely from funds generated from operations. The Company's cash and short-term investments balance at December 31, 1985 was $38.2 million. The Company believes that the proceeds of this offering, together with existing cash balances and funds generated from operations, will be sufficient to meet its cash requirements through fiscal 1987.

EXHIBIT A-1   Microsoft prospectus (*Continued*).

BUSINESS

Microsoft designs, develops, markets, and supports a product line of systems and applications microcomputer software for business and professional use. The Microsoft Software Product Line chart inside the front cover of this Prospectus illustrates the evolution and diversity of the Company's product line. Microsoft markets over 40 software products, including three operating systems, computer language products in six computer languages, and business applications software in the following categories: word processing, spreadsheet, file management, graphics, communications, and project management. The Company's products are available on 8-bit, 16-bit and 32-bit microcomputers domestically and internationally, including IBM, Tandy, Apple (Macintosh and Apple II series), COMPAQ, Olivetti, AT&T, Zenith, Wang, Hewlett-Packard, DEC, Siemens, Philips, Mitsubishi, and NEC.

Microsoft MS-DOS, introduced in 1981 as a 16-bit operating system for Intel microprocessor architectures, is running on approximately four million IBM PC and IBM compatible microcomputers, according to industry publications. The Company believes that more of the widely used business applications programs run on Microsoft MS-DOS than on any other 16-bit microcomputer operating system. Microsoft XENIX, a UNIX-based multi-user 16-bit operating system for microcomputers, is designed to accommodate transaction oriented data processing tasks. The Company's first product, Microsoft BASIC Interpreter, which was introduced in 1975, and newer versions of Microsoft BASIC Interpreter are running on an estimated eight million microcomputers, according to industry publications. The Company also markets compiler products in the following computer languages: BASIC, "C", FORTRAN, COBOL, and Pascal, and machine language assembler products. Microsoft Word, a word processing program introduced in 1983, Microsoft Multiplan, an electronic spreadsheet introduced in 1982, and Microsoft Chart, a graphics product introduced in 1984, are business applications products which run on Microsoft MS-DOS-based computers and on the Apple Macintosh. Microsoft Excel, an integrated spreadsheet introduced in 1985, and Microsoft File, a file management product also introduced in 1985, run on the Apple Macintosh. Microsoft Access, a communications tool released in 1985, and Microsoft Project, a project management product introduced in 1984, are MS-DOS applications.

Microsoft develops most of its software products internally using proprietary development tools and methodology. As of December 31, 1985 the Company employed 271 persons in software product development.

Microsoft markets and distributes its software products domestically and internationally through both the OEM and retail channels. In the OEM channel Microsoft generally provides an OEM with master copies of the software and documentation and the OEM duplicates, packages, and distributes them, although there is increasing OEM marketing of Microsoft's packaged language and applications products. The Company's domestic OEM sales force of approximately 20 has an active technical and business information relationship with approximately 100 OEM customers. Domestic retail marketing involves the distribution of Microsoft's packaged software products primarily through independent distributors, large volume dealers, corporate key dealers, and other dealers, and direct marketing to corporate customers, government agencies, and colleges and universities. International OEM and retail marketing and distribution of domestic and foreign language versions of the Company's systems software and applications software are conducted through seven foreign subsidiaries and several independent sales representatives. International Operations maintains an active technical and business information relationship with approximately 80 OEM customers.

The Company also designs and markets Microsoft® Mouse pointing and editing devices. Microsoft Press has published 27 books since it commenced operations in 1983, including **Running MS-DOS**®, by Van Wolverton and **The Peter Norton Programmer's Guide to the IBM PC**, by Peter Norton.

EXHIBIT A-1   Microsoft prospectus (*Continued*).

Company Organization

Microsoft's business strategy emphasizes the development of a product line of microcomputer software marketed through multiple channels of distribution. To this end, the Company is organized into seven operating groups: Systems Software, Applications Software, Press, Hardware, OEM Sales, Retail Sales, and International Operations. The Systems Software and Applications Software groups are responsible for the design and development of products and the management of the marketing efforts for those products. Microsoft Press publishes computer books and manages the marketing and distribution. The Hardware group designs hardware products, subcontracts their production, and manages the marketing. The OEM Sales group is responsible for the marketing of systems, applications, and hardware products through the domestic OEM channel. The Retail Sales group performs marketing and distribution through the domestic retail channel, including the marketing of Microsoft Press books. The International Operations group markets and distributes systems and applications products, both domestic and foreign language versions, and hardware products in foreign countries. The Company has recently formed a new group—CD ROM Software—to pursue the research and development of this technology. See "Business—Product Development."

The following table sets forth the percentage contribution to net revenues for each of the Company's product groups and channels of distribution for the year ended June 30, 1985.

Product Groups		Channels of Distribution	
Systems	54%	Domestic OEM	31%
Applications	38	Domestic Retail	36
Hardware and Books	8	International OEM	19
Total	100%	International Retail	13
		Press	1
		Total	100%

Products

There are two basic categories of microcomputer software: systems software and applications software. Systems software can be divided into two subcategories: operating systems and languages. Operating systems control the hardware, allocate computer memory, schedule the execution of applications software, and manage the flow of information and communication among the various components of the microcomputer system. Microcomputer language programs, which contain instructions regarding the syntax and rules of a particular computer language, allow the user to write programs in a particular computer language and translate programs into a binary machine-readable set of commands which activate and instruct the hardware. Common microcomputer languages include BASIC, "C", FORTRAN, COBOL, Pascal, and machine languages.

Applications software provides the microcomputer with instructions for the performance of end user tasks. General or "horizontal," as contrasted with specific or "vertical," applications software is designed for use by a broad class of end users, regardless of business, industry, or market segment. Primary examples of general applications software are word processing programs and spreadsheet programs.

The chart inside the front cover of this Prospectus shows the ten year evolution of Microsoft's software product line. Microsoft has developed most of the current versions of the products shown on the chart.

EXHIBIT A-1   Microsoft prospectus (*Continued*).

Systems Software

OPERATING SYSTEMS

Microsoft markets three proprietary operating systems for microcomputers: Microsoft MS-DOS, Microsoft XENIX, and Microsoft MSX-DOS®. Microsoft MS-DOS is today a single-user, single-tasking operating system designed initially for the IBM PC microcomputer with its 16-bit Intel® 8088 microprocessor chip. Since its introduction in 1981, it has been modified for newer Intel microprocessor chips, for the accommodation of additional peripheral hardware devices, and to meet the needs of applications software developers. Recent versions of MS-DOS support file sharing and networking between microcomputers. The current version of Microsoft MS-DOS includes a file system, a program loader, a memory manager, user utilities, and a BASIC Interpreter program.

Management believes that more of the widely used business applications programs run on Microsoft MS-DOS than on any other 16-bit microcomputer operating system. According to industry publications, Microsoft MS-DOS is running on over four million microcomputers as of December 31, 1985. Microsoft MS-DOS is available on IBM, Tandy, COMPAQ, Olivetti, AT&T, Zenith, Wang, Hewlett-Packard, DEC, and other IBM compatible microcomputers. Microsoft has adapted the product to support certain foreign language character types, including European, Chinese, Kanji and Hangeul.

In November 1985, Microsoft began shipping Microsoft Windows, a graphical operating environment which runs on the Microsoft MS-DOS operating system. As an extension of MS-DOS, Microsoft Windows manages such hardware as the keyboard, screen, and printer. This product allows new applications programs to present themselves in a standard and graphical manner that is independent of video or other output devices. Microsoft is encouraging independent software developers to create applications programs which will take advantage of Microsoft Windows graphical user interface features. Lotus Development recently announced its intent to pursue the development of applications products that will run on Windows. Microsoft's own new applications software will be based on Microsoft Windows. It is too early in the life of Microsoft Windows to determine what level of acceptance it will attain in the marketplace.

Microsoft Networks, shipped in 1984, is a local area networking program which enables the end user to share files, disks, printers, and other devices within a networked Microsoft MS-DOS operating system environment.

Microsoft also has developed and markets Microsoft XENIX, which is a UNIX-based multi-user microcomputer operating system designed for the type of tasks traditionally undertaken by a minicomputer system. These include transaction oriented data processing tasks such as payroll systems and accounts receivable management. Microsoft XENIX is also used in a single-user fashion by scientists, engineers and programmers. As is the case with Microsoft MS-DOS, Microsoft has modified XENIX several times since its 1980 introduction to take advantage of newer 16-bit and 32-bit microprocessors.

Microsoft introduced its third operating system, Microsoft MSX-DOS, in 1984. Microsoft MSX-DOS is a single-user operating system which works in conjunction with an 8-bit computer whose hardware and software specifications have been established by Microsoft. The MSX® computers have been sold primarily in the Japanese home computer market. The Microsoft MSX-DOS operating system runs on an optional disk drive unit which can be attached to an MSX computer.

LANGUAGES

Microsoft has developed and markets numerous microcomputer language products. These products come in the form of interpreters and compilers. An interpreter stores a condensed version of the source code in memory and interprets it each time it executes the program. A compiler translates in a line-by-line manner programs written in human readable or source code form into instructions in binary machine readable or object code form. Compiled programs run faster and generally occupy less

EXHIBIT A-1   Microsoft prospectus (*Continued*).

space in memory than interpreted programs. Users can write, edit, and debug programs interactively with an interpreter and then compile the final product for faster execution.

The Company's first product, which the Company believes was the first commercially available computer language program written for a personal computer, was a BASIC Interpreter developed in 1975 for the MITS ALTAIR microcomputer. BASIC is a general-purpose microcomputer programming language. The Microsoft BASIC Interpreter has been enhanced from its original 8-bit implementation to 16-bit versions for MS-DOS and XENIX operating systems and the Apple Macintosh.

First shipped in 1979, the Microsoft BASIC Compiler has also been enhanced through the years. In 1981 the Microsoft® GW-BASIC® Compiler, with its enhanced graphics capabilities, was introduced. In 1985 the Company shipped its newest BASIC product, Microsoft QuickBASIC Compiler, which is faster than earlier versions and can take advantage of the extended features of the newer versions of MS-DOS.

"C" is a language often used by professional programmers to write operating systems and other systems software and applications programs. Microsoft began marketing a C compiler in the Spring of 1983 and in early 1985 began shipping an enhanced version of a Microsoft developed product. The Company uses its C Compiler extensively for developing its software products.

The Microsoft FORTRAN Compiler is used primarily in scientific and engineering work because of its ability to manage complicated numerical calculations. Introduced in 1977 as an OEM product and in 1980 as a retail product, Microsoft FORTRAN Compiler has been enhanced and runs on the MS-DOS and XENIX operating systems. Microsoft also markets a FORTRAN product for the Apple Macintosh.

COBOL is a programming language most often used in commercial data processing and other transaction processing applications. Microsoft introduced its Microsoft COBOL Compiler in the Fall of 1978 for 8-bit microcomputers and has developed newer versions for 16-bit systems using the MS-DOS and XENIX operating systems.

Pascal was created as a language to teach good programming practices and its greater control structures facilitate a structured programming method useful for creating larger programs. Microsoft introduced the Microsoft Pascal Compiler in 1981 and its current version, released in the Fall of 1985, runs on the MS-DOS and XENIX operating systems.

Microsoft Macro Assemblers, machine language products, allow a user to write programs in machine-readable instruction form, thus permitting flexibility in programming and utilization of a machine's particular capabilities. Microsoft markets a Macro Assembler which generates machine-readable code for Zilog Z-80® and Intel 8080 microprocessor-based machines and another which generates such code for Intel 8086/8088 and 80186/80286 microprocessor-based machines.

Applications Software

Microsoft offers general, or "horizontal," business applications software in each of six business applications categories: word processing, spreadsheet, file management, graphics, communications, and project management. Certain Microsoft business applications products running on MS-DOS can share data, such as Multiplan and Chart or Multiplan and Access. All Microsoft business applications running on the Apple Macintosh can share data with each other.

Word Processing. Microsoft Word, a graphics-based word processing product, runs on the Microsoft MS-DOS and XENIX operating systems and the Apple Macintosh. Introduced in 1983, the product is also available in seven European language versions for the MS-DOS operating system and the Apple Macintosh. Microsoft Word Version 2.0 supports the latest and most advanced output devices, including laser printers, graphics cards, and monitors. It gives the user access to multiple windows, allowing simultaneous access to more than one document. It can be used with a mouse for editing. Its formatting capabilities facilitate organization and assembly of documents. The network

EXHIBIT A-1   Microsoft prospectus (*Continued*).

version of Microsoft Word allows the sharing of word processing capabilities and files among networked microcomputers.

Spreadsheets. Microsoft Multiplan is available on over 70 different microcomputers and has been translated into 13 foreign languages. It was introduced in the Summer of 1982 and over one million copies had been distributed through December 31, 1985. Microsoft Multiplan is designed to create and process large amounts of information quickly. The product can be used with a mouse pointing device, linked to Microsoft Chart to generate presentation quality graphics, and can directly read and write Lotus® 1-2-3® files. Multiplan allows the linking of several spreadsheets and offers 49 mathematical, statistical, trigonometric and financial functions. In October 1985 Microsoft began shipping Version 2.0, which has a number of new features, including a macro capability that allows users to automate complex tasks.

In October 1985 Microsoft introduced Microsoft Excel, a spreadsheet integrated with database and business graphics modules for use on the Apple Macintosh computer. Microsoft Excel's charting capabilities can be linked to its spreadsheets to allow simultaneous changes to charts as changes are made to the spreadsheets. Microsoft Excel offers 85 mathematical, statistical, trigonometric and financial functions. Its data base module has sorting and searching capabilities. Extensive formatting capabilities allow the user to highlight any entry. The product is available in European language versions as well.

File Management. Microsoft File for the Apple Macintosh allows the user to create text and graphics files, prepare reports and forms, display information from the files, and search and sort up to nine items simultaneously. Microsoft File allows the sharing of data between other Macintosh software programs such as Microsoft Multiplan, Microsoft Chart and Microsoft Word. This product was introduced in January 1985 and three European language versions were introduced in the Spring of 1985. In December 1985 the Company began distributing Microrim® Rbase 5000™, a data base management product, in the European market under the name Microsoft Rbase.

Graphics. Microsoft Chart offers a wide variety of chart types, patterns and colors and runs on a substantial number and variety of printers and plotters. The product can be linked to share data with widely used spreadsheet and database software programs. Microsoft Chart has been translated into two European languages for the MS-DOS operating system and into five languages for the Apple Macintosh.

Communications. Microsoft Access, a business information access program for use on MS-DOS based microcomputers, conducts electronic communications with other computers in asynchronous mode, including information retrieval systems such as Dow Jones News/Retrieval®, Compuserve®, and NewsNet®. Microsoft Access allows information sharing between computer programs and provides windows which allow the user to view information in eight spaces simultaneously. The product also provides custom menus to simplify the interface of many major commercial information services and permits the user to create menus for specialized communications. Microsoft shipped this product in August 1985.

Project Management. Microsoft Project is a critical path method ("CPM") project scheduling and resource allocation program designed for use on Microsoft MS-DOS-based computers. The product can perform as a budgeting, monitoring and cost estimating tool for large projects and as a critical path and schedule planning tool. Microsoft Project can be used with a mouse for editing and can share data with other software programs such as Microsoft Multiplan, Microsoft Chart and Lotus 1-2-3. Microsoft introduced this product in April 1984 for the IBM PC and enhanced it in December 1985 to include PERT charting and computer-based training, among other new features.

Hardware

The Company's major hardware product is the Microsoft Mouse, a handheld pointing device which facilitates editing of text on the screen. It can be used with MS-DOS based machines and works with many Microsoft applications products. It also has been adapted to be used with other companies'

EXHIBIT A-1 Microsoft prospectus (*Continued*).

software products such as Lotus 1-2-3. The mouse for the IBM PC was introduced in the Spring of 1983 and several newer versions have been released.

Microsoft has marketed memory expansion boards (RAMCard®) for the Apple II and IIe and the IBM PC and PCjr and a co-processor card (SoftCard®) for the Apple II, IIe and III, but does not foresee significant future distribution of those products.

Hardware products accounted for less than 10% of the Company's revenues and earnings in fiscal 1985.

Books

Founded in 1983, Microsoft Press publishes books about the products of Microsoft and other software developers and about current developments in the microcomputer industry. The 27 books published as of December 31, 1985 include **Running MS-DOS®**, by Van Wolverton; **The Peter Norton Programmer's Guide to the IBM PC**, by Peter Norton; and **The Apple Macintosh Book**, by Cary Lu.

Books published by Microsoft Press are typically written and copyrighted by independent authors who submit their manuscripts to the Company for publication and who receive a royalty from the Company which is tied to the book's sales.

Marketing and Distribution

Microsoft markets its software and hardware products through four primary channels of distribution: domestic OEM, domestic retail, international OEM, and international retail.

Domestic OEM Distribution

The Company's operating systems are marketed primarily to OEMs, under agreements which grant the OEM the right to make copies of the product and distribute the copies with the OEM's microcomputer. The Company also markets its language and application programs to OEMs under similar arrangements. In addition, the Company sells its standard packaged products to OEMs for resale to buyers of the OEMs' computers. In almost all cases, the products are distributed under Microsoft trademarks. The OEM generally pays the Company based on the number of copies of the product it makes or the number of microcomputers it ships, with an initial minimum commitment fee. The Company has OEM agreements covering one or more of its products with virtually all of the major domestic microcomputer OEMs, including IBM, Tandy, COMPAQ, Olivetti, AT&T, Zenith, Wang, Hewlett-Packard, and DEC.

Domestic Retail Distribution

Distributors and Dealers. The Company markets its products in the retail channel through independent distributors and dealers, large volume dealers such as Computerland and Businessland, and dealers who emphasize large business customers. A majority of the Company's distribution is through five independent, non-exclusive distributors — Softsel Computer Products, First Software, Ingram Software Distribution Services, Micro D, and Gates Distributing. Certain dealers who commit to take specified actions to target large business end user customers are eligible to participate in the Company's Corporate Key Dealer Program, under which they obtain products directly from the Company and are given incentives in return for their commitments to train and support these customers.

Microsoft has a network of field sales representatives and field support personnel who solicit orders from dealers and distributors, provide product training to dealers and large business customers, and provide sales support. As of December 31, 1985, Microsoft had five regional offices in operation in the United States, staffed with 45 field sales and support personnel.

Direct Marketing. In recognition of the importance of obtaining large orders from corporate customers, Microsoft has established a National Accounts Group to coordinate with Corporate Key

EXHIBIT A-1   Microsoft prospectus (*Continued*).

Dealers to market applications products directly to those customers. While several contracts have been signed recently, to date no significant revenues have been generated by the program. The Company has structured a similar program to coordinate with value added resellers to sell products to various government agencies. The Company also markets its applications products to colleges and universities. These institutions can market the products to their students, professors, and other employees. The Company had entered into agreements with 30 colleges and universities as of December 31, 1985.

International OEM Distribution

The Company distributes to and maintains an active business and technical information relationship with a number of Japanese microcomputer manufacturers, including NEC, Mitsubishi, Matsushita, Tokyo Sanyo, Fujitsu, Kyocera, Epson, and Toshiba. In fiscal 1985, customers in Japan accounted for approximately 12% of the Company's net revenues, mostly from Japanese OEMs who shipped Microsoft products with their microcomputers. The Company markets its products in Japan and South Korea through exclusive sales representative arrangements. The Company's independent sales agent in Japan is ASCII Corporation ("ASCII"), and in South Korea it is QNIX Microsoft. A former officer and director of the Company is a major shareholder and officer of ASCII. See "Certain Transactions." The agents receive commissions for sales in their respective territories. ASCII represents the Company for both OEM and retail sales, while QNIX Microsoft handles only OEM sales.

The Company's exclusive sales representative agreement with ASCII terminates on or before March 17, 1986. Microsoft formed a wholly-owned subsidiary in Japan, Microsoft K.K., in February 1986 involving start-up costs of approximately $2,000,000. The subsidiary will handle the existing OEM business and potential retail business in Japan. The Company and ASCII have entered into an agreement for retail business during a transition period ending June 30, 1986 and are negotiating for a transition agreement for OEM business. It is possible that this transition will cause a disruption in the Company's Japanese business which will adversely affect net revenues in Japan.

OEM marketing, and business and technical relations with European OEMs, including Siemens, Philips, Ericsson, Triumph Adler, ACT, Bull Micral, and SMT Goupil, are primarily handled by the Microsoft subsidiaries in their respective territories, who are assisted by the International Operations group at Company headquarters. Headquarters personnel also handle the Company's OEM marketing efforts to Southeast Asia, Latin America, and other markets.

The Company bills its international OEM customers in U.S. dollars and therefore payment is not subject to currency exchange fluctuations.

International Retail Distribution

In general, retail distribution has been the Company's larger source of revenue in Europe, Canada, and Australia and only a relatively minor revenue generator in the Far East and other areas. Microsoft has a practice of "localizing" its retail products, including user messages and documentation, for distribution in those countries. Thus, in France all user messages and documentation are in French and all monetary references are in French francs, and in the United Kingdom monetary references are in pounds and user messages and documentation reflect certain British conventions. Various Microsoft products have also been localized for distribution in West Germany, Italy, Spain, Portugal, Scandinavia, the Netherlands and Latin America. See the Microsoft Software Product Line chart inside the front cover page of this Prospectus for an indication of which products have been localized.

The Company has established marketing, distribution, and support subsidiaries in Canada, the United Kingdom, West Germany, France, and Australia and has marketing and support subsidiaries in Sweden and Italy. In addition to retail marketing activities, the subsidiaries also deal directly with OEMs in their territories, as discussed in the preceeding section. Another subsidiary operates a manufacturing facility in Dublin, Ireland which supplies packaged products for the Company's European operations. The Irish manufacturing facility shipped its first products in December 1985.

EXHIBIT A-1   Microsoft prospectus (*Continued*).

The Company's international operations, both OEM and retail, are subject to certain risks common to foreign operations in general, such as governmental regulations and import restrictions. For further information with respect to the Company's international revenues, see Note 8 of the Notes to Consolidated Financial Statements.

Microsoft Press

Microsoft Press contracts with an independent commercial printer for the manufacture of its books. Harper & Row Publishers, Inc. acts as the Company's fulfillment house in the United States, maintaining the majority of the inventory of Microsoft Press books. Books are marketed to the traditional book trade by independent sales representatives and by Microsoft Press sales personnel. Sales to non-traditional channels — primarily computer stores — are handled by the Company's software retail sales force. Internationally, Microsoft Press has agreements with publishers in France, Germany, Italy, the Netherlands, Sweden, Spain, and Japan for the worldwide distribution of its books in the respective foreign languages. Microsoft Press has granted to a publisher in England the right to distribute English language versions of its books in all countries except the U.S. In most cases, Microsoft Press provides each publisher with a book's manuscript and the publisher arranges for its translation, and the printing, distribution, and marketing of the translated version.

Customers

The Company believes that most of its end user customers are individuals in businesses, both small and large, representing a variety of industries, government agencies, and educational institutions. These end users obtain Microsoft products primarily through distributors, dealers, and OEMs who include certain Microsoft products with their hardware. See "Business — Marketing and Distribution." No single customer accounted for more than 10% of the Company's revenues in fiscal 1985.

Product Development

The microcomputer software industry is characterized by rapid technological change, which requires a continuous high level of expenditures for the enhancement of existing products and the development of new products. The Company is committed to the creation of new products and intends to continue the enhancement of its existing products.

Most of the Company's software products are developed internally. Product documentation is also created internally. Internal development enables Microsoft to maintain closer technical control over the products and gives the Company the freedom to designate which modifications and enhancements are most important and when they should be implemented. The Company has created a substantial body of proprietary development tools and has evolved a development methodology for the creation and enhancement of its products. These tools and methodology are also designed to simplify a product's portability among different operating systems or computers.

The Company believes that a crucial factor in the success of a new product is getting it to market quickly to respond to a new user need or an advance in hardware design, without compromising product quality. The Company strives to become as fully informed as possible at the earliest possible time about technological advances and changing usage patterns. The Company recently hired a Vice President, CD ROM Software to direct the Company's exploration of the potential of CD ROM (Compact Disk Read Only Memory) technology in the microcomputer industry. See "Management—Certain Transactions." CD ROM technology may never generate revenue or profit for the Company, but may allow the Company to produce products incorporating that technology if and when such a market emerges.

As of December 31, 1985, the Company employed 271 persons engaged full time in software development. During fiscal 1983, 1984 and 1985, the Company spent approximately $7,021,000, $10,665,000, and $17,108,000, respectively, on product development and enhancement activities. Those amounts represented approximately 14%, 11%, and 12%, respectively, of net revenues in each of those

EXHIBIT A-1   Microsoft prospectus (*Continued*).

years. Management presently anticipates that product development and enhancement expenditures will continue at approximately the present level as a percentage of net revenues.

When the Company licenses a software product from an independent author, it typically pays the author a percentage royalty based on net revenues generated by the product. Royalties to independent software authors totalled $3,222,000, $2,801,000, and $3,736,000 in fiscal 1983, 1984, and 1985, respectively. The bulk of those payments related to the XENIX operating system and the Company's Flight Simulator game product. Microsoft XENIX is based on AT&T's UNIX operating system, which the Company licenses from AT&T. Microsoft has customized UNIX for, primarily, Intel microprocessor architecture and enhanced it for office use.

The specifications for the Company's hardware products are typically created internally, while production is subcontracted.

Employees

As of December 31, 1985, the Company employed 998 people, 840 domestically and 158 internationally. Of the total, 326 were in product development, 402 in sales, marketing and support, 113 in manufacturing and distribution, and 157 in finance and administration. Microsoft's success is highly dependent on its ability to attract and retain qualified employees. Competition for employees is intense in the software industry. To date the Company believes it has been successful in its efforts to recruit qualified employees, but there is no assurance that it will continue to be successful in the future. None of the Company's employees is subject to collective bargaining agreements. The Company believes that relations with its employees are good.

Competition

The microcomputer software market is highly competitive and has been subject to rapid change, which can be expected to continue. The Company's competitors include many independent software vendors, such as Lotus Development, Ashton-Tate, Software Publishing, and Borland International, as well as a number of microcomputer manufacturers which are devoting significant resources to creating microcomputer software, notably IBM, AT&T, and Apple Computer. Many of the Company's competitors have financial, marketing, and technological resources which exceed those of the Company.

Microsoft markets its operating systems products primarily to OEMs. The Company competes for that business with other independent systems software vendors, such as Digital Research and AT&T, and with the OEMs themselves to the extent that they may be developing their own systems software. The Company believes that the principal competitive factors in marketing to OEMs are the product's reputation, product features and functions, timeliness of delivery, product reliability, and availability and quality of support services.

Microsoft's language products are primarily marketed through the retail distribution channel. Most of the Company's language products, including Microsoft FORTRAN, Microsoft C, and Microsoft BASIC Compilers, are relatively high-priced in relation to languages offered by competitors, and are directed at end users who demand a high degree of functionality from a language product and will pay for the extra features. There is and will continue to be price pressure on these products as lower priced competing offerings become more fully featured. Other language products, such as Macro Assembler, QuickBASIC, and MacBASIC, are lower priced versions for end users who do not need all of the features available in the Company's other language products. The market for these products is quite price sensitive.

The Company's application products are also marketed primarily through the retail channel. All of the Company's applications products are opposed in the marketplace by competing products offering many similar features. The Company believes that the principal competitive factors in the applications products market include product features and functions, ease of understanding and operating the

EXHIBIT A-1   Microsoft prospectus (*Continued*).

software, product reliability, price/performance characteristics, name recognition, and availability and quality of support and training services.

To date price competition has not been a major factor in the microcomputer software market. It seems likely to management, however, that price competition, with its attendant reduced profit margins, will emerge in the next few years as a significant consideration. The recent increase of "site licenses" (permitting copying of the program and documentation) and discount pricing for large volume retail customers is evidence of such competition.

Microsoft also competes with other companies in the microcomputer software market for distributors, dealers, and other channels of product distribution. In addition to the factors listed above, the principal considerations for distributors and dealers in determining which products to offer include profit margins, product support and service, and credit terms.

Manufacturing

The Company has manufacturing facilities located in the United States and the Republic of Ireland. The Company's manufacturing operations involve the duplication of diskettes, assembly of purchased parts, and final packaging. Quality control tests are performed on purchased parts, duplicated diskettes, and finished products. The chief materials and components used in Microsoft products include diskettes, plastic boxes, binders, and multi-color printed materials. The Company is often able to acquire component parts and materials on a volume discount basis. The Company has multiple sources for raw materials, supplies, and components.

Disk duplicating and labeling are highly automated. Final assembly of the products is labor intensive. All manufacturing operations are equipped with computerized inventory, manufacturing, management, and financial control systems.

Properties

The Company's executive offices are located at 16011 NE 36th Street, Redmond, Washington, in four adjacent leased buildings having a total of 240,000 square feet of space. The land and buildings are leased under a 15 year lease, with two five-year options to renew. The Company also has a 73,000 square foot manufacturing, assembly, and shipping facility at another site in Bellevue, a 25,000 square foot product distribution center in nearby Kirkland, Washington, and a 36,000 square foot manufacturing, assembly, and shipping facility in Dublin, Ireland. All of these facilities are leased.

In addition, the Company leases office space in 24 locations in the United States and in 7 foreign countries (Australia, Canada, England, France, Italy, West Germany and Sweden). These locations function primarily as sales, training, and field service centers for their regions.

All of the Company's properties are leased from unaffiliated third parties.

The Company believes that its new headquarters complex is adequate for its present needs. A contiguous site is under option for expansion.

See Note 6 of Notes to Consolidated Financial Statements for information regarding the Company's obligations under leases.

Product Protection

Microsoft regards its software as proprietary and attempts to protect it with copyrights, trade secret laws, and internal nondisclosure safeguards, as well as restrictions on disclosure and transferability that are incorporated into its software license agreements. The Company licenses its software products to customers rather than transferring title. Despite these restrictions, it may be possible for competitors or users to copy aspects of the Company's products or to obtain information which the Company regards as trade secrets. Computer software generally has not been patented, and existing copyright laws afford limited practical protection. Monitoring and identifying unauthorized use of

EXHIBIT A-1   Microsoft prospectus (*Continued*).

such a broadly disseminated product as microcomputer software is difficult, and software piracy can be expected to be a persistent problem for the packaged software industry. These problems may be particularly acute in international markets. For that reason, most of the Company's products distributed internationally have electronic copy protection methods embedded in the disks.

Microsoft seeks patent protection on new products in appropriate circumstances, and has two patent applications pending.

Legal Proceedings

Microsoft was served in January 1986 with a summons and complaint in an action commenced by Seattle Computer Products, Inc. ("SCP") in the Superior Court for King County, Washington. This action arises out of an agreement entered into in 1981 under which SCP sold to Microsoft SCP's rights in a disk operating system which Microsoft developed into MS-DOS. SCP seeks the following relief: (i) a judicial declaration that under the agreement SCP has an assignable, perpetual, royalty-free worldwide license from Microsoft for MS-DOS in its current and future versions; (ii) an injunction against Microsoft prohibiting alleged interference with SCP's attempts to sell its business and requiring Microsoft to honor SCP's interpretation of the agreement; and, in the alternative, (iii) judgment against Microsoft for damages "believed to exceed $20,000,000" or $60,000,000 when trebled or a rescission of the agreement, a return of the rights granted thereunder, and an accounting for the payment to SCP of all revenues received from Microsoft's marketing of MS-DOS. The Company believes that SCP's interpretation of the agreement is erroneous and intends to vigorously defend this action. In the opinion of the Company, were SCP to prevail on its requested declaratory or injunctive relief (see items (i) and (ii) above), such a result would not have a material adverse effect on the Company's financial condition or results of operations. Although the outcome of litigation can never be predicted with certainty, the Company further believes that it is unlikely that SCP could obtain the relief sought with respect to damages or rescission of the contract (see item (iii) above).

EXHIBIT A-1   Microsoft prospectus (*Continued*).

MANAGEMENT

Directors and Executive Officers

The directors and executive officers of the Company are as follows:

Name	Age	Position With Company
William H. Gates III	30	Chairman of the Board, Chief Executive Officer
Jon A. Shirley	47	President and Chief Operating Officer; Director
Francis J. Gaudette	50	Vice President, Finance and Administration, Chief Financial and Administrative Officer
Steven A. Ballmer	29	Vice President, Systems Software
Ida S. Cole	38	Vice President, Applications Software
James W. Harris	42	Vice President, OEM Sales
Thomas M. Lopez	42	Vice President, CD ROM Software
William H. Neukom	44	Vice President, Law & Corporate Affairs
Scott D. Oki	37	Vice President, International Operations
Jean D. Richardson	49	Vice President, Corporate Communications
Gerald A. Ruttenbur	42	Vice President, Retail Sales
Portia Isaacson	43	Director
David F. Marquardt	37	Director

All directors hold office until the next annual meeting of stockholders and the election and qualification of their successors. Directors receive no compensation for serving on the Board except for reimbursement of reasonable expenses incurred in attending meetings. Officers are elected annually by the Board of Directors and serve at the discretion of the Board.

Mr. Gates was a founder of the Company and has been its Chief Executive Officer and Chairman of the Board since the Company's predecessor partnership was incorporated in 1981. From 1975 to 1981, Mr. Gates was a partner with Paul Allen, Microsoft's other founder, in the predecessor partnership. Mr. Gates is responsible for technical development including product design and internal development and review.

Mr. Shirley joined Microsoft as President, Chief Operating Officer, and a director in August 1983, after 25 years with Tandy Corporation. At Tandy, Mr. Shirley was Vice President, Computer Merchandising, from 1978 until 1983, and prior to 1978 held a variety of positions at Tandy in sales, merchandising, manufacturing, and international operations. Tandy Corporation is a leading supplier of personal computers and consumer electronics products.

Mr. Gaudette joined Microsoft in September 1984 as Vice President, Finance and Administration. Mr. Gaudette joined Microsoft from C3, Inc., where he served as Vice President, Finance and Administration from 1981 to 1984. Prior to C3, Gaudette was with Informatics General, where he served as Vice President, Business Operations, of the Information Services Group. In addition, he has held senior management positions with Computer Network Corporation (COMNET); Rexnord, Inc.; Rockwell International; and Frito-Lay, Inc.

Mr. Ballmer has been Vice President, Systems Software since 1984. Since joining the Company in 1980, Mr. Ballmer has also served as Assistant to the President, Vice President, Corporate Staffs, and Vice President, Marketing. Before coming to Microsoft, Mr. Ballmer worked in marketing for The Procter & Gamble Company.

Ms. Cole joined Microsoft as Vice President, Applications Software in February 1985. Prior to joining the Company, Ms. Cole spent four years at Apple Computer. At Apple, her most recent position was Director of New Product Development, and she also served as Director of Marketing for Apple II and III product lines, Director, Applications Software, and Manager, Applications Software Development.

EXHIBIT A-1   Microsoft prospectus (*Continued*).

Mr. Harris joined Microsoft in January 1983 as General Manager, OEM Sales and was promoted to Vice President, OEM Sales shortly thereafter. Prior to joining the Company, Mr. Harris was Marketing Manager in the Software Distribution and Support Operation at Intel Corporation, a position he held from 1980 to 1982. From 1982 to 1983, Mr. Harris was chairman of Intel's Strategic Business Section, where he was responsible for strategic business and product planning.

Mr. Lopez joined the Company in January 1986. From November 1984 until joining Microsoft, Mr. Lopez was President and founder of Cytation, Inc., which was involved in the development of CD ROM applications products. From 1981 until 1984, Mr. Lopez was employed by Activision, Inc., first as Vice President, Editorial Development and later as Senior Vice President. Prior to that, he was Director of Strategic Planning for J. Walter Thompson Company, an advertising agency.

Mr. Neukom joined the Company in December 1985 as Vice President, Law and Corporate Affairs. Mr. Neukom formerly was a member of the Seattle law firm of Shidler McBroom Gates & Lucas, the Company's general counsel. He served as the Company's senior outside counsel from 1979 until 1985. He engaged in the private practice of law from 1968 until joining the Company.

Mr. Oki has served as the Company's Vice President, International Operations since 1983. He was hired by Microsoft in 1982 as Marketing Manager, Special Accounts. From 1980 to 1982, Mr. Oki was Vice President for Product Development with Sequoia Group, Inc., a developer of turnkey computer systems for physicians. Six months after Mr. Oki joined Microsoft, Sequoia Group filed a petition in bankruptcy. Prior to 1980, he held marketing positions with Hewlett-Packard.

Ms. Richardson joined Microsoft as Vice President, Corporate Communications in February 1985 after eight years with Apple Computer. Ms. Richardson joined Apple in 1978 as Marketing Services Manager and was responsible for the creation of its Marketing Communications Group. In 1982 she became Apple's Director of Marketing Communications.

Mr. Ruttenbur joined Microsoft in March 1984 as Vice President, Retail Sales. Mr. Ruttenbur came to Microsoft from Koala Technologies Corporation, a producer of hardware and software for microcomputers, where he was Vice President of Sales from 1982 to 1984. From 1980 to 1983, Mr. Ruttenbur was Director of National Sales for Atari's Home Computer Division. Prior to 1982, Mr. Ruttenbur spent 12 years with M&M Mars Distributing in various sales and marketing positions.

Ms. Isaacson has been a director of the Company since December 1985. She is currently Chairman and Chief Executive Officer of Intellisys Corporation, a home automation software system company and is also head of Isaacson, Incorporated, a merger and acquisition firm. In 1981 Ms. Isaacson founded Future Computing, a market research company, and was its Chief Executive Officer until October 1985, when she became its Vice Chairman of the Board.

Mr. Marquardt has been a director of the Company since 1981. Since 1980, Mr. Marquardt has been a general partner of TVI Management, TVI Management-2, and TVI Management-3, which are general partners of Technology Venture Investors, Technology Venture Investors-2, and Technology Venture Investors-3, venture capital limited partnerships. He has been with TVI Management since 1980. He is also a director of Archive Corporation and Sun Microsystems, Inc.

EXHIBIT A-1   Microsoft prospectus (*Continued*).

Executive Compensation

The following table sets forth the cash compensation paid by the Company to its five highest paid executive officers, and to all executive officers as a group, during the year ended December 31, 1985:

Name	Capacity in Which Served	Cash Compensation (1)
Jon A. Shirley	President and Chief Operating Officer; Director	$ 228,000
William H. Gates III	Chairman of the Board, Chief Executive Officer	133,000
Francis J. Gaudette	Vice President, Finance and Administration, Chief Financial and Administrative Officer	109,000
William S. Roland(2)	Vice President/General Manager, Peripherals and Hardware Development	96,000
Steven A. Ballmer	Vice President, Systems Software	88,000
All executive officers as a group (12 persons)(3)		$1,127,000

(1) Includes bonuses awarded under a bonus program for salaried employees. Messrs. Shirley and Gates do not participate in the bonus program. Bonuses of up to 15% (20% in the case of one executive officer) of base earnings are awarded on a discretionary basis.

(2) Mr. Roland has resigned effective February 1986.

(3) Includes two persons whose employment with the Company ended in March 1985.

1981 Stock Option Plan

All present and future employees who, at the time the options are granted, are regular full-time employees of the Company are eligible to participate in the Option Plan. As of January 15, 1986, there were options outstanding to purchase 2,681,457 shares of Common Stock and 39,896 shares remained available for future grants. At its January 28, 1986 meeting the Board of Directors voted to increase shares available for future grants by 200,000. The option price is determined by the Board of Directors, subject to the provisions of the Option Plan. For incentive stock options, the option price cannot be less than the fair market value of the stock on the date of grant. For one year following the date of this Prospectus, the Company has agreed not to grant stock options at a price less than 85% of the fair market value of the Common Stock on the date of grant. The Board of Directors determines the size of each option and the vesting schedule. Options expire five years after grant, or following termination of employment.

An option may be exercised by paying the option price in cash, in shares of Common Stock, or in any combination of cash and shares. When a non-qualified option is exercised, the option holder must also pay related taxes.

In calendar year 1985, the following executive officers were granted stock options under the Option Plan for the indicated number of shares: Jon A. Shirley, 150,000 shares at an average exercise price of $5.50 per share; Francis J. Gaudette, 15,000 shares, average exercise price of $5.50 per share; all executive officers as a group (12 persons), 302,499 shares, average exercise price of $4.51 per share.

In calendar year 1985, the following executive officers exercised stock options granted under the Option Plan. The dollar amounts in parentheses indicate the net value of the shares purchased (market value as of the exercise date less option price): Jon A. Shirley, 22,500 shares (net value of $65,000); all executive officers as a group (12 persons), 45,312 shares (net value of $99,218).

1986 Employee Stock Purchase Plan

The 1986 Employee Stock Purchase Plan allows all full-time employees to authorize payroll deductions at a rate of 2, 4, 6, 8, or 10% of base pay (including bonuses) to be applied toward purchases of Common Stock. There are 300,000 shares of Common Stock reserved for issuance under the Purchase Plan. The Purchase Plan will end on December 31, 1990.

EXHIBIT A-1   Microsoft prospectus (*Continued*).

Each offering period is six months, and new offerings commence on January 1 and July 1 of each year. An employee must authorize a payroll deduction before the start of an offering in order to participate in that offering, and if the employee has not withdrawn from the offering before its last business day he will be deemed to have exercised the option to purchase as many shares as his payroll deductions will allow, at the option price. The option price is the lesser of 85% of (i) the fair market value of the Common Stock on the first business day of the offering, or (ii) the fair market value on the last business day of the offering.

The Company anticipates that the first offering under the Purchase Plan will commence on or after July 1, 1986.

Certain Transactions

In 1981, an executive officer and certain employees of the Company purchased Common Stock from the Company at a price less than the fair market value on the purchase date. The Company made loans to these individuals to enable them to pay their income tax liability on the below-market purchases. The loans bear interest at 7% per annum and are due and payable in July 1988. The following table includes Mr. Ballmer's obligation to the Company pursuant to such a loan.

Certain executive officers of the Company have entered into stock purchase agreements with the Company whereby they have purchased Common Stock from the Company at the then-current fair market value, as determined by independent appraisal, with the purchase price due and payable seven years from the date of the agreement. The unpaid purchase price bears interest at 9% per annum. The following table includes Mr. Shirley's obligation under such a stock purchase agreement.

Since January 1, 1985, the following directors and executive officers have purchased the indicated number of shares of Common Stock at the indicated prices: Ida S. Cole, Scott D. Oki, and Jean D. Richardson, 16,667 shares, 6,667 shares, and 11,667 shares, respectively, at $3.00 per share; Portia Isaacson, Thomas M. Lopez, and Jean D. Richardson, 10,000 shares, 7,500 shares, and 8,000 shares, respectively, at $5.50 per share, and William H. Neukom, 35,000 shares at $17.50 per share. In all cases, the purchase price was determined by independent appraisal.

The Company has made loans to employees for the purchase of stock and for the payment of taxes in connection with stock purchases, and at times has made loans to new employees, primarily for the purpose of assisting in the employee's relocation. The following executive officers owed the Company in excess of $60,000 at some time since the beginning of fiscal 1983:

Name of Executive Officer	Largest Amount Owed from 7/1/82 to 12/31/85	Balance Owed at 12/31/85	Interest Rates(%)
Jon A. Shirley	$810,751	$608,501	9
Francis J. Gaudette	143.888	89.664	9, 12
Steven A. Ballmer	533,711	533,711	7
Scott D. Oki	198,711	56,211	9, 12
Jean D. Richardson	305,170	55,170	9, 12
Gerald A. Ruttenbur	131,723	23,241	9, 12

Kazuhiko Nishi, a former director and executive officer of the Company, owed the Company $509,850 as of December 31, 1985, pursuant to loans in the principal amounts of $100,000 and $275,000 made in 1981 and 1983. Both loans bear interest at 12% per annum. The Company doubts repayment and has accordingly fully provided for the uncollectibility of these loans. Mr. Nishi is a principal of ASCII Corporation ("ASCII"), the Company's exclusive sales representative in Japan. The Company is in the process of terminating that relationship. See "Business — Marketing and Distribution — International OEM Distribution." The Company's agreement with ASCII, which has been in effect for a number of years, provides for the payment to ASCII of a 30% commission on OEM sales in its territory. Until recently, ASCII's territory was the Far East, but it was limited to only Japan in September 1985. ASCII also handles the retail distribution, including manufacturing, of Microsoft

EXHIBIT A-1 Microsoft prospectus (*Continued*).

products in its territory and pays Microsoft 30% of those revenues. In fiscal 1983, 1984, and 1985, Microsoft paid OEM commissions to ASCII in the amount of $2,090,000, $4,377,000, and $5,179,000, respectively, and received less than $1,000,000 in each of those years as its portion of ASCII's retail Microsoft product revenues.

On January 6, 1986, when the Company hired Thomas M. Lopez as its Vice President, CD ROM Software, it purchased from Mr. Lopez and one other individual all of the outstanding stock of a two-employee CD ROM research and development company founded by Mr. Lopez. The acquired company's major asset was a CD ROM-related product which is in development. Mr. Lopez received $81,600 for his stock, plus 1.8% of the revenues earned by Microsoft on any sales of the acquired company's product during the four years ending January 5, 1990. Mr. Lopez is entitled to a minimum of $30,000 in royalties during the four-year period.

Mr. Gates' father is a member of Shidler McBroom Gates & Lucas, the Company's general counsel since 1978. In fiscal 1983, 1984, and 1985, the law firm received legal fees and reimbursement of expenses from the Company in the amounts of $154,833, $216,932, and $536,532.

Loans outstanding at the present time have been approved by the majority of the disinterested and independent directors. All future loans to officers, directors or employees will be approved by a majority of the disinterested and independent directors. In the future the Company will not enter into any transactions with affiliated parties unless the disinterested and independent directors determine that the terms of such transactions are at least as favorable to the Company as if made with unaffiliated parties.

EXHIBIT A-1   Microsoft prospectus (*Continued*).

PRINCIPAL AND SELLING STOCKHOLDERS

The following table sets forth certain information regarding the ownership of the Company's Common Stock as of January 15, 1986, (i) by each person who is known by the Company to own beneficially more than 5% of the outstanding shares of the Common Stock, (ii) by each of the Company's directors, (iii) by all directors and officers as a group, and (iv) by each Selling Stockholder. Unless otherwise indicated below, the person or persons named have sole voting and investment power:

Directors, Officers, and 5% Stockholders	Shares Beneficially Owned Prior to Offering		Shares To Be Sold	Shares Beneficially Owned After Offering(1)	
	Number	Percent		Number	Percent
William H. Gates III(2)(3) Microsoft Corporation 16011 NE 36th Street Redmond, WA 98073-9717	11,222,000	49.2%	80,000	11,142,000	44.8%
Paul G. Allen(3) Asymetrix Corporation 110-110th Avenue NE Suite 617 Bellevue, WA 98004	6,390,000	28.0	200,000	6,190,000	24.9
Steven A. Ballmer Microsoft Corporation 16011 NE 36th Street Redmond, WA 98073-9717	1,710,001	7.5	30,000	1,680,001	6.8
Technology Venture Investors 1, 2 & 3 3000 Sand Hill Road Menlo Park, CA 94025	1,378,901(4)	6.1	294,893	1,084,008(4)	4.4
Jon A. Shirley	400,000	1.8	60,000	340,000	1.4
David F. Marquardt(5)	21,099(5)	.1	5,107	15,992(5)	.1
Portia Isaacson	10,000	—	—	10,000	—
All Officers and Directors as a Group (13 Persons)	13,521,099(5)(6)	59.1	175,107	13,345,992(5)(6)	53.6
Other Selling Stockholders					
William H. and Mary M. Gates	114,000(7)	.5	33,000	81,000(7)	.3
William H. Neukom, Trustee for Kristianne Gates	20,000	.1	20,000	—	—
Charles Simonyi	305,667	1.3	10,000	295,667	1.2
Gordon Letwin	293,850	1.3	40,000	253,850	1.0
Frederic H. Ballmer	36,666	.2	15,000	21,666	.1
Merritt Family Trust	34,000	.1	7,000	27,000	.1

(1) Assuming no exercise of the Underwriters' over-allotment option.

(2) By reason of his position with the Company and his beneficial ownership of Common Stock, Mr. Gates may be deemed to be a "parent" of the Company within the meaning of the Securities Act of 1933.

(3) Messrs. Gates and Allen were partners in the Company's predecessor partnership, and may be deemed to be "promoters" of the Company within the meaning of the Securities Act of 1933. They received their Common Stock in exchange for their transfer to the Company of all of the assets and liabilities of the predecessor partnership. Mr. Allen was the Company's Executive Vice President from its inception until 1983, and also served as a director from inception through April 1985.

(4) The shares listed for Technology Venture Investors 1, 2 and 3 takes into account the automatic conversion of Preferred Stock into 985,710 shares of Common Stock as of the date of this Prospectus.

(5) Mr. Marquardt is a general partner in TVI Management 1, 2, and 3 which are the general partners in the limited partnerships Technology Venture Investors 1, 2, and 3. The shares listed opposite Mr. Marquardt's name takes into account the automatic conversion of Preferred Stock into 14,290 shares of Common Stock. All shares listed for Mr. Marquardt are owned by TVI Management 1, 2, and 3.

(6) Includes 77,914 shares subject to options which are exercisable within 60 days of January 15, 1986.

(7) Includes 40,000 shares held in trust for the benefit of Mr. and Mrs. Gates.

EXHIBIT A-1   Microsoft prospectus (*Continued*).

SHARES ELIGIBLE FOR FUTURE SALE

Immediately after the offering pursuant to this Prospectus, 21,996,017 shares of Common Stock will continue to be held by existing stockholders. All such shares of Common Stock, and shares to be issued under outstanding stock options, were or will be acquired in reliance upon the "private placement" exemption under the Securities Act of 1933 (the "Act") (such outstanding shares of Common Stock being referred to as "Restricted Shares"). Of those Restricted Shares, 20,542,086 shares are owned by persons who may be deemed to be affiliates of the Company. Restricted Shares may not be sold unless they are registered under the Act or are sold pursuant to an applicable exemption from registration, including an exemption under Rule 144. Beginning 90 days after the date of this Prospectus, Restricted Shares may be sold in accordance with Rule 144 if the conditions of that Rule have been met. Restricted Shares may not be sold under Rule 144 unless they have been fully paid for and held for two years. After such two-year holding period, the shares may be sold in brokers' transactions in an amount in any three months not in excess of the greater of 1% of the number of shares of Common Stock then outstanding or the average weekly trading volume for a four-week period prior to each such sale. After they have been paid for and held for more than three years, Restricted Shares held by persons who are not affiliates of the Company may be sold without limitation. However, under Rule 144, Restricted Shares held by affiliates must continue, after the three-year holding period, to be sold in brokers' transactions subject to the volume limitations described above. The above is a summary of Rule 144 and is not intended to be a complete description thereof. Approximately 230,000 Restricted Shares will be eligible for sale pursuant to Rule 144 as of the date of this Prospectus.

A total of 2,921,353 shares of Common Stock are reserved for issuance under the Option Plan. See "Management — 1981 Stock Option Plan." In addition, 300,000 shares of Common Stock are reserved for issuance under the Purchase Plan. See "Management — 1986 Employee Stock Purchase Plan." The Company intends to file registration statements under the Act to register shares to be issued pursuant to such plans approximately 90 days after the date of this Prospectus, to become effective as promptly thereafter as practicable. Shares issued upon exercise of outstanding stock options under the Option Plan and Purchase Plan after the effective date of such registration statement generally may be sold in the open market.

The Company, and the Selling Stockholders, officers, and directors, holding in the aggregate approximately 21,070,000 shares of Common Stock, have agreed with the Underwriters not to offer, sell, or otherwise dispose of any shares of Common Stock for a period of 120 days after the date of this Prospectus without the prior written consent of the Representatives, except that the Company may, without such consent, grant options, or issue stock upon exercise of outstanding options, pursuant to the Option Plan, and issue stock pursuant to the Purchase Plan.

Prior to this offering, there has been no market for the Common Stock, and no precise predictions can be made of the effect, if any, that market sales of shares or the availability of shares for sale will have on the market price prevailing from time to time. Nevertheless, sales of substantial amounts of the Common Stock in the public market could adversely affect prevailing market prices.

DESCRIPTION OF COMMON STOCK

The Company is authorized to issue up to 60,000,000 shares of Common Stock, par value $.001 per share. As of January 15, 1986, there were 22,791,017 shares of Common Stock outstanding, held of record by 181 stockholders. The Common Stock is not entitled to any preemptive rights. The Common Stock is neither redeemable nor convertible. Upon liquidation, the holders of Common Stock are entitled to share ratably in the entire net assets of the Company, after payment in full to all creditors of the Company. All outstanding Common Stock is, and all Common Stock offered hereby will be, when issued, fully paid and nonassessable. The holders of the Common Stock are entitled to dividends when and as declared by the Board of Directors, out of funds legally available therefor. Each

EXHIBIT A-1   Microsoft prospectus (*Continued*).

holder of Common Stock is entitled to one vote for each share of Common Stock held of record on all matters submitted to a vote of stockholders, including the election of directors.

Registrar and Transfer Agent

The registrar and transfer agent for the Common Stock is The First Jersey National Bank, Jersey City, New Jersey.

EXHIBIT A-1 Microsoft prospectus (*Continued*).

UNDERWRITING

Subject to the terms and conditions set forth in the Underwriting Agreement, the Company and the Selling Stockholders have agreed to sell to each of the Underwriters named below, and each of the Underwriters, for whom Goldman, Sachs & Co. and Alex. Brown & Sons Incorporated are acting as Representatives, has severally agreed to purchase from the Company and the Selling Stockholders the respective number of shares of Common Stock set forth opposite its name below.

Underwriter	Number of Shares	Underwriter	Number of Shares
Goldman, Sachs & Co.	440,500	Kleinwort, Benson Incorporated	15,000
Alex. Brown & Sons Incorporated	440,500	Ladenburg, Thalmann & Co. Inc.	15,000
ABD Securities Corporation	15,000	Cyrus J. Lawrence Incorporated	6,000
Advest, Inc.	15,000	Lazard Frères & Co.	42,000
Allen & Company Incorporated	15,000	Legg Mason Wood Walker Incorporated	15,000
Arnhold and S. Bleichroeder, Inc.	15,000	McDonald & Company	15,000
Robert W. Baird & Co. Incorporated	15,000	Merrill Lynch, Pierce, Fenner & Smith Incorporated	42,000
Baker, Watts & Co.	6,000	Montgomery Securities	42,000
Banque de Neuflize, Schlumber, Mallet	15,000	Moore & Schley Capital Corporation	6,000
Barclays Merchant Bank Limited	6,000	Morgan Grenfell & Co. Limited	15,000
Bateman Eichler, Hill Richards Incorporated	15,000	Morgan Keegan & Company, Inc.	6,000
Bear, Stearns & Co. Inc.	42,000	Morgan Stanley & Co. Incorporated	42,000
Sanford C. Bernstein & Co., Inc.	15,000	Moseley, Hallgarten, Estabrook & Weeden Inc.	15,000
Birr, Wilson & Co., Inc.	6,000	Needham & Company, Inc.	6,000
William Blair & Company	15,000	Neuberger & Berman	6,000
Blunt Ellis & Loewi Incorporated	15,000	W. H. Newbold's Son & Co., Inc	6,000
Boettcher & Company, Inc.	15,000	Newhard, Cook & Co. Incorporated	6,000
J. C. Bradford & Co., Incorporated	15,000	The Nikko Securities Co. International, Inc.	6,000
Brean Murray, Foster Securities Inc.	6,000	Nomura Securities International, Inc.	6,000
Butcher & Singer Inc.	15,000	The Ohio Company	15,000
Cable, Howse & Ragen	42,000	Oppenheimer & Co., Inc.	15,000
Carolina Securities Corporation	6,000	PaineWebber Incorporated	42,000
Cazenove Inc.	6,000	Parker/Hunter Incorporated	6,000
The Chicago Corporation	6,000	Pictet & Cie.	6,000
Cowen & Co.	15,000	Piper, Jaffray & Hopwood Incorporated	15,000
Credit Commercial de France	15,000	Prescott, Ball & Turben, Inc.	15,000
Dain Bosworth Incorporated	15,000	Prudential-Bache Securities Inc.	42,000
Daiwa Securities America Inc.	6,000	Rauscher Pierce Refsnes, Inc.	15,000
D.A. Davidson & Co. Incorporated	6,000	Raymond, James & Associates, Inc.	6,000
Deutsche Bank Capital Corporation	15,000	Robertson, Colman & Stephens	42,000
R. G. Dickinson & Co.	6,000	The Robinson-Humphrey Company, Inc.	15,000
Dillon, Read & Co. Inc.	42,000	Rotan Mosle Inc.	15,000
Doft & Co., Inc.	6,000	Rothschild Inc.	15,000
Donaldson, Lufkin & Jenrette Securities Corporation	42,000	L. F. Rothschild, Unterberg, Towbin, Inc.	42,000
Drexel Burnham Lambert Incorporated	42,000	R. Rowland & Co., Incorporated	6,000
Eberstadt Fleming Inc.	15,000	Sal. Oppenheim Jr. & Cie.	6,000
A. G. Edwards & Sons, Inc.	15,000	Salomon Brothers Inc	42,000
Eppler, Guerin & Turner, Inc.	15,000	J. Henry Schroder Wagg & Co. Limited	15,000
EuroPartners Securities Corporation	15,000	Seidler Amdec Securities Inc.	6,000
First Albany Corporation	6,000	Shearson Lehman Brothers Inc.	42,000
The First Boston Corporation	42,000	Sogen Securities Corporation	15,000
First Manhattan Co.	6,000	Stephens Inc.	15,000
First Southwest Company	15,000	Stifel, Nicolaus & Company, Incorporated	15,000
Furman Selz Mager Dietz & Birney Incorporated	15,000	Sutro & Co. Incorporated	15,000
Gruntal & Co., Incorporated	15,000	Swergold, Chefitz & Sinsabaugh, Inc.	6,000
Hambrecht & Quist Incorporated	42,000	Swiss Bank Corporation International Securities Inc.	15,000
Hill Samuel & Co. Limited	15,000	Thomson McKinnon Securities Inc.	15,000
J. J. B. Hilliard, W. L. Lyons, Inc.	6,000	Tucker, Anthony & R. L. Day, Inc.	15,000
Hoare Govett Limited	6,000	UBS Securities Inc.	15,000
Howard, Weil, Labouisse, Friedrichs Incorporated	15,000	Underwood, Neuhaus & Co. Incorporated	15,000
E. F. Hutton & Company Inc.	42,000	Vereins-und Westbank A.G.	6,000
Interstate Securities Corporation	15,000	Wedbush, Noble, Cooke, Inc.	6,000
Investment Corporation of Virginia	6,000	Wertheim & Co., Inc.	42,000
Janney Montgomery Scott Inc.	15,000	Wheat, First Securities, Inc.	15,000
Johnson, Lane, Space, Smith & Co., Inc.	6,000	Dean Witter Reynolds Inc.	42,000
Johnston, Lemon & Co. Incorporated	6,000	Yamaichi International (America), Inc.	6,000
Josephthal & Co. Incorporated	15,000	Total	2,795,000
Kidder, Peabody & Co. Incorporated	42,000		

EXHIBIT A-1   Microsoft prospectus (*Continued*).

Excluding shares subject to the over-allotment option, each of the Underwriters is to purchase from the Company and each of the Selling Stockholders, respectively, that number of shares which bears the same proportion to the total number of shares to be sold by the Company and the Selling Stockholders as the total number of shares to be purchased by such Underwriters bears to the total number of shares to be purchased by all of the Underwriters.

Under the terms and conditions of the Underwriting Agreement, the Underwriters are committed to purchase all the shares offered hereby, if any are purchased.

There has been no previous market for any of the Company's securities. The major factors considered by the Company, the Selling Stockholders, and the Representatives in determining the public offering price of the Common Stock, in addition to prevailing market conditions, were historical performance, estimates of the business potential and earnings prospects of the Company, the present state of the Company's development, an assessment of the Company's management, and the considera-tion of the above factors in relation to market valuations of comparable companies. Based on the initial public offering price, and assuming that the Underwriters' over-allotment option is not exercised, the aggregate market value of shares outstanding after the offering will be approximately $519,017,373.

The Underwriters propose to offer the shares in part directly to the public at the initial public offering price set forth on the cover page of this Prospectus and in part to certain securities dealers at such price less a concession of $0.75 per share. The Underwriters may allow, and such dealers may reallow, a concession not in excess of $0.10 per share to certain brokers and dealers. After the shares are released for sale to the public, the public offering price and other selling terms may from time to time be varied by the Representatives.

The Company has granted the Underwriters an option exercisable for 30 days after the date of this Prospectus to purchase up to an aggregate of 300,000 additional shares of Common Stock to cover over-allotments, if any. If the Underwriters exercise their over-allotment option, the Underwriters have severally agreed, subject to certain conditions, to purchase approximately the same percentage thereof that the number of shares to be purchased by each of them as shown in the foregoing table bears to the 2,795,000 shares of Common Stock offered hereby. The Underwriters may exercise such option only to cover over-allotments made in connection with the sale of the 2,795,000 shares of the Common Stock offered hereby.

The Representatives have informed the Company that they do not expect sales to discretionary accounts by the Underwriters to exceed five percent of the total number of shares of Common Stock offered by them hereby and that sales to discretionary accounts by the Representatives will be less than one percent of the total number of shares of Common Stock offered by them hereby.

The Company, and the Selling Stockholders, officers, and directors, holding in the aggregate approximately 21,070,000 shares of Common Stock, have agreed not to offer, sell, or otherwise dispose of any shares of Common Stock for a period of 120 days after the date of this Prospectus without the prior written consent of the Representatives, except that the Company may, without such consent, grant options, or issue stock upon exercise of outstanding options, pursuant to the Option Plan, and issue stock pursuant to the Purchase Plan.

The Company and the Selling Stockholders have agreed to indemnify the Underwriters against certain civil liabilities, including liabilities under the Act.

LEGAL MATTERS

The validity of the shares of Common Stock offered hereby will be passed upon for the Company by Shidler McBroom Gates & Lucas, Seattle, Washington, and for the Underwriters by Sullivan & Cromwell, Los Angeles, California. Sullivan & Cromwell may rely upon the opinion of Shidler McBroom Gates & Lucas as to matters of Washington law. Members of Shidler McBroom Gates & Lucas beneficially owned 114,000 shares of Common Stock prior to this offering. See "Manage-ment—Certain Transactions" and "Principal and Selling Stockholders."

EXHIBIT A-1 Microsoft prospectus (*Continued*).

The consolidated financial statements included in this Prospectus, and the related supplemental schedules included elsewhere in the Registration Statement as of June 30, 1984 and 1985 and for each of the three years in the period ended June 30, 1985, and the consolidated financial statements as of June 30, 1982 and 1983 and for the year ended June 30, 1982, from which the Selected Consolidated Financial Data included in this Prospectus have been derived, have been examined by Deloitte Haskins & Sells, independent public accountants, as stated in their opinions appearing herein and elsewhere in the Registration Statement. Such consolidated financial statements, supplemental schedules, and Selected Consolidated Financial Data have been so included in reliance upon such opinions given upon the authority of that firm as experts in accounting and auditing.

ADDITIONAL INFORMATION

The Company has filed with the Securities and Exchange Commission, Washington, D.C., a Registration Statement under the Act, as amended, with respect to the Common Stock offered hereby. This Prospectus does not contain all of the information set forth in the Registration Statement and the exhibits and schedules thereto. For further information with respect to the Company and the Common Stock, reference is hereby made to such Registration Statement, exhibits, and schedules, copies of which may be obtained from the Commission's principal office in Washington, D.C., upon payment of the fees prescribed by the Commission.

EXHIBIT A-1   Microsoft prospectus (*Continued*).

OPINION OF INDEPENDENT PUBLIC ACCOUNTANTS

Microsoft Corporation:

We have examined the consolidated balance sheets of Microsoft Corporation and subsidiaries as of June 30, 1984 and 1985, and the related consolidated statements of income, stockholders' equity, and changes in financial position for each of the three years in the period ended June 30. 1985. Our examinations were made in accordance with generally accepted auditing standards and, accordingly, included such tests of the accounting records and such other auditing procedures as we considered necessary in the circumstances.

In our opinion, such consolidated financial statements present fairly the financial position of Microsoft Corporation and subsidiaries at June 30, 1984 and 1985 and the results of their operations and the changes in their financial position for each of the three years in the period ended June 30, 1985, in conformity with generally accepted accounting principles applied on a consistent basis.

We have also previously examined, in accordance with generally accepted auditing standards, the consolidated balance sheets as of June 30, 1982 and 1983 and the related consolidated statements of income, stockholders' equity, and changes in financial position for the year ended June 30, 1982 (none of which are presented herein); and we expressed unqualified opinions on those consolidated financial statements. In our opinion, the information set forth in the selected financial data for each of the four years in the period ended June 30, 1985 appearing on page 9 is fairly stated in all material respects in relation to the consolidated financial statements from which it has been derived.

DELOITTE HASKINS & SELLS

Bellevue, Washington
August 15, 1985
(January 29, 1986 as to Notes 4 and 9)

EXHIBIT A-1 Microsoft prospectus (*Continued*).

MICROSOFT CORPORATION

CONSOLIDATED BALANCE SHEETS

ASSETS

	June 30,		December 31,
	1984	1985	1985
			(Unaudited)
	(In thousands, except share data)		
Current assets:			
Cash and short-term investments	$ 3,282	$18,948	$38,158
Trade accounts receivable — net of allowance for doubtful accounts of $1,964, $2,288 and $2,860.................	23,566	25,273	33,893
Inventories (Note 2)	9,770	5,919	5,730
Other (Note 7)	1,329	1,926	2,386
Total current assets	37,947	52,066	80,167
Property and equipment — net (Note 3)	8,076	11,190	12,661
Other assets...	1,614	1,808	1,610
	$47,637	$65,064	$94,438

LIABILITIES AND STOCKHOLDERS' EQUITY

	June 30,		December 31,
Current liabilities:			
Accounts payable	$ 4,954	$ 2,497	$ 4,533
Customer deposits	3,709	2,757	3,892
Royalties and commissions payable	1,460	1,315	3,220
Deferred income taxes	4,108	1,251	6,872
Other...	2,258	2,804	4,076
Total current liabilities	16,489	10,624	22,593
Long-term debt (Note 5)	436	—	—
Commitments and contingencies (Notes 4, 6 and 9)			
Stockholders' equity (Note 7):			
Convertible Preferred Stock — $.01 par value; shares authorized and outstanding 500,000; liquidation preference $1,000,000; to be automatically converted to 1,000,000 shares of Common Stock upon completion of a public offering of the Company 's Common Stock	5	5	5
Common Stock — $.001 par value; shares authorized 60,000,000; issued and outstanding before 1,000,000 shares from conversion of preferred stock—21,260,227, 21,533,353 and 21,715,113	21	22	22
Paid-in capital	4,873	5,101	5,277
Retained earnings...................................	25,873	49,974	67,092
Translation adjustment	(60)	(662)	(551)
Total stockholders' equity..........................	30,712	54,440	71,845
	$47,637	$65,064	$94,438

See accompanying notes.

EXHIBIT A-1   Microsoft prospectus (*Continued*).

MICROSOFT CORPORATION

CONSOLIDATED STATEMENTS OF INCOME

	Year Ended June 30,			Six Months Ended December 31,	
	1983	1984	1985	1984	1985
				(Unaudited)	
	(In thousands, except per share data)				
Net revenues	$ 50,065	$ 97,479	$140,417	$ 62,837	$ 85,050
Costs and expenses:					
Cost of revenues	15,773	22,900	30,447	15,507	18,270
Research and development	7,021	10,665	17,108	7,414	8,720
Sales and marketing	11,916	26,027	42,512	18,268	24,429
General and administrative	4,698	8,784	9,443	3,831	6,980
Total costs and expenses	39,408	68,376	99,510	45,020	58,399
Income from operations	10,657	29,103	40,907	17,817	26,651
Non-operating income (loss) (Note 1)	407	(1,073)	1,936	402	2,397
Income before income taxes	11,064	28,030	42,843	18,219	29,048
Provision for income taxes (Note 4)	4,577	12,150	18,742	8,223	11,930
Net income	$ 6,487	$ 15,880	$ 24,101	$ 9,996	$ 17,118
Net income per share	$ .29	$ .69	$ 1.04	$ .43	$ .72
Shares used in computing net income per share	22,681	22,947	23,260	23,253	23,936

See accompanying notes.

EXHIBIT A-1 Microsoft prospectus (*Continued*).

MICROSOFT CORPORATION

CONSOLIDATED STATEMENTS OF STOCKHOLDERS' EQUITY

	Preferred Stock		Common Stock		Paid-In Capital	Retained Earning	Treasury Stock		Translation Adjustment	Total Stockholders' Equity
	Shares	Amount	Shares	Amount			Shares	Amount		
					(In thousands, except share data)					
Balance, June 30, 1982	500,000	$ 5	21,830,566	$22	$4,766	$ 3,506				$ 8,299
Sale of stock to employees			1,000							
Purchase of treasury stock							(997,366)	$ (732)		(732)
Amortization of deferred compensation					573					573
Net income for year ended June 30, 1983						6,487				6,487
Foreign currency translation adjustment									$ 11	11
Balance, June 30, 1983	500,000	5	21,831,566	22	5,339	9,993	(997,366)	(732)	11	14,638
Sale of stock to employees			426,027		26					26
Retirement of treasury stock			(997,366)	(1)	(732)		997,366	732		(1)
Amortization of deferred compensation					240					240
Net income for year ended June 30, 1984						15,880				15,880
Foreign currency translation adjustment									(71)	(71)
Balance, June 30, 1984	500,000	5	21,260,227	21	4,873	25,873			(60)	30,712
Sale of stock principally to employees			273,126	1	145					146
Amortization of deferred compensation					83					83
Net income for year ended June 30, 1985						24,101				24,101
Foreign currency translation adjustment									(602)	(602)
Balance, June 30, 1985	500,000	5	21,533,353	22	5,101	49,974			(662)	54,440
Sale of stock principally to employees (Unaudited)			181,760		176					176
Net income for the six months ended December 31, 1985 (Unaudited)						17,118				17,118
Foreign currency translation adjustment (Unaudited)									111	111
Balance, December 31, 1985 (Unaudited)	500,000	$ 5	21,715,113	$22	$5,277	$67,092			$(551)	$71,845

See accompanying notes.

337

EXHIBIT A-1   Microsoft prospectus (*Continued*).

MICROSOFT CORPORATION

CONSOLIDATED STATEMENTS OF CHANGES IN FINANCIAL POSITION

	Year Ended June 30,			Six Months Ended December 31,	
	1983	1984	1985	1984	1985
				(Unaudited)	
			(In thousands)		
Working capital provided:					
Operations:					
Net income	$ 6,487	$15,880	$24,101	$ 9,996	$17,118
Depreciation	1,007	2,068	3,462	1,423	2,403
Other	1,190	(684)	83	—	—
Total from operations	8,684	17,264	27,646	11,419	19,521
Common stock issued	—	591	368	43	207
Long-term borrowings	—	848	—	—	—
Total working capital provided	8,684	18,703	28,014	11,462	19,728
Working capital used:					
Additions to property and equipment — net	3,230	5,837	6,576	3,531	3,874
Reduction of long-term debt	—	413	436	—	—
Loans to stockholders — net	(159)	534	213	19	52
Purchase of treasury stock	732	—	—	—	—
Translation adjustment	(11)	72	602	635	(111)
Other	245	341	203	19	(219)
Total working capital used	4,037	7,197	8,030	4,204	3,596
Increase in working capital	$ 4,647	$11,506	$19,984	$ 7,258	$16,132
Changes in elements of working capital:					
Current assets — increase (decrease):					
Cash and short-term investments	$ 15	$ 53	$15,666	$ 7,460	$19,210
Trade accounts receivable	5,789	13,518	1,707	4,537	8,620
Inventories	1,341	5,225	(3,851)	(2,964)	(189)
Other	89	438	597	804	460
Current liabilities — (increase) decrease	(2,587)	(7,728)	5,865	(2,579)	(11,969)
Increase in working capital	$ 4,647	$11,506	$19,984	$ 7,258	$16,132

See accompanying notes.

EXHIBIT A-1   Microsoft prospectus (*Continued*).

MICROSOFT CORPORATION

NOTES TO CONSOLIDATED FINANCIAL STATEMENTS

1. SIGNIFICANT ACCOUNTING POLICIES

Business — The Company's principal business activity is the design, development and distribution of microcomputer software along with the distribution of related books and hardware peripheral devices.

Principles of Consolidation — The consolidated financial statements include the accounts of Microsoft and its wholly-owned subsidiaries. Significant intercompany transactions and balances have been eliminated.

Revenue Recognition — Revenue from sales of software and hardware consumer products to distributors or retail dealers is recognized when the product is shipped.

Software products are sold to original equipment manufacturers under license agreements which generally provide for a commitment fee payable over a minimum commitment period of one to three years. When the product is accepted, the commitment fee is recognized as revenue ratably over the minimum commitment period or on a per-system or per-copy basis if sales exceed the commitment fee level. Subsequent to the minimum commitment period, revenue based upon the number of systems shipped or copies sold is recognized as earned. Commitment fees received prior to product acceptance are recorded as customer deposits.

Short-term Investments — Short-term investments are carried at cost which approximates market.

Inventories — Inventories are valued at the lower of cost or market. Cost is determined using the first-in, first-out method.

Property and Equipment — Property and equipment are stated at cost and depreciated using straight-line and declining-balance methods over their estimated useful lives of from 5 to 7 years.

Warranties and Exchanges—The Company warrants certain products against certain defects and has policies permitting dealers and distributors to exchange products under certain circumstances. The Company's policies do not permit return of products for credit or refund. Estimated liabilities for warranties and exchanges at June 30, 1984 and 1985 and December 31, 1985 were not material.

Software Research and Development Costs — The majority of the Company's products are developed internally. Costs related to research and development and to production of software product masters are expensed as incurred. In August 1985; the Financial Accounting Standards Board issued a statement requiring capitalization of certain costs of producing software product masters beginning in the Company's year ending June 30, 1987. Had these new guidelines been applicable to the accompanying financial statements, income from operations may have been higher than amounts reported by an indeterminable amount.

Cost of revenues include royalties paid to authors of certain software products made under license agreements. Such royalties, which are based on net revenues were $3,222,000, $2,801,000, and $3,736,000 for the years ended June 30, 1983, 1984 and 1985 and $2,037,000 and $2,684,000 for the six months ended December 31, 1984 and 1985.

Non-operating income — Non-operating income includes interest income of $407,000, $427,000 and $952,000 for the years ended June 30, 1983, 1984 and 1985 and $402,000 and $1,151,000 for the six months ended December 31, 1984 and 1985. In addition, in 1984 the Company realized a short-term capital loss of $1,500,000 from the write-off of the entire value of a minority interest in a closely held company. In 1985 the Company realized a short-term capital gain of $984,000 upon the sale of marketable equity securities. During the six months ended December 31, 1985 the Company realized a

EXHIBIT A-1   Microsoft prospectus (*Continued*).

MICROSOFT CORPORATION

NOTES TO CONSOLIDATED FINANCIAL STATEMENTS (Continued)

foreign currency transaction gain of $1,245,000 resulting from the repayment of debt from certain international subsidiaries.

Income Taxes — Certain items of income and expense included in the financial statements are reported in different years in the tax returns in accordance with applicable income tax laws. The resulting difference between the financial statement income tax provision and income taxes currently payable is reported in the financial statements as deferred income taxes. Investment and other tax credits are accounted for as a reduction of tax expense in the year in which the credits reduce taxes payable (flow-through method).

Foreign Currency Translation — Assets and liabilities denominated in foreign currencies are translated at the exchange rate on the balance sheet date. Revenues, costs, and expenses are translated using an average rate. Translation adjustments are shown separately in stockholders' equity.

Net Income Per Share — Net income per share is computed on the basis of the weighted average number of common and common equivalent shares outstanding and is adjusted for the assumed conversion of preferred shares and shares issuable upon exercise of stock options. The computation assumes the proceeds from the exercise of stock options were used to repurchase common shares at the independently appraised value of the Company's common stock in each period. Had the computation been made assuming that Common Stock issued during the twelve months ended December 31, 1985 was outstanding in all periods and assuming that proceeds from the exercise of stock options issued during the twelve months ended December 31, 1985 were used to repurchase common shares at the price of shares offered for sale by this Prospectus, net income per share would not have been significantly less than that presented for each period.

Interim Financial Information — The financial statements at December 31, 1985 and for the six month periods ended December 31, 1984 and 1985 are unaudited but, in management's opinion, reflect all adjustments (consisting only of normal recurring adjustments) necessary for a fair presentation.

2. INVENTORIES

Inventories at June 30, 1984 and 1985, and at December 31, 1985 were as follows:

	June 30,		December 31,
	1984	1985	1985
	(In thousands)		
Finished goods	$1,507	$3,414	$3,398
Raw materials	8,263	2,505	2,332
Total	$9,770	$5,919	$5,730

EXHIBIT A-1   Microsoft prospectus (*Continued*).

MICROSOFT CORPORATION

NOTES TO CONSOLIDATED FINANCIAL STATEMENTS (Continued)

3. PROPERTY AND EQUIPMENT

Property and equipment at June 30, 1984 and 1985, and at December 31, 1985 were as follows:

	June 30,		December 31, 1985
	1984	1985	
	(In thousands)		
Computer equipment...........................	$7,007	$11,574	$14,241
Office furniture and equipment.................	2,899	4,306	5,143
Leasehold improvements	1,658	2,260	2,630
	11,564	18,140	22,014
Less accumulated depreciation	3,488	6,950	9,353
Property and equipment — net	$8,076	$11,190	$12,661

4. INCOME TAXES

The provision for income taxes is composed of:

	Year Ended June 30,		
	1983	1984	1985
	(In thousands)		
Current	$3,325	$11,549	$17,363
Deferred	1,252	601	1,379
Total	$4,577	$12,150	$18,742
The provision for deferred income taxes is composed of:			
Cash basis tax accounting	$ 35	$ 2,270	$ 2,309
Deferred compensation	(264)	(111)	(38)
Inventory adjustment................................	—	(850)	(714)
DISC	1,323	(12)	(282)
Other-net	158	(696)	104
Total	$1,252	$ 601	$ 1,379

EXHIBIT A-1   Microsoft prospectus (*Continued*).

MICROSOFT CORPORATION

NOTES TO CONSOLIDATED FINANCIAL STATEMENTS (Continued)

The Company's effective tax rate differs from the federal rate as follows:

	1983		1984		1985	
	Amount	% of Pre-Tax Income	Amount	% of Pre-Tax Income	Amount	% of Pre-Tax Income
			(In thousands)			
Federal income taxes at statutory rate	$5,090	46.0%	$12,893	46.0%	$19,708	46.0%
State income taxes net of federal tax benefit	—	—	500	1.8	1,194	2.8
Unrealized tax benefit of foreign operating losses	251	2.3	534	1.9	516	1.2
Unrealized (realized) tax benefit of capital loss carryforward	—	—	690	2.5	(453)	(1.1)
DISC/FSC benefit	—	—	(1,754)	(6.3)	(1,247)	(2.9)
Tax credits.........................	(846)	(7.6)	(1,368)	(4.9)	(2,007)	(4.7)
Other-net...........................	82	.7	655	2.3	1,031	2.4
Total	$4,577	41.4%	$12,150	43.3%	$18,742	43.7%

In 1984 the Company reversed Domestic International Sales Corporation (DISC) deferred taxes as a result of federal legislation to permanently exempt certain DISC earnings from taxation.

At June 30, 1985 the Company had capital loss carryforwards of $516,000 which expire in 1989 and unused foreign operating loss carryforwards of $2,906,000, available to offset future foreign taxable income, which expire as follows: 1988, $354,000; 1989, $602,000; 1990, $591,000; 1991, $133,000; 1992, $380,000; indefinitely, $846,000.

In the course of a current examination of the years ended June 30, 1983 and 1984 by the Internal Revenue Service, a field agent has proposed that the Company is subject to the personal holding company ("PHC") tax. The PHC penalty tax applies to a corporation that meets two tests: (1) more than 50% of the outstanding stock is owned by five or fewer individuals, and (2) at least 60% of its adjusted ordinary gross income, as defined in Section 543 of the Internal Revenue Code, is from passive sources such as interest, dividends, rents, and royalties. The law was designed to discourage the accumulation of passive income by closely-held corporations and is generally not applied to active operating corporations. However, in September 1984 the Internal Revenue Service issued a private letter ruling holding that income from license fees and maintenance fees received by a developer of custom software which it licensed, relying on trademark and trade secret protection, to a limited number of large companies and governmental agencies was "personal holding company income" under Section 543 of the Internal Revenue Code. The Company meets the stock ownership requirement and is expected to continue to meet that test after the offering. However, the Company believes that its business significantly differs from the corporation discussed in the private letter ruling and that its retail sales of mass produced packaged software products are sales of tangible personal property and should not be classified as PHC income.

The PHC tax is 50% of after-tax income and through December 31, 1985 could be as much as approximately $30,000,000 plus interest. At its option, a corporation subject to the PHC tax may declare a "deficiency dividend" to its stockholders of record at the time such a dividend is declared in an amount equal to the corporation's undistributed PHC income. For the Company this could be as much as approximately $60,000,000 as of December 31, 1985. The payment of a deficiency dividend avoids a PHC tax to the corporation (but not the related interest) but is taxable to the shareholders. If a PHC tax were to be assessed and the Company elected to pay the tax, the payment of tax would be

EXHIBIT A-1 Microsoft prospectus (*Continued*).

MICROSOFT CORPORATION

NOTES TO CONSOLIDATED FINANCIAL STATEMENTS (Continued)

recorded as a charge to operations and would reduce net income accordingly. If a PHC tax were to be assessed and the Company elected to declare a deficiency dividend, retained earnings would be reduced by the amount of such a dividend.

The 1985 Tax Reform Bill passed by the House of Representatives in December 1985 and currently under consideration in the Senate, contains a safe-harbor provision specifically for software royalty income. Congress has amended the PHC tax provisions at least 20 times, generally to alleviate harsh treatment of an active industry that happened to fall within the mechanical test of the PHC tax. In a few instances, the amendment has been retroactive. Retroactive enactment of the computer software provision is actively supported by some members of Congress. If passed, the proposed change would remove the Company from personal holding company status. Regardless of whether corrective legislation is passed and regardless of whether such legislation is retroactive, the Company believes that its retail sales are greater than 40% of adjusted ordinary gross income for all significant periods through December 31, 1985 and that such sales are not PHC income, and intends to vigorously contest any PHC tax assessment.

Although management and counsel presently believe that there is a small risk that the Company might have to either pay the PHC tax or declare a deficiency dividend, they believe that it is more likely than not that neither payment of a material tax nor a material deficiency dividend will be required. Because the total amount of any PHC tax that might be assessed could vary significantly based upon the specific year for which such an assessment might occur and other facts and circumstances and because management and counsel presently believe that it is more likely than not that neither a material payment of a PHC tax nor a material deficiency dividend will be required, management has not formulated specific intentions as to how the Company will proceed in the event such a tax is assessed.

5. LONG-TERM DEBT

	June 30,	
	1984	1985
	(In thousands)	
12% Long-term note payable	$705	$650
Less current portion	269	650
Total	$436	—

The current portion of long-term debt is included in other current liabilities in the financial statements. At December 31, 1985 the Company had no long-term debt.

6. LEASES

In July 1985, the Company entered a lease for a new corporate campus. The Company will occupy the facility upon completion of construction scheduled for the Spring of 1986. The noncancelable operating lease expires in 2001 with renewal options through 2011. The Company also leases various other facilities and equipment under operating leases that expire through 1988. Rental expense was approximately $926,000, $2,373,000 and $3,012,000 for the years ended June 30, 1983, 1984 and 1985 and $1,210,000 and $1,925,000 for the six months ended December 31, 1984 and 1985.

Minimum lease commitments including the new corporate campus, for years subsequent to June 30, 1985, are as follows: 1986, $4,329,000; 1987, $4,244,000; 1988, $3,900,000; 1989, $3,383,000; 1990, $3,485,000; thereafter, $55,874,000.

EXHIBIT A-1   Microsoft prospectus (*Continued*).

MICROSOFT CORPORATION

NOTES TO CONSOLIDATED FINANCIAL STATEMENTS (Continued)

7. STOCKHOLDERS' EQUITY

Authorized Capital and Common Stock Split — During 1984, the number of shares of authorized $.001 par value common stock was increased from 20,000,000 to 60,000,000 and a 2 for 1 common stock split was effected in the form of a stock dividend. All share and per share information has been restated to give effect to the stock split.

Preferred Stock — Preferred stock is convertible into 1,000,000 shares of common stock (subject to adjustment in certain events) at the option of the holder, or automatically upon sale of the Company's common stock in a public offering in which aggregate cash proceeds are at least $5,000,000. The Company has reserved 1,000,000 shares of common stock for conversion. Preferred stock is redeemable in whole, but not in part, at the option of the Company at any time after receipt of written consent from the holders of two-thirds of the then outstanding preferred stock or at any time after May 1, 1986. The redemption price is $2 per share plus declared but unpaid dividends (none to date) to the date of redemption. In the event of voluntary or involuntary liquidation, holders of preferred stock are entitled to $2 per share plus declared but unpaid dividends.

Preferred shares have the same voting rights as common stock and are entitled to dividends as declared by the Board of Directors. No dividends may be paid on common stock unless the preferred stock, at the same time or prior thereto, receives a dividend of an equal or larger amount per share.

Employee Stock Purchases — In 1982, certain shares of common stock were sold to employees at prices below fair value as independently appraised. The excess was charged to compensation during the period that related services were performed. At June 30, 1984 unamortized deferred compensation expense of $83,000 was recorded as an offset to paid-in-capital. Such deferred compensation was fully amortized during the year ended June 30, 1985. Other assets included 7% loans to stockholders of $746,000 and $736,000 at June 30, 1984 and 1985 and $757,000 at December 31, 1985 originally made to employees to enable them to pay personal income taxes arising from this transaction. Stock purchase agreements with these employees provide the Company with the right of first refusal to repurchase employee's shares and, in 1983, 997,366 shares of common stock were purchased from terminated employees.

During the years ended June 30, 1984 and 1985 and the six months ended December 31, 1985, 353,335, 58,335 and 8,000 shares of common stock were issued to employees at independently appraised fair values for 9% notes receivable of $540,000, $175,000 and $44,000. Such notes have been recorded as a reduction of paid-in-capital. Payments under these notes, due from 1991 to 1993, will be credited to paid-in-capital as received.

Employee Stock Purchase Plan — In January 1986, the Company established an employee stock purchase plan for all employees. Employees may contribute up to 10% of their compensation to purchase the Company's common stock at fair market value. The Plan will commence in July 1986 and terminate December 1990. The Company has reserved 300,000 shares of common stock for the plan.

Stock Option Plan — The Company has a stock option plan for officers and key employees which provides for nonqualified and incentive options. The Board of Directors determines the option price (not to be less than fair market value for incentive options) at the date of grant. The options generally expire five years from the date of grant and are exercisable over the period stated in each option.

EXHIBIT A-1   Microsoft prospectus (*Continued*).

MICROSOFT CORPORATION

NOTES TO CONSOLIDATED FINANCIAL STATEMENTS (Continued)

	Reserved Shares	Outstanding Options Number	Outstanding Options Price Per Share
Balance, June 30, 1982	3,020,000	900,598	$ .475
Granted	—	532,000	$ 1.50
Exercised	(1,000)	(1,000)	$ .475
Expired...	—	(54,342)	$ .475
Balance, June 30, 1983	3,019,000	1,377,256	$.475–$1.50
Granted	—	733,615	$1.50–$3.00
Exercised	(72,692)	(72,692)	$.475–$1.50
Expired...	—	(109,464)	
Balance, June 30, 1984	2,946,308	1,928,715	$.475–$3.00
Granted	—	652,715	$ 3.00
Exercised	(214,153)	(214,153)	$.475–$3.00
Expired...	—	(219,726)	$.475–$3.00
Balance, June 30, 1985	2,732,155	2,147,551	$.475–$3.00
Additional shares reserved..............................	200,000	—	
Granted	—	848,865	$3.00–$5.50
Exercised	(160,398)	(160,398)	$.475–$3.00
Expired...	—	(168,157)	$.475–$5.50
Balance, December 31, 1985	2,771,757	2,667,861	$.475–$5.50

Of the options granted during the six months ended December 31, 1985, 150,000 were nonqualified options. All other options granted were incentive options.

At December 31, 1985, options for 547,118 shares were exercisable and 103,896 shares were available for future grants under the Plan.

EXHIBIT A-1   Microsoft prospectus (*Continued*).

MICROSOFT CORPORATION

NOTES TO CONSOLIDATED FINANCIAL STATEMENTS (Continued)

8. FOREIGN SALES AND OPERATIONS

	United States	Foreign Subsidiaries	Eliminations	Consolidated
		(In thousands)		
Year ended June 30, 1983:				
Net revenues:				
United States	$ 39,944	$ —	$ —	$ 39,944
International	9,635	637	(151)	10,121
Total	$ 49,579	$ 637	$ (151)	$ 50,065
Income from operations	$ 11,289	$ (552)	$ (80)	$ 10,657
Identifiable assets	$ 24,556	$ 281	$ (509)	$ 24,328
Year ended June 30, 1984:				
Net revenues:				
United States	$ 75,576	$ —	$ (7,572)	$ 68,004
International	22,469	8,555	(1,549)	29,475
Total	$ 98,045	$ 8,555	$ (9,121)	$ 97,479
Income from operations	$ 29,204	$ (1,169)	$ 1,068	$ 29,103
Identifiable assets	$ 49,093	$ 8,152	$ (9,608)	$ 47,637
Year ended June 30, 1985:				
Net revenues:				
United States	$109,612	$ —	$(13,895)	$ 95,717
International	27,972	19,745	(3,017)	44,700
Total	$137,584	$ 19,745	$(16,912)	$140,417
Income from operations	$ 42,937	$ (378)	$ (1,652)	$ 40,907
Identifiable assets	$ 71,163	$ 12,119	$(18,218)	$ 65,064

Cost of revenues includes commissions of $2,090,000, $4,377,000 and $5,179,000 during the years ended June 30, 1983, 1984 and 1985 and $2,544,000 and $2,453,000 for the six months ended December 31, 1984 and 1985 paid to a foreign company whose major stockholder is a former director of the Company. The Company is in the process of terminating its relationship with this foreign company.

9. SUBSEQUENT EVENT

Subsequent to December 31, 1985 Microsoft was served with a summons and complaint in an action commenced by Seattle Computer Products, Inc. ("SCP") in a Washington state court. This action arises out of an agreement entered into in 1981 under which SCP sold to Microsoft SCP's rights in a disk operating system which Microsoft developed into MS-DOS. The complaint, which has not yet been filed with the court, seeks the following relief: (i) a judicial declaration that under the agreement SCP has an assignable, perpetual, royalty-free worldwide license from Microsoft for MS-DOS in its current and future versions; (ii) an injunction against Microsoft prohibiting alleged interference with SCP's attempts to sell its business and requiring Microsoft to honor SCP's interpretation of the agreement; and, in the alternative, (iii) judgment against Microsoft for damages "believed to exceed $20,000,000" or $60,000,000 when trebled or a rescission of the agreement, a return of the rights

EXHIBIT A-1   Microsoft prospectus (*Continued*).
MICROSOFT CORPORATION

NOTES TO CONSOLIDATED FINANCIAL STATEMENTS (Continued)

granted thereunder, and an accounting for the payment to SCP of all revenues received from Microsoft's marketing of MS-DOS. The Company believes that SCP's interpretation of the agreement is erroneous and intends to vigorously defend this action. In the opinion of the Company, were SCP to prevail on its requested declaratory or injunctive relief (see items (i) and (ii) above), such a result would not have a material adverse effect on the Company's financial condition or results of operations. Although the outcome of litigation can never be predicted with certainty, the Company further believes that it is unlikely that SCP could obtain the relief sought with respect to damages or rescission of the contract (see item (iii) above).

EXHIBIT A-1   Microsoft prospectus (*Continued*).

Microsoft:
A sample of new products from 1985

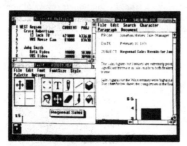

Microsoft® Windows. An operating environment that sits between the MS-DOS® operating system and applications programs, Windows provides a graphical interface for end users and allows them to run several programs concurrently.

Microsoft® Word. During 1985, Microsoft introduced both a network version and a new single-user version of this word processing product. Word allows the user to work with text in multiple windows and supports advanced output devices such as laser printers.

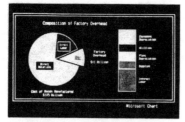

Microsoft® Chart. Designed to work with more than 60 printers and plotters, Microsoft Chart Version 2.0 can produce a wide selection of chart types, patterns, and colors. This is a sample of a slide generated by the program.

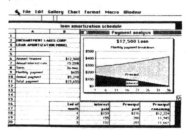

Microsoft™ Excel. Designed for the Apple® Macintosh™, Microsoft Excel is a spreadsheet integrated with business graphics and database capabilities. Charts can be linked to spreadsheets so that when the numbers change, the graphs change automatically.

Microsoft® Mouse. The newest version of the Microsoft Mouse pointing and editing device works with many applications products from Microsoft and other companies.

EXHIBIT A-1   Microsoft prospectus (*Continued*).

The following trademarks are used in this Prospectus:

APPLE is a registered trademark of, and Macintosh is a trademark licensed to Apple Computer, Inc.

AT&T is a registered trademark of American Telephone & Telegraph Co.

COMPAQ is a registered trademark of COMPAQ Computer Corp.

COMPUSERVE is a registered trademark of Compuserve Corporation.

CP/M is a registered trademark of Digital Research Inc.

DEC is a registered trademark of Digital Equipment Corporation.

DOW JONES NEWS/RETRIEVAL is a registered trademark of Dow Jones & Company.

IBM is a registered trademark of International Business Machines Corporation.

INTEL is a registered trademark of Intel Corporation.

LOTUS and 1-2-3 are registered trademarks of Lotus Development Corporation.

MICRORIM is a registered trademark of Microrim, Inc.

MICROSOFT, MS-DOS, MSX-DOS, MSX, XENIX, GW-BASIC, RAMCARD, SOFTCARD and MULTIPLAN are registered trademarks of Microsoft Corporation.

MITSUBISHI is a registered trademark of Mitsubishi Electric Corporation.

NEWSNET is a registered trademark of NewsNet, Inc.

NEC is a registered trademark of NEC Corporation.

OLIVETTI is a registered trademark of Ing. C. Olivetti.

PHILIPS is a registered trademark of Philips International B.V.

Rbase 5000 is a trademark of Microrim, Inc.

TANDY is a registered trademark of Tandy Corporation.

TRIUMPH is a registered trademark of Triumph Adler AG.

UNIX is a registered trademark of AT&T Information Systems Inc.

ZENITH is a registered trademark of Zenith Radio Corporation.

ZILOG and Z-80 are registered trademarks of Zilog, Inc.

EXHIBIT A-2   Worlds of Wonder prospectus.

TABLE OF CONTENTS

4,700,000 Shares

WORLDS OF WONDER'

Common Stock

PROSPECTUS

June   , 1986

Smith Barney,
Harris Upham & Co.
Incorporated

Dean Witter Reynolds Inc.

EXHIBIT A-2   Worlds of Wonder prospectus (*Continued*).

As filed with the Securities and Exchange Commission on May 13, 1986

Registration No. 33- *5627*

SECURITIES AND EXCHANGE COMMISSION
Washington, D.C. 20549

FORM S-1
REGISTRATION STATEMENT
UNDER
THE SECURITIES ACT OF 1933

35 29 4508

WORLDS OF WONDER, INC.
(Exact name of registrant as specified in its charter)

California	5042	94-2960825
(State or other jurisdiction of incorporation or organization)	(Primary standard industrial classification code number)	(I.R.S. employer identification number)

RECEIVED

MAY 1 5 1986

Bechtel Information Services
Gaithersburg, Maryland

4209 Technology Drive
Fremont, California 94538
(415) 659-4300
(Address, including zip code, and telephone number, including area code,
of registrant's principal executive offices)

DONALD D. KINGSBOROUGH
Chairman of the Board, President and
Chief Executive Officer
WORLDS OF WONDER, INC.
4209 Technology Drive
Fremont, California 94538
(415) 659-4300
(Name, address, including zip code, and telephone number,
including area code, of agent for service)

RECD S.E.C.

MAY 1 3 1986

FEE 34

Copies of communications to:

LARRY W. SONSINI, ESQ.
WILSON, SONSINI, GOODRICH & ROSATI
A Professional Corporation
2 Palo Alto Square, Suite 900
Palo Alto, California 94306

M. PETER LILLEVAND, ESQ.
ORRICK, HERRINGTON & SUTCLIFFE
600 Montgomery Street
San Francisco, California 94111

Approximate date of commencement of proposed sale to the public: As soon as practicable after the Registration Statement becomes effective.

If any of the securities being registered on this Form are to be offered on a delayed or continuous basis pursuant to Rule 415 under the Securities Act of 1933 check the following box. ☐

CALCULATION OF REGISTRATION FEE

Title of Each Class of Securities to be Registered	Amount to be Registered(1)(2)	Proposed Maximum Offering Price Per Share(3)	Proposed Maximum Aggregate Offering Price(3)	Amount of Registration Fee(3)
Common Stock, without par value	5,475,000 shs.	$16.00	$87,600,000	$17,520

(1) Includes 705,000 shares which the Underwriters have an option to purchase to cover over-allotments, if any.

(2) Includes 70,000 shares not included in the offering being registered for sale by a shareholder.

(3) Estimated solely for the purpose of computing the registration fee pursuant to Rule 457 under the Securities Act of 1933.

The Registrant hereby amends this Registration Statement on such date or dates as may be necessary to delay its effective date until the Registrant shall file a further amendment which specifically states that this Registration Statement shall thereafter become effective in accordance with Section 8(a) of the Securities Act of 1933 or until the Registration Statement shall become effective on such date as the Commission, acting pursuant to said Section 8(a), may determine.

This Is Page One of 813 Pages

Exhibit Index Is Located On Pages 61+62

EXHIBIT A-2   Worlds of Wonder prospectus (*Continued*).

WORLDS OF WONDER, INC.

Cross-Reference Sheet between Items of
Form S-1 and Prospectus

Form S-1 Item	Prospectus Heading
1. Forepart of the Registration Statement and Outside Front Cover Page of Prospectus	Facing Page of Registration Statement; Outside Front Cover Page
2. Inside Front and Outside Back Cover Pages of Prospectus	Inside Front Cover Page and Outside Back Cover Page
3. Summary Information, Risk Factors and Ratio of Earnings to Fixed Charges	Prospectus Summary; The Company; Risk Factors
4. Use of Proceeds	Use of Proceeds
5. Determination of Offering Price	Underwriting
6. Dilution	Dilution
7. Selling Security Holders	Principal and Selling Shareholders; Management; Certain Transactions
8. Plan of Distribution	Front Cover Page; Underwriting
9. Description of Securities to be Registered	Description of Capital Stock
10. Interests of Named Experts and Counsel	Legal Matters; Experts
11. Information with Respect to the Registrant	Front Cover Page: The Company; Dividend Policy; Capitalization; Selected Financial Data; Management's Discussion and Analysis of Financial Condition and Results of Operations; Business; Management; Certain Transactions; Principal and Selling Shareholders; Description of Capital Stock; Consolidated Financial Statements
12. Disclosure of Commission Position on Indemnification for Securities Act Liabilities	Not Applicable

EXHIBIT A-2   Worlds of Wonder prospectus (*Continued*).

INTRODUCTORY NOTE

This Registration Statement contains two forms of front and back cover pages. The first form of such is intended for use in connection with the initial public offering of the Company's Common Stock. The second form of each is intended for use in connection with the sale of 70,000 shares of the Company's Common Stock by a shareholder of the Company, which sale is contingent upon the completion of such offering.

EXHIBIT A-2   Worlds of Wonder prospectus (*Continued*).

PRELIMINARY PROSPECTUS DATED MAY 13, 1986

PROSPECTUS

4,700,000 Shares

WORLDS OF WONDER®

Common Stock

Of the Common Stock offered hereby 3,100,000 shares are being sold by Worlds of Wonder, Inc. (the "Company") and 1,600,000 shares are being sold by certain shareholders of the Company the "Selling Shareholders"). The Company will not receive any of the proceeds from the sale of shares by the Selling Shareholders.

Prior to this offering there has been no public market for the Company's Common Stock. It is currently estimated that the initial public offering price will be between $13 and $16 per share. See "Underwriting" for information relating to the method of determining the initial offering price to the public.

Prospective investors should carefully consider the factors set forth under "Risk Factors."

THESE SECURITIES HAVE NOT BEEN APPROVED OR DISAPPROVED BY THE SECURITIES AND EXCHANGE COMMISSION NOR HAS THE COMMISSION PASSED UPON THE ACCURACY OR ADEQUACY OF THIS PROSPECTUS. ANY REPRESENTATION TO THE CONTRARY IS A CRIMINAL OFFENSE.

	Price to Public	Underwriting Discounts and Commissions(1)	Proceeds to Company(2)	Proceeds to Selling Shareholders(2)
Per Share	$	$	$	$
Total(3)	$	$	$	$

(1) See "Underwriting" for indemnification arrangements with the Underwriters.

(2) Before deducting expenses payable by the Company estimated at $

(3) The Selling Shareholders have granted the Underwriters an option exercisable within 30 days after the date hereof to purchase up to 705,000 additional shares to cover over-allotments, if any. See "Underwriting." If all such shares are purchased, the total Price to Public, Underwriting Discounts and Commissions and Proceeds to Selling Shareholders will be increased to $,$ and $, respectively. Does not include 70,000 shares which are not included in the offering but are being registered for future sale by a shareholder of the Company. See "Description of Capital Stock—Shares Eligible for Future Sale."

The shares of Common Stock are being offered by the several Underwriters named herein subject to prior sale, when, as and if accepted by them and subject to certain conditions. It is expected that the certificates for the shares of Common Stock will be available for delivery on or about June   , 1986 at the office of Smith Barney, Harris Upham & Co. Incorporated, 110 Wall Street, New York, New York 10005.

Smith Barney, Harris Upham & Co. Dean Witter Reynolds Inc.
Incorporated

June   , 1986

EXHIBIT A-2   Worlds of Wonder prospectus (*Continued*).

PRELIMINARY PROSPECTUS DATED MAY 13, 1986

PROSPECTUS

70,000 Shares

WORLDS OF WONDER®

Common Stock

This Prospectus covers 70,000 shares of the Common Stock of the Company to be sold by Equus Investment I, Ltd. ("Equus")   Such shares will be sold in one or more transactions at the prevailing market price for such shares in normal brokerage transactions. The Company will not receive any of the proceeds from the sale of shares by Equus.

Prospective investors should carefully consider the factors set forth under "Risk Factors."

THESE SECURITIES HAVE NOT BEEN APPROVED OR DISAPPROVED BY THE SECURITIES AND EXCHANGE COMMISSION NOR HAS THE COMMISSION PASSED UPON THE ACCURACY OR ADEQUACY OF THIS PROSPECTUS. ANY REPRESENTATION TO THE CONTRARY IS A CRIMINAL OFFENSE.

This Prospectus, except this cover page and the back cover page, is also being used for a public offering of the Company's Common Stock by the Company and certain Selling Shareholders. Sales by Equus are contingent on the completion of such offering. The sections herein entitled "Use of Proceeds" and "Underwriting" are included only in connection with such offering, and the Underwriters of such offering have no responsibility or liability with respect to the offering made by this Prospectus. Dean Witter Reynolds Inc., one of the Underwriters of such offering, is an investment advisor to Equus, but will not participate in sales of shares of Common Stock by Equus.

The date of this Prospectus is June   , 1986

EXHIBIT A-2   Worlds of Wonder prospectus (*Continued*).

TEDDY RUXPIN,® the
animated, storytelling
toy whose mouth, nose
and eye movements are
synchronized to his voice.

The Company intends to furnish its shareholders with annual reports containing audited financial
statements examined by an independent public accounting firm and quarterly reports containing unaudited
financial information for the first three quarters of each fiscal year.

IN CONNECTION WITH THIS OFFERING, THE UNDERWRITERS MAY OVER-ALLOT OR EFFECT
TRANSACTIONS WHICH STABILIZE OR MAINTAIN THE MARKET PRICE OF THE COMMON STOCK .
OF THE COMPANY AT A LEVEL ABOVE THAT WHICH MIGHT OTHERWISE PREVAIL IN THE OPEN
MARKET. SUCH STABILIZING, IF COMMENCED, MAY BE DISCONTINUED AT ANY TIME.

EXHIBIT A-2   Worlds of Wonder prospectus (*Continued*).

SNOOPY®* and CHARLIE BROWN* will tell stories and sing songs about the Peanuts® gang. WOODSTOCK* will chirp and flap his wings. Twelve colorful storybooks and tapes are scheduled for release.

v
reg

The Talking Mother Goose™* will move her eyes and beak and turn her head. Twelve traditional fairy tales with tapes are scheduled for release.

The Talking Mickey M
©The Walt Disney Con

*Shown are prototypes only. Production is scheduled to begin in the summer of 1986.
**Plush representation of the character only. Prototype is under development. Production is scheduled to begin in late 1986.

EXHIBIT A-2   Worlds of Wonder prospectus (*Continued*).

3y

The Land of Pleasant Dreams®
keepsake cloth animals,* five
different characters in all.

Pamela™
The Living Doll.™®
When you touch
her face or talk to
her, she'll talk back.
Six voice cards and
sticker books are
scheduled for
release.

rLyte™®
or.™®

EXHIBIT A-2   Worlds of Wonder prospectus (*Continued*).

PROSPECTUS SUMMARY

The following information is qualified in its entirety by the more detailed information and financial statements appearing elsewhere in this Prospectus. All share numbers and per share amounts throughout this Prospectus have been adjusted for a 3-for-2 stock split of the outstanding Common Stock effective as of May 8, 1986.

The Company

Worlds of Wonder, Inc. is engaged in the design, development, marketing and distribution of toy products. During its first fiscal year ended March 31, 1986, the Company produced and sold one product line, THE WORLD OF TEDDY RUXPIN, which has as its central character an animated story-telling plush toy named TEDDY RUXPIN. TEDDY RUXPIN "comes to life" through an electromechanical animation technology which synchronizes eye, nose and mouth movements to a corresponding speech pattern utilizing a pre-programmed cassette tape. From its initial shipment in August 1985 to March 31, 1986 the Company shipped approximately 1.4 million units of TEDDY RUXPIN and recorded net sales from the product line of approximately $93 million.

The Company has announced several new product lines, including the electromechanical animation of THE TALKING MOTHER GOOSE, SNOOPY, CHARLIE BROWN and MICKEY MOUSE. The Company also has announced other new product lines, including LAZER TAG incorporating infrared light technology and the PAMELA doll incorporating digital speech technology. The Company expects the manufacture of certain of these products to begin in the summer of 1986 with initial shipments of all of these products to retailers staggered from summer through the 1986 Christmas season.

In addition to toy products, the Company is exploring other opportunities to adapt proven technologies to innovative entertainment and leisure products that can be promoted and distributed through mass market channels. Although it has not announced any such products, the Company continues to evaluate non-toy products consistent with this strategy.

The Offering

Common Stock offered	4,700,000 shares, of which 3,100,000 shares will be sold by the Company and 1,600,000 shares will be sold by the Selling Shareholders (1)
Common Stock to be outstanding..............	21,117,435 shares
Proposed NASDAQ symbol	WOWI
Use of proceeds by the Company	Repayment of subordinated debt and short-term bank debt

Summary Financial Data
(in thousands, except per share data)

	First Quarter	Second Quarter	Third Quarter	Fourth Quarter	Fiscal Year Total
			Fiscal Year Ended March 31, 1986		
Income Statement Data:					
Net sales	$ —	$ 2,695	$45,800	$44,592	$93,087
Operating costs and expenses	1,622	5,063	34,086	35,120	75,891
Income (loss) before taxes on income	(1,666)	(2,614)	11,288	8,266	15,274
Net income (loss)	(1,666)	(2,614)	7,852	4,530	8,102
Net income (loss) per share	(.09)	(.14)	.42	.24	.43

	March 31, 1986	
	Actual	As Adjusted(2)
Balance Sheet Data:		
Working capital.................................	$ 3,209	$
Total assets......................................	70,261	
Short-term debt.................................	23,739	(3)
Long-term debt.................................	—	—
Shareholders' equity...........................	11,624	

(1) Assumes the Underwriters' over-allotment option to purchase up to 705,000 shares from the Selling Shareholders is not exercised. See "Underwriting."

(2) Adjusted to reflect the sale of the Common Stock offered hereby and the application of the net proceeds of this offering. See "Use of Proceeds."

(3) As of May 9, 1986 the outstanding short-term debt was approximately $27 million. The Company anticipates that outstanding short-term debt will not be fully repaid by the proceeds of the offering.

EXHIBIT A-2   Worlds of Wonder prospectus (*Continued*).

THE COMPANY

Worlds of Wonder, Inc. ("Worlds of Wonder" or the "Company") is engaged in the design, development, marketing and distribution of toy products. During its first fiscal year ended March 31, 1986 the Company produced and sold one product line, THE WORLD OF TEDDY RUXPIN, which has as its central character an animated story-telling plush toy named TEDDY RUXPIN. From its initial shipment in August 1985 to March 31, 1986, the Company shipped approximately 1.4 million units of TEDDY RUXPIN and recorded net sales from the product line of approximately $93 million.

TEDDY RUXPIN "comes to life" through an electromechanical animation technology which synchronizes eye, nose and mouth movements to a corresponding speech pattern utilizing a pre-programmed cassette tape. The Company has positioned TEDDY RUXPIN with a character background and ongoing storyline, building a product line including related characters, storybooks, cassette tapes, clothing and various accessories around the main character. The Company believes that the marketing of these related items, which accounted for approximately 33% of net sales in the year ended March 31, 1986, will help extend the life cycle of the product line.

The Company has announced several new product lines, including the electromechanical animation of THE TALKING MOTHER GOOSE, SNOOPY, CHARLIE BROWN and MICKEY MOUSE. The Company also announced three other product lines: LAZER TAG, incorporating infrared light technology; PAMELA, a doll incorporating digital speech technology; and PLEASANT DREAMS, a line of old-fashioned rag doll animals. Each new product line will consist of related toy items and/or a range of accessories. The Company expects the manufacture of certain of these products to begin in the summer of 1986 with initial shipments of all of these products to retailers staggered from summer through the 1986 Christmas season.

In addition to toy products, the Company is exploring other opportunities to adapt proven technologies to innovative entertainment and leisure products that can be promoted and distributed through mass market channels. Although it has not announced any such products, the Company continues to evaluate non-toy products consistent with this strategy.

Worlds of Wonder was incorporated under the laws of California in March 1985. Its corporate headquarters are located at 4209 Technology Drive, Fremont, California 94538. The Company's telephone number is (415) 659-4300. Its products come under Standard Industrial Classification (SIC) Code Number 5042.

TEDDY RUXPIN and FOBs are registered trademarks, and THE WORLD OF TEDDY RUXPIN and GRUBBY are trademarks, of Alchemy II, Inc. WORLDS OF WONDER is a registered trademark of the Company, and the WOW logo, THE TALKING MOTHER GOOSE, LAZER TAG, STARLYTES and PAMELA are trademarks of the Company. PEANUTS, SNOOPY, CHARLIE BROWN and WOODSTOCK are registered trademarks of United Features Syndicate. MICKEY MOUSE and GOOFY are registered trademarks of The Walt Disney Company. PLEASANT DREAMS is a registered trademark of Anthony Paul Productions.

USE OF PROCEEDS

The net proceeds from the sale of the Common Stock offered by the Company are estimated to be $ Approximately $3.7 million of the net proceeds will be applied to the repayment to certain shareholders of outstanding subordinated debt used for working capital purposes. See "Certain Transactions." The remaining net proceeds will be applied to repay a portion of the outstanding short-term bank debt used by the Company to fulfill general working capital needs. See "Management's Discussion and Analysis of Financial Condition and Results of Operations—Liquidity and Capital Resources."

The Company will not receive any of the proceeds from the sale of shares of Common Stock offered by the Selling Shareholders.

EXHIBIT A-2   Worlds of Wonder prospectus (*Continued*).

RISK FACTORS

Prospective investors should carefully consider the following factors before purchasing the shares of Common Stock offered by this Prospectus.

Short Operating History. The Company has a short operating history, having commenced operations in April 1985. Although the Company achieved approximately $93 million in net sales and was profitable during its first fiscal year ended March 31, 1986, its operations are subject to a number of risks, some of which are summarized below. Accordingly, there can be no assurance that the Company will continue to experience rapid growth in net sales or remain profitable.

Dependence on Single Product Line; New Product Introductions. To date, the Company has marketed products from a single product line, THE WORLD OF TEDDY RUXPIN. The product life cycle of a toy line is generally relatively short. Successful new products and product lines may therefore be crucial to the success of the Company's business. The Company expects to introduce six new product lines during the current fiscal year, including three product lines employing the electromechanical animation technology used in TEDDY RUXPIN. Although such products have been announced, tooling is not yet completed and none of the products has yet been manufactured. The Company has only limited experience in product introductions, and product line expansion will place great demands on management and other Company resources. If the TEDDY RUXPIN product line loses market acceptance and is not replaced successfully with new products, or if new product introductions are unsuccessful, the Company's business would be affected adversely. In addition, if animated talking toys should lose market acceptance, the Company could be affected adversely. See "Business—Products" and "Business—Product Development and Design."

Dependence on Foreign Contract Manufacturers. The Company conducts substantially all of its manufacturing operations through unaffiliated contract manufacturers in Hong Kong, the People's Republic of China, Taiwan and Korea. Foreign manufacturing is subject to a number of risks, including transportation delays and interruptions, political and economic disruptions, labor strikes, the imposition of tariffs and import and export controls, and changes in governmental policies. In addition, three manufacturers accounted for approximately 95% of the production of TEDDY RUXPIN units, representing approximately 63% of net sales for the year ended March 31, 1986. Although the Company has increased the number of manufacturers it will use in fiscal 1987, it expects to continue to use a limited number of contract manufacturers and accordingly will continue to be dependent upon sources outside the Company for timely production and quality workmanship. There can be no assurance that unusual delays or quality control problems of such manufacturers may not delay product deliveries or result in product returns, resulting in losses of revenues and goodwill. Although the Company believes other contract manufacturers would be available upon acceptable terms if the need were to arise, the Company's operations could be adversely affected by a substantial delay in locating acceptable substitutes or increasing the production of alternative manufacturers. See "Business—Manufacturing."

Limited Mold and Component Sources. The Company has used multiple outside sources to create the plastic and foam molds for the manufacture of a majority of its products; however, a large percentage of such molds are fabricated by a single vendor. There can be no assurance that this vendor will continue to provide services sufficient to meet the Company's needs. Additionally, any significant business problems encountered by this vendor could adversely affect the Company's operations. Certain parts and electronic components included in the Company's electromechanical talking toys are available from a single source or limited sources. In certain instances, the Company has arranged for the sole suppliers of the parts to carry additional inventories. However, interruption in the supply of components could adversely affect the Company. See "Business— Manufacturing."

Dependence on Key Personnel and New Employees. The Company believes its success will depend to a significant extent on the efforts and abilities of certain of its senior management, in particular those of Donald Kingsborough, its Chairman of the Board, President and Chief Executive Officer. The loss of Mr. Kingsborough's services or of certain other key employees could have a material adverse effect on the

EXHIBIT A-2   Worlds of Wonder prospectus (*Continued*).

Company. The Company's success also depends upon its ability to attract and retain qualified employees. Hiring to meet anticipated Company operations will require the Company to assimilate large numbers of new employees in a relatively short period of time. See "Business—Employees" and "Management."

Competition. The toy industry is highly competitive. Among the Company's competitors are toy companies and toy divisions of large diversified companies with greater assets and resources than those of the Company, as well as hundreds of smaller domestic and foreign toy manufacturers, importers and marketers. The relatively low barriers to entry into the toy industry also permit new competitors to easily enter the industry. The Company believes it has enjoyed limited competition to its TEDDY RUXPIN product line. Due to the success of TEDDY RUXPIN, however, the Company anticipates other companies will introduce talking toy products that will compete with TEDDY RUXPIN and other new products announced by the Company. Such entrants might force price reductions or cause the Company to lose market share, which events may adversely affect the Company. The Company's new products may face more immediate and significant competition than that faced by the TEDDY RUXPIN product line. See. "Business—Competition."

Dependence on Independent Designers. Three of the Company's six anno·nced new product lines employ characters created by outside designers. The Company intends to continue to seek product ideas and licenses from third parties. The inability to secure these licenses on reasonable terms could adversely affect the Company. THE WORLD OF TEDDY RUXPIN was created by Alchemy II, Inc ("Alchemy"), a privately-owned product design and development company, and is licensed to the Company pursuant to a Development and Marketing Agreement with Alchemy. All of the Company's animated talking toys employ technology licensed from Alchemy. Alchemy has advised the Company of differences in the interpretation of certain elements of the Development and Marketing Agreement. See "Business —Product Development and Design—Alchemy."

Seasonality; Quarterly Results. Sales of toys are highly seasonal, with a majority of retail sales occurring during the Christmas season. Although indications of interest are provided by retailers early in the year, orders are generally cancellable without penalty. The seasonality of sales may cause operating results to vary significantly from quarter to quarter. The Company anticipates that net sales for the quarter ended June 30, 1986 will be less than those for the prior quarter and, as a result, the Company expects to report a loss for the quarter. See "Management's Discussion and Analysis of Financial Condition and Results of Operations." There can be no assurance that the Company can maintain sufficient flexibility with respect to its working capital needs, manufacturing capacity and supplies of raw materials, tools and components to be able to minimize the adverse effects of an unanticipated shortfall in demand. See "Business—Seasonality and Backlog."

Capital Requirements. The Company's cash flow from operations, together with the proceeds of this offering, are not expected to be sufficient to provide the working capital required for its anticipated growth. The Company anticipates that the net proceeds of this offering will not be sufficient to fully repay the outstanding short-term bank debt. Accordingly, the Company must obtain additional working capital from expanded bank borrowings or through additional debt or equity financings. If the Company is unable to obtain adequate working capital from these sources on acceptable terms, its operations would be adversely affected. See "Use of Proceeds" and "Management's Discussion and Analysis of Financial Condition and Results of Operations—Liquidity and Capital Resources."

Product Diversification. The Company has derived all of its net sales to date from toy products and expects to derive substantially all of its net sales for the fiscal year ending March 31, 1987 from toy products. However, the Company intends to develop products other than toys that can be effectively promoted and distributed through mass market channels. Developing such products will involve significant senior management time and Company resources. Future products may utilize different technologies and require knowledge of markets in which the Company does not presently participate. See "Business—Product Development and Design."

EXHIBIT A-2   Worlds of Wonder prospectus (*Continued*).

CAPITALIZATION

The following table sets forth the capitalization of the Company as of March 31, 1986, and as adjusted to reflect the sale of the shares of Common Stock offered by the Company hereby and the application of the net proceeds thereof.

	March 31, 1986	
	Actual	**As Adjusted**
Short-term bank debt (1)	$20,088,000	$ —
Subordinated debt (2)	3,651,000	—
Total short-term debt	$23,739,000	$ —
Long-term debt	$ —	$ —
Shareholders' equity:		
Preferred Stock; 1,000,000 shares authorized; no shares outstanding	—	—
Common Stock; 50,000,000 shares authorized; 18,017,435 outstanding(3); 21,117,435 shares outstanding as adjusted	3,547,000	
Shareholder note receivable	(25,000)	(25,000)
Retained earnings	8,102,000	8,102,000
Total shareholders' equity	11,624,000	
Total capitalization	$11,624,000	$

(1) As of May 9, 1986 the outstanding short-term bank debt was approximately $27 million. The Company anticipates that such debt will be significantly larger on the effective date of this offering, and that the net proceeds of this offering will not be sufficient to fully repay the short-term bank debt. See "Management's Discussion and Analysis of Financial Condition and Results of Operations—Liquidity and Capital Resources."

(2) See "Certain Transactions" for a discussion of the terms of the subordinated notes which are to be repaid from the proceeds of this offering.

(3) Does not include 1,985,000 shares of Common Stock reserved for future issuance pursuant to the 1985 Incentive Stock Option Plan, of which 1,028,250 shares were subject to outstanding options as of March 31, 1986. See "Management—1985 Incentive Stock Option Plan."

DIVIDEND POLICY

The Company has never paid cash dividends, and currently intends to retain all earnings for the foreseeable future for use in the Company's business. The Company's ability to declare and pay dividends is currently prohibited by financial covenants in its bank credit agreement. See Note 4 of Notes to Consolidated Financial Statements.

EXHIBIT A-2   Worlds of Wonder prospectus (*Continued*).

DILUTION

The net tangible book value of the Company at March 31, 1986 was $10,301,000, or $.57 per share. Net tangible book value per share is determine... by dividing the tangible net worth of the Company (total tangible assets less total liabilities) by the number of shares of Common Stock outstanding. Without taking into account any changes in such net tangible book value after March 31, 1986, other than to give effect to the sale by the Company of 3,100,000 shares of Common Stock offered hereby, the pro forma net tangible book value of the Company at March 31, 1986 would have been $, or $ per share of Common Stock. This represents an immediate increase in net tangible book value of $ per share to existing shareholders and an immediate dilution of $ per share to new investors. The following table illustrates the dilution of a new investor's equity in a share of Common Stock at March 31, 1986:

Public offering price(1)			$
Net tangible book value before offering.............................	$	.57	
Increase attributable to new investors	___		
Pro forma net tangible book value after offering(2)			
Dilution to new investors..			$ ___

___

(1) Offering price before deduction of Underwriters' discounts and commissions and offering expenses.

(2) After deduction of Underwriters' discounts and commissions and estimated offering expenses.

The following table summarizes as of March 31, 1986 the difference between the number of shares of Common Stock purchased from the Company, the total consideration paid and the average price per share paid by the investors purchasing new shares and by existing shareholders (without giving effect to the exercise of the Underwriters' over-allotment option):

	Shares Purchased	Percent of Total Common Stock	Consideration Paid	Percent of Total Consider- ation Paid	Average Price of Common Stock
New investors		%	$	%	$ (1)
Existing shareholders(2)	18,017,431	___	3,547,000	___	
Total...		100%	$ -	100%	

___

(1) Offering price before deduction of Und.rwriters' discounts and commissions and offering expenses.

(2) Sales by Selling Shareholders in this offering will reduce the number of shares held by existing shareholders to   or   % of the total shares of Common Stock outstanding, and will increase the number of shares held by new investors to   or   % of the total shares of Common Stock outstanding after the offering. If the over-allotment option is exercised in full, sales by Selling Shareholders in this offering will reduce the number of shares held by existing shareholders to   or   % of the total shares of Common Stock outstanding, and will increase the number of shares held by new investors to   or   % of the total shares of Common Stock outstanding after the offering.

As of March 31, 1986, there were outstanding options to purchase 1,028,250 shares of Common Stock under the Company's 1985 Incentive Stock Option Plan. The exercise prices of the outstanding options ranged from $1.67 to $3.33 per share with a weighted average price of $2.47 per share. See "Management—1985 Incentive Stock Option Plan."

EXHIBIT A-2 Worlds of Wonder prospectus (*Continued*).

SELECTED FINANCIAL DATA

The selected financial data presented below should be read in conjunction with the Company's consolidated financial statements and related notes and with Management's Discussion and Analysis of Financial Condition and Results of Operations included elsewhere herein. The quarterly data has been derived from the Company's unaudited interim financial statements which, in the opinion of management, include all adjustments (consisting of normal recurring accruals) necessary for a fair presentation. The fiscal year totals and the March 31, 1986 balance sheet data have been derived from the annual consolidated financial statements for the fiscal year ended March 31, 1986, which statements have been examined by Deloitte Haskins & Sells, independent public accountants, as indicated in their opinion included elsewhere herein.

	First Quarter	Second Quarter	Third Quarter	Fourth Quarter	Fiscal Year Total
Income Statement Data:					
Net sales	$ —	$ 2,695	$45,800	$44,592	$93,087
Operating costs and expenses:					
Cost of sales	191	2,117	25,853	24,540	52,701
Advertising and promotion	376	1,299	4,420	5,707	11,802
Selling and distribution	215	507	2,727	2,595	6,044
General and administrative	840	1,140	1,086	2,278	5,344
Total operating costs and expenses	1,622	5,063	34,086	35,120	75,891
Income (loss) from operations	(1,622)	(2,368)	11,714	9,472	17,196
Interest expense	42	147	329	784	1,302
Other expense	2	99	97	422	620
Income (loss) before taxes on income	(1,666)	(2,614)	11,288	8,266	15,274
Taxes on income	—	—	3,436	3,736	7,172
Net income (loss)	$(1,666)	$(2,614)	$ 7,852	$ 4,530	$ 8,102
Net income (loss) per share(1)	$ (.09)	$ (.14)	$ .42	$ .24	$ .43
Shares used in computing net income (loss) per share(1)	18,876	18,876	18,876	18,876	18,876

Fiscal Year Ended March 31, 1986 (in thousands, except per share data)

	March 31, 1986 (in thousands)
Balance Sheet Data:	
Working capital	$ 3,209
Total assets	70,261
Short-term bank debt	20,088
Subordinated debt(2)	3,651
Long-term debt	—
Retained earnings	8,102
Shareholders' equity	11,624

(1) See Note 1 of Notes to Consolidated Financial Statements for information concerning the per share calculations.

(2) See "Certain Transactions" for a discussion of the terms of the subordinated notes.

EXHIBIT A-2   Worlds of Wonder prospectus (*Continued*).

MANAGEMENT'S DISCUSSION AND ANALYSIS OF FINANCIAL CONDITION AND RESULTS OF OPERATIONS

Results of Operations

Worlds of Wonder commenced operations in April 1985. During the period from April through August the Company concentrated its efforts on staffing key positions, developing its initial product line, marketing and promoting the product line, obtaining sales orders, securing supply and manufacturing commitments and obtaining financing. Net sales for the first two quarters of fiscal 1986 were not material. The following table sets forth, for the periods in the 1986 fiscal year indicated, the relative percentage of net sales represented by certain income and expense items:

	Fiscal Third Quarter	Fiscal Fourth Quarter	Fiscal Year Total
Net sales	100.0%	100.0%	100.0%
Operating costs and expenses:			
Cost of sales	56.4	55.0	56.6
Advertising and promotion	9.7	12.8	12.7
Selling and distribution	6.0	5.8	6.5
General and administrative	2.4	5.1	5.7
Total operating costs and expenses	74.5	78.7	81.5
Income from operations	25.5	21.3	18.5
Interest expense	.7	1.8	1.4
Other expense	.2	.9	.7
Income before taxes on income	24.6	18.6	16.4
Taxes on income	7.5	8.4	7.7
Net income	17.1%	10.2%	8.7%

In September, the first full month of shipping, approximately 41,000 units of TEDDY RUXPIN were shipped, and the Company recorded sales of approximately $2.6 million for the character and related accessories. In the third quarter, net sales increased rapidly. The Company recorded monthly net sales of $9.2 million, $18.1 million and $18.5 million for the months of October, November and December, respectively. In addition to the seven storybooks and tapes released with the introduction of TEDDY RUXPIN, an additional six storybooks and tapes were released in late October.

Pre-Christmas sales were constrained by limited production capacity. Many retailers experienced out-of-stock positions during the entire Christmas season. Consequently, the demand for the product line remained high after Christmas, and the Company recorded fourth quarter net sales of $44.6 million, or 97% of third quarter net sales. A price increase of approximately 5%, effective January 1, 1986, was largely offset by a concurrent 5% "early buy" discount offered to retailers. In the fourth quarter, the Company also released the character GRUBBY and six additional TEDDY RUXPIN storybooks and tapes and began selling products for distribution into Canada and Australia.

For the entire 1986 fiscal year, net sales were approximately $93 million, of which approximately 33% were derived from sales of accessories. Net sales represent product revenues reduced by trade discounts and estimated product returns. The Company anticipates that trade discounts will remain relatively constant as a percentage of product revenues for the present fiscal year and that product returns for its existing product line will be favorably affected by recent product modifications. See "Business—Product Warranty."

The major components of cost of sales are direct contract manufacturing product costs, freight to the United States, royalties, manufacturing administration and quality control. Costs of sales as a percentage of net sales decreased 1.4% from the third quarter to the fourth quarter, representing primarily a decrease in freight costs offset in part by an increase in direct product cost. During the third quarter a substantial

EXHIBIT A-2   Worlds of Wonder prospectus (*Continued*).

portion of the Company's products were shipped from the Far East by air rather than ocean freight to reach the United States market in time for Christmas. Direct product costs increased as a percentage of net sales in the fourth quarter due to price increases from the Company's contract manufacturers and initial international shipments of approximately $3.7 million at lower per unit prices. The Company's international sales are made at lower per unit prices to offset marketing, distribution and certain warranty costs and expenses assumed by foreign distributors.

The Company believes that demand for its products is sensitive to advertising and promotion and expended significant amounts in this category in fiscal 1986. In addition, TEDDY RUXPIN received significant media attention during fiscal 1986 which increased the visibility of the Company's products. Advertising and promotion expense increased as a percentage of net sales in the fourth quarter primarily due to expenses related to the annual American International Toy Fair ("Toy Fair") in New York City in February, increased personnel expense and marketing activity in support of new products. The Company expects to continue to support products through significant advertising and promotion, including amounts for television productions and point of purchase displays which are expensed over their useful lives.

General and administrative expense includes product design and development, corporate and legal, finance, human resource and administration expenses. Such expenses increased approximately $1.2 million in the fourth quarter principally due to engineering efforts relating to new products to be introduced in fiscal 1987. expansion of facilities and increases in personnel.

The Company incurred interest expense during the year on borrowings under its bank line, on subordinated debt, on certain payables and on standby letters of credit issued to certain vendors. Interest expense increased in the fourth quarter principally as a result of an increase in average bank borrowings from approximately $4.8 million to approximately $12.3 million.

The effective income tax rate for the third quarter was 32%, reflecting tax benefits of the cumulative loss for the first six months of the year. The overall rate for the year was 47%, reflecting certain tax credits and the effect of foreign tax rates. See Note 5 of Notes to Consolidated Financial Statements.

A majority of retail toy sales occur in the four months prior to Christmas. Although the Company's net sales in the quarter ended March 31, 1986 were favorably affected by unsatisfied Christmas demand, the Company would generally expect reduced levels of net sales in the first half of the calendar year. Certain toy companies attempt to increase sales in the first half of the calendar year by shipping products on extended terms that allow payment at the end of the Christmas season. The Company, however, attempts to match product shipments more closely to the retail sales cycle and ships all of its products on terms requiring relatively prompt payment. In the quarter ending June 30, 1986, which precedes the Christmas sales season and the initial shipments of its new products, the Company anticipates lower retail sales levels and lower shipments to retailers. The Company therefore anticipates that net sales for the quarter ended June 30, 1986 will be less than those for each of the two prior quarters and, as a result, the Company expects to report a loss for the quarter.

Liquidity and Capital Resources

Since its inception, the Company's internally generated cash flow has not been sufficient to finance accounts receivable, inventory and capital equipment needs, as well as support growing operations. The Company has met its capital requirements to date primarily through borrowings under secured bank lines of credit, the private sale of equity securities and borrowings under subordinated notes payable to shareholders

The Company can borrow up to $35 million under its current bank line, which expires in September 1987. A bank, as agent for a syndicate of other banks, has committed to provide a $50 million line of credit upon execution of the required agreements, which is expected in late May 1986. The borrowing limits under this line will be increased as follows: (i) to $75 million, upon the Company obtaining an additional $10 million in subordinated debt or equity financing; and (ii) to $110 million, upon the Company obtaining an additional $20 million (for an aggregate of $30 million) in subordinated debt or equity financing. A $9 million standby letter of credit provided by a shareholder collateralizes the bank line. This letter of credit will expire upon the closing of this public offering.

EXHIBIT A-2   Worlds of Wonder prospectus (*Continued*).

The Company believes the aggregate $30 million financing requirements referred to above will be satisfied by the proceeds from the sale of the Common Stock offered hereby. In the event the proceeds are not sufficient to meet such financing requirements, the Company will have to augment its capital resources through subordinated debt or equity financing. After retiring the Company's subordinated debt of approximately $3.7 million, the net proceeds from the sale will be used to repay a portion of outstanding short-term borrowings (which aggregated approximately $27 million as of May 9, 1986 and which are expected to be approximately $50 million by June 30, 1986) under the bank line.

In addition to the operating line, the Company has a $16 million import financing line (subsequently increased to $18.8 million by mutual agreement of the parties) which expires on June 30, 1986. The Company is negotiating a renewal of this credit facility and anticipates an increase in the line to $35 million.

Based on its current plan of operations, management anticipates that the above-mentioned credit facilities and the proceeds from this offering, together with funds from operations, will be sufficient to meet the Company's short-term cash requirements. There are currently no significant commitments for capital expenditures.

EXHIBIT A-2   Worlds of Wonder prospectus (*Continued*).
BUSINESS

Worlds of Wonder is engaged in the design, development, marketing and distribution of toy products. During its first fiscal year ended March 31, 1986 the Company produced and sold one product line, THE WORLD OF TEDDY RUXPIN, which has as its central character an animated story-telling plush toy named TEDDY RUXPIN. From its initial shipment in August 1985 to March 31, 1986, the Company shipped approximately 1.4 million units of TEDDY RUXPIN and recorded net sales from the product line of approximately $93 million.

TEDDY RUXPIN "comes to life" through an electromechanical animation technology which synchronizes eye, nose and mouth movements to a corresponding speech pattern utilizing a pre-programmed cassette tape. The Company has positioned TEDDY RUXPIN with a character background and ongoing storyline, building a product line which includes related characters, storybooks, cassette tapes, clothing and various accessories around the main character. The Company believes that the marketing of these related items, which accounted for approximately 33% of net sales in the year ended March 31, 1986, will help extend the life cycle of the product line.

The Company has announced several new product lines, including the electromechanical animation of THE TALKING MOTHER GOOSE, SNOOPY, CHARLIE BROWN and MICKEY MOUSE. The Company also announced three other product lines: LAZER TAG, incorporating infrared light technology; PAMELA, a doll incorporating digital speech technology; and PLEASANT DREAMS, a line of old-fashioned rag doll animals. Each new product line will consist of related toy items and/or a range of accessories. The Company expects the manufacture of certain of these products to begin in the summer of 1986 with initial shipments of all of these products to retailers staggered from the summer through the 1986 Christmas season.

In addition to toy products, the Company is exploring other opportunities to adapt proven technologies to innovative entertainment and leisure products that can be promoted and distributed through mass market channels. Although it has not announced any such products, the Company continues to evaluate non-toy products consistent with this strategy.

The World of Teddy Ruxpin

During the fiscal year ended March 31, 1986 the Company produced and sold products solely from THE WORLD OF TEDDY RUXPIN line. The feature character in the line, TEDDY RUXPIN, is an animated story-telling plush character. TEDDY RUXPIN employs an electromechanical animation technology which, through a pre-programmed medium, synchronizes facial movements to the toy's corresponding speech patterns. The medium used by TEDDY RUXPIN is a dual track cassette tape played on a specifically modified cassette player built into the product. One track on the cassette contains the audio dialogue, including TEDDY RUXPIN's voice, other characters' voices, music and sound effects. The second track contains digital information that is electronically converted into electromechanical movement, causing the eyes, nose and mouth to be synchronized with the voice on the tape.

THE WORLD OF TEDDY RUXPIN encompasses several other characters. These characters were featured in fiscal 1986 in a series of 19 adventures recorded on cassette tapes accompanied by storybooks. TEDDY RUXPIN's best friend GRUBBY is a plush "octopede." When alone, GRUBBY is inanimate, but an electronic cord which attaches to TEDDY RUXPIN allows the two characters to have animated conversations. Other accessories to the line include FOBs (plush hand puppets) and five additional clothing outfits for TEDDY RUXPIN. The Company is expanding the TEDDY RUXPIN line for fiscal 1987 through the introduction of other non-animated characters from THE WORLD OF TEDDY RUXPIN, the addition of six new cassette tapes and storybooks, other accessories, and the introduction of cassette tapes and storybooks in several foreign languages.

The Company has recently signed a number of licensing agreements allowing third parties to manufacture and distribute merchandising and promotional goods (including clothing for children, linens and novelty items) depicting THE WORLD OF TEDDY RUXPIN characters. The Company will receive

EXHIBIT A-2   Worlds of Wonder prospectus (*Continued*).

royalties based on sales of these products, although payments to date have been insignificant. Generally, these agreements have terms of two years, provide for initial cash payments to the Company as nonrefundable advances against royalties, and require certain minimum annual royalty payments.

The characters in THE WORLD OF TEDDY RUXPIN and the talking toy technology are licensed by the Company on an exclusive basis from Alchemy II, Inc. ("Alchemy"). See "Product Development and Design—Alchemy."

New Products

The product life cycle of a toy line is generally relatively short. Accordingly, the Company's success will be dependent in large part on its ability, as to which there can be no assurance, to introduce new products in a timely and efficient manner and to extend the life cycle of existing products.

The Company's new product lines for the 1986 Christmas season are based on three distinct technologies: electromechanical animation, infrared light and digital speech. The Company made its first appearance at the Toy Fair this year to announce the new product lines. Since the announcement of the new product lines, the Company has refined the product designs, contracted for the required molds and executed contracts for the manufacture of certain of these products. The Company expects the manufacture of most of these products to begin in the summer of 1986 with initial shipments of all these products to retailers staggered from the summer through the 1986 Christmas season. The new products announced for the 1986 Christmas season are as follows:

Electromechanical Animation Products

THE TALKING MOTHER GOOSE. Positioned for a slightly younger audience than that of TEDDY RUXPIN, THE TALKING MOTHER GOOSE is an animated story-telling plush goose which will recite fairy tales and nursery rhymes through its built-in, specifically modified cassette player. In addition to synchronized movements of her eyes and beak, the goose's head will periodically move from side to side (as if she were addressing an audience). The Company plans to introduce 12 accessory storybooks and tapes of classic fairy tales for THE TALKING MOTHER GOOSE for the 1986 Christmas season.

PEANUTS characters. The Company has acquired the exclusive, worldwide rights to develop, manufacture and sell electromechanical plush versions of characters from the syndicated comic strip PEANUTS by Charles M. Schultz. See "Product Development and Design—Character Licenses." The Company has announced SNOOPY (with a built-in, specifically modified cassette player), his companion CHARLIE BROWN (with an electronic cord which attaches to SNOOPY), and WOODSTOCK. In addition to synchronized eye, nose and mouth movements, SNOOPY's ears will also perk up periodically in imitation of a live dog's movements when he hears something of interest. As in the cartoon strip, WOODSTOCK will not talk, but will chirp, open and close its beak, flap its wings, and blink its eyes when squeezed. The Company plans to introduce 12 accessory storybooks and tapes for these characters for the 1986 Christmas season.

DISNEY characters. The Company has acquired the exclusive rights to manufacture and sell mechanical talking plush toy versions of the Disney characters in the United States. The first two characters announced by the Company are MICKEY MOUSE (with a built-in, specifically modified cassette player) and his companion GOOFY (with an electronic cord which is attached to MICKEY MOUSE). Initial shipments of GOOFY are not expected to be made until after the 1986 Christmas season. Under the Company's agreement with The Walt Disney Company, storylines for ten storybooks and cassette tapes are to be created by Disneyland-Vista Records for the 1986 Christmas season. See "Product Development and Design—Character Licenses."

Lazer Tag

The game of LAZER TAG is set far in the future, when all conflict is resolved by playing LAZER TAG. The game is played with hand-held STARLYTES that emit a harmless infrared light beam. This beam is aimed at sensors which are either stationary targets or worn by participants. If the light beam hits

EXHIBIT A-2   Worlds of Wonder prospectus (*Continued*).

a sensor, a sound and a display register a "tag." Each sensor also has a bank of oscillating displays for visibility and a variable heartbeat sound which accelerates with each tag. The Company intends to market a full complement of sensors, targets and accessories for LAZER TAG.

Pamela

PAMELA is a doll incorporating digital speech technology through a custom microcontroller which contains a proprietary method of speech synthesis. A resident memory of 64K ROM allows the storage of up to 50 words digitally programmed with the word sounds as well as variations in pitch, intonation and duration. More than 60 sentences are developed with these words and also stored in memory. When spoken to, PAMELA responds with a randomly selected sentence. In addition, when one of the six sensors on her face is touched, she speaks a randomly selected sentence related to the facial feature touched.

PAMELA is designed to accept specially produced voice cards, of which six are expected to be distributed for the 1986 Christmas season. These cards change her vocabulary, allowing the development of additional sentences adapted to specific themes (e.g., PAMELA goes to school, the beach, a party).

Pleasant Dreams

As a complement to the talking toys discussed above, which are generally expected to retail for approximately $40 to $80, the Company announced at Toy Fair its PLEASANT DREAMS line. PLEASANT DREAMS consists of five animals of old-fashioned rag doll design, each of which is expected to retail for $20 to $30. Each animal is accompanied by its own storybook and cassette tape for use with a standard cassette player. Six additional storybooks and tapes about these characters are expected to be introduced for the 1986 Christmas season.

Product Development and Design

The Company's product development strategy encompasses the use of independent designers, character and technology licenses and internal development. The Company also periodically evaluates the prospects of acquiring or participating in joint ventures with other companies which are developing products compatible with the Company's product strategy.

To date the Company's product development and design activities have principally been confined to toys and have been derived from the following sources:

Alchemy

THE WORLD OF TEDDY RUXPIN and the related talking toy technology were developed by Alchemy, a privately-owned design and production company based in Chatsworth, California. Under a Development and Marketing Agreement with Alchemy, the Company acquired exclusive worldwide manufacturing and distribution rights to the talking toy technology and the characters in THE WORLD OF TEDDY RUXPIN. Alchemy receives royalties on sales from articles using talking toy technology and from products using THE WORLD OF TEDDY RUXPIN characters. The Agreement is effective through December 1995, with an option by the Company to renew for an additional ten years. The Agreement also provides the Company with a right of first refusal to manufacture, market and distribute any other products targeted for the retail market, developed, or to be developed by Alchemy during the term of the Agreement. See Note 2 of Notes to Consolidated Financial Statements.

In June 1985 the Company acquired from Alchemy's former technology partners a 50% undivided interest in the electromechanical animation technology developed by Alchemy, which included the talking toy technology, modular animation technology and walk around costume technology, as well as the related patents, patent applications, know-how and trade secrets (the "Technology"). The Company also agreed to contribute $220,000 towards the repayment of a debt owed by Alchemy to a third party. The Company and Alchemy formed a corporation, Gray Ventures, Inc. ("Gray Ventures"), in October 1985. The Company and Alchemy each own 50% of the outstanding capital stock of Gray Ventures, and the Company has the right to elect a majority of the Board of Directors. In exchange for its shares in Gray

EXHIBIT A-2   Worlds of Wonder prospectus (*Continued*).

Ventures, the Company assigned its then recently acquired interest in the Technology to Gray Ventures. Similarly, in return for its shares, Alchemy transferred to Gray Ventures all of its rights to the Technology. The purpose of Gray Ventures is to exploit the Technology subject to the Company's exclusive rights with respect to the talking toy technology as set forth in the Development and Marketing Agreement. To date, no applications have been developed by Gray Ventures and all electromechanical product introductions have been made pursuant to the terms of the Development and Marketing Agreement.

Alchemy assisted in the development of the prototype of THE TALKING MOTHER GOOSE, based on the Company's product concept, in return for talking toy technology and character license fees on the sale of the product and accessories. Alchemy will also receive talking toy technology license fees on the sale of the PEANUTS and DISNEY character products.

In May 1986 certain issues arose concerning the interpretation of the Development and Marketing Agreement. These issues include responsibility for the payment of certain graphics costs, applicability of royalty fees to cassette tapes to be used in the PEANUTS and DISNEY characters, responsibility for the payment of certain mechanical royalties, interpretation of a definition used to compute a port: n of the royalty due on products and Alchemy's role in the Company's product development for the talking toy technology. The Company believes that the resolution of these issues will not have an adverse impact on the operations of the Company.

Other Independent Designers and Consultants

Under a licensing agreement entered into in December 1985 with Anthony Paul Productions, the Company acquired the exclusive rights to commercially exploit the PLEASANT DREAMS characters and related products. The licensor agreed to design, create and develop storylines, story concepts, scripts, lyrics, music a d dialogue using the characters and will receive royalties on the sale of the characters and related cassette tapes and storybooks during the license period which expires December 1990. The licensor has agreed to develop additional characters adaptable to toys and games, which the Company has the right of first refusal to produce and market.

The Company has arrangements with several other independent contractors to assist in the design and development of new products and accessories, artwork and graphics, packaging and television production. The Company believes that the use of independent contractors provides a valuable, cost-effective means of supplementing internal resources and intends to continue utilizing such services.

Character Licenses

The Company's product lines have also been expanded through adaptation of product ideas and technologies to existing well-known characters. Under a sublicense agreement, the Company acquired from United Features Syndicate and Determined Productions the exclusive worldwide rights, except in Brazil, to manufacture and sell electromechanical plush versions of characters from the PEANUTS comic strip in exchange for royalties based upon net sales. The initial term of the agreement ends on June 30, 1987, and will be automatically renewed for three one-year terms provided the Company achieves certain sales levels of the PEANUTS characters and related accessories.

Under license agreements with The Walt Disney Company and Disneyland-Vista Records, the Company has acquired the exclusive right to manufacture and sell in the United States mechanical talking plush toys using certain Disney characters as well as cassette tapes, storybooks and other related accessories in exchange for royalties based on net sales. The license agreements are for an initial term ending October 31, 1987 and grant the Company three consecutive one-year renewal options provided the Company pays certain advances against future royalties.

EXHIBIT A-2   Worlds of Wonder prospectus (*Continued*).

Internal Development

Internal product design and development is a joint effort between the Company's marketing and engineering groups. The Company spends considerable time and effort in concept development, product design and research. To date these efforts have led the Company to create and develop two new product lines, LAZER TAG and PAMELA, and create the concept for THE TALKING MOTHER GOOSE. In addition, the Company pre-tests product concepts and prototypes through consumer market research techniques, including focus groups and in-home use tests. All such research is conducted by independent third parties.

The Company continually explores opportunities to adapt proven technologies to innovative entertainment and leisure products that can be promoted and distributed through mass market channels. In April 1986 the Company acquired the assets of Intraview Systems Corporation, a privately held corporation which was engaged in the development of interactive audio/video products.

Marketing and Sales

The Company's products are sold for resale throughout the United States by independent manufacturers' representatives on a commission basis and directly by Company sales personnel to toy stores, toy distributors, catalog showrooms, mass merchants, department stores and discount stores. Toys "R" Us, Inc., the largest toy store chain in the United States, was the Company's largest customer in fiscal 1986, accounting for approximately 16% of the Company's net sales. No other customer accounted for more than 10% of net sales. The Company anticipates a broader retail distribution of its products in fiscal 1987 primarily due to increased production capacity and greater acceptance of the Company by retailers. While the Company anticipates an expanded retail distribution, the Company expects that a limited number of customers will continue to account for a significant percentage of its net sales.

The Company sells its products internationally through its Hong Kong-based subsidiary to distributors in various foreign markets. The first international shipments were made in November 1985 pursuant to a distributorship agreement whereby Charan Industries sold products in Canada. In March 1986 the Company shipped products to Australia under a territorial distributorship agreement with Mattel, Inc. The agreement with Mattel also covers most of Western Europe and New Zealand. The Company also entered into an arrangement with Kong King for distribution in Hong Kong with shipments to commence in fiscal 1987. The distributorship agreements generally cover two-year periods commencing with the first shipment of product, provide that the cost of translating the cassette tapes and storybooks into foreign languages shall be shared between the Company and the distributor and commit the distributors to minimum annual purchase quantities. The distributorship agreements extend to products from THE WORLD OF TEDDY RUXPIN and certain other products as agreed to by the Company and the distributors. Mattel has agreed during the term of its distributorship agreement not to sell toys in Western Europe, Australia and New Zealand which compete with THE WORLD OF TEDDY RUXPIN product line. In addition, Mattel has the first opportunity for distribution rights in all other countries in which the Company has distribution rights not currently committed, provided that Mattel has a subsidiary or joint venture operation in such country. Mattel also has the first opportunity to distribute present and future Company products in the countries in which Mattel has distribution rights, as well as in those countries in which the Company presently has distributors after the present distributorship agreements expire. The Company's current plans are to distribute primarily the TEDDY RUXPIN line outside the United States in fiscal 1987.

The Company's advertising and promotion strategy utilizes point-of-purchase displays and emphasizes advertising and public relations oriented toward the retail trade, adults as well as children. To introduce the TEDDY RUXPIN product line, the Company incurred costs of approximately $10 million through March 31, 1986 for television advertising, co-operative advertising with retailers, public relations and point-of-purchase promotions. Product advertising was augmented with the production of two 30-minute television specials featuring THE WORLD OF TEDDY RUXPIN. A concerted publicity campaign resulted in extensive coverage in the trade, business and general press, and contributed to the placement of significant orders before the start of production and to widespread consumer recognition of THE WORLD OF TEDDY RUXPIN by the 1985 Christmas shopping season. Although the Company

EXHIBIT A-2   Worlds of Wonder prospectus (*Continued*).

intends to continue a strategy of extensive advertising and promotional activities with respect to the introduction of its new products in fiscal 1987, there can be no assurance that such products will receive extensive coverage in the trade, business and general press.

To assist in the promotion of its product lines, the Company intends to produce two animated television series. One series would consist of 65 episodes of the Adventures of Teddy Ruxpin. The Company has signed a letter of intent whereby Lexington Broadcast System ("LBS") would distribute the series subject to certain broadcast distribution criteria. Additionally, LBS and the station group would bear a portion of the estimated $12 million production cost. The Company, LBS and the station group would share profits from the program after the production and certain other costs have been recovered. The first 10 of these episodes are expected to be broadcasted on syndicated television in two five-part mini series starting in the fall of 1986. In the fall of 1987, all 65 episodes are expected to be broadcasted weekdays for a period of 13 weeks. The second series is based on LAZER TAG. The Company has an oral commitment from NBC to run the program weekly on Saturdays starting in September 1986. It is anticipated that the series will run for a minimum of 13 weeks. Under the arrangement NBC would have an option to broadcast new episodes produced over the next two years.

Point-of-purchase displays are an important element of the Company's marketing program. The TEDDY RUXPIN display is approximately three feet long and generally is placed at the end of an aisle of toys. When a customer walks within approximately 10 feet of the front of the display unit, TEDDY RUXPIN is activated and, through a specially programmed cassette tape, gives a three to four minute description of himself and other products in the line. The Company believes these displays have provided and will continue to provide strong inducements to buy since they clearly and quickly demonstrate the product. Prototypes of displays for THE TALKING MOTHER GOOSE, SNOOPY, LAZER TAG and PAMELA have been developed. The Company delivered approximately 4,500 point-of-purchase displays to retailers in fiscal 1986 for TEDDY RUXPIN and, because of an expected increase in retail distribution and the introduction of new products in fiscal 1987, plans to install a significantly larger number of additional displays in fiscal 1987.

The Company believes that gauging customer demand is critical to its long-term success. To assist in this, the Company has initiated a National Merchandising Program designed to put merchandising representatives retained by the Company on a part-time contract basis in direct field contact with retailers to obtain "sell-through" information. By monitoring inventory levels at selected outlets, the Company will attempt to avoid inventory buildups or shortages at the retail level. The merchandisers will also service and repair the Company's point-of-purchase displays, participate in product promotions, and monitor and enhance Company presence at the retail level.

Seasonality and Backlog

The demand for toys is highly seasonal with a majority of toy retail sales taking place during the Christmas season. Toy Fair and major regional toy shows generally occur in January and February each year, and a significant percentage of toys to be shipped each year are ordered by the end of April for scheduled delivery throughout the rest of the year. As a result, the Company expects to receive orders early in the year for products that are generally not scheduled for delivery until late in the year and for which there is not yet any significant public demand. Retailers generally may cancel all or part of the orders prior to shipment without penalty. Therefore, the Company generally will not build to such orders until consumer demand for the products is demonstrated. Due to the ability of retailers to cancel orders without penalty, the Company believes its order backlog at any point in time may not be indicative of actual sales for any succeeding period.

EXHIBIT A-2   Worlds of Wonder prospectus (*Continued*).

Manufacturing

Manufacturing Strategy

The Company's present strategy is to contract for all its manufacturing requirements, maintaining only a product engineering and development facility at its headquarters in Fremont, California. The Company's toys are presently manufactured to its specifications by unaffiliated contract manufacturers who have facilities in Hong Kong, the People's Republic of China, Taiwan and the United States. Three of the manufacturers accounted for 95% of the TEDDY RUXPIN units produced, representing 63% of net sales, during the year. To meet its expected manufacturing requirements for fiscal 1987 and to avoid increasing its dependence on its existing manufacturers, the Company plans to use a greater number of contract manufacturers to produce TEDDY RUXPIN and the Company's other products. It has recently negotiated contracts with additional manufacturers with facilities in Korea as well as in Hong Kong and the People's Republic of China.

Decisions related to the choice of manufacturer are based on price, quality of merchandise, reliability and the ability of a manufacturer to meet the Company's timing requirements for delivery. Manufacturing contracts generally have a one-year term and provide for delivery of finished products based upon rolling 90-day production schedules provided by the Company, composed of non-cancellable orders for the first 30-day period, non-cancellable but reschedulable orders for the next 30-day period, and a cancellable estimate of needs for the last 30-day period. The Company may terminate the contract upon 60 days' notice to the manufacturer. These terms allow the Company to adjust production volumes with relatively short notice to reflect changes in demand.

Management believes that its strategy to contract for all manufacturing requirements provides the Company with financial flexibility and the most efficient use of its capital. However, since the Company does not have its own manufacturing facilities, it is dependent on close working relationships with its contract manufacturers for the supply and quality of its products. See "Risk Factors—Dependence on Foreign Contract Manufacturers."

Transportation

The Company depends on sea and air transport to bring its products to local markets and, as a result, may be subject to labor disruptions, particularly in the maritime shipping industry, as well as to limitations on the availability of air cargo space for the shipment of items in certain circumstances. To date, the Company has not been materially affected by any such disruptions or constraints. Cargo management, importation and distribution services are provided by Sears World Trade, Inc. under an import services agreement which expires June 30, 1986. The agreement is currently under negotiation for an extension of its term. Should the agreement not be extended, the Company believes such services will be readily available from a number of other organizations.

Molds and Components

The Company contracts the design and fabrication of all its molds with companies in Hong Kong, the United States and Taiwan. The completed molds, which remain the property of the Company, are then consigned to designated manufacturers. The Company expects that a large percentage of its 1987 mold requirements will be fulfilled by one company. There can be no assurance that this company will continue to provide services sufficient to meet the Company's needs, and any significant business problems encountered by this enterprise could adversely affect the Company's operations.

The cassette mechanism, molded foam, certain integrated circuits, potentiometers and servomotors incorporated in certain of the Company's products have been available from single sources or in limited quantities. To address these limitations, the Company has contracted with additional manufacturers of cassette mechanisms and molded foam and is in the process of obtaining a second source for servomotors. The Company has also arranged for the sole suppliers of the integrated circuits and potentiometers to carry additional inventories. If the Company is not able to obtain any of these components in sufficient quantities, the results of its operations may be adversely affected.

EXHIBIT A-2   Worlds of Wonder prospectus (*Continued*).

Quality Control and Assurance

The Company maintains a quality control and quality assurance program. The Company has identified certain components in its products which its contract manufacturers are allowed to purchase only from designated approved suppliers. Each contract manufacturer submits samples from early production runs to independent testing laboratories to determine whether the manufacturer is producing to certified safety and product standards. On an ongoing basis, random samples are drawn from each manufacturer for full-scale testing.

The Company has established inspection and test criteria for each of its products. These test criteria are applied by the Company or its agents regularly to product samples in each manufacturing location prior to shipment. Once the products arrive in the United States, samples are subject to another inspection prior to distribution.

In order to source a variety of raw materials and components, provide quality control and administer contracts related to goods delivered to the Company's manufacturers on location, the Company has used the services of Sourcing International Limited ("SIL") in Hong Kong. In February 1986 the Company purchased all the outstanding shares of SIL in order to insure priority access to such services. SIL will continue to provide such services to the Company, as well as to a limited number of other customers.

Product Warranty

The Company's current products carry a 90-day replace-or-repair warranty for sales in the United States. On international sales, warranty periods vary by country according to law or custom, and warranty costs are shared between the Company and its distributors.

The Company developed and introduced TEDDY RUXPIN in the short period of time between commencement of operations in April 1985 and first product deliveries in August 1985. While the Company was aware that the electromechanical components of the product made it a relatively complex toy, initial versions of TEDDY RUXPIN experienced levels of product returns in excess of expected levels. The Company attributes a majority of such returns to failures in the built-in cassette player. The Company commenced shipments in late December 1985 of a modified version of TEDDY RUXPIN intended to correct the problem. The Company has experienced reduced returns of the modified version. The Company continues to modify and refine its TEDDY RUXPIN product, and expects to incorporate these modifications into all of its electromechanical talking toys. Although there can be no assurance, the Company believes that the changes incorporated into TEDDY RUXPIN will lead to lower returns on new electromechanical talking toy products.

Competition

The toy industry is highly fragmented with over 700 domestic toy companies and over 85 product categories as defined by the Toy Manufacturers of America, an industry trade group. No one competitor accounts for more than 15% of industry sales. The industry is, however, influenced by five major firms—Hasbro Bradley, Inc.; Mattel, Inc.; Coleco Industries, Inc.; Fisher Price and Kenner Parker Toys, Inc. Together, they accounted for approximately 43% of 1985 toy sales in the United States. Virtually all competitors select several categories in which to compete, and no competitor offers products in every category.

The Company believes it had the predominant share of the animated talking toy market in calendar 1985. As happens with any successful toy, the Company expects a number of competitive products for the 1986 Christmas season, which will result in a decreased market share for the Company within this market segment. This competition may also result in reduced gross margin due to price pressure.

With respect to any new toy product, the Company may compete with several larger and many smaller domestic and foreign toy manufacturers, importers and distributors. Many of its competitors have greater assets and resources than the Company. Furthermore, new competitors may enter the market with relative ease. Product innovation, quality, product identity through marketing and promotion, and strong distribution capabilities are all important elements of competition in the toy industry. The Company believes that it compares favorably with other toy companies on these factors.

EXHIBIT A-2   Worlds of Wonder prospectus (*Continued*).

Government Regulation

The Company is subject to the provisions of the Federal Hazardous Substances Act and the Federal Consumer Product Safety Act. Those laws empower the Consumer Product Safety Commission (the "Commission") to protect children from hazardous toys and other articles. The Commission has the authority to exclude from the market articles which are found to be hazardous and can require a manufacturer to repurchase such toys under certain circumstances. In the pre-production stages and periodically thereafter, the Company causes sample toys to be sent to independent laboratories to test for compliance with the Commission's Rules and Regulations, as well as with the voluntary product standards of the Toy Manufacturers of America. Similar laws exist in some jurisdictions in the United States as well as in certain foreign countries. To date, the Company has not experienced any material safety or governmental compliance problems with respect to its products.

The United States Government has established a Generalized System of Preferences which affords duty-free status to certain of the Company's products that are imported into the United States. The United States Government is now, by statutory mandate, reviewing the Generalized System of Preferences, and, because Hong Kong and Taiwan are considered to be more advanced economically than other countries, they may lose the duty-free benefits conferred by the Generalized System of Preferences, effective July 1, 1987. In such case, products imported from those countries into the United States would be subject to duties ranging from 5.8% to 14%. The loss of such duty-free benefits could have a negative impact on the Company.

Licenses, Patents, Trademarks and Copyrights

The Company's sales to date have been derived from products under patent, know-how, trademark and copyright licenses from third parties. The Company anticipates that a significant portion of future revenues will continue to be derived from licensed product lines. See "Product Development and Design."

The Company generally attempts to obtain patent, trademark or copyright protection on products not covered by licenses with others. It owns or is the beneficiary of patents or applications for many United States and foreign patents, copyrights and trademarks covering its proprietary products as well as mechanisms used in both licensed and proprietary products.

The Company believes that its license rights, patents, trademarks and copyrights are of significant value, and the loss of these rights for particular products or product lines might have a material adverse effect on the Company's business. The Company is not aware of any pending challenges to the validity of its or its licensors' rights.

Facilities

The Company's principal executive offices are located in Fremont, California, wh it occupies 112,000 square feet of office and engineering space and 57,000 square feet of warehouse space in three adjacent buildings. These facilities are leased under three separate leases which expire from April 1990 to February 1991 and are renewable for additional five-year periods. The Company leases an additional 35,000 square foot warehouse in Fremont, California on a month-to-month basis. The Company also leases 6,000 square feet of office space in Hong Kong under a three-year lease expiring April 1989. The Company believes its facilities are adequate and generally suitable for its business needs at the present time and for the immediate future. See Note 6 of Notes to Consolidated Financial Statements for information regarding the Company's obligations under leases.

Employees

At March 31, 1986, the Company had 131 full-time employees composed of 15 in sales, 15 in marketing, 44 in manufacturing and engineering, 24 in operations administration, and 33 in financial and corporate administrative activities. Of such employees, 21 were located in Hong Kong and Taiwan. The Company also retains a significant number of temporary employees. The Company anticipates hiring a substantial number of additional full-time employees in all areas during the next year. There can be no assurance, however, that the Company will be able to attract and retain qualified personnel in sufficient numbers to meet its needs. None of the Company's employees is covered by a collective bargaining agreement. The Company considers its employee relations to be good.

EXHIBIT A-2   Worlds of Wonder prospectus (*Continued*).

MANAGEMENT

Executive Officers and Directors

The executive officers and directors of the Company are as follows:

Name	Age	Title
Donald D. Kingsborough	39	Chairman of the Board, President and Chief Executive Officer
Angelo M. Pezzani	44	Executive Vice President, Chief Operating Officer, Director and Secretary
Stephen M. Race	36	Executive Vice President—Corporate Development
M. Robert Goldberg	38	Executive Vice President—Marketing
Mark Bradlee	37	Executive Vice President—Sales
Larry C. Lynch	47	Executive Vice President—Manufacturing and Engineering
Brian M. Wong	32	Executive Vice President—Administration
Don L. Hawley	37	Executive Vice President and Chief Financial Officer
John B. Howenstine	45	Director
Barry H. Margolis	40	Director

Donald D. Kingsborough is the principal founder of the Company and has served as Chairman of the Board, President and Chief Executive Officer since the Company's inception. Prior to founding the Company, Mr. Kingsborough consulted with various companies from 1984 to 1985. He was Executive Vice President, Sales and Marketing and a Division President of Atari, Inc., which was at the time a video game and computer manufacturer, from 1983 to 1984. Mr. Kingsborough founded Software Knowledge Unlimited, a national distributor of software and peripherals for personal computers, where he served as President and Chief Executive Officer from 1982 to 1983. From 1976 to 1983, he was President and Chief Executive Officer of DK Marketing, an electronics manufacturers' representative firm.

Angelo M. Pezzani joined the Company in May 1985 as Executive Vice President-Legal and was named Chief Operating Officer in February 1986. Mr. Pezzani performed consulting services for various start-up companies from 1984 to 1985. From 1982 to 1984, Mr. Pezzani was Vice President-Divisional General Counsel of Atari, Inc., providing legal counsel on technology licensing, trademarks and copyrights, domestic and international joint ventures and general corporate legal matters, as well as managing outside legal support. From 1973 to 1982, Mr. Pezzani was Vice President-Law, Associate General Counsel and Assistant Secretary of Chromalloy American Corp. in St. Louis, Missouri, a publicly-traded multinational company.

Stephen M. Race joined the Company in May 1985 and served first as Executive Vice President-Marketing, then as Managing Director of WOW International Limited until he was named Executive Vice President-Corporate Development in February 1986. From 1984 to 1985 he was self-employed. From 1982 to 1984, Mr. Race was with Atari, Inc., where he served as Vice President of Marketing and Communications for the International Division, responsible for developing distribution to and coordinating software development for the international market. Prior to joining Atari, Mr. Race was a consultant for five years for Arthur D. Little, Inc., a management consulting firm located in San Francisco, California, and Cambridge, Massachusetts.

M. Robert Goldberg joined the Company as Executive Vice President-Marketing in December 1985. Prior to joining the Company, Mr. Goldberg was President of The Learning Company, a computer software publisher. Mr. Goldberg spent two years, 1984 and 1985, at Software Knowledge Unlimited, a computer software distributor, as Vice President of Marketing responsible for all purchasing, merchandising, advertising and product development. From 1972 to 1983, Mr. Goldberg was employed by CBS Specialty Stores as Director of Computer Specialty Stores.

EXHIBIT A-2   Worlds of Wonder prospectus (*Continued*).

Mark Bradlee has served as Executive Vice President-Sales since the Company's inception. Prior to joining the Company, Mr. Bradlee co-founded National Sales Group, a manufacturers representative organization for the distribution of home microcomputer software packages, where he served as President from 1984 until National Sales Group was purchased by the Company (see "Certain Transactions"). Mr. Bradlee founded and was Vice President of Sales for Flagship Software Systems of Santa Clara, California, a software distributor, from 1983 to 1984. From 1981 to 1983, he served as Vice President of Sales for Imagic, Inc., a video game manufacturer which he co-founded. Prior to co-founding Imagic, Mr. Bradlee served as National Accounts Manager for Atari, Inc. from 1980 to 1981.

Larry C. Lynch has served as Executive Vice President-Manufacturing and Engineering since June 1985 and as Vice President-Manufacturing and Engineering since the Company's inception. Prior to joining the Company, Mr. Lynch was Product Development Director of Nellcor, Inc., a manufacturer of medical instrumentation, from 1984 to 1985. Mr. Lynch was Vice President of Operations Engineering—Consumer Products for Atari, Inc. from 1980 to 1984, and was responsible for test engineering, automation, industrial engineering, project management, licensee operations and manufacturing documentation. Prior to joining Atari, Mr. Lynch was Manager of Manufacturing, Engineering and New Product Introduction and then Quality Assurance Director for Fairchild Test Systems, a division of Fairchild Semiconductor Corporation.

Brian M. Wong has served as Executive Vice President-Administration for the Company since its inception. From 1981 to 1985, he was with Atari, Inc., serving in several positions, including Director of Operations, Director of Sales Planning and Director of Supply and Demand. Prior to his tenure at Atari, Mr. Wong held several financial management positions at Intel Corporation, a semiconductor manufacturer, from 1978 to 1981, including Finance Manager for both the Memory Systems and Corporate Divisions.

Don L. Hawley joined the Company as Executive Vice President and Chief Financial Officer in April 1985. From 1984 to 1985 he was self employed. From 1981 to 1984 he co-founded and was President and Chief Operating Officer of Westar Sporting Goods Inc., as well as two other sporting goods manufacturers acquired by Westar Sporting Goods Inc. Prior to that, Mr. Hawley was with Sunset Designs, Inc., a needlecraft products company, where he served as Controller from 1975 to 1978 and Director of Finance from 1978 to 1981.

John B. Howenstine has served as a director of the Company since its inception. In 1976 he joined J.S. Abercrombie Interests and became the President of J.S. Abercrombie Mineral Company in 1983. In addition, he serves as an officer and representative for various other Abercrombie entities and investments. Prior to joining J.S. Abercrombie Interests, Mr. Howenstine was engaged in various business interests including real estate development. Prior thereto, Mr. Howenstine was on the management consulting staff of Ernst & Ernst in Cleveland and Los Angeles. Mr. Howenstine is also currently a director of First City Bank of Bellaire, Texas.

Barry H. Margolis has served as a director of the Company since August 1985. Since 1977, he has been the Managing Partner of Margolis, Phipps & Co., a public accounting firm in Houston. Prior to 1977, Mr. Margolis was a tax manager for Deloitte Haskins & Sells in Houston. Mr. Margolis also currently serves as a director of Allied Bank of Texas in Houston

Directors of the Company are elected to one-year terms and serve until their successors are duly elected and qualified. Mr. Kingsborough is entitled to be appointed a director during the term of his employment agreement. See "Executive Compensation." Officers serve at the discretion of the Board of Directors. The Board of Directors intends to expand the Board with additional outside members.

EXHIBIT A-2   Worlds of Wonder prospectus (*Continued*).

Executive Compensation

The following table sets forth the cash compensation of each of the Company's five most highly compensated executive officers whose cash compensation exceeded $60,000, and the aggregate cash compensation of all executive officers as a group for the fiscal year ended March 31, 1986:

Name of Individual	Capacities in Which Served	Cash Compensation(1)(2)
Donald D. Kingsborough	Chairman of the Board, President and Chief Executive Officer	$ 332,641
Angelo M. Pezzani	Executive Vice President, Chief Operating Officer, Director and Secretary	203,591
Mark Bradlee	Executive Vice President—Sales	199,096
Larry C. Lynch	Executive Vice President—Manufacturing and Engineering	199,096
Brian M. Wong	Executive Vice President—Administration	167,243
All executive officers as a group (8 persons)		$1,447,224

(1) The Company has no pension, retirement, annuity, savings or similar benefit plan.

(2) Includes bonus payments received in April 1986 for the fiscal year ended March 31, 1986.

In February 1986, the Board of Directors authorized five-year employment agreements with Donald Kingsborough and Angelo Pezzani, officers and directors of the Company. The agreements provide for initial annual salaries of $400,000 and $200,000, respectively, and subsequent salary increases of at least ten percent annually. In the event they die or become permanently disabled, they (or their heirs or assigns) shall be entitled to receive their then current salaries over the remainder of the term of the agreement. In the event they are terminated without cause, the Company is obligated to pay in a lump sum an amount equal to the greater of two years' salary or the amount due for the balance of the employment term. If the Company is acquired or substantially alters its principal line of business, they shall be entitled to terminate their employment and shall be paid an amount equal to one year's salary. If the Company fails to elect Mr. Kingsborough as President and Chairman of the Board or fails to elect Mr. Pezzani as Executive Vice President, they shall be entitled to terminate their employment and shall be paid in a lump sum an amount equal to the salary payments which would have been paid for the remainder of the employment terms. Pursuant to these agreements, the Company has purchased five-year term life insurance policies in the face amount of $1,000,000 for each of Messrs. Kingsborough and Pezzani, and has given them the right to designate the beneficiary of any proceeds thereof. The Company will pay all state and federal income taxes attributable to the premiums paid by the Company. In addition, the Company maintains an insurance policy on the life of Mr. Kingsborough, the proceeds of which are payable to the Company.

The Company has executed employment agreements with terms ranging from two to four years with each of the Executive Vice Presidents, providing for minimum base salaries, salary continuation for a period of six months in the event of illness or disability, and termination for employment only for cause as defined in the agreements.

Commencing in fiscal 1987, the Company has adopted a policy to pay all outside directors an annual fee of $25,000 payable in quarterly installments and to reimburse them for their actual expenses incurred in attending meetings of the Board.

1985 Incentive Stock Option Plan

The Company's 1985 Incentive Stock Option plan (the "Plan") was adopted by the Board of Directors in November 1985 and approved by the shareholders in December 1985, initially reserving 1,500,000 shares of Common Stock for issuance thereunder. In April 1986 the Board of Directors adopted, and the shareholders approved, an amendment to the Plan to increase the number of shares reserved thereunder to 2,000,000. The Plan provides for the grant to employees or consultants of either "incentive stock options" within the meaning of Section 422A of the Internal Revenue Code or nonstatutory stock options. As of March 31, 1986, options to purchase 1,028,250 shares of Common Stock at an average per share exercise price of $2.47 were outstanding, options for 15,000 shares had been exercised, and 956,750 shares remained available for future grant.

EXHIBIT A-2   Worlds of Wonder prospectus (*Continued*).

The Plan is administered by the Board of Directors, or a committee appointed by the Board, which determines the terms of options granted under the Plan, including the exercise price, number of shares subject to the option, and the exercisability thereof. The exercis · price of options granted under the Plan must be at least equal to the fair market value of the Common Stock on the date of grant, and the maximum term of each option may be no longer than 10 years. With respect to any participant who may own stock possessing more than 10% of the voting rights of the Company's outstanding capital stock, the exercise price of any incentive stock option must be at least equal to 110% of fair market value on the date of grant and the term may be no longer than five years. The aggregate fair market value of the Common Stock (determined at the date of the option grant) for which any employee may be granted incentive stock options in any calendar year may not exceed $100,000, plus certain carry-over allowances from the previous three years.

Of the executive officers named in the table under "Executive Compensation" above, Mr. Kingsborough was granted an option to purchase 49,500 shares at an exercise price of $2.33 per share, Mr. Pezzani was granted options to purchase an aggregate of 150,000 shares at an average exercise price of $2.83 per share, Mark Bradlee was granted an option to purchase 30,000 shares at an exercise price of $3.33 per share, and Brian M. Wong was granted an option to purchase 30,000 shares at an exercise price of $3.33 per share, during the fiscal year ended March 31, 1986. Executive officers as a group (7 persons) were granted options to purchase an aggregate of 379,500 shares at an average exercise price of $2.67 per share during the fiscal year ended March 31, 1986. No executive officer exercised an option during the year.

CERTAIN TRANSACTIONS

In March 1985, the Company sold 5,953,500 shares of Common Stock to Donald D. Kingsborough, Chief Executive Officer of the Company, for consideration consisting of cancellation of indebtedness of the Company and cash aggregating $49,000 and the assignment to the Company of all of Mr. Kingsborough's rights, valued by the Board of Directors at $10,000, Mr. Kingsborough's approximate cost, under that certain Marketing and Development Agreement dated March 28, 1985 with Alchemy II, Inc., as amended, relating to technology and character rights for TEDDY RUXPIN. See "Business—Product Development and Design—Alchemy."

In March 1985, the Company sold 6,196,500 shares of Common Stock to John B. Howenstine, a director of the Company, as nominee for J.S. Abercrombie Interests ("JSA") for $204,000 cash. In July 1985 the Company issued 1,620,000 shares of Common Stock to JSA in consideration of the issuance by JSA of an irrevocable standby letter of credit in the amount of $9,000,000 for use by the Company. The Board of Directors valued the letter of credit at $53,333, its cost to JSA.

In July 1985, Mr. Kingsborough and JSA converted loans to the Company into Subordinated Notes in the amounts of $151,000 and $3,500,000, respectively, bearing interest payable quarterly at the rate of 10% per annum or such greater rate as shall be necessary to avoid the imputation of interest by the Internal Revenue Service. The principal amount of the Notes are payable upon the earlier of two years or the initial public offering by the Company. The Notes are fully subordinated to all present and future bank debt of the Company, which shall not exceed $25 million unless approved by the Board of Directors.

Pursuant to agreements entered into in March, April and May 1985, the Company sold an aggregate of 1,783,500 shares of Common Stock in October 1985 at a cash per share price of $.10 to certain executive officers and other employees pursuant to stock purchase agreements which provide the Company with an option to repurchase such shares at the original sales price in the event of termination of the shareholder's employment within a four year period from the date of the shareholder's initial employment. The Company's option terminates at the rate of 25% per year, or terminates with respect to all of the shares upon the closing of this offering. In addition, the agreements provide that, in the event of a proposed transfer of such shares, the Company shall have the right to purchase such shares at the proposed transfer

EXHIBIT A-2   Worlds of Wonder prospectus (*Continued*).

price less $.57 per share. Pursuant to these agreements, the following executive officers purchased the following numbers of shares:

Name	Title	Number of Shares
Larry C. Lynch	Executive Vice President—Manufacturing and Engineering	300,000
Mark Bradlee	Executive Vice President—Sales	300,000
Brian M. Wong	Executive Vice President—Administration	217,500
Stephen M. Race	Executive Vice President—Corporate Development	187,500
Don L. Hawley	Executive Vice President and Chief Financial Officer	187,500
Angelo M. Pezzani	Executive Vice President and Chief Operating Officer	178,500

In October 1985, Mr. Kingsborough transferred 346,500 shares to Mr. Pezzani and 75,000 shares to Mr. Lynch at a per share price of $.10 pursuant to agreements which, in the event of a proposed transfer of such shares by Messrs. Pezzani or Lynch, provide Mr. Kingsborough the right to purchase such shares at the proposed transfer price less $1.13 per share.

In February 19.5, the Company purchased the assets of National Sales Group ("NSG"), a manufacturers' representative for home microcomputer software, from Mr. Mark Bradlee, an executive officer of the Company, and another individual, an officer of the Company. Under the terms of the purchase agreement, the sellers received cash of $20,000 and will receive 50% of the net profits from the continuing operations of NSG until March 31, 1987.

The Company has obtained various company insurance policies from various underwriters through insurance agencies with which Mr. Kingsborough's wife, Rebecca Kingsborough, was affiliated as a sales agent. Mrs. Kingsborough received compensation for insurance policies written by such agencies for the Company until February 1986 when she discontinued such affiliation. Management believes the terms and rates of such insurance policies were reasonable and competitive with those offered by other insurance agencies. In December 1985, the Board of Directors passed a resolution to reimburse Mrs. Kingsborough for the cost of her reasonable travel expenses when accompanying Mr. Kingsborough on Company business trips. The amounts reimbursed to Mrs. Kingsborough during the fiscal year ended March 31, 1986 aggregated $18,300. In April 1986, the Board determined to discontinue the reimbursement of such expenses.

EXHIBIT A-2 Worlds of Wonder prospectus (*Continued*).

PRINCIPAL AND SELLING SHAREHOLDERS

The following table sets forth certain information regarding ownership of the Company's Common Stock as of March 31, 1986 (i) by each person who is known by the Company to own beneficially more than five percent of the Company's Common Stock, (ii) by each of the Company's directors, (iii) by each Selling Shareholder, and (iv) by all officers and directors as a group.

Name(1)	Shares beneficially owned prior to offering		Shares to be sold(2)	Shares beneficially owned after offering	
	Number	Percent		Number(2)	Percent
Donald D. Kingsborough 4209 Technology Drive Fremont, CA 94538	4,918,356	27.3%	289,520	4,628,836	21.9%
J S. Abercrombie Mineral Co. 5005 Riverway, Suite 500 Houston, TX 77056	2,876,496	16.0	200,528	2,675,968	12.7
JSA Ventures, Ltd. 5005 Riverway, Suite 500 Houston, TX 77056	2,400,000	13.3	167,456	2,232,544	10.6
Josephine E. Abercrombie 5005 Riverway, Suite 500 Houston, TX 77056	1,620,000	9.0	113,072	1,506,928	7.1
W.O.W. Shares Partnership 3731 Briar Park, Suite 200 Houston, TX 77042	1,297,284	7.2	290,077	1,007,207	4.8
John B. Howenstine 3731 Briar Park, Suite 200 Houston, TX 77042	1,110,000(3)	6.2	52,272	1,057,728(3)	5.0
Angelo M. Pezzani	525,000	2.9	38,096	486,904	2.3
Barry H. Margolis	273,597(4)	1.5	67,177(4)	212,420(4)	1.0
Ayrshire Corporation	243,243	1.4	54,393	188,850	.9
General Electronics	225,000	1.2	50,311	174,689	.8
Henry J. A. Taub, II	202,703	1.1	45,325	157,378	.7
Other Selling Shareholders who each individually own less than 1% of the outstanding shares of Common Stock (38 persons)	1,378,925	7.7	298,950	1,079,975	5.1
All directors and executive officers as a group (9 persons)	8,094,453(3)(4)	44.9%	456,313	7,638,140	36.2%

(1) The persons named in the table have sole voting and investment power with respect to all Common Stock beneficially owned by them, subject to community property laws where applicable and the information contained in the footnotes to the table.

(2) Assumes the Underwriters' over-allotment option to purchase up to 705,000 shares from the Selling Shareholders is not exercised.

(3) Does not include shares held by J.S. Abercrombie Mineral Co. in which shares Mr. Howenstine may be deemed to have a beneficial interest by virtue of his employment relationship with such entity. See "Management—Executive Officers and Directors." Mr. Howenstine disclaims beneficial ownership as to such shares. Includes certain shares held of record by JSA Ventures, Ltd. in which Mr. Howenstine has a beneficial interest.

(4) Represents shares held of record by W.O.W. Shares Partnership in which Mr. Margolis has a beneficial interest. Does not include remaining shares held of record by W.O.W. Shares Partnership, in which shares Mr. Margolis may be deemed to have a beneficial interest by virtue of his position as Managing Partner thereof. Mr. Margolis disclaims beneficial ownership as to such shares.

EXHIBIT A-2   Worlds of Wonder prospectus (*Continued*).

DESCRIPTION OF CAPITAL STOCK

The Company's authorized capital stock consists of 50,000,000 shares of Common Stock and 1,000,000 shares of Preferred Stock.

Common Stock

As of March 31, 1986, 18,017,435 shares of Common Stock were outstanding and were held by 60 shareholders. The holders of Common Stock are entitled to one vote for each share held of record on all matters submitted to a vote of shareholders and, upon giving notice required by law, may cumulate their votes in the election of directors. Subject to the dividend preferences applicable to any outstanding shares of Preferred Stock, holders of Common Stock are entitled to receive ratably such dividends as may be declared by the Board of Directors out of funds legally available therefor. In the event of liquidation, dissolution or winding up, holders of the Company's Common Stock are entitled to share ratably among themselves in all assets of the Company legally available for distribution and remaining after payment of liabilities and any preferential amounts payable in respect of the Preferred Stock. See "Preferred Stock" below. The outstanding Common Shares are fully paid and non-assessable.

Preferred Stock

The Board of Directors has the authority to issue Preferred Stock in one or more series and to fix the rights, preferences, privileges and restrictions, including the liquidation preferences and the dividend, conversion, voting, redemption (including sinking fund provisions) and other rights, and the number of shares constituting any series and the designations of such series, without any further vote or action by the shareholders. Because the terms of the Preferred Stock may be fixed by the Board of Directors without shareholder action, the Preferred Stock could be issued quickly with terms calculated to defeat a proposed take-over of the Company, or to make the removal of management more difficult. Under certain circumstances this could have the effect of decreasing the market price of the Common Stock.

The Company has no outstanding Preferred Stock and does not presently contemplate the issuance of any Preferred Stock.

Shares Eligible for Future Sale

Upon completion of this offering, the Company will have outstanding 21,117,435 shares of Common Stock. Of these shares, the 4,700,000 shares sold in the offering made hereby (assuming no exercise of the Underwriters' over-allotment option) will be freely tradeable without restriction or registration under the Securities Act of 1933, as amended (the "1933 Act"). In addition, 70,000 shares of Common Stock held by one shareholder are being registered with the Securities and Exchange Commission concurrently with the shares offered hereby and may be sold within 90 days after commencement of the offering. After such sale, such shares will also be freely tradeable without restriction under the 1933 Act. The remaining shares (the "Restricted Shares") were issued by the Company in private transactions between March 1985 and January 1986. The Restricted Shares will be eligible for public sale if registered under the 1933 Act or sold in accordance with Rule 144 thereunder. The Restricted Shares will initially be eligible for sale in the public market in reliance upon Rule 144 under the 1933 Act beginning at the earliest upon expiration of a two year holding period commencing with their date of purchase. For a description of the Company's agreements with various shareholders to register their Common Stock under the 1933 Act, see "Outstanding Registration Rights" below.

Stock Transfer Restrictions

An aggregate of 15,753,912 shares of Common Stock are subject to stock transfer restrictions until the closing of the Company's initial underwritten public offering of shares. The Company has the right of first refusal to purchase the shares at appraised value. Should the Company not elect to purchase the shares, Donald Kingsborough and John B. Howenstine as Nominee for J.S. Abercrombie Interests have the option and preferential right to purchase the offered shares at appraised value. These rights also terminate upon the closing of the Company's initial underwritten public offering.

EXHIBIT A-2   Worlds of Wonder prospectus (*Continued*).

Rights of First Refusal

The holders of 2,432,432 shares of Common Stock have a 20-day right of first refusal to purchase, pro rata, all or part of any "Share Rights" which the Company may propose to issue and sell. The term "Share Rights" means any share of Capital Stock whether or not presently authorized, rights, options or warrants to purchase Capital Stock, or securities convertible into Capital Stock, but does not include: (i) securities sold in a registered public offering, or (ii) a specified number of securities issued to key employees or officers of the Company or issued pursuant to any incentive stock option plan or other stock plan approved by the shareholders. The right terminates upon the consummation by the Company of a firm commitment underwritten public offering by the Company registered under the 1933 Act.

Outstanding Registration Rights

The holders, or their transferees, of an aggregate of 16,202,432 shares of Common Stock (the "Holders") are entitled to certain registration rights with respect to such shares under the 1933 Act. The Holders may request that the Company file a registration statement under the 1933 Act with respect to such shares, and the Company shall use its best efforts to effect such registration, subject to certain conditions including a requirement that the aggregate proposed public offering price of the securities to be sold is at least $4,000,000 with respect to a registration on Form S-1 or S-2, and $2,000,000 with respect to a registration on Form S-3. Furthermore, whenever the Company proposes to register any of its securities under the Act, either for its own account or on account of other security holders exercising registration rights, the Company is required in each such instance to notify each Holder and include all shares of Common Stock which such Holders may request to be included in such registration; provided, among other things, that an underwriter of the offering has the right to limit the number of such shares being registered. ...e Selling Shareholders have agreed not to exercise their registration rights without the permission of the Underwriters for a period of 180 days after the commencement of this offering.

Transfer Agent and Registrar

Bank of America NT & SA serves as the Company's transfer agent and registrar.

EXHIBIT A-2   Worlds of Wonder prospectus (*Continued*).

UNDERWRITING

Under the terms and subject to the conditions contained in the Underwriting Agreement, the Underwriters named below have severally agreed to purchase an aggregate of 4,700,000 shares of Common Stock from the Company and the Selling Shareholders, each Underwriter having agreed to purchase the number of shares set forth opposite its name below:

Name	Number of Shares
Smith Barney, Harris Upham & Co. Incorporated	
Dean Witter Reynolds Inc.	
Total	4,700,000

The Company has been advised by Smith Barney, Harris Upham & Co. Incorporated and Dean Witter Reynolds Inc., as Representatives of the Underwriters, that the Underwriters propose to offer part of the shares of Common Stock purchased by them directly to the public at the initial public offering price set forth on the cover page of this Prospectus and part of such shares to certain dealers at a price which represents a concession not in excess of $ per share below the price to the public. The Underwriters may allow, and such dealers may reallow, a concession not in excess of $ per share to certain other dealers. The nature of the Underwriters' obligations is such that they are committed to purchase and pay for all of the Common Stock offered hereby if any shares are taken. The Underwriters have advised the Company that they do not intend to confirm sales of the Common Stock offered hereby to any account over which they exercise discretionary authority.

If the Underwriters purchase any of the additional 705,000 shares of the Common Stock which are subject to the over-allotment option granted to the Underwriters by the Selling Shareholders, each of the Underwriters will be committed, subject to certain conditions, to purchase approximately the same percentage thereof which the number of shares to be purchased by it as shown in the foregoing table bears to 4,700,000. The Underwriters may purchase such shares only to cover over-allotments made in connection with the sale of the 4,700,000 shares shown in the foregoing table.

EXHIBIT A-2   Worlds of Wonder prospectus (*Continued*).

Prior to this offering there has been no established public market for the Common Stock of the Company. The public offering price set forth on the cover page of this Prospectus has been determined by negotiation between the Company and the Representatives of the Underwriters. Among the factors considered in determining the public offering price were the history of and prospects for the business in which the Company operates and an assessment of the Company's management, its past and present operations, its past and present earnings and the trend of such earnings, the prospects for earnings of the Company, the general condition of the securities markets at the time of the offering, and the market prices and earnings of similar securities of somewhat comparable companies at the time of the offering.

The Underwriters are not purchasing 70,000 shares of Common Stock held by a shareholder of the Company which are being registered with the Securities and Exchange Commission concurrently with the shares offered hereby. Such shares may be sold within 90 days after the commencement of the offering.

The Company has agreed to indemnify the Underwriters against certain liabilities, including liabilities under the Securities Act of 1933.

LEGAL MATTERS

The legality of the issuance of the shares of Common Stock offered hereby will be passed upon for the Company by Wilson, Sonsini, Goodrich & Rosati, a Professional Corporation, 2 Palo Alto Square, Suite 900, Palo Alto, California 94306. Orrick, Herrington & Sutcliffe, 600 Montgomery Street, San Francisco, California 94111, is acting as legal counsel for the Underwriters in connection with certain legal matters relating to the sale of the Common Stock offered hereby.

EXPERTS

The consolidated financial statements of the Company as of March 31, 1986 and for the year then ended included in this Prospectus and related supplemental schedules included elsewhere in the Registration Statement have been examined by Deloitte Haskins & Sells, independent public accountants, as stated in their opinions appearing herein and elsewhere in the Registration Statement and have been so included in reliance upon such opinions given upon the authority of that firm as experts in accounting and auditing.

ADDITIONAL INFORMATION

The Company has filed with the Securities and Exchange Commission, Washington, D.C., a Registration Statement on Form S-1 under the Securities Act of 1933 with respect to the Common Stock being offered hereby. For further information about the Company and the securities offered hereby, reference is made to the Registration Statement and to the financial statements, schedules and exhibits filed as a part thereof. Statements contained in this Prospectus as to the contents of any contract or any other document are not necessarily complete, and in each instance, reference is made to the copy of such contract or document filed as an exhibit to the Registration Statement, each such statement being qualified in all respects by such reference. The Registration Statement, including exhibits thereto, may be inspected without charge at the Commission's principal office in Washington, D.C., and copies of all or any part thereof may be obtained from such office after payment of the fees prescribed by the Commission.

EXHIBIT A-2   Worlds of Wonder prospectus (*Continued*).

OPINION OF INDEPENDENT PUBLIC ACCOUNTANTS

Worlds of Wonder, Inc.:

We have examined the consolidated balance sheet of Worlds of Wonder, Inc. as of March 31, 1986 and the related consolidated statements of income, shareholders' equity and changes in financial position for the year then ended. Our examination was made in accordance with generally accepted auditing standards and, accordingly, included such tests of the accounting records and such other auditing procedures as we considered necessary in the circumstances.

In our opinion, such consolidated financial statements present fairly the financial position of the Company at March 31, 1986 and the results of its operations and the changes in its financial position for the year then ended, in conformity with generally accepted accounting principles.

Deloitte Haskins & Sells

DELOITTE HASKINS & SELLS
Oakland, California
May 9, 1986

EXHIBIT A-2 Worlds of Wonder prospectus (*Continued*).

WORLDS OF WONDER, INC.

CONSOLIDATED STATEMENT OF INCOME

For the Year Ended March 31, 1986

Net sales	$93,087,000
Operating costs and expenses:	
Cost of sales (Note 2)	52,701,000
Advertising and promotion	11,802,000
Selling and distribution	6,044,000
General and administrative	5,344,000
Total operating costs and expenses	75,891,000
Income from operations	17,196,000
Interest expense (Notes 3, 4)	1,302,000
Other expense	620,000
Income before taxes on income	15,274,000
Taxes on income (Note 5)	7,172,000
Net income	$ 8,102,000
Net income per share (Note 1)	$.43
Shares used in computing net income per share (Note 1)	18,876,000

See notes to consolidated financial statements.

EXHIBIT A-2 Worlds of Wonder prospectus (*Continued*).

WORLDS OF WONDER, INC.

CONSOLIDATED BALANCE SHEET

March 31, 1986

ASSETS

Current assets:

Cash	$ 1,361,000
Accounts receivable—net (Note 8)	45,925,000
Inventories	12,259,000
Prepaid expenses	2,176,000
Total current assets	61,721,000
Property—net (Note 8)	6,267,000
Other assets	2,273,000
	$70,261,000

LIABILITIES AND SHAREHOLDERS' EQUITY

Current liabilities:

Bank lines of credit (Notes 4, 10)	$20,088,000
Accounts payable	18,299,000
Income taxes payable (Note 5)	8,419,000
Accrued liabilities (Note 2)	8,055,000
Subordinated notes payable to shareholders (Notes 3, 10)	3,651,000
Total current liabilities	58,512,000
Deferred income taxes	125,000

Commitments (Notes 6, 9)

Shareholders' equity (Notes 3, 10):

Preferred stock—no par value, 1,000,000 shares authorized, no shares outstanding	—
Common stock—no par value, 50,000,000 shares authorized, 18,017,435 shares outstanding	3,547,000
Less shareholder note receivable	(25,000)
	3,522,000
Retained earnings	8,102,000
Shareholders' equity	11,624,000
	$70,261,000

See notes to consolidated financial statements.

EXHIBIT A-2   Worlds of Wonder prospectus (*Continued*).

WORLDS OF WONDER, INC.

CONSOLIDATED STATEMENT OF SHAREHOLDERS' EQUITY

For the Year Ended March 31, 1986

| | Common Stock | | Shareholder Note Receivable | Retained Earnings |
	Shares	Amount		
Common shares issued for:				
Cash	11,877,935	$3,431,000		
Development and marketing rights	4,488,000	10,000		
Standby letter of credit	1,620,000	53,000		
Compensation	16,500	28,000		
Exercise of stock options	15,000	25,000	$(25,000)	
Net income				$8,102,000
Balances, March 31, 1986	18,017,435	$3,547,000	$(25,000)	$8,102,000

See notes to consolidated financial statements.

EXHIBIT A-2   Worlds of Wonder prospectus (*Continued*).

WORLDS OF WONDER, INC.

CONSOLIDATED STATEMENT OF CHANGES IN FINANCIAL POSITION

For the Year Ended March 31, 1986

Operations:	
Net income	$ 8,102,000
Items not requiring working capital:	
Depreciation and amortization	1,360,000
Deferred income taxes	125,000
Working capital provided by operations	9,587,000
Effect of changes in:	
Receivables	(45,925,000)
Inventories	(12,259,000)
Prepaid expenses	(2,176,000)
Accounts payable	18,299,000
Income taxes payable	8,419,000
Accrued liabilities	8,055,000
Cash used by operations	(16,000,000)
Financing activities:	
Common stock issued	3,522,000
Subordinated notes payable to shareholders	3,651,000
Borrowings on bank lines of credit	20,088,000
Cash provided by financing activities	27,261,000
Investment activities:	
Purchases of property	(7,405,000)
Investment in other assets	(2,495,000)
Cash used for investment activities	(9,900,000)
Cash, March 31, 1986	$ 1,361,000

See notes to consolidated financial statements.

EXHIBIT A-2   Worlds of Wonder prospectus (*Continued*).

WORLDS OF WONDER, INC.

NOTES TO CONSOLIDATED FINANCIAL STATEMENTS

1. *Operations and Significant Accounting Policies*

Operations—Worlds of Wonder, Inc. (the "Company"), a California corporation, is engaged in the design, development, marketing and distribution of toy products. Operations commenced on April 1, 1985, and product shipments began in August 1985.

Principles of consolidation—The consolidated financial statements include the Company and its wholly-owned subsidiaries.

Inventories, consisting primarily of finished goods, are stated at lower of first-in, first-out cost or market.

Property is stated at cost and depreciated using the straight-line method over estimated useful lives of three to five years for machinery and equipment and five years for furniture and fixtures. Product graphics and tape production costs are amortized on a straight-line basis over the anticipated market lives of the related product lines. The costs of promotional equipment and of tools, dies and molds are depreciated over the shorter of their useful lives or the estimated market lives of the related product lines.

Sales are recognized upon shipment, net of estimated returns and allowances.

Product warranties—Provision is made at the time of sale for the estimated costs to repair or replace products covered by the Company's stated warranties.

Income taxes—Deferred income taxes are provided for income and expense items which are recognized in different years for tax purposes than for financial reporting purposes. Investment tax credits reduce income tax expense in the year the related asset is placed in service.

Net income per share is computed on the basis of the outstanding number of common shares and common share equivalents (shares issuable upon exercise of stock options). The computation assumes that common shares issued and stock options granted during fiscal 1986 were outstanding during the entire year and that proceeds from the assumed exercise of stock options were used to repurchase common shares at the estimated offering price for the shares to be sold in the Company's initial public offering (see Note 10).

2. *Transactions with Alchemy*

In February 1985, Donald D. Kingsborough, the Company's Chairman, negotiated a Development and Marketing Agreement with Alchemy II, Inc. ("Alchemy"); the Agreement was subsequently assigned to the Company (see Note 3). This Agreement, as amended, granted the Company exclusive worldwide manufacturing and distribution rights to present and future retail products incorporating Alchemy's electromechanical animation technology and to products incorporating certain characters developed by Alchemy. In exchange, the Company granted Alchemy separate royalties on sales of articles using the technology and of products using the characters.

Coincident with the amendment of the Agreement, the Company purchased certain remaining interests in the electromechanical animation and related technologies from unrelated third parties. The Company and Alchemy each contributed their rights to these technologies to Gray Ventures, Inc. ("Gray"), and each became a 50% owner in Gray; Alchemy's right to receive royalties under the amended Development and Marketing Agreement was not contributed to Gray.

Cost of sales includes $5,755,000 of royalty expense to Alchemy, of which $2,721,000 (net of advances to Alchemy of $2,374,000) was payable at March 31, 1986.

During fiscal 1986, the Company paid Alchemy $862,000 for the production of story cassette tapes and the development of specified products. In addition, the Company advanced $800,000 to Alchemy to finance the production in fiscal 1986 of television shows based on the licensed characters.

EXHIBIT A-2   Worlds of Wonder prospectus (*Continued*).

WORLDS OF WONDER, INC.

NOTES TO CONSOLIDATED FINANCIAL STATEMENTS—(Continued)

Substantially all of Alchemy's assets, including its interest in Gray, are pledged to the Company as collateral for certain of the advances made to Alchemy.

In May 1986, Alchemy advised the Company of differences in the interpretation of certain elements of the Development and Marketing Agreement. The Company believes that the resolution of these issues will not have an adverse impact on the operations of the Company.

3. *Capital Financing*

During fiscal 1986, the Company issued a total of 13,770,000 common shares to its founders in exchange for $253,000 in cash, the assignment of the Development and Marketing Agreement with Alchemy, and assistance in obtaining bank financing; such assistance was in the form of a $9 million standby letter of credit made available in August 1985 by a shareholder for the Company's use. The shares issued to the founders for such agreement and financing assistance were recorded at the founders' approximate cost.

Subordinated notes payable to shareholders, issued in conjunction with the above issuance of stock, bear interest at 10% and are due at the earlier of June 1987 or the initial public offering of the Company's common stock (see Note 10).

During fiscal 1986, the Company also sold 2,432,435 common shares for $3,000,000 to unrelated parties and 1,783,500 restricted common shares for $178,000 to officers pursuant to employment agreements. Each officer's shares are subject to various restrictions, including the right of the Company to repurchase declining percentages of the shares at issuance price during the four-year period following the issuance if the officer's employment is terminated; such right terminates upon the initial public offering of the Company's common stock (see Note 10).

All share amounts reflect the 8.1-for-1 and 3-for-2 stock splits in August 1985 and May 1986, respectively.

4. *Bank Lines of Credit*

At March 31, 1986, the Company has borrowings of $20,088,000 under a $25 million bank operating line bearing interest at prime plus 1¼%. The line is secured by the Company's assets and a $9 million irrevocable standby letter of credit made available by a shareholder (see Note 3). Under the terms of the bank credit agreement, the Company may not declare any dividends on its outstanding stock.

In May 1986, the bank extended this operating line through September 30, 1987 and increased available borrowings under the line to $35 million. The bank, as agent for a syndicate of other banks, has committed to provide a $50 million line of credit, upon execution of the required agreements (expected in late May 1986). The borrowing limits under this line will be increased as follows: (i) to $75 million, upon the Company obtaining an additional $10 million in subordinated debt or equity financing; and (ii) to $110 million, upon the Company obtaining an additional $20 million (for an aggregate of $30 million) in subordinated debt or equity financing. The standby letter of credit collateralizing the line will expire upon the infusion of an aggregate of $20 million in financing. See Note 10.

At March 31, 1986, the Company also had outstanding standby letters of credit totaling $16,299,000 under an $18.8 million import financing line. The line, which expires on June 30, 1986, bears interest at 1½% and is secured by inventories and receivables.

EXHIBIT A-2   Worlds of Wonder prospectus (*Continued*).

WORLDS OF WONDER, INC.

NOTES TO CONSOLIDATED FINANCIAL STATEMENTS—(Continued)

5. *Taxes on Income*

The provision for taxes on income is as follows:

Currently payable:	
Federal	$ 6,651,000
State	1,521,000
Foreign	232,000
	8,404,000
Deferred:	
Federal	(1,114,000)
State	(118,000)
	(1,232,000)
Total	$ 7,172,000

The components of the deferred tax provision are as follows:

Warranty and returns reserves	$ (839,000)
State taxes	(700,000)
Cooperative advertising allowances	(525,000)
Point of purchase displays	533,000
Depreciation	125,000
Other	174,000
Total	$(1,232,000)

The provision for income taxes differs from the amount computed at the U.S. Federal statutory income tax rate (46%) as follows:

Federal income tax at statutory rate	$7,026,000
State taxes, net of Federal income tax benefit	758,000
Effect of foreign tax rates	(341,000)
Investment and research and development tax credits	(308,000)
Other	37,000
Provision for taxes on income	$7,172,000

No provision has been made for taxes on the undistributed earnings of subsidiaries not consolidated for U.S. income tax purposes since it is the Company's intention to reinvest such undistributed earnings ($1,240,000 at March 31, 1986) in the foreign location.

6. *Operating Leases*

The Company leases office and warehouse facilities and equipment under operating leases. Rental expense was $625,000 for fiscal 1986. Future minimum rental commitments are as follows:

Year ending March 31:	
1987	$1,520,000
1988	1,516,000
1989	1,513,000
1990	1,377,000
1991	1,005,000
Total	$6,931,000

EXHIBIT A-2   Worlds of Wonder prospectus (*Continued*).

WORLDS OF WONDER, INC.

NOTES TO CONSOLIDATED FINANCIAL STATEMENTS—(Continued)

7. *Stock Option Plan*

During fiscal 1986, the Company adopted an Incentive Stock Option Plan ("Plan") and reserved 1,500,000 shares of common stock for issuance under the Plan. The Plan provides for the grant of nonqualified and incentive options. The Board of Directors determines the option price (not to be less than fair market value or, for shareholders with more than a specified percentage of shares, no less than 110% of fair market value) at the date of grant. The options expire five to 10 years from the date of grant and are exercisable over the period stated in each option. During fiscal 1986, options for 1,043,250 shares were granted at exercise prices ranging from $1.67 to $3.33 per share. Options for 15,000 shares at $1.67 per share were exercised; no other options became exercisable, were exercised or canceled during fiscal 1986. In April 1986, the number of shares of common stock issuable under the Plan was increased to 2,000,000, and options for 500 shares at $5.33 per share were granted.

8. *Additional Financial Statement Information*

Accounts receivable consists of:

Trade accounts receivable	$48,880,000
Other receivables	28,000
	48,908,000
Less allowances for doubtful accounts and estimated returns	(2,983,000)
Receivables—net	$45,925,000

Property consists of:

Product graphics and tape production	$ 1,496,000
Promotional equipment	2,475,000
Tools, dies and molds	1,155,000
Machinery and equipment	140,000
Furniture and fixtures	2,138,000
	7,404,000
Less accumulated depreciation and amortization	(1,137,000)
Property—net	$ 6,267,000

During fiscal 1986, one customer accounted for approximately 16% of the Company's net sales.

9. *Commitments*

The Company is a party to various contracts and commitments and subject to various claims in its normal course of operations, including those related to contract manufacturing and media advertising. These commitments, which may be substantial at various times during the fiscal year, amounted to approximately $13,000,000 at March 31, 1986. The Company has also entered into character license agreements (other than those with Alchemy), which provide for royalties based on sales of specified products scheduled for release in fiscal 1987.

The Company has employment contracts with certain individuals with total minimum obligations of $1,600,000 per year in decreasing amounts through February 1991. Certain of the contracts provide for severance pay equal to the amounts due under the remaining contract terms for termination without cause, severance pay of lesser amounts for terminations under certain other conditions, and/or payments through the remaining contract terms in the event of disability or death.

In May 1986, the Company signed a letter of intent with a television syndicator and received an oral commitment from a television network for the production of two separate animated television series, which are planned to be aired beginning in the fall of 1986. The letter of intent is subject to certain broadcast distribution criteria which must be met by the syndicator. The cost of producing the two series is estimated

EXHIBIT A-2   Worlds of Wonder prospectus (*Continued*).

WORLDS OF WONDER, INC.

NOTES TO CONSOLIDATED FINANCIAL STATEMENTS—(Concluded)

at approximately $15 million, of which $9 million is to be provided by the syndicator and the network. The Company expects to recover its remaining investment through broadcast revenues and the sale of foreign, home video and cable distribution rights.

10. *Proposed Initial Public Offering*

In April 1986, the Company commenced preparations to sell newly-issued common shares of the Company as well as shares held by certain existing shareholders in an initial public offering scheduled for fiscal 1987. The Company anticipates that the net proceeds from such offering will satisfy the financing conditions of its $110 million bank operating line (see Note 4). Because the subordinated notes payable to stockholders (see Note 3) must be retired from the proceeds of such an offering, these notes have been classified as current.

11. *Subsequent Acquisition*

In April 1986, the Company purchased certain assets of Intraview Systems Corporation for approximately $300,000 plus royalties based on future sales from products using the interactive video technology developed by the seller. Had the acquisition taken place at the beginning of fiscal 1986, the consolidated results of operations of the Company would not have been significantly different.

EXHIBIT A-2   Worlds of Wonder prospectus (*Continued*).

Teddy Ruxpin and his friend Grubby talk and sing together when connected with an animation cord.

Prototype of new Teddy Ruxpin and Grubby™ animated point-of-purchase display.

Plush hand puppets. Foo™ and prototype of the Anythings™, Tweeg,™ Wooly What's-It,™ and L.B. the Bounder.™

Prototype of the Airship™ Toy Model created for Teddy Ruxpin's adventures.

Teddy Ruxpin Adventure Outfits.

Prototype of the Land of Grundo™ Map Play Area, shown with prototypes of poseable miniatur[

Teddy Ruxpin storybooks and tapes take children on eighteen different adventures. Six more scheduled for release.

EXHIBIT A-3   Standard & Poor's recommendation on Microsoft.
(From Standard & Poor's **Emerging & Special Situations,** *February 14, 1986.*
Copyright © 1986 by The McGraw-Hill Companies.)

Spotlight recommendation

Microsoft

This premiere software company's greatest claim to fame is its MS-DOS operating system, which is used in virtually all IBM and IBM-compatible personal computers. The company receives a royalty on every IBM PC shipped that includes this and other of its operating system software. In addition, Microsoft also provides other operating systems software (ie. XENIX for the IBM PC-AT), computer language products such as its BASIC Interpreter, which is included in over eight million PCs, and business applications software for word processing, spreadsheet analysis, file management and graphics. In November 1985, the Excel integrated spreadsheet package was introduced for use on the Apple Macintosh computer. For the fiscal year ended June 30, 1985, systems software accounted for 54% of net revenues, applications packages 38%, and hardware and books 8%. The distribution channel breakdown was 50% OEM, 49% retail and 1% print. Foreign sales accounted for 32% of revenues, versus 30% in FY '84-5.

This is an extremely profitable company. The net margin during the first half of the current fiscal year was a very high 20%. Microsoft's challenge will be to leverage its revenue stream from the MS-DOS operating system to develop new applications products to offset lower future margins on current applications software due to site licensing and increased use of volume discounts as well as reduce its dependence on MS-DOS revenues. Although future revenue growth

> *Underwriters: Goldman Sachs; Alex. Brown. Offering: 2,500,000 shares (2,000,000 by company; 500,000 by selling stockholders). Anticipated price: $16 to $19. Shares to be outstanding: 24,715,113. Minimum market cap.: $395,441,808. Proposed symbol: MSFT.*

from MS-DOS software will not come close to equalling that of the recent past, there is so much applications software now available on MS-DOS that it will be hard for it to be displaced as the operating system of choice for personal computers. Sales and earnings growth are quite likely to slow from the torrid pace of the last few years, but revenues should climb by a healthy 15% annually, with earnings rising somewhat in excess of that rate, aided by a newly implemented change in accounting for the cost of software research and development. For all of FY '85-6, we are estimating EPS of $1.60 on sales of $195 million. Based on the indicated range and our projection of FY '85-6 results, the stock's price to sales ratio will fall between 2.0 and 2.4, which, in our view, is a reasonable valuation, given the firm's current high margins and growth prospects.

There are some negatives. It is possible that stockholders equity may have to be reduced by some $60 million, paid out in a cash dividend to stockholders as a way of avoiding personal holding tax penalties; personal computer sales growth is slowing; site licensing or volume dis-

(cont'd on following page)

Selected financial data

	1982	1983	1984	1985	1984	1985
		Year ended June 30			6 mos. to Dec. 31	
Revs. ($000s)	24,486	50,065	97,479	140,417	62,837	85,050
Net Inc. (loss) ($000s)	3,507	6,487	15,880	24,101	9,996	17,118
Earn. (loss) Per Sh. ($)	.17	.29	.69	1.04	.43	.72

EXHIBIT A-3   Standard & Poor's recommendation on Microsoft *(Continued)*.

Spotlight recommendation

counts could gradually reduce margins on mature applications products; and most importantly, co-founder and now departed Paul G. Allen seems poised to become the Steve Jobs (or Mitch Kapor) of Microsoft, systematically selling his over six million share holdings over time, whenever market conditions are favorable.

Nonetheless, we believe that the MS-DOS operating program is well-entrenched in its target market and the company has a good chance of achieving, if not exceeding, our sales and earnings projections over the next few years. **Selling at just 10–12X projected FY '85–6 EPS, we recommend purchase of the stock.**

EXHIBIT A-4 Standard & Poor's recommendation on Worlds of Wonder. *(From Standard & Poor's* Emerging & Special Situations, *June 13, 1986. Copyright © 1986 by The McGraw-Hill Companies.) (Continued).*

New and noteworthy

Worlds of Wonder

Out of the ashes of Atari has come . . . Teddy Ruxpin. Parents who drove miles to find a Teddy Ruxpin talking bear for their child are well aware of the unsatiated demand for this cassette tape programmed electro-mechanical talking teddy. When Ruxpin speaks (via cassette) his eyes, nose and mouth are synchronized to the words expressed. Mr. Ruxpin was one of the most popular items (at $65 and up) last Christmas. Since toys like these usually sell well for at least two holiday seasons, Ruxpin is likely to generate sales well in excess of last year's $93.1 million for FY '85-6. We are estimating $150 to $175 million. Add that to sales likely to be generated from similar Mickey Mouse and Snoopy talking dolls, modest sales of a Pamela random sentence voice-card doll which will compete with a similar Lewis Galoob product that has caught Wall Street's fascination, and more importantly, a lazer tag game which will compete with a like product made by LJN, and total sales could approach $300 million. There is also some talk of creating talking sales manikins using Ruxpin's technology.

Unfortunately, given the vagaries of the toy business, a sales decline of rapid proportions could also occur as competing electronic toys steal the spotlight. Most of management have been on this kind of roller coaster ride before, having come from Atari, the former video game leader.

The offering has been priced in line with Lewis Galoob, a stock which has more than doubled since early this year

> *Underwriters: Smith Barney; Dean Witter. Offering: 4,700,000 shares (3,100,000 by company; 1,600,000 by selling stockholders). Anticipated price: $13 to $16. Shares to be outstanding: 21,117,435. Minimum market cap.: $274,526,655. Proposed symbol: WOWI.*

on promising prospects for its random speech doll and bear lines. Based on its current stock price, Lewis Galoob, with a more diversified product line, is capitalized at roughly $120 million. Worlds of Wonder, with a preliminary IPO price of $16, will have a market cap of $340 million and both companies will be sporting multiples well in excess of the historical average for a toy company. Nonetheless, using a $300 million sales level, net margins of 10% (an appropriate margin for lightly taxed Worlds of Wonder), and using Galoob's current multiple on '86 EPS, one comes up with an offering price of $15.

Despite the fact that upper management will walk away with millions just based on the shares they are selling through this offering and that they are selling 15% of an embryonic company for over $40 million (more than what Interleaf is getting for a greater percentage of the firm), this is a hot deal and the shares could easily go to 20 in initial trading. **Nonetheless, this is likely to be a very volatile holding, and we advise against maintaining a position in these shares for any extended period of time.**

Selected financial data:

	Q1	Q2	Q3	Q4	Total
		Year ended March 31, 1986			
Revs. ($000s)	—	2,695	45,800	44,592	93,087
Net Inc. (loss) ($000s)	(1,666)	(2,614)	7,852	4,530	8,102
Earn. (loss) Per Sh. ($)	(.09)	(.14)	.42	.24	.43

Index

ABOUT THE AUTHOR

Robert Natale is a Managing Director at Bear Stearns Asset Management, Portfolio Manager for the Bear Stearns S&P STARS Portfolio Fund, and a well-known expert on small-cap stocks and IPOs. For more than a decade, Natale has edited Standard & Poor's *Emerging and Special Situations* newsletter, one of the investment world's leading publications covering new issues and small-capitalization stocks. He is a regular guest on *CNBC* and *Bloomberg Business,* and has appeared on the *Nightly Business Report.* He is often quoted in business publications, including the *Wall Street Journal, Business Week, Investors Business Daily,* and the *New York Times.*